JOURNAL FOR THE STUDY OF THE OLD TESTAMENT SUPPLEMENT SERIES
260

Sheffield Academic Press

Troubling Jeremiah

edited by
A.R. Pete Diamond,
Kathleen M. O'Connor
and Louis Stulman

Journal for the Study of the Old Testament
Supplement Series 260

Copyright © 1999 Sheffield Academic Press

Published by
Sheffield Academic Press Ltd
Mansion House
19 Kingfield Road
Sheffield S11 9AS
England

Typeset by Sheffield Academic Press
and
Printed on acid-free paper in Great Britain
by Biddles Ltd
Guildford, Surrey

British Library Cataloguing in Publication Data

A catalogue record for this book is available
from the British Library

ISBN 1-85075-910-3

CONTENTS

Part II
READER-CENTERED READINGS OF JEREMIAH

Part III
THEOLOGICAL CONSTRUCTION

Part IV
RESPONSE

ABBREVIATIONS

AB	Anchor Bible
ABD	David Noel Freedman (ed.), *The Anchor Bible Dictionary* (New York: Doubleday, 1992)
AnBib	Analecta biblica
ANQ	*Andover Newton Quarterly*
AOAT	Alter Orient und Altes Testament
ASTI	*Annual of the Swedish Theological Institute*
ATANT	Abhandlungen zur Theologie des Alten und Neuen Testaments
BA	*Biblical Archaeologist*
BBB	Bonner biblische Beiträge
BDB	Francis Brown, S.R. Driver and Charles A. Briggs, *A Hebrew and English Lexicon of the Old Testament* (Oxford: Clarendon Press, 1907)
BEATAJ	Beiträge zur Erforschung des Alten Testaments und des Antiken Judentums
BETL	Bibliotheca ephemeridum theologicarum lovaniensium
BHS	*Biblia hebraica stuttgartensia*
BHT	Beiträge zur historischen Theologie
BibInt	*Biblical Interpretation: A Journal of Contemporary Approaches*
BibOr	Biblica et orientalia
BJS	Brown Judaic Studies
BKAT	Biblischer Kommentar: Altes Testament
BWANT	Beiträge zur Wissenschaft vom Alten und Neuen Testament
BWAT	Beiträge zur Wissenschaft vom Alten Testament
BZ	*Biblische Zeitschrift*
BZAW	Beihefte zur *ZAW*
CBC	Cambridge Biblical Commentary
CBQ	*Catholic Biblical Quarterly*
CRBS	*Currents in Research: Biblical Studies*
DJD	Discoveries in the Judaean Desert
EBib	Etudes bibliques
EvT	*Evangelische Theologie*
FAT	Forschungen zum Alten Testament

FRLANT	Forschungen zur Religion und Literatur des Alten und Neuen Testaments
GCT	Gender, Culture, Theory
GKC	*Gesenius' Hebrew Grammar* (ed. E. Kautzsch, revised and trans. A.E. Cowley; Oxford: Clarendon Press, 2nd edn, 1980 [1910])
HALAT	Ludwig Koehler *et al.* (eds.), *Hebräisches und aramäisches Lexikon zum Alten Testament* (5 vols.; Leiden: E.J. Brill, 1967–1995)
HAR	*Hebrew Annual Review*
HAT	Handbuch zum Alten Testament
HBT	*Horizons in Biblical Theology*
HSM	Harvard Semitic Monographs
IB	*Interpreter's Bible*
ICC	International Critical Commentary
Int	*Interpretation*
ITC	International Theological Commentary
JAAR	*Journal of the American Academy of Religion*
JBL	*Journal of Biblical Literature*
JJS	*Journal of Jewish Studies*
JNES	*Journal of Near Eastern Studies*
JNSL	*Journal of Northwest Semitic Languages*
JPSV	*Jewish Publication Society Version*
JSJSup	*Journal for the Study of Judaism*, Supplement Series
JSOT	*Journal for the Study of the Old Testament*
JSOTSup	*Journal for the Study of the Old Testament*, Supplement Series
JSS	*Journal of Semitic Studies*
JTS	*Journal of Theological Studies*
KAT	Kommentar zum Alten Testament
KHAT	Kurzer Hand-Kommentar zum Alten Testament
KHCAT	Kurzer Hand-Commentar zum Alten Testament
KJV	King James Version
LD	Lectio divina
MSu	Mitteilungen des Septuaginta-Unternehmens
NCBC	New Century Bible Commentaries
NEB	*New English Bible*
NICOT	New International Commentary on the Old Testament
NJPS	New Jewish Publication Society
NRSV	New Revised Standard Version
OBO	Orbis biblicus et orientalis
OTE	*Old Testament Essays*
OTG	Old Testament Guides
OTL	Old Testament Library
OTP	James Charlesworth (ed.), *Old Testament Pseudepigrapha*
OTS	Oudtestamentische Studiën

OTWSA	Ou-Testamentiese Werkgemeenskap in Suider-Afrika
RB	*Revue biblique*
RevQ	*Revue de Qumran*
SBL	Society of Biblical Literature
SBLDS	SBL Dissertation Series
SBLMS	SBL Monograph Series
SBT	Studies in Biblical Theology
SEÅ	*Svensk exegetisk årsbok*
SJOT	*Scandinavian Journal of the Old Testament*
SJT	*Scottish Journal of Theology*
ST	*Studia theologica*
STDJ	Studies on the Texts of the Desert of Judah
TA	*Tel Aviv*
TS	*Theological Studies*
TTod	*Theology Today*
VT	*Vetus Testamentum*
VTSup	*Vetus Testamentum*, Supplements
WBC	Word Biblical Commentary
WMANT	Wissenschaftliche Monographien zum Alten und Neuen Testament
WO	*Die Welt des Orients*
ZAW	*Zeitschrift für die alttestamentliche Wissenschaft*

LIST OF CONTRIBUTORS

John Barton, Oriel College, Oxford University, UK

Angela Bauer, Episcopal Divinity School, Cambridge, MA, USA

Alice Ogden Bellis, Howard Divinity School, Washington, DC, USA

Lawrence Boadt, Washington Theological Union, Washington, DC, USA

Walter Brueggemann, Columbia Theological Seminary, Decatur, GA, USA

Mary Chilton Callaway, Fordham University, New York, NY, USA

Robert P. Carroll, Glasgow University, Glasgow, UK

A.R. Pete Diamond, Adult Education Coordinator, All Saints Episcopal Church, Santa Barbara, CA, USA

William R. Domeris, University of the Witwatersrand, Johannesburg, South Africa

John Hill, Yarra Theological Union, Melbourne, Australia

Else K. Holt, University of Aarhus, Aarhus, Denmark

Martin Kessler, Danville, PA, USA

Nancy C. Lee, Elmhurst College, Chicago, IL, USA

Kathleen M. O'Connor, Columbia Theological Seminary, Decatur, GA, USA

Dennis T. Olson, Princeton Theological Seminary, Princeton, NJ, USA

Thomas W. Overholt, University of Wisconsin-Stevens Point, Stevens Point, WI, USA

Leo G. Perdue, Brite Divinity School, Texas Christian University, Fort Worth, TX, USA

Raymond F. Person, Jr, Ohio Northern University, Ada, OH, USA

Louis Stulman, University of Findlay, Findlay, OH, USA

Marvin A. Sweeney, Claremont School of Theology and Claremont Graduate University, Claremont, CA, USA

Roy D. Wells, Jr, Birmingham-Southern College, Birmingham, AL, USA

INTRODUCTION

A.R. Pete Diamond

Biographical Prescript

'Why is a raven like a writing-desk?'
(The Mad Hatter, from *Alice's Adventures in Wonderland*)

An intractable riddle, indeed!

Jeremiah has proved equally so for the interpretative guild. Armed with or against its Bernhard Duhm, Jeremiah studies has rushed toward the end of the twentieth century into impasse after impasse on almost every major point of the agreed agenda set for reading and resolving the problems of the Jeremiah tradition. The figure of Jeremiah remains troubled and troubling for the professional interpretative community.

The papers collected within this volume all carry out their readings conscious of this troubling shadow. They reflect the work of the Composition of the Book of Jeremiah Group of the SBL where they were originally presented.[1]

The circumstances of the papers and the work of the group were ironic. For when the group began it was heir to the recent wealth of English language commentary on Jeremiah. In short order volumes by Carroll, Holladay, McKane, Overholt, Brueggemann, Clements were appearing—a learned and creative community of Jeremiah readers! Their readings represented and represent a major capstone for an era of Jeremiah scholarship as well as a major transition. Ironically, the Jeremiah represented in these commentaries so profoundly differs that it was reasonable to ask if each were actually reading the same book!

The present collection reflects a decided shift in reading strategy that

---

1. The papers by Mary Chilton Callaway, 'Black Fire on White Fire', and Kathleen O'Connor, 'The Tears of God', are exceptions to this, though both consciously interact with the work of the group.

can be understood best only against the backdrop of the accomplish-
ments and impasses alluded to above. In other words, this recent spate
of English language commentary offers the primary intertextual field
for the present volume. For the work of the group had set itself the
experimental task of generating new paradigms for reading the troubled
and troubling Jeremiah tradition.

For those familiar with the intellectual ferment represented in the
dialogues and debates between modernity and postmodernity, some of
the moves of these collected papers will be recognizable. For those
unaware of that ferment or lately come to it, the shift in reading strategies may seem surprising, quixotic, even mad (but then the Cheshire
Cat would say 'we're all mad here ... ').

There are, however, theoretical subtexts offering clarity to readers of
these readings. It is my task to surface such subtexts and thus make a
map.

Framing the Issues

'Would you tell me please which way I ought to go from here?'
(Alice, from *Alice's Adventures in Wonderland*)

Given the appearance of multiple up-to-date commentaries on Jeremiah,
how shall further research proceed? What more can be done within the
existing theoretical and critical frameworks that have generated these
commentaries and guided Jeremiah studies to the present juncture? Or
stated more appreciatively, what has current commentary on Jeremiah
enabled us to see about the task of reading the prophetic book that
represents indispensable gain? Yet what, at the same time, indicates we
cannot simply continue within the framework of those reading strategies if we are to capitalize on the very insights they have made possible? It is not a question of repudiating the past achievements in the
academic study of Jeremiah; rather how do we build and go forward?
Will minor adjustments in the practice of 'normative' exegesis in Jeremiah suffice? Or should we attempt a major paradigmatic shift?

Talk of paradigms and prophets, of cabbages and kings, and other
fancy interpretative pursuits, however, requires attention to the accompanying subtext of contemporary hermeneutic debate—namely, where
does the privilege of meaning lie in the interpretation of a text: in the
author, the text, or the reader? As the following map will argue, the
enclosed papers all commit acts of reading deeply implicated in the

hermeneutic debate currently playing itself out in the interpretative guild.

Historical-critical Method: The Travail of Author-centered Assumptions

'... but it's *rather* hard to understand!' ...
'Somehow it seems to fill my head with ideas—only I don't exactly know what they are! However, *somebody* killed *something*: that's clear, at any rate—.'
(Alice, from *Alice through the Looking Glass*)

In a review of recent commentaries on Jeremiah, Helga Weippert[2] makes three crucial interrelated observations regarding the current paradigms used in the study of Jeremiah. First, faced with the problem of making sense of the diversity, complexity and apparent contradictions within the Jeremiah tradition, recent commentaries, whatever their disagreements, do agree that a historical-critical perspective provides *the* perspective for working out a reading of the prophetic book. This agreement is so fundamental that it has 'gone without saying'. Viewed in the light of the contemporary debate in hermeneutics, these commentaries negotiate the meaning of the text against the realities of author–text–reader by privileging the historical author or more broadly formulated the extrinsic realities that produced the book of Jeremiah.

The tradition of critical biblical studies solves the problem of the literature by reconstructing its genesis correlated with the phase(s) of the history of Israelite religion within which it emerged. For exegesis of Jeremiah, this has meant the quest for the historical prophet, by and large. The *historical person* of the prophet provides the anchor point for interpreting the disparate materials collected in the book. From this perspective, such diverse interpreters as Bernhard Duhm and William Holladay are in basic agreement. The origin point in the historical mission of Jeremiah is accorded crucial interpretative priority for reading the resultant prophetic tradition. It is just that Duhm is a minimalist while Holladay is a maximalist in relation to the retrievable authentic kernel in the tradition.

On this score, even Carroll is in accord hermeneutically. I mean the Robert Carroll of the 1986 commentary. For there he anchors meaning

---

2. Helga Weippert, '*Hieremias quadruplex*: Vier neue Kommentare zum Jeremiabuch' (unpublished paper, n.d.).

and the strategy for reading extrinsically, by reference out of the work to its historical agents—instead of the critically reconstructed historical Jeremiah, it is the critically reconstructed editors/communal voices of the late exilic/early postexilic period. Reading the work in the historical-critical interpretative paradigm is a matter of reading the text as a source of, even allegory of, information about the historical agents of the work. Valid interpretation is viewed as the probable historical meaning of the text as this expresses the intentions of those historical agents in their specific cultural contexts.

Given such *koinōnia* of hermeneutic, whence all the vigorous fire of debate? Weippert's comment isolates for me a second crucial observation: It is not the 'type of exegesis', that is, historical-critical principles, which produces this diversity of commentary. Rather, it is the very different models employed to conceptualize the dynamics of literary process and production in the first millennium BCE. For Holladay and Carroll, the extreme polls in the orientation of current commentary, the debate is constituted, on the one hand, between a relatively short, intensely complex period of compositional activity under the control of the historical prophet and/or his close associate with historical and biographical intention (so Holladay). And, on the other, the compositional activity is conceptualized as a chronologically extended, complex, non-centralized process, under control of diverse factional agents, freely and creatively handling the tradition for their own ideological ends, who felt no need to provide an overarching coherent orientation to the 'rolling corpus' of traditional material (so Carroll).

The difficulty of adjudicating these diverse models or some compromise between the two poles is only exacerbated by the fatal vacuum of direct, non-biblical, non-traditional, concrete, extrinsic information about any of the postulated historical agents, and/or literary stages in the production of the prophetic book (barring whatever aid can be invoked from LXX and MT relationships). The text in its final form is not just the prime datum for adjudicating the contending models; it is the only datum. Historicist interpretative pre-commitments must hope that as a mirror of reality the work offers no systemic, serious, fundamental distortions of reality or at least none that is insurmountable, or incapable of correction.

This brings me back to contemporary debate over meaning in literary theory and to a third observation by Weippert. These historical-critical contributions to commentary on Jeremiah do not explicitly engage the methodological debate or better the choice offered interpretation of privileging either the historical-critically reconstructed genetic process or the book in its final form. To read Jeremiah oriented to genetics is really an act of reading compositional history. To read Jeremiah oriented to the final form is really an act of reading with literary competency tuned to the poetics of the extant work. The failure explicitly, strenuously and rigorously to engage this choice may prevent paradigmatic advance until some fortunate happenstance significantly alters the vacuum of hard data in regard to the extrinsic circumstances and agents of the Jeremiah tradition.

To be sure, in his argument with the historical-biographical reading of Jeremiah, Carroll raised the issue of genre in a comprehensive and effective manner to expose historicist assumptions that raise the question: Do the traditions represent historiography or fictive, legendary portrayal? And though differing in significant ways from him, other commentary is replete with expression of skepticism about historical referentiality and the viability of recovering the vaunted desideratum of the historical-biographical quest—that is, the originating oral setting of the tradition (cf. Overholt, and especially McKane). At the least, it is profoundly cognizant in practice about the difficulty of offering significantly controllable readings of the tradition in reference to its originating moments (cf. Brueggemann and Clements).

Nevertheless, this lack in historical-critical commentary provides the starting point for more extended reflection on the choice between historicist and non-historicist literary critical method. The possibility of viewing the tradition as a symbolic, imaginative construct emerges—therefore, issuing in a fundamental shift from a hermeneutics that is author-centered to one that is text-centered. In other words, to privilege the nexus of author–text–reader as imaginative, text-immanent constructs and then proceed to analyze the phenomena for reading not as data for the reconstruction of a compositional history but rather, to inquire about the underlying network of codes that have generated the present text as a semiotic structure. To take this option is to take the route of critical literary theory that runs from New Criticism/Practical Criticism through Russian Formalism and the Saussurean revolution into Structuralism/Post-Structuralism.

If we are seriously going to consider potential candidates for new paradigms, do we not owe it to ourselves to look long and carefully at both the advances and regressions of broader literary theory and debate currently under way? To do so is also to do justice to the necessarily interdisciplinary reality of academic biblical studies. Furthermore, should we not say that such a move to non-historical approaches has good historicist warrants? For as studies in the redaction of tradition and the canonical process suggest, there was a de-historicizing impulse in the management of it, contemporizing and typologizing it, rendering it serviceable and vital to community interests. To make sense of a literature so produced do we not have to crack the code(s) that make such literary acts possible? Does not this 'datum' of historical-critical research now require non-historicist theory and method to capitalize upon it?

The Turn to Literary Readings: Text-centered Assumptions

'—so long as I get *somewhere* ...', said Alice.
'Oh, you're sure to do that,' said the Cat, 'if you only walk long enough.'

(Alice's Adventures in Wonderland)

It is precisely the reorientation toward poetics that characterizes the majority of essays in this volume. They have made the decisive turn from reading for extrinsic agency behind the text to an intrinsic reading for an immanent and meaningful form. It is a turn already forcefully broached in the commentary of Walter Brueggemann, which opted for a literary-sociological-theological reading of the text (a shift also begun in Ronald Clements's commentary). For Brueggemann and his inter-texts in this volume, there is a turn away from, a de-centering of extrinsic, and historicist preoccupation to the intrinsic, imaginative world of the text as constituting its own coherent hermeneutic system and por-trait. From a literary-critical perspective, they rely heavily on the 'close reading' techniques familiar to us from the practice of rhetorical and canonical criticism. The difficulty for such strategies has been that they may never rise above a 'pure' formalism; as a result, they cannot suc-cessfully address the inconcinnities of the Jeremiah tradition that so trouble such (close) readers as Carroll or McKane. In such cases the effort to produce an overarching coherent reading of the book opens itself to the criticism of 'over-reading' beyond any demonstrable rhetor-ical rationale or structure to connect what is not explicitly connected; and still, at times, even the will to 'over-read' has had to prescind from the attempt by confessing no discernible coherent form.

To speak, for the sake of discussion, in terms of post-Saussurean literary theory, a literary theory capitalizing on Saussure's distinction between *langue* and *parole* (language system/individual speech act), a 'pure' formalism is not properly structuralist. A network of codes generated the surface expression of the text—competency in these codes is crucial for the negotiation of textual meaning for both author and reader. Only as we discover the semiotic grammar creating the symbolic, surface structure of the book of Jeremiah can we successfully demonstrate that there is a coherent system of meaning structured by the book—in short, that the final form of the book, even in its contradictions, is readable. In the context of contemporary literary theory, if the turn, even in moderate fashion, from a historicist paradigm (also an over-reading of the traces of anonymous agency!) is to achieve self-absolution, then it must make its turn beyond close readings to poetics of a post-Saussurean type—that is, the study of meaning in the intersection of author–text–reader as *code generated*, text-immanent, imaginative, symbolic constructs.

Having said this, however, these collected papers illustrate that a uniform method for getting at those codes is not to be expected.

Nevertheless, it is in its effort to surface the underlying codes of the Jeremiah tradition that the present collection attempts to offer its 'new', its 'advance' over preceding Jeremianic intertexts even where they take up familiar close-reading tactics.

Three of the papers, taken together, look at the structure of the entire collection. Thus Louis Stulman exposes the structuring, mapping function of the prose speeches in Jeremiah 1–25. He envisions the 'C' material as reader, midrashist, reperformer and domesticator taming the indeterminacy and inconcinnity of the poetry. Theological (ideological) desires attend this literary artistry—that is, dismantling the dominant symbol system and domain assumptions of the state religion. Of similar scope, that is, in elucidation of *codes generative of unity and coherence*, Martin Kessler evaluates the structuring role of Jeremiah 25, 50–51. Jeremiah 25 offers a hinge for the whole prophetic collection, summarizing the material in the preceding 24 chapters and anticipating the climax of the tradition in 50–51 with the demise of Babylon. The coherence of the tradition is found in its myth of the (struggle for the?) sovereignty of Yahweh which begins in the judgment of Judah and moves out over the surrounding nations finally to climax in the punishment of Babylon. Jeremiah 50–51 offers the great reversal. Babylon the subjugator now becomes the subjugated; Judah the subjugated and punished becomes the liberated and restored.

Robert Carroll enters the synchronic arena constructed by the final form of Jeremiah 25 to show that such *unifying, coherence-generating codes* (like those elucidated by Stulman or Kessler) are ideologically inspired impositions of transformative and subversive effect, illustrative of the deconstructive tenor of the composition. Indeed, Jeremiah 25 is a 'Janus text', looking back to the beginning and looking forward to the end of the book with resumptive summations and proleptic anticipations. Yet it constructs a 'canonical' reading of the tradition that is 'counter-ideological to whatever may have been represented originally by the prophetic and textual voice'. For in the 'discourse of blame' (25.1-7) communal destruction resulted from the failure to heed the prophetic mission, yet 23.9-40 had already laid fault on the prophetic mission itself. And if 'true' prophecy effects communal repentance (23.22), does not Jeremiah's failed mission of repentance (25.1-7) deconstruct Jeremiah's prophetic legitimacy? Similarly the transfiguration of Nebuchadrezzar from beast (cf. 4–6, 50–51) to divine servant (25.8-14) transforms the rhetoric of Jerusalem's perpetual shame and reproach (2–24) into a temporary 70-year moment, and Babylonian hegemony as the mechanism of Judah's ultimate redemption. The Jeremianic rhetoric of absolute and inescapable destruction has been subverted and overcome. For the oracles against the nations (25.15-29) rewrite prophecy as a word of salvation rather than judgment and critique, the apocalyptic destruction of the world as the inauguration of Israel's final salvation (25.30-38).

Remaining papers broadly but not exclusively text-centered in turn take up passages of more restricted scope.

Nancy Lee explores the presence of subtle, hidden subtexts as intertextual codes at play in the tradition. It is the insinuations of the Cain and Abel narrative in Jeremiah 2 and 14 that Lee uses to lay bare the polysemantic strategies of the composition.

Kathleen O'Connor and I are concerned with the symbolic grammar underlying the imagery of female infidelity in 2–3 (4.2), exploring its rhetorical (persuasive) function and intertextual reception. Jeremiah's metaphor of the broken marriage functions as a root metaphor that unifies and narratizes the disparate material in these chapters. Intertextual performance and reperformance (between Hosea and Jeremiah, between Jer-LXX and Jer-MT) re-encode the marriage metaphor to serve new circumstances and create a new configuration of readers.

John Hill examines the construction of time within the metaphorical world of the text. Jeremiah 25 appears as his test case. Both definite and indefinite temporal indicators have taken on symbolic rather than 'literal' chronological function. Temporal distance between the events of 605 and 587 BCE is collapsed. Jeremiah 25 constructs a symbolic 'in-between' period, placing itself between the beginning of divine cosmic judgment (with Jerusalem; cf. Kessler above) and its full realization in some indefinite future. For Hill this opens up a *metaphoric* space for readers to see their current situation *as* an exile. The revelatory and transformative desires of the world in the text are thus exposed (a Ricoeurean process of narrative refiguration!).

In her examination of Jeremiah 37–44, Else Holt invokes Roland Barthes' reflection on the nature of texts as textures, as a weaving together of different types of codes. Holt's task is to unravel the texture of Jeremiah 37–44 into its symbolic threads. Four threads attract her attention: (1) the physical location of the prophet as a code for hostile treatment of the word of God; (2) citizenship (Judahite vs. Foreigner) of key actors as a code for contrasting (ironically) and evaluating proper piety vis-à-vis God and the prophetic mission; (3) mirroring king and prophet (as opposites and as complements of each other) as a code structuring personal fate; (4) the prophet as mediator and, therefore, personified code for the word of God.

Mary Callaway's study on 37–38 refigures narrative inconcinnities that have frustrated readings of these narratives as coherent compositions into guides productive of a midrash-like reading strategy. Callaway discerns narrative voices immanent in the textual plane of the composition that cannot be identified merely with its historical agents, nor viewed simply as the sum of the redactional parts. These voices press readings of the final form in two directions: (1) an annalistic voice represents the traditions as realistic historical accounts; (2) a second deconstructs the first and propels the developing prophetic traditions out of the framework of political history into its new context of Torah.

Callaway posits in this second voice the loosing of Jeremiah from his historical context and thus the subtext for the permutations of the figure of Jeremiah eventually enacted outside the book of Jeremiah. It remains for John Barton's essay to trace these transformations of Jeremiah into the late Second Temple period from historical figure into seer, wonder-worker, mystagogue and eschatological figure.[3]

His descriptive analysis holds in equipoise issues of author–text–reader. In a sense, he offers a *history* of Jeremianic representations that are both rewritings and rereadings of the prophet! Barton's effort to navigate the permutations and inconcinnities of Jeremianic transfiguration raises the interesting question: had these disparate traditions been found gathered into a single collection, would they have posed a problem of readability any worse than that posed by our extant scroll of Jeremiah! Barton dramatizes a need everywhere felt and quested for in our collected papers—to surface the cultural and aesthetic codes which produce 'writings' of the sort that Jeremiah, the scroll, offers. In short, we theorize 'writing' prophecy in ancient Israel.

Finally in this section of the collected papers, Alice Bellis offers a counter-text to prior readings of Jeremiah 50 which saw in the collection only non-order and thematic incoherence. Her close reading surfaces three independent unified poems, distinguishable by theme, image and structure (50.1-20; 50.21-33; 50.34-38). Jeremiah 50.39-46 represent intertextual re-citations, re-formations and adaptations of OAN oracular material whose function is to bind the three preceding poems into a unified whole.

Taken as a subset of the whole collection, these papers dramatize an impulse toward dehistorization within the tradition (as true for the traditions within the scroll as those without as Barton's essay shows) not sufficiently plumbed or reckoned with in earlier historicist preoccupation with the prophetic book. How future historicist concerns are to proceed from the hints and allegations of history still retained in the tradition remains unclear. The composition has profoundly refigured its traditions.

Also interesting are the fortunes of McKane's envisioned 'rolling corpus', fragmentary, non-systematic, textually localized, and discontinuous of agency. For as diverse as these papers are in the ways they tease out the network of codes at play in the tradition, they all offer counter-texts to McKane's proposal, at least as offers overcoming some of the inconcinnity McKane has sensed afflicting the tradition. As

---

3.   Because of its focus upon the traditions *outside* the book of Jeremiah about the prophet, Barton's essay occupies a distinct place among the essays. We have set his paper, therefore, after the text-centered and at the end of the reader-centered subsections but before Part III, which is focused on the consequences for theological interpretation posed by new readings of the prophet.

exceptions, Barton's paper, on the other hand, might be taken as offering an external demonstration of processes already operative within the formation of the Jeremiah scroll, while Carroll's assessment of the synchronic consequences of Jeremiah 25 lays bare subversive and deconstructive internal processes, and thus both offer corroboration of McKane's model.

Whether a reader is of historicist bent or de-historicist, it seems that the trace of history retained within Jeremiah's texture will make itself felt and seek to reassert its day. Or as Thomas Overholt will want to remind us, 'we will always be troubled by the specter of "history"'.[4] So it is that Marvin Sweeney offers a voice in dissent with the de-centering of history practiced in the preceding readers. He offers a Redaction Critical analysis of Jeremiah 2–6; and recovers authentic Jeremianic oracles preached during the reign of Josiah in service of political reunification interests with the defunct northern monarchy. Following Josiah's death in 609, the prophet will re-edit the oracles to serve the circumstances of his continuing mission to Judah early in the reign of Jehoiakim. Unrepentant historicism? Maybe. But what brings Sweeney's paper into dialogue with the preceding essays is his contention that it is precisely a careful literary reading of the tradition that will open up the literary seams upon which the historicist critic can play to recover the history of composition and even more history than that! The turn to literary readings with their text-centered assumptions apparently cannot prevent the return to history (Holladay as intertext insinuates its presence!).

The Turn to Discourse: Reader-centered Assumptions

'When I use a word,' Humpty-Dumpty said ... 'it means just what I choose it to mean—neither more nor less.'

(Alice through the Looking Glass)

The will to power of a reader toward meaning emerges! Lament it or laud it. If interpretation is to proceed, that will must be exercised. Cultural desires and ideological interests perennially circulate through the nexus of author–text–reader. At each point of that nexus readers emerge, for at each point readings are enacted. And where it is a matter of readings at work, the nexus of author–text–reader for Jeremiah is

---

4. Unpublished remarks given at the Composition of the Book of Jeremiah Consultation (SBL/AAR Annual Convention, 1992).

exposed as a symbolic arena where the discourse of the tradition is perennially performed (whether literally rewritten or only metaphorically reconceived) toward the satisfaction of rhetorical (persuasive) desire.

In the hermeneutic world that is post-Saussure *and post-structural*, reader-centered discussion of meaning is unavoidable.

Hence the problematics of reader-response literary analysis and ideological critique press themselves on the guild troubled and troubling with Jeremiah. The choice of reader-centered strategies represents the second major turn of this collection. A second subset of new readings presents itself devoted to those problematics (see also some of the papers in the previous subset which also exhibit this turn). But the issues were already inscribed in prior intertexts of the interpretative guild.

Recall for example the competing visions of Jeremiah in commentary by Walter Brueggemann and Robert Carroll. When Brueggemann shifts our attention to the persona of the prophet constituted in the text he reads that figure as an authoritative voice, legitimating a way of life termed 'covenantal', against all opposing voices, termed 'ideological'. Covenantal reality promotes liberating human and societal existence, opposed to elite monopolization of power and its consequent marginalization of the weak/poor. Carroll, on the other hand, can discern no such unitary figure or conception. Instead there are a plurality of conflicted characterizations of the prophet, sustaining a plethora of theopolitical ideologies, backed by a diversity of party factions. Both readings reconceptualize the text as a social symbol, re-constitute the prophetic book as 'rhetoric', and force an exigent question—what kind of a political document is a prophetic book?

The agenda for troubling Jeremiah expands. It appears, the work and the prophet, Jeremiah, are born out of the myth(s) of Israel, the symbolic battlefield of competing readers, and feeds back on that myth(s). The link between poetics and power has been broached but not connected to a clearly articulated social theory of literature (though one should acknowledge Overholt's attentiveness to recovering the social processes at play in Israelite prophecy). Addressing this problem is more than providing a reconstruction of the 'historical reader' and setting that reader in the social history of Israelite society or religion. To do so without a clearly reasoned social theory of literature raises the question of how a text, as social symbol, relates to reality. To act as if a unilinear correspondence is the only possible mode of correlation simply repeats the inadequacies of a naïve historical method, recreating the cul-de-sac of *Sitz im Leben* as this was conceptualized by form criticism. In the hermeneutical world that is *post-Saussure* and post-structural, there can be no turn to the reader unless this is a turn through the text as coded discourse in which 'somebody says something about something to somebody'.

Recognition of Jeremiah as a social symbol demands the development of an explicit social theory of literature executed hermeneutically as a turn to the text as coded discourse. Fittingly, Robert Carroll appears here (on this side of the commentary) to make just such a proposal. Bakhtinian literary theory focuses on the dialogical character of texts, which constitutes their intertextuality, an open chain of rereadings and, therefore, necessarily raises the question of ideology (cf. his essay on Jer. 25 above). Who determines a specific reading under what conditions and to what sociopolitical ends? This question provides the heuristic entry for meditation on the textuality (texture) of Jeremiah. Carroll dramatizes the high degree of intertextual anxiety in Jeremiah (both within the scroll and between other writings). The scroll of Jeremiah weaves in and out of other scrolls; it is a 'reading of readings' gathered around the destruction of Jerusalem as their attracting mythological topos. One text has provided the occasion for another rather than some historical referent (approving the usefulness of McKane's rolling corpus). Jeremianic intertextuality represents a 'dissenting voice' in the intertextuality offered by the Bible—that is, since it so often undoes, 'writes off', themes and topoi in its dialogue partners. The polyphony is also within as 'traces' of hope and protest dramatize voices set over against the dominant impulse to a theodicy which writes off Judah's past. Querying the necessary and sufficient conditions for the production of such textuality, Carroll appeals to scribal activity within the second temple period (preferably in the Hellenistic period) where a temple elite generate a legitimization literature for temple cult, its lands and the elites wielding power. Jeremianic intertextuality thus inscribed, with traces of the ideological commitments of the tradition's writers, editors, authorizers and readers, presses upon contemporary interpretation a quest for ethical readings of the book.

The remaining four essays tease out further aspects of reader and ideology circulating through the Jeremianic tradition and in so doing expose multiple senses in which readers can be said to be present to the tradition. William Domeris employs the sociolinguistic categories of 'antisociety' and 'antilanguage' to evaluate Jeremianic discourse (cf. the sociolinguist M.A.K. Halliday on the social semiotic functions of language). The figure of Jeremiah represents an antisociety, in this case, the Yahweh-alone party. The rhetoric of the text is an antilanguage designed to subvert the dominant ideologies of popular Israelite religion and establish a counter-identity over against them. The scroll of Jeremiah has become a distorting mirror since it misconstrues its ideological opponents in the service of its own cultural interests. The reality it offers us is the projected reality of its agents. The alternative Yahwisms of varying official and popular religion are caricatured in the effort to bolster the 'monist' position. Modern guilds of readers mistake metaphor and myth for social reality where they remain insensitive to the heavily relexicalized prevailing language register at play in the tradition—both newly coined terms and old terms in new contexts.

Ray Person widens this gap between readers in antiquity and those in the present by contrasting the sense of textuality for cultures still predominantly oral versus the highly literate. Examples from the contemporary study of oral traditions (esp. the work of J.M. Foley) provide the comparative analogy for his discussion. The debate between competing models of composition (rolling corpus versus systematic redaction) for Jeremiah is re-evaluated in light of the comparative analogies. The relationship between LXX-Jer and MT-Jer provides the delimiting case. An entire class of textual variants (additions of titles, proper names, adjectives, adverbs, divine names and epithets, standard prophetic formula) are reinterpreted as reflections of the largely oral matrix of the ancient Israelite scribe; in keeping with difference in the *perception of variability* in an oral matrix, the ancient scribe may not have viewed such verbal variants (our perception!) as changes effecting the meaning of the tradition. Units of meaning as perceivable by them allowed for variation within those units. Consequently, Person offers qualified support to McKane's rolling corpus model and more importantly suggests that 'our' sense of arbitrariness, inconsistency and incoherence represents a projection of textuality on the tradition uninformed by an oral mentality.

Roy Wells engages LXX and MT relationships to different ends. He examines the MT rewriting/rereading of Jeremiah 40–44 in order to expose editorial tendencies at play and thus the way in which concrete social realities come to expression in texts. MT rereads its 'finished' form of the Jeremianic tradition; through endorsement, amplification and supplementation it enhances a picture of the complete religious and communal collapse of the remnant of Judah (into which MT manages to include all Diasporan Jewish communities except for the Babylonian groups) and its forfeiture of any claim to land and identity as Israel. Thus Wells detects within the very textual history of the tradition the early stages of an ideological development that accords with Carroll's thesis—that is, that central to the mythic construction of the Bible is ideological concern over land tenure. Any claimants to a future in Palestine other than the Babylonian exiles are effectively erased from the tradition. Wells treats us to a glimpse of an ideological rewriting of the past, to the domestication of the tradition in service of the interests of the present, and to the practice of selective amnesia inscribed into the composition. He thereby offers an additional example in support of Domeris's discovery of the book of Jeremiah as distorting mirror in the interest of social processes of legitimization and critique.

From the reader-centered analyses of Carroll, Domeris and Wells emerges a Jeremiah as an 'unsafe' social symbol whose construction of reality merits a high degree of hermeneutic suspicion. So too Angela Bauer's feminist reading of Jer. 4.29-31 and the construction of women (metaphorical or otherwise) across the book adds to the deconstructionist impulse, latent, at least, if not explicit in these reader-centered readings. Bauer detects traces of female social reality subjected by the tradition to metaphorical reductionism. Polar stereotypes serve rhetorical needs in context of either vilifying or glorifying 'the woman'— depending on the need to legitimize the destruction of Jerusalem or beatify her social restoration. The only desirable 'woman' is the chaste virgin of the inaccessible past or the 'woman' of the not-as-yet-realized future. For the present, the community is embodied in vilified female experience. The shifting polarization of the female stereotypes embodies the shifting theological fate of the community. Bauer raises in this context the problem such metaphorical codes raise for contemporary (readers') retrievals of a biblical theology of Jeremiah (cf. the complementary thesis in the essay by O'Connor and Diamond above).

The five essays introduced in this subsection have taken up the challenge of Jeremiah as a social symbol by configuring readers as ideological agents. In each case, the readers to whom they attend are the diverse historical readers extrinsic to the tradition, whether ancient or modern or both. Among these five, to greater and lesser degrees, socio-historical reconstruction reappears—only now retuned by conversation with contemporary social, cultural and literary theory and method. Each has had to make their turn to reader-centered approaches by looking through the text of Jeremiah as coded social discourse. Thus text-centered strategies insinuate themselves in these reader-centered approaches. And in their way, they represent counter-readings of suspicion to the intertexts provided by Brueggemann and Clements—especially where the latter emphatically practice theological retrieval in their engagement with Jeremiah. But then Walter Brueggemann will want to remind us (justly) that suspicion and retrieval are dialectical practices, intertwined modalities of every reading. Adjudicating the two modalities, it seems, is a question of where a reader needs to get.[5]

But more than extrinsic readers circulate through the Jeremiah tradition. Readers as imaginative constructs inside the world of the text can also be inferred and recovered. A glance back to the papers of the previous section surfaces readings relevant on this score. For example, Lee's excavation of semantic polyphony projects a fictive generic reader sufficiently competent in such subtleties of intertextual play. O'Connor and Diamond detect nuanced figurations of an encoded reader in service to the rhetorical (persuasive) interests of the symbolic grammar operative in the marital imagery. Stulman identifies the so-called 'C' material as an ideological reader who domesticates the poetic tradition to its symbolic regime. In similar fashion, Mary Callaway's paper discerns narrative voices immanent in the 'spaces' between the contradictions transforming the context for reading Jeremianic tradition.

Thus the two sections of essays are porous toward each other in their choice of hermeneutical orientation and reading strategy; the effort to interrupt (if only moderately or temporarily) historical method in order to escape its inadequacies and dead-ins has required a turn both to text-centered and reader-centered hermeneutical paradigms.

Troubling Jeremiah: The Travail of Theology in the De-centering of History

'If I did *fall*,' he went on, '... *The King has promised me—with his very own mouth—*to—to' ...

---

5. Unpublished remarks given at the Composition of the Book of Jeremiah Consultation (SBL/AAR Annual Convention, 1992).

'to send all his horses and all his men,' Alice interrupted ...
(Humpty Dumpty, from *Alice through the Looking Glass*)

The edifice of theological construction dependent upon the foundation of historicist critical method must surely feel itself under severe threat caught as it is within the debates, the hints and allegations, enacted between the modern and its postmodern progeny! So it is fitting that the work of the group should turn to the implications for theological reflection in Jeremiah consequent to new readings, text- and reader-centered in assumption and exegetical practice. What future project for the Yahweh(s) immanent in Jeremiah where reader-centered interpreters might discern in Jeremiah's god-talk discourse masking Israel's negotiations for cultural power, where one group's Yahweh is pitted against another and where text-centered interpreters might discern in the tropes of that talk a symbolic battlefield where 'Yahweh' does not transcend the ontology of Near Eastern divinity? Does Jeremiah's Yahweh become a 'broken cistern' within the plural and fragmented horizons of postmodernity?

To stage the beginnings of conversation on such problems, we offer a panel discussion gathered around Leo Perdue's book *The Collapse of History*,[6] and the implications of that 'collapse' for reading Jeremiah theologically. Perdue summarizes his analysis of contemporary theological strategies and offers a revised though still modernist plea against an uncontrolled, pluralist theological vision. Lawrence Boadt expresses his substantial endorsement of Perdue's thesis with his own plea that the Jeremianic tradition sustained generative power for faith communities by virtue of its rootedness in historical memory. Dennis Olson critiques Perdue's quest for a unifying, transcendent theological criteriology as an unworkable abstraction doing disservice to the (desirable) particularity of localized interpretative communities. Thomas Overholt analyzes Perdue's proposed criteria for the evaluation of biblical theological constructions but finds they do not escape a fundamental and necessary ambiguity thus preventing the privileging of one Old Testament theology over others.

Beyond the theoretical reflections of these panelists, yet troubling them all the same, we offer two experiments in the practice of a

---

6. Leo Perdue, *The Collapse of History: Reconstructing Old Testament Theology* (Minneapolis: Fortress Press, 1994).

theological reading of Jeremiah carried out in the shadow of text- and reader-centered approaches to interpretation.

In the effort to elucidate the canonical shape and the hermeneutic of the canonical process, Walter Brueggemann reads the figure of Baruch (43.1-7) as a cipher and symbol of the extrinsic social voices and interests who have capitalized on Jeremianic Yahwistic poetry. In the figures of 'Jeremiah' and 'Baruch', Brueggemann traces the relationship between a poet whose work is 'metapolitical' and the deeply politically vested 'users' of that poetry. Brueggemann discerns a canonizing process that is deeply ideological in motivation, yet, which cannot be reduced to the service of mere *Realpolitik*, for ideology is deeply implicated in utopian impulses. In Jeremiah's (the scroll) case, 'it is Yahweh's sovereignty that prevails and causes the text to run beyond more managed horizons'. Politics has succumbed to a 'theological vision'.

Kathleen O'Connor analyzes the construction of Yahweh in chs. 2–9 as a non-unified, de-stabilized, 'radically multiple' character negotiated across figures of god as husband, military general and weeping deity. In the latter, O'Connor discerns a semiotics of divine tears that radically deconstructs divine transcendence, impassibility and power.

Postscript

Taken together the essays in this volume press for an end to 'innocent' readings of Jeremiah—that is, to the extent that regnant models prove inadequate for troubling the very Jeremiah they have already helped to reveal. The literary readings press this on traditional historicist approaches, just as the latter had already pressed this on the 'innocence' inhabiting pre-critical readings. And the turn to Jeremiah as a social semiotic discourse presses for an end to 'innocent' biblical theology readings that have companioned historical-critical orthodoxy in one fashion or another. No doubt, one 'innocence' gives way to 'naïveté' yet to be surfaced.

Now whether or not the troubled namesake of this prophetic scroll has been eased by these new approaches remains undecideable. What can be observed, however, is the opening up of new space for troubling the meaningfulness of the Jeremianic corpus.

> 'If there's no meaning in it,' said the King, 'that saves a world of trouble, you know, as we needn't try to find any.'
>
> (*Alice's Adventures in Wonderland*)

Part I

TEXT-CENTERED READINGS OF JEREMIAH

THE PROSE SERMONS AS HERMENEUTICAL GUIDE
TO JEREMIAH 1–25: THE DECONSTRUCTION OF
JUDAH'S SYMBOLIC WORLD[*]

Louis Stulman

The beginning of the modern discussion of the literary and historical problems involved in the composition of the book of Jeremiah is usually associated with the work of B. Duhm[1] and S. Mowinckel.[2] Both Duhm and Mowinckel identified three types of material in the book— two as primary literary strata, poetic oracles and biographical prose, and the third as a later residual or supplementary category. This latter material was identified, primarily by Mowinckel, as prose speeches that reflect a distinctive style, language and structure similar to such rubrics in the Deuteronomistic History and the book of Deuteronomy.

Since the beginning of the present century, scholars have spent considerable time describing the literary character of the prose sermons (the so-called 'C' material) in Jeremiah. In particular, attention has focused on diachronic and historical-critical concerns related to the origins of the prose sermons in Jeremiah's complex history of transmission. Research along these lines is well known and is perhaps still most thoroughly outlined by William Holladay in the second volume of his Hermeneia commentary.[3] In reviewing this history of research one discovers a dearth of significant work on the role and function of the 'C'

*   This essay is an abridged version of Chapter 1, 'A Contextual Reading of the Prose Sermons in Jeremiah 1–25: Death and Dismantling of Judah's Sacred World', in my *Order amid Chaos: Jeremiah as Symbolic Tapestry* (The Biblical Seminar, 57; Sheffield: Sheffield Academic Press, 1998), pp. 23-55.

1.   B. Duhm, *Das Buch Jeremia* (Tübingen: J.C.B. Mohr [Paul Siebeck], 1901).

2.   S. Mowinckel, *Zur Komposition des Buches Jeremia* (Kristiania: Jacob Dybwad, 1914).

3.   W.L. Holladay, *Jeremiah 2: A Commentary on the Book of the Prophet Jeremiah, Chapters 26–52* (Hermeneia; Minneapolis: Fortress Press, 1989), pp. 10-95.

material in the overall structure of the book of Jeremiah.[4] The near consensus of a century of scholarship is that the prose sermons contribute
well to the book's seemingly 'chaotic appearance'.[5] Accordingly, they
have been described as intrusive, extremely disjointed, randomly placed
in their present literary settings, haphazardly located, and scattered
irregularly throughout the book. Such descriptions present the dominant
voice in twentieth-century Jeremiah scholarship.

Speeches or sermons outside Jeremiah, however, have long been recognized as playing a seminal role in Hebrew narrative. They are rarely
present in a book without good contextual and teleological reasons.
They often provide important rhetorical, literary and ideological clues
for understanding narratorial strategies. Prose speeches in the Deuteronomistic History (Dtr), as is well known, mark important transitions in
the work, and they reveal salient points of authorial/textual intention
(*Tendenz*). Over 20 years ago, H.W. Wolff examined the prose
speeches in Dtr to determine the theological or kerygmatic intention of
the editor,[6] though it was M. Noth who first argued that 'at all the
important points in the course of the history, Dtr brings forward the
leading personages with a speech, long or short, which looks forward
and backward in an attempt to interpret the course of events, and draws
the relevant practical conclusions about what people should do'.[7]
E. Janssen's form-critical examination of the prose speeches of Dtr discovered a structural pattern that includes an introduction, recital of
God's acts, a description of disobedience and threats or promises, which
according to Janssen in many respects encapsulates Deuteronomistic
theology.[8]

4.   See for recent review of the history of research, L. Stulman, *The Prose Sermons of the Book of Jeremiah: A Redescription of the Correspondences with the
Deuteronomistic Literature in the Light of Recent Text-Critical Research* (SBLDS,
83; Atlanta: Scholars Press, 1986), pp. 7-32.

5.   J. Bright, *Jeremiah: A New Translation with Introduction and Commentary*
(AB, 21; Garden City, NY: Doubleday, 1965), p. lx.

6.   H.W. Wolff, 'The Kerygma of the Deuteronomic Historical Work', in
W. Brueggemann and H.W. Wolff (eds.), *The Vitality of Old Testament Traditions*
(trans. F.C. Prussner; Atlanta: John Knox Press, 1975), pp. 83-100.

7.   M. Noth, *The Deuteronomistic History* (JSOTSup, 15; Sheffield: JSOT
Press, 1981), p. 5.

8.   E. Janssen, *Juda in der Exilszeit: Ein Beitrag zur Frage der Entstehung des
Judentums* (Göttingen: Vandenhoeck & Ruprecht, 1956), pp. 105-10.

The crucial role played by prose discourses in Dtr and the well-established points of correspondences between Dtr and the prose sermons in Jeremiah elicit further investigation as to whether the latter enjoy strategic and significant locations within the overall structure of Jeremiah.[9] The present contextual reading of chs. 1–25 seeks to elucidate the literary and symbolic function of the Jeremiah prose speeches in the macro-structure of the later and longer Hebrew text (MT).[10] It asks how the so-called 'C' material functions contextually and rhetorically in chs. 1–25. Do these prose sermons make a distinctive ideological/theological contribution to these chapters? If so, do they enjoy a meaningful and teleological presence in the overall structure of Jeremiah 1–25? Furthermore, the present chapter explores the function (not origins) of prose discourse (*Kunstprosa*)[11] in a largely poetic context. Does the shift from prose to poetry (and the reverse) reveal definitional shifts and transformations in social and symbolic meanings? The focus of this essay is not upon the literary growth and development of the prose sermons or the external world in which the material took shape; instead, the text is treated here *as text* giving expression to *its* own focal concerns, dominant attitudes, and functions in the present *Sitz im Buch*.[12]

9. See Stulman, *Prose Sermons*, pp. 7-48.

10. An analysis of the shorter, more pristine LXX and its (reconstructed) LXX *Vorlage* would no doubt yield very important results. While there are several dissenting voices, the common opinion of recent scholarship is that the MT of the book of Jeremiah is only one line of text tradition that can be recovered and that the other line—surviving in a few Hebrew fragments and in the ancient Greek versions—escaped a significant number of expansions that are present in the MT; see Stulman, *Prose Sermons*, pp. 49-118, and the major commentaries on Jeremiah, including R.P. Carroll, *Jeremiah: A Commentary* (OTL; Philadelphia: Westminster Press, 1986); Holladay, *Jeremiah 2*, pp. 2-8; W. McKane, *A Critical and Exegetical Commentary on Jeremiah. I. Introduction and Commentary on Jeremiah I–XXV* (ICC; Edinburgh: T. & T. Clark, 1986).

11. See Helga Weippert, *Die Prosareden des Jeremiabuches* (Berlin: W. de Gruyter, 1973), p. 78.

12. Although the present study attempts to focus upon the present form of the text of Jeremiah, it is nonetheless impossible (or for that matter desirable) to divorce entirely diachronic from synchronic concerns. As such, this chapter accepts as well established, for example, the following 'historical-critical' claims: The prose sermons (1) reflect a distinct genre in the book—set apart from poetic material and perhaps the biographical prose (see M.J. Williams, 'An Investigation of the Legitimacy of Source Distinctions for the Prose Material in Jeremiah', *JBL* 112

Recent Macro-Structural Analyses of Jeremiah 1–25

An examination of the prose sermons *in context* is dependent to a large extent on assessments of the macro-structures of the book itself, and for the purposes of this essay, particularly Jeremiah 1–25. Although it is quite common to hear the book of Jeremiah described as 'a hopeless hodgepodge thrown together without any discernible principle of arrangement at all',[13] large *composite* structures or collections of shorter 'books' have long been recognized. Chapters 46–51, for instance, comprise an intentional corpus of material commonly called the 'Oracles Against the Nations' (henceforth, OAN).[14] In the opinion of many scholars, chs. 37–44 (45) constitute an identifiable literary grouping, although its plot development and storyline are much disputed.[15] Less clear are other macro-units including the so-called 'Book of Consolation' in chs. 30–33[16] or the prose cycle associated with prophets (Jer. 27–29). The first 25 chapters in their present form (Jer. 1.1–25.14 [15–38]) are commonly viewed as a composite macro-unit embracing several long and short groupings each with a complex redaction history. These chapters are often placed under the heading 'Judgment Oracles Against Judah and Jerusalem'.[17]

While the presence of macro-structural units is undeniable, modern

---

[1993], pp. 193-210)—and (2), as a whole, enjoy a relationship that is closer to Dtr than any other prophetic literature. The precise nature of this relationship, however, is fraught with difficulties given the current available data. (3) Moreover, the prose sermons represent a later development of the text, most probably a development of the earlier poetry. Again, the nature of this growth is difficult to ascertain at the present juncture of Jeremiah studies.

13. Bright, *Jeremiah*, p. lvi.

14. See the recent work of Alice Ogden Bellis, *The Structure and Composition of Jeremiah 50.2–51.58* (Lewiston, NY: Edwin Mellen Press, 1995).

15. In this volume, Brueggemann, 'The "Baruch Connection"', pp. 367-86.

16. See the recent work of B.A. Bozak, *Life 'Anew': A Literary-Theological Study of Jer. 30–31* (Rome: Pontificio Istituto Biblico, 1991).

17. See, e.g., W. Rudolph, *Jeremia* (Tübingen: J.C.B. Mohr [Paul Siebeck], 1947), who describes 1–25 as 'Judgment Sayings Against Jerusalem and Judah'; also W. Brueggemann, *To Pluck Up, To Tear Down: A Commentary on the Book of Jeremiah 1–25* (Grand Rapids: Eerdmans; Edinburgh: Handsel Press, 1988), who places the material under the rubric 'The Pluck Up, and Tear Down'; and also D.R. Jones, *Jeremiah* (NCBC; Grand Rapids: Eerdmans, 1992) who employs the title 'Prophetic Criticism and Warnings Against Judah and Jerusalem'.

Jeremiah scholarship has, for the most part, held that these composite blocks of material do not reflect a literary organization that is meaningfully executed.[18] That is to say, the majority holds that the book of Jeremiah is not *readable* in its present forms (MT and LXX). Jeremiah is, as one has recently noted, just 'too bumpy' to be read as a coherent literary piece.[19] McKane has made the most sustained argument for this position. The notion of a rolling *corpus* (always italicized because, according to McKane, it is not a corpus per se) provides the key to McKane's understanding of the compositional history of the book and its resultant forms.[20] By rolling *corpus* he means 'that small pieces of pre-existing text trigger exegesis or commentary. MT is to be understood as a commentary or commentaries built on pre-existing elements of the Jeremianic *corpus*.'[21] As a consequence of this process of 'triggering', the book of Jeremiah in its present shape has a 'piecemeal character'. Accordingly, Jeremiah 1–25 is not a 'well-ordered literary whole, with accumulative teleological significance'.[22] For McKane there is no evidence of a dominant editorial hand with a discernible theological *Tendenz*. Instead, one is confronted with a 'complicated, untidy accu-

---

18. There are a few notable exceptions. See, e.g., the recent work of Brueggemann, 'The "Baruch Connection"'; R.E. Clements, 'Jeremiah 1–25 and the Deuteronomistic History', in A.G. Auld (ed.), *Understanding Poets and Prophets: Essays in Honor of George Wishart Anderson* (JSOTSup, 152; Sheffield: Sheffield Academic Press, 1993), pp. 93-113; A.R. Diamond, *The Confessions of Jeremiah in Context: Scenes of Prophetic Drama* (JSOTSup, 45; Sheffield: JSOT Press, 1987); K.M. O'Connor, *The Confessions of Jeremiah: Their Interpretation and Role in Chapters 1–25* (SBLDS, 94; Atlanta: Scholars Press, 1988); M.S. Smith, *The Laments of Jeremiah and their Contexts: A Literary and Redactional Study of Jeremiah 11–20* (SBLMS, 42; Atlanta: Scholars Press, 1990); and R.R. Wilson, 'Poetry and Prose in the Book of Jeremiah', in Robert Chazan *et al.* (eds.), *Ki Baruch Hu: Ancient Near Eastern-Biblical and Judaic Studies in Honor of Baruch A. Levine* (Winona Lake, IN: Eisenbrauns, forthcoming). All have examined sections of the book of Jeremiah and argued for a purposeful editorial hand.

19. E.F. Campbell, 'Relishing the Bible as Literature and History', *Christian Century* 109 (1992), pp. 812-15. In his review of R. Alter's *The World of Biblical Literature*, Campbell argues that attempts to arrive at literary coherence sometimes do violence to the inherent tensions in the biblical text which is 'intentionally not coherent' (p. 814).

20. McKane, *Jeremiah*, I.

21. McKane, *Jeremiah*, I, p. lxxxiii.

22. McKane, *Jeremiah*, I, p. li.

mulation of material, extending over a very long period and to which many people have contributed'.[23]

McKane's starting point is the conviction that the short piece of poetry lies at the very center of the exegetical task. Prophetic *speech* or oral discourse is assumed as the primary locus of interpretation. With this assumption, McKane follows the lead of modern research on the prophets in giving speech precedence over writing. R.E. Clements notes in this regard that 'the goal of critical interpretation ever since the work of J.G. Herder and J.G. Eichhorn has been to "hear" the word of prophecy as it was originally proclaimed'.[24] While it is probably true that oracular speech is the 'essence of prophecy',[25] prophetic texts in the Bible have been preserved as *literature* and not merely as discrete oracular discourse (see, for instance, the neo-Assyrian oracle texts or prophetic texts from Mari). The movement from orality to writing has removed prophecy from its original settings in life (*Sitze im Leben*) and recontextualized it in literary settings (*Sitze im Buch*). Clements has argued convincingly that the 'complexity of this transition from orality to literacy is everywhere evident in the prophetic writings of the Old Testament, and it is vitally important to reflect that such a collection of written prophecy is a unique legacy from the ancient world'.[26]

The implications of the transition from orality to writings are complex and wide-ranging and well beyond the scope of this essay. For our purposes, however, I suggest only that the present shape of these texts bears witness to (1) a wide range of hermeneutical strategies that are not governed primarily by referential or mimetic restraints, as well as (2) a resultant literary organization that often conveys some final theological *Tendenz*.

23. McKane, *Jeremiah*, I, p. xlviii.

24. R.E. Clements, 'Prophecy as Literature: A Re-Appraisal', in D.G. Miller (ed.), *The Hermeneutical Quest: Essays in Honor of James Luther Mays on his Sixty-Fifth Birthday* (Allison Park, PA: Pickwick Press, 1986), pp. 59-76 (59). See also E.W. Conrad's *Reading Isaiah* (Philadelphia: Fortress Press, 1991), pp. 3-33, for an excellent discussion of the interpretive strategies shared by historical-critical scholarship, especially as these strategies pertain to Isaiah studies.

25. R.P. Carroll, 'Prophecy and Society', in R.E. Clements (ed.), *The World of Ancient Israel: Sociological, Anthropological and Political Perspectives* (Cambridge: Cambridge University Press, 1989), pp. 203-25 (207).

26. R.E. Clements, 'Israel in its Historical and Cultural Setting', in *idem* (ed.), *The World of Ancient Israel: Sociological, Anthropological and Political Perspectives* (Cambridge: Cambridge University Press, 1989), pp. 3-16 (13).

One might note in this regard the 'historical' introductions and salvific endings present in most prophetic writings. In addition to introducing speaker, setting and familial background, editorial colophons, for example, often locate oracular speech and other prophetic genres within a carefully designed 'theology of history' frame of reference. These superscriptions present the divine world invading space and time to reveal the divine will and purpose to a particular target audience. That is to say, the headings introduce God as One who is actively involved in world affairs. Salvific words at the end of many prophetic books, among other things, seem to serve as *heilsgeschichtliche* (salvation-historical) alternatives for later readers who stand chronologically at some distance from the historical perimeters of the earliest oral or written community.[27] Beginnings and endings of prophetic books are only two indications that such writings are not simply collections of oral (or, written) materials preserved in a disinterested manner or only for referential interests; instead, they reflect a wide range of ideological strategies, complex structural patterning, and the hermeneutical process of reinterpretation and adaptation.[28] Whether attempting to authorize changes in existing systems of control, prove the authenticity of a prophet, or validate apparent incongruities in prophecies,[29] the process of literary development was apparently purposeful and 'technological'[30]—an effort to recast the *traditum* to address the matrix of needs,

27. See Stulman, *Order amid Chaos*, pp. 115-19.

28. See, e.g., the work of R.E. Clements, 'Jeremiah 1–25', pp. 93-113; B.S. Childs, *Introduction to the Old Testament as Scripture* (Philadelphia: Fortress Press, 1979), pp. 46-106; C.R. Seitz, *Isaiah 1–39, Interpretation: A Bible Commentary for Teaching and Preaching* (Atlanta: John Knox Press, 1993).

29. See Brian Peckham, *History and Prophecy: The Development of Late Judean Literary Traditions* (Garden City, NY: Doubleday, 1993), p. 301.

30. G. Baumann, *The Written Word: Literacy in Transition* (Oxford: Clarendon Press, 1986). Contemporary studies of language such as Baumann's have made us more aware that the transition from orality to writing involves symbolic shifts and transformations. 'Writing is a technology that restructures thought. Writing is not merely an exterior tool, but a practice that alters human consciousness to the degree to which it is..."interiorized"' (*The Written Word*, p. 3). For an incisive treatment of the oral and written word in ancient Israel, see Susan Niditch, *Oral World and Written Word: Ancient Israelite Literature* (Louisville, KY: Westminster/John Knox Press, 1996).

focal concerns, and imaginative possibilities (and impossibilities) of subsequent communities.[31]

Following the direction of contemporary scholarship, which has in recent years become increasingly attentive to the importance of the shift from orality to writing for the overall structure of prophetic writings, C.R. Seitz has made a persuasive case that the book of Jeremiah is itself amenable to final form readings. He understands the literary structure of Jeremiah to be meaningfully executed, with the intention of giving some final theological message. Seitz has suggested that a Deuteronomic representation of Moses as the 'first' prophet 'amidst the wilderness generation provides the major thematic force at work on the final redactors of the Book of Jeremiah'.[32]

Convinced that McKane's idea of a rolling *corpus* leaves the actual ordering of the material too much to a random (or accidental) process, Clements has also discerned clear signs of structural units within the book, especially within chs. 1–25. Without supposing that these larger

---

31. As P.R. Ackroyd describes it, the Old Testament is witness to 'the living application of the recognized word of God…to the ever new needs of a community sensitive to the vitality of that word' ('The Vitality of the Word of God in the Old Testament', *ASTI* 1 [1962], pp. 7-23). Clements observes in this regard that 'in preserving a collection of written prophecies, the scribes and editors who have done so were endeavoring to serve a wider range of concerns and religious purposes than simply to observe a kind of biographical exactitude which ensured that each literary unit matched precisely the occasion in the prophet's activity in which it had originated' (Clements, 'Prophecy as Literature', p. 72). The 'written' text was involved in a long and varied process of transmission in which the authoritative *traditum* and its network of meanings were employed to address and engage the particular network of meanings present in subsequent communities. Somewhat differently, Fishbane notes that 'inner-biblical exegesis…takes the stabilized literary formulation as its basis and point of departure' (M. Fishbane, *Biblical Interpretation in Ancient Israel* [Oxford: Clarendon Press; New York: Oxford University Press, 1985], p. 7). Unlike tradition-history criticism which moves from the written sources to the oral traditions, 'inner-biblical exegesis starts with the received Scripture and moves forward to the interpretations based on it' (Fishbane, *Biblical Interpretation in Ancient Israel*, p. 7). Likewise, Childs suggests that 'the heart of the canonical process lay in transmitting and ordering the authoritative tradition in a form which was compatible to function as scripture for a generation which had not participated in the original events of revelation' (Childs, *Introduction to the Old Testament as Scripture*, p. 60).

32. C.R. Seitz, 'The Prophet Moses and the Canonical Shape of Jeremiah', *ZAW* 101 (1989), pp. 3-27 (27).

ideological blocks of material were always evident and left undisturbed, he suggests that the final shaping of chs. 1–25 has been organized with a discernible theological design. Clements contends that the macro-structures of Jeremiah 1–25 correspond very closely to the Deuter-onomistic reflection on the downfall of the Northern Kingdom in 2 Kgs 17.7-23 (which, of course, is a principal homily in Dtr according to Martin Noth in *The Deuteronomistic History*), with its distinctive emphasis upon the role of the prophet as mediator of the covenant, and Israel's rejection of this prophetic mediation.[33] Marked off by the opening section in Jer. 1.1-19 (an introductory call and commissioning of the prophet) and the concluding section in Jer. 25.1-14 (a synopsis of Jeremiah's prophecies [esp. vv. 3-7]), the large composite structures of Jeremiah 1–25 which correspond to Dtr, and specifically to 2 Kgs 17.7-23, are as follows:

1. Jer. 2.1–6.30: Judah's Culpability is Greater than Israel's.
2. Jer. 7.1–10.16: An Accusation of Idolatry and the Predicted Destruction of the Jerusalem Temple.
3. Jer. 11.1–20.18: Judah's Rejection of Jeremiah as God's Covenant Mediator and its Consequence.
4. Jer. 21.1–24.10: The Condemnation of the Davidic Dynasty for Breach of Covenant: A Conditional Interpretation of the Royal Office.[34]

Here Clements breaks new ground. He works with *both* structural arti-fices and intentional ideological strategies. The Dtr editor of Jeremiah, according to him, has not simply parroted well-established Deuterono-mistic themes but has in effect employed the shaping of these macro-units for 'accommodating, interpreting and applying Jeremiah's prophe-cies'[35] to a different network of meaning present in subsequent communities.

While Clements may overread some of the incongruities present in the extant text, the basic outline of his structural analysis is argued cogently and serves as the point of departure for the present study. Clements (with others) is clearly correct in seeing chs. 1 and 25 as an

33. Clements, 'Jeremiah 1–25', pp. 94-95, 107-108.
34. Clements, 'Jeremiah 1–25', pp. 94-107.
35. Clements, 'Jeremiah 1–25', p. 108.

editorial framework for Jeremiah 1–25.[36] Moreover, he has made a strong case for his four major composite divisions. The present study, however, follows a slightly different division of macro-structural units in Jeremiah 1–25 and a distinct reading of the material. It suggests that the first 25 chapters of the book map out the dismantling of Judah's symbolic universe, that is, its basic perception of life and reality.

Jer. 1–25: The Dismantling of Judah's 'First Principles'

Jer. 1.1-19: The Functional Introduction: God's Sovereign Plan Regarding Judah's Newly Defined Place Among the Nations

Jer. 2.1–6.30: Macro-Unit One. Judah's Departure From Yahweh: The Basis for Guilt and Penalty of Death

Jer. 7.1–10.1-25: Macro-Unit Two. Dismantling of Temple Ideology

Jer. 11.1–17.27: Macro-Unit Three. Dismantling of Covenant Ideology

Jer. 18.1–20.18: Macro-Unit Four. Dismantling of Insider–Outsider Understandings

Jer. 1.1–24.10: Macro-Unit Five. Dismantling of Royal Ideology

Jer. 25.1-38: The Functional Closure: The Fulfillment of God's Sovereign Plan Regarding Judah's Newly Defined Place among the Nations

The primary difference between Clements's structural analysis and the one proposed in this study revolves around the way Jer. 11.1–20.18 is treated. Whereas Clements reads this unit as a distinct macro-structural unit with its own integrity, I see Jer. 11.1–20.18 as comprised of two distinct (but integrally related) units. This particular reading is based on the following observations: (1) Jer. 7.1; 11.1; 18.1; 21.1 constitute the most basic indicators of structural divisions for Jeremiah 1–25 and as such should be treated as having their own integrity; (2) Jer. 7.1–8.3; 11.1-17; 21.1-10; and 18.1-12 share the rubric, 'The word that came to Jeremiah from Yahweh' (הדבר אשר היה אל ירמיהו מאת יהוה), the distinctive prose style and diction akin to Dtr, as well as a corresponding literary structure.[37] (3) Jer. 7.1–8.3; 11.1-17; 21.1-10, and Jer. 18.1-10

---

36. See also T.R. Hobbs, 'Some Remarks on the Composition and Structure of the Book of Jeremiah', *CBQ* 34 (1972), pp. 257-75.

37. This structure includes an introductory word from Yahweh (7.1; 11.1; 18.1;

serve an analogous literary and symbolic function in the *Sitz im Buch*. As for this latter point, it is necessary only to say here that these prose speeches function as an internal reading map for chs. 1–25. Finally, it is worth noting that this assignment of texts—Jer. 7.1–8.3; 11.1-17; 18.1-12; 21.1-10—as markers of each macro-unit, is essentially identical to that of Mowinckel's 'C' stratum; it is slightly smaller than Rudolph's, and somewhat larger than others. Consequently, the structural organization proposed here fits well within the contours of modern Jeremiah scholarship.

I agree with Seitz and Clements, therefore, that Jeremiah 1–25 is amenable to final form readings and does not reflect a random placement of materials. However, I wish to show that it is the so-called 'C' material, the prose sermons, and the introductory and concluding chapters of Jeremiah 1–25, that provide the ideological grid and the narratorial structure for this composition executed with the intent to convey a final theological message.

The Prose Framework of Chapters 1–25

In order to clarify this narratorial edifice and its significance I now turn to an examination of Jeremiah 1 and 25, which perform a clear and discernible purpose in the overall structure of the book. Chapters 1 and 25 provide the functional framework to Jeremiah 1–25—the so-called 'first scroll'.[38] Chapter 1 serves as an introduction to the book by presenting its major themes in cryptic and anticipatory terms.[39] Chapter 25 brings closure to the 'corpus' by poignantly announcing the fulfillment of Yahweh's word and its devastating effects upon Judah and all

---

21.1), an imperative addressed to the prophet to act or speak (7.2; 11.2; 18.2; 21.2), and the content of the action or message communicated (7.3-15; 11.3-13; 18.5-11; 21.3-7).

38. See K.M. O'Connor, 'Do Not Trim a Word: The Contribution of Chapter 26 to the Book of Jeremiah', *CBQ* 51 (1989), pp. 617-30. My reference to 'first scroll' is not to be taken as an allusion to a possible *Urrolle* associated with the story in Jer. 36. I would suggest, however, that at some point in the development of the text the broad outlines of Jer. 1–25 may have enjoyed an existence independent of Jer. 26–52.

39. See O'Connor, *The Confessions of Jeremiah*, pp. 118-23; E.W. Nicholson, *Preaching to the Exiles: A Study of the Prose Tradition in the Book of Jeremiah* (New York: Schocken Books, 1970), pp. 113-15. See also the commentaries of Brueggemann, Carroll and McKane for a similar view.

nations. Together they provide a temporal edifice for the punctiliar poetry (and prose) of chs. 2–24. Accordingly, the poetry and prose sections are presented within a structured pattern of history that is governed by Yahweh's controlling goal: the realization of God's just rule over the nations through and in spite of Babylonian subjugation and control.

Chapter 1 and its superscription employ temporal and spatial categories to focus on the onslaught of the word of Yahweh. As the book's point of departure, the introductory heading (vv. 1-3) affirms that Yahweh's potent word 'impinges upon the royal reality'[40] during a period of great turmoil and upheaval, as Judah's kingdom (associated in the first place with the reign of Josiah) and its domain assumptions begin to unravel and disintegrate.

The call or ordination report proper (vv. 4-10) takes shape as a rather simple account of the reception of the word of Yahweh which gives birth to the mission and destiny of Jeremiah. This passage presents Jeremiah as one who is chosen (before [his] time) to be instrumental in God's predetermined program for the nations. His role and function as prophet extend beyond national boundaries, as do the sovereign purposes of God (vv. 5, 10). Furthermore, the word placed in the mouth of the prophet by God (in v. 9) apparently functions as a sign demonstrating both the empowerment and election of Jeremiah and the divine authority of the 'book'.[41]

With the reception of the word comes the summary of the written tradition's major motifs—'to pluck up and to pull down [to destroy and to overthrow], to build and to plant' (v. 10bc) (see also in the prose sections 1.14-17; 18.7-10; 24.5-7), followed by the assurance that God will fulfill the dynamic prophetic word (vv. 11-12). The chapter continues with a holy convocation of northern forces—couched in cryptic language—ushering in disaster on account of Judah's infidelity and idolatry (vv. 13-16). Jeremiah, moreover, is warned that he too should prepare for war; however, unlike Judah, his enemies will originate from inside the boundaries and the combat be waged by the established social and religious hierarchy—bad insiders (vv. 17-19). Notwithstanding the

---

40. Brueggemann, *To Pluck Up, To Tear Down*, p. 21.

41. Nicholson and others have observed that the call narrative is shaped by the 'deuteronomistic conception of the role and function of prophecy in Israel' (*Preaching*, p. 115), thus representing Jeremiah as a spokesperson who stands in the prophetic succession which originated with Moses, the prophet *par excellence*.

onslaught of internal forces, the prophet is not to fear, for he is given
the assurance of the divine presence (vv. 8, 19) amid the hostility and
dissolution of Jerusalem.

Emerging from the introductory chapter, therefore, are motifs that are
not only present in chs. 1–25 but are their principal reference points.
That is to say, ch. 1 reads as a thematic microcosm of the first scroll. It
includes the following motifs: the proclamation of the word of Yahweh
by one who is a 'prophet like Moses', the reliability of this word and its
assertion of God's sovereign rule over Judah and all nations (i.e. the
claim that geopolitics is governed by God and not human ingenuity and
power), the rejection of the prophetic message and the resultant dismantling of all social and symbolic supports by a northern barbarian, a
war waged against Jeremiah from within by the upper tiers of the social
hierarchy, and the cryptic hope of salvation in the midst of the destruction and undoing of all social and symbolic supports. All of these
motifs foreshadow and encapsulate the dominant literary themes that
are located in the first part of the book.

Jeremiah 25 closes the *written account* of the first phase of Jeremiah's public life. Not unlike ch. 1, the text presents the word coming
to the prophet at a most critical juncture of Judah's conceptual world: at
the end of one epoch—the crumbling of the state with its established
domain assumptions—and at the beginning of another, in which Judah
is now a displaced or dislocated community within the great neo-
Babylonian empire. The chapter takes shape as a 'textual' synopsis of
Jeremiah's oracles and Judah's ill-fated history. 'For twenty-three
years, from the thirteenth year of King Josiah son of Amon of Judah, to
this day, the word of Yahweh has come to me, and I have spoken
persistently to you, but you have not listened' (v. 3). Here the amalgam
of voices from chs. 2–24 converge and speak with utter perspicuity that
the end of Judah's symbol and social system is the culminating result of
an entire history of obduracy and disobedience to prophetic words.
With one bold stroke 23 years of prophetic speech are reduced to 'not
hearing' (שמעו לא). Judah has refused the invitation to 'return' (שוב)—
an invitation previously accompanied by the prospect of continued land
occupation—and as a result is rejected by Yahweh, redefined, and
reduced to the status of vassalage. With the same stroke Jeremiah is
vindicated as a true prophet: while his message goes unheeded, his
written words are nonetheless fulfilled (Deut. 18.22; Jer. 25.13). Verses
1-7 in particular accentuate collective blame and prophetic vindication.

The remainder of the chapter describes the newly emergent world imagined by the text. First, Judah's status as a privileged people is radically redefined. Judah is now placed alongside and actually in front of all the rejected nations that must drink Yahweh's cup of wrath (25.15-18). As a result, it is to be without land and king and subservient to Babylon and its ruler. Second, it becomes clear that the cryptic reference to disaster from the north (in ch. 1) is now manifest in the person of King Nebuchadrezzar, who, although 'speechless' and underdeveloped in character presentation, enjoys the honored title 'servant of Yahweh' (עבד יהוה in v. 9). (In the MT the reference to the 'fourth year of Jehoiakim' is almost eclipsed by the appositional 'the first year of Nebuchadrezzar of Babylon.') However, not unlike the domestication of Pharaoh (see Exod. 1–15), the king of Babylon is thoroughly tamed and subjugated, he is depicted as Yahweh's vassal who is instrumental *only* in establishing moral symmetry and retributive justice for Judah. Nebuchadrezzar's rule and Babylonian hegemony are merely theopolitical realities demonstrating the sovereign rule of Yahweh. Third, the text's coherent symbol system cannot tolerate Babylon, the symbol of raw and indiscriminate power, to go unchecked and unpunished. Consequently, God's moral judgment is also directed against Babylon and its king. 'I am going to punish the king of Babylon and that nation, the land of the Chaldeans, for their iniquity, says the Lord, making the land an everlasting waste' (v. 13). The king of Babylon will be the last to drink from the wrathful cup in Yahweh's hand (v. 26). The great *imperium* of Babylonia will end in ruin, as did Judah's own little regime (proleptically in 626; see v. 3); indeed every idolatrous nation must drink from the cup of Yahweh's anger, for God alone is supreme ruler. Chapter 25, thus, heralds God's rule over all nations; and Jeremiah emerges in this symbol system as the 'prophet to the nations' (1.5), balancing and filling in the cryptic ideological gaps of ch. 1.

Chapters 1 and 25, therefore, serve as 'bookends' that proclaim in bold and unflinching terms the reign of God over Judah and all nations. As such, these framing chapters apparently function as an interpretive guide that establishes congruent and symmetrical arrangements for the reader. While providing textual validation for the prophetic word, Jeremiah 1 and 25 demonstrate that written (and oral) prophecy opens the geopolitical arena to new and transcendent understandings of reality beyond ordinary spatial and temporal categories.

*The Function and Theological Contribution of the Prose Sermons
in Chapters 1–25: A Contextual Reading*

Jeremiah 1 and 25 frame five macro-structural units, of which four are introduced by prose sermons ('C' material). The only exception (Jer. 2–6) is the poetic introduction to the first scroll which apparently serves to establish the charge of guilt and the penalty of death. The goal of this section is to identify the literary structure of each of the five units with special attention given to the function and theological contribution of the prose speeches in context.

*The Poetic Introduction, Jeremiah 2–6: The First Macro-Structural
Unit*
Jeremiah 2–6 has long been recognized as a composite macro-structural unit with a probably long and complex redaction history. This large block is introduced in ch. 2 with a calculated and somewhat dispassionate indictment against Judah and Jerusalem for infidelity and apostasy. The introductory chapter, often referred to as a lawsuit oracle, is a reasoned apology for Yahweh's innocence and Jerusalem's culpability (2.1). Yahweh is faithful husband and provider; betrayer Israel is a faithless bride, a stubborn beast, a wild vine, a guilt-stained person, a wild ass in heat (2.20-25).

As the indictments develop in Jer. 3.1–4.4, they become more scathing and passionate. The prophetic speech portrays the depth of Judah's guilt and depravity, which is often defined as cultic abuse. The nation is accused of engaging in practices that are understood to be the worst sort of violation of the religious order (note, e.g., the priestly language employed in this section: 'pollute', 'bare heights', 'abominations', 'circumcise', 'god of shame'). In this jumbled and 'messy' literary and symbolic world, Yahweh responds to betrayal as a devastated and distraught lover (reminiscent of the image of God in Hosea). Pulsating with passion and throbbing with pain, Yahweh longs for reunion and embrace (chs. 3–4) while lashing out in rage and vengeance (chs. 5–6). The language of shame, the dark and terrible musings of death, still mingled with longing and imagined hope (e.g. 3.22b-23), is voiced with force and pathos.

In Jer. 4.5–6.30 imagined hope and (missed) opportunities give way to destruction, devastation and total abrogation of Judah's symbolic world and social order (see, e.g., the images of chaos, mourning, darkness, invading barbarians, labor pains in 4.23-31). Yahweh declares war and becomes Judah's adversary. As a result, disaster and death loom on the horizon, the inescapable and total dismantling of life and all infrastructural supports. Invasion and the ravaging effects of war are depicted poignantly. Duhm was certainly correct that these early chapters are grounded in danger and the dirge. Notwithstanding the language of siege and imminent disaster (רעה), Judah remains stubborn, smug and secure (e.g. 5.20-24; 6.10-12; 6.13-17).

A Contextual Reading of Jeremiah 7.1–8.3: The Second Macro-Structural Unit, Jeremiah 7.1–10.25

Jeremiah 7.1–8.3—a composite block of prose material with a complex history of composition that is held together by its attention to cultic abuses—is often viewed as intrusive and disruptive to its poetic setting. Consequently, the pericope is frequently interpreted as a part of the scattered Deuteronomistic 'C' material rather than as indispensable to its immediate literary environment, and there is certainly good reason for such readings.

The picture of Judah that emerges from 7.1-15 is a radical departure from that drawn in the preceding chapters. In the first macro-block of poetry, Judah (Jer. 2–6) is depicted as having totally abandoned Yahweh for other gods, which then becomes the basis for the charge of guilt and penalty of death. In the so-called 'Temple Sermon', the Judah portrayed by the text is one that clings tenaciously to the Jerusalem temple (MT) and its cultus and not to 'other gods' (אלהים אחרים) for life and security (see, however, Jer. 7.9).

A contextual reading, however, would suggest little disparity. Jeremiah 7.1-15 is a prose homily using the preceding poetry as subtext. This prose pericope comments on and must be read as a response to Jeremiah 2–6. In the sermon we discover that the confidence and smugness exuded by Judah in chs. 2–6 derives in part from its temple ideology. That is to say, the picture emerging from this prose 'commentary' is that of Judah using the temple *as a sanctuary from the devastating indictment pronounced in chs. 2–6.*

> Do not rely upon deceptive words such as,
> 'This the temple of Yahweh, the temple of Yahweh,
> the temple of Yahweh...
> Will you steal, murder, commit adultery, swear falsely,
> burn incense to Baal, and go after other gods whom you
> do not know? And then will you come and stand before me in this

house by which my name is called, and say, "We have sanctuary",
so that we can do all these abominations?' (Jer. 7.4, 9-10).

In the temple precincts, the community seeks shelter and protection
from Yahweh who has become its dangerous adversary. With considerable force, the prose sermon shows the absurdity and futility of
such attempts. 'You know, I, too, am watching, says Yahweh' (v. 11b).
Attempts to circumvent Yahweh's sovereign word and the resultant
redefinition of Judah's status are doomed to failure. Loss of land and
shrine are imagined as approaching shifts in the symbolic arrangements
of the universe. Even the great Jerusalem temple and its ideological grid
of invincibility cannot save the people from imminent disaster (vv. 1-
15); nor can the intercession of the prophet (vv. 16-20; 11.14; 15.1).
There is indeed 'no mercy for Judah this side of judgment'.[42]

As midrash, or commentary, on the preceding collection of oracles,
Jer. 7.1–8.3 not only summarizes 'the early oracles by way of focusing
on the cult and denouncing the practices found there',[43] but also punc-
tuates and reperforms the poetry. This reperformance occurs as the
polyphonic and dissonant poetry is sublimated by univocal and congruent prose.[44] In the prose homily, for example, it becomes crystal clear
that (1) Judah's cultic behavior is reprehensible, a cardinal violation of
its internal boundaries and symbol system, and that (2) the community's culpability is evident at present (7.8-20) and throughout holy
history (7.21-26). Moreover, it also becomes evident that (3) Yahweh is
an 'untamed' and dangerous reality that can neither be controlled nor
manipulated by Judah's games (see 7.1-15 esp.). Therefore, (4) as a
result, the death and dismantling of Judah's old social system and hierarchical arrangements—*particularly those associated with Judah's temple ideology*—are absolutely necessary and inevitable.[45]

42. J.G. McConville, *Judgment and Promise: An Interpretation of the Book of
Jeremiah* (Winona Lake, IN: Eisenbrauns, 1993), p. 51.

43. Carroll, *From Chaos to Covenant*, p. 84.

44. Rather than viewing this and other prose sermons as adaptation (or reperformance) with an integrity of their own, Duhm, Mowinckel, Hyatt and Rudolph (to
a lesser degree) all treat the 'C' materials with some disdain. Thus, Mowinckel
could assert, for instance, that Jeremiah is transformed into *Schattfigur* (shadowy
figure) by the Deuteronomistic writer (Mowinckel, *Komposition*, p. 22).

45. 'The function of the material collected and presented in 7.1–8.3 is to show
the cultic behaviour of the Jerusalem community to have been so corrupt that the

Jeremiah 7.1–8.3 functions not only as midrash on chs. 2–6 but also chs. 8–10. The prose discourse serves as a seam or hinge holding together the two mostly poetic blocks of material. This pivotal role is possible largely because chs. 2–6 and chs. 8–10 share many of the same images and motifs. The major part of this poetry depicts Judah as a desperate and faithless community engaged in false worship and on its way to death. Moreover, it 'demonstrates that Judah, and not Yahweh, is guilty of abandoning covenant. As a result, judgment will come, either in the form of invasion, destruction and death, or exile.'[46]

Jeremiah 7.29–8.3 depicts Judah's guilt in the most gruesome light and the resultant divine judgment with graphic and grotesque imagery. Consequently, the pericope sets the panic-stricken topos for Jeremiah 8–10.

> Hear, O women, the word of Yahweh,
> listen to the word of my mouth;
> teach your daughters a dirge,
> and every neighbor a lament.
> For death has come up to our window,
> and it has entered our palaces,
> to cut off the children from the streets,
> and the young men from the squares.
> Speak! Thus says Yahweh,
> the corpses of men shall fall
> like dung in the field
> like sheaves behind the reaper,
> with no one gathering them (Jer. 9.19-21).

As death draws closer, the poetry becomes more jumbled and the voices more blurred. With Yahweh and Jeremiah, Judah is now a grief-stricken participant in the dialog (see, e.g., 8.14-17). Although there are still traces of indifference and confidence (8.4-9), the voices of fear, pain and profound sadness converge with force at the certain prospect of Judah's downfall.

> Why should we sit still?
> Assemble together; let us go to the fortified
> cities and be silent there;
> for Yahweh our God has silenced us by giving us

---

destruction of city and people was entirely justified' (Carroll, *From Chaos to Covenant*, p. 90).

46. Brueggemann, *To Pluck Up, To Tear Down*, p. 82.

poisoned water to drink,
because we have sinned against Yahweh (Jer. 8.14).

My joy is gone, grief has overwhelmed me,
my heart is sick (Jer. 8.18).

Only Jer. 10.1-16 interrupts this language of siege and desperation. This poem is almost always seen as intrusive and more congruent with the *Weltanschauung* (world-view) of 2 Isaiah than that of the book of Jeremiah.[47] While admittedly its ideological world is (most likely later and) different than that of the rest of Jeremiah, it has been appended to Jer. 7.1–9.26 and perhaps Jer. 1.1–9.26 with a discernible literary-theological purpose. Against the turbulent and dangerous geopolitical terrain—which Judah might be tempted to interpret as evidence of an abrogation of Yahweh's power—this appendix celebrates in liturgical form the absolute sovereign rule of Yahweh over all nations and the utter impotence (הבל in vv. 3, 8, 15) and falsehood (שקר in v. 14) of their symbol systems.[48] It proclaims Yahweh as the incomparable 'king of the nations' (מלך הגוים in v. 7) in whom trust is due. In contrast, the gods of the nations are said to be unable to 'speak, walk, or do either harm or good' (see v. 5); they are nothing, impotent, and not to be trusted. Yahweh is heralded as the one in control of Judah's destiny as well as that of the nations.

Such discourse echoes the rhetoric of chs. 1, 7 and 25. First, as is apparent in chs. 1 and 25, Jeremiah 10 affirms that Yahweh's sovereign rule extends over Judah and the nations (see, e.g., the remarkably high concentration of the word גוי in 1.5, 10; 25.11, 12, 13, 14, 15; 10.2, 7, 10; cf. 10.25). This poem, not unlike the concluding chapter (25) of the first scroll, focuses attention on the broad theopolitical terrain and intimates that Judah's destruction has nothing at all to do with the ravaging and invading nations and their gods: instead it has everything to do with Yahweh, 'the true God', ' the living God', ' the everlasting God' whose wrath rocks the earth (v. 10). Second, the polemic against the gods of the nations parallels the indictment against Judah for its reliance on the temple and its cultus in ch. 7. Both the idols of the nations and Judah's trust in the temple are considered 'falsehood' (שקר, 10.14 and 7.4, 8). The temple and its ideological constructions, like those of the nations

---

47. Carroll, *Jeremiah*, pp. 252-59.
48. Brueggemann has called Jer. 10.1-16 'a litany of contrasts between the true God and false gods' (*To Pluck Up, To Tear Down*, p. 98).

(10.2-3), are unreliable and unable to save Judah from the God who refuses to don the straitjacket of perverse and controlling systems. Indigenous and foreign cults alike serve as foil for the supremacy of Yahweh.

A Contextual Reading of Jeremiah 11.1-17: The Third Macro-Structural Unit, Jeremiah 11.1–17.27
Jeremiah 11.1–17.27 forms another long composite unit comprised of poetic and prose material, including three of the five main Jeremianic Confessions. It is noteworthy that this section is bracketed by prose discourses—addressed to the 'people of Judah and those who live in Jerusalem' (11.2, 17.20, although the latter includes מלכי יהודה)—which serve as a midrash on covenant-observance (Jer. 11.1-13, 17.19-27). As such, these prose sermons provide a covenant framework for the macro-unit as a whole.[49]

This framework, which portrays Jeremiah as covenant mediator, serves at least two contextual functions. First, as introduction, Jer. 11.1-17 sets the portentous tone for the unit by invoking a Deuteronomic curse upon those who are disobedient to the covenant and by integrally relating continued land-occupation and the election tradition to obedience (vv. 3-5; cf. 17.27). As noted by Holladay and O'Connor, Jeremiah's recital of a Deuteronomic curse formula ominously prefigures the future fate of Judah.[50] Jeremiah again proclaims that the present community is no better than the ancestral community (see 7.21-26): both are guilty of covenant-breaking and both must suffer the consequences for non-compliance (11.8, 11). Jeremiah insists, therefore, that the Sinai covenant (or prophetic intercession [v. 14]) cannot avert the threat of imminent 'disaster' (רעה in vv. 11, 12, 14, 17 [twice]). Like the temple, the 'covenant' (ברית הזאת) cannot save the community from a radical redefinition of status required by exile. The text destabilizes and ultimately deals a death-blow to any hope for protection and security associated with covenant ideology. Instead, the presentation of covenant in this introductory prose sermon serves as an apology for

49. This macro-unit has received extensive contextualized treatment by Diamond, *The Confessions of Jeremiah*; W.L. Holladay, *The Architecture of Jeremiah 1–20* (Lewisburg: Bucknell University, 1976); O'Connor, *The Confessions of Jeremiah*.
50. See Holladay, *Architecture*, pp. 160-62; and O'Connor, *The Confessions of Jeremiah*, p. 131.

Yahweh's righteous acts in light of Judah's blatant failure.

Second, the prose framework brings literary coherence to intermediate chapters laden with anomie and dissymmetry. Chapters 12–17 are replete with images of war and devastation: drought, hunger, dishonored death, rape and utter hopelessness. The voice of the dirge—now rarely mingled with hope—is deafening. God laments over the ravaging of Judah (12.7-13). Judah laments over its inevitable fate (14.1-9). And Jeremiah laments over his own painful ordeal.

Accordingly, the prophet suffers unjustly at the hands of the community. He is attacked, ostracized, ridiculed and rejected. Such treatment gives rise to raw expressions of rage and poignant doubts about the justice of God and the orderly arrangements of the universe (Jer. 12.1-6; 15.15-18). Jeremiah, however, never responds to the adversity penitentially but incessantly declares his innocence and prays for the restoration of moral symmetry (e.g. 17.14-18). And it is the prose framework that tames the raging counter-coherence and produces moral symmetry. *In context*, the prophet's rejection and abuse now serve to accentuate Judah's guilt. Whereas Yahweh suffers rejection in chs. 2–10, in chs. 11–18 it is Yahweh's covenant mediator who is spurned and despised, thus establishing the community's wrongdoing. 'Now the figure of Jeremiah, typified in his rejection, serves to make plain that Israel has not kept the covenant and must suffer the inevitable curse spelled out in Jer. 11.1-8.'[51] The prose framework therefore creates a symbolic and literary representation of social and cosmic cohesion. This newly emergent world of the text is moral and stable. Jeremiah is vindicated as true prophet, and the community is threatened with ruin, with no hope for mediation, since it has not heeded (לֹא שָׁמַע; see 11.6-8; 12.7; 13.11; 17.27) Yahweh or Yahweh's covenant mediator, Jeremiah.

A Contextual Reading of Jeremiah 18.1-12 (13): The Fourth Macro-Structural Unit, Jeremiah 18.1–20.18
Jeremiah 18.1-11 (12) is the prose introduction to the fourth macro-block of material in chs. 1–25 (18.1–20.18).[52] It begins with the customary 'coming of the word of the Lord to Jeremiah' and reflects the diction and style often referred to as Deuteronomistic. As usual, the

51. Clements, 'Jeremiah 1–25', p. 102.
52. Chapters 18–20 have long been recognized as a 'separate redactional unit' because of their introductory heading and unifying theme (although disputed), which sets it apart from the larger literary context.

introductory heading is followed by a divine command issued to Jeremiah ('stand' 7.2, 'hear and speak' 11.2, 'arise and go down' 18.2; cf. 'please inquire' asked by Pashhur on behalf of King Zedekiah in 21.2), to which a sermon/prose oracle is attached with a description of the community's disobedience and a threat of imminent judgment. The theme of the unit, as usual, is encapsulated in the prose discourse. That is to say, the prose report, Jer. 18.1-12, introduces the cycle's dominant themes and redefines yet another of Judah's domain assumptions or first principles: Judah's status as chosen and blessed. Such insider-status, the text asserts, is not an unconditional claim. Because of persistent infidelity and recalcitrance, Judah has forfeited its privileged position and will face the fate once reserved for the nations. This announcement is accentuated by offering the once-rejected nations an imagined opportunity to enjoy the position once reserved only for Judah.

In Jer. 18.2 the prophet is commanded to 'go down' (ירד) to the potter's workshop where he will receive (שמע [hi.]) the message of the Lord (a message that will go unheeded [לבלתי שמע בקולי in v. 10] by Judah; in Jer. 18.19 Jeremiah begs Yahweh to 'hear' [שמע] his case against his adversaries; much of this macro-unit apparently revolves around the question, 'who is listening?'). Jeremiah obeys the command (v. 3) and witnesses there spoiled clay being reworked by the potter (v. 4). Accompanying the 'sign' is its meaning in vv. 5-11. Like the potter, Yahweh is utterly at liberty to shape or remold the clay at his discretion. At any time (רגע in vv. 7, 9) Yahweh can 're-form' the destiny of Israel and the nations based on their conduct and response to prophetic speech. Using the language of the call narrative in ch. 1, this prose report announces that Yahweh enjoys the utter freedom to reverse the good fortune of a nation—which we discern contextually as a reference to the people of Judah and the inhabitants of Jerusalem—on account of its 'evil' (רעה). In the topsy-turvy world of the text 'insiders'—once chosen, protected, and blessed, that is to say, those who were 'built and planted'—can become 'outsiders' who are rejected, judged and punished. Conversely, outsiders, if responsive to the word of Yahweh (שוב), can be transformed into insiders.

In v. 12 a blanket rejection of Yahweh is placed in the mouth of the people of Judah (see in v. 11 the reference to איש יהודה ועל יושבי ירושלם as antecedent of ואמרו in v. 12), making it altogether clear that they have missed yet another opportunity to 'return' to God. In other words, as the text develops (in v. 12), the community's response to the

invitation becomes clear and unequivocal: 'It is no use. We will follow
our own plans, and each of us will act according to the stubbornness of
our evil will.' Consequently, Judah can no longer rely upon and appeal
to the election tradition for security and safety. Though once chosen,
Judah is now rejected by Yahweh.[53]

The following poetic oracle (vv. 13-17) invites the *nations* to enter
the dialogue. It is quite interesting to observe that the once rejected
nations are first to be interrogated regarding Judah's preposterous act of
forsaking God (שְׁכֵחֻנִי and יְקַטֵּרוּ in v. 15; see also in 19.4 עֲזָבֻנִי and
יְקַטְּרוּ), and, ironically, they are first to witness the resultant termination
of Judah's special status.

In the fourth lament of Jeremiah (18.18-23), the prophet emerges as
witness to and participant in the rejection of Yahweh by Judah. Prophetic intercession for the people (prohibited by Yahweh in 7.16; 11.4;
15.1) is replaced by the prayer of judgment because the community
persists in its non-compliance to the prophetic word (cf. 10.25). Again,
all symbolic supports, indeed all support systems, have been shattered.

In ch. 19, the potter/pottery motif continues to take shape.[54] It
becomes transparent now that the 'clay jar' (יוֹצֵר חֶרֶשׂ in v. 1, הַבַּקְבֻּק in
v. 10, and כְּלִי הַיּוֹצֵר in v. 11) is no longer amenable to 're-formation'
(cf. 18.1-10) but must be shattered and destroyed. 'I will break this
people and this city, as one breaks a potter's vessel, so that it can never

53. K.M. O'Connor has argued cogently that 18.1-12 'marks the turning point
in the story of Israel's fate recounted in cc. 1–25. The last exhortation to repent
appears here when Yahweh demands, "Turn back, each of you from your evil way
and make good your doings" (18.11). The people answer with a dramatic and
definitive no' (*The Confessions of Jeremiah*, pp. 143-44). The text's emphasis on
Judah's 'last chance' is eclipsed in importance, I think, by the 'signed and sealed'
abrogation or revocation of its elect status (in v. 12 and in the appeal itself in vv. 7-
11a). While the meaning of 18.1-11 is far from unambiguous (see, e.g., commentaries by McKane, Carroll and Holladay), especially in light of Thiel's analysis of
the text's growth (W. Thiel, *Die deuteronomistische Redaktion von Jeremia 1–25*
[WMANT, 41; Neukirchen–Vluyn: Neukirchener Verlag, 1973], pp. 210-18), the
allegory of the potter *and* its interpretation signal the *forfeiture* of Judah's 'election,' to which a final invitation to שׁוּב is appended. The prose introduction again
sets the tone for the macro-unit as a whole: Judah has committed an unthinkable act
of abandoning Yahweh and annulling its relationship with God. As a result, Judah
now emerges as a nation with no special claim upon God.

54. Jer. 19.1-15 has apparently undergone a complex redaction history and now
appears to be a conflation of at least two originally independent accounts (see Stulman, *Prose Sermons*, p. 76, for a brief discussion).

be mended' (v. 11). Brueggemann observes in this regard that 'the broken flask is a parabolic assault on imagination. The coming judgment is a firm resolve on the part of God. That resolve is all the more ominous because "it can never be mended" (v. 11). This is the point of no return.'[55] A horrific picture of siege and devastation, the undoing of all social and symbolic supports, is graphically painted in ch. 19. Both chs. 18 and 19 are replete with Yahweh's intent to do evil (רעה) to Judah (see the word in 18.8, 10, 11 [twice], and v. 12 הרע; 19.3, 15), but the latter chapter more graphically depicts Judah's approaching death.

With no disturbance to the storyline (see the *Stichwort* [catchword] שמע) Jer. 20.1-6 narrates the violent response to the word of Yahweh proclaimed by Jeremiah: the prophet is imprisoned, rejected and scorned by the high priest Pashhur on account of his message (echoing the response of Judah to Yahweh in chs. 2–10 and not unlike the response of King Jehoiakim to the scroll in ch. 36).

Chapter 20 concludes the macro-unit with an account describing an attack on Jeremiah's life by the *religious hierarchy* and an accompanying lament and petition for retribution against the prophet's enemies. By the end of this 'act,' several new ideas are introduced: (1) Jeremiah is persecuted and rejected explicitly by a representative of the upper tiers of the religious hierarchy (serving as a transitional link to the final macro-structural unit); (2) Babylon—the once rejected and now accepted nation—is mentioned for the first time by name as the instrument of God's judgment against Judah and as the faraway place of Judah's captivity; as such, disaster looms even closer on the horizon; (3) finally, if Holladay is correct, this passage contributes to 'a total reversal of *Heilsgeschichte*' and in particular 'the overturning of the covenant with the patriarchs'.[56]

Chapters 18–20 therefore continue to elucidate the complete undoing of Judah's domain assumptions and sacred canopy: its temple ideology, its covenant traditions (both Sinai and ancestral covenant), and its status as protected insider with clear and well-defined boundaries. The only 'first principle' not yet addressed and dismantled is the community's royal-dynastic theology, which is the focus of attention in the final macro-block.

55. Brueggemann, *To Pluck Up, To Tear Down*, p. 169.
56. W.L. Holladay, 'The Covenant with the Patriarchs Overturned: Jeremiah's Intention in "Terror on Every Side" (Jer. 20:1-6)', *JBL* 91 (1972), pp. 305-20.

A Contextual Reading of Jeremiah 21.1-10: The Fifth Macro-Structural Unit, Jeremiah 21.1–24.10

Chapters 21–24 comprise the final macro-unit of the first scroll. This complex cycle of material takes up matters related to the royal Davidic dynasty and other upper-tiered positions in the sociopolitical hierarchy (e.g. 23.9-40). Following an introduction in Jer. 21.1-10, Jer. 21.11–22.30 accentuates the *conditional* nature of the Davidic dynasty as well as its utter failure and imminent judgment. The old systems of governance—falling miserably short of acceptable Torah standards of justice—are to be dissolved and dismantled as they were once known. In their place, God promises to appoint new shepherds and to establish an ideal ruler of David's line who will govern with justice, wisdom and righteousness (Jer. 23.1-8). Despite the promise of future restoration for David's dynasty, the focus of the macro-structure as a unit is on the termination of the old symbolic structures and conventional social categories. The text can no longer envisage the continuation of those networks of meanings—especially ones associated with the dominant power structures of the social hierarchy—that are perceived as architect and *causa causans* of the community's anomie and disorientation (see also Jer. 23.9-40).[57]

Chapter 24 concludes this macro-unit with the vision of the fig baskets. As is well known, in this prose report, which is associated in form with Jer. 1.11-13 and perhaps Jer. 13.1-11, God promises mercy and salvation to the *golah* in Babylon while rejecting unequivocally King Zedekiah and those who remain with him in the land. Exile to distant Babylon apparently represents (for the community residing in Babylonia) the kind of total abrogation of the past—with all its understandings of reality—that is necessary for the introduction of new beginnings and radical shifts in the community's symbolic arrangements.

The macro-unit is introduced by a prose discourse, Jer. 21.1-10, which is most often associated with the 'C' tradition, even though it admittedly deviates at points from the customary rubrics.[58] The diction, style and theology of the passage betray marked points of correspondence with Jer. 7.1-15, 11.1-14, 18.1-12, 25.1-14. The passage begins with the conventional introductory formula (v. 1a), and it exhibits the

---

57. The unit's ambivalence regarding the institution of kingship is not unlike that of Deuteronomy.

58. See Stulman, *Prose Sermons*, pp. 80-81.

'verbose' style and alternative speech form which are characteristic of the Jeremiah prose tradition.

In the prose narrative Zedekiah sends Pashhur and the priest Zephaniah to request from Jeremiah an oracle of the Lord on his behalf. The request for a hearing is granted, but the petition for divine intervention on Zedekiah's behalf is flatly denied. Jeremiah declares that Yahweh is waging 'holy war' *against* Zedekiah and the royal city (see v. 4 [הזאת העיר]; v. 7 [הזאת בעיר הנשארים ואת]; vv. 9-10). The conflation and inversion of the credo and holy war traditions are stunning: Yahweh's 'outstretched hand and mighty arm' are no longer anchored in the ancient confession celebrating Yahweh's victorious act of judgment against Egypt on Israel's behalf; now Yahweh's 'outstretched hand and mighty arm' allude to his declaration of holy war against the Davidic monarch and the inhabitants of the royal city (vv. 5-7).[59] Yahweh will deliver Zedekiah to King Nebuchadrezzer of Babylon who is the instrument of divine judgment. The traditional and conventional claims of dynastic immutability have been subverted; hope is no longer extended to the historical dynasty or the royal city.

The fateful oracle against Zedekiah is followed by an 'alternative' *Prophetenaussage* (prophetic message) setting forth a choice between life and death: life for (obedience that is expressed in) surrender to Babylonian rule, or death for (disobedience that is expressed in) continued residence in 'this city' (i.e. Jerusalem). Brueggemann is no doubt correct that the reference to 'this city' includes 'the social ideology and policy of the throne and temple, and the power arrangements that sustain that ideology and policy'.[60] Nonetheless, while the royal ideology stands under Yahweh's *Unheil* (disaster), the inhabitants of 'the city' are offered a way out, if they 'go out' and 'surrender' to the Chaldeans.

This introductory prose discourse functions contextually in ways that are markedly similar to other 'Deuteronomistic' prose sermons in Jeremiah 1–25. First, Jer. 21.1-10 serves as a *hinge* holding together rhetorical units that denounce priest, prophet, shepherd (king) and sage, that is to say, the major power brokers in the old world order (see, e.g., Jer. 18.18–20.18 and 21.11–23.40). The claim is thereby made that those wielding the most power in the social and literary world of Jeremiah are most culpable of skewing the stability of the established symbolic

59. See the erudite treatment in Brueggemann, *To Pluck Up, To Tear Down*, pp. 181-87.

60. Brueggemann, *To Pluck Up, To Tear Down*, p. 183.

arrangements of the universe. The survival of Jeremiah and Judah is placed in grave danger by these groups who enjoy leading positions in the community.[61]

Second, Jer. 21.1-10 introduces and encapsulates the major theological motifs present in the macro-unit as a whole. In particular, the prose introduction announces the collapse of the royal ideology with its power arrangements and networks of meaning. The rejection of Zedekiah, the last king of the Davidic line in Jerusalem, represents the failure and categorical cessation of the historical dynasty.[62] Furthermore, Jer. 21.1-10 announces that Babylon's invasion of the royal city is a theopolitical reality sanctioned and initiated by Yahweh to punish a wayward and idolatrous Judah that has become Yahweh's adversary.

Finally, the prose discourse declares that the destiny of Judah as a reimaged community depends in large measure on its response to Babylonian subjugation, which, as we have seen, is couched in theopolitical terms representing Yahweh's sovereign rule over Judah and the *gôyim*.

These three themes—the announcement of the categorical cessation of the historical dynasty, the role of Babylon as Yahweh's instrument of judgment, and preferential place afforded the *golah* in Babylon over the remnant in Jerusalem—are again taken up as the principal motifs in the closure of this final macro-unit (Jer. 24.1-10). Thus the prose introduction and the concluding chapter 24 function contextually as a thematic *inclusio* that completes the undoing of Judah's sacred canopy and the redefinition of the community's *raison d'être*. Nothing can save Judah: neither temple, covenant, its status as an elect people, nor Davidic king. All security systems of the former world order are dreadfully inadequate and ineffectual. Judah must look elsewhere for its newly defined categories of existence as a reimaged community in the neo-Babylonian empire.

61. See Carroll, *Jeremiah*, pp. 406-407, for a helpful discussion of the two Pashhurs in chs. 20 and 21. This antiroyal sentiment is reminiscent of the antimonarchic musing in Amos in the years immediately prior to the end of national independence (see, e.g., Amos 9.15 where all of Israel's wickedness is associated with Gilgal, the site of Saul's coronation).

62. Clements, 'Jeremiah 1–25', pp. 103-107. This conviction is echoed in the litany of failures and accusations against the Davidic kings in ch. 22. Any hope for David's line transcends historical particularities and depends now on the decisive act of God (Jer. 23.1-6). In contrast to Dtr, Jer. 21–24 (and perhaps the book as whole) attaches no hope to Jehoiachin or any other Davidic ruler.

The Theological Tendenz *of the Prose Sermons in Context:*
A Conclusion

The greatest danger inherent to any contextual and formal approach is the risk of glossing the text's inconcinnities. Jeremiah 1–25 is unquestionably an 'untidy' book that reflects profound tensions and conflictual encounters. The first and lasting impression rendered by the Jeremianic poetry of the first scroll is its jumbled and dissonant character. It is wild, untamed verse that testifies to the disintegration of social and cosmic structures.

I have tried to demonstrate in this essay that the so-called 'C' material of Jeremiah 1–25 introduces equilibrium and stabilization into this messy world and witnesses univocally to order and *nomos* (while at the same time reflecting its own sense of contingency and danger). As such, 'C' functions not only as writer but also as reader who fills in literary and symbolic 'gaps of indeterminacy' that present themselves in the poetry. Accordingly, 'C' acts as midrash, which introduces, clarifies and encapsulates poetic motifs of blame; that is to say, it echoes and enunciates notes that are present in its immediate literary setting. 'C' also reperforms the absonant language of the poetry by sublimating it with univocal prose. As a result, 'C' tames and 'codifies' the wild and multiphonic voices of the poetry, not unlike 'the composer and the improvisational musician…[who] must contain the dissonance within a frame that holds the audience's attention until resolution is found'.[63] In all these various functions, the sermonic prose of the first scroll creates structural unity and cohesion by providing literary and symbolic *seams* that hold together a symbol system and imagined world replete with counter-coherence and *anomie*.[64]

Furthermore, the prose discourses of chs. 1–25 'clean up' their jumbled poetic context by providing (with their introductory and concluding chapters that function as bookends to the *corpus*) a literary artifice and an intentional theological strategy that aims at dismantling the state

---

63. Ronald A. Heifetz, *Leadership without Easy Answers* (Cambridge, MA: Harvard University Press, 1994), p. 6.

64. Since the 'C' material does not exist in a literary or ideological vacuum, it should perhaps no longer be viewed as a distinct literary tradition/stratum divorced at least synchronically from its *Sitz im Buch*. See also Clements, 'Jeremiah 1–25,' p. 109.

religion's major symbol system and domain assumptions.[65] This process of undoing all conventional constructions of reality is not executed on a flat, linear plane, without progression and development. Instead, each prose sermon in sequence broadens and intensifies the scope of Judah's crumbling world until it culminates in the indictment against the upper tiers of the community's social hierarchy (in chs. 21–24).

The narratorial construction presented by 'C' makes three major claims. First, it insists that Judah has *rejected the prophetic word* spoken by Jeremiah, who is represented as the last in the succession of spokespersons that originated with Moses. In doing so, the community acts in conjunction with its ancestors who have incessantly rebelled against Yahweh. As a result, Judah's infidelity and disobedience testify to its own culpability before God. In this regard, the prose discourses of Jeremiah 1–25 echo the poetic indictment of blame. Judah, not Yahweh, is at fault.

Second, Judah's rejection of Jeremiah's prophetic word results in impending and unequivocal judgment, a punishment that is just and well deserved. Consequently, the vision of the desolate end of life, often cast in the *qînah* form in the poetry, is set squarely by the prose sermons within symmetrical and orderly cosmic arrangements. As such, Judah's dissolution—and the amalgam of poetic voices of siege, destruction and chaos—now produces cohesion rather than counter-coherence. 'C's' ideology of the *prophetic word* places the whole of chs. 1–25 within a context of reciprocal justice, thereby domesticating the turbulent and unrestrained poetry. In this way, it provides order and congruence to a symbol system and literary environment laden with asymmetry. It is interesting to note in this regard that Dtr often deals with 'mess' by the prophetic presence and word; that is to say, one of the narratorial functions of prophets in Dtr is to bring coherence to its *Weltanschauung* when 'embarrassed' by dissymmetry (especially when apparently historical and ideological concerns are at odds; see, e.g., 2 Kgs 14.23-29; 1 Kgs 21.25-29; cf., however, 2 Kgs 2.28-30).

Finally, the prose sermons in context reimage the existence of Judah by providing strategies for survival and redefinition in a newly emergent theopolitical world. The *Unheil* inflicted by the northern foe and the resultant destabilization of the whole complex of 'self-evident'

---

65. See William R. Domeris, 'Jeremiah and the Religion of Canaan', *OTE* 7 (1994), pp. 7-20, who argues that Jeremiah achieves this end by his use of 'anti-language'.

assumptions and social meanings shared by the community prior to the first quarter of the sixth century pave the way for definitional shifts and transformations in Judah's symbol system. The prose sermons testify that nothing from the old world order can save Judah—neither the temple and its *Weltanschauung* of permanence (ch. 7), the 'old' covenant (ch. 11; cf., however, Jer. 31.31-34), an appeal to election or the privileged insider–outsider distinction (ch. 18), nor the royal ideology and the imperial modes of reality (ch. 21). All cosmic and social supports of the former symbolic system are inadequate, both for sixth-century Judah as well as later interpretive communities. The old paradigms and domain assumptions of the state religion are gone forever. Judah's sacred canopy has been dismantled decisively by the prose sermons. In fact, all its sacred pillars—temple, covenant, election and Davidic dynasty—no longer provide support but now testify that immunity from disorientation and its disfranchised place in the new world order governed by Yahweh will not be granted.

The end of the old system, this cosmic crumbling, however, prepares the groundwork for a newly emergent community. In other words, God shatters Judah's 'little' categories of control and its illusion of certainty in order to create a counter-community with fresh imaginative possibilities. This newly constructed community is to be defined in part by an adherence to written prophecy, the belief in God's intrusive and unrestrained rule over all nations, an ethic of hospitality extended to the poor (e.g. 7.5-7), the condemnation of idolatry, a Torah piety of justice and compassion and a future hope that is (re)focused upon divine promises to David.

While these symbolic shifts toward reorientation are certainly present in 'C' in context, they *do not* give Jeremiah 1–25 its distinctive character. This scroll focuses more intently on the end of one epoch than upon the imagined possibilities of another.[66] As such, chs. 1–25 set the literary stage and provide symbolic underpinnings for the second scroll (chs. 26–52). There it becomes increasingly clear how this revivified community—without temple, cultus, land and Davidic ruler, and with redefined understandings of covenant and election—will take shape in its cultural milieu among the nations. Only beyond the literary perimeters of Jeremiah 1–25 does the reader more fully enter the world of new beginnings and the partial construction of life beyond exile.

---

66. Contra S. Herrmann, *Die prophetischen Heilserwartungen im Alten Testament* (BWANT, 5; Stuttgart: W. Kohlhammer, 1965).

THE FUNCTION OF CHAPTERS 25 AND 50–51
IN THE BOOK OF JEREMIAH

Martin Kessler

It may be fair to say that Jeremiah scholarship has not arrived at a satisfactory solution concerning the structure of the book as a whole. Robert Carroll's comments are quite typical, as he laments the untidiness and therefore incomprehensibleness of the book.[1] The task which historical critics have undertaken, namely, the discovery of the *ipsissima verba* of the prophet and, by extension, the understanding of the historical Jeremiah, has done its share to contribute to the situation.

This essay offers a modest contribution to a solution by focusing on three chapters which function like pillars in a structure, namely, chs. 1, 25 and 50–51, and their role in the composition of the book (without claiming that these chapters necessarily form the sole key to the composition of Jeremiah).

We first turn to Jeremiah 25. This chapter, which Brueggemann labels 'an odd and unexpected unit in the Jeremiah tradition',[2] is rather one of the keys of the compositional riddle of the book, as I have shown in detail in a paper now published in *ZAW*.[3]

---

1. 'To the modern reader the books of Isaiah, Jeremiah, and Ezekiel are virtually incomprehensible as *books*. This is especially the case with Isaiah and Jeremiah... Often the material lacks apparent order or arrangement, does not have the kind of contextualizing information necessary for interpretation...' (Robert P. Carroll, *Jeremiah: A Commentary* [OTL; Philadelphia: Westminster Press, 1986], p. 38). See also Martin Kessler (ed.), *Reading the Book of Jeremiah* (not yet published) which contains 11 essays which, each in its own way, tries to argue the coherence of the book of Jeremiah.

2. W. Brueggemann, *To Pluck Up, To Tear Down: A Commentary on the Book of Jeremiah 1–25* (Grand Rapids: Eerdmans; Edinburgh: Handsel Press, 1988), p. 212. This comment is strange since other oracles, whether directed to Israel and Judah or to foreign nations, are equally harsh.

3. Martin Kessler, 'Jeremiah 25:1-29: Text and Context. A Synchronic Study', *ZAW* 109 (1997), pp. 44-70.

Jeremiah 25.1-18 is a double oracle of judgment. Verses 1-7 form the motivation (invective speech) triggering both oracles; in fact, the first oracle with its motivation, as has often been pointed out, may be viewed as a summary of chs. 2–24. As a retrospective piece it focuses on 'the word' that 'happened' (again and again) to a prophet who was sent to communicate it. In this, the links with the call narrative are obvious as well:

> ... to all to whom I send you you shall go,
> and whatever I command you you shall speak (1.7).

Though the fundamental aim of the prophetic message was repentance,[4] the people of Judah did not 'hear' (obey); this is of course the drawn-out story of chs. 2–24. The prophet experienced recalcitrance even to the point of receiving violence from his audience (Jer. 38.6) as the divine word went unheeded. This is behind the first (absolute) judgment oracle, 25.8-11, which announces (certain, not contingent) punishment to be meted out by the tribes of the north, specified as 'king Nebuchadrezzar of Babylon'.

The keyword 'send' (שׁלח) is employed meaningfully: because the people have not heard the prophets YHWH *sent*, he will *send* punishment to be meted out by 'all the tribes of the north'.

As the judgment oracle runs on, it takes an unexpected turn in vv. 11b, 12 (the hinge):

> ... these nations shall serve the king of Babylon seventy years. Then
> after seventy years are completed, I will punish the king of Babylon and
> that nation, the land of the Chaldeans, for their iniquity, says YHWH.

After 70 years, the punisher will himself be punished. Rather than detailing that punishment, the writer summarily refers to what 'Jeremiah prophesied against all the nations' (25.13). Evidently, this functions as a pointer to the Jeremiah OAN ('Oracles Against the Nations') collection, chs. 46–51.[5]

---

4. A distinction needs to be made between oracles which are 'absolute', whose fulfilment is indicated, quite likely in the imminent future, and 'contingent' oracles, which depend on the people's response. Some 'oracles' offer 'two ways', the way of life, and the way of death; the people are urged to do the will of YHWH and choose life (Jer. 26.2-6; 36.2-3). Also, in the kind of divine speech that sounds like a 'divine lament', it is clear that repentance is the goal of prophetic preaching; cf. Jer. 2.2-3: 'I remember the devotion of your youth, your love as a bride, how you followed me in the wilderness ...'

5. In the Greek text, the OAN follow at this point.

Summarizing, 25.8-14 contains two judgment oracles: *the first* (which had presumably already taken place) refers to Judah and her neighbors (vv. 8-11); *the second*, presented as a future event, announces judgment on Babylon (vv. 12-14).

After the judgment oracles follows the 'cup of wrath' pericope (25.15-29) presented as a symbolic act to be performed by the prophet (though, strictly speaking, it is a literary construct). This section ties in explicitly with the call narrative:

> See, I have set you this day over nations and kingdoms,
> to pluck up and to break down,
> to destroy and to overthrow,
> to build and to plant (1.10; cf. 25.12).[6]

The list of nations, which ties together the oracles against Judah with those against foreign nations, is headed by Judah and Jerusalem (25.18),[7] then Egypt (the nation of the exodus), and apparently all the other known peoples of the ancient Near East. After Elam and Media, the writer seems to pause, but the rhetorical effect is *suspense*, leaving the contemporary hearer/reader with the question: *What about Babylon?* The writer obliges: 'And after them, the king of Sheshak shall drink' (25.26).[8]

Commentators are still puzzling about the role of chs. 26–45 (MT). It may well be the most vexing problem in Jeremiah studies. A provisional structural outline might be:

Aa   Word of YHWH to Judah, 1–25
X   Hinge (ch. 25)
Ab   Word of YHWH functioning in Judah, 26–45
B'   Word of God to the Nations, 46–51.

The intricacies of M versus G structure are clearly a huge problem on their own, beyond the scope of this paper.[9] Suffice it to say that the

---

6. It might be tempting to suggest that the first double infinitive refers to Judah, the second to 'the nations', and the third to Judah again.

7. Israel/Judah is the 'firstborn' of the nations; in the oracle against Babylon, that nation is called 'the last of the nations' (50.12).

8. It seems typical for a list of 'the nations' to begin with Egypt, and end with Babylon, for Israel's political life was played out chiefly vis-à-vis the superpowers of the Nile valley and Mesopotamia (Assyria and Babylon).

9. Bright comments on 25.1: 'The words in parentheses [in his translation] are omitted by LXX and may be a gloss, but a correct one' (John Bright, *Jeremiah: A*

placing of Babylon, the superpower of the age, *at the conclusion*, both in the cup pericope and in the OAN collection, seems quite preferable to G which has Babylon somewhere in the middle of its listing.[10]

Now we turn to Jeremiah 50 and 51. The paradox with the Jeremian oracles against Babylon is that, although they have suffered from scholarly neglect, they remain crucial for an understanding of the book as a whole. Even among other prophetic books which have OAN collections (such as Amos, Isaiah and Ezekiel), no other book has anything like the oracular literature of Jeremiah 50–51. These oracles call attention to themselves for a variety of reasons:[11]

1. Quantitatively, they occupy almost one half of the total volume of OAN material in the book of Jeremiah (a total of 104 verses).

2. While some nations have some *shālôm* promises appended to judgment oracles,[12] the tone of the oracles against Babylon is so fierce, that such a possibility appears unworthy of consideration in those oracles.

3. The oracles against Babylon contain a stunning profusion of literary genres (or genre elements: *Gliedgattungen*), formulas, litanies, narrative descriptions, unlike any other OAN. It is truly the 'mother of oracles'. The oracles against Israel/Judah are

New Translation with Introduction and Commentary [AB, 21; Garden City: Doubleday, 1965], p. 160). Holladay begins his comments on Jer. 25 with the following statement: 'Analysis of this passage presents great difficulty; the contrast between *G* and *M* for these verses and the rhetoric of both forms of text make it clear that the passage has undergone much redactional activity' (*Jeremiah 1: A Commentary on the Book of the Prophet Jeremiah, Chapters 1–25* [Hermeneia; Philadelphia: Fortress Press, 1986], p. 664). It should also be said, however, that M, taken in itself, offers a coherent and intelligible text.

10. The role of Babylon in Israel's history is quite different from that of Egypt, which is the nation of slavery and exodus. Babylon is presented as the land of the patriarchs' origin (at least, Abram's!), the land of idols, out of which the people were called, to follow the true God. In a sense, it is the land of the 'first exodus', to be replayed as Judean exiles are urged to flee to their own land (in the oracles against Babylon).

11. It has also been suggested that the original OAN collection may not have included any anti-Babylon oracles.

12. See, e.g., Jer. 46.26b (Egypt): 'Afterward Egypt shall be inhabited as in the days of old, says YHWH.' That scholars should baulk at the *shālôm* oracle directed to Israel in Amos 9.11-15 is surprising, since the original message of judgment for Israel/Judah, always changes to *shālôm*.

essentially different: they were originally given[13] as calls to repent and later, as pieces of theodicy, or, even more so, as examples of applied Torah (*haftarot!*).

A fundamental aspect that ties chs. 1, 25, 50–51 together is the emphasis on the prophetic persona.[14] Older scholars refused to focus on these chapters as a unit, since they stumbled on the historicity question. But we are not involved in the search for '*the historical Jeremiah*' and even less, with what words might actually derive from him and which do not. We are dealing with *literature, not history*—literature with a theological *Tendenz*, a kerygmatic thrust.

If one looks at the book as we have it, it may be possible to bring some increased understanding. Jeremiah 1, 25 and 50–51 in their present form, share a common emphasis on the office of the prophet, who was sent by YHWH to speak the word. Since the word was rejected (given in much detail in chs. 2–24, and *in nuce* in 25), *the contingent judgment oracles were fulfilled*: the threatened 'enemy from the north' was eventually particularized in the text of Jeremiah, and identified as Babylon and its king Nebuchadrezzar.

But the book of Jeremiah did not leave it there. When Judah's punishment was complete (70 years), a drastic change in fortune occurred for Babylon: she could not avoid drinking from the same cup of wrath that all other nations (beginning with Judah) had been forced to drink.

In ch. 25 we do not have a foreign philosophy or a novel ideology, which is out of step with prophetic teaching elsewhere; rather, this is *a stunning example of YHWH's exercise in world sovereignty or imperium*, completely in line with the prophetic call in ch. 1. On the surface, Jeremiah 25 in itself is about universal judgment—beginning with Judah and ending with Babylon. But the oracles against Babylon, while they describe Babylon's fall (and the fall of her gods) in graphic

13. Regardless of the possibility that there may have been a (historical or cultic) *Sitz im Leben* for such oracles, before they found their place in a literary setting. We are more concerned with their *Sitz in der Literatur*.

14. Since the Hebrew Bible is our only source for the life of the historical Jeremiah, and since the literature in which his story is embedded does not have the goal of presenting us with 'history' in the modern sense—since this literature was written with a theological/ideological purpose, or, to state it differently, since it is kerygmatic, it seems better to abandon the search for a 'historical Jeremiah'. The only Jeremiah we have is the man the book with his name presents us. That Jeremiah is a persona: the 'Jeremiah of the Scriptures'.

detail, go one significant step further. *Babylon's defeat enables Israel to flee to her land and to Zion.* The repeated 'calls to flee' are indirectly announcements of freedom, of redemption. There are also echoes here of the Egyptian exodus and the covenant at Sinai.[15] Jeremiah 31.31-33 predicted a new covenant, which would, unlike the old covenant, not be broken: ' ... I will be their God, and they shall be my people' (v. 33). In 50.4, 5 the people of Israel and Judah (jointly!) ask for the way to Zion, to 'join themselves to YHWH by an everlasting covenant that will never be forgotten' (v. 5).

In Isa. 40.2 where a prophet categorically declares that Jerusalem 'has served her term, that her penalty is paid, that she has received from YHWH's hand double for all her sins', so God himself will carry his people out of exile, as incompetent sheep (Isa. 40.11); but in Jeremiah 50 the people are urged to take an active part: to flee, to take the initiative in vacating Babylon (v. 8).

Once more: in all three places (chs. 1, 25, 50–51), the role of the faithful prophet is heightened: memories of Jeremiah, a faithful prophet of YHWH, were marshalled to convey a 'philosophy of history' to the community after 586 BCE, the declaration that the word of YHWH had come true, and therefore, merits to be heard for what it has to say for the present.

In Jeremiah 1, the prophet is called and commissioned to hear and pass on YHWH's word 'to the nations', that is, not only to Judah but to all known peoples. Jeremiah 25, as a hinge chapter, reflects the circumstance that that word had been given to Judah and her neighbors, and carried into fulfilment, through the instrumentality of Babylon, the (temporary) 'servant of YHWH', and that it (yet) needed to be fulfilled against Babylon as well. In this, a reference of the Babylon oracles seems entirely appropriate (from the standpoint of the book as a whole).

Jeremiah 50–51 provides the final step. Judah is forgiven, YHWH's mercy is about to be granted in full measure, and the people are urged to take advantage of their new opportunity for freedom by returning to the land of God's promise.

Neither is this turn of events unique. The brief *shālôm* message at the end of Amos's book, often rejected, follows the same pattern. The book

---

15. But there is also an analogy to Abram's call, out of Ur, to an unknown land, that YHWH would show him. Here, they already know the land; they only need to bring it to mind (51.50b: 'Remember YHWH from afar, and let Jerusalem come into your mind').

of Isaiah, full of doom oracles amply spells out redemption (beginning with ch. 40). The same is true for Jeremiah, though in its own unique form. This is, incidentally, an argument for the MT sequence of oracles. The G version incorporates the *shālôm*-thrust somewhere midway in the oracle collection, which one would expect to stand at the conclusion of the OAN. The MT order emphatically underscores the point that the oracles against Babylon constitutes the climax, the 'great reversal'. There was a time when Babylon, as a world power, inflicted punishment on Judah; now, Babylon herself is punished, which spells redemption for Judah.

Two specific historical references may be adduced to make a further point. When Nebuchadrezzar took Judah, he appointed a benevolent governor Gedaliah (Jer. 39.14; 40.5) to represent him, but perversely, the people murdered him (41.1, 2): an indication that their rebellion continued, climaxing in their hasty descent to Egypt, in spite of the prophet's warnings against such action. On the other hand, there is, at the very end of the book of Jeremiah, the brief notice that when Evil-merodach took the throne of Babylon, he moved Judah's exiled king Jehoiachin out of prison and let him dine at the king's table (52.31-34): thus the book ends with an act of great symbolic significance. It may be seen as a historical reflex of YHWH granting mercy to his people, *announced in the oracles against Babylon, and now being fulfilled.* Thus the book closes with a philosophy of history come full circle:[16]

1. Judah, *a lost sheep*, Jer. 23.1 (where kings are blamed), Jer. 50.6, 7; see also Isa. 53.6a: 'All we like sheep have gone astray, we have all turned to our own way'.
2. Judah *punished* (as was Israel, at the hand of the Assyrians). The report of how the judgment, threatened in the oracular material of Jeremiah 2–24, was fulfilled, is given in chs. 37–39.
3. Finally, Judah *redeemed*, and offered the opportunity to go home again: 'Flee from Babylon, and go out of the land of the Chal-

---

16. This scheme is based on Northrop Frye's writing. See his *Anatomy of Criticism: Four Essays* (Princeton, NJ: Princeton University Press, 1957), p. 56, where he writes: 'The "literary critics" of the Bible are not literary critics, and we have to make the suggestion ourselves that the Book of Isaiah is in fact the unity it has always been traditionally taken to be, *a unity not of authorship but of theme,* and that theme in epitome the theme of the Bible as a whole, as the parable of Israel lost, captive, and redeemed' (emphasis added).

deans' (50.8a). 'I will restore Israel to its pasture, and it shall feed on Carmel and in Bashan, and on the hills of Ephraim and in Gilead its hunger shall be satisfied' (50.19).

The ideology of the book of Jeremiah is spelled out in detail in the hinge chapter, Jeremiah 25, which looks *backward* (when Babylon was YHWH's servant, meting out his punishment on Judah and her neighbors) and *forward* (when, by means of punishing Babylon, Judah would be set free). Both perspectives are illustrated in the cup of wrath pericope.

While the first doom oracle ties in with the first half of the book (oracles against Judah, chs. 2–24), the second oracle is echoed, as it were, in the anti-Babylon oracles. That Babylon is threatened with punishment is not nearly as important as the result of the change of affairs: namely, *that the people of Judah are granted the opportunity to return to their land*:

> Come out of her, my people!
> Save your lives, each of you, from the fierce anger of YHWH! (51.45).

Clearly, the anti-Babylon oracles are not some late, irrelevant, non-Jeremian appendix, but are among the supporting columns that support the total structure of the book of Jeremiah.

Readers tend to be overwhelmed by the tenor of the language of chs. 50–51: the repetition, the shifting between present, past and future, the focusing not only on Babylon, but also on her enemies, and on Judah, both pacific pastoral scenes and a sorely besieged city, etc. Even commentators who should know better, claim that there is little new material in ch. 51, that we are are not making progress. That may appear to be the case, but a more concentrated reading will force one to conclude otherwise.

It all hangs together. If we wish to make value judgments on part or on all of this material, we may do so, as long as we remember that this is typical prophetic theology, with a firm Deuteronomic stamp upon it. It invites its readers to hear and apprehend its message—not to give us historical data, but to nurture the faith communities of synagogue and church.

Finally, a few summarizing methodological comments:

1. The book of Jeremiah is not history in the modern sense.[17] As far as we know, the Medes never conquered Babylon. Neither was there, as far as we know, a battle fought in Babylon such as described in the oracles against Babylon.

2. Because this is not history, it will be more fruitful if we de-emphasize historical questions. The most we can expect is some historical reflexes, which illustrate the general milieu of the period. At the same time, it makes no sense to try to 'clean it up', by 'picking and choosing' so that we have a modern, 'reliable' historical account, or, as now is becoming popular, to overlay the text with ideological schemes. Instead of being helpful, that actually does violence to the text. If we wish to serve the faithful community best, we should try to shape the picture that is consistent with the literature itself, let the text speak for itself and refrain from value judgments or overlay the text with extrinsic ideologies, whatever their label may be.

3. We cannot arrive at the prophet's *ipsissima verba*, or paint a portrait of the historical Jeremiah. Reading numerous commentaries and their judgments about what is 'authentic' and what is not, or what could be Jeremiah speaking, and what could not possibly be him, becomes not only tiresome, it provides no help in understanding the text.

---

17. There are of course scholars who take the historicity of the biblical account very seriously, or subject it to historical critique in order to get a true historical picture. Bright and Holladay are two prominent examples. The position taken here is that this literature should be taken to convey a theological thrust, for the communities who have accepted this as Scripture.

HALFWAY THROUGH A DARK WOOD:
REFLECTIONS ON JEREMIAH 25

Robert P. Carroll

Nel mezzo del cammin di nostra vita
mi ritrovai per una selva oscura,
che la diritta via era smarrita.

Dante Alighieri[1]

These reflections were first mooted at the 1994 Annual Meeting in Chicago when working with a one-sheet-of-paper set of notes which were in turn based on my original 1986 commentary on Jeremiah, updated by further work and reflection.[2] Too much work is regularly being published in Jeremiah studies for any past piece of work not to require rewriting in order to be kept up to date. In the expanded form of those 1994 reflections this revised and expanded paper (written in September 1998) owes a considerable debt to John Hill's work on the role of Babylon in the book of Jeremiah.[3]

1. *The Divine Comedy: Text with Translation* (trans. Geoffrey L. Bickersteth; Oxford: Basil Blackwell, 1981 [1965]), Canto 1, lines 1-3 (p. 2). Among the most famous lines in *The Divine Comedy*, Bickersteth translates them as 'At midpoint of the journey of our life / I woke to find me astray in a dark wood, / perplexed by paths with the straight way at strife' (p. 3). I would settle for reading the lines to include the notion of 'being lost in a dark wood midway through our life' because it catches my own life's existential experience quite well in relation to writing my commentary on Jeremiah.

2. The sheet was written on 5 September 1994 and submitted to the Consultation committee thereafter. The reflections therein were based on Robert P. Carroll, *Jeremiah: A Commentary* (OTL; London: SCM Press; Philadelphia: Westminster Press, 1986), pp. 489-508, and R.P. Carroll, 'Synchronic Deconstructions of Jeremiah: Diachrony to the Rescue? Reflections on Some Reading Strategies for Understanding Certain Problems in the Book of Jeremiah', in J.C. De Moor (ed.), *Synchronic or Diachronic? A Debate on Method in Old Testament Exegesis* (OTS, 34; Leiden: E.J. Brill, 1994), pp. 39-51 (on Jer. 25.3-7 and 25.9).

3. See John Hill, 'Friend or Foe? The Figure of Babylon in the Book of

My 1994 sheet offered reflections on Jeremiah 25 in four paragraphs corresponding to the topics of vv. 1-7, 8-14, 15-29, 30-38 and following my commentary.[4] These four topics are: The Discourse of Blame; Domesticating the Beast as Servant of YHWH; Wine-Bearer to the Nations; World Judgment (*Weltgericht*). Whatever some purists may imagine about the text of Jeremiah, it is not a seamless robe running from 1.1 to 52.34 requiring a synchronic reading without punctuation. We all live in a real world constructed from culturally determined conventions, so we all read Bibles whose texts are *now* marked by divisions into chapters and verses. My OTL commentary was based on the English translation of the biblical text known as the Revised Standard Version.[5] It was not intended to be a reading of the MT minus chapter and verse divisions. Hence my reading of Jeremiah 25 follows the chapter and verse divisions which are now the conventional property of English translations. Of course I could have read the chapter and commented on it as a totality, but for convenience's sake I followed the break-up of sections as topical elements. All four sections feed into one another and have a linked focus. They also represent a proleptic ending of the tradition, having links with both ch. 1 and ch. 52. Situated virtually in the middle of the book (or scroll), the material in Jeremiah 25 looks both forward to the end of the scroll and backward to its beginning (a Janus text, as it were). In the commentary I treated 25.1-14 as the 'summary' of chs. 1–25 and 25.15-38 as the introduction to the 'oracles against the nations', thus indicating the Janus-like structure of

Jeremiah MT' (DTh dissertation, Melbourne College of Divinity, 1997) and its forthcoming publication in the *Biblical Interpretation* series (Leiden: E.J. Brill, 1999). I am extremely grateful to John Hill for sending me a copy of his thesis long before its publication.

4. The doyen of Jeremiah commentaries, William McKane, also follows the same division in his magisterial commentary: see McKane, *A Critical and Exegetical Commentary on Jeremiah*. I. *Introduction and Commentary on Jeremiah I–XXV* (ICC; Edinburgh: T. & T. Clark, 1986), pp. 618-58; cf. for an almost similar division see Walter Brueggemann, *A Commentary on Jeremiah: Exile and Homecoming* (Grand Rapids: Eerdmans, 1998), pp. 220-28 (vv. 1-14, 15-29, 30-38) under the general heading 'The Cup of Wrath (25: 1-38)'.

5. Carroll, *Jeremiah*, p. 82. I have been amazed by the number of reviewers and readers of my commentary who give the impression that the English text used in the commentary is somehow my own translation rather than that of the RSV. The public text in the commentary is the RSV, balanced in the Textual Notes by my use also of the NEB and JPSV as textual comparators.

the chapter.[6] Differences between the MT and the LXX at this juncture are of the essence in exegeting the distinctive textual traditions represented by these two rather different versions of the Jeremiah tradition, but I shall resist the temptation here to pursue such a scholarly luxury.

Intrepid commentators on Jeremiah find themselves midway through the task when they arrive at ch. 25. The reason I have entitled this essay on Jeremiah 25 'halfway through a dark wood' is simply that because being halfway through any task always puts me in mind of the paradox that one can only go *halfway* into a wood before one begins to come out of that wood. By the time I got to ch. 25 my own sense of lostness when working on the Jeremiah commentary was such as to conjure up for me Dante's immortal words with which the *Commedia* opens. Halfway through his life he found himself lost in a dark wood. The words will do for my own endeavours in the matter of commentating on Jeremiah. Whatever the more sanguine commentators on Jeremiah may say and think, I am still of the opinion that the book of Jeremiah is a very difficult, confused and confusing text. *I refuse not to be confused by it.* So I found (and find) working my way through the text a very difficult task and very similar to working my way through a dark wood (*selva oscura*). Writing the commentary on Jeremiah was for me a Dantean experience: a journey through a wood darker than I had ever imagined it would or could be.

Jeremiah 25.1-7: The Discourse of Blame

I think one of the strongest elements running through the poems and narratives of Jeremiah 2–24 is *a discourse of blame* directed against the country, the people and the city of Jerusalem. The targets of that blaming discourse vary considerably from poem to poem and section to section. Many different groups are singled out for blame and are accused of being the cause of Jerusalem's destruction: kings, priests and prophets, the wise, the people and, of course, specific named kings

6. When I wrote the commentary (1981–85) there was far less written on the 'oracles against the nations' material than is available now: see Alice Ogden Bellis, *The Structure and Composition of Jeremiah 50:2–51:8* (Lewiston, NY: Edwin Mellen Press, 1995); Beat Huwyler, *Jeremia und die Völker: Untersuchungen zu den Völkerspruchen in Jeremia 46–49* (FAT, 20; Tübingen: Mohr Siebeck, 1997); David J. Reimer, *The Oracles against Babylon in Jeremiah 50–51: A Horror among the Nations* (San Francisco: Mellen Research University Press, 1993).

(Manasseh, Jehoiakim, Zedekiah). It is not permitted among the prophetic writings for YHWH to be blamed for what has happened, though
4.10 may hint at such an explanation without any degree of developed
articulation (the writers of the book of Jeremiah do not measure up to
the calibre of the writers of the book of Job). Guilty parties must be
found, identified and blamed. If the prophets *en masse* are identified in
23.9-40 as the ones to blame for the corruption and destruction of Jerusalem, in the reprise and conclusion to 1–24 in 25.1-7 it is the people
themselves who are to blame because of their persistent refusal to listen
to the prophets (cf. 18.11-12). But surely not their refusal to listen to the
prophets of 23.9-40? How can the people be blamed for failing to listen
to the prophets who were spreading corruption throughout the land?
How could they be blamed both for listening to the prophets and for
refusing to listen to the prophets (cf. Lam. 2.14)? How is such a
contradiction in the tradition possible?

In my reading of the book of Jeremiah such contradictions become
clues as to how the book should be read rather than matters to be
glossed over in the *best possible reading* which will not ruffle any
feathers anywhere.[7] I am deeply conscious of just how much and how
many commentators on Jeremiah disagree fundamentally and violently
(metaphorically of course, thank Marduk) with my reading of the book
of Jeremiah.[8] The annual meetings of the SBL Consultation on the

7.   I would need to hear much more argument about *who* decides *which* is the
best reading, *how*, *for what* and *for whom* before I could go along with the demand
which uses the aesthetic notion of the 'best work of art' or which insists on the
magisterium of an imagined religious community: see Dale Patrick and Allen Scult,
Rhetoric and Biblical Interpretation (JSOTSup, 82; Sheffield: Almond Press,
1990), pp. 84-85, 127-39.

8.   I will not here provide a lengthy roll-call of those who have spoken out so
strongly in print or especially at the Consultation meetings against my interpretation
of Jeremiah, but those who do not know the tradition may consult the writings of
the following, especially my arch-critic Walter Brueggemann, 'Jeremiah: Intense
Criticism/Thin Interpretation', *Int* 42 (1988), pp. 268-80; also Douglas R. Jones,
Jeremiah (NCBC; London: Marshall Pickering, 1992), pp. 62-63; and especially
Jeremiah Unterman, *From Repentance to Redemption: Jeremiah's Thought in
Transition* (JSOTSup, 54; Sheffield: JSOT Press, 1987) (*passim*). For rational,
argued and modulated criticism of my reading of Jeremiah which I find quite
acceptable see McKane's two volumes on Jeremiah, especially vol. 2 (*A Critical
and Exegetical Commentary on Jeremiah*. II. *Commentary on Jeremiah XXVI–LII*
[ICC; Edinburgh: T. & T. Clark, 1996]). From this kind of 'friendly' criticism I can
learn; from the other hostile kinds, however, I cannot learn because they are utterly

Composition of Jeremiah group have made me bitterly aware of just how strong and virulent that opposition constantly has been throughout the 1990s—I never thought that I would have to learn to internalize the point made by Jer. 15.10—as individual after individual at meeting after meeting has found it necessary to rise to their feet and denounce me in the strongest terms possible for my reading of Jeremiah.[9] And yet I must persist in my folly and in my integrity (as Job might say) and insist that the problem lies with the text of Jeremiah rather than with me. I simply do not understand how readers can follow the arguments of Jer. 23.9-40 that 'the prophets of Jerusalem' are to blame for the destruction of the people and then when they arrive at Jer. 25.1-7 not *see* the blatant contradiction that is entailed in the claim that the people's destruction is due to their not listening to the prophets! So my reading of 25.1-7 inevitably must put that claim alongside the rather different claim of 23.9-40 and read both pericopae intertextually. It has to be said that at this point the book of Jeremiah once again collapses under the weight of its own internal contradictions. Such is my reading of the ongoing text as it unfolds. A similar point could be made about ch. 24, but only 25.1-7 need detain us at this stage of the argument.[10]

As I said in Chicago in my one-page treatment: 'A close comparison of 23.22 and 25.3-7 would deconstruct the notion of a prophet turning the nation as evidence of the prophet's standing in the divine council.

---

dismissive, destructive and oppositional, whereas McKane knows how to be critically constructive—that is, agreeing and disagreeing where appropriate but always with a balanced voice.

9. My experience at every meeting of the Consultation has inevitably left me silenced by the strength of the vociferous opposition to me, though I think the Chicago meeting was especially vicious in the attacks on me and my reading of Jeremiah—or so I remember it (I recall that even my erstwhile most strident critic Jeremiah Unterman had to protest against the intemperate terms of the verbal onslaught on me). It has all been a most salutary lesson to me about the ideological nature and depth of the Guild's political opposition to non-conforming voices in the contemporary discipline of biblical studies. I include this note of protest here just for the record of my perception and experience of the Consultation meetings (my skin is too thick, thank Marduk, for any serious or long-lasting damage to have been done to my psyche).

10. The point could not be simpler: among the rotten figs in Jerusalem which will be destroyed by YHWH must be counted *the rotten fig which is his servant the prophet Jeremiah*! What levels of unawareness and lack of reflection are posited by this confusion or indeed of the failure of commentators to see the obvious?

Theodicy, intertextuality and deconstruction of prophets are all inscribed
in this opening section.' Some four years later I cannot think of a
convincing argument which would make me dissent from that judgment
made then. It does seem to me that a prophet who is judged to have
spoken 23.22 as a critique of the prophets of Jerusalem for their failure
to convert the people and cause them to repent of (turn from: *šûb*) their
evil ways and then who has to make confession that all YHWH's
servants the prophets have failed to make the people listen to them or
turn from their evil ways is himself a prophet who stands under his own
judgment as one who has not stood in the divine council.[11] I think the
logic is impeccable, even though most other commentators prefer not to
read it that way. I shall stick to my own reading and treat Jeremiah as a
false prophet *by his own logic*. False or, on the other hand, hypocritical
and hypercritical, confused and confusing: readers must make their own
choice of nouns for describing how they read the intertextualities here.
A synchronic reading of Jeremiah leaves the reader with little option
but to accept that logic. Alternative accounts of the book's composition
may get readers off the hook, but I do not think it is the contemporary
commentator's task to make the text conform to our own values or to
protect the text from critique. The book of Jeremiah is a strange and
alienating text, quite discrete and different from our own contemporary
values. That is how it should be because it comes to us from an ancient
and alien time and culture. It is not part of my remit to save the appear-
ances of the text, to make it conform to my expectations or to yield
comfort to my prejudices.[12]

Jeremiah 25.8-14: Domesticating the Beast as Servant of YHWH

This section reprises 1.13-15 and so forms a closure (*inclusio*) to the
first part of the book of Jeremiah (that is, chs. 1–25). The MT develops a

---

11. I made a similar point in Carroll, 'A Non-cogent Argument in Jeremiah's
Oracles against the Prophets', *ST* 30 (1976), pp. 43-51; cf. Carroll, 'Synchronic
Deconstructions of Jeremiah', pp. 41-46 (on Jer. 23.22 and 25.3-7).

12. Somewhere in that sentence are to be found the beginnings of a hermeneutics of Bible reading, but I shall not cash it out here. Alien texts from alien
times ought to alienate us today: I tried to make that point with my *Wolf in the
Sheepfold: The Bible as Problematic for Theology* (London: SCM Press, 1997).
That book was, of course, reviled by some of those critics who also reviled my
approach to Jeremiah!

simpler text than the LXX by identifying the foe from the north with Nebuchadrezzar and the Babylonians. So it historicizes the mythical foe (of chs. 4–6 and 50–51) and identifies it with the destroyer of Jerusalem (cf. 36.29). Similar textual activities can be seen in Isaiah 40–55 where the Persian emperor Cyrus becomes the *māšîaḥ* (that is, YHWH's anointed leader) and in Ezra where Cyrus the Persian emperor effectively becomes the temple builder. All these textual traditions follow the same interpretative principle: the alien, foreign emperors have become YHWH's representative (vicar?) on earth, replacing the Davidic king, and thereby domesticating the hostile forces ranged against Judah-Jerusalem. In treating Nebuchadrezzar as YHWH's servant (cf. the focus on this figure in Isa. 40–55), the text has quite effectively domesticated the Nebuchadrezzar who is depicted as the Beast (or dragon), who in Jer. 51.34 has devastated Jerusalem (the 'washing up dishes' images of 51.34 I shall leave unexegeted). Beast and Servant: Nebuchadrezzar has become YHWH's oxymoron! YHWH's *stupid cow* we might say in modern parlance.

Acknowledging that the LXX does not read or represent Nebuchadrezzar as a servant in its version of the Jeremiah tradition, I must admit that my exegesis here only works for the Hebrew version of Jeremiah and for all those English translations for which the Hebrew is a warrant. One strand of the tradition however will suffice as the basis for my argument here. Not only does the MT domesticate Nebuchadrezzar the Beast *as* the servant of YHWH, it also incorporates him and his imperializing, destructive enterprise against Jerusalem into a Judaean triumphalist ideology. This incorporation into Judaean ideology has the effect of periodizing the Babylonian hegemony and therefore reversing its long-term effects. Babylon in the form of YHWH's servant Nebuchadrezzar is transformed by this domestication into an item or element in Judaean ideology. Hence the destructive force of the Babylonian hegemony becomes but *a moment* in YHWH's positive treatment of Jerusalem and Judah. In the twinkling of an eye, a mere *70 years*, and Babylon itself will be destroyed. Thus the terrifying destruction of Jerusalem by fire which will bring *permanent* reproach and *perpetual* shame (cf. 21.12b; 23.39-40) will be effectively extinguished by this *forecast* destruction of Babylon (reading the book of Jeremiah synchronically). Reading the section this way underlines the subversive nature of the pericope about Nebuchadrezzar, servant of YHWH. He inaugurates a moment in Judah's history rather than terminates that history. The Babylonian story is itself incorporated into and swallowed by the Judaean story. This appropriation is a lovely example of how subversive weakness can be and how its rhetoric can reverse the hegemonic role of empire by incorporation of that hegemonic force into the conquered territory's own story. The severe critique of chs. 2–24 has been toned down considerably by this coda to the text and the constant reiteration of judgment by the prophet Jeremiah subverted into a negative moment within an ongoing tradition of Judaean triumphalism.

The trope of Nebuchadrezzar as YHWH's servant may be read as the representation of the Babylonians as a friendly force in the Jeremiah tradition (cf. Jer. 27–29; 39–40). This is one of the most positive representations of Babylon in the biblical traditions, certainly in the book of Jeremiah. The presentation of Jeremiah's Nebuchadrezzar is rather like Joshua, the servant of YHWH (Josh. 24.29), a leader in YHWH's wars of extermination.[13] Various oppositions, binary and otherwise, are represented in the book of Jeremiah to such an extent that it is very difficult for modern readers to produce a consistent reading of the text. Too much has been incoprorated into the text to provide a simple, consistent reading of the book without any surplus. As with so much else, these matters are all relative. From the point of view of the destruction of Jerusalem and the concomitant butchery of men, rape of women and murder of children, Babylon was a dragon, monster and beast destroying the people (see Lamentations for rhetorical details). But from a rather different perspective, say, the provision of diasporic employment and protection elsewhere or the maintenance of good order in the land, Babylon could be viewed as YHWH's servant. That is, as part of YHWH's ongoing provision for his people, positive and/or negative. The so-called diaspora novellas, such as Daniel, Esther, Judith, Tobit, show a Babylon (or Persia) which is friendly disposed towards the diasporic Jews, providing them with golden opportunities to advance their careers in the operations of the empire. In 25.8-14 the destruction of city and land is incorporated into the cycle of redemption and punishment which characterizes the deuteronomistic representation of the history of Israel. It becomes one more element within the series of elements constituting YHWH's dealings with his people.

One might also read Jer. 25.1-14 in terms of the two occurrences of the motif 'servant': the prophets who were YHWH's servants in 25.4,

---

13. See Hill, 'Friend or Foe?', pp. 142, 269.

to whom the people did *not* listen, and Nebuchadrezzar in 25.9, the servant to whom the people will have no choice but to listen when he destroys land and inhabitants. If the prophets will not be listened to, then a servant of YHWH will come who will make the people hear what YHWH is saying to them. That may be an oversubtle way of reading the text, but modern readings of the biblical text are nothing if not subtle—they have to be or else be lost in the intertextualities of the Hebrew Bible. YHWH sends two types of servants: his servants the prophets and his servant the Beast! This dual way of reading the tradition reminds me of Martin Luther's dual reading of the role of the Turk in his time: if God is behind the Turk you should fear the Turk because it represents God's coming against you in judgment, but if God is not behind the Turk then the Turk is not to be feared! A neat way of reading the times which allowed for some subtlety of interpretation, while calling for genuine discernment of the times. So the Jeremiah tradition may be read in a similar way: if you will not heed the prophets who are YHWH's servants, then YHWH will send his servant the Beast against you. Him you will listen to, hear and obey.

Behind the redactional material in 25.8-14 may be a larger programmatic account of events in the fortunes of Judah-Jerusalem (cf. Jer. 1.12). The destruction of Babylon (25.12-14) *is* the restoration of Judah: a point which is implicit in 25, I think, and quite explicit in Jer. 50–51. Looking backward to ch. 1 and forward to chs. 50–51, the destructive moment which was Babylon is but an element in a series which moves towards the redemption of Judah. This aspect of the tradition is made fully explicit in chs. 50–51 where the destruction of Babylon is the vindication of Zion (51.10). In my judgment, a synchronic reading of the book of Jeremiah will always associate Babylon with Judah-Jerusalem's vindication and will read 25.8-14 as the turning-point in the tradition. Whatever the redactional history of the book of Jeremiah may be imagined to have been, the (original?) Jeremiah's preaching of destruction has here been converted into the proclamation of long-term victory against Babylon. While I also think that the different placements of the 'oracles against the nations' sections indicated by the MT and the LXX create space for varying discussions of the rhetorical shape of the Jeremiah tradition, I suspect that in the long run it does not make very much difference how we read those placements. The logic of the 'oracles against the nations' is invariably the redemption of Judah-Jerusalem, so the first-half of the book of Jeremiah ends with a series of takes on that motif of redemption by means of the destruction of Babylon and of all the other nations (*all flesh*).

Jeremiah 25.15-29: Wine-Bearer to the Nations

In this section of the chapter Jeremiah the symbolist bears the cup of wine, that is YHWH's wrath, around the nations and thereby transforms the motif of Jerusalem's destruction into a taxonomy of the universal destruction of the nations. The annihilation of Judah-Jerusalem's ene-mies is a tacit acknowledgment of the ultimate vindication of Judah-Jerusalem, or is tantamount to saying that Judah-Jerusalem will be redeemed. It also is a complete transformation of the thrust of Jere-miah's oracles in chs. 2–24. The word of judgment has been trans-formed into the word of salvation. Biblical prophecy symbolizes the triumph of the Judaean nation (or Jerusalem), whatever the minutiae of the texts may appear to proclaim. To state the obvious in a somewhat different way: a canonical reading of the prophets makes them bearers of the word of salvation rather than proclaimers of critique and judg-ment. Canon is counter-textual because it reads texts at a macro-level rather than at a micro-level.[14] What in the oracles of Jeremiah was a highly focused gaze at Judah-Jerusalem in terms of *destruction*, a specificity of voice and vision, has become in the oracles against the nations a much more generalized message of Judah-Jerusalem's *salva-tion* rather than destruction. Thus is the prophetic voice subverted and transformed. The biblical prophets have been coopted into the national triumphalist dream of ultimate and long-term vindication. It is in such a transformation of prophecy that I find the redactional and canonical activities of subsequent receivers of the tradition to have been quite subversive of prophecy. In my judgment the canonical ideologizes the tradition in such a way that the canonized texts become counter-ideo-

---

14. On such subversive aspects of canon see Gerald L. Bruns, 'Canon and Power in the Hebrew Bible', in *idem*, *Hermeneutics: Ancient and Modern* (New Haven: Yale University Press, 1992), pp. 64-82; Joseph Blenkinsopp, *Prophecy and Canon: A Contribution to the Study of Jewish Origins* (University of Notre Dame Center for the Study of Judaism and Christianity in Antiquity, 3; Notre Dame: University of Notre Dame Press, 1977); cf. Robert P. Carroll, 'Clio and Canons: In Search of a Cultural Poetics of the Hebrew Bible', in S.D. Moore (ed.), *The New Historicism* (*BibInt* 5 [1997]), pp. 300-23 (esp. 315-21).

logical to whatever may have been represented originally by the prophetic and textual voices.[15]

At the same time I think a reading of 25.15-38 shows that the motif of the divine act of judgment against Judah-Jerusalem (the subject-matter of chs. 2–24) has been transformed into something approximating to *the apocalyptic vision* of the destruction of the nations (*Weltgericht*). The symbolic action of bearing wine around the nations, which is itself part of a larger strand of material running throughout the book of Jeremiah (the prophet as actor), here becomes a moment of reflective transformation of the Jeremiah tradition itself.[16] The topos of destruction is turned into a symbol—the motif of the distribution of wine, with its inevitable trace of inverted eucharistic grace for Christian readers, provides a premature parody of the eucharist for a canonical (Christian) reading of Jeremiah—and then extended across the known universe to take in the destruction of all the nations (a patterned transformation of the 'oracles against the nations' genre). The apocalyptic dimension is never very far from the surface of the redacted prophetic traditions in the Hebrew Bible.[17] In fact, in my opinion, it keeps being intruded into the text by the redactors because it represents a more positive tradition than the prophetic critique. The absolute word of judgment of an Amos or a Jeremiah inscribes a categorical negative against the tradition, whereas the redactional affirmation of the future reinscribes that which the prophetic voice had undermined and critiqued. Thus the sword that was summoned by Jeremiah against Judah-Jerusalem is now summoned against 'all the inhabitants of the earth' (25.29) and the destruction of Jerusalem becomes the first event in a series which has replaced the original event of Jerusalem's destruction.

15. Walter Brueggemann would make the relation of ideology to canon the flip side of the coin: see 'Recent Jeremiah Study', in Brueggemann, *A Commentary on Jeremiah*, pp. viii-xiv.

16. On the stratum of symbolic actions in Jeremiah see W. David Stacey, *Prophetic Drama in the Old Testament* (London: Epworth Press, 1990), pp. 129-70 (148-51 on 'the cup of wrath' passage); cf. Robert P. Carroll, *From Chaos to Covenant: Uses of Prophecy in the Book of Jeremiah* (London: SCM Press, 1981), pp. 130-35 ('the prophet as actor'); *Jeremiah*, pp. 497-508.

17. On the apocalpytic in Jeremiah see Daniel C. Olson, 'Jeremiah 4. 5-31 and Apocalyptic Myth', *JSOT* 73 (1997), pp. 81-107. On the relation between prophecy and apocalyptic in general see Stephen L. Cook, *Prophecy and Apocalypticism: The Postexilic Social Setting* (Minneapolis: Fortress Press, 1995).

The past has been redeemed by incorporation into a bigger, better and different scheme of things.

Jeremiah 25.30-38: World Judgment (Weltgericht)

YHWH's quarrel (*rîb*) with his people (2.9) has been transformed in the course of the tradition's redaction into a divine quarrel (*rîb*) with the nations (25.31). Starting with Jerusalem divine judgment spreads out to incorporate the whole world (cf. 1 Pet. 4.17) and becomes positively apocalyptic in its range and scope. So Part 1 of the book of Jeremiah ends on a note of world destruction, a note which may also be read as triggering the word of hope dormant in ch. 1. The synchronic mode of reading a biblical text such as Jeremiah will inevitably entail reading the topos of the destruction of the world as the initiation of the salvation of Judah-Jerusalem or Israel. Within 25.30-38 is to be found a complex reinscription of many phrases and motifs from the proclamation of Jeremiah in the oracles against Judah-Jerusalem, but then it is now a well-known and amply recognized fact that the redaction of the prophetic books in the Hebrew Bible has entailed considerable re-use of traditional and conventional material.[18] Critique of Judah-Jerusalem has become apocalyptic judgment of the nations, and in such a transformation of a domestic issue Judah-Jerusalem escapes ultimate destruction because in the context of, and against a background of the destruction of the nations, Judah-Jerusalem's fate is invariably one of ultimate salvation. YHWH's vindication of Jerusalem is coded in the motifs of the apocalyptic judgment of the nations. As an indicator of how such a code works I would point out the conventional phrase 'from his *holy habitation* [he will] utter his voice' (25.30; cf. Amos 1.2; Joel 3.16-17), where the allusion to Zion and its *holy* temple (not a point made in Amos) takes up a notion almost foreign to Jeremiah's critique in chs. 2–24. Whatever may be one's point of view on the relationship of the material in 2–24 to an imagined original Jeremiah, few readers are

---

18. This phenomenon is now referred to as 'intertextuality': see discussion and bibliographical details in R.P. Carroll, 'Jeremiah, Intertextuality, and *Ideologie-kritik*', *JNSL* 22.1 (1996), pp. 15-34, and its updated version 'The Book of J: Intertextuality and Ideological Criticism' in this volume; cf. Robert P. Carroll, 'Intertextuality and the Book of Jeremiah: Animadversions on Text and Theory', in J. Cheryl Exum and David J.A. Clines (eds.), *The New Literary Criticism and the Hebrew Bible* (JSOTSup, 143; Sheffield: JSOT Press, 1993), pp. 55-78.

likely to assert that the 'original Jeremiah' or even any of the voices expressed in the text (with the possible exception of 17.12-13) identified Jerusalem or its temple with holiness in the Jeremiah tradition.[19] It is the corruption of the temple by the people's lives which constitutes one of the strongest indictments of the nation in 2–24, so to encounter an allusion to 'his holy habitation' in 25.30 is a little startling and disruptive (in the opinion of this reader).[20]

I think of the motif of the destruction of the nations as being invariably metonymic of the salvation of Israel or of Judah-Jerusalem (cf. 50–51), so I see in ch. 25 (especially in vv. 8-38) a great transformation of the Jeremiah tradition whereby the redaction has adjusted the harsh voice associated with the prophet Jeremiah and aligned it with the larger ideology of ultimate salvation for YHWH's people. As the pivotal chapter in the unfolding book of Jeremiah (unrolling scroll), all that follows in chs. 26–51 is troped by these poems of YHWH's judgment against the nations (against all flesh 25.31). That is how I read this chapter and also how I read the book of Jeremiah in its present state (whether in Hebrew or English). Of course I do recognize that other readers will read the chapter and the book quite differently from me. That is fine by me—the more readings the better, because every reading is a rereading which affords all other readers a further opportunity for insight, rethinking, reflection or whatever is entailed in any reading of a text. That is, every reading is a new encounter with the text. But as these are my own particular reflections on ch. 25 so, although they follow closely what I wrote in my commentary so many years ago, I would want to stand by them even now as the century ends and a new millennium dawns. Halfway through the book of Jeremiah it is a case of 'darkness at noon', but there is also a trace of or anticipation of 'light at the end of the tunnel' in ch. 25. The plot will thicken yet awhile, but ultimately everything will work out right for Judah-Jerusalem: 'there is hope for your children' (31.16).

Readers, working their way through the book (scroll), now know that,

---

19. As a counter-voice I would have to acknowledge Walter Brueggemann's insistence on Jeremiah as 'the utterance of holiness in the midst of disruption, sounds about the Holy One, sounds from the Holy One' (*A Commentary on Jeremiah*, p. xiv). It is not how I would read the tradition (Isaiah or Ezekiel seem to have better claims than Jeremiah for the topos of holiness).

20. See McKane, *Jeremiah*, I, p. 648, for other points of view on where YHWH is thought to dwell in this verse.

although Judah-Jerusalem will be put to the sword and fire by Babylon, in 70 years' time 'all will be well and all manner of thing will be well'. I wonder what 'the original Jeremiah' might have thought about such a transformation of his work, but that is an idle question well beyond the resources available for assaying a rational answer. As I belong to that minority of readers of Jeremiah who regard the book (as we now have it) as *either* a radical transformation of the original *traditum* (whatever that may have been) in such ways that the original voice of Jeremiah has been buried by the tradition beyond our capacity to recover it *or* as a betrayal or subversion of the text in this matter—or as *both* transformation and subversion—I would regard the subversion of the tradition as being now beyond recall. We may regret that it is so, but we must learn to live with it (or deal with it). While truth is not a matter of statistics to be decided by counting heads or noting the number of battalions, it is still a minority voice crying in the wilderness of contemporary Jeremiah studies. Speaking for myself the wood remains dark, nor are we out of it yet!

EXPOSING A BURIED SUBTEXT IN JEREMIAH AND LAMENTATIONS: GOING AFTER BAAL AND ... ABEL

Nancy C. Lee

I more than suspect already that he is deeply conscious of being in the wrong—that he feels the blood of this war, like the blood of Abel, is crying to heaven against him.

Abraham Lincoln[1]

... the blood of the innocent cries up from the ground
... the voices crushed in the woods and under the fresh pavements of Europe press upward. The new plants that cover the places where corpses were buried in mass pits carry blood in their dew.

Cynthia Ozick[2]

For each man in his time is Cain ...

Elton John[3]

... For three transgressions of all people,
For four, I will not forgive ...
For forgetting what it means to be all alone,
shunned by every nation in your hour of need ...
For the blood cries out from the ground,
the corpses are many in every place, and silence is cast about ...

Rabbi Michael Strassfeld, 'Prayer for Bosnia'[4]

---

1. From Lincoln's 'Mexican War Speech', delivered when he was still a congressman in 1847. In his book *Lincoln at Gettysburg*, historian Garry Wills says Lincoln's rhetoric in this speech was against President James K. Polk, who led the United States in the war against Mexico to secure new territory for slavery (New York: Simon & Schuster, 1992), pp. 177-78.

2. 'Of Christian Heroism', *Partisan Review* 59 (1992), pp. 44-51 (45).

3. Bernie Taupin and Elton John, *The One*, cassette MCAC 10614, MCA (1992).

4. The full poetic text by M. Strassfeld of Temple Ausche Chesed, New York, appeared in Sarajevo and the former Yugoslavia in *Bilten: Herald of Jewish Community of Bosnia and Herzegovina* (1994), pp. 14-15.

A speech, an essay, a song, a prayer suggest the enduring influence of the story[5] of Cain and Abel in the human imagination to address social wrong. How the story has been interpreted since its biblical rendition is a topic in two recent works. In *Narrative in the Hebrew Bible*, David M. Gunn and Danna Nolan Fewell summarize diverse interpretations of the Genesis 4 narrative from Philo to Mosala.[6] In *The Changes of Cain*, Ricardo Quinones traces the transformations of the character Cain through literature from Philo to Paz.[7] The present study proposes that even *Jeremiah's speech*, presenting both formulaic and unique cadences within the biblical prophets, uses fragments of 'the'[8] Cain and Abel story (like those above) to depict and critique social reality.[9] This rhetoric of Cain and Abel then reappears in a striking way in the book of Lamentations.

The general thesis is that Jeremiah's use of rhetorical fragments from

5.   The term 'story' for the Genesis text of Cain and Abel is used here merely for the sake of simplicity. See Phyllis Trible's discussion in *Rhetorical Criticism: Context, Method, and the Book of Jonah* of the need for standard terminology in naming the genre of a given text (Minneapolis: Fortress Press, 1994), p. 83. I am more concerned with what is the most accurate term to use for the Cain and Abel fragments in Jeremiah and Lamentations. In this study I will refer to the fragments by two terms: *subtext* and *aggadic* rhetoric. Subtext refers to the *location* of the fragments of the Cain and Abel story within the larger text. *Aggadic* is the more comprehensive term, because it refers to what the subtext is, a latent *retelling* (*aggadah*) of the story in new, poetic form and context. For a seminal discussion and definition of *aggadah* as biblical narrative, see S. Sandmel, 'The Haggadah within Scripture', *JBL* 80 (1961), pp. 105-22.

6.   New York: Oxford University Press, 1993.

7.   *The Changes of Cain: Violence and the Lost Brother in Cain and Abel Literature* (Princeton, NJ: Princeton University Press, 1991). Examples of the Cain and Abel story in modern literature include John Steinbeck's *East of Eden* (New York: Penguin Books, 1952) and N. Scott Momaday's Pulitzer novel, *House Made of Dawn* (1966) in which the main character is a Navaho Indian named Abel (New York: Harper & Row, 1968).

8.   'A' story as opposed to 'the' story, since we certainly cannot assume that the story in Gen. 4 was the only version of it known to Jeremiah. I do assume Jeremiah was drawing upon oral tradition of the story stable enough to be recognized by the community.

9.   On the 'critiquing' and 'energizing' role of the biblical prophets' and Jeremiah's speech, see Walter Brueggemann, *The Prophetic Imagination* (Philadelphia: Fortress Press, 1978), pp. 19-21, 44-61: 'Bringing hurt to public expression is an important first step in the dismantling criticism that permits a new reality, theological and social, to emerge' (p. 21).

a Cain and Abel story creates a somewhat hidden *subtext* in the book. The subtext of Cain and Abel is hidden primarily because one of its Hebrew wordplays, residing in the root הבל in 2.5 (see below), is not readily seen nor heard by speakers of other languages, and thus not translated. This essay aims to expose this hidden or 'buried' meaning by attending to matters Everett Fox has recently stressed following the Buber-Rosenzweig method of translation. That is, wordplay and multiple root meanings should be rendered, if possible, into the target language.[10]

Jeremiah's use of Cain and Abel imagery I call a 'subtext' for two reasons. The first reason lies in the nature of *poetry*, and language in general, to suggest layers of meaning (see methodology below). Second, the term subtext is used because this rhetoric will be seen to function like a *parable* that sneaks up on the listening Judean audience and their leaders to identify them with Cain. The subtext's element of surprise works much like Nathan's parable indicting David (2 Sam. 12). Abraham Lincoln (quoted above) used the imagery of the cry of Abel's blood as a kind of identifying parable, in a more overt manner, to accuse a political leader of his own time.[11]

Identification of Subtext

Jeremiah's subtext with Cain and Abel initially appears in the first speech in the book's canonical order (Jer. 2.1-9).[12] The subtext calls

10. '*The Five Books of Moses*' in *The Schocken Bible*, I (New York: Schocken Books, 1995), pp. ix-x, xv.

11. Note that in both Lincoln's speech and Elton John's song above, the use of *names* (Cain or Abel) are utilized within the rhetorical fragment or lyric to invoke the larger story. In Cynthia Ozick's *narrative* essay, as with Michael Strassfeld's prophetic 'prayer', it is the imagery or theme of the blood crying out that invokes the larger story. On the tragic exploitation of the Cain and Abel story by Christian interpreters who promoted anti-Judaism, see Rosemary Radford Ruether, *Faith and Fratricide: The Theological Roots of Anti-Semitism* (New York: Seabury, 1974), pp. 133-34.

12. The two poetic texts, Jer. 2.1-9 and 14.1-10, comprising the subtext, are still widely agreed by scholars as belonging to the 'A-material' (Mowinckel) of the book, and thus attributed to the prophet himself, leaving room of course for a redactor's final shaping. For a discussion see John Bright, *Jeremiah: A New Translation with Introduction and Commentary* (AB, 21; New York: Doubleday, 1965), pp. lv-lxxxv, and L. Perdue and B. Kovacs (eds.), *A Prophet to the Nations: Essays in Jeremiah Studies* (Winona Lake, IN: Eisenbrauns, 1984), pp. 175-91, 213-28.

attention to itself by its peculiar wordplay in Hebrew at 2.5 which
suggests the name, or appellative, Abel, הבל:

וילכו אחרי ההבל ויהבלו

'They went after ההבל and became הבל.'[13] The subtext appears again
later in 14.1-18. There it is identified in two ways—in the book's larger
structural level, and at the *lexical* level. First, in the dramatic development of the book, ch. 14 marks an important larger climax, since there
the people are presented as finally speaking to YHWH *for the first time*
in answer to YHWH's many accusing questions. Second, and more
specifically, the subtext appears in 14.10 where the people are characterized, both with the use of another wordplay, this time with Cain's
name (קין = כן), and with the use of the key term *wander* (נוע) especially used to describe Cain in Gen. 4.12, 14. Finally, the Cain and Abel
subtext is not restricted to the book of Jeremiah. As will be seen, the
subtext resurfaces most fully and clearly in Lam. 4.12-19.[14] A close
reading of Jeremiah 2 and 14 below aims to show how the subtext is
embedded in and functions in the surrounding text.

General Purpose of the Subtext

Why are fragments of the Cain and Abel story embedded within the
book's rhetoric? First, the subtext with Cain and Abel is just one of the
prophet's many rhetorical vehicles for *accusing* Judah within YHWH's
larger dispute (ריב) with the people in chs. 2–25. And second, the
intertextual connection is drawn because that rather tight story of Gen.
4 holds some of the same dramatic elements, in terms of plot and character, also at work with the people of Judah in their context. This rich
convergence of stories produces persuasive power for the prophet. The
specific convergences in the text will be traced below.

---

13.   The translations used in this study will be noted when not the author's. The
wordplay utilizes both the noun form and the qal imperfect consecutive verb of the
root, הבל.

14.   I argue in my dissertation that the Lam. 4 text suggests two distinct voices,
that of the people and that of Jeremiah, whose voice can be consistently traced in
Lamentations as one among several.

Methodology

While the basic methodology here is rhetorical,[15] this study tries to integrate matters of rabbinic and aggadic analysis, biblical poetry, sociological context, and theology. First, I point to Samuel Sandmel[16] and Michael Fishbane[17] among many others who discuss a traditional rabbinic claim that every text carries several levels or dimensions of meaning. In addition to 'plain sense' (simple, obvious) meanings at the *peshat* level, meanings are conveyed on other levels by intertextualities,[18] contexts, motifs, wordplay and memory.[19] It is out of these levels

15. See Trible's detailed treatment of rhetorical approaches in *Rhetorical Criticism*, pp. 25-87, building on the pioneering work of James Muilenburg. My own use of rhetorical method is integrated from several scholars, but has been shaped most by my teacher, Walter Brueggemann (also a student of Muilenburg) for whom I originally wrote this paper as a master's thesis, and by my Hebrew teacher, B. Elmo Scoggin. I am much indebted as well to Mishael M. Caspi for his insights about this essay and for his approach to oral poetry with its balancing embrace of tradition and fluid new renderings in diverse, contemporary contexts.

16. Samuel Sandmel gives four rabbinic levels of interpretation as *p'shat* or simple, plain meaning; *remez* or hinted at overtones and inferences; *derash* or sought for meaning; and *sod* or hidden meaning (*Judaism and Christian Beginnings* [New York: Oxford University Press, 1978], pp. 115-16).

17. In *The Garments of Torah*, Fishbane elaborates that the *remez* dimension produces meaning *extrinsically* through intertextuality, context, and the interpreter's own frames of reference. On the other hand, the *derash* dimension contains more *intrinsic* constructs such as motifs and wordplay (Bloomington: Indiana University Press, 1989), pp. 112-20. See also David Weiss Halivni, *Peshat and Derash* (New York: Oxford University Press, 1991).

18. My definition of the Cain and Abel subtext makes it an 'intertext' of course; however, I prefer the term 'aggadic' to convey the intertextual dimension, since aggadic is a less general term and rooted in Hebrew interpretation. For recent 'intertextual' studies of the Bible, see especially D. Nolan Fewell (ed.), *Reading Between Texts: Intertextuality and the Hebrew Bible* (Louisville, KY: Westminster/John Knox Press, 1992), and Timothy K. Beal's helpful essay therein ('Ideology and Intertextuality', pp. 27-39) referring to Julia Kristeva who coined this modern phrase (1969), influenced by Bakhtin; see also D. Boyarin, *Intertextuality and the Reading of Midrash* (Bloomington: Indiana University Press, 1990); J. Neusner, 'Intertextuality and the Literature of Judaism', *American Journal of Semiotics* 7 (1990), pp. 153-82; W.S. Green, 'Romancing the Tome: Rabbinic Hermeneutics and the Theory of Literature', *Semeia* 40 (1987), pp. 148-68; T. Morgan, 'Is There an Intertext in This Text?', *American Journal of Semiotics* 3 (1985), pp. 1-40.

19. Fishbane, *Garments*, pp. 116-20.

that I identify a 'subtext'[20] with Cain and Abel in the book of Jeremiah.

Another basis for analyzing this subtext in Jeremiah may be found in scholarship on *aggadic* elements in the Bible. Sandmel's seminal article 'The Haggada within Scripture' (1961)[21] helped move modern scholarship beyond source-critical methodology. In 1963 Nahum Sarna employed 'inner biblical exegesis' to analyze Psalm 89.[22] Michael Fishbane employed his teacher's approach comprehensively across biblical texts, and developed a definition of 'inner biblical aggadic exegesis'.[23] In these approaches, an old biblical tradition or story (*aggadah* from the verb *nâgad*, to tell) is retold and reused for a new time and place. With exhaustive examples, Fishbane shows how aggadic exegesis 'characteristically draws forth latent and unsuspected meanings' from the old tradition.[24] The present study is informed by his approach but leans away from the premise that biblical traditions were reformulated through *exegesis,* but rather reformulated *as rhetoric*, along the lines of oral poetry and narrative.

Aggadic rhetoric of Cain and Abel would further fall into a subcategory that Fishbane calls 'typological'. Several prophets draw on stories compiled in Genesis for typologies in order to speak *aggadically* about the social relationships of 'brothers'. Consider Amos's rhetoric: 'Alas for those who lie on beds of ivory ... and eat lambs from the flock ... but are not grieved over the ruin of Joseph!' (6.4-6, NRSV). In Hosea 12, that prophet re-employs the story of Jacob (Gen. 25.11–35.22):

> ... the sibling rivalry between Jacob and Esau, as well as other instances
> of Jacob's deceptions and deeds, form the basis of a trenchant diatribe
> against latter-day Israel. Thus, as a species of typological exegesis,
> the ... deceptions ... of corporate Israel are represented as a national reit-

---

20.   I regard the above rabbinic categories as helpful for analysis while at the same time recognizing that they describe interrelated, inseparable realities. I am indebted to Mary Chilton Callaway for her suggestive 1993 SBL paper, 'Historical Context and Literary Subtext in Jeremiah 37–39'.

21.   *JBL* 80 (1961), pp. 105-22.

22.   'Psalm 89: A Study in Inner Biblical Exegesis', in A. Altmann (ed.), *Biblical and Other Studies* (Brandeis Texts and Studies; Cambridge, MA: Harvard University Press, 1963), pp. 29-46.

23.   'Inner biblical aggadic exegesis' also pays attention to layers of meaning, to the *sensus plenior* of the text (*Biblical Interpretation in Ancient Israel* [Oxford: Clarendon Press, 1985], pp. 283, 376-79).

24.   Fishbane, *Biblical Interpretation*, p. 283.

eration of the behavior of their eponymous ancestor, Jacob-Israel ... .
That the prophet fully intended this conclusion is also evident from the
way he has exegetically linked Jacob's biography to the later history of
'Jacob' through a series of deft verbal associations and puns [e.g. מרמה,
'deceit', and עקב, 'to supplant'] ... . As in so many matters, the prophet
Jeremiah echoes many motifs found first with Hosea ... . Thus, in Jer.
9.3-5 numerous key terms are adapted from the Jacob Cycle to stress that
the new Israel is like the old ... . [Jeremiah] says, 'Be wary of your
neighbor, and do not trust your brother ... for every brother (אח) is a
deceitful supplanter (עקוב יעקב) ... .'[25]

It is important to note that Jer. 9.3-5 (Heb.) does not literally use the
name of Jacob; it is *hidden* in the Hebrew of the wordplay above.
Jeremiah is more subtle than Hosea in this regard. While Jeremiah
echoes several of Hosea's poetic motifs, I would propose that Jeremiah
is inspired by another old story about siblings—Cain and Abel—to
forge unique *aggadic* rhetoric of his own.[26]

It also must be emphasized that, as with Hosea's use of Jacob, so

---

25. *Biblical Interpretation*, p. 283. My colleague at Union (VA), Kurt Noll,
after he read this paper, discovered another piece of the Cain and Abel subtext here
in Jer. 9.3, which echoes and transforms Cain's speech, 'Am I my brother's
keeper?'

איש מרעהו השמרו ועל־כל־אח אל־תבטחו
כי כל־אח עקוב יעקב

> 'Each one against his neighbor *keep guard*!
> and put no trust in *any brother*!
> For *every brother* surely supplants [like Jacob] ...' (Jer. 9.3).

The NRSV translation excises the subtext, and associated meanings, by translating
'brother' as 'kindred'.

26. Fishbane notes, it is 'precisely because certain features ... predominate in
the imagination and memory ... that they are reused in aggadic exegesis' (*Biblical
Interpretation*, pp. 282-83). I prefer the terms '*aggadic* rhetoric' or 'subtext' over
'allusion', since allusion is not large enough to explain the phenomenon at work
here. See R. Alter for allusion in the Bible (*The World of Biblical Literature* [New
York: Basic Books, 1992], pp. 107-30; *The Art of Biblical Poetry* [New York:
Basic Books, 1985], pp. 123, 153). Neither is the present study promoting the older
type of 'allegorizing' exegesis, which was often 'decontextualizing', as James Barr
has put it, but attempts rather, in his words, 'a theological understanding of a text
that already in itself ["in the original writing of it"] has some sort of allegorical
character' as well as an understanding which is 'contextually defensible' ('The Literal, the Allegorical, and Modern Scholarship', *JSOT* 44 [1989], pp. 3-17 (13, 15).

with Jeremiah's use of Cain and Abel, most of the story is not retold in the poetry. In fact we are only given poetic fragments (in Jer. 2. and 14) suggestive of the whole. The hearers'/readers' recognition is triggered by the choice use of a few key terms. They/we are expected to know characters and stories and imaginatively fill in the gaps with contemporary events in mind. This filling in of the gaps of this subtext is evident later in Lamentations 4, as will be seen. James Sanders has observed that 'the more common and well-known a biblical concept was, the less likely the community was to cite it in its final written form and the more likely they were to assume that the ... community would know it'.[27]

Finally, Jeremiah's rhetoric engages in constructing (and sometimes deconstructing) the *worlds* of his listeners.[28] This socio-rhetorical approach follows Brueggemann's method and view of the prophet as 'a destabilizing presence' who challenges a constructed world.[29]

All these methodological factors are at work in the following analysis of Jeremiah's use of a subtext with Cain and Abel. The investigation will now proceed with close attention to the two texts in which the subtext appears, Jeremiah 2 and 14. This will be followed by a concluding look at the subtext's appearance in Lamentations 4 where it depicts destruction and exile in relation to the Babylonian invasion.

Jeremiah 2.1-9

> What does one do when confronted by a difficult and obscure text? One reads it again and again, and discovers another layer beneath the visible, another dimension, another meaning ...
>
> Elie Wiesel[30]

27. *Torah and Canon* (Philadelphia: Fortress Press, 1972), p. xiv.

28. As reflected in YHWH's commissioning Jeremiah: 'Now I have put my words in your mouth. See, today I appoint you over nations and over kingdoms, to pluck up and to pull down, to destroy and to overthrow, to build and to plant' (Jer. 1.9b-10, NRSV).

29. *A Social Reading of the Old Testament: Prophetic Approaches to Israel's Communal Life* (Minneapolis: Fortress Press, 1994), pp. 221-22. For Brueggemann's fuller methodology, see *Israel's Praise* (Philadelphia: Fortress Press, 1988), pp. 1-53; *Old Testament Theology: Essays on Structure, Theme, and Text* (Minneapolis: Fortress Press, 1992), pp. 74, 77.

30. *Five Biblical Portraits* (Notre Dame: University of Notre Dame Press, 1981), p. 117.

The wordplay in 2.5 signaling the subtext is transliterated below:

1. The word of YHWH came to me, saying:
2. 'Go and proclaim in the ears of Jerusalem,
   "Thus says YHWH:
   'I've remembered your youthful devotion,
           your bridal love,
           your following me in the wilderness,
              in a land not sown.
3.   Set apart is Israel for YHWH,
           first fruits of his harvest,
           all eating it will be held guilty;
             trouble will come upon them,'
               says YHWH.
4. 'Hear the word of YHWH, O house of Jacob,
   and all the families of the house of Israel,
5. thus says YHWH':
       "What injustice did your ancestors find against me
         that they went far away from me?
           They went after *haheḇel*,
             wayyehbālû.
6. They did not say,
     'Where is YHWH?
   the One who brought us up from the land of Egypt,
   the One who led us in the wilderness,
           in a land of deserts and pits,
           in a land of drought and deathshadow,
           in a land no one had passed through,
           and where no human had dwelt.'
7. Then I brought you into the garden-land,[31]
           to eat its fruit and its goodness,
   But you came in and defiled my land,
         and my heritage you made abhorrent.
8. The priests did not say,
   'Where is YHWH?'
   The handlers of the law ignored me,
   the rulers rebelled against me, and
   the prophets prophesied by Baal,
           and went after things that do no good.[32]
9. Therefore, I still have a dispute with you,"
         says YHWH, "and with your children's children
       I have a dispute.' "'

---

31. Following BDB, pp. 501-502. Hebrew: ארץ הכרמל. Cf. Jer. 4.26.
32. Following JPSV.

Most commentators identify the genre of Jeremiah 2 as a kind of legal dispute YHWH is bringing against Jerusalem and Judah (ריב at v. 9). Jeremiah 2.1-9[33] introduces this large dispute ranging across chs. 2–25; the indictment here serves as a warning since the prophet is calling the people to turn back to YHWH while there is still time.

There is narrative flow across 2.1-9 by a movement from the wilderness setting,[34] or desert, to the land. Across ch. 2 is a recurring *Leitwort*:[35] the people 'go after' (הלך + אחרי) or 'follow' various

33. Following the limit at 2.9 by R.P. Carroll (*Jeremiah: A Commentary* [OTL; Philadelphia: Westminster Press, 1986], pp. 121-25) primarily because of the parallel between 'fathers' in v. 4 and 'children' in v. 9; contra J. Bright who sets the limit at v. 13 and rearranges the texts in ch. 2 in order to harmonize the shifts in persons of address (*Jeremiah*, p. 17); thus also E. Nicholson (*The Book of the Prophet Jeremiah* [Cambridge: Cambridge University Press, 1973], p. 31) and J. Thompson (*The Book of Jeremiah* [Grand Rapids: Eerdmans, 1980], p. 166). W.L. Holladay (*Jeremiah 1: A Commentary on the Book of the Prophet Jeremiah, Chapters 1–25* [Hermeneia; Philadelphia: Fortress Press, 1986], p. 68) also puts the limit at v. 9; however, I disagree with his view that Jeremiah originally preached 2.4-9 as an oracle to the north. Although v. 4 ('Hear ... O house of Jacob') is a 'summons to the accused' (H. Huffmon, 'The Covenant Lawsuit in the Prophets, *JBL* 78 [1959], pp. 285-95 [286-88]), it serves here as a *rhetorical* strategy to persuade Judah rather than as a remnant, literal setting of the address. Is it not because of Judah's *analogous experience* to the northern kingdom that this rhetoric is placed here? The rhetoric is highly ironic since YHWH summons the people of the northern kingdom, which no longer exists, now to be witnesses against Judah for committing similar transgressions. The speech in vv. 1-3 is included in this analysis due to its sharing the *Leitwort* of 'going after' that appears throughout ch. 2.

34. Cf. Shemaryahu Talmon's comprehensive discussion of the use of the wilderness motif in the Bible and his convincing refutation of the scholarly claim of a 'desert ideal' ('The "Desert Motif" in the Bible and in Qumran Literature', in A. Altmann [ed.], *Biblical Motifs: Origins and Transformations* [Cambridge, MA: Harvard University Press, 1966], pp. 31-63). Talmon says there are two basic themes suggested by the wilderness motif: YHWH's leadership of the people in the wilderness and the people's disobedience and punishment there. Both themes are utilized in Jer. 2. In addition, Jeremiah continues to use Hosea's 'marital love image', which is, according to Talmon, an 'infusion [by Hosea] into the desert motif of initially unrelated themes' (p. 53). I would propose that Jeremiah also infuses a new element into the wilderness motif: a Cain and Abel subtext. This subtext furthers the 'disobedience and punishment' theme. See also Julia O'Brien's study on the marriage metaphor in Malachi and other prophets ('Judah as Wife and Husband: Deconstructing Gender in Malachi', *JBL* 115 [1996], pp. 241-50).

35. M. Buber's term, '*Leitwort* Style in Pentateuch Narrative' (orig. lecture,

things.[36] The prophet's rhetoric begins with YHWH fondly addressing Judah:

> I've remembered your youthful devotion,
>   your bridal love,
>   your *going after* me in the wilderness,
>   in a land not sown (2.2b-c).

The wilderness imagery where YHWH was engaged in a new relationship with a people, creating a people in 'a land *not* sown', calls to mind another place and time 'when no plant of the field was yet in the earth and no herb of the field had yet sprung up' (Gen. 2.4b-7; NRSV), where YHWH was forming *hā'ādām* from the dust of the ground, planting a garden, and putting humans there. Along with the imagery of wilderness and the marriage metaphor appears an unfolding layer of associated meaning with Genesis traditions. The rhetoric continues:

> 'Set apart is Israel for YHWH,
>   first-fruits of his harvest,
> all eating it will be punished [אשם];
>   evil will come upon them', says YHWH (2.3).

Jacob Milgrom suggests this text refers to the 'consequential meaning' of אשם and that 'Jeremiah, then, applies the law of trespass upon sancta metaphorically to Israel's enemies. It is Aggadic midrash ... on D's concept of the holiness of all Israel ...'[37] But who are Israel's enemies? *Anyone* eating first-fruits set aside for YHWH will be held responsible.[38] This includes not only Jerusalem's outside enemies, but also its own priests, who may be violating their prerogative of receiving the first-fruits set aside for YHWH. Indeed, this text begins to suggest the failings of the priesthood in Jeremiah's time (see 2.8), but as will be

---

'The Bible as Storyteller', 1927) in *Scripture and Translation* (Bloomington: Indiana University Press, 1994), pp. 114-15, 120-21.

36. Noted by Holladay (*Jeremiah 1*, p. 96) and Brueggemann (*To Pluck Up, To Tear Down: A Commentary on the Book of Jeremiah 1–25* (Grand Rapids: Eerdmans; Edinburgh: Handsel Press, 1988], pp. 33-34).

37. *Leviticus 1–16* (AB, 3; New York: Doubleday, 1991), pp. 340, 358.

38. While Holladay suggests the prophet's use of cultic language to envisage Israel is surprising, his comment is suggestive: 'Priests who are disobedient fail to make a distinction between what is appropriate to Yahweh ... and what is fit only for ordinary use ...' (*Jeremiah 1*, p. 84). Carroll notes that mention of the first-fruits requirement emphasizes Israel's protected status, ironic in light of Jerusalem's eventual fate (*Jeremiah*, p. 120).

seen, the failing is not only about the integrity of worship. The improper appropriation of YHWH's offering, the abuse of the cult, leads to social violations of YHWH's people, as the larger text will eventually show.

Anyone eating first fruits set aside by YHWH also invites the Genesis layer of associations of negative examples, in the garden of Eden, and in Cain's bringing an unacceptable offering wherein (it is implied) he brought before YHWH not the *first* fruits, nor the first of the flock, like Abel brought, which YHWH looked upon with favor (Gen. 4.3-5). In that story, Cain was indignant (and perhaps hurt) by YHWH's indifferent response to his offering.

Here in Jer. 2.5, YHWH, perhaps with a 'willingness to admit fault' in this legal dispute, next asks a striking question (Holladay):[39]

> What injustice did your ancestors find in me
> > that they went far away from me?
> > > They went after *hahebel* (ההבל),
> > > > *wayyehbālû* (ויהבלו).

'What injustice did your ancestors find in me ... that they went after[40] "the one who vanishes [is evanescent, like a breath—ההבל—Abel/futility]", and they themselves vanished [like Abel]/became futile?'[41] This initial, cumbersome translation aims to elicit root or 'primal' meanings of the Hebrew wordplay, and associated meanings of biblical names,

---

39. Holladay says Jeremiah 'by his rhetorical question forces the listener to conceive the inconceivable—that Yahweh might have a defect'. This 'willingness to admit fault' is 'hinted at again in the new covenant passage (31.31-34), that Yahweh has learned from the failure of the earlier covenant and will plug the loopholes the next time ...' (*Jeremiah 1*, pp. 85-86)!

40. In no other Jeremiah text does הבל occur as the object of what is 'gone after'. While the construction הלך אחרי often suggests a general or abstract 'following', there are also instances where it means a more graphic 'pursuing' of someone. In Exod. 14.19, the angel of the Lord moves and 'goes after' Israel to protect it from the rear. In Gen. 37.17, Joseph 'goes after' his brothers, looking for them. In Judg. 19.5, the Levite gets up and 'goes after' his concubine. The preposition אחרי without a verb can mean to follow just behind someone, as in Judg. 5.14 where the people fall in and follow Benjamin marching into battle. אחרי also often appears with a number of other verbs meaning 'to chase' or 'pursue', such as רדף.

41. Or, 'They went after the Transient One (Abel) and became transient themselves'. Another translation that captures a meaning of the double root is, 'They went after vapor and evaporated'.

rather than a smooth translation which is reductionistic.[42] Note the exceptional use of the definite article with הבל in 2.5, unusual in poetry,[43] and *nowhere else* used by Jeremiah with this term.[44] The article normally suggests definiteness or identity[45] beyond the noun's

42. Following the Buber-Rosenzweig-Fox method, *'The Five Books of Moses'*, pp. x-xvi.

43. Scholars have shown that poetic texts do not typically make use of the definite article as often as non-poetic texts, see especially D.N. Freedman (*Pottery, Poetry, and Prophecy* [Winona Lake, IN: Eisenbrauns, 1980], pp. 2-3); F. Andersen and A. Forbes (' "Prose Particle" Counts of the Hebrew Bible', in C. Meyers and M. O'Connor [eds.], *The Word of the Lord Shall Go Forth* [Winona Lake, IN: Eisenbrauns, 1983], pp. 165-75 [165-67]). But see also James Barr's discussion of the insufficiencies of grammar books in defining functions of the article (' "Determination" and the Definite Article in Biblical Hebrew', *JSS* 34 [1989], pp. 307-35).

44. See Jer. 8.19; 10.3, 8, 15; 14.22; 16.19; 23.16; and 51.18. Yet the article is used across 2.5-8 to indicate certain individuals: '*the* one who brought us up', '*the* one who led us', '*the* priests', '*the* handlers of the law', '*the* shepherds', '*the* prophets', '*the* Baal'. The definite article with the singular of הבל is used only three times in the Old Testament: (1) here in Jer. 2.5; (2) in 2 Kgs 17.15, which appears to quote Jeremiah's phrase verbatim; and (3) in Ps. 78.33, which ironically falls within a description of the people's rebellion *in the wilderness*. Ps. 78.33 holds a key to understanding this exceptional construction.

45. While proper names do not take the definite article (B. Waltke and M. O'Connor, *An Introduction to Biblical Hebrew Syntax* [Winona Lake, IN: Eisenbrauns, 1990], pp. 230-41), there are three usages of the article which support a reading of ההבל as Abel. First, Waltke and O'Connor say, 'there is one major class of exceptions. Sometimes, through usage, the article not only points out a particular person or thing, but it also elevates it to such a position of uniqueness that the *noun + article* combination becomes the equivalent of a *proper name*' (p. 249). An example is 'the river', meaning the Euphrates, or 'the baal', meaning Baal. This exception allows for names to be constituted. Certainly the prophets, especially Isaiah and Hosea, are depicted as constituting names (e.g. Isa. 7.14, 8.3-4; Hos. 1.6, 9). How then might a previous name be '*re*constituted' if, in fact, it was not a 'name' so much as an appellative' (like הבל) suggestive of other meanings? I propose that by adding the startling definite article, Jeremiah momentarily deconstructs these other meanings and reconstructs a referent for the character Abel from the old story.

Second, while Abel in Gen. 1–4 does not occur with a definite article, there is a precedent for this kind of construction. 'Adam' often occurs with a definite article in Gen. 1–4 (across 'sources') as האדם. Both אדם and האדם occur in Gen. 1–4. While *hā'ādām* occasionally refers to a generic human, it especially points to *the male character in the narrative*. One may see a later example of these two usages of אדם even in this Jeremiah text. In Jer. 2.6, אדם refers to the generic human, 'where no one lives' (NRSV). This reading is supported by the use of איש in parallel with it.

general class, thus the proposed Abel.[46]

A piece of evidence suggestive of Jeremiah's *aggadic* image is found in the *Midrash Haggadol,* passed down from the Jewish community that probably migrated to Yemen after the exile. In it, an *aggadah* on Genesis 4 reads:

> When Abel ... began to shepherd the flock, Cain *chased after* him [רדף אחריו] from mountain to valley and from valley to mountain, until he seized him ... but Abel overpowered Cain and he fell under him ... [emphasis added].[47]

In Jer. 2.5, if one reads/hears beyond a tone of anger in YHWH's wistful question, 'What injustice did your ancestors find in me?', it expresses even greater pathos when heard through the Cain and Abel subtext: your ancestors 'went away from me', and they went after 'their

---

Yet, in Jer. 4.25 in the noted undoing of creation, האדם is used to point back to the human character created in Genesis, thus: 'I looked, and behold! there was no Adam' (NRSV misses this distinction by rendering 'no one').

Third, Barr highlights an overlooked demonstrative or 'deictic' function of the article ה. Following J. Lyons, *Semantics* (Cambridge: Cambridge University Press, 1977), p. 648, he suggests an early meaning of ה is 'Look!' or 'There!' ('"Determination"', pp. 321-22) which seems to function like הנה. Thus in Jer. 2.5 we might be able to translate: 'your ancestors ... went after—look!—Abel!' In fact, since the article at 2.5 is its first appearance in this rhetorical passage, it would have a startling effect on the hearer (especially when followed by the noted string of articles, not to mention a strong assonance in 2.5-8 of the h-sound). Jer. 2.5 then becomes very similar to the verse just mentioned, Jer. 4.25: 'I looked, and behold! [הנה] there was no Adam [האדם]!' Genesis subtexts are evident in Jeremiah's rhetoric.

46. The definite article with a noun suggesting an abstract state may occasionally create a generic usage, such as 'faithfulness' (Waltke and O'Connor, *Introduction*, pp. 244, 246). However, abstract meanings of הבל as a generic usage appear elewhere in Jeremiah *without* the article, e.g. 10.3, 16.19.

47. *Midrash Haggadol* (Jerusalem: Mossad Harav Kook, 1975 [Heb.]). Van der Heide suggests that 'in the *Midrash ha-Gadol* and other *yalqutim* the Yemenites had preserved many forgotten and unknown midrashim, a considerable part of which dated back even to Tannaitic times, with the result that on their discovery a notable gap in our knowledge of the midrash was filled' (*The Yemenite Tradition of the Targum of Lamentations* [Leiden: E.J. Brill, 1981], p. 8). Perhaps Jeremiah referred to a popular aggadah of the Cain and Abel story in Jer. 2.5. Furthermore, Lam. 4 (discussed below) uses a similar piece of rhetoric to convey the subtext, perhaps also borrowing from the above *aggadah*. The people, likened to Abel say: 'They dogged our steps ... our pursuers were swifter than the eagles in the heavens; they chased us on the mountains ...' (Lam. 4.18a, 19a).

brother' (ההבל), and they also were destroyed (like Abel). The question of YHWH's possible injustice or unfairness becomes a point of discussion in the history of interpretation on Genesis 4 and is conveyed by a midrash on Cain and Abel. Cain says to YHWH:

> True, I slew him, but Thou didst create the evil inclination in me. Thou guardest all things; why, then, didst Thou permit me to slay him? Thou didst Thyself slay him, for hadst Thou looked with a favorable countenance toward my offering as toward his, I had had no reason for envying him, and I had not slain him.[48]

At least in this verse within the legal dispute, the subtext strikingly suggests YHWH's distress at the loss of the ancestors and of the northern kingdom (in exile/death),[49] as well as the divine sense of responsibility in losing them and allowing their destruction. Upon closer inspection, the dispute, therefore, in Jeremiah 2 is not completely one-sided in YHWH's favor.

That YHWH destroyed some of the ancestors in the wilderness, as well as brought the northern kingdom to an end, is also presented in Ps. 78.33. That text, too, is set in the wilderness, and it too makes use of a very similar wordplay which may have influenced Jeremiah's rhetoric. After a description of the people's rebellion *in the wilderness*, Ps. 78.33-34a reads:

> So YHWH destroyed their days *bahebel* (in a breath/with Abel), and
>   their years *babbehālāh* (with terror);
> When YHWH killed them, then they sought him and returned.

---

48. See Louis Ginzberg's *The Legends of the Jews* for the citation (New York: Simon & Schuster, 1956), p. 57. Obviously, since the chronology of the 'story-world' in Gen. 4 is before the giving of the Law of Moses, Cain may be defended as ignorant of the first-fruits requirement. Also, Cain might well have claimed, 'Even if my offering was not as favorable, you did not favor me. How is your response any different from mine?' The people will say in effect to YHWH in Jer. 14.7-9 (see below), 'We wandered from you, but you in turn have wandered from us. How is your response any different from ours?' In both cases, YHWH's rejection in which the punishment matches the transgression is questioned as not good enough.

49. Cf. the Jer. 2.5 wordplay appearing verbatim in 2 Kgs 17.15. It falls within a description of the actions of the northern kingdom in the Syro-Ephraimite war resulting in its exile. Perhaps the subtext is suggestive of Israel's actions. When Israel with Rezin of Damascus turned against Judah, Israel 'went after Abel' like Cain going after his brother. The immediate historical result was that the northern kingdom disapeared, some of Israel 'became like Abel', and some of Israel went into exile, like Cain.

The meaning of intended violence by YHWH is clear,[50] even though
the rationale appears to be to intimidate the surviving people into obedience.[51] Note the sound similarities to the wordplay in Jer. 2.5.

> *way^{e}kal-bahebel ...*   *babbehālāh* (Ps. 78.33)
> *wayyēl^{e}kû 'ahrê hahebel ...*   *wayyehbālû* (Jer. 2.5b)

Psalm 78 may have influenced Jeremiah's rhetoric. Psalm 78 depicts
YHWH as killing the people. The text also depicts YHWH relenting:
'Yet he, being compassionate, forgave their iniquity, and did not
destroy them; often he restrained his anger, and did not stir up all his
wrath. He remembered that they were but flesh, a wind that passes [not
a הבל but a רוח] and does not come again' (Ps. 78.38, NRSV).

On the other hand, the subtext of Jeremiah 2 implies that it was the
ancestors of the people who killed their brother/sibling *in the wilderness* and then were destroyed themselves. Nevertheless, Jer. 2.1-9 also
suggests YHWH's self-questioning and complicity in the destruction.

The wordplay in Jer. 2.5 is a 'polysemantic pun'.[52] It suggests at least

---

50.   However, this meaning is glossed over by a weak NRSV translation: 'So
YHWH made their days vanish like a breath'. While 'made vanish' captures the
causative sense of the piel verb, כלה, it does not capture a piel meaning of the verb
'to destroy' (BDB, p. 478). The NRSV also amends the MT's preposition 'with' to
'like'. Read instead a wordplay, 'So YHWH destroyed/ended their days in a vapor/
with the one, Abel, who so vanishes, and their years with terror'.

51.   Yet, later in this text when the northern kingdom rebelled, YHWH 'gave
the people to the sword' (78.62, NRSV).

52.   W.G.E. Watson defines a 'polysemantic pun' as one in which a word can
have two or more meanings; these meanings are purposefully exploited by the poet
for effect. Often such wordplays are referred to as having 'double meaning' (*Classical Hebrew Poetry* [Sheffield: Sheffield Academic Press, 2nd rev. edn, 1995], pp.
238-42). Wordplay, which the ancients and rabbinic tradition were well aware of, is
increasingly being noticed by modern scholars across a range of biblical Hebrew
poetry; Scott B. Noegel (*Janus Parallelism in the Book of Job* [JSOTSup, 223;
Sheffield: Sheffield Academic Press, 1996] and other scholars would counter
Watson's claim that this kind of wordplay is uncommon in Ugaritic or Akkadian
poetry, where they have found a growing number of examples of 'Janus parallelism'. This is a type of wordplay where a single word 'faces' in two semantic
directions. In Cyrus Gordon's definition, Janus parallelism 'hinges on the use of a
single word with two entirely different meanings: one meaning paralleling what precedes, and the other meaning, what follows' (quoted in Watson, *Classical*, p. 159).
Watson points out an example of this in the larger Jeremiah text under consideration in 2.14-15 which begins, 'Is Israel a slave ... why has he become a *contempt/*

two primary meanings or usages of the root הבל: (1) the appellative of the person *Abel* (הבל),[53] suggestive of one who disappears, like a breath, vapor, who has a short, fleeting, even futile, life;[54] and (2) the more abstract 'evanescence, futility, worthlessness', often used as a metonymy for 'idols'.[55] NRSV thus translates this second meaning:

spoil ...' The word בז, means 'contempt' in terms of the first part of the text, but 'spoil' in terms of the last part referring to lions (p. 159).

53. Mishael Caspi conveyed regarding the birth of Abel in Gen. 4 (private communication): 'There is nearly always a giving meaning to the name of the newborn. By comparison, there is no meaning for naming Dinah, and right after the rape she is not mentioned again. By not being presented a meaning to the name of *Hevel*, the reader is presented with a hidden concept that this person will have a short role. The reader is aware of the meaning of the word *hevel* as "vapor", a mist which is seen and disappears at almost the same time.' Watson notes the frequent use of puns on proper names in the Hebrew Bible (*Classical*, pp. 244-45). See H. Fisch's study of Hosea: 'The Naming of Names is the Very Matter of Hosea's Prophecy' (*Poetry with a Purpose* [Bloomington: Indiana University Press, 1988], pp. 136-57 [144]).

54. Gen. 4 commentators usually note that Abel's name itself suggests 'breath, nothing, futility' or the like. 'An explanation of this name is not given, but everyone who hears it thinks of the other Hebrew word *hebel* ("breath", "futility") [!] and takes this connotation as a somber allusion to what follows' (G. von Rad, *Genesis* [OTL; Philadelphia: Westminster Press, 1961], p. 100); 'puff, vanity', E.A. Speiser, *Genesis* (AB, 1; Garden City, NY: Doubleday, 1964), p. 30; 'he is named "Breath, Nothingness" ', C. Westermann, *Genesis: A Practical Commentary* (Grand Rapids: Eerdmans, 1987), p. 32, and, 'it is an appellative rather than a proper name ...' *Genesis 1–11* (Minneapolis: Augsburg, 1984), p. 292; 'Abel's name is "vapor, noth-ingness", without the possibility of life', Walter Brueggemann, *Genesis* (Interpreta-tion; Atlanta: John Knox Press, 1982), p. 56; 'breath, nothingness ... the fleeting nature of life', N. Sarna, *Genesis* (JPS Torah Commentary; Philadelphia: Jewish Publication Society of America, 1989), p. 32; 'the significance of Abel's name, "futility", lies in the story itself and cannot derive from any other source, such as a genealogy', John Van Seters, *Prologue to History* (Louisville, KY: Westminster/ John Knox Press, 1992), p. 137; 'the name suggests "something transitory" ', Fox, *'The Five Books of Moses'*, p. 25. In a recent study of the word הבל in Ecclesiastes, Michael Fox proposed a new translation for the term there: 'absurdity'. Yet, in his wider biblical word study, he neglects to mention its usage in Gen. 4, 'The Meaning of *Hebel* for *Qoheleth*', *JBL* 105 (1986), pp. 409-27. If most commentators readily regard the name Abel in Gen. 4 as suggesting the above meanings, is it not also possible that when the term appears elsewhere it may suggest Abel?

55. In the Hebrew Bible, הבל occurs about 76 times, and except for Genesis, occurs in overwhelmingly *poetic* texts: Gen. 4.2 (2×), 4 (2×), 8 (2×), 9, 25; Deut. 32.21; Isa. 30.7, 49.4, 57.13; Lam. 4.17; Zech. 10.2; 1 Kgs 16.13, 26; 2 Kgs 17.15;

'They went after worthless things and became worthless.' Added to these meanings of the הבל wordplay in 2.5 should be added John Bright's proposal of a likely wordplay, more subtle, with Baal who appears later in 2.8.[56]

Among some of the rhetorical devices favored by Jeremiah which William Holladay identified,[57] two are found here with הבל: the double occurrence of a root in its noun and verbal forms, and the use of 'double meanings'. Holladay notes:

> Jeremiah often achieves pure sorcery in his plays on words. His ringing of the changes on *šûb* comes to mind; he loves to play on the variety of meanings which this verb offers ... There are other instances in which he seems deliberately to exploit two contrasting meanings of a word. In 8.13 we are uncertain as to whether *'āsap* means 'gather' or 'destroy'. But must we choose? Jeremiah surely had both in mind.[58]

Jon. 2.9; Prov. 13.11, 21.6, 31.30; Pss. 31.7; 39.6, 7, 12; 62.10, 11; 78.33; 94.11; 144.4; Job 7.16; 21.34; 27.12; 35.16; Qoh. 1.2 (2×), 14; 2.1, 11, 15, 17, 19, 21, 23, 26; 3.19; 4.4, 7, 8, 16; 5.6, 9; 6.2, 4, 9, 11, 12; 7.6 (2×), 15; 8.14; 9.9 (2×); 11.8, 10; 12.8 (from Solomon Mandelkern, *Veteris Testamenti Concordantiae* [Jerusalem: Sumptibus Schocken, 1955], p. 307, except the Genesis texts which he does not include). The *only* other occurrence of the word in the Pentateuch, besides Gen. 4, is Deut. 32.21. There the word suggests 'idols' in parallel with gods (NRSV; NJPS fn.). Thus one finds both the meaning 'idol' as well as 'Abel' in moderately early texts. One may conclude that Jeremiah's use of הבל could refer to Abel and its connotations crystallized in the old story in Gen. 4 as well as to 'idols'.

56. Bright is one of the few scholars whose translation takes into account the definite article possibly functioning to create an appellative. However, his translation of ההבל in 2.5 as 'Lord Delusion' oversteps the meanings of הבל. Bright also suggests v. 8 (והנביאים נבאו בבעל ואחרי לא־יועלו הלכו) ('by Baal they prophesied and followed 'the useless ones') and v. 11b ('Lord Useless') contain plays on Baal (*Jeremiah*, pp. 10, 15). The term יעל means 'to profit, benefit' and plays on the meanings of Baal, 'to possess' or 'own' (BDB, p. 127; *Jeremiah*, pp. 10, 15).

57. These include the use of chiasmus, assonance, irony, and abrupt changes of speaker, 'Style, Irony, and Authenticity in Jeremiah', *JBL* 81 (1962), pp. 44-54.

58. Holladay, 'Style', p. 45. R. Gordis has identified this use of double meaning, which the rabbis called *talḥin*, in Lamentations and Job. He defines it as 'the choice of a particular word because it not only carries a primary significance appropriate to the context, but also a secondary meaning. Unlike paranomasia, where only one meaning is intended, in *talḥin* both are present in the consciousness of the poet and the reader' (*The Song of Songs and Lamentations* [New York: Ktav, 1954], pp. 122-23). Trible calls this technique 'antanaclasis' (*Rhetorical Criticism*, p. 126).

Holladay suggests Jeremiah will often 'heighten vocabulary' in this way. A word used in a certain context Jeremiah stretches to fit a wholly unexpected context.[59] Such is the case in Jer. 2.5. With one stroke of the chord, several notes reverberate: the people go after Abel and after idols, bringing consequences *both* futile and fatal.[60] The second meaning of the wordplay suggests that the ancestors pursued the idols of the nations around them and their pursuit came to nought (cf. Deut. 32.21; 1 Kgs 16.13, 26). This meaning Jeremiah texts also utilize; however, they do *not* have the article with הבל (Jer. 8.19, 10.3, 8, 15; 14.22; 16.19; and 51.18).

A notable and rare verbal use of הבל (hi. participle) occurs in Jer. 23.16: 'Do not listen to the words of the prophets who are prophesying to you; *they* are making you הבל.' This occurrence has more in common with the Jer. 2.5 text's use of the verb, as here it suggests that the prophets, in their deceptive words that lead the people astray, may cause them to become like Abel. (May this text suggest an oral tradition in which Cain lured Abel out to the field with deceptive words?) In Jer. 23.16 the prophets are analogous to Cain, and should be avoided. This meaning clearly emerges again in Lam. 4.15 where the priests and prophets are likened to Cain in graphic imagery (see below).

Moreover, after the prophets are likened to Cain in Jer. 23.16, at v. 23 this subtext is corroborated by evidence, again, from the *Midrash Haggadol*. In the midrash on Genesis 4, Cain comes before YHWH after killing his brother and pretends to know nothing. The midrash has YHWH *confront Cain* by quoting YHWH's own words of accusation found in *Jer. 23.23 against Judah*:

59. Holladay, 'Style', p. 46.

60. David Handy has a helpful discussion of the echoes of intertextuality in terms of musical overtones in his dissertation, 'The Gentile Pentecost: A Literary Study of the Story of Peter and Cornelius (Acts 10.1–11.18)' (PhD dissertation, Union Theological Seminary and Presbyterian School of Christian Education, 1998), pp. 38-39. He suggests that by holding down a piano key without playing it, in order to allow the strings to vibrate, and then playing that note an octave lower, 'the sound waves of the lower note strike the strings an octave higher and set them in motion through "sympathetic vibration" ... In a similar way, one biblical passage can "strike a chord" in us by causing another passage buried in our memory to start ringing by a sort of mental "sympathetic vibration".' One might add that repeated striking of sympathetic notes across a text can create a sustained undertone or *subtext*.

> Am I a God nearby, and not a God far off?
> Who can hide in secret places so that I cannot see him?

In this midrash, YHWH is speaking at once to both Cain and Judah.

Returning to Jeremiah 2, YHWH continues the description of the ancestors:

> They did not say,
> 'Where is YHWH?
> the One who brought us up from the land of Egypt,
> the One who led us in the wilderness,
> > in a land of deserts and pits,
> > in a land of drought and deathshadow,
> > in a land no one had passed through,
> > and where no human had dwelt' (Jer. 2.6).

YHWH's dispute with Judah began with concern for the cult and the suggestion of the misuse of offerings (2.3). Here, the prophet's rhetoric suggests a *failure of speech* in the cult. The question 'Where is YHWH?' apparently was used at the beginning of litanies to introduce YHWH's former saving actions (see this pattern in Isa. 63.11-12, just as Jeremiah presents the formula here, with the same question followed by a litany that was, however, *not* spoken by the priests of old).[61] The question also appears a few times in prophetic accusation speech, as below in Jeremiah's highly ironic speech in 2.28 against Judah: '*Where are your gods* that you made for yourself?'[62] More important than the absence of the initial question is the absence of the recounting of YHWH's saving deeds, with which both psalms of lament and praise traditionally, implicitly confirmed and invoked YHWH's *present* power. In Jeremiah 2, YHWH laments and misses hearing the expected litany, the regular conversation. The prophet's rhetoric suggests a neglect of YHWH, even as the cult proceeds, and an assumption that YHWH is not really present. The *Leitwort* of the people's earlier, blissful 'going after' YHWH is no more. As in the garden of Eden, and as with Cain, there is an analogy that the people believed their actions in the 'garden-land' were without consequence when they came to meet YHWH in conversation (i.e. worship).

---

61. That this question does not appear regularly in the liturgy of the Psalms raises the possibility that it was an antiphonal line used only by the priests in worship. In Ps. 42 the lamenter's enemies use the question as a taunt, 'Where *is* your God?' and in Ps. 79.10 the enemy nation also says, 'Where is their God?'

62. See the question also used in Hos. 13.10; Mic. 7.10; Joel 2.17; Mal. 2.17.

Perhaps because the wilderness was traditionally the place of the Hebrews' rebellion and 'wandering' (נוע, Num. 32.13) imposed by YHWH, this *Leitwort* of 'wandering' allows Jeremiah to use the Cain and Abel subtext there to foreshadow the danger lying ahead in Judah's future, as it was for Cain. For YHWH, the recurring, destructive pattern of the people's transgression is not only cause for anger, but anguish, for YHWH has a past that includes allowing violence to run its course against the people. Leaving behind past failings, YHWH now shifts to address directly this generation of Judah in 2.7a:

> Then I brought *you* into the garden-land,
>> to eat its fruit and its goodness ...
> But you came in and defiled (טמא) my land,
>>> and my heritage you made abhorrent (2.7b).

That Jeremiah's term here, 'garden-land' (ארץ הכרמל), aims to suggest the garden or fertile vegetation of Genesis is evident in his rhetoric of 4.23-26.[63]

> I looked on the earth, and behold! waste and void (תהו ובהו)!
> and to the heavens, and no light! ...
> I looked, and behold! no human (האדם)!
> and all the birds of the air had fled (נדד);
> I looked, and behold! the garden-land (כרמל) a desert (המדבר)! ...

Back to Jer 2.8, the accused 'you' of the text is now made explicit:

> The priests did not say,
>> 'Where is YHWH?'
> The handlers of the law ignored me,
> The rulers rebelled against me, and
> The prophets prophesied by Baal,
>> and went after things that do no good (2.7-8).

The *defilement* of the land is being caused by the actions of the cultic, legal and political leaders. In this piercing critique, they defile the land, not only by the pursuit of false gods, but by *the shedding of blood* (see Num. 35.33-34),[64] suggesting internal social violence and oppression.

How descendants of the exiles in the Babylonian synagogue read the Jeremiah 2 text suggests the text's concern for defilement of the land by

---

63. Jer. 2.7 seems to borrow from the creation traditions of Gen. 1 and 2–3.

64. Holladay lists all the potential actions that defile the land: sexual transgressions, child sacrifice (Lev. 18.19-30), murder (Num. 35.34), and by leaving the corpse of a criminal hung on a tree overnight (Deut. 21.23) (*Jeremiah 1*, p. 88).

bloodshed. The synagogue began a liturgical tradition of reading Jer. 2.4-28 with Numbers 33–36 (also concerned with defilement of the land by bloodshed) as a *haftorah* in worship just before the ninth of Ab (to commemorate the destruction of Jerusalem). They read these texts together because of their accordance in themes.[65] The Numbers text is also set *in the wilderness* and concerns the Hebrews *entering the land*.[66] It focuses on the Levitical towns, the cities of refuge for a murderer, and the avenger of blood. A portion reads:

> You shall not pollute [חנף] the land in which you live, for blood pollutes the land, and no expiation can be made for the land, for the blood that is shed in it, except by the blood of the one who shed it. You shall not defile [טמא] the land in which you live, in which I also dwell (Num. 35.33-34b).

Given this theme in Jeremiah 2, Richard Nelson Boyce's analysis of the cry of Abel's blood is suggestive of why a Cain and Abel subtext serves Jeremiah's legal dispute (ריב) here:

> The blood of the murdered innocent does not cry out once and stop; it characteristically keeps on crying out until it is heard ... Abel, now dead, can obviously not represent himself at the trial of his own murder. It is therefore left to his blood to appeal for such a hearing, a 'testimonial' function elsewhere in evidence (e.g., Job 16.18-19) ... Following a murder ... the cry functions ... as a cry for *vengeance* ... for an 'avenger of blood', *go'el haddam* (Num. 35.19; Deut. 19.6; Josh. 20.3; etc.) ... Here it seems is a special type of legal appeal properly directed toward the king or YHWH, an appeal they both were especially obligated to hear.[67]

Moreover, in light of the defilement of the land by bloodshed, it is inaccurate to conclude that the text is *primarily* concerned with 'apos-

---

65.   Thus C. Roth and G. Wigoder (eds.), 'Torah, Reading of', in *Encyclopaedia Judaica*, XV (Jerusalem: Keter Publishing House, 1971), pp. 1247-51. The Jeremiah and Numbers texts can be found in A. Cohen (ed.), *The Soncino Chumash* (Hindhead, Surrey: Soncino Press, 1947), pp. 971-87, or J. Hertz (ed.), *The Pentateuch and Haftorahs* (London: Soncino Press, 1968), pp. 725-26. Hertz notes that Jer. 2.4-28 (and 3.4; 4.1-2) is the second of the three 'Haftorahs of Rebuke' read on successive Sabbaths just before the ninth of Ab, the anniversary of the destruction of Jerusalem (pp. 702-54).

66.   Cf. Num. 34.2 with Jer. 2.7b.

67.   *The Cry to YHWH in the Old Testament* (Atlanta: SBL, 1988), pp. 44-45. For a discussion of ancient traditions about blood defiling the land, see J.G. Frazer, *Folklore in the Old Testament* (New York: Avenel Books, 1923), pp. 33-45.

tasy', as many commentators do. That generalist reading supports an interpretation of the wordplay in 2.5 as being only about going after idols and misses the subtext's subtle but serious concern for social abuse. The phrase 'going after' is suggestive of more than merely a 'religious' problem. It is concerned with more of the commandments, so to speak, than just the first. As the text repeats over and again, the people have committed *two* evils, forsaking YHWH *and* pursuing other things (in vv. 8, 13, 17-18, 28, 31). Indeed, by 2.34, there is the overt accusation: 'Also on your hands is discovered the *lifeblood of the inno-cent*.'[68] Brueggemann is one of the few commentators who observes that the text reflects 'deep social conflict…[in] the divided Jerusalem community'.[69]

In Jer. 2.10-37, YHWH's anguish turns to anger, suggested by the series of metaphors denouncing Judah's 'roaming' behavior (as a bride, a slave, an ox, a whore, a wild vine, a thief and a murderer). Then at 2.23b YHWH implores Judah, '*Know* what *you have done*!' This is a 'frustrated' imperative form of the question YHWH asks Cain after he kills his brother: '*What have you done*?' (Gen. 4.10). Cain had responded with apparent denial, 'I did not *know* I was my brother's keeper' (Gen. 4.9). Again (Jer. 2.31), YHWH raises another striking, self-critical question: 'Have I myself been a *wilderness* to Israel…why do my people say, "We roam about;[70] we will not come to you any more"?'

Robert Carroll points to YHWH's words just before this: 'In vain have I smitten your children, they took no correction…' (Jer. 2.30). Carroll raises an essential point here: the people could justifiably respond by saying, 'a God who destroys his own people is a thick dark-ness, a desert and a demoniacal force'.[71] The people have forgone any

---

68. Following the Septuagint.

69. *To Pluck Up, To Tear Down*, p. 13. For the sociopolitical use of the Cain and Abel story in Talmudic literature and the use of 'Cain' as a subterfuge or code name for the Roman Empire, see D. Hirsch and N. Aschkenasy, *Biblical Patterns in Modern Literature* (BJS, 77; Chico, CA: Scholars Press, 1984), pp. 1-2.

70. Since there are several variant readings, *BHS* proposes amending the MT's רדנו 'we roam' (from רוד), to נדנו 'we wander' (from נוד), drawing evidence from the use of this verb in 4.1. However, emendation is not necessary; רוד likely carries connotations of wandering (BDB, p. 923). As becomes apparent, the book of Jere-miah presents a range of images and terms to fill out the leitmotif 'wandering' (see discussion of Jer. 14.18 below).

71. 'Small wonder that the people should shun him' (*Jeremiah*, p. 138). Yet

desire to be in YHWH's presence, even though it is requisite for dwelling in the 'garden-land'.

The subtext of Cain and Abel, as *aggadic* rhetoric, draws forth the latent motif of Cain's *wandering* away from YHWH. Upon YHWH's corresponding punishment in making him a 'fugitive and wanderer' banished from Eden, Cain vociferously laments that that punishment is too great to bear, to be separated from the soil, and hidden from YHWH's face. In contrast, *Judah does not lament* its 'roaming' existence apart from YHWH—Judah *prefers* it. Here Jeremiah has taken the story of Cain a step further: the people have grown to love their 'cursed' existence.[72] Yet the troubling suggestion remains that there is something about YHWH's behavior that drives them away.

The key rhetorical purposes of the Cain and Abel subtext in Jeremiah 2 may now be summarized. The subtext begins as a vehicle of accusation for YHWH against Judah (and their ancestors, including the northern kingdom) whose actions are parallel to Cain. More specifically, the following elements of plot begin to act as an unfolding parable in serving the prophet's persuasive task. First, the story of Cain and Abel contains a turning point in the plot where Cain is presented with the possibility (and warning) of choosing to do good or not. This open-endedness in the story, where Cain faces a moment of decision which will determine his future, also marks where Judah is before YHWH in

---

Carroll says, 'However, that is not the intention of the speaker: it is not Yahweh's behavior which is being questioned but the people's religious affiliations. That the speaker is unaware of the theological difficulties raised by vv. 30-31 (contrast the lament psalms or the book of Job) reveals just how ideologically committed the discourse is to a one-dimensional interpretation of the exilic disaster' (Carroll, *Jeremiah*, p. 138). To the contrary, I think, the speaker *is* raising the theological difficulty of YHWH's behavior, and it is through YHWH's self-critical speech! Indeed, Carroll's ideological reading on this text is 'one-dimensional' in so far as it completely takes the side of the people against YHWH and the 'speaker'. A closer reading of the text reveals a more complex and complete picture: Jeremiah's rhetoric negatively critiques *both* YHWH and people, yet also, in later texts, conveys empathy for both the people and YHWH. Perhaps this is in line with the genre of the רִיב, though granted, the people's side of the argument will not be presented until Jer. 14 (below). The text is large enough, one trusts, to critique YHWH as well, and that YHWH is large enough for self-criticism. Indeed, the critique of YHWH is a key point carried by the vehicle of the Cain and Abel subtext.

72. See Kathleen O'Connor's analysis of the movement toward curse across Jer. 11–25 (*The Confessions of Jeremiah: Their Interpretation and Role in Chapters 1–25* [SBLDS, 94; Atlanta: Scholars Press, 1988], pp. 154-55).

Jeremiah 2. Second, the story is primarily concerned with the violent action of one sibling against another, of internal, familial and social conflict, matters with which Jeremiah is concerned (see Jer. 5.1; 5.26; 6.6-7; 7.9, 8.10; 9.4-5, 22.3-4) in his indictment of Judah. The twofold meaning of the wordplay gives voice to the cry of the blood of Abel in the ריב against Judah, along with the accusation of the pursuit of other gods and their idols. The land is defiled not only by idols, but by the shedding of blood. Third, the Cain and Abel story also contains a striking divine–human confrontation and a dialogue of mutual dispute and denial (Gen. 4.9-10). Fourth, the plots of Genesis 4 and Jeremiah 2 depict the movement from an idyllic state (Eden/garden-land) to banishment (east of Eden/exile). And fifth, there is the questioning of YHWH's justice in responding to Cain and Judah, raising theological dilemmas about divine mercy, forgiveness and human freedom.

Larger Structure of rîb/dispute to Jeremiah 14

YHWH's side of the dispute, begun in ch. 2, goes on across the text for the next 13 chapters. Any speech by the people of Judah is only quoted from Yahweh's point of view. Finally, after a long silence (implying avoidance?), the people speak. It is a climactic moment analogous to YHWH's confrontation with Cain. Precisely here, in Jeremiah 14, the subtext surfaces again.

The Subtext in Jeremiah 14.1-10

While scholars largely refer to the people's *communal lament*[73] beginning at v. 7, the text does not give the people the first word.[74] The text

73. Scholars who generally identify Jer. 14 as containing communal lament include Bright (*Jeremiah*, p. 102); Westermann (*Praise and Lament in the Psalms* [Atlanta: John Knox Press, 1981], p. 60; *Basic Forms of Prophetic Speech* [Louisville, KY: Westminster/John Knox Press, 1991], p. 91); W. McKane, *A Critical and Exegetical Commentary on Jeremiah*. I. *Introduction and Commentary on Jeremiah I–XXV* (ICC; Edinburgh: T. & T. Clark, 1986), p. 316; Carroll (*Jeremiah*, p. 308); Holladay (*Jeremiah 1*, pp. 425, 427); E. Gerstenberger (*The Forms of Old Testament Literature*. XIV. *Psalms, Part One* [Grand Rapids: Eerdmans, 1988], pp. 9-10); Brueggemann (*To Pluck Up, To Tear Down*, p. 128); and R. Clements, *Jeremiah* (Interpretation; Atlanta: John Knox Press, 1988), p. 89.

74. For the general dramatic and dialogical nature of Jer. 14, see R. Gordis (*Poets, Prophets, and Sages* [Bloomington: Indiana University Press, 1971],

opens, rather, with a *non-human* point of view, a third-person description of the distress and dying of Jerusalem and the land of Judah, its creatures and towns.

1. The word of the Lord that came to Jeremiah concerning the matters of the hardships.[75]
2. Judah mourns and her gates [cities] languish,
    They grow dark to the ground, and the cry of Jerusalem goes up;
3.   Their nobles send their servants for water;
    They come to the pools, they do not find water,
    their vessels return empty;[76]
    They are ashamed and humiliated, and cover their heads.
4.   For the earth is in terror—
    because there is no rain in the land—
    The farmers are ashamed, they cover their heads.
5.   For even the doe in the field gives birth and forsakes,
    because there is no grass.

p. 117); W. Beuken and H. van Grol, 'Jeremiah 14,1–15,9: A Situation of Distress and its Hermeneutics. Unity and Diversity of Form-Dramatic Development', in P.-M. Bogaert (ed.), *Le livre de Jérémie: Le prophète et son milieu, les oracles et leur transmission* (Leuven: Peeters, 1981), pp. 297-342 (297); and Y. Gitay ('Rhetorical Criticism and the Prophetic Discourse', in D.F. Watson (ed.), *Persuasive Artistry: Studies in New Testament Rhetoric in Honor of George A. Kennedy* (JSOTSup, 50; Sheffield: JSOT Press, 1991), pp. 13-24.

75. Or distresses, dearths (KJV). That the plural of בצר at 14.1 conveys not only 'drought' (thus NRSV still and many scholars), *but also* the 'siege' (or cutting off) of the city and land is very evident. This striking plural term in 14.1 is its only occurrence in the entire Hebrew Bible. Yet, NRSV has translated *the same feminine word in the singular* in Ps. 9.10 (and Ps. 10.1) as 'trouble'. Yet later in this unit, Judah's speech uses the phrase 'its time of trouble' (NRSV) (בעת צרה); consider the possibility that if those two terms were joined, with the last term plural, one might get הבצרות. Thus I propose that the term refers to the 'matters of (the time of) the hardships' including siege and drought. Is this a signal indicating the beginning of the siege and destruction of Jerusalem in 587? Note 2 Kgs 25.2's important reference to the simultaneous state of siege (במצור) into which Jerusalem 'entered' while being 'seized' by famine (רעב) at the second deportation in 587. Note also in 14.18, those in the fields outside the city are being slain, while those in the city are suffering from famine, due perhaps to drought, but also to the cutting off of food sources, common in a siege. Importantly, other terms are also used for drought in Jeremiah (חרב) in 50.38, and ציה in 2.6. In Jeremiah texts, בצר and צור *usually* have the connotation of 'cutting off' or 'siege' (6.9; 10.17; 19.9; 21.4, 9; 32.2; 37.5; 52.5). The rationale for maintaining 'drought' alone as the translation of הבצרות in 14.1 is weak. See also Beuken and van Grol ('Jer. 14,1–15,9', pp. 322, 325, 336).

76. Following Holladay (*Jeremiah 1*, p. 430).

6.   And the wild asses stand on the bare hills;
they pant for air like jackals, their eyes fail,
because there is no herbage (14.1-6).

Jeremiah 14.1-6 renders a cry going up from Jerusalem, giving voice
to one who is *dying*, Jerusalem personified. The image of Jerusalem in
the throes of death[77] casts a scene from which the subtext, with the
slaying of Abel, will emerge below (14.17-18). The genre of 14.1-6 is a
communal dirge.[78] Yet, Jeremiah's rhetoric, unlike other prophetic
instances of communal dirge which describe death/destruction as an
accomplished fact or image, here depicts death as an *unfolding process*.[79] This may give credence to the possibility that the text is
describing the beginning of siege in 587 (see n. 76 above). The *warning*
element of YHWH's accusation is still at work, at the zero hour, desperately pointing the people to the danger signs of imminent death—
languishing cities, powerless nobles, lack of water, parched land and
lack of food for dying animals.

In the first verse, the verb אבל, to mourn, sets the tone for the
communal dirge.[80] Verses 1-6 give a last glimpse of the land of Judah.
And Jerusalem (like הבל), having cried out and now resigned and
laboring under death, lifts its dimmed eyes *to the people* and looks for
a response. If ever there was a place in the text for a strong word

77.   Brueggemann notes the emphasis on death in vv. 7-9 and 19-22 (*To Pluck
Up, To Tear Down*, p. 128).

78.   Dirge elements in this text include a description of crisis, an outcry or
wailing, mourning by Judah, and expressions of shame by covering heads with dust.

79.   See Ferris's discussion of the neo-Sumerian city-state Laments as being
overwhelmingly 'retrospective' in outlook (*The Genre of Communal Lament in the
Bible and the Ancient Near East* [SBLDS, 127; Atlanta: Scholars Press, 1992],
p. 161).

80.   The sound of the term is suggestive of the name, הבל. Professor Bruegge-
mann first suggested to me the association of these words. Jewish tradition associ-
ated the name הבל with אבל, to 'mourn'. L. Ginzberg quotes Josephus who said,
'Abel ... signifies sorrow' (*Ant.* 1.2.1; cited in L. Ginzberg, *The Legends of the
Jews*, V [Philadelphia: Jewish Publication Society of America, 1953], p. 135).
Ginzberg says this is 'a midrashic explanation which is based on the similarity of
sound ... this is already found in Philo' (*De Migr. Abrah.* 13.74; cited in *Legends*,
V, p. 135). The similarity of sound is probably reflected in the textual variant of
Deut. 32.21 (referred to above), where the Samaritan Pentateuch has באבליהם
instead of the MT's בהבליהם (idols) (referred to in E. Tov, *Textual Criticism of the
Hebrew Bible* [Minneapolis: Fortress Press, 1992], p. 96).

signaling confession, here it is. But no—the people begin their long-awaited speech, surrounded by the throes of death, with an '*if*'!

> *Even if* our iniquities speak against us,[81]
> O Lord, act for the sake of your name (7a).

The particle 'if' (אם) in Jeremiah usually marks a question or conditional clause. Here it is concessive. Finally responding, the people first relegate their sin to a concessive clause which may not be all that 'confessive'.[82] They quickly cast the responsibility back onto YHWH with an imperative to 'act!', which is the real stress of the sentence. In the people's speech is also an angry and aggressive reply. In the overall rhetoric of Jer. 2–14, YHWH has been using 'if' (אם) in a flurry of accusing questions fired at the people. Now the people turn this stinging little word (אם) they've heard so often from the prophet back on YHWH in preparation for their own attack.[83] Note that the speaking voice is not specified as a particular group (priests, prophets or king; cf. YHWH's response in v. 11: 'this people!'). The people offer a quick confession:

> For many are our turnings;
> Against you we have sinned (v. 7b).

Then, instead of answering YHWH's avalanche of questions, the people boldly stand firm in their turn to speak, not only with mere confession in communal lament, but with stinging accusation against YHWH whom they look upon as utterly powerless to help them.[84]

---

81. The use is concessive (noted by Holladay, *Jeremiah 1*, p. 432; also N. Kessler, 'From Drought to Exile: A Morphological Study of Jer. 14.1–15.5', *SBL Proceedings 1972* [Missoula, MT: Scholars Press], p. 505). The angry tone of the use of אם in 15.1 ('*Even if* Moses and Samuel stood before me …') only raises a hypothetical possibility to be dashed by YHWH's negative response.

82. Beuken and van Grol ('Jer. 14,1–15,9', p. 327), suggest the people's answer is 'ambiguous' and becomes a 'reproach' of YHWH. They see the people's stance as part of 'temple theology', hinted at by their reference to YHWH's 'name' in vv. 7 and 9.

83. As Brueggemann has shown, Jeremiah's prevalent use of questions elsewhere (with מדוע, ה and אם) works to 'establish the basis of consensus between covenant partners … [and] creates an entry for the accusation' ('Jeremiah's Use of Rhetorical Questions', *JBL* 92 [1973], pp. 358-74 [362-63]).

84. As such, YHWH becomes the people's *enemy*. The communal lament genre of this text bears this sense, wherein the expected elaboration of confession is replaced suddenly by elaboration about the enemy–YHWH. YHWH *as enemy*

8. Hope of Israel,
    Its Savior in time of trouble,
    Why are you being like a sojourner in the land?
                    like a wayfarer stretching out for the night?
9. Why are you being like a man confused?[85]
                    like a warrior with no power to save?
    But you are in our midst, Lord;
    By your name we are called—do not abandon us! (14.7-9).

Judah takes God's initial complaint in 2.5: 'They did not ask, "Where is YHWH? the one bringing us up from the land of Egypt ..." ' and *asks now: 'Where is YHWH?!'* turning God's hoped for litany of praise into a litany of ridicule.[86] Judah turns the tables and accuses YHWH of wandering aimlessly, of not being YHWH.[87] God had asked the people earlier, 'Have I been a wilderness to Israel?' The people now answer, 'Yes!' Here, the people take the Cain and Abel subtext and turn it back on God, virtually accusing YHWH of being like Cain. The people are justified in their critique. YHWH is destroying them, relinquishing the land (and defiling it) by allowing the deadly consequences of their sin to go forward fully, by not intervening. One must ponder the people's

overrides the expected YHWH as 'Savior' in times past and 'Hope' in the present. For this reason, Jer. 14 bears close connections to the rhetoric of Lamentations, which also accuses YHWH of being the enemy. Westermann's view that Jer. 14 is a 'variation' of the communal Lament genre (*Praise and Lament*, p. 174) misses the anger, perhaps even sarcasm, of the people's accusations against YHWH as enemy; the text is more a 'violation' of the genre than a 'variation' (see below). The people have seized on the lament form in order to express their ריב complaint against YHWH. As such the genre carries the ambiguity: first people, then YHWH, are depicted at serious fault.

85. NRSV.

86. The insult of YHWH here is indicated by how the Targum of Jeremiah changes the abrasive language in vv. 8-9 so that *the people* become the subject of these verbs rather than YHWH (trans. R. Hayward [Wilmington, DE: Michael Glazier, 1987], p. 90). For a reading of a sarcastic *tone* of the people's voice in a biblical text, see B. Elmo Scoggin's analysis of Mic. 6.6-8 ('An Expository Exegesis: Micah 6.6-8', *Faith and Mission* 2 [1985], pp. 50-58).

87. Beuken and van Grol also see the larger text dealing with accusations back and forth about who is doing the 'wandering' ('Jer. 14,1–15,9', p. 333). K. Noll suggests that the people's criticism that YHWH is 'not being YHWH' is in fact also a criticism of YHWH *being YHWH*, the One who, after all, wanders about in the wilderness in a tent and a tabernacle. As such, the people's critique perhaps reveals their stance in Zionist theology (private communication).

haunting questions: is not YHWH also culpable like Cain? The ambiguity and theological dilemma of the situation is enormous. Nevertheless, Jeremiah's whole rhetoric indicates that the people's critique does not diminish their own culpability nor the fact of YHWH's anguish.[88]

YHWH does not entertain Judah's accusation but responds in v. 10 in distant third person with a climactic indictment using another wordplay with a name—this time *not* הבל:

> Thus (*kēn*)—they have *loved to wander* (*nûᵃ*; נוע),
> they have not restrained their feet,
> and YHWH does not accept them
> now he will remember their iniquity and punish their sin (v. 10).

Like Cain (*qayin*), 'Thus (*kēn*), they have loved to wander.' I propose that 'thus' (*kēn*, כן) is a wordplay with 'Cain' (*qayin*, קין)[89] in conjunction with the key term, 'wander' (נוע), descriptive of Cain. Jeremiah echoes Hosea's style. Hosea uses *this same formula* (the perfect of אהב plus the infinitive construct) in his aggadah indicting Israel who is like Jacob:

> A trader, in whose hands are false [מרמה] balances—
> he *loves to oppress* [לעשק] (Hos. 12.8, NRSV).

While other terms for the wandering leitmotif have appeared, this climactic utterance of נוע in Jer. 14.10 is the real *Leitwort* of the subtext, triggering the connection of Judah with Cain. According to Martin Buber, the *Leitwort* is a 'word root that is meaningfully

> repeated within a text or sequence of texts ... [producing] a meaning of
> the text revealed or clarified, or ... made more emphatic ... The overall

---

88. If one reads YHWH's *tone* later in 15.5-6 as one of anguish, even 'confession' (more than anger), the tragedy and pathos of the situation is greatly enlarged: 'Who will have pity on you, O Jerusalem, or who will bemoan you? Who will turn aside to ask about your welfare? ['as I have done', is the implication] You have rejected me ... so I have stretched out my hand against you and destroyed you—I am weary of relenting ... I have bereaved them, I have destroyed my own people ...' Beuken and van Grol well state: '[YHWH] would have wished to be the comforter, but [Jerusalem] rejected him. Finally [YHWH] also disappears from the picture ... no less lonely than [Jerusalem] ...' ('Jer. 14,1–15, 9', p. 323).

89. Cf. the use of כן in Gen. 4.15 when Cain expresses concern that he will be killed. The MT has YHWH respond with לכן, 'therefore', which would be unusual in the context. The Septuagint and several other versions rendered this particle as though it were לא כן: 'not so, a sevenfold vengeance will come upon anyone killing Cain'. However, in Jer. 14, YHWH's response to the people is 'כן!'

dynamic effect ... is in a way a *movement* ... This may involve ... paronomasia *at a distance*, working not in immediate juxtaposition but over an extended stretch of text ... The meaning to be stated is portrayed without any tacked-on moral, i.e., without any disruption or distortion of the ... narrative ... Investigating such a narrative can make us feel that we have discovered a hidden, primordial midrash in the biblical text itself; and we may then be dubious. But the correspondences are so exact, and fit so perfectly into the situation as a whole, that we have to accept the idea: that the roots of the 'secret meaning' reach deep into the earlier layers of tradition.[90]

It is most significant that Buber immediately follows this explanation of *Leitwort* with an example of it: precisely the *deception* (מרמה) by *Jacob* depicted in Jer. 9.3 and Hos. 12.4![91] The 'extended stretch of text' that includes the Cain and Abel subtext is from Jer. 2.5 to 14.10 to Lam. 4.14-15, where the *Leitwort* of *wandering* (root נוע) reappears with graphic and stunning imagery of Cain (see below).

In the Septuagint of Jer. 14.10, the Greek appears to try to capture the wordplay. The Greek drops out the initial 'thus' of the Hebrew (כן) and has 'they have loved to wander (*kineîn*)'. The infinitive construct *kineîn* approximates the name *Káin*.[92]

Finally, the Jeremiah 14 text marks a significant turning point in the movement of the book. The people have reached a point of no return in regard to coming exile. Jeremiah offers a plea of defense for the people (14.13; note the possible shift to *prose* which nevertheless continues the narrative begun in the poetry). He accuses the false prophets of leading the people astray.[93] But YHWH ignores his plea, ignores the people's

90. M. Buber, in M. Buber and F. Rosenzweig, *Scripture and Translation* (trans. L. Rosenwald with E. Fox; Bloomington, IN; Indiana University Press, 1994), pp. 114-15, 120-21. Fox notes Buber's understanding that one cannot 'prove' a biblical reading based on *Leitwort*, but rather one must 'demonstrate plausibility' (Fox, *'The Five Books of Moses'*, p. xxii).

91. Buber and Rosenzweig, *Scripture*, pp. 120-21.

92. I am grateful to A.R. Pete Diamond for calling my attention to this reading.

93. Jeremiah's attempt at intercession here in 14.13 is brief and muted. But it is important to remember, as K. O'Connor points out, that Jeremiah meanwhile, in his laments, is besieging and critiquing YHWH with ריב language in his own dispute with YHWH (*Confessions of Jeremiah*, pp. 90-91). Jeremiah's plea in 14.13, critiquing the prophets, picks up on his theme in 2.8 of the prophets' transgressions. Critique of the prophets continues in Jer. 23.16, employing the term הבל: 'They [the prophets] are making you הבל.' K. O'Connor's study of Jeremiah's laments shows their concern to legitimate Jeremiah as a true prophet over against the false

lament, their fasting, and bringing offerings. Beuken and van Grol note
that the people make recourse here to cultic activity, already identified
as a key problem, to alleviate their suffering.[94] YHWH tells Jeremiah to
stop praying for the people.

Instead, Jeremiah, *as though hearing the cry of Jerusalem*, resumes
immediately with a communal *dirge* for the beloved one who *has been
killed* (14.17-18, now in *perfect* tense), and for *all* those killed:[95]

17.   ... 'Let my eyes run down with tears night and day,
             and let them not cease,
         For the virgin Daughter—My People—
             is struck down with a crushing blow,
             with a very grievous wound.
18.   If I *go out into the field*,
             look![96] those killed by the sword!

prophets within the larger literary development of the book (*Confessions of Jeremiah*, p. 4). If Jeremiah's Cain and Abel subtext identifies the prophets and priests
with Cain, then Jeremiah, as one who suffers from their persecution—even from
members of his own family and village—*identifies himself with Abel*. Note O'Connor's analysis of Jeremiah's general preoccupation with his enemies, cries for
vengeance, and his description of their *attack on his life* in his very first confession
(*Confessions of Jeremiah*, pp. 102-103).

94.   Yet Beuken and van Grol also note that through current temple theology, 'it
was precisely this complex of ideas which offered the people a false refuge and
prevented a realistic view of their own guilt' ('Jer. 14,1–15,1', p. 331). In 14.15-16,
YHWH gives the announcement of judgment describing the deaths of the prophets
and people who listened to them, saying there shall be 'no one burying' them. In
regard to the subtext, many legends developed around how Cain tried to hide
Abel's body by burying it (see J. Gutmann's 'Cain's Burial of Abel: A Jewish Legendary Motif in Christian and Islamic Art', *Eretz-Israel* 16 [1982], pp. 92-98). Yet,
here in Jer. 14 the people's bodies, evidence of their death, will *not* be hidden or
buried (thus violating Deut. 21's injunction), perhaps to serve as an 'example' of
their actions which have led to total destruction and death (cf. Jer. 8.2-3 where
YHWH says the bones of all the leaders and people will be removed from their
tombs and laid out for all to see).

95.   Following Holladay, *Jeremiah 1*, p. 436.

96.   Note the striking, related use of the exclamation here in Jeremiah's speech
and in previous texts:

'Your ancestors ... went after *ha! hebel* ... (Jer. 2.5c) [reading the article
     deictically]
        'I looked and *hinnēh*! no *hā'ādām*' (Jer. 4.25a) [context of creation]
     'If I go out to the field, *hinnēh*! those killed by the sword!' (Jer. 14.18)
         [Jeremiah's dirge]

And if I enter the city, look! those sick with famine!
For even prophet and priest journey[97] to a land they do not *know*.'

The text continues the subtext, extending the imagery of the Cain and Abel scenario. Cain said to Abel, 'Let us go out to the field' (Gen. 4.8),[98] and he killed him there. Jeremiah is pictured here going out to the field and finding the one slain, the virgin Daughter—My People. Again the priests and prophets appear as the figure Cain, wandering, to a strange land they do not know (see the same image below in Lam. 4).

Jeremiah's last intervention at 14.13 is rebuffed by YHWH who speaks in anger at 15.1: 'Even if Moses and Samuel stood before my face [לפני], my *nefesh* is not toward this people! Send them away from my face [מעל-פני, 'out of my sight'], and let them go!' Note the subtext's connection. Cain, upon hearing his punishment, said, in part, 'Look! You have driven me today away from the face [מעל-פני] of the ground, and from your face [ומפניך] I will be hidden ... Then Cain went out from the face [מלפני] of the Lord and dwelled in the land of Nod, east of Eden' (Gen. 4.14a, 16).

In summary, Jeremiah 14 depicts the people's critical, first speech to YHWH. Yet, their speech is embedded within a larger text (vv. 1-16) shaped by a litany of negative particles (*lô, 'ên, 'ênennî*) occurring 20 times across poetry and prose. A tone of *denial* and rejection from the land, the people, and from YHWH, pervades the text. Although the earlier 'no-conversation' pattern (with the distant people merely quoted by YHWH) is telescoped here for the first time into a 'face-to-face' confrontation, the text's reluctant *form* pictures the people and YHWH drawing near, yet rejecting one another with a harangue of accusations.

Dénouement: Lamentations 4

Finally, the subtext becomes explicit in the book of Lamentations.[99] In Lamentations 4 the people and Jeremiah,[100] in the midst of siege and

97. In fact, *wander* would well render the term סחר; cf. BDB, 'go around about, travel about in ... to go to and fro' (p. 695).

98. Cain's line is maintained in the Septuagint, Samaritan Pentateuch, and the Syriac.

99. The Qumran texts on Lam. 4 may be found in M. Baillet, J.T. Milik and R. de Vaux, 'Les "Petites Grottes" de Qumrân', in DJD, III, pp. 174-78.

100. I argue in my dissertation that one of the speaking voices in Lamentations

destruction of Jerusalem, narrate their fateful *aggadah*. Significantly, they utilize the communal dirge genre similar to Jeremiah 14. The first speaker in Lamentations 4, whom I take to be Jeremiah, continues to rest the blame for the devastation not upon the Babylonians, but on YHWH as the people did earlier in Jeremiah 14, and also now on the people themselves; but most poignantly, he points to the injustices of the *priests and prophets* as the primary cause, whom prophet and people now visualize *as Cain*.[101] As the Babylonians, the enemies from without, burst through the city gates, the real enemies are already residing within:

12.   The kings of the land did not believe,
          nor all the inhabitants of the world,
             that foe or enemy could enter the gates of Jerusalem.
13.   It is for the *sins* of her prophets
          and the *iniquities* of her priests,
          who *shed blood* in her midst,
             blood of the righteous.
14.   They *wander* [נעו][102] blindly in the streets,
          so defiled with *blood*[103]
          no one is able to touch their clothes.
15.   'Turn aside! Unclean!' people call at them,
          'Away! Away! Do not touch!'
          Therefore, they flee—even *wander as fugitives* [נצו גם־נעו]![104]

is Jeremiah's and that it can be consistently traced through the book. Here it appears in Lam. 4.1-16 and 21-22.

101.   Some Lamentations commentators note the parallel with Cain/Gen. 4 to Lam. 4.15: W. Rudolph (*Die Klagelieder* [KHAT; Stuttgart: Gütersloher Verlagshaus, 1962], p. 249) following K. Budde and M. Haller; H. Gottlieb (*A Study of the Text of Lamentations* [Århus: Acta Jutlandica, 1978], p. 66); T. Meek (in *IB*, VI, p. 33); N. Habel (*Jeremiah–Lamentations* [St Louis: Concordia Publishing House, 1968], p. 413); and W. Reyburn (*A Handbook on Lamentations* (New York: United Bible Society, 1992], p. 122). But quite a few commentators do not note the connection. I have yet to find a modern commentator who sees (or hears) 4.17 continuing the subtext by its reference to הבל.

102.   The verb is נעו from נוע.

103.   'so defiled', thus NRSV.

104.   Jeremiah's Hebrew, נצו גם־נעו, aggadically renders the old story's phrase, 'I shall be a fugitive and a wanderer' (נע ונד). The rhetorical technique is called a *farrago* (see J. Sasson, 'Time ... to Begin', in M. Fishbane and E. Tov [eds.], *Sha'arei Talmon: Studies in the Bible, Qumran and the Ancient Near East Presented to Shemaryahu Talmon* [Winona Lake, IN: Eisenbrauns, 1992], pp. 183-94 [188]). NRSV must see the connection with Cain and Abel in Lam. 4.15, for it

Among the nations, it is said,
'They no longer sojourn'.

16. *The face* of the Lord scatters them
and will no longer look upon them,
The faces of the priests are not *lifted up*,[105]
and the elders show no mercy.

(4.12-16; italicized words also in Gen. 4)

As if this weren't enough, in the next verse (17), the people finally speak for the first time in the book of Lamentations. They speak *as the people of the dying city*, sinking to its knees so to speak, in the *persona of Abel*, struck down by a crushing blow:

17. 'Still *our* eyes grew weak looking for help—Abel (הבל) futility—[106]
keeping watch for a nation not saving.

18. They dogged our steps,
so we couldn't go in our streets.
Our end drew near,
our days were finished,[107]
for our end had come.

19. Our pursuers were swifter
then the eagles in the heavens;
They *chased us on the mountains*,[108]
they lay in wait for us *in the wilderness* … ' (v. 19, NRSV).

Aggadah and history are one. Slain Abel cries out, Cain is banished from Eden, behind him the flaming swords of cherubim—exiles flee, leaving behind the flaming ruins of Jerusalem. Shall YHWH respond

---

translates this phrase as though it were exactly the same as that in Gen. 4.12 and 14. My translation attempts to capture the ring of the familiar phrase as well as its *aggadic* modification. The Hebrew's stunning rhetorical stroke, after all, must effect an impact on the hearer.

105. An ironic dénouement with great pathos, in light of how Cain's face fell, and for whom YHWH *did* show mercy in his banishment, in his escape from death.

106. הבל appears here with pausal lengthening as it does in Gen. 4.2 when the character is first introduced. NRSV's translation is questionable as it renders the term הבל as though it were an adverb modifying how the people watched. Again, the term is a wordplay, this time suggestive of Abel and of the other 'futile' nations gone after for help. Here הבל is the pivotal term in a Janus parallelism and needs two terms for its translation.

107. Translate 'finished' here rather than NRSV's 'numbered'.

108. Recall the *Midrash Haggadol*'s account: 'When Abel … began to shepherd the flock, Cain *chased after* him [רדף אחריו] from mountain to valley and from valley to mountain …'

any longer to this agonistic *aggadah*? Jeremiah's contemporary, Ezekiel,[109] suggests it is so:

> ... the presence of YHWH left the platform of the house and stopped above the cherubim. And I saw the cherubim lift their wings and rise from the earth, with the wheels beside them as they departed; and they stopped at the entrance of the eastern gate of the house of YHWH, with the presence of the God of Israel above them ... The Presence of YHWH ascended from the midst of the city, and stood on the hill east of the city. Then the spirit lifted me up and brought me in a vision by the spirit of God into Chaldea, to the exiles ...
>
> Ezek. 10.18-19; 11.23-24a (foll. JPSV).

---

109. Note another element of the Cain and Abel subtext in Ezek. 9.4. At the moment YHWH's presence rises from the cherubim in the temple to leave the city, YHWH calls forth for a man to 'go through the city, through Jerusalem, and put a mark on the foreheads of those who sigh and groan over all the abominations that are committed in it'. To the others he said ... 'Pass through the city after him, and kill ... but touch no one who has the mark ... the land is full of bloodshed' (NRSV).

UNFAITHFUL PASSIONS: CODING WOMEN CODING MEN IN JEREMIAH 2–3 (4.2)*

A.R. Pete Diamond and Kathleen M. O'Connor

Introduction

Contemporary ideological and theological criticism stumbles over the violent and pornographic in the use of female imagery in the Jeremiah traditions. Ancient Israel's national-religious tradition, a contemporary 'icon', 'our classic text', offends moral sensibility. Normal ethnocentric impulses for domestication of the classic seem to run aground. Ironically, contemporary processes of reading biblical texts reveal a text utterly alien, locked within a past whose moral discourse and rhetoric no longer seem sustainable.

Verbal art,[1] especially of the sacred, which touches the foundations of a culture's world-view and self-identity, elicits overpowering impulses to ethical evaluation and poses the problem of censorship. We like to find ourselves in our texts. But what do you do when the text will not serve? Aspects of contemporary literary theory, however, indicate that symbols are context dependent, intention relative, polyvalent to point of view. A tangle of wide-ranging theoretical problems arise: If the classic symbols seem to have gone awry, can the classic be rehabilitated? How can symbolic obsolescence be overcome to maintain the generative authority of the sacred text? In short, how do we understand the symbolic processes that enable communities to negotiate 'new worlds' with old texts?[2] What can exegesis contribute, if anything, to the discussion?

---

*   Previously published as 'Unfaithful Passions: Coding Women Coding Men in Jeremiah 2–3 (4:2)', in *BibInt* 4.3 (1996), pp. 288-310, and is reproduced here by kind permission of E.J. Brill.

1.   That is, the classic literary tradition as a creative, imaginative, symbolic construction of reality.

2.   Suggested by analogy to the exploration of the new world and the comment

In this study, we refocus exegesis by making a turn to poetics in our critical methodology. This need not entail a doctrinaire, anti-historical posture, though it does require movement beyond the limitations of an uncritical historicism. In so doing, we assume analogous difficulties for the custodian's of Israel's sacred traditions who also lived in a matrix of symbols and symbolic processes. After all, historical exegesis reveals that the managers of prophetic tradition did not share the historical-critical project—that is, the reconstruction of the 'original' meaning of the text. Rather, prophetic traditions are already religious symbols, icons, whose vested, contemporary rereading to address community issues of identity and destiny was uppermost. Thus for any historical reader of this literature the blended cultural realities of poetics and power are at play. And because they are 'at play', the questions, methods and interests of poetics become vitally relevant to our critical task of investigating Jeremiah's rhetoric in 2–3 (4.2). Within what network of codes did the rhetoric of female sexual infidelity function? We investigate the problem of reading constituted by the Jeremiah tradition—more specifically by its use of gender imagery—for Israel's 'symbol handlers'.

As a preliminary probe, the study seeks to reconstruct the symbolic grammar in which the imagery of female sexual infidelity is embedded in Jeremiah 2–3 (4.2) in order to assess its rhetorical function and reception. Reader-response theory, in part, provides perspective and orientation for the study. Methodologically, the study proceeds from a close reading of the text in its final form, through analysis of MT and LXX *Vorlage* variants (hereafter LXX*V*) to broader cultural intertexts. All of these, we argue, shape the encoded reader's performance of the marital metaphor.

We claim that the marital metaphor functions as a root metaphor, organizing the disparate pieces of the composition and providing a narrative frame designed to guide the reader in the management of the

---

of the Jesuit explorer José de Acosta in Anthony Grafton's recent book: 'I will describe what happened to me when I passed to the Indies. Having read what poets and philosophers write of the Torrid Zone, I persuaded myself that when I came to the Equator, I would not be able to endure the violent heat, but it turned out otherwise ... What could I do then but laugh at Aristotle's *Meteorology* and his philosophy? For in that place and that season, where everything, by his rules, should have been scorched by the heat, I and my companions were cold' (Anthony Grafton, *New Worlds, Ancient Texts* [Cambridge, MA: Harvard University Press, 1992], p. 1).

twists and turns of the tradition. Further, we argue that the two forms of
the Jeremiah tradition represented in MT and LXXV offer alternative
performances of the tradition. The intertextual character of the root
metaphor and its alternative performances illustrate both symbolic plia-
bility and rhetorical suppleness as the encoded reader acquires multiple
'faces' in the text. This 'play' in an ancient symbolic grammar of
female sexual infidelity offers ideological threat in a world of new
readers and, at the same time, perhaps, offers promise of how such
threat might be overcome.

Analysis

Defining Terms and Categories: What Reader? Reading What?
The nature of the issues raised by the gender imagery in Jeremiah highlights the methodological importance of focusing upon the reader. This,
of course, shifts our investigation of poetics in the direction of reader-
response theory. But that is not to say very much, for the varieties of
reader response are legion.[3]

Encoded textual constructs: what reader? It is common in the analysis
of narrative to speak of a series of textual levels between the 'world'
inside and the 'world' outside the text.[4] We use a reader-response criticism that focuses upon the 'reader' as an encoded textual construct.
Since our text consists of speeches in poetry and prose, these textual
levels of reader-response criticism can be illustrated in our text:

---

3.   For an excellent introductory survey see Susan R. Suleiman, 'Introduction:
Varieties of Audience-Oriented Criticism', in Susan R. Suleiman and Inge Crosman
(eds.), *The Reader in the Text* (Princeton, NJ: Princeton University Press, 1980), pp.
3-45. Additional bibliography and discussion can be found in Terry Eagleton, *Literary Theory: An Introduction* (Minneapolis: University of Minnesota Press, 1983).

4.   (extrinsic to the encoded text) historical poet/writer/redactor—(intrinsic
textual constructs) implied author—narrator ‖ narratee—implied audience—(extrinsic to the encoded text) historical audience. For theoretical analysis and explanation
of these distinctions see S. Rimmon-Kenan, *Narrative Fiction* (London: Methuen,
1983); Seymour Chatman, *Story and Discourse: Narrative Structure in Fiction and
Film* (Ithaca, NY: Cornell University Press, 1978). Although these categories
originated in study of narrative, we use them to study speeches in poetry and prose
because we find a narrative thread organizing the composition. See below.

Table 1. *Textual Levels for Jeremiah 2–3*

Outside the Text	Inside the Text
Historical poet/writer/redactor—anonymous	Implied speaker/poet—prophet Jeremiah
Historical audience—late exilic early postexilic Jewish communities	Dramatic speaker—husband Yhwh Dramatic addressee—wife Israel Implied audience—Jerusalem's citizenry/ Israel's progeny

In sum, we are interested in the construction of the implied audience encoded in Jeremiah 2–3 (4.2) and that audience's competency as reader of the gender symbolism.

Root metaphor, organizing metaphor: reading what? Our focus on the marital metaphor in Jeremiah 2–3 raises the concept of root or organizing metaphor. We have in view 'dominant metaphors' which have the ability to 'assemble subordinate images', 'engendering and organizing a network'. We evaluate the broken marriage metaphor in Jeremiah 2–3 as an example of such a root metaphor, assembling a cascade of other metaphors and images, formal elements and characters into itself thereby forming a narrative whole.[5]

Beginning at the Surface: Close Reading Data from the Final Form (MT)
Introduction. Although interpreters have long noted the presence of the metaphor of God's marriage to Israel in Jeremiah 2–3 (4.2), they disagree about both its scope and significance. William L. Holladay, for instance, sees the marital metaphor as only one figure among 'a variety of rhetorical twists and turns' that articulate the theme of disloyalty.[6] William McKane finds 'the thread upon which the different parts of the chapter are strung'[7] not in the marriage metaphor but in the word שוב

---

5. The theoretical formulation is Paul Ricoeur's (*Interpretation Theory: Discourse and the Surplus of Meaning* [Fort Worth: Texas Christian University Press, 1976], p. 64).

6. *Jeremiah 1: A Commentary on the Book of the Prophet Jeremiah, Chapters 1–25* (Hermeneia; Minneapolis: Fortress Press, 1986), pp. 130-31.

7. *A Critical and Exegetical Commentary on Jeremiah. I. Introduction and Commentary on Jeremiah I–XXV* (ICC; Edinburgh: T. & T. Clark, 1986), p. 82.

and its derivatives. For Michael de la Roche the 'harlotry cycle' predominates rather than the marriage metaphor,[8] whereas Mark E. Biddle subordinates the marriage material to generational divisions.[9] In the commentaries of Robert P. Carroll[10] and Walter Brueggemann[11] the marriage metaphor looms larger. Carroll observes that 'much of chs. 2–6 describes the breakdown in marital terms'. Though Brueggemann does not find a sustained argument, he does note that 'the decisive metaphor [in ch. 2] is that of marriage and infidelity'.[12] Investigations that study the metaphor itself appear chiefly in feminist works. These are less concerned with the metaphor's role in Jeremiah than with its symbolic power in shaping the lives of women.[13]

In this study we propose that the metaphor of the broken marriage functions as a root or foundational metaphor[14] that formally, thematically and narratively unifies the diverse materials collected in chs. 2–3. We argue further, that in a process of intertextual transformation, Jeremiah adapts or re-encodes the marriage metaphor borrowed from

8. 'Jer 2.2-3 and Israel's Love for God during the Wilderness Wanderings', *CBQ* 45 (1983), pp. 364-76.

9. *A Redaction History of Jeremiah 2.1–4.2* (ATANT, 77; Zürich: Theologischer Verlag, 1990), p. 82.

10. *Jeremiah: A Commentary* (OTL; Philadelphia: Westminster Press, 1986).

11. *To Pluck Up, To Tear Down: A Commentary on the Book of Jeremiah 1–25* (Grand Rapids: Eerdmans; Edinburgh: Handsel Press, 1988), pp. 38-39.

12. *To Pluck Up, To Tear Down*, pp. 38-39; Carroll, *Jeremiah*, p. 123.

13. Tikva Frymer-Kensky, *In the Wake of the Goddesses: Women, Culture and the Biblical Transformation of Pagan Myth* (New York: Fawcett Columbine, 1992), pp. 144-52; Kathleen M. O'Connor, 'Jeremiah', in Carol H. Newsom and Sharon H. Ringe (eds.), *The Women's Bible Commentary* (Louisville, KY: Westminster/ John Knox Press, 1992), pp. 170-71; Gale A. Yee, 'Hosea', in Newsom and Ringe (eds.), *The Women's Bible Commentary*, pp. 198-200; Renita J. Weems, 'Gomer: Victim of Violence or Victim of Metaphor', *Semeia* 47 (1989), pp. 87-104. But see Nelly Stienstra, *YHWH is the Husband of his People: Analysis of a Biblical Metaphor with Special Reference to Translation* (Kampen: Kok, 1993), for a study of the metaphor using cognitive theories.

14. On metaphor, see Paul Ricoeur, *The Rule of Metaphor: Multidisciplinary Studies of the Creation of Meaning in Language* (Toronto: University of Toronto Press, 1975) and *Interpretation Theory*, pp. 45-69; Janet Martin Soskice, *Metaphor and Religious Language* (Oxford: Clarendon Press, 1985); Frank Burch Brown, *Transfiguration: Poetic Metaphor and the Languages* (Chapel Hill: University of North Carolina Press, 1983); Sallie McFague, *Metaphorical Theology: Models of God in Religious Language* (Philadelphia: Fortress Press, 1982).

Hosea. The result is a cultural[15] and literary intertext[16] that serves three principal functions: it provides ideological support for returnees from Babylon, serves as a theodicy for the nation's fall, and involves God in the scapegoating and abuse of women.

Jeremiah 2–3 (4.2). To study the literary structure of the two chapters, we use the gender of persons addressed in the text as a heuristic device. In the introductory poem (2.1-3), Husband/Yhwh addresses Israel as a bride (v. 2), and then shifts inexplicably to address Israel as male (v. 3). This juxtaposition of direct address to female and male personae functions to identify them with one another and to highlight their symbolic equivalence. Both the bride (v. 2) and male Israel (identified as the 'first-fruits of the harvest', v. 3)[17] are 'totally devoted to'[18] and the exclusive property of Yhwh. Jeremiah 2.1-3, therefore, introduces the collection of poems in chs. 2–3 by equating male Israel with bride Israel. The two personae are one.

Attention to the shifts in gender of addressee in the following poems reveals a literary composition structured as a drama enacting the marriage metaphor. The drama has two acts: Act 1, 'The Divorce' (2.1–3.5); and Act 2, 'The Aftermath' (3.6-25; 4.2[19]).

1. *Act 1, 'The Divorce': Structure.* This includes the introductory poem (2.1-3), followed by four poems, similar in form and theme. These poems alternate in addressing male (2.4-16; 2.26-32, 2nd m. sing./pl.) and female Israel (2.17-25; 2.33–3.5, 2nd f. sing.):

---

15. See Vincent B. Leicht, *Cultural Criticism, Literary Theory, Post Structuralism* (New York: Columbia University Press, 1992).

16. See Michael Fishbane, *Biblical Interpretation in Ancient Israel* (Oxford: Clarendon Press, 1985).

17. Fishbane (*Biblical Interpretation*, p. 300) also sees v. 3 as an explication of Israel's fidelity in v. 2, although the syntactical relation of the two verses is not clear.

18. Brueggemann, *To Pluck Up, To Tear Down*, p. 32.

19. The first two verses of ch. 4 continue the address to the children, and repeat the term שׁוּב that occurs frequently in the marital metaphor.

Table 2. *Structure*

Addressee: Female	Male and Female	Male
	Introduction 2.1-3	
		Poem 1, 2.4-16
Poem 2, 2.17-25		
		Poem 3, 2.26-32
Poem 4, 2.33–3.5		

This alternation continues the identification of the male and female personae with one another.

Rhetorical devices. Formally, all the poems in Act 1 prolong the husband's first-person monologue of accusation and of shaming that begins in 2.1-3. The monologue employs three poetic devices in fairly even distributions across all four poems.

Table 3. *Rhetorical Devices*

Male Israel (2nd m. sing./pl.)	Female Israel (2nd f. sing.)
Direct Address:	
Poem 1, 2.4b-13	Poem 2, 2.17-25
Poem 3, 2.28-31	Poem 4, 2.33–3.5
Rhetorical questions:	
Poem 1, 2.5, 6, 8, 14	Poem 2, 2.17, 18, 21, 23, 24
Poem 3, 2.28, 29, 31, 32	Poem 4, 3.1, 4
Quotation of the accused:[20]	
Poem 1, 2.6, 8	Poem 2, 2.20, 23, 25
Poem 3, 2.27, 31	Poem 4, 2.35, 3.4-5

Each of these formal elements builds up the harangue of the injured speaker. He addresses, interrogates and quotes both male and female Israel to build a massive legal case against them and to show by their own words that divorce is amply deserved and inevitable. These devices conjure up the mute and guilty presence of male/female Israel, in order to make the implied readers witnesses to the husband's fury. Readers become sympathetic friend of the speaker, and, by implication, they participate in the metaphor as jury and judge.

Themes. Although the poems use different imagery to express the husband's accusations, the themes of the four poems are similar. Of

20. On quotations in Jeremiah see Thomas W. Overholt, 'Jeremiah 2 and the Problem of Audience Reaction', *CBQ* 41 (1979), pp. 262-73.

most importance, they explicitly reverse themes announced in the introductory poem (2.1-3): the love of the bride for her husband (2.2a, theme
A) and her exclusive loyalty as she followed him alone in the wilderness (2.2b, theme B). In the four subsequent poems, Yhwh accuses both
male and female addressees of abandonment (theme A—) and of
pursuing other relationships (theme B—).

Table 4. Development of Themes

Poem 1 (2.4-16) Male Israel (sing. and pl.)

A— What wrong did your ancestors find in me (2.5a)

B— that they went after worthless things? (2.5b)

A— Priests did not say, where is the Lord; those who handle the law did
not know me (2.8ab)

B— Prophets prophesied by Ba'al and went after worthless things (2.8c).

A— they have forsaken me, the fountain of living water (2.13a).

B— dug cisterns out for themselves that cannot hold water (2.13b).

Poem 2 (2.17-25) Female Israel (2nd f. sing.)

A— Have you not brought this upon yourself by forsaking the Lord your
God? (2.17).

B— What did you gain by going to Egypt to drink the waters of the
Nile? ... (2.18).

A— Know that it is evil ... for you to forsake the Lord your God (2.19b).

A— You broke your yoke ... 'I will not serve' (2.20).

B— How can you say, 'I have not gone after the Baals?' (In 2.23-24 a
series of animal metaphors accuse her of adultery.)

B— You said, 'It is hopeless, for I have loved strangers and after them I
will go' (2.25).

Poem 3 (2.26-32) Male Israel (2nd m. sing./pl., 3rd m. pl.)

B— [rulers] say to a tree, 'You are my father', and to a stone, 'You gave
me birth.' For they have turned their backs to me ... (2.27).

B— ... You have as many gods as you have towns, O Judah (2.28).

A— ... You have rebelled against me (2.29)

A— Why do my people say 'We are free, we will come to you no more'?
(2.31).

A— Can a girl forget her ornaments, or a bride her attire? Yet you have
forgotten me ... (2.32).

Poem 4 (2.33–3.5) Female Israel (2nd f. sing.)

B— How well you direct your course to seek lovers (2.33).

B— You have played the whore with many lovers and would you return to
me? (3.1cd).

B— Where have you not been lain with? By the wayside you have sat
waiting for lovers (3.2ab).

Thematically, therefore, the four poems accuse male and female Israel of analogous crimes. Male Israel (sing./pl.) abandons Yhwh, goes after worthless things, other gods, empty cisterns. Female Israel abandons her husband, pursues other lovers and plays the whore. Both betray Yhwh and turn to others, but only female Israel's infidelities are domestic and sexual.

Plot. The metaphor exhibits narrative progress in Act 1. The husband recalls longingly the mutual devotion and fidelity of the honeymoon in the wilderness (2.2), and the protection he gave to Israel, 'the first-fruits of his harvest' (2.3). In the next four poems, he accumulates evidence against male/female Israel of abandonment for other objects of devotion that turns the idyllic period of the honeymoon upside down.

In the first poem (2.4-16), husband/Yhwh announces to male Israel his shock and pain at the ancestors' treatment of him. He recounts his generosity in bringing them to the land for which male Israel returned only ingratitude and betrayal. Punishment at the hands of the Egyptians becomes unavoidable.

Female Israel brings punishment upon herself in the second poem (2.17-25) by trading Yhwh for Egypt and Assyria. Sexual language of wanton harlotry and unrestrained animal lust quickly replaces language of political infidelity. Her husband quotes her to show that she is totally committed to following strangers (2.25).

The third poem (2.26-32) compares the shame of male Israel to a thief and to idolaters who relate in covenant loyalty to stones and trees. They turn their back on Yhwh and resist correction. Yhwh defends himself and accuses male Israel of forgetfulness more astonishing than that of a bride forgetting her ornaments.

Husband/Yhwh again addresses female Israel (2.33–3.5) with scathing accusations of sexual infidelities that she compounds by teaching them to other women. He characterizes her as a murderer of the innocent poor, promising to shame her for denying her sin (2.34-36). In the second part of the fourth poem (3.1-5), judgment comes in the form of an irreversible divorce. Will a husband return to his wife after a divorce? No (3.1).[21] And 'would you [2nd f. sing.] return to me'? No. The marriage is over.

---

21. See Holladay, *Jeremiah 1*, pp. 112-13, and McKane, *Jeremiah*, I, pp. 58-59, for discussions of the translation difficulties of this rhetorical question. For an alternative reading see Stienstra, *YHWH is the Husband*, pp. 223-26.

In Act 1, form, theme and poetic device conspire to create a drama of a destroyed relationship, told as a monologue of a jealous and bereft husband. Rhetorically, the metaphor of the broken marriage allows the poet to introduce the female persona and, thereby, to heap upon her the more intimate, sexual, demeaning, aggressive and animal-like infidelities. Hence, the text encodes her as evil, dirty and faithless in order to encode male Israel as a woman and a wicked one. In the ancient world male Israel could be no more shamed.

2. *Act 2, 'The Aftermath': Structure.* Formal confusion characterizes the literary materials that create 'The Aftermath' (3.6-25):

Table 5. *Structure*

Prose	Poetry
3.6-12a	3.12b-14
3.15-18	3.19-23
3.24-25	

Rhetorical devices. These formal divisions in Act 2, however, do not correspond to shifts in addressee. Direct address of female (3.12b-13; 3.19) and male (3.20) Israel continues, but other characters hardly noticed in Act 1 become more important here. Jeremiah, mentioned only in the superscription of 2.1, becomes part of the narrative in 3.6-12 as sympathetic friend who listens to the husband's complaints and intercedes with the first wife. A second wife appears, though she is not addressed (3.7-10). Of most importance, male children, heretofore mentioned only in 2.30, assume the central and climactic role in 'The Aftermath'. They are addressed in 3.14-18, spoken about in 3.21, addressed again in 3.22a, and then themselves become the speaker in 3.22b-25, addressing Yhwh directly:

Table 6. *Addressee*

Jeremiah	Female	Male/Female Israel	Male children	Yahweh
3.6-12				
	3.12-13			
			3.14-18	
		3.19-20		
			3.(21)-22a	
				3.22b-25

These rhetorical devices strangely evoke the confusion and pain that follow divorce itself, and draw attention away from male/female Israel to the children.

Themes. Themes from Act 1 of abandonment (A—) and pursuit of others (B—) also appear in Act 2, but like the rhetorical devices they undergo change, reverting back to love (A) and exclusive loyalty (B):

> Have you seen faithless Israel, how she went upon every high hill and under every green tree and played the whore? (3.6, B—).
> … and her false sister, Judah, played the whore (3.8, B—),
> … and did not return (3.10, B-).
> … I thought you would [but she does not] call me 'My Father' (3.19, A—),
> and return and follow me (3.19, B-).
> They [the children] have forgotten the Lord their God (3.21, A—).

Yhwh's commands to return, addressed to female Israel (3.12b) and to the children (3.14, 22), raise the hope that she might return. The children, however, not the mother, accept the invitation and the original themes sounded in the opening poem reappear:

> Here we come to you; (B) for you are the Lord our God (A; 3.22b).

The children reject other lovers:

> Truly the hills are an illusion, the orgies on the mountains (B). Truly in the Lord our God is the salvation of Israel (A, 3.23).

Plot. Despite the structural and thematic complexity of Act 2, a narrative thread unifies these passages and connects them to Act 1. The appalled husband turns to Jeremiah in 3.6-12a with a rhetorical question that blames the wife for the broken marriage, 'Have you seen what she did …?' (3.6). Separation appears final. But readers receive a shock when the husband admits he has a second wife who also cuckolded him and whose infidelities make those of the first wife less heinous. The husband sends Jeremiah to invite her back, on condition that she take the blame for abandoning him (A—) and for pursuing other lovers (B—, 3.13).

The text narrates no response from her. Instead, the husband turns his attention to the children. He invites them to return (3.14), but to them he presents no preconditions. Yet his unfaithful wife lingers in his thoughts as he muses about his past plans for her and for their relationship (3.19). At this bitter moment, the divine speaker steps out of the role of husband to elucidate the meaning of the marital metaphor. 'As a faithless wife leaves her husband, so you have been O house of

Israel' (3.20). Female and male Israel are still one.

In the following poem (3.21-22), the children are weeping because they have forgotten their God (A—). Unlike their mother, they grieve over and repent of their sins. The husband/father calls them a second time and utters words the mother never heard, 'I will heal your faithlessness' (3.22). The narrative closes with a dramatic reunion of father and children. The father does not quote the children; rather, for the first time characters other than Yhwh speak and Yhwh, in turn, becomes the addressee. 'Here we come to you; for you are our God' (theme A, 3.22b). In Act 2, monologue has become dialogue.

Summary. The broken marriage metaphor in Jeremiah 2–3 organizes the material of the entire two chapters. In a story spun from metaphor, the children encode the implied audience, while male/female Israel encode the previous generation. Rhetorically, the metaphor interprets the fall of the nation as a theodicy in which Yhwh, broken-hearted and bitter, angry and shamed, remained faithful despite appalling lack of response from his spouse. Language of woman as an aggressive, sexual animal encodes female Israel as unreliable and dangerous. She, in turn, encodes male Israel as a person with no status, that is, as a woman, and not only a woman, but the worst sort of treacherous, adulterous woman.

As a root metaphor, Jeremiah's broken marriage assembles a cascade of other metaphors, images, formal elements, themes and characters into itself to form a narrative whole, on the one hand, and to create a new version of Israel's history, on the other. In the process, Jeremiah rearranges Israel's set of symbols to serve the new context of return from Exile.

Alternative Performances: Patterns in the MT and LXX Vorlage *Variants*[22]

In light of the rescensional character of the variants between the MT and the *Vorlage* of the LXX,[23] it is striking to observe in Jeremiah 2–3 that

---

22. The concept of 'alternative performances', derived from analogy to Folklore analysis of traditional literatures, aids us in moving critical perception beyond the theoretical limits of redaction criticism. Often the latter focuses upon disparate, discreet editorial layers reading diachronically, at times, not doing full service to the potential integrity of and synchronic effect on the whole composition. The language of performance also aids us in our effort to shift critical interest to elucidation of the poetics shaping prophetic rhetoric.

23. The basic argument for the rescensional quality of MT and LXX relationships

the majority of variants cluster in sections where feminine singular dramatic addressee is present. Whether one views the MT as a second edition to the LXXV or leaves this question open, considering them as equally alternative performances of the tradition, we have the opportunity to discern the implied audience/reader making their presence felt amidst the twists and turns of the textual variants.

Two central actions and operations characterize this implied reader's attention to the gender imagery. We summarize those operations at the outset, and then, follow with specific illustration. The first operation of the reader can be styled as *parsing the marital parable*.[24] Throughout the composition it is the alternating identity of the dramatic addressee (from male to female) which plays a large part in 'telling' the reader (implied audience) to treat the marital story as a national, religious parable. This remains constant between the MT and the LXXV. What one finds are attempts to parse the marital parable by stitching and bridging the 'gaps' between poems with the female addressee and poems with the male, thus furthering the national application and import of the marital image. This is largely, though not exclusively, an operation from LXXV to MT.

Parsing the Marital Parable: Illustrations. Jeremiah 2.1-2a. The literary context plus generous use of oracular formulae emphatically signal that the identity of the implied poet is the prophet Jeremiah. Similarly, the identity of the main dramatic speaker, Yhwh, husband of wife Israel, is not in doubt. The MT additions or plusses (ויהי דבר־יהוה אלי לאמר הלך וקראת באזני ירושלם לאמר): 2.1-2a, not only concretize the setting of the speech but draw the prophet and his audience into the dramatic scene making explicit the latter's identity as Jerusalem's

is in Emanuel Tov, *The Text-Critical Use of the Septuagint in Biblical Research* (Jerusalem: Simor, 1981) and canvassed in the recent commentaries by William Holladay, R.P. Carroll and William McKane. Further literature can be found on the topic in these works. Helpful evaluations of the textual models are in Sven Soderlund, *The Greek Text of Jeremiah: A Revised Hypothesis* (Sheffield: JSOT Press, 1985), and David J. Reimer, *The Oracles against babylon in Jeremiah 50–51: A Horror among the Nations* (San Francisco: Mellen Research University Press, 1993).

24. The grammatical term 'parse' is used figuratively. As one parses (explains, analyzes) the grammar of a sentence, so we suggest one operation of the textual variants between LXXV and MT is to parse the symbolic grammar of the root metaphor which shapes the composition.

citizens, parsing, in advance, the significance of the following marital metaphor in political terms. This effort to signal the presence of the implied audience and register for them the significance of the marital metaphor occurs again at 2.31. For the LXX*V*, 'Hear the word of Yhwh, thus says Yhwh' (normal oracular formulae; cf. LXX*V* שמעו דבר־יהוה כה אמר יהוה), MT supplies 'you are the generation, acknowledge the oracle of Yhwh' (הדור אתם ראו דבר־יהוה). We suggest this is an apostrophe to the implied audience applying the force of the accusations to them.[25]

Jeremiah 2.2. Reference to the Exodus-wilderness trek is a MT plus (לכתך אחרי במדבר בארץ לא זרועה:). LXX*V*, by contrast, makes no mention of it: 'How you followed me, oracle of Yhwh' (לכתך אחרי נאם יהוה:).[26] MT parses the bridal imagery. The implied reader construes the marital metaphor of the dramatic situation as an allegory of the national myth, linking a specific period of the 'marriage' to a specific period in national history. The history of the marriage and the history of the nation are paralleled.

Jeremiah 2.16. This verse rationalizes the nation's political misfortunes and failure by citing national apostasy from Yhwh. Verse 16 lists damage administered to Yhwh's spouse by Egypt. MT, '[they] have grazed/broken the crown of your head' (ירעוך קדקד:), contrasts with

25. This reconfigures the general perception of 2.31a as a marginal gloss while taking seriously its intrusive or editorial character. See the commentaries which generally drop the clause. On this understanding, there is also no need to emend vocalization and word order to produce a more meaningful clause as Holladay seeks to do (Holladay, *Jeremiah 1*, pp. 55, 107). McKane conjectures that LXX reflects an attempt to normalize the unusual reading of MT rather than a different *Vorlage* (McKane, *Jeremiah*, I, p. 52). Perhaps, but LXX is literal in its approach to translation (Tov, *The Text-Critical Use of the Septuagint*) and normally represents oracular formulae accurately when they are present in its *Vorlage*. Statistics: ἀκούσατε λόγον κυρίου (10× Jer.). Apart from 2.31 the MT has שמעו דבר יהוה. τάδε λέγει κύριος (64× Jer.). The MT has כה אמר יהוה, excluding the current text. The messenger formula is represented variously by the LXX: 70×—οὕτως εἶπε κύριος. 14×—a zero variant. 4×—οὕτως λέγει κύριος.

26. LXX: τοῦ ἐξακολουθῆσαί σε τῷ ἁγίῳ Ισραηλ λέγει κύριος. Though possible, it is unlikely that the epithet קדוֹש ישׂראל was present in LXX*V* (the epithet occurs 2× in Jer. MT, 50.29, 51.5). It is more likely that LXX interprets the pronoun on the preposition since it refers to the deity (cf. Jer. 3.16 MT—ברית־יהוה/LXX—διαθήκης ἁγίου Ισραηλ; and 3.21 MT—יהוה אלהיהם/LXX—θεοῦ ἁγίου αὐτῶν. Statistics: ἅγιος—6× קֹדֶשׁ, 2× קָדוֹשׁ. ἅγιος Ισραηλ—4× (2.2, 3; 3.16; 28[51].5). θεὸς ἅγιος—2× (3.21; 27[50].29).

LXX*V*, '[they] have known and trifled with you' (יִדְעוּךְ וַיִּתְהַלְּלוּ:).[27] While LXX*V* performs the tradition in service of the gender metaphor, constructing the picture of a woman, sexually used then forsaken, MT adjusts the image in harmony with the picture of political destruction, seeing in the introduction of 'crown of the head' a reference to the monarchy.[28]

Jeremiah 3.1-5. The last unit of the composition in which husband Yhwh directly addresses his bride, shifts the temporal setting of the dramatic situation after the divorce and raises the issue of a reconciliation or remarriage. The husband's question 'would you return to me?' casts an image of her from his perception that projects upon her a desire to return. Deut. 24.1-4 acts as the legal intertext influencing the terms of the speech for both MT and LXX*V*.[29] For MT the legal problem focuses upon the threat of pollution to the land (חָנֹף תֶּחֱנַף הָאָרֶץ הַהִיא) in contrast to the LXX*V* focus upon the polluted woman (הָאִשָּׁה הַהִיא).[30] Again, in v. 3, MT depicts the consequences of the wife's infidelity on the land (וַיִּמָּנְעוּ רְבִבִים וּמַלְקוֹשׁ לוֹא הָיָה, 'the showers have been withheld, and the spring rain has not come') over against the LXX*V* performance: 'your many shepherds have been your snare' (וְלֹךְ רֹעִים רַבִּים לְמוֹקֵשׁ לָךְ).[31]

---

27. LXX: ἔγνωσάν σε καὶ κατέπαιζόν σου. Statistics: γινώσκω—in Jer. 45× ידע, 1× בין. καταπαίζω—3× in Old Testament (Jer. 2.16; 9.5[4] תלל hi.; 2 Kgs 2.23 קלס htp.).

28. So Holladay, *Jeremiah 1*, p. 95, and other commentators (cf. Jer. 48.45). In light of the composition's interest in invoking Josiah (3.6), a more specific allusion to Josiah's death may be in view. In this regard the MT plus in the next verse (2.17), 'while he led you in the way' (בְּעֵת מוֹלִיכֵךְ בַּדֶּרֶךְ) could represent code for the religious reform sponsored by that same ruler (contrast LXX*V*; עָזְבֵךְ אֹתִי נְאֻם יהוה אֱלֹהָיִךְ 'by forsaking me, oracle of Yhwh your god'). For earlier suggestions of the allusion to Josiah's death see Holladay, *Jeremiah 1*, p. 95, McKane, *Jeremiah*, I, p. 37; and contrast Carroll, *Jeremiah*, pp. 129-30, who argues against historical specificity for any of the political allusions throughout the passage.

29. See further Fishbane, *Biblical Interpretation*, pp. 307-12.

30. LXX: ἡ γυνὴ ἐκείνη.

31. LXX: καὶ ἔσχες ποιμένας πολλοὺς εἰς πρόσκομμα σεαυτῇ. What ἔχω represents in its *Vorlage* is unclear. In Jeremiah it often reflects an idiomatic attempt to render stative, intellectual states, and/or nominative sentences. In the rest of the Old Testament it also reflects a variety of idioms with the most frequent being the representation of the *preposition* אצל with the stock translation of the active middle ptc. (25×). Statistics: ἔχω—7× (1× שׂים, 1× נאמן, 1× בטח, 1× סלולה לא, 2× דאג and 1× in 18.15, where its *Vorlage* is uncertain). ποιμήν—20× רעה. πολύς—15× (רב), in OT 318×. πρόσκομμα—occurs only here in Jeremiah, in Old Testament 5× (2×

These alterations suggest a bilateral move by both performances of the tradition to parse the marital image politically.[32] 'Your many shepherds' preserves with the political, the image of multiple paramours.

Summary. Evaluation of MT and LXX*V* variants as alternative performances of the composition detects the presence of an implied reader shaped and schooled to parse the marital symbolism by reference to the national myth of Israel. The function of this operation is to sharpen the political import of the metaphor in the juxtaposition of alternating gender poems.

Performing the Female: Illustrations. The second operation of alternative performances, we call *performing the female.* These variants configure and reconfigure the female persona. The issue is one of shifting the details of her characterization to a common end, that is, to portray her as an incurably wanton source of danger. The operation is bidirectional between the LXX*V* and MT.

Citing the accused. As husband Yhwh proceeds through the trial, he periodically cites statements of the accused as further evidence of her guilt. MT and LXX*V* variously manipulate those citations in their effort to characterize Yhwh's faithless spouse in her own self-incriminating words. 2.20-25 rehearses the history of the marriage, documenting a series of failed attempts on the part of the husband to secure the adulterous wife's fidelity. At v. 20, the LXX*V* explicitly extends the length of the citation 'I will not serve' with 'Indeed, I will go up on every high hill and under every luxuriant tree, there will I "spread" in my harlotry' (ותאמרי לא אעבד כי אלך על־כל־גבעה ותחת כל־עץ רענן שם אתצעה בזנותי).[33]

מוקש, 1× נף, 1× קוש). Cf. the retroversion offered by Bernhard Duhm, *Das Buch Jeremiah* (Tübingen: J.C.B. Mohr [Paul Siebeck], 1901), p. 34: רבים למוקש לך היו ורעים.

32. Cf. v.1 MT ואת זנית רעים רבים to LXX*V* ואת זנית רעים רבים. LXX: καὶ σὺ ἐξεπόρνευσας ἐν ποιμέσι πολλοῖς. ποιμήν in Jeremiah consistently renders רעה. See the previous note for statistics. רע is represented variously: 15× πλησίος, 2× φίλος, 2× πολίτης, 1× σύνειμι.

33. The harlot-wife brazenly announces her intentions, in detail (with iterative force, note the htp. צעה) to her husband. LXX: καὶ εἶπας οὐ δουλεύσω, ἀλλὰ πορεύσομαι ἐπὶ πάντα βουνὸν ὑψηλὸν καὶ ὑποκάτω παντὸς ξύλου κατασκίου, ἐκεῖ διαχυθήσομαι ἐν τῇ πορνείᾳ μου. At two points the retroversion is problematic. The htp. of צעה is suggested by translation with the aorist passive and the assumption of alternative divisions of the consonantal text. But this is the only time

At v. 25 the LXX*V* reports the wife's response to her husband's summons to turn with one word; the remainder has become an explanatory
clause: 'and she said, "useless", for she loves strangers and after them
she walks' (ותאמר נואש כי־אהבה זרים ואחריהם ילכה).[34] This time MT
extends the citation putting the incriminating explanation on the lips of
the accused: 'and you said, "useless, no, for I love strangers after them I
will walk" ' (ותאמרי נואש לוא כי־אהבתי זרים ואחריהם אלך).

Cosmetic alteration of the accused. Different descriptors of the
accused's behavior create alternative cosmetic visions of the harlot-
wife. At 2.23-24, MT offers the notorious image of the faithless wife
who possesses the animal sexual appetite of the she-camel, and the wild
she-ass in the desert (בכרה קלה משרכת דרכיה: 2.24 פרה למד מדבר).[35]
LXX*V* takes a different direction: 'In the evening she cries, she enlarges

---

διαχεώ is used to represent צעה in the Old Testament (14× פשׂה, 1× נטשׁ, 1× שׁקה,
1× פרשׂ, 1× פוץ, 1× פזר). πορνεία in Jeremiah normally represents זנות (3×; in the
rest of the Old Testament 7×). In Jeremiah πόρνη is the translation equivalent for
זנה (2×) but the latter only occurs a total of 3× in Jeremiah.

The MT offers a citation and a *kethib/qere* problem: 'I will not serve' or 'I will
not pass over' (לא אעבד [אעבור]). Perhaps the *qere* can be accounted for (apart
from resh/daleth confusion) in association with the preceding bi-colon. The verbs
are morphologically ambiguous representing archaic 2nd fem. sing. or 1st pers.
sing. forms. Read as the latter, *qere* understands a reference to the Exodus ('I broke/
I tore off') and the citation of the woman-Israel as an oath of fidelity ('I will not
transgress'; cf. BDB, p. 717, §1i which has proved false (cf. Targum and Cairo
Geniza fragment which follow the *qere*, see *BHS* apparatus).

34. LXX: ἡ δὲ εἶπεν Ἀνδριοῦμαι. ὅτι ἠγαπήκει ἀλλοτρίους καὶ ὀπίσω αὐτῶν
ἐπορεύετο. The retroversion of ἀνδρίζω is problematic. Elsewhere in the Old
Testament it represents חזק (10×) or אמץ (6×). But again at Jer. 18.12 the ni. ptc. is
rendered with the same Greek verb. Perhaps LXX etymologizes the root יאשׁ in
relation to אישׁ. In any case the translator understands the interjection to be one of
defiance rather than despair. See further Holladay, *Jeremiah 1*, p. 102; McKane,
Jeremiah, I, p. 44; and Roy D. Wells, Jr, ' "Your Ways in the Valley": The LXX of
Jer. 2.20-25' (unpublished paper, SBL, Southeastern Section, 1984). The Hebrew is
represented variously elsewhere in the Old Testament: ἀνίημι (1 Sam. 27.1), ἀνέχω
(Job 6.26), ἀποτάσσω (Qoh. 2.20), παύω (Isa. 57.10).

35. On the complicated correlation of the behavior described in the text with
that of 'real' she-camels and she-asses, see Holladay, *Jeremiah 1*, pp. 100-101. The
problem for the text's discourse is whether both animals contribute the note of
sexual passion or only the she-ass. If the she-camel's reproductive behavior is
described, then the depiction is contrary to fact! See further, Kenneth E. Bailey and
William L. Holladay, 'The "Young Camel" and "Wild Ass" in Jeremiah ii 23-25',
VT 18 (1968), pp. 256-60.

her ways by the waters in the desert' (בערב קלה היליל דרכיה הרחיבה
למי מדבר).[36] What the latter means is not clear. We suggest perhaps a
reference to the site of her adulterous trysts and compare it to the motif
in love poetry where the desert as uninhabited territory provides the
place for erotic adventures (Song 8.5, cf. 3.6).[37] In any case, the MT
performance gains in its depiction of the wife's bestial depravity.

At 2.33, MT makes of her a 'madam' of whores (לכן גם את־הרעות
[למדתי] למדת את־דרכיך:, 'so that even to wicked women you have
taught your ways'), while LXX*V* provides a general characterization of
her wickedness (לא כן כי אם ואת־הרעות לטמא את־דרכיך, ' "not so!"
except you acted wickedly by defiling your way').[38]

The two wives of the husband introduced in 3.6-20 (בגודה אחותה
יהודה/ה/משבה ישראל) receive in MT an additional characterization as
sisters; LXX*V* consistently lacks that designation (3.7, 8, 10). It is attrac-
tive to see another intertextual connection—that is, the Ezekiel allegory
of the two sisters (16.46-63). The two faithless wives of LXX*V* have
become Ezekiel's lewd wife-sisters. The reader perceives in Jeremiah 3
a narratizing compositional strategy in connection with the marital
metaphor—albeit with gaps—which can be managed by filling those
gaps with the aid of intertexts of Israel's national myth under the sign
of marital politics.

36. LXX: ὀψὲ φωνὴ αὐτῆς ὠλόλυξεν τὰς ὁδοὺς αὐτῆς ἐπλάτυνεν ἐφ᾽ ὕδατα
ἐρήμου. ὀψὲ = ערב (1×), בין הערבים (1×), נשף (1×) in Old Testament. If one
assumes some similarity between the MT and LXX*V*, then ὀψέ might represent כבר
or better כברה with the latter understood adverbially—'at length'. ὀλολύζω = pre-
dominately the hi. of ילל (18×; in Jeremiah 2×). πλατύνω = hi. רחב (10×), qal (1×),
רחב (1×, Jer. 28[51].58) unless LXX repoints MT הרחבה as a ho. verb (cf. ἐπλα-
τύνθη), פחה (3×), פון (1×). See also Wells, 'Your Ways in the Valley', pp. 4, 9.

37. Another possibility is suggested by Wells, 'Your Ways in the Valley', p. 14.
He detects an allusion to illicit female mourning rites in the desert, comparable, for
example, to weeping for Tammuz. Also, for Wells, there may be association with
Lilith imagery, effecting the hint of lurid demonic overtones to the woman's portrayal. None of these associations for the imagery may be mutually exclusive.

38. LXX: οὐχ οὕτως ἀλλὰ καὶ σὺ ἐπονηρεύσω τοῦ μιᾶναι τὰς ὁδούς σου. οὐχ
οὕτως = ואנך (3× in Jeremiah). ἀλλὰ = כי אם (13× of 24). πονηρεύω = רעע (3× of
4; 21× in rest of Old Testament). μιαίνω = טמא (3×; 93× in rest of Old Testament),
חנף (3×; 1× in rest of Old Testament). On this reading, we still understand MT
את־הרעות as a reference to 'wicked women' (RSV, NEB). Recent commentators
prefer a more abstract understanding, 'evil deeds'. See Carroll, *Jeremiah*, p. 139;
McKane, *Jeremiah*, I, p. 53; Holladay, *Jeremiah 1*, pp. 109-110, emends and reconstructs the MT in a way that blends the MT and LXX*V* variants.

Summary. Evaluation of MT and LXX*V* variants as alternative performances of the composition detects the presence of an implied reader shaped and schooled to perform and reperform the female figure. It is a performance designed to ruin her image and, thus, vindicate her husband's treatment of her. It remains to assess the significance of both operations for tracing the full outline of the encoded reader figured in the text.

Performing Cultural Intertexts: Jeremiah Recoding Hosea's Metaphor
Jeremiah neither invents the broken marriage metaphor nor originates its network of symbolic meanings. He inherits it from Hosea 1–3, adapts it, and transforms it. In the process, he changes its narrative shape, recasts its characters and, thereby, re-encodes the reader and alters the metaphor's rhetorical import. Scholars have long pointed to the many similarities between Jeremiah 2–3 and Hosea 1–3, but most observe connections at the level of vocabulary and image.[39] Jeremiah's borrowings from Hosea, however, are far more drastic. From Hosea he adopts narrative structure (particularly Hos. 2) and an authoritative tradition that he will remold. Rather than reiterate similarities between the two versions of the metaphor, we offer examples of alterations Jeremiah makes in his Hosean legacy:

1. In Hosea there are two marriages: Hosea's marriage to Gomer and God's marriage to Israel. Jeremiah presents one marriage, enabling him to concentrate on the husband's pain and the spouse's guilt.
2. Jeremiah alters the wife's motivation for pursuing other lovers, thereby, creating a more monstrous character. In Hos. 2.7 (Hebrew), she is merely searching for security and fertility, but in Jeremiah raw, animal lust drives her (Jer. 2.20-25).
3. Jeremiah changes the husband's behavior toward his wife. No longer does Yhwh seek merely to withhold fertility and to shame her publicly (Hos. 2.11-12); now he casts her away by divorcing her (Jer. 3.1-5).
4. Unlike Hosea (2.18-25), Jeremiah does not restore the marriage. To restore the marriage, the wife must accept blame (3.13) which

---

39. See William L. Holladay, *Jeremiah 2: A Commentary on the Book of the Prophet Jeremiah, Chapters 26–52* (Hermeneia; Minneapolis: Fortress Press, 1989), pp. 45-47, for a thorough catalogue of linguistic connections.

she does not do. Jeremiah can blame her, therefore, both for destroying the marriage and for refusing to return.

5. Jeremiah repositions the children from the beginning of the story (Hos. 2.3-5) to the end where they become survivors of the family tragedy, and meet the conditions set for their mother (Jer. 3.22-25).

Jeremiah reads an old metaphor and writes a new narrative. He omits elements of his inherited set of symbols, rearranges narrative structure, and adds new features to reanimate and re-encode the metaphor for a new audience. Jeremiah's intertextual alterations create a new configuration of readers. Symbolized by the children, readers are called to return wholeheartedly to their father and then they will be secure in their land.

Implications

The Ancient Text: Character, Competencies and Rhetorical Needs of the Encoded Reader

If we are correct about the identity of the implied audience as the citizens of Jerusalem, dramatized explicitly as such, and metaphorically as the children of Yhwh's faithless wives, then this community is addressed as a male collective. Patterned variants between MT and LXX*V* lavish effort upon the gender symbolism to control the way this implied reader accesses that imagery. The composition is at pains to school its 'reader'. The sons are led through their father's rehearsal of the past. But throughout this rehearsal the encoded reader is repeatedly 'replaced', 'refigured' according to diverse rhetorical needs. As recipient of a theodicy argument, the reader is offered a rhetoric of sympathy for husband Yhwh, figuring the implied reader as 'male'. As object/subject of restoration, the reader is offered a rhetoric of perennial erotic dangers, refiguring the encoded reader as 'female'.

The surface of the marital metaphor addresses men about women. Gender symbols are parsed repeatedly in reference to political and religious realities; yet these remain subordinate to the rhetoric of sexual politics. The composition 'figures' an implied reader in need of a theodicy for the destruction of Judah, but codes that reader as 'male' in its exploitation of the gender symbols. The composition constructs a rhetoric of sympathy for husband Yhwh. The performance of the female also serves this intent. Given her unsympathetic representation, the children must side with their father.

But as children of the divorced woman, subject once again to a renewed initiative of reconciliation from their father, the implied reader is 'refigured' as female. The composition constructs a rhetoric of erotic dangers. Though the encoded readers function as observers of the trial, their inclusion as dramatized objects of restoration after the divorce replaces them into the structural location of the woman—'you are the generation'. The encoded reader also relives the crisis of the woman's unfaithful passions. Her passions not only vindicate her treatment by the betrayed husband but threaten perennially to break out within her children (4.1-2). This rhetorical re-placement of the reader keeps the ethos of crisis/danger alive.

A New World: Feminist Ideological Critique
Leaving the horizon of the ancient text to reread it in a feminist context creates new problems. A feminist critique asks how Jeremiah's portrayal of female Israel related to the lives of historical women. In ancient Israel women caught in adultery risked stoning; women's status and security derived from their husbands and sons. Given such constraints, what women in that society would leave husbands for other lovers? For the metaphor to be effective, such behavior had to be imaginable. Perhaps a woman might abandon her husband for others if she were mentally ill and, hence, impervious to social and moral constraints on her actions. Perhaps a woman might be in such desperate circumstances within her marriage that it would be worth any risk to escape.

But if we admit that such behavior by women would have been rare in ancient Israel, other considerations arise. First, though women are portrayed in Jeremiah's text, they are neither present in it nor addressed by it, nor are they assumed to be among its readers. Rather the text presents a fictional representation of women to address its male audience. Second, if the text does not present circumstances of real women, then it contains a male projection of betrayal and evil onto women. The primary image of sin used in Jeremiah's metaphor is that of an unfaithful, nymphomaniac wife. She is the principle tool used in a rhetoric of shaming to encode the infidelities of male Israel.[40]

40. See Phyllis Bird, ' "To Play the Harlot": An Inquiry into an Old Testament Metaphor', in Peggy L. Day (ed.), *Gender and Difference in Ancient Israel* (Minneapolis: Fortress Press, 1989), pp. 75-94; Mary Joan Winn Leith, 'Verse and

Psychological factors such as male fears of female sexuality, betrayal and loss of control over their wives that might contribute to such projection are beyond the scope of this inquiry. What can be said with certainty is that the metaphor reflects 'regimes of reason'[41] that prevailed in ancient Israel. Because women were among the weakest members of the society, held little status, and were thought to be 'other', this metaphor can use them to shame the strong. But the metaphor descends even further by choosing a faithless woman, a crazed and dirty woman, to accomplish its ends. In achieving them, it creates new knowledge. Like all good metaphors, it puts into the public domain new images,[42] in this case of women, women out of control, women driven like beasts, to prey upon innocent men (2.23; 3.2) and who pollute the earth (3.3) and teach other women to follow suit (2.33). Besides shaming men, therefore, Jeremiah's metaphor cautions men about women in a rhetoric of fear. By making God a husband, it also elevates husbands to the role of God.[43]

The metaphor weaves a narrative in which the monologue of the injured husband alone is our source of information about this marriage. As often happens in divorce, it may be that the husband exaggerates the crimes of his spouse, blames her for everything wrong in the relationship, and makes as a condition of her return her acceptance of that blame. We hear him interrogate her belligerently and accuse her with his version of her words. We learn, to our surprise, that he had a second wife who treated him even worse. Put this way, we become suspicious of the husband and his version of events. Another account of this marriage lies hidden in the recesses of the metaphor.

What would happen if female Israel told the story? Would she tell of her husband's verbal abuse, his foolish jealousy, his despicable exaggerations, his claims to have 'planted her as a choice vine' (2.21), his continual distrust of her and her sexuality? Would she recount how loving he had been and tell how he had become more and more controlling and demanding? We cannot know, of course, because in this

Reverse: The Transformation of the Woman Israel in Hosea 1–3', in Day (ed.), *Gender and Difference*, pp. 95-108.

41. A term of Vincent Leicht, *Cultural Criticism*, pp. 3-4.

42. See Ricoeur, *The Rule of Metaphor*; Mary Gerhart and Allan Russell, *Metaphoric Process: The Creation of Scientific and Religious Understanding* (Forth Worth: Texas Christian University Press, 1984), pp. 112-15.

43. O'Connor, 'Jeremiah', p. 171.

case, the husband is God, and not such a nice god, even if broken-hearted.

What we do know about this metaphorical woman, though, is that she makes a moral and religious choice. She does not return to him despite the safety and social status a return might provide. She refuses to speak the words he demands of her: 'Only acknowledge your guilt ...' (3.13). She will not accept blame for the failure of the marriage, and she will not reject the gods and goddesses whom she loves. She accepts the price of her autonomy. By contrast, the children in this dysfunctional family behave the way their father expects them to behave.

As a model of divine–human relationship Jeremiah's metaphor is immensely problematic for male and female readers in certain cultures today. Despite the metaphor's sympathetic portrayal of the deity who suffers deeply and longs for his beloved, the metaphor undermines itself by reinforcing cultural images of a punishing unjust God, of punishing unjust husbands, and of wicked independent women.

THE CONSTRUCTION OF TIME IN JEREMIAH 25 (MT)

John Hill

The stimulus for this essay has come from two sources. One has been the series of consultations at the annual SBL meeting, entitled 'New Readings of Jeremiah'. A further stimulus was an article by Walter Brueggemann sharply critical of recent Jeremiah scholarship, which he believes has been dominated by two questions inherited from the work of Duhm and Mowinckel: (a) what is early and late material in the book of Jeremiah? (b) what is genuine to the prophet Jeremiah and what is an addition?[1] A preoccupation with issues of chronology and historical context has meant that many literary and theological aspects of the final form of the text have been often overlooked. As an attempt at a newer reading of the book of Jeremiah, this essay will explore the world of the text of one chapter in the book, and so lead to suggestions about the theological concerns not only of the particular chapter, but of the book's MT edition.

Jeremiah 25 (MT) has been chosen for such an exploration because it is regarded by a number of critics as marking the end of the first part of the book, and as such is important for our understanding of the shape of the book as a whole.[2] Furthermore, because most studies of it are text-

---

1. Walter Brueggemann, 'Jeremiah: Intense Criticism/Thin Interpretation', *Int* 42 (1988), pp. 268-80 (269). While acknowledging Brueggemann's criticism, it is also important to note the appearance of some recent studies that have explored the literary and theological aspects of the book, especially the confessions of Jeremiah: e.g., A.R. Pete Diamond, *The Confessions of Jeremiah in Context: Scenes of Prophetic Drama* (JSOTSup, 45; Sheffield: JSOT Press, 1987); Mark Smith, *The Laments of Jeremiah and their Contexts* (ed. Adele Yarbro Collins and E.F. Campbell; SBLMS, 42; Atlanta: Scholars Press, 1990); T. Polk, *The Prophetic Persona: Jeremiah and the Language of the Self* (JSOTSup, 32; Sheffield: JSOT Press, 1984).

2. E.g. J.A. Thompson, *Jeremiah* (NICOT; Grand Rapids: Eerdmans, 1980), p. 128. Winfried Thiel, *Die deuteronomistische Redaktion von Jeremia 1–25*

critical or redaction-critical, little attention has been given to its final form.[3] The essay has its specific focus on the construction of time because the book's temporal references have been evaluated primarily from the point of view of their historical accuracy, with the result that their significance in constructing the world of the text has been over-looked. The focus of the essay is not the world behind the text, but the explication of 'the type of being-in-the-world unfolded *in front of the text*'.[4]

The Shape of Jeremiah 25 MT

The MT of ch. 25 can be divided into three larger sections (vv. 1-14; vv. 15-26; vv. 27-38), each capable of further division into smaller units.[5] Verses 1-14 are a modified prophetic judgment speech which can be divided into an introduction (vv. 1-2); a reason for judgment expressed in summary form (vv. 3-7); the messenger formula (v. 8a); an announce-ment of judgment against Judah and Babylon (vv. 8b-14). Verse 1 also functions as an introduction to the whole chapter. What we have here is

(WMANT, 41; Neukirchen–Vluyn: Neukirchener Verlag, 1973), p. 44.

3. The neglect of the chapter's final shape is reflected in the arrangement of Robert P. Carroll's commentary (cf. his *Jeremiah: A Commentary* [OTL; Philadel-phia: Westminster Press, 1986], pp. 86-88). He divides the book into part one (Jer. 1.1–25.14), part two (25.15-28; chs. 46–51), part three (26–36), epilogue (52.1-34). A similar presentation of the book's contents is given by Wilhelm Rudolph, *Jere-mia* (HAT, 3; Tübingen: J.C.B. Mohr, 1968), p. 1. William McKane (*A Critical and Exegetical Commentary on Jeremiah*. I. *Introduction and Commentary on Jeremiah I–XXV* [ICC; Edinburgh: T. & T. Clark, 1986], pp. 618-58) treats the chapter as four separate units, and does not attend to its overall shape.

4. Paul Ricoeur, 'The Hermeneutical Function of Distanciation', in John B. Thompson (ed. and trans.), *Hermeneutics and the Human Sciences: Essays on Lan-guage, Action and Interpretations* (Cambridge: Cambridge University Press, 1981), p. 141 (italics his). This is not to imply the irrelevance of the history of the text or its inaccessibility in the interpretive process. For the purposes of this study the question is one of emphasis. What will be explored is this overlooked aspect of the interpretation of Jer. 25 MT rather than the text's history, which can often be reduced to discussion about the reliability of the LXX vis-à-vis the MT. One example of the latter approach is McKane, *Jeremiah*, I.

5. It may be noted here that the use of form-critical categories is purely functional: they provide a convenient way of describing the structure and function of a passage and/or its subunits. The essay is not attempting to suggest any conclu-sions about the prehistory of units or their *Sitz im Leben*.

a prophetic judgment speech with two modifications. The first is the general nature of the accusation, which Westermann sees as evidence of the breakdown of the form of the prophetic judgment speech.[6] The second is that the judgment speech is directed against both Judah and Babylon. Verses 1-14 then are a judgment speech directed first against Judah and its neighbours (v. 9) and subsequently against Babylon (v. 12).

Verses 15-26 centre on a prophetic symbolic action and are held together by the theme of judgment symbolized by the drinking of the cup of wine. These verses constitute a report of a symbolic act: in vv. 15-26 is the command to perform the symbolic action (v. 15); v. 16 a description of its consequences; v. 17 the performance of the action; vv. 18-26 a list of those who must drink.[7] Verses 15-26 amplify vv. 1-14 by describing the judgment in symbolic terms and giving a detailed list of nations and groups. In this respect it is more specific than vv. 1-14, and describes the submission of Babylon as the climax of the judgment process (v. 26).[8]

---

6. According to his analysis (Claus Westermann, *Basic Forms of Prophetic Speech* [London: Lutterworth Press, 1967], pp. 206-207), the elements of the prophetic judgment speech can be seen in these verses as follows: vv. 1-2 introduction; vv. 3-7 reason; v. 8a messenger formula; vv. 8b-11, 13 announcement of judgment. His analysis requires modification here because he omits vv. 12 and 14 from his considerations.

E.W. Nicholson (*Preaching to the Exiles: A Study of the Prose Tradition in the Book of Jeremiah* [Oxford: Basil Blackwell, 1967], pp. 55-57) sees vv. 4-11 as patterned on 2 Kgs 17.13-18. There is however a notable difference between 2 Kgs 17.13-18 and Jer. 25.4-11. The former uses predominantly third-person speech to describe the threat of divine punishment, whereas the latter uses first-person speech. The use of לכן to introduce the announcement of judgment (v. 8a) further supports the claim that Jer. 25.1-14 is better classified as a prophetic judgment speech. It may be further noted that Nicholson does not give an examination of the whole passage. Claus Rietzschel (*Das Problem der Urrolle: Ein Beitrag zur Redaktionsgeschichte des Jeremiabuches* [Gütersloh: Gerd Mohn, 1966], pp. 29-42) also analyses only parts of the passage. He finds a *Scheltrede* in an original kernel of vv. 3-7 (viz. vv. 3, 5, 7). Verses 8-11 are regarded as a *Drohrede*, and vv. 12-14 as later additions.

7. Cf. W. Eugene March, 'Prophecy', in John H. Hayes (ed.), *Old Testament Form Criticism* (San Antonio: Trinity University Press, 1977), pp. 141-77 (172), for the elements of this genre.

8. The unique position of Babylon is highlighted by the syntax of v. 26b, where the king of Babylon is the the subject of the clause: ומלך ששך ישתה אחריהם.

Verses 27-38 contain proclamations of punishment and laments. Verses 27-29, in the form of a prediction of disaster, deal with the possibility of the refusal to drink.[9] Both vv. 27-29 and vv. 30-31 begin with an instruction to the prophet. In v. 30 ואמרת אליהם is preceded by another instruction, ואתה תנבא, perhaps to underline Jeremiah's role as a prophet to the nations. The passage comprises two units, vv. 30-31 and 32-38. Although vv. 30-31 show similarities to the theophany in Amos 1.2, they are better understood here as a prophetic oracle, as their introduction (ואתה תנבא) and conclusion (נאם־יהוה) would suggest.[10]

Verses 32-36 begin with the the introductory כה אמר יהוה צבאות. Form critically, they may be best described as a prophetic oracle, containing the language of lament and death. Here, imagery used earlier in the book to describe Yahweh's activity against Judah is now employed in a new context. The theme of evil brought by Yahweh against the people of Judah, which is particularly common in the earlier chapters of the book (e.g. 1.14; 4.6; 6.1; 11.11; 19.3), is now universalized in 25.32. The association of Yahweh's anger with a storm, an image used in a diatribe against the prophets (23.18), is also found in 25.32. The imagery of death and desecration (v. 33) is found earlier: v. 33b repeats 8.2b. References to wailing and lamenting because of Yahweh's promised destruction (vv. 34, 36) are also in 6.26; 9.16-18 (MT). The expression מפני חרון אפו (25.38) is found earlier in 4.26. Other references to the divine anger (also in 25.37) are found in passages such as 2.35; 4.8; 7.20.

Verses 27-38 continue the theme of judgment against the nations. What is different here is the presence of language previously found in chs. 4–6 where it was used in the speeches against Judah. The use here, in the judgment on the nations, of language previously found in the judgment against Judah signifies the inevitable fulfilment of what is threatened. Just as certainly as Judah was destroyed (v. 18), the same fate awaits all the nations.

The syntax of vv. 18-26a uses the accusative case with the object marker for the nations who are to submit to the divine judgment.

9. So Westermann, *Basic Forms*, p. 156.

10. The similarity between v. 31 and Amos 1.2b is noted by William L. Holladay, *Jeremiah 1: A Commentary on the Book of the Prophet Jeremiah, Chapters 1–25* (Hermeneia; Philadelphia: Fortress Press, 1986), p. 679.

The Text's Construction of Time

By the use of both definite and indefinite temporal indicators, the chapter constructs its own time. What follows then is (1) an examination of the significance of the definite temporal indicators (i.e. chronological references) in 25.1; (2) an examination of other such indicators and their function within the book of Jeremiah (viz. 24.1; 26.1; 32.1), the purpose of which is to show that these indicators signify more than just chronological information; (3) the indefinite temporal indicators 'seventy years' (vv. 11, 12), עולם (vv. 5, 9, 12), 'as at this day' (v. 18), and 'on that day' (v. 33).

1. The expression 'the fourth year of Jehoiakim' is found in three other places in the book: 36.1; 45.1; 46.2. These are important points in the book. As Marion Ann Taylor has suggested, 'the significance of the fourth year of Jehoiakim goes far beyond historical specificity'.[11] The first reference for consideration is in ch. 36, which portrays the rejection of the prophetic word by Jehoiakim. Like ch. 25, there is a retrospective aspect regarding the prophet's preaching (36.2).[12] According to this chapter, the prophetic message is definitively rejected, punishment is proclaimed and there is no further offer of repentance. It is the end of an era in Judah's history.

The sense of an endpoint is strengthened when we look at the role of the prophet in ch. 36. He is the focus of attention in the early verses as he dictates the scroll, but then he fades from the scene as the scroll occupies centre stage. We are witnessing a shift in emphasis from the person of the prophet to the written word. The rejection of the prophetic word by Jehoiakim is followed by the realization of God's judgment in chs. 37–44.

The next reference is in ch. 45, which refers back to the writing of the scroll (cf. 45.1). This text also represents a shift in focus away from the person of the prophet to that of Baruch, whom the text casts in the likeness of Jeremiah. The complaint of the former in 45.3 reflects that of the latter in 15.10, 18; 20.18. Chapter 45 marks the end of a phase in which Jeremiah is sole bearer of the prophetic tradition.[13] In 45.5 it is

---

11. Marion Ann Taylor, 'Jeremiah 45: The Problem of Placement', *JSOT* 37 (1987), pp. 79-98 (88).

12. As noted by Thiel, *Die deuteronomistische Redaktion*, pp. 270-71.

13. On this, see Carroll, *Jeremiah*, p. 745.

Baruch who is given the promise of survival. By means of its references to breaking down and uprooting the land (originally found in 1.10), the text reinforces the sense that we are at an endpoint. The final reference to the fourth year of Jehoiakim is in 46.2. Here it is in the context of Egypt's history. The oracles against Egypt are introduced by a reference to Nebuchadnezzar's defeat of the Pharaoh Neco. Verses 2 and 13 link the impending demise of Egypt to the battle of Carchemish. For Egypt also, the fourth year of Jehoiakim signifies the end of an era.

Jeremiah 25.1 also refers to the first year of Nebuchadnezzar. One function of this regnal citation is to foreshadow his appearance later in the chapter.[14] A further function relates to the significance of dual chronologies. There is only one other place in the book where we find the use of dual chronologies. In 32.1 the account of Jeremiah's purchase of the field is set in the tenth year of Zedekiah, the eighteenth of Nebuchadnezzar. The year is of course particularly significant—587. Nebuchadnezzar is even more so the ruler of Judah than is Zedekiah. As in 32.1, the reference to his reign indicates that he had control of Judah's destiny.[15] While, as a number of scholars have pointed out, the question of the control of Syria was not settled in 605, the function of the chronological references in 25.1 is to indicate the end of an era or phase in Judah's history.[16] As Taylor writes, the fourth year of Jehoiakim functions 'as a code word for judgement'.[17]

2. A number of other definite temporal indicators in the book have a further function than just imparting chronological information. The setting of ch. 32 is the time of the siege of Jerusalem in 587. The theological significance of this is recognized by critics. At the very point of the nation's total collapse a future is promised. A comparison between the respective visions of the future contained here and ch. 24 is instructive. In ch. 32, the future embraces both those outside the land (vv. 37-41) and the land itself (and by extension, its inhabitants). In ch. 24, whose setting is the time after the first deportation of 597, a future is promised to the exiles only and the land is a place of death for those left

14. Cf. Thiel, *Die deuteronomistische Redaktion*, pp. 269-70.

15. This point is made by F. Nötscher, *Das Buch Jeremia: Die Heilige Schrift des Alten Testaments 7,2* (Bonn: Hanstein, 1934), p. 187.

16. For further discussion of the question of the extent of Babylonian control in Syria-Palestine, see Christopher R. Seitz, *Theology in Conflict: Reactions to Exile in the Book of Jeremiah* (BZAW, 176; Berlin: W. de Gruyter, 1989), pp. 87-91.

17. Taylor, 'The Problem of Placement', p. 88.

behind. The year 587 is thus associated not simply with the fall of Jerusalem but with the promise of a future for both those outside of the land and those in the land. The year 597 is associated with a future for the exiles only.

An examination of the significance of the reference in 26.1 to 'the beginning of the reign of Jehoiakim' is also useful. This chapter is set in the year 609. It contains an account of the prophet's preaching which is set at an earlier stage than that found in ch. 25. In 26.4-6 we find two key elements of the Summons to Repentance, that is, the accusation (vv. 4-5) and the threat (v. 6).[18] The prophetic message described here is related to listening. As 26.3 has it, אולי ישמעו וישבו. The account of the prophet's preaching in 25.3-7 refers back to a period when the people were summoned to listen but refused.

The significance of these definite temporal indicators in the book of Jeremiah can be further appreciated if their significance is compared with a purely annalistic listing of the relevant dates and events.[19]

Annalistic Listing	*The Book of Jeremiah*
609 death of Josiah accession and deposition of Jehoahaz II Accession of Jehoiakim	609 preaching of repentance— 'It may be that they will listen' (26.3)
605 the Babylonians defeat the Egyptians at the battle of Carchemish	605 preaching of judgment against Judah—'Because you have not obeyed my words, I will send for the tribes of the north ...' (25.8)
	announcement of judgment against all the nations, including Babylon (25.17-26)
	Jerusalem and the cities of Judah desolate (25.18)

---

18. For this analysis of the Summons to Repentance, see Thomas M. Raitt, *A Theology of Exile: Judgement/Deliverance in Jeremiah and Ezekiel* (Philadelphia: Fortress Press, 1977), pp. 37-40.

19. My understanding of 'annalistic listing' is derived from Hayden White's description of the annal as 'a list of events ordered in chronological sequence' (*The Content of the Form: Narrative Discourse and Historical Representation* [Baltimore: The Johns Hopkins University Press, 1987], p. 5).

<table>
<tr><td></td><td></td><td></td><td>the rejection of the prophetic message of the scroll and the announcement of judgment (36.27-32)</td></tr>
</table>

597	Jerusalem surrenders to the Babylonians; the first deportation	597	a future promised to the exiles; for those in the land, death and dispersion (24.4-7, 8-10)
587	Jerusalem again capitulates to the Babylonians; the second deportation	587	a future promised both to exiles and for the land (32.36-41, 42-44)

A comparison with the Deuteronomistic history's interpretation of the events of 597 and 587 highlight the peculiar perspective of the Jeremiah tradition. According to 2 Kgs 24.1-7 events which culminated in the first siege and deportation (597) were interpreted as divine punishment for the sins of Manasseh, and the events of 587 are linked to the evil of Zedekiah (24.18-20). The Jeremiah tradition also recognizes the guilt of Manasseh (15.1-4) as a potential cause for divine retribution, but it links the sins of Manasseh with the second Babylonian siege and deportation (587). The differences here between DtrH (Deuteronomistic history) and the Jeremiah tradition are significant. For DtrH the year 597 signifies only disaster. In Jeremiah 24 the year 597 signifies both disaster and a future, while Jeremiah 32 associates a more expansive future with 587. In the book of Jeremiah the year 605 has a number of meanings attached to it, whereas DtrH mentions it only obliquely (2 Kgs 24.1) and identifies Jehoiakim's rebellion against Nebuchadnezzar as the catalyst for divine punishment. While the year 605 functions as a code-word for judgment, other major events are likewise given a theological interpretation. What is different with the year 605 is that a number of theological judgments are associated with it.

3. Verses 1-14 also contain the expression 'seventy years', which is said to be the duration of Babylon's domination (vv. 11, 12).[20] This expression stands in some tension with the indefinite temporal indicator עולם which is used to describe both the fate of Judah in v. 11 (לחרבות עולם) and Babylon in v. 12 (לשממות עולם). One use of the word עולם is to describe a time 'the beginning or end of which is either uncertain or

---

20. The extensive literature on the meaning of this expression is detailed by Peter R. Ackroyd, *Exile and Restoration: A Study of Hebrew Thought of the Sixth Century B.C.* (London: SCM Press, 1968), p. 240 n. 27.

else not defined'.[21] The pairing of 'seventy years' with עולם indicates that the former term is not to be understood chronologically. Rather, it indicates a period which is of unknown length but at the same time finite, as v. 12 makes clear.

עולם also appears in v. 5, which describes the gift of the land to the ancestors as ומן־עולם ועד־עולם. While this precise expression is found only in Jer. 7.7, texts such as Gen. 13.15 and 17.8 use עולם when referring to the promise of the land.[22] In 25.5 it is the finite dimension of עולם that is significant: the period of indefinite possession is about to end. There is also a lack of specificity in v. 14. Like that of Judah, Babylon's punishment is described as desolation of the land (שממות עולם) and subjugation to some unnamed hostile powers. Again we have the indefinite עולם. The use of this word stands in some tension with vv. 1-3. The text has moved from what seems precise chronological information to the indefinite and the non-specific. According to the world of the text we are still in the year 605, the fourth of Jehoiakim.

The next temporal indicator is the expression in v. 18, 'as at this day' (כיום חזה). The context is the narrative in which the nations are to drink the cup of wrath. The first to drink are 'Jerusalem and the cities of Judah, its kings and princes' (v. 18). The result is that they will become 'a desolation and a waste, a hissing and a curse as at this day'. The words 'desolation' (שממה), 'ruin' (חרבה) and 'hissing' (שרקה) occurred in v. 9 and serve to link vv. 15-26 with what precedes. However, the most striking feature of v. 18 is its statement that the promised judgment has already happened. Jerusalem and the cities of Judah are already in ruins. In the world of ch. 25 'as at this day' refers to the year 605. The chapter has collapsed the chronological distance between 605 and 587, so that the promised judgment becomes immediately realized.

The final temporal indicator for consideration, 'on that day' (ביום ההוא) in v. 33, is part of the prophetic oracle of vv. 32-36. Here the language of lament and death, used previously in the book to describe God's judgment against Judah, is now employed in a new context. The theme of evil brought by Yahweh against the people of Judah, which is particularly common in the earlier chapters of the book (e.g. 1.14; 4.6;

21. See S. Tregelles, *Gesenius' Hebrew-Chaldee Lexicon to the Old Testament* (Grand Rapids: Eerdmans, 1980), p. 612.

22. In Gen. 13.15, the land is promised to Abraham and his descendants עד־עולם; in 17.8 it is promised as an 'everlasting possession' (לאחזת עולם).

6.1; 11.11; 19.3), is now universalized in 25.32. The association of Yahweh's' anger with a storm, an image used in a diatribe against the prophets (23.18), is also found in 25.32. The imagery of death and desecration (v. 33) is found earlier: v. 33b repeats 8.2b. References to wailing and lamenting because of Yahweh's promised destruction (vv. 34, 36) are also in 6.26; 9.16-18 (MT). The expression מפני חרון אפו (25.38) is found earlier in 4.26. Other references to the divine anger (also in 25.37) are found in passages such as 2.35; 4.8; 7.20.

The chapter differentiates between 'this day' and 'that day'. At 'this day' the judgment against Jerusalem and the cities of Judah has been realized, but the divine judgment against the whole world belongs to 'that day' in the undefined future. The chapter presents us with an in-between phase. The judgment has been partially realized, but there is more to come—judgment on a cosmic scale which however will not necessarily initiate the restoration of Judah.

Significance of the Text's Construction of Time

The world constructed in Jeremiah 25 M T collapses the temporal distance between the years 605 and 587. The chronological information in 25.1 signifies two things. The reference to the reign of Nebuchadnezzar indicates that he was as much (or more so) the ruler of Judah as was Jehoiakim; the reference to the 'fourth year of Jehoiakim' that an endpoint has been reached. The events of 587—the date more usually associated with the end of an era—are then associated with 605.

The chapter then presents its understanding of this end-point. It questions Judah's self-understanding as a divinely chosen people. This is done in the judgment speech of vv. 3-14, which links Judah and Babylon together as recipients of divine punishment. The speech contains no suggestion that Babylon's demise will foreshadow Judah's restoration. In vv. 15-26 Judah then appears as one of a list of nations to undergo divine judgment. The narrative of the cup of wrath situates Judah as no different to any of the nations who must undergo judgment. This is the same phenomenon as found in the OAN ('Oracles Against the Nations') of the book of Amos, where the repeated use of the prophetic judgment speech portrays both Israel and Judah as no different to the other nations that are condemned. The expanded accusation in the speech against Israel simply indicates that its guilt and thus its consequent punishment will be greater. Israel's belief in itself as God's elect is subverted in these oracles, as it is later in Amos.[23] It contains no suggestion that the impending judgment against the nations will imply salvation or restoration for Judah.

The order of the nations in vv. 15-26 points to another of the text's theological interests. According to v. 17 'the cup of the wine of wrath' is to be given to 'all the nations to whom I send you', and these are specified by the list in vv. 18-26. The list begins 'Jerusalem, the cities of Judah, its kings and princes'. The effect of the list is to reinforce what was suggested in vv. 8-14: Judah is just one of the גוים. The list then details Judah's neighbours (vv. 18-22) and extends more broadly to embrace other nations of the region (vv. 23-25).[24] Then we find generic groups mentioned—'all the kings of the north, far and near, one after another' and 'all the kingdoms of the world'. The list ends with the king of Babylon. In vv. 18-25 all of those who drink the cup are the grammatical object of ואשקה (v. 17) as are the generic groups in v. 26a.

The portrayal of a judgment process, which begins in Jerusalem and extends to all the nations, is found also in 25.28-29. There is in v. 28 an implied refusal by unnamed nations or groups to accept the cup. The response is twofold. First, a command to drink is given, couched in an emphatic form (שְׁתוּ תשׁתו—v. 28). Secondly, the process of judgment is identified as beginning with Jerusalem and extending to all the earth: 'For behold, I begin to work evil at the city which is called by my name ... for I am summoning a sword against all the inhabitants of the earth.' An irony in the passage is that the nation most guilty of refusing the divine word is Judah. The image of judgment beginning in Jerusalem and extending from there to the whole world stands in stark contrast to the vision of Jerusalem in the psalms of Zion (e.g. 46.1-8 [MT]). The overthrow of Zion theology is also suggested in ch. 1, according to which foreign kings will set up their thrones at the gates of Jerusalem (v. 15), and the only city with divinely guaranteed protection is Jeremiah (v. 18).[25] Jerusalem is now a place of death, not life and blessing.

---

23. ' "Are you not like the Ethiopians to me, O people of Israel?" says the Lord. "Did I not bring up Israel from the land of Egypt, and the Philistines from Caphtor and the Syrians from Kir?" ' (Amos 9.7).

24. Holladay, *Jeremiah 1*, pp. 672-73.

25. See Harry P. Nasuti, 'A Prophet to the Nations: Diachronic and Synchronic Readings of Jeremiah 1', *HAR* 10 (1986), pp. 249-86, and especially the section of his study entitled 'Jeremiah and Jerusalem: A Tale of Two Cities' ('A Prophet to the Nations', pp. 258-62).

Central to the world of the text created in Jeremiah 25 is an understanding of Judah's God as active on the world stage. Defeated Judah and conquering Babylon are equally under the power of this God who can designate as 'my servant' not only great figures of Judah's history—Moses, Joshua, David—but Babylon's king also (25.9).[26] While this understanding is not new, what is new is the position in which Jeremiah 25 locates itself—that is, between the execution of divine cosmic judgment, begun by the destruction of Jerusalem, and its full realization at some indefinite time in the future.

This in-between position of ch. 25 is also reflected in the arrangement of the Jeremiah MT, which differs significantly from that of the book of Ezekiel which situates the oracles against the nations (chs. 25–32) immediately after the oracles against Judah and Jerusalem (chs. 1–24). After the news of the fall of Jerusalem (33.21-22), the book takes a far more optimistic note which climaxes in the vision of the restored temple (chs. 40–48). The reader of the book of Ezekiel is led through the period of judgment, first against Judah and then against the nations, to the promise of a future. By way of contrast, at the end of the book of Jeremiah MT the reader is left in exile. As Rosenberg's analysis of the its structure shows, the contents of the book are enclosed in what might be called an exilic envelope.[27] Jeremiah 1.1-3 contains chronological information leading up to the exile, while ch. 52 begins with the events of 587. Apart from the disputed suggestion of a muted hope in 52.31-34, neither passage speaks about a future.

A reticence about the future is found in other places in the book. Promises about the restoration are like small oases of hope in a large desert of judgment speeches. The promise of 16.14-15 is hedged around by threats of punishment. The promises found in 23.1-8 are subverted by the threats. The promised future for the exiles in 24.4-7 is submerged by what follows—ch. 25 and its threat of a universal judgment.

---

26. While עבדי in 25.9 might indicate only a relationship of vassalage, as argued by Ziony Zevit ('The Use of עֶבֶד as a Diplomatic Term in Jeremiah', *JBL* 88 [1969], pp. 74-77), its meaning in 27.5-7 signifies that Nebuchadnezzar is more than just an instrument or vassal of Judah's God.

27. The framing effect of 1.1-3 and ch. 52 are brought out by Rosenberg's analysis of the book's structure. See Joel Rosenberg, 'Jeremiah and Ezekiel', in Robert Alter and Frank Kermode (eds.), *The Literary Guide to the Bible* (Cambridge: Belknap Press, 1990), pp. 184-206 (190-91).

The book of consolation (chs. 30–31) may well represent the centre-point of the book, as Rosenberg maintains.[28] However, its message of hope, continued into chs. 32–33 is subverted by ch. 36 with its belief in the inevitability of impending doom. Even the oracles which tell of the defeat of Babylon (50.1–51.58) are not allowed to stand as the final word in the book. There is a future, but it is a long way off.[29]

Given the above, is it possible to say anything about the function of the MT edition of the book of Jeremiah in the postexilic community? The elements of answer lie in recognizing the book's final form, which suggests that it is addressed to an audience who are in exile (i.e. liter-ally) or should consider themselves to be in exile (i.e. metaphorically). Given the general agreement that the book reached its final form in the postexilic period, the investigation of a metaphoric understanding of exile seems preferable. What occurs in this mode of interpretation is a process of refiguration, which Ricoeur describes as 'the power of reve-lation and transformation achieved by narrative configurations when they are "applied" to actual acting and suffering'.[30] The effect in a nar-rative or metaphoric text is to produce a 'seeing as... ' In the case of the MT edition of Jeremiah, this process enables the reader to see his or her current situation as an exile and to interpret it in the light of the tradi-tion's fundamental experience of exile—namely, the complex of events which we know as the Babylonian exile.[31]

The literature of second temple Judaism contains a large number of metaphorical references to the community in Judah as still in exile.[32] Two passages can serve as examples: Dan. 9.2; Tob. 14.3-7. The first passage refers to Daniel's attempt to interpret the meaning of the Jeremian 'seventy years'. The book portrays Daniel seeking to under-stand when the community's exile would end. What is significant for this essay is that this exilic situation is a fiction of the book, which uses

28. See Rosenberg, 'Jeremiah and Ezekiel', pp. 192-93, for his analysis of the book's structure.

29. As noted by Rosenberg, 'Jeremiah and Ezekiel', p. 192.

30. Paul Ricoeur, 'Narrated Time', in Mario J. Valdés (ed.), *A Ricoeur Reader: Reflection and Imagination* (Toronto: University of Toronto Press, 1991), pp. 338-54 (339).

31. 'Seeing *as* ... is the Spirit [*âme*] common to metaphor and narrative' (Ricoeur, 'Narrated Time', p. 350).

32. These instances are documented by N.T. Wright, *The New Testament and the People of God, Christian Origins and the Question of God* (2 vols.; London: SPCK, 1992), I, pp. 268-72.

the event of the exile as a way of understanding the community's situation in the Maccabean period. 'Seventy years' is interpreted as 'seventy weeks of years', so that the date of its realization 'was thus well beyond the imminent and meaningful historical horizon of our apocalyptic writer'.[33] The second passage (Tob. 14.3-7) is also from a post-exilic composition which also constructs an exilic setting for itself: in this instance, Nineveh. In v. 5 Tobit expresses the hope that the people's exile will end and the house of God rebuilt. As indicated by the use of the expressions ἕως πληρωθῶσιν καιροὶ τοῦ αἰῶνος and εἰς πάσας τὰς γενεὰς τοῦ αἰῶνος (v. 5), the passage suggests that the restoration will happen in the indefinite future.[34]

At the level of its reception, a text has both a revelatory and transforming function.[35] Expressed in broad, thematic terms, what is revelatory in the book of Jeremiah is that the 'present' is an exile, which has come about because of the judgment of God in response to the community's sin. There is a promised future, but its realization is in the indefinite future. The transformative function, again expressed in broad terms, relates to an acceptance of the interpretation of the text's revelatory dimension: the acceptance of the exile as divine justice and judgment, a willingness to repent, and the abandonment of a glib hope which sees an imminent end to the exile.

Conclusion

At the beginning this essay described itself as exploratory and as an attempt to articulate one possible new reading of the book of Jeremiah. The interpretation suggested above is nascent and provisional, requiring further reflection and precision. It is offered with the hope of provoking

33. Michael Fishbane, *Biblical Interpretation in Ancient Israel* (Oxford: Clarendon Press, 1991), p. 483.

34. The temporal expressions cited above are from the BA recension of the book. Only the first of these expressions occurs in the S recension and in an expanded form: καὶ οὐχ ὡς τὸν πρῶτον, ἕως τοῦ χρόνου, οὗ ἂν πληρωθῇ ὁ χρονος τῶν καιρῶν.

35. These qualities, which Ricoeur sees as part of the reception process of any narrative, are especially applicable to the use of biblical texts. A text is revelatory in that 'it brings out into the open the traits dissimulated but already sketched out at the heart of our practical and empathetic experience' ('Narrated Time', p. 350). The transforming dimension means that 'a life thus examined is a life changed' (Ricoeur, 'Narrated Time', pp. 350-51).

further critical discussion about ways of interpreting the book of Jeremiah which take us beyond those articulated by the long-established approaches of source- and redaction criticism.

THE POTENT WORD OF GOD: REMARKS ON THE COMPOSITION
OF JEREMIAH 37–44[*]

Else K. Holt

My interest in Jeremiah 37–44 is not an interest in the historical incidents before and under the Babylonian defeat of Jerusalem in 587 BCE or in the *Leidensgeschichte* (passion narrative) of Jeremiah but in the literary tools of the author of this fine novella. And, even more than that, it is an interest in the theology of this particular part of the book of Jeremiah.[1] This theology, however, will first be comprehensible when we have examined the literary tools used by the author—a person to whom I shall return in a moment. It is indeed to the literary tools that I shall call attention, for it is obvious that the author uses catchwords and catch-concepts in a skillful manner in order to accentuate his theological focus.

---

* Paper read at the SBL Annual Meeting, New Orleans November 1996, slightly revised.

1. When speaking of a particular part of the book of Jeremiah, I refer to the fact that the book of Jeremiah is a book of many theologies, among which the Deuteronomistic theology is a very important one. This is to be seen at the surface level (composition) as well as on the ideological and the semantic level; see, among others, E.W. Nicholson, *Preaching to the Exiles: A Study of the Prose Tradition in the Book of Jeremiah* (Oxford: Basil Blackwell, 1970); W. Thiel, *Die deuteronomistische Redaktion von Jeremia 1–25* (WMANT, 41, Neukirchen–Vluyn: Neukirchener Verlag, 1973); *idem, Die deuteronomistische Redaktion von Jeremia 26–45: Mit einer Gesamtbeurteilung der deuteronomistischen Redaktion des Buches Jeremia* (WMANT, 52, Neukirchen–Vluyn: Neukirchener Verlag, 1981); R.P. Carroll, *Jeremiah: A Commentary* (OTL; London: SCM Press, 1986). Conversely, chs. 37–44 have been considered a Jeremiah biography, written by Baruch; so, e.g., H. Kremers, 'Leidensgemeinschaft mit Gott im Alten Testament', *EvT* 13 (1953), pp. 122-40; G. Wanke, *Untersuchungen zur sogenannten Baruchschrift* (BZAW, 122; Berlin: W. de Gruyter, 1971), pp. 91-133. See also G. Keown *et al., Jeremiah* (WBC, 27; Dallas: Word Books, 1995), pp. 209-11.

The Composition of the Book of Jeremiah

As we all know, the composition of the book of Jeremiah is far from being as arbitrary as claimed by older scholarship, for example, by Sigmund Mowinckel in 1914.[2] As demonstrated by Martin Kessler in 1968,[3] the aim of its composition is to present the divine word as spoken by Jeremiah and to illustrate the reception, or rather, the non-reception of this divine word. The important thing is the dynamic relationship between 'doom' and 'salvation'. In 'book' one, chs. 1–25, the divine word is presented as a collection of oracles and acts which illustrate the contents of the divine message. Book two consists of the 'Oracles Against the Nations' (OAN), chs. 26–32 in the first edition of Jeremiah.[4] Thus, in 'books' one and two, the word of God is aptly presented, and what follows in 'book' three is the history of the reception of the word. The third 'book' has been divided into two complexes, chs. 26–36 and 37–45.[5] The first complex is concerned with the dialogue engendered by Yahweh's word, as proclaimed by Jeremiah. This complex, Kessler says,

> needed a sequel, for the 'word' as faithfully communicated by Jeremiah was not heard (implied: obeyed) and therefore the question as to whether it would be fulfilled is yet unanswered. The conception that Yahweh's word was potent and creative and in no wise 'empty' dictated such a sequel.[6]

These considerations bring us to the narrative account of the fate of Jeremiah, and accordingly, the fate or history of the word of Yahweh during the siege and fall of Jerusalem (37–45). These chapters are seen

---

2. S. Mowinckel, *Zur Komposition des Buches Jeremia* (Kristiania: Jacob Dybwad, 1914).

3. M. Kessler, 'Jeremiah Chapters 26–45 Reconsidered', *JNES* 27 (1968), pp. 81-88. Kessler's three-part division has been followed and amplified in, e.g., Carroll, *Jeremiah*.

4. Cf. E. Tov, 'L'incidence de la critique textuelle sur la critique littéraire dans le livre de Jérémie', *RB* 79 (1972), pp. 189-99; *idem*, 'Some Aspects of the Textual and Literary History of the Book of Jeremiah', in P.-M. Bogaert (ed.), *Le livre de Jérémie: Le prophète et son milieu, les oracles et leur transmission* (Leuven: Leuven University Press, 1981), pp. 145-67; J.G. Janzen, *Studies in the Text of Jeremiah* (HSM, 6; Cambridge, MA: Harvard University Press, 1973).

5. So also among others, Carroll, *Jeremiah*.

6. Kessler, 'Jeremiah', p. 84.

by Kessler as the narrative of 'history which vindicated the rejected word by relating its fulfilment in historical events'.[7] And more than that: these chapters are the ultimate justification of the terrible events that led to the destruction of the temple, the city and the people of God. Not even during the punishment did the leaders of Jerusalem understand and submit to the will and the wrath of God.

We shall now try to find and follow some of the means of composition used by the author of chs. 37–44. The word 'author' will not be used as the emblem of Baruch the Scribe or any other person known to us, but as the emblem of the Deuteronomistic writer who composed the traditions of Jeremiah and the last days of Jerusalem into a well-told narrative.[8]

The Literary Tools

The message is communicated through a skillfully composed narrative, opening with the pericope Jer. 37.1-10. Here the *dramatis personae*, King and Prophet, are introduced. In v. 3 Jeremiah is depicted as a mediator: 'Intercede on our behalf with the LORD our God', the royal emissaries say. The political and military situation is presented, and the total devastation of the city is foreseen, and this creates the scenario for the ensuing accounts. Together with the concluding Deuteronomistic sermon of ch. 44, Jer. 37.1-10 forms an *inclusio*, underlining the justice of the punishment.

Inside this thematic *inclusio* we find literary tools, or *codes*, of different sorts. The formulation of these codes and some of the codes themselves vary from the beginning of the narrative—the chapters that describe what took place before the fall of Jerusalem—to the end of the narrative. One code is that of *the situation of Jeremiah*. Another one is *the code of ethnicity*, which draws on the contrast between the foreigner who obeys God and the stubborn, obstinate princes and people of Judah who do not obey him. Finally, a third code to be mentioned is *the relationship between King and prophet*. Through the entire narrative as a leitmotif runs the picture of Jeremiah as a mediator and as the

7. Kessler, 'Jeremiah', p. 84.
8. That the author/redactor of Jer. 37–45 was a Deuteronomist was called into question by T. Römer in his paper: 'How Did Jeremiah Become a Convert to Deuteronomistic Ideology?', SBL Annual Meeting 1996.

personified word of God. This role is presented in the introduction in 37.1-10, and it remains important until the closing sermon of ch. 44.

The Situation of Jeremiah

Throughout the first chapters of the novella the situation of Jeremiah forms the literary basis. We meet the theme for the first time in 37.1-10, where the royal deputies are seeking an oracle from Jeremiah: 'At that time Jeremiah was free to come and go among the people; he had not yet been thrown into jail.' The word of God is still openly demanded, but this is quickly changed. In the rest of the narrative the situation is the opposite.

'So Jeremiah remained in the court of the guard-house', we are told (37.16, 21; 38.13, 28). This sentence has been used by scholarship as a form-critical device to separate the various parts of the narrative into separate anecdotes and accordingly to create a 'historical' sequence.[9] The sentence, however, is better viewed as a code: The prophet—and that is the word of Yahweh—was hostilely treated. The prophet, the word of God, was put away and not heard. The leaders of Jerusalem tried to close God's mouth, so to speak. During the final, crucial days of the Davidic dynasty and the appointed city of God, his word was kept out of the way by the leaders.

It should be noted that Jeremiah's prisons are not places of no importance or a random choice. First, Jeremiah is in the house of Jonathan the Scribe. Later, with the intercession of the king, he is moved to the court of the guardhouse. These are public places, belonging to the ruling party (which is not Deuteronomistic[10]). With the code of the imprisoned Jeremiah, the guilt of Jerusalem is emphasized and the justice of the divine punishment acknowledged.

The code of Jeremiah's whereabouts continues after the fall of Jerusalem. In 39.11 Jeremiah is taken care of by Nebuzaradan, the Babylonian captain of the guard, who takes him from the court of the guard.

---

9. E.g. Kremers, 'Leidensgemeinschaft'; and Wanke, *Untersuchungen*.

10. The significance of family names in the book of Jeremiah should not be underestimated. Most of Jeremiah's helpers seem to belong to 'old' Deuteronomistic families, such as the Shaphan family (Jer. 26.24; 29.3; 36.10; 39.14; 40.5, 9, 11; 41.2; 43.6; cf. 2 Kgs 22), while his opponents belong to other families, such as the Ma'aseja family (Jer. 29.21, 25; 35.4; the Ma'aseja of Jer. 37.3 seems to belong to yet another family).

He entrusts him to Gedaliah to be brought home, and we are told: 'So he stayed with his own people.' Here the formulaic use of the code of Jeremiah's whereabouts tentatively ends, but as a part of the narrative flow we are told that at his own wish he goes to stay with Gedaliah (40.4, 6). After having been away from the narrative in one-and-a-half chapters Jeremiah returns as a mediator at the beginning of ch. 42 and is taken by the Judeans to Egypt, where the story and the book ends.[11]

So in the first part, chs. 37–38, we see an attempt to silence Jeremiah, the word of God. But you cannot tell Yahweh to shut up. There are ways for him to make his will known. When the king asks him questions, he will get his answer. When sitting in public prison Jeremiah continues his loud spoken sermons to the people of Jerusalem, not caring for the hushes of the guards. When thrown into the courtyard of Šeol—and that is the coded content of the muddy pit, so we learn from the book of Psalms[12] and so the story stresses—the true friend of God, the foreigner Ebed-Melech, has him pulled up again.

In the second part, however, after the fall of Jerusalem, the divine word is set free, never to be silenced again. Actually, the book of Jeremiah ends with a complete sermon (ch. 44)! The word of God conquers in the end.

The People of Šeqer

This word of God is a word to be believed. The messenger Jeremiah is not a treacherous person. When Jeremiah is about to leave Jerusalem to go to the Benjaminite territory, the officer of the guard accuses him of going over to the Chaldeans (37.11-16). This accusation is refuted by Jeremiah with the word *šeqer* (treachery). People talking against Yahweh are talking *šeqer*. And when they accuse him of discouraging the soldiers and everyone on the street by prophesying the demolition of Jerusalem (38.1-6), *we* know that he was right and they were wrong. They are the people of the Covenant with *šeqer*, not Jeremiah.

Judean treachery is also an important part of the incidents after the Chaldean seizure of power, as Gedaliah, the Chaldean governor, is killed by treachery by a Judean guerilla leader (41.1-3), while Jeremiah

---

11. The following chapters, the Oracles Against the Nations (OAN), have been transferred to this place in the second edition of the the book of Jeremiah, after that the story was written and redacted.

12. Pss. 28.1; 30.4; 40.3; 88.5, 7; 143.7; cf. Isa. 38.18.

and Baruch the Scribe on their side are accused of lying, talking *šeqer*, before the Judean refugees force them to go with them to Egypt (43.2-3).

So, the Judeans are demonstrated to be the people of *šeqer*. The point is most profoundly affirmed through the lengthy narrative of the Ethiopian eunuch Ebed-Melech and the 3 (or 30) men who drag the prophet from the cistern (38.7-13). The story is told in such an elaborate way that it must be something more than just an account of how Jeremiah escaped death. Here we find the code of Jeremiah's quarters coinciding with the code, which we have labeled 'the code of ethnicity'.

The Code of Ethnicity

The people of *šeqer* are the Judeans—conversely the Ethiopian Ebed-Melech is the man of God. His foreign origin is mentioned three times in 38.7-13 and again in the blessing which he receives in ch. 39. In 39.15-18, Yahweh promises him that when the day of ruin comes for Jerusalem he will preserve him from the sword, and from the men he fears. The wrath of Yahweh will not befall the Ethiopian—'because you have trusted in me'—as opposed to the faithless city, and he will be rescued from his opposers, the princes, we surmise, whom he stood up against.

That ethnicity is an important code is also confirmed by the speech in ch. 40 by the Babylonian captain of the guard, Nebuzaradan. He makes a perfectly Yahwist (and Deuteronomistic) speech to Jeremiah:

> The LORD your God threatened this place with this disaster; and now the LORD has brought it about, and has done as he said, because all of you sinned against the LORD and did not obey his voice. Therefore this thing has come upon you (40.2-3).

Here a foreigner, the victorious enemy of Judah, repeats the words of Jeremiah, that is, the words of the will of God. Since Nebuzaradan appears as the savior of Jeremiah, offering him protection after the flight and capture of the king, he is portrayed as a good man, as a man of God. So here again we find the foreigners as the chosen people—and the chosen ones as the men of *šeqer*.

The code of ethnicity is one of the means used by the author to underline the complete sin of the originally chosen people. Those from whom they had been set apart through Election and Covenant in the end became the elected instruments of the God of the Covenant. This theme, of course, is not alien to the Old Testament, especially in an exilic context, but here there is more to it than just that of the 'necessary idiots', to quote Lenin. Here the foreigners frame the offenses of the native people.

King and Prophet

Until now we have seen how the author uses harsh contrasts to promote his message. In his presentation of the relationship between Jeremiah and the unfortunate King Zedekiah we find a more delicate mode of expression.

First of all, Zedekiah is portrayed as a weak man, a king without power and genuine influence. When the princes tell him that Jeremiah has to be executed he answers: 'Here he is; he is in your hands; for the king is powerless against you' (38.5). When Jeremiah calls him to surrender to the Chaldeans to save the city he refuses, saying: 'I am afraid of the Judeans who have deserted to the Chaldeans, for I might be handed over to them and they would abuse me' (38.19). And at the end of the second meeting with Jeremiah Zedekiah is the one to ask for reticence (38.24-26).

Zedekiah is a man without a firm course. The picture of him drawn by the author is that of a man swaying to and fro. He is not an enemy of God, nor a villain like the good-for-nothing king Jehoiakim ben Josiah, who cut the scroll of Jeremiah's oracles into pieces and burned it without fearing or renting his clothes (ch. 36). Zedekiah seems to be beyond responsibility. Nothing he can do will prevent the divine disaster.

We do not know why the picture of the king looks like this. It seems that nothing would have been easier to the author than laying the ultimate blame on this last Davidic king of Jerusalem.[13] But that is not done—and one even gets to pity Zedekiah for his gruesome fate: when captured by the Babylonians after taking flight from the palace, his sons are killed before his very eyes and he himself is blinded and taken in fetters to Babylon (39.6-7).

Leaving this issue aside for a moment we will ask: 'What is the king's relationship to Jeremiah—that is, to the word of Yahweh?' An analysis of the structure of the two stories about the encounters of

13. Cf. 2 Kgs 24.20.

Jeremiah and Zedekiah (37.11-21; 38.14-28) will lead towards an understanding of that relationship:

37.11-21:

A   The situation of Jeremiah: Accusation and imprisonment

B   The king sends for Jeremiah to consult him

C   Jeremiah presents his plea to the king.

D   New situation: The king complies with Jeremiah's request—and Jeremiah sits in the court of the guardhouse.

38.14-18:

A   The situation of Jeremiah: Accusation and imprisonment

B   The king sends for Jeremiah to consult him

C   The king presents his plea to Jeremiah.

D   New situation: Jeremiah complies with the king's request—and Jeremiah sits in the court of the guardhouse.

A and B are alike, while C and D are converses. The structure of the two *inclusios*, however, is analogous. It seems reasonable to see king and prophet as opponents and at the same time complementing one another. This becoms clear from C: In ch. 37 Jeremiah implores the king to save his life, whereas in ch. 38 the king asks Jeremiah to tell a lie to save his.

And what is the content of the king's lie? It is that Jeremiah presented a petition to the king not to send him back to the house of Jonathan. But this is exactly what Jeremiah asked for at their first encounter. So it seems fair to claim that Jeremiah's lie was supposed to save the king and not, as it seems at first sight, the prophet himself. It is the king who initiates the lie and he seems to be the one feeling threatened at the time. In ch. 37 the possibility of a violent death for Jeremiah is stressed, if the king will not help him. In ch. 38 the stress is on the death of the king, and how to avoid it.

The reflecting of Jeremiah and Zedekiah crystallizes in the concept of *mud*. Jeremiah is thrown into the cistern, where there was no water, only mud (38.6). Over Zedekiah the lament will be sung:

> Your trusted friends have seduced you
> and have overcome you;
> Now that your feet are stuck in the mud,
> they desert you (38.22).

The word for mud is not the same in the two instances (38.6: *ṭîṭ*; 38.22: *boṣ*). But nevertheless the future of Zedekiah, misled by his own friends is the reflection of Jeremiah, who was saved by a foreigner.

The motive of this reflection seems to be to compare the two persons: The king could have surrendered to Yahweh and thereby saved his life, but he chose not to. Jeremiah, in return, was rescued from death by Ebed-Melech because he is the personification of the word of God.[14] Somehow, for once, a person gets into focus as a *person*: Zedekiah, who could have saved himself but didn't. The fate of Jerusalem and Judah was already sealed by Jehoiakim who destroyed and burned the word of God (36.20-26). The fall of Jerusalem was inevitable.

Zedekiah as a person, however, could have saved himself. He got the offer, and he wanted to accept it, but he was too weak. Somehow, one cannot help but speculating that what really happened (knowing that the words 'really happened' is almost taboo nowadays) in the near past made schematizing more or less impossible to the author.

Jeremiah and Zedekiah confront each other, reflect each other, complement each other. But that couldn't have been in the case that Zedekiah had been the ultimate foe of Yahweh as king Jehoiakim was. Jeremiah and Jehoiakim never met. Jeremiah and Zedekiah *did* meet. They mutually helped each others. Zedekiah saved Jeremiah's life just as Jeremiah tried to save Zedekiah's. And so Zedekiah is enlisted among the helpers of God. Zedekiah becomes an almost modern figure among the kings of the Deuteronomist.[15] He is not either/or—he is both/and. He is weak—and that seals his sad end.

Coda

The means of making the stories of Jeremiah and his contemporaries into a narrative of the rejected word of God are not haphazard. Some would argue that the search for the name and ideas of the author is futile. To this objection one might answer: In this instance the ideas of the author present themselves so strongly and with such artistic skill that there must have been a real author of flesh and blood at work. Somebody wrote the novella of the rejected word of God, compiling it out of transmitted fragments of fact, narrative and fantasy. Somebody

14. So E.W. Nicholson, *Jeremiah 26–52* (CBC; Cambridge: Cambridge University Press, 1975).

15. Another example is Ahaz, king of Israel; see my article ' "Urged by His Wife Jezebel"—A Literary Reading of 1 Kgs 18 in Context', *SJOT* 9 (1995), pp. 83-96.

wanted to obtain something. And this 'somebody', whom I would call the Deuteronomist, placed himself so ponderously on the material that his contour was left on it.

BLACK FIRE ON WHITE FIRE: HISTORICAL CONTEXT
AND LITERARY SUBTEXT IN JEREMIAH 37–38

Mary Chilton Callaway

In the course of reflecting on the seven things that preceded the creation
of the world, *Midrash Tehillim* provides an intriguing description of the
origins of Torah: 'And How was the Torah written? With black fire
upon white fire as it rested on the knee of the Holy One, blessed be
He.'[1] In joining the human image of an author with his work on his
knee with the mystical image of black fire on white fire the midrash
invites the reader to ponder the complex nature of the Torah as both a
text written by an author and so subject to rules of interpretation and as
a mystical reality that stands beyond human comprehension. Written
with black fire on white fire the Torah burns but is not consumed; it is
always changing yet never altered. The author of the midrash notes that
the texts he interprets are fire, and will always elude his best efforts at
making their dancing letters stand still.

In the current situation of multiple and often irreconcilable
approaches to the book of Jeremiah I find the midrashic image to be
especially evocative, for it is humbling in its understanding of the limits
of interpretation, and challenging by its requirement of multi-dimen-
sional thinking. There is no returning to an Eden of pre-critical reading;
the rich and hard-won results of the historical-critical methods have
provided precious insights into these mysterious texts. These approaches
potentially give discipline to our exegesis, pointing us away from
indulgent readings and opening our eyes to interests not particularly
relevant to our own agenda. Yet such methods are far from objective or
free of ideology, were such a thing possible.[2] Historical-critical exegesis

1.   William G. Braude (trans.), *Midrash Tehillim* (2 vols.; New Haven: Yale
University Press, 1959), I, p. 94.
2.   See especially Jon D. Levenson, *The Hebrew Bible, the Old Testament, and
Historical Criticism* (Louisville, KY: Westminster/John Knox Press, 1993).

has properly lost its hegemony, but not its value, and it is in complicating our readings with new angles of vision that I think we will live more faithfully with what Northrop Frye called 'this huge, sprawling, tactless book sit[ting] there inscrutable in the middle of our cultural heritage, like the "great Boyg" or sphinx in *Peer Gynt*, frustrating all our efforts to walk around it'.[3]

The story of the meeting between Jeremiah and Zedekiah during the last days of Jerusalem is a good case study for testing new readings, because it is in certain respects unreadable. On the one hand, the language of the narrative is so full of detail and technical terms that many scholars believe it could only have been written by an eyewitness. In fact some of the vocabulary is so specific to its time and place that already the LXX translators had difficulty with it. It bears many of the marks of reliable historical memoir. On the other hand, the structure of the narratives consistently blocks our well-intentioned 'straightforward' reading of them as a chronologically coherent account of Jeremiah's last days in Jerusalem. As many readers ancient and modern have recognized, these chapters are made up of episodes which do not at all follow smoothly upon each other, but are temporally and spatially disorienting. The narrative jumps backwards and forwards in time, and moves in and out of a variety of prisons and dungeons. A compelling proposal for how these chapters came to their present chaotic state has been put forward by Christopher Seitz, who argues that they comprise two perspectives on the fall of Jerusalem, reflecting competing interests.[4] The older is an account of the last days of Jerusalem and the life of the Judahites, composed by scribes (notice what good press scribes get in these chapters) who remained in the land under the Babylonian-appointed Gedaliah. Throughout this narrative Jeremiah counseled surrender and saw continued life in Judah under Babylonian rule as the best option. This narrative found its way to Babylon after the murder of Gedaliah, where it was edited by exiles, who saw themselves as the true remnant of Israel. In this exilic redaction, the original scribal narrative was disrupted by additions (largely prophetic words from other contexts) underscoring the inevitability of

    3.   Northrop Frye, *The Great Code* (New York: Harcourt, Brace, Jovanovich, 1982).
    4.   Christopher R. Seitz, *Theology in Conflict: Reactions to the Exile in the Book of Jeremiah* (BZAW, 16; Berlin: W. de Gruyter, 1989).

Jerusalem's fall and the exile of the inhabitants. The peculiar shape of the narrative as we have it reflects, therefore, the conflict between the exiles in Babylon, who thought they were the only true remnant, and the Judahites who remained in the land under Babylonian occupation.

Seitz's theory of redaction offers a coherent reading of how this disjointed set of narratives came to be, and an admirably clear account of the two historical voices intertwined in the narratives. It allows us to see how these narratives are similar to other complex cycles in the Hebrew Bible in which several strands representing different political positions are evident. The Saul narratives in 1 Samuel are a good example of the results of this kind of redactional process. Yet our understanding of the historical contexts of these chapters still leaves us with an unreadable text. Do we view chs. 37–38 as a somewhat botched redaction, in which the exilic redactors failed to cover their tracks and to smooth out their narrative? Or might we conclude that the criteria for coherence were different in the culture of the redactors than for later readers?

Let me suggest that for a few minutes we attend to the tensions within these chapters not as a problem to be solved, but as a potential guide to our reading. The bumpy surface of these narratives may provide a new point of entry into the ancient stories. Often it is the most perplexing aspect of a text, the place where it seems most unyielding to a modern reader, that gives us our best opportunity of being tutored by the ancient witnesses. In literary terms, it is at the impasse where the contract between reader and narrator breaks down and the reader can no longer follow where the narrator is leading that a breakthrough in understanding can occur. To continue, the reader must try to abandon his or her own perspective and attend more closely to the voice(s) in the text. It is possible to discern in these chapters voices that do not represent the intentions of competing historical groups, but which we might say are the by-product of the process of redaction. The exilic redactors may have intended to press their understanding of the true Israel, but the richly textured result of their redaction in fact points readers in other directions. As the midrash suggests, behind the letters on the scroll other letters made of fire shimmer; we cannot make them stand still, but we can glimpse them dancing about between the letters written in ink.

One way of articulating the problem of the narrative is that both its detail-rich texture, and its overtly linear structure, moving from Nebuchadnezzar's attack on Jerusalem in 588 to the final siege in 587, encourage a historical reading; at the same time, however, the repetitions and contradictions in chronology frustrate such a reading. The narrative sets the reader up for a historical account while at the same time undermining such a reading. The problem presented by these internal contradictions is not one of competing political viewpoints, but rather of different narrative modes. I propose understanding these two aspects of the narrative as two voices, which create a different dimension from the ones presented by the Scribal Chronicle and its Exilic redactors.

The first voice is that of a chronicler reporting the events of the last days of Jerusalem. Three literary traits characterize this voice. First, it speaks in the language of the annalist, carefully dating the events:

> Zedekiah the son of Josiah, whom King Nebuchadrezzar of Babylon made king in the land of Judah, reigned instead of Coniah the son of Jehoikim (37.1).
>
> The army of Pharaoh had gone out from Egypt, and then when the Chaldeans who were besieging Jerusalem heard the report of them, they withdrew from Jerusalem (37.5).
>
> Now when the Chaldean army had retreated from Jerusalem before the army of Pharaoh, Jeremiah went out from Jerusalem to go to the land of Benjamin ... (37.11-12).
>
> And they gave Jeremiah a loaf of bread from the bakers' street daily until all the bread in the city was gone (37.21).
>
> And Jeremiah remained in the court of the guard until the day Jerusalem was captured (38.28).

By anchoring the narratives about the prophet in public and verifiable events, the voice of the chronicler interprets Jeremiah's story as part of Judah's political history. The second noteworthy characteristic of this voice is its frequent use of technical terms for places, for example, the 'dungeon' (37.16), the bakers' street (37.21), the royal storage of old garments (38.11), the third gate of the Temple (38.4). Such terminology evokes the voice of a narrator who is contemporaneous with the events being reported, and assumes the same familiarity on the part of his audience. Finally, the voice is characterized by its tendency to name the characters fully and to present them as identifiable members of Temple and court, again lending an air of historical authority to the account. This first voice overlaps the boundaries of Seitz's Scribal Chronicle and its Exilic Redaction, incorporating parts of both; but it reflects the political concerns of neither. It is rather a quality of the narrative that guides the reader to understand the stories as a realistic historical account of the last days of Jerusalem.

There is another, quieter voice embedded in these chapters, whose accents are not nearly as clear as those of the first, yet which proves to be none the less compelling. If the first voice is heard in the details of the narratives, especially their highly particular vocabulary, the second is evident in their structure. The attempt to follow the first voice and read these stories as historical accounts is confounded by the way the seven scenes are structured into a single narrative. The chronological markers in the narratives confuse rather than clarify. Why would Jeremiah be charged with deserting to the Babylonians if he went to Benjamin when they had retreated? The most troubling transition for most commentators is the one between chs. 37 and 38, 'and Jeremiah remained in the court of the guard' (37.21); 'Now Shephatiah son of Manan, Gedaliah son of Pashhur, Jucal son of Shelemiah, and Pashhur son of Malchiah heard the words that Jeremiah was saying to all the people ...' (38.1). How could Jeremiah speak treasonous words to all the people if he had been shut up in the court of the guard? The story in ch. 38 presents a second tale of arrest and imprisonment as though the first had not occurred. Similarly, the story of Zedekiah summoning Jeremiah to the third gate of the Temple (38.14) is unconnected to the account that immediately precedes it, in which Jeremiah is said to remain in the court of the guard. The disturbed chronology has led some readers to conclude that far from being a historical account, these chapters present an elaboration of a single episode in the prophet's life.[5]

While the first voice seems to encourage reading the vignettes of Jeremiah and Zedekiah as historical accounts whose significance is in their relation to the events of 587, the second voice suggests another hermeneutic for the narratives. This second voice—or perhaps it is the sound of silence—is present in the spaces between the scenes of the narrative. It is what makes the narrative unreadable by disrupting linear chronology. What I am suggesting is that instead of seeing the disturbed chronology as a lack, to be explained as redactive, we hear the absence

---

5. See the discussion of Skinner, Bright and Thompson in William Holladay, *Jeremiah 2: A Commentary on the Book of the Prophet Jeremiah, Chapters 26–52* (Hermeneia; Minneapolis: Fortress Press, 1989), p. 282. Holladay rejects the proposal that the accounts are based on a single episode, while Carroll accepts it. See Robert P. Carroll, *Jeremiah: A Commentary* (OTL; Philadelphia: Westminster Press, 1986), pp. 672-73.

of chronology as a voice, as present as the other voice, which is nudging us toward finding a different context for understanding the stories. At the same time that one voice seems to be anchoring the stories in the particularity of history, the other voice is quietly removing the anchor, allowing the stories to bob freely against each other. In fact this paratactic arrangement is characteristic of many larger narrative units in the Bible, though not always with such problematic chronology as we see here.[6] Paratactic arrangement of the individual narratives about Jeremiah creates a linear account of the prophet's last 18 months in Jerusalem, while at the same time creating a disturbed chronology and a pattern of repeated tropes that invites a different hermeneutic.

In the episodes narrated in Jeremiah 37–38 two related themes repeatedly emerge, giving the chapters a circular structure that contravenes its tenuous linear structure. The themes are familiar in the traditions of Israel, especially in the prophetic narratives in the books of Kings. The first is the theme of confrontation between king and prophet. In Jeremiah 37–38 this theme is represented by the repeated circumstance of the king hopefully summoning the prophet for a word from Yahweh, only to hear words of doom. The scene is reminiscent of the confrontation between Balak and Balaam in Numbers 22–24, Saul and Samuel in 1 Samuel 28, and Jeroboam with Ahijah in 1 Kings 14, to name a few. In Jeremiah 37–38 three episodes are narrated in which Zedekiah initiates contact with Jeremiah:

> Zedekiah sends two emissaries to ask Jeremiah 'to intercede with Yahweh on our behalf'. The prophet delivers an oracle of doom (37.3-10).

> Zedekiah secretly summons Jeremiah from his dungeon to ask for a word from the Lord, and Jeremiah delivers a condensed version of the same message: you will be given into the hand of the king of Babylon (37.17-21).

6.   So for example the individual stories of the Primeval History in Gen. 2–11, or of the Abraham cycle in Gen. 12–25. The problems of consistency arising from linking independent narratives into a single chronology have provided material for centuries of exegesis and midrash. But the question of where Cain found a wife, how Noah knew which animals were clean and unclean or why Isaac is called Abraham's only son in Gen. 22.1 did not seem to bother the redactors of these cycles. Closer to the problem of Jer. 37–38 is the thrice-told wife-sister story of Gen. 12, 20 and 26. The similarity in structural arrangement between the narratives of Jer. 37–38 and that of the Torah bears more investigation.

Zedekiah again sends for Jeremiah, this time confiding his fears to the
prophet, but the message is the same: surrender and live, resist and be
captured (38.14-28).

The repetition of the scene highlights the tradition of confrontation
between king and prophet, with its tropes of royal desperation and
prophetic truth-telling, and so it blurs the sharp edges of the
straightforward historical account told in the first voice.

The second tradition, often linked with the first, is the physical persecution of the prophet. In Jeremiah 37–38 three episodes are narrated in
which 'the princes' physically harm Jeremiah, clearly seeking his death:

The princes arrest Jeremiah leaving Jerusalem, beat and imprison him in
a dungeon where he cannot survive (37.13-16).

A contingent approaches Zedekiah to demand that Jeremiah be put to
death for his treasonous words. Zedekiah hands him over, and he is
lowered into a muddy cistern, to certain death (38.1-6).

The princes approach Jeremiah about his conversation with the king, for
which they intend to kill him (38.27).

The pattern is clear: the prophet speaks the word of Yahweh, and the
officials try to silence him by violence. Jezebel's murder of the prophets
(1 Kgs 18.13) and her attempt on Elijah's life come to mind, as does the
story of Micaiah ben Imlah's rough treatment at the hands of King
Ahab (1 Kgs 22). The repetition of scenes of violence against Jeremiah
tends to highlight this traditional pattern.

The major commentaries debate the historicity of these accounts,
some assuming that the three are an elaboration of a single event, others
arguing that Jeremiah was actually arrested three times.[7] I am suggesting an alternate way of reading these chapters, a way which does not
seek to reconcile the problems by addressing the 'actual events' behind
the text or separating out layers of redaction, but which seeks coherence
from the conflicts within the narratives. The two voices, which do not
coincide with sources or redactions, speak of two Jeremiahs: the Jeremiah of the last 18 months of Jerusalem, and the Jeremiah of the developing prophetic tradition. The first voice locates a unique prophetic
figure firmly in the particular politics of Zedekiah's last days, while the

---

7. So, for example, John Bright in *Jeremiah: A New Translation with Introduction and Commentary* (AB, 21; Garden City, NY: Doubleday, 1965), p. 233, and
Carroll, *Jeremiah*, pp. 672-73, argue that the accounts are duplicates. Holladay, on
the other hand, 'rules out the suggestion', in *Jeremiah 2*, pp. 282 and 289.

second voice echoes themes of other times and places. While the first urges the unique aspects of Jeremiah's story, the second limns its ancient tropes. Hence the structural features that make chs. 37–38 problematic—especially the disjointed chronology and the unlikely repetitions of events—are not an unfortunate aspect to be quickly dispatched, but a significant voice. The voice of the historical chronicler is joined by another voice, one that makes the context of these stories about Jeremiah not political history but Torah.

The *Nachleben* of Jeremiah probably developed in part out of the subtext of these narratives, from the voice that loosened Jeremiah from his historical context. Midrash *Lamentations Rabbah*, for example, linked Jeremiah with Joseph and Daniel because all three spoke the truth and were thrown into a pit to die.[8] Perhaps our suggestion of a new way of making sense of these narratives in Jeremiah is related to a very old way.

---

8.   *Midrash Lamentations Rabbah* (trans. Maurice Simon; New York: Soncino, 1981), on Lam. 3.52. On the traditions about Jeremiah's martydom see Louis Ginzberg, *The Legends of the Jews*, VI (New York: Jewish Publication Society of America, 1968), pp. 39-400.

POETIC STRUCTURE AND INTERTEXTUAL LOGIC
IN JEREMIAH 50[*]

Alice Ogden Bellis

Biblical scholars generally agree that Jeremiah 50 (and 51) is a poorly organized collection which lacks thematic development.[1] Although many have offered suggestions about how the material should be divided into poetic units, some more confidently than others,[2] no proposal has met universal acceptance. Nevertheless, it is my contention that Jeremiah 50 consists of three poems—50.2-20, 50.21-32 and 50.33-38—and a series of scriptural additions at the end. These poems are clearly distinguished from one another by theme, imagery and structure. Although the overall concern of all of the poems in Jeremiah 50 is the fall of Babylon, the theme of the first poem is God's forgiveness and restoration of God's people, who are described as sheep. The second poem focuses on the rebellion and punishment of Babylon who is characterized as an insolent woman. The theme of the third poem is Israel's complaint against Babylon. Legal imagery is utilized here.

Following these poems is a series of skillfully adapted scriptural additions. The scriptural texts found in Jer. 50.39-46 are Isa. 13.19-22; Jer. 6.22-24; and 49.18-21. These texts extend the thought of the third poem and of the series, even providing an inclusion for Jer. 50.2-46. Isaiah 13 is a prophecy of doom on Babylon. Jeremiah 6.22-24 is part

---

*   Sections of this article have previously appeared in Alice Ogden Bellis, *The Structure and Composition of Jeremiah 50:2–51:58* (Lewiston, NY: Edwin Mellen Press, 1995). The publishers acknowledge with gratitude permission from Edwin Mellen Press to reproduce this material.

1.   Robert P. Carroll, *Jeremiah: A Commentary* (OTL; Philadelphia: Westminster Press, 1986), p. 815.

2.   For bibliography, see William L. Holladay, *Jeremiah 2: A Commentary on the Book of the Prophet Jeremiah, Chapters 26–52* (Minneapolis: Fortress Press, 1989), p. 401.

of an oracle of doom originally pronounced on Jerusalem. Babylon's destruction of Jerusalem in 587 fulfilled that prophecy. Here it is ironically reapplied to Babylon. Jeremiah 49.18-21 was in its original setting a prophecy of doom on Edom. It is used here because of its emphasis on Yahweh's involvement in the coming destruction. In addition the pastoral imagery links with that in the first poem, but in reverse. In 50.2-20 the Israelites are sheep pursued by Babylonian lions. Here God is the lion and the enemies of Israel the sheep. Finally, the words in 49.21 provide an inclusion for Jer. 50.2-46, tying the whole bundle together.

The literary genre of the oracles in Jeremiah 50 is that of prophecies against the nations. In the whole Hebrew Bible this genre has perhaps been paid the least attention.[3] The reason is understandable. The hatred and bloodthirst displayed in these oracles is an embarrassment to the more humane sensibilities of modern believers, both Christian and Jewish.

However, a close reading of these oracles, which involves a painstaking analysis of the structure of the individual poems, makes clear that they have well-developed thought patterns of both literary and theological merit.[4] In addition, the scriptural additions at the end of Jeremiah 50 are rationally chosen and contribute to the overall message.

A word needs to be said about the text of this material. The MT is longer than the LXX and probably is a later version than the Hebrew

---

3. Michael Cahill ('The Oracles Against the Nations: Synthesis and Analysis for Today', *Louvain Studies* 16 [1991], pp. 121-36) agrees with P.C. Beentjes ('Oracles Against the Nations: A Central Issue in the "Latter Prophets" ', *Bijdragen: International Journal in Philosophy and Theology* 50 [1989], pp. 203-209) about the need for study of the OAN material. For similar judgments see also B. Margulis ('Studies in the Oracles Against the Nations' [dissertation, University of Brandeis, 1967], p. 1) and M. Kessler ('Rhetoric in Jeremiah 50 and 51', *Semitics* 3 [1973], pp. 18-35 [18]). For further bibliography on the OAN genre, see Y. Hoffman ('From Oracle to Prophecy: The Growth, Crystallization, and Disintegration of a Biblical Gattung', *JNSL* 10 [1982], pp. 75-81) and the literature cited in Cahill ('The Oracles Against the Nations'), Beentjes ('Oracles Against the Nations'), and J. Vermeylen (*Du prophète Isaïe à l'apocalyptique: Isaïe, I–XXXV, miroir d'un demi-millénaire d'expérience religieuse en Israël* [2 vols.; Paris: Gabalda, 1977–78], I, p. 355 n. 3).

4. Space does not permit printing the poems arranged in poetic lines with full textual notes in this article. For this see my *The Structure and Composition of Jeremiah 50:2–51:58* (Lewiston, NY: Edwin Mellen Press, 1995).

Vorlage of the LXX.[5] It is not the purpose of this paper to determine the earliest form of the poems in Jeremiah 50. Undoubtedly additions exist in the MT. However, the basic structures of the poems are not affected by these additions. Nevertheless, when material from Jeremiah 50 is quoted, the words and phrases that are not in the Old Greek will be enclosed in parentheses.

The First Poem:
'I Shall Forgive the Remnant I Preserve'

The first poem, Jer. 50.2-20, shares in common with the other poems in the series the theme of the fall of Babylon. This is not the central focus of the poem, however. The major concern of the poet is rather the problem of the Hebrews' apostasy (vv. 6-7), the need for divine forgiveness (vv. 4, 20) and the establishment of a covenant which will not be abandoned as the old one was (v. 5). The poem is primarily an attempt at a theological explanation of the events of 587 and a resolution of the problem created by the destruction and exile of Yahweh's own people by the Babylonians. It builds up to the climax in the last colon of v. 20, which is also the final colon of the poem, where Yahweh declares that he will forgive the remnant which he has determined to preserve.

5.　See J.G. Janzen, *Studies in the Text of Jeremiah* (HSM, 6; Cambridge, MA: Harvard University Press, 1973), and E. Tov, *The Septuagint Translation of Jeremiah and Baruch: A Discussion of an Early Revision of the LXX of Jeremiah 29–52 and Baruch 1:1-38* (HSM, 8; Missoula, MT: Scholars Press, 1976); *idem*, 'L'Incidence de la critique textuelle sur la critique littéraire dans le livre de Jérémie', *RB* 79 (1972), pp. 189-99; *idem*, 'Exegetical Notes on the Hebrew Vorlage of the LXX of Jeremiah 27 (34)', *ZAW* 91 (1979), pp. 73-93; *idem*, 'Some Aspects of the Textual and Literary History of the Book of Jeremiah', in P.-M. Bogaert (ed.), *Le livre de Jérémie: Le prophète et son milieu, les oracles et leur transmission* (BETL, 54; Leuven: Leuven University Press, 1981), pp. 145-67; *idem*, 'The Literary History of the Book of Jeremiah in the Light of its Textual History', in Jeffrey H. Tigay (ed.), *Empirical Models for Biblical Criticism* (Philadelphia: University of Pennsylvania Press, 1985), pp. 213-37.

The Old Greek of Jeremiah is best represented by the manuscripts B–S. They are the earliest available form of the Greek text which has not yet been adjusted in the direction of the MT, as have the later LXX recensions. These manuscripts, B–S, are in general the basis of J. Ziegler's edition (*Septuaginta, Vetus Testamentum Graecum auctoritate Societatis Litterarum Gottingensis editum. XV. Ieremias–Baruch–Threni–Epistula Ieremiae* [Göttingen: Vandenhoeck & Ruprecht, 1957]). This is the text of the Old Greek that I use in this study.

Because this is the most important point in the poem, I have appropriated this final colon for use as the English title of the poem.

In addition to the major theme of Yahweh's forgiveness of his people, two secondary themes are developed in the poem. Yahweh will bring about the fall of Babylon (vv. 2-3, 9-10, 12-16, 18) and return his people to their homeland (vv. 5, 19). These two themes are related to the major theme and to each other. Because Yahweh forgives his people (v. 20), he returns them to Palestine (v. 19). The Hebrews are able to leave Babylon (v. 8), because Yahweh arouses an enemy against Babylon, which will bring about her demise (vv. 3, 9-10, 14-16) and allow the foreign residents to go home (v. 16).

The poet uses contrast and juxtaposition to a high degree in developing the two secondary themes. The contrast between the current good fortune of Babylon and the Babylonians (v. 11) and the current misfortune of the Israelites (vv. 6-7) is stark. The Babylonians are described as merry and exultant and through simile as calves frisking on the grass and snorting stallions (v. 11). The Israelites are pictured as scattered sheep (v. 6) devoured by enemies (v. 7). The present conditions of both Babylon and Israel, however, will be reversed. The contrasts between Babylon's present glee and future doom (vv. 2-3, 9-10, 12-13, 14-16, 18), on the one hand, and between Israel's present dismal state (vv. 6-7, 17) and future prosperity (vv. 19-20), on the other, are equally striking. The contrast between Babylon's and Israel's futures, which are a reversal of their present situations, completes the multiple contrasts the poet sets up. By juxtaposing the present and future situations of Babylon and Israel in a variety of ways through the poem, the poet emphasizes the double secondary theme. The poem includes eight sections which are summarized in the chart below.

Section	Description	Category
I (vv. 2-3)	Instructions to announce the fall of Babylon at the hands of an army from the north	A
II (vv. 4-5)	The return of the exiles to Yahweh and Jerusalem	B
III (vv. 6-7)	The present dire situation of Israel and its consequences	C
IV (vv. 8-10)	Instructions to the exiles to leave Babylon and description of the army that will destroy her	D

V	(vv. 11-13)	The present happy situation of the Babylonians and Yahweh's threat	C'
VI	(vv. 14-16)	Instructions to the army to attack Babylon and description of the inhabitants' flight	D'
VII	(vv. 17-18)	Israel's plight as the reason for the fall of Babylon and the fall of Assyria as the guarantee of the fall of Babylon	A'
VIII	(vv. 19-20)	The return of Israel to Palestine and Yahweh	B'

As is evident from the chart, the poem has a concentric structure. The first two sections (vv. 2-3, 4-5), labeled A and B, deal with Babylon's fall (A) and Israel's restoration to Yahweh and Jerusalem (B). They are paralleled by the last two sections (vv. 17-18, 19-20), which deal with Babylon's fall and Israel's restoration to Yahweh and Palestine and thus are labeled A' and B'. The third section (vv. 6-7) describes the *present* dire situation of Yahweh's people. This section is labeled C. It is paralleled to some degree by the fifth section (vv. 11-13), which describes the *present* happy situation of the Babylonians. Section V also responds to the statement in Section III that the Israelites' enemies, that is, the Babylonians, devoured them (v. 7). In v. 13 we read that because of Yahweh's anger (and it is implied that Yahweh is angry with the Babylonians for their actions against his people), Babylon will become an uninhabited desert. Thus, the fifth section is labeled C'. The fourth section (vv. 8-10) begins with *instructions* to the Israelite exiles to leave Babylon. Then the poet gives the reason that they will be able to flee: Yahweh is stirring up an enemy army to destroy Babylon. This section is labeled D. It is paralleled to some extent by the sixth section (vv. 14-16), which begins with *instructions* to the enemy army to attack Babylon (vv. 14-15) and ends with a description of the Babylonians' flight in response to the attack (v. 16). This description of *flight* links up with the instructions to the exiles to *flee* in v. 8. Thus, the sixth paragraph is labeled D'.

The poetic development of the twofold theme differs from what one would expect in prose. In prose the progression of thought would run something like this: Israel's leaders abdicated their responsibility for leadership and, in fact, misled the Israelites. Israel abandoned Yahweh and the covenant and began worshipping other gods. The Hebrews were then highly vulnerable before the great empire centered in Babylon. Just as previously Israel fell victim to Assyria, Judah also later fell before Babylon's might. Yahweh will forgive his people, however, and raise up an army to destroy Babylon so that Israel may return to its own land. The Jews will again seek Yahweh and their homeland, repenting of having abandoned their God. The logic of the poetry is not linear, but the message is clear.

Although the poem has an internal cohesion resulting from the development of the bipartite theme and the use of animal imagery (Israel = sheep, Babylon = lions), the repetition of several key words in the second and final sections[6] underscores this unity. In v. 4 we are told that

> *In those days and at that time*—(oracle of Yahweh)[7]—
>> the *Israelites* will come,
>> they and the *Judahites* together.
> Walking and weeping they will proceed,
>> *seeking* Yahweh their God.

In the final lines of the poem we read (v. 20):

> *In those days and at that time*—(oracle of Yahweh)—
>> the iniquity of *Israel* will be *sought*
>> and there will be none;
> And the sins of *Judah*,
>> and none will be found,
>> for I shall forgive the remnant I preserve.

The repetition of 'In those days and at that time', 'Israel', 'Judah' and the verb 'seek' (בקשׁ) at the beginning of the second and end of the last paragraphs forms an inclusion which helps mark the limits of the poem.

Although the repetition of these three words and one phrase is probably a rhetorical device used by the poet to mark the limits of this poem, the primary means of discerning the end of the poem is through understanding how the final section (vv. 19-20), and especially the final colon 'for I shall forgive the remnant I preserve' function as the climax of the thematic development and the finale of the poem.

---

6.   Carroll (*Jeremiah*, p. 821) views vv. 4 and 20 as prose. Holladay (*Jeremiah 2*, pp. 391-93) reads vv. 4 and 20 as poetry, though he believes 'In those days and at that time, oracle of Yahweh' and 'they and the children of Judah together' should be omitted. He also omits the first line of v. 20, 'In those days and at that time, oracle of Yahweh'. Of this line and the identical line in v. 4 he writes, 'These words add nothing to the poem'. Perhaps, but maybe that view comes from an insufficient understanding of the poetry.

7.   Words in parentheses are omitted in Old Greek.

A number of prominent features in this poem distinguish it from the rest of the material in Jeremiah 50. The double theme of Babylon's doom and Israel's restoration and the alternation between these two themes provide a structural framework quite distinct from that of any of the rest of the material in this chapter. The imagery of Yahweh as the Hebrews' divine shepherd is absent elsewhere in Jeremiah 50–51. The motif of the Israelites' apostasy and the need for a new covenant, which would not be abandoned, unlike the old one, also distinguishes this poem from the remainder of Jeremiah 50.

I maintain that Jer. 50.2-20 is a poem with a rational argument, structure and image patterns. It is also a poem with a theological message that was certainly pertinent to its time, both challenging and comforting the exiled Israelites with the conviction that their God was indeed the Lord of history and would soon bring their exile to an end.

The Second Poem:
'The Rebellion and Punishment of Ms. Insolence'

The second poem in Jeremiah 50 (vv. 21-32) could aptly be given the English title 'The Rebellion and Punishment of Ms Insolence' because of the emphasis on the rebellion against Yahweh of Babylon, personified as a queenly figure[8] and named Insolence in vv. 31-32,[9] and on Yahweh's plans to punish Babylon. Whereas the first poem in Jeremiah 50 (50.2-20) focuses on Israel's apostasy and the need for Yahweh to forgive and establish a new covenant and to return Israel to Zion in Palestine, this second poem focuses on Babylon's sins and Yahweh's response to them.

In the opening line of the poem (v. 21) two Babylonian districts are named which represent the whole of the Babylonian homeland. The districts of Merathaim and Peqod are chosen for this purpose, because of the play on words their Hebrew root letters make possible. Merathaim, 'Double Rebellion'[10] in Hebrew (מרה), refers to Marratu of

---

8. See A. Fitzgerald, 'The Mythological Background of Jerusalem as a Queen and False Worship as Adultery in the OT', *CBQ* 34 (1972), pp. 403-16.

9. In these verses Babylon is treated grammatically as a masculine figure because זדון is a masculine noun. Nevertheless, in the poem as a whole Babylon is a feminine figure. See, e.g., the feminine pronouns in vv. 26-27, 29.

10. Given the form of the Babylonian toponym, the Hebrew form should be

southern Babylonia. Peqod, 'Punish' in Hebrew, refers to Puqudu of eastern Babylonia.[11]

Babylon's rebellion is described in terms of her challenging (התגרית) Yahweh (v. 24b) and of her insulting (זדה) him (v. 29b). The root זיד means to insult, act insolently, presumptuously or *rebelliously*. In vv. 31-32 Babylon is addressed and referred to as 'Ms *Insolence*' (זדון).

The punishment of Babylon and the Babylonians is described using the root פקד in vv. 27b and 31. These two verses are similar. The former speaks of the Babylonians' time of punishment (עת פקדתם); the latter, of the time when Yahweh will punish Babylon (עת פקדתיך). Babylon's punishment is also referred to in vv. 28-29 in terms of divine revenge (נקמה, v. 28) and divine retribution (שלמו לה כפעלה ככל אשר עשתה עשו לה, v. 29).

In vv. 24-25, Babylon's punishment comes by means of a divine counterattack. Babylon had challenged Yahweh (התגרית, v. 24), and Yahweh responded (פתח יהוה את אוצרו ויוצא את כלי זעמו, v. 25).

Much of the poem is devoted to instructing the army that Yahweh employs in the counter-attack on Babylon. The opening lines of each section (vv. 21, 26-27, 29-30) are addressed to the army. These instructions are in an indirect way part of the theme of Yahweh's punishment of Babylon.

The poem can be divided into three sections, each of which opens with orders to the army (vv. 21, 26-27, 29-30). The structure of these sections is presented in summary fashion in the following chart.

---

regarded as a real dual. Cf. F.E. König, *Historisch-Kritisches Lehrgebraüde der hebräischen Sprache* (3 vols.; Leipzig: Hinrichs, 1881–97), II, part 2, §257c. It is possible to compare the colloquial Arabic greeting *marḥabatên* = 'twice welcome'. See *HALAT*, p. 604. In Akkadian *marratu* means '(bitter, salty) sea' (Akk. *marāru*; Heb. מרר). As a toponym it can refer to the marshland of southern Babylonia. See S. Parpola, *Neo-Assyrian Toponyms* (AOAT, 6; Neukirchen–Vluyn: Neukirchener Verlag, 1970), p. 240, map at end; E. Michel, 'Die Assur-Texte Salmanassars III (858–824)', *WO* 1 (1947–52), pp. 68-69 n. 5. For a similar deformation of a name, see Judg. 3.8, 10: כושן רשעתים, 'Kushan of double wickedness' (*HALAT*, p. 445).

11. *Puqūdu* is a district in east-central Babylonia. See Parpola, *Neo-Assyrian Toponyms*, p. 280, map at end.

The First Section: Babylon's Challenge, Yahweh's Response

Verses	Description	Category
21	Instructions to the army	A
22	Sounds (קוֹל) of war	B
23-25	Mock Dirge as in Isaiah 14[12]	C

The Second Section: Yahweh's Revenge

Verses	Description	Category
26-27	Instructions to the army	A
28	Sounds (קוֹל) of returning exiles declaring Yahweh's revenge	B

The Third Section: Yahweh's Challenge to Ms Insolence

Verses	Description	Category
29-30	Instructions to the army	A
31-32	Yahweh's challenge to Ms Insolence = declaration of war	D

Each of the three sections begins with instructions to the army (A). In the first two sections this is followed by a sound-oriented piece (B). In the first section the audience is asked to imagine the sounds of war (v. 22); in the second section, the sounds of the returning exiles declaring in Zion Yahweh's revenge (v. 28). After B the first section continues with a mock dirge in which Babylon's fall is sarcastically lamented (vv. 23-25). This is labeled C. The third section has nothing that corresponds to either B or C. Rather, it concludes with Yahweh's challenge to Ms Insolence (vv. 31-32). This is labeled D.

This second poem (50.21-32) is bound together as a poetic unity, thematically and structurally. In addition an inclusion helps delineate the unit. The root פקד occurs in each of the three sections (vv. 21, 27, 31). In the first section (vv. 21-25) it is in the first line; in the third section (vv. 29-32) it is at the beginning of Yahweh's challenge to Babylon (v. 31) which concludes the poem. These first and last occurrences form an inclusion which both emphasizes one of the main themes and marks the beginning and end of the poem.

The last occurrence of פקד would be even nearer the end of the poem

---

12. See H. Jahnow, *Das hebräische Leichenlied im Rahmen der Völkerdichtung* (BZAW, 36; Giessen: Alfred Töpelmann, 1923), pp. 239-53.

if the last line (v. 32b), which is very similar to 21.14,[13] is a redactional addition. Jeremiah 21 is an oracle of doom on Jerusalem spoken to King Zedekiah when King Nebuchadrezzar of Babylon was threatening Zion. That oracle was fulfilled with the Babylonian destruction of Jerusalem. However, now Yahweh is doing a new thing. The redactor probably added 21.14b to the end of this poem because it afforded him the opportunity to indicate that the destruction of Jerusalem was not God's final word. He may also have chosen this particular line because 21.14a says, 'I will *punish* you according to the fruit of your doings ...' Just as Yahweh previously punished Jerusalem, now Yahweh will punish Babylon.

Although it is possible that the original author of this second poem (50.21-32) is responsible for the inclusion of 21.14b rather than a redactor, the line is literarily anticlimactic, though theologically sound. It is not unreasonable to imagine that the same hand that added a number of adapted scriptural passages after the third poem in Jeremiah 50 is also responsible for the use of 21.14b here.

This second poem (50.21-32), read with or without the final line, is clearly distinguished from the first one (50.2-20), structurally and thematically. The structure of the two poems is quite different. The first poem uses the method of contrast, juxtaposing the present and future conditions of Babylon and Israel. Babylon is temporarily lush and green, but will become an uninhabited desert. The Israelites have wandered away from their native pasture, but God will return them to himself, who is their real pasture, as well as to their native land, and they will eat their fill. The second poem focuses primarily on the rebellion and punishment of Babylon who is personified as Ms Insolence. The first poem has much greater variety in its sections in order to present the desired contrasts. All three sections in the second poem begin with orders to the army.

The primary focus of the first poem, the apostasy of the Israelites and the need for a new covenant with Yahweh that will not be broken, is

---

13. For MT בעריו, the Old Greek reflects ביערו, 'her [lit. his] forest', and 21.14 reads ביערה, 'her forest'. It is difficult to determine on purely text-critical grounds whether the MT or the Old Greek of 50.32 represents the superior reading. However, context may be helpful here. Except for the date palms that grew along the waterways in Babylonia, trees (especially in the form of forests) were very rare. This suggests that the MT reading 'her cities' is an alteration made to adapt this text to its new context.

absent in the second poem. The double theme of the second poem, Babylon's rebellion and punishment, is present in the first poem to a very limited degree. Babylon's rebellion against God is for the most part implicit rather than explicit, however.

One exception which occurs in v. 14, 'for she sinned against Yahweh', is missing in the Old Greek. Prophetic clichés are often added in MT Jeremiah.[14] Perhaps the redactor felt the need to make this theme explicit. Perhaps this concern also explains why the second poem follows the first. We may also note v. 11 of the first poem where the Babylonians are called 'plunderers of my (Yahweh's) property'. Thus all of Babylon's actions against the Israelites constitute actions against Yahweh. See also v. 15 where the poet speaks of Yahweh's revenge.

In contrast to these indirect references to Babylon's rebellion in the first poem, the theme of Babylon's rebellion is set in the first line of the second poem with the appropriation of the name of the Babylonian district Merathaim, 'Double Rebellion' in Hebrew, to represent, along with Peqod, 'Punishment', the whole of Babylonia. We also find explicit statements in the second poem that Babylon challenged Yahweh (v. 24) and insulted him (v. 29). Babylon is even called 'Ms Insolence' (vv. 31-32).

The theme of punishment appears once in the first poem, when in v. 18 Yahweh says that he will punish Babylon, just as he punished Assyria. But the root פקד occurs three times in the second poem, which is less than half as long as the first poem. This kind of overlapping in poems that have in common the theme of Babylon's doom must be expected. What distinguishes these poems is their differences, which are major. The surprise is how little overlapping we do find in poems devoted to the doom of the same city and empire.

The Third Poem:
Israel-Judah's Complaint against Babylon

The focus of the third poem (vv. 33-38) is the conflict between Babylon and Israel-Judah. Babylon has oppressed the Hebrews (v. 33), but Yahweh will champion their cause so that they will find relief from this intolerable situation (v. 34). The resolution of the conflict is, of course, that Babylon is doomed to destruction (vv. 35-38).

---

14. See Janzen, *Studies in the Text of Jeremiah*, pp. 82-84.

The third poem might well be called 'Israel-Judah's Complaint against Babylon' because the basic conflict in this poem is between Israel-Judah and Babylon. In the first poem (50.2-20) the focus is on the Hebrews' sins of apostasy against Yahweh and the need for repentance and divine forgiveness; in the second poem (50.21-32), on Babylon's rebellion against Yahweh and Yahweh's punishment of Babylon. In this third poem the focus is on Babylon's sins against Israel-Judah. Yahweh is the Hebrews' divine kinsman (v. 34) and therefore will champion their cause. Nevertheless, the fundamental conflict in this poem is between Israel-Judah and Babylon.

Verses 33-38 can be isolated as an individual poem on the basis of their distinct literary form and the distinctive legal language of vv. 33-34, the first section. By form vv. 33-38 are a literary imitation of the language of the process of law in ancient Israel. Adaptations have been made, of course, because Yahweh himself takes part in the proceedings. Thus there is, for example, no jury or judge or witnesses. Yahweh himself performs all their functions.[15] The language of v. 33b, 'All their captors hold them fast, refusing to let them go' (pi. שלח), is reminiscent of the exodus. The exodus theme may be seen to extend into the second section, vv. 34-38, where the 'sentence' in the lawsuit is a series of חֶרֶב's suggestive of the plagues and the final חֹרֶב אֶל מֵימֶיהָ (v. 38) which reminds the reader of the drying up of the sea.

This third poem is distinguished from the other two poems in Jeremiah 50 by its focal conflict, imagery, structure and theme. The primary focus is on the oppression of the Hebrews by the Babylonians, which is the source of their complaint. Though Yahweh is involved and his help is essential to the Hebrews, the primary conflict is a horizontal one between two equals, in the sense that humans are involved—Babylon and Israel.

The primary conflicts in the first two poems are vertical, that is, between unequal parties, Yahweh and Israel on the one hand (Poem One, vv. 2-20) and Yahweh and Babylon on the other (Poem Two, vv. 21-33). The focus of the first poem (vv. 2-20) is Israel's apostasy and Yahweh's forgiveness; the focus of the second poem (vv. 21-33), Babylon's rebellion against Yahweh and Yahweh's punishment of Babylon. In the first two poems, therefore, the focal relationship involves Yahweh. Both Israel and Babylon had sinned against Yahweh in different

15. See K. Nielsen, *Yahweh as Prosecutor and Judge: An Investigation of the Prophetic Lawsuit (Rîb-Pattern)* (JSOTSup, 9: Sheffield: JSOT Press, 1978).

ways. However, Israel repented and Yahweh forgave. Babylon did not repent, and Yahweh meted out the severest punishment, annihilation. But the picture is not complete until it is also seen that Babylon had sinned against Israel. She was in conflict not only with Yahweh, but also with Israel. Although this aspect of the total situation is not omitted altogether from the other poems, it is the primary focus of the third poem. The foci of the three poems form a kind of triangle.

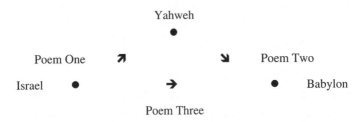

The structure of the three poems is also quite different. The first poem (50.2-20) has a concentric arrangement of sections in which sections I–II parallel VII–VIII and III–IV parallel V–VI; the second poem (50.21-32) has three sections, each of which begins with orders to an army; and third poem (50.33-38), two sections, the first of which poses the problem and the second of which provides the solution.

The imagery in each of the three poems is also different. The first poem (50.2-20) is dominated by pastoral imagery, in which Yahweh is the divine shepherd, the Hebrews are sheep, and the Babylonians are lions. The second poem (50.21-32) utilizes the image of Babylon as 'Ms Insolence', a queenly figure who has insulted Yahweh and whose challenge Yahweh must answer. The imagery of the third poem (50.33-38) is that of the exodus and the lawsuit.

To this point the logic with which the three independent poems in Jeremiah 50 have been ordered has been the focus. The three poems, though they are filled with traditional language, give every indication of being original creations collected here according to plan by an editor. It is true that here and there it is possible to detect a certain tendency toward expansion on the basis of other Old Testament texts. But that does not negate the fact that fundamentally the editor has gathered original material. The one possible exception is 50.32b which may have been adapted from 21.14b. This situation changes with 50.39-46, which cites extensive materials from Isa. 13.19-22, Jer. 49.18-21 and Jer. 6.22-24.

Scriptural Additions at the End of Jeremiah 50

This adapted material is present in the OG, and so is at least as early as that version of Jeremiah 50. The important point is that the materials have been adapted to their new context in such a way that they form a conclusion for Jer. 50.33-38, but also for the whole of Jer. 50.2-38, and they fit into the plan of the chapter. It is possible, of course, that there is involved here a second editorial hand, or even several stages in the redaction of Jeremiah 50, but I see no reason to postulate more than one redactional stage for the chapter as a whole. That, of course, is not meant to exclude minor changes, like those reflected in the MT when compared with the LXX.

Jeremiah 50.39-46 contains three sections. The first, 50.39-40, has parallels with Isa. 13.19-22 and Jer. 49.18, although it is shorter and in a different order than the similar material in Isa. 13.19-22. The second section, Jer. 50.41-43, is very similar to Jer. 6.22-24. The differences are primarily a result of the different contexts of the prophecies. In Jer. 6.22-24 Zion is the subject of the prophecy of doom; in Jer. 50.41-43, it is Babylon, of course, with whom the prophecy is concerned. The third section, Jer. 50.44-46, is very similar to Jer. 49.19-21. As in the second section, the different contexts require some differences in the wording, especially in place names. In Jer. 49.19-21 Edom is the one who is doomed; in Jer. 50.44-46 it is Babylon. There are also additional differences between the final line, Jer. 50.46, and its parallel in Jer. 49.21, which cannot be explained in this way. These differences will be examined below.

In order to understand why an editor appended these particular scriptural passages to the end of the poems in Jer. 50.2-38, we will examine each of the three sections. The first section, Jer. 50.39-40, is a shortened, reordered and revised version of Isa. 13.19-22 with the last part of v. 40 coming from Jer. 49.18. The editor has reworked the material from Isa. 13.19-22 much more extensively than any of the other passages. The reasons for the reworking will be considered later.

The usage of the material from Isaiah 13 is appropriate for several reasons. First of all Isaiah 13 is a prophecy of doom on Babylon. By drawing on a few key lines in Isaiah 13, the editor recalled to his readers' minds the entire prophecy. Both Isaiah 13 and Jer. 50.33-38 describe the threat of an attack upon Babylon in which Babylon becomes a desert. Isaiah 13.19-22 describes the fate of Babylon after the attack: Babylon is a desert without human inhabitants, inhabited only by desert beasts and demons.

The reasons for the reordering and adaptation of Isa. 13.19-22 will now be considered. A comparison of Jer. 50.39-40 and Isa. 13.19-22 follows.

Jeremiah 50.39-40		*Isaiah 13.19-22 (reordered)*
39.	לכן ישבו ציים את איים	21.	ורבצו שם ציים ...
	וישבו בה בנות יענה		ושכנו שם בנות יענה ...
		(22.	(וענה איים באלמנותיו ...
	ולא תשב עוד לנצח	20.	לא תשב לנצח
	ולא תשכן עד דור ודור		ולא תשכן עד דור ודור ...
40.	כמהפכת אלהים את סדם	19.	כמהפכת אלהים את סדם ...
	ואת עמרה ...		ואת עמרה

The word אימים, 'terrors, shocking (gods)' in 50.38, may have suggested the connection with Isa. 13.22. For this, the OG's *Vorlage* apparently had איים. Both MT אימים, in 50.38, and MT איים, in 50.39, it renders νήσοις. The OG rendering in both cases is certainly wrong, but it seems clear that the איים of 50.39 must be derived from the אִיִּים of Isa. 13.22, where the OG (ὀνοκένταυροι) has interpreted more or less accurately. Either איים (probably a copyist's error) or אימים (most probably the preferable reading) in Jer. 50.38 could have called to mind Isa. 13.22 (איים), reminded the editor of Isaiah 13, and suggested that by incorporating Isa. 13.19-22 here in abbreviated fashion, he could not only get into Jer. 50.33-38 the threat of an attack (50.35-38), but also its results (Isa. 13.19-22). This immediately gives us the explanation why the editor, though he does not cite Isa. 13.22 in full, lifts איים out of Isa. 13.22, inserts it in a convenient place in Isa. 13.21, and then immediately continues Jer. 50.38 with the citation of the adapted Isa. 13.21.

It is also clear why Isa. 13.19 ends the materials cited from the text. Isa. 13.19 is echoed by the opening of Jer. 49.18-21, the next text the editor intended to incorporate, and the verbal connection again played a role in bringing Jer. 49.18-21 into Jeremiah 50. The following series of comparisons will clarify this.

Isa. 13.19	כמהפכת אלהים את סדם ואת עמרה ...
Jer. 49.18	כמהפכת סדם ועמרה ...
Jer. 50.40	כמהפכת אלהים את סדם ואת עמרה ...

The first part of Jer. 50.40 follows the Isa. 13.19 wording. The last part of Jer. 50.40 follows Jer. 49.18 with two minor exceptions. A comparison of the last part of Jer. 49.18 and 50.40 follows.

Jer. 49.18   ושכניה <u>אמר</u> יהוה לא ישב שם איש ולא יגור בה בן אדם

Jer. 50.40   <u>ואת</u> שכניה <u>נאם</u> יהוה לא ישב שם איש ולא יגור בה בן אדם

Jer. 50.40 adds an את before שכניה to make it parallel to the other two verbal objects which are preceded by את, following the wording of Isa. 13.19. Jeremiah 50.40 also reads נאם rather than אמר, a minor variation perhaps caused by faulty memory or a variant text tradition.

The point being made here is that the reconstructed version of Isa. 13.21 heads the quotation from Isaiah 13, because it echoed אימים / איים of Jer. 50.38. The citation from Isa. 13.19 closes the quotation from Isaiah 13, because it matched the opening of Jer. 49.18-21, with which the editor planned to continue his unit. The rest of the citation from Isa. 13.20 could only be set in the middle.

The second section in Jer. 50.39-46, Jer. 50.41-43, is very similar to Jer. 6.22-24. These three verses, 50.41-43, are inserted between Jer. 50.40 = 49.18 and 50.44-46 = 49.19-21. The reasons for the placement of this material at this point will be discussed below. The reason the editor wanted to use this material is that Jer. 6.22-24 was part of an oracle of doom pronounced originally on Jerusalem. Babylon's destruction of Jerusalem in 587 fulfilled that prophecy. But here the editor is reapplying that prophecy of doom to Babylon. Thus the attempt is made to put the words of 6.22-24 in a new context. It is true that Yahweh threatened Jerusalem with doom in 6.22-24, and it is true that Yahweh's threat was fulfilled. But the Jerusalem of 6.22-24 was an unrepentant, disloyal Jerusalem. That situation has now been changed and thus it is time to reverse and so genuinely understand 6.22-24. Now Babylon will be destroyed, and in the context of the whole of Jeremiah 50 Jerusalem will be restored. There is irony in the reinterpretation of Jer. 6.22-24, which fits in well with the contrasts in the first poem (vv. 2-20) between Israel's and Babylon's reversed fates. Divine retribution is also implied, which fits in with the theme of the second poem (vv. 21-32), especially v. 29.

A number of minor changes have been made in 6.22-24 to make these verses fit their new context. A comparison of 50.41-43 and 6.22-24 follows. Variations in the two versions will be underlined.

Jeremiah 50.41-43		Jeremiah 6.22-24	
41.	הנה עם בא <u>מצפון</u>	22.	... הנה עם בא <u>מארץ צפון</u>
	וגוי גדול		וגוי גדול
	<u>ומלכים רבים</u>		
	<u>יערו</u> מירכתי ארץ		<u>יעור</u> מירכתי ארץ
42.	קשת וכידון יחזיקו	23.	קשת וכידון יחזיקו
	אכזרי <u>המה</u> ולא ירחמו		אכזרי <u>הוא</u> ולא ירחמו
	קולם כים יהמה		קולם כים יהמה
	ועל סוסים ירכבו		ועל סוסים ירכבו
	ערוך כאיש למלחמה		ערוך כאיש למלחמה
	עליך בת <u>בבל</u>		עליך בת <u>ציון</u>
43.	<u>שמע מלך בבל את שמעם</u>	24.	<u>שמענו את שמעו</u>
	ורפו <u>ידיו</u>		רפו <u>ידינו</u>
	צרה <u>החזיקתו</u>		צרה <u>החזיקתנו</u>
	חיל כיולדה		חיל כיולדה

The first change occurring in 50.41, the omission of אֶרֶץ, is insignificant. The phrase from 6.22 was probably accommodated to גוי מצפון in 50.3, though 50.9 also offers קהל גוים (גדולים) מארץ צפון.

The second change, also in v. 41, the addition of מלכים רבים was occasioned by the different historical situation. See the semantically similar 50.9: אנכי מעיר (ומעלה) על בבל קהל גוים (גדולים) מארץ צפון. When Jeremiah predicted Jerusalem's doom in Jer. 6.22-30, the 'nation coming from the northern land' and the 'great people' were the Babylonians. At the time when these poems were probably written (between 562 and 550[16]), the anticipated enemy of Babylon was the Medes (see 51.11, 27), an empire composed of many peoples, each of which had its own ruler or king. The expectation that the Medes would be the ones whom Yahweh used to defeat Babylon is perhaps reflected in 50.9 as well where the poet speaks of 'a band of great nations'.

16.   The fact that nowhere in any of the poems in Jer. 50–51 is Cyrus mentioned suggests that they were written prior to his overthrow of the Median king Astyages in 550 which was the beginning of his spectacular rise to power. The mention of the Medes in 51.11 and 51.28 (though these verses are probably additions) and to Ararat, Minni, and Ashkenaz in 51.27, provinces which Cyaxares II had conquered and incorporated into the Median empire (See W. Culican, *The Medes and the Persians* [Ancient Peoples and Places, 42; New York: Praeger, 1965], p. 15) suggests that the Medes were the ones expected to overthrow Babylon, not the Persians.

The expectation of the Babylonians' imminent overthrow seen throughout these poems suggests that they were written after the death of Nebuchadrezzar in 562. Following his death there were four kings in seven years. This political unrest may well have raised hopes for Babylon's imminent demise.

The next changes, occurring in 50.41-42, are the shift from הוא to
המה and יעור to וערו, due to the insertion of מלכים רבים, and the
substitution of Babylon for Zion. There are a number of minor changes
in 50.43 required by the change from 'we' to the 'king of Babylon' as
subject. The reason the editor may have chosen to revise to 'king of
Babylon', rather than the more parallel 'inhabitants of Babylon', is, perhaps, to be traced to the reference to the king of Babylon (מלך בבל) in
50.18.

The reasons the editor chose to adapt Jer. 6.22-24 for use in Jeremiah
50 have been considered, and the logic behind the particular changes in
the text based on the changed context has been presented. The reasons
for inserting this material so soon after he had made the transition from
the reworked section of Isa. 13.19-22 to Jer. 49.l8 can only be considered after the third section in this block of scriptural plusses, Jer. 49.19-
21, has been examined in a preliminary way.

The third section, Jer. 50.44-46 = Jer. 49.19-21, was in its original
setting a prophecy of doom on Edom in which Yahweh declares that the
coming destruction is a result of the plans he made against them. The
reasons why the editor wanted to use this passage will be considered
later in detail. The focus here is on the general tenor of the passage and
how it links up with the other passages. The following list of the passages in Jeremiah 50, beginning with the third poem (vv. 33-38), and
the import of each of them will reveal the progression of thought the
editor achieved by ordering the passages as he did.

Verses 33-34. The Hebrews have been oppressed by Babylon, but
Yahweh is their kinsman who will find relief for his people.

Verses 35-38. Yahweh pronounces sentence upon Babylon—Babylon
will be attacked and end up a desert (חרב אל מימיה).

What does this mean? What are the implications?

Verses 39-40. Babylon will be a desert inhabited by desert beasts and
demons; no one will ever dwell there.

But what events will lead up to this result?

Verses 41-43. A people from the north and many kings will come
from the north and attack Babylon.

What is Yahweh's role in this?

Verses 44-46. Yahweh will join the attack. It is his plans that have
brought it about. Thus, the attack on Babylon is a combination of
human enemies led by Yahweh. This combining of human and divine
activity is seen throughout Jeremiah 50. The human side is emphasized

in vv. 3, 9-10, 14-16, 21, 26-27, 29; the divine, in vv. 25, 31-32. But the divine participation in the attacking force is nowhere so explicit as in 50.44. And the divine participation is the culmination of the thought progression.

The problem of the separation of Jer. 49.18 = Jer. 50.40 from Jer. 49.19-21 = Jer. 50.44-46, when the sources were combined in ch. 50, was alluded to above. The principle of verbalism immediately connects Isa. 13.19 = Jer. 50.40, up to עמרה, to Jer. 49.18 = Jer. 50.40, everything following עמרה.

Isa. 13.19	כמהפכת אלהים את סדם ואת עמרה
Jer. 49.18	כמהפכת סדם ו עמרה ושכניה
	אמר יהוה לא ישב שם איש ולא יגור בה בן אדם
Jer. 50.40	כמהפכת אלהים את סדם ואת עמרה ואת שכניה
	נאם יהוה לא ישב שם איש ולא יגור בה בן אדם

But why is the immediately continuing text of Jer. 40.18 = Jer. 50.40, that is, Jer. 49.19-21 = Jer. 50.44-46, separated in the combined sources in ch. 50, by the insertion of Jer. 6.22-24 = Jer. 50.41-43? If Jer. 50.41-43 = 6.22-24 had been appended to Jer. 50.44-46 = 49.19-22, rather than inserted between Jer. 50.40 = Isa. 13.19/Jer. 49.18 and Jer. 50.44-46 = 49.19-21, it would have disturbed the logical thought progression outlined above.

The principle of verbalism may again be at work as well. Jeremiah 6.22-24 = 50.41-43, which begins with הנה, was prefixed to Jer. 49.19 = 50.44, which also begins with הנה. These passages in their new context were then viewed as introducing the human army and Yahweh into the attack on Babylon.

A more detailed consideration of the third section in the block of scriptural additions in Jer. 50.39-46, Jer. 50.44-46 = 49.19-21 will now be presented. A comparison of the texts will show the changes the editor has made. Changes will be underlined.

Jeremiah 50.44-46		*Jeremiah 49.19-21*	
44.	הנה כאריה יעלה	19.	הנה כאריה יעלה
	מגאון הירדן אל נוה איתן		מגאון הירדן אל נוה אתן
	כי ארגעה <u>אריצם</u> מעליה		כי ארגיעה <u>אריצנו</u> מעליה
	ומי בחור אליה אפקד		ומי בחור אליה אפקד
	כי מי כמוני		יכ מי כמוני
	ומי יועדני		ומי יעידני
	ומי זה רעה		ומי זה רעה
	אשר יעמד לפני		אשר יעמד לפני

45.	לכן שמעו עצת יהוה	לכן שמעו עצת יהוה
	אשר יעץ אל <u>בבל</u>	אשר יעץ אל <u>אדום</u>
	ומהשבותיו אשר חשב	ומחשבותיו אשר חשב
	אל <u>ארץ כשדים</u>	אל <u>ישבי תימן</u>
	אם לא יסחבום צעירי הצאן	אם לא יסחבום צעירי הצאן
	אם לא ישים עליהם <u>נוה</u>	אם לא ישים עליהם <u>נוהם</u>
46.	מקול <u>נתפשה בבל</u>	21. מקול <u>נפלם</u>
	<u>נרעשה הארץ</u>	<u>רעשה הארץ</u>
	<u>וזעקה בגוים נשמע</u>	צעקה בים סוף נשמע <u>קולה</u>

The first change, from the suffix ‏אריצנו‎ to ‏אריצם‎ in the second line, was a result of the change in focus from Edom to the Babylonians. The changes in v. 45, from ‏אדום‎ to ‏בבל‎ and from ‏ישבי תימן‎ to ‏ארץ כשדים‎, were also a result of the change in focus. See also ‏ארץ כשדים‎ in 50.1, 8, 25. The difference between ‏נוה‎ and ‏נוהם‎ at the end of 49.20 = 50.45 is probably to be attributed to a dittography in 49.20 or haplography in 50.45.

The changes in 50.46 = 49.21 are of a different magnitude and will be dealt with below, as a part of the consideration of why the editor chose to use this passage from Jer. 49.19-21. We have already seen how the poet linked this passage with the one from Isa. 13.19-22, by means of the common image of Yahweh's overthrow of Sodom and Gomorrah and the shared desert motif (49.18); but this linkage is not sufficient explanation of the use of this passage. The use of Isa. 13.19-22 was particularly apt, since it is a prophecy of Babylon's doom. The passage from Jer. 6.22-24 was appropriate, because of the irony involved in reinterpreting the prophecy of doom on Jerusalem, which was fulfilled by Babylon's action against Jerusalem, as a prophecy directed against Babylon. But the passage from Jer. 49.19-21 is a part of an oracle of doom on Edom, bearing no direct or indirect relationship on the coming fall of Babylon. However, two aspects of 49.19-21 may have suggested the use of the passage to the editor. The first is the pastoral language found in these verses which links up with that in 50.2-20. The imagery of the lion and sheep is almost the reverse of what is found in the first poem (50.6, 7, 17). In the first poem, the Babylonians are the lions that drove out the Hebrew sheep. In Jer. 49.19-21, as revised in 50.44-45, Yahweh acts as a lion, and the hunted sheep are now Babylonians, rather than Israelites. This reversal fits in with the contrast between the fates of Israel and Babylon found in the first poem.

Secondly, the poet chose to use Jer. 49.19-21, because of the ease with which he could alter the final line, in order to recall the opening line of the first poem in Jer. 50.2-20, thus providing a kind of inclusion for the entire collection. Jeremiah 49.21 did not need to be changed at all to fit into the new context in ch. 50. Nevertheless, the editor made extensive changes. That the changes are a result of the editor's desire to provide an inclusion for the entire chapter will be seen through a comparison of Jer. 50.46 with 49.21 and 50.2.

Jeremiah 49.21	*Jeremiah 50.46*
מקול נִפְלָם רעשה הארץ	מקול נִתְפְּשָׂה בָּבֶל נרעשה הארץ
צעקה בְּיַם סוּף נשמע (קולה)	וזעקה בַּגּוֹיִם נשמע

The significant differences between 49.21 and 50.46 are underlined. When 50.46 is compared with 50.2, it can be seen that the changes the editor made were a result of his desire to provide an inclusion for the chapter.

Jeremiah 50.46	*Jeremiah 50.2*
מקל נִתְפְּשָׂה בָּבֶל נרעשה הארץ	הגידו בַגּוֹיִם הַשְׁמִיעוּ ...
וזעקה בַּגּוֹיִם נִשְׁמַע	נִלְכְּדָה בָבֶל

Although the verbs נלכדה, 'captured', and נתפשה, 'taken', are different, they are synonyms. The phrases נלכדה בבל / נתפשה בבל, בגוים and השמיעו / נשמע form a multiple inclusion.

The plusses beginning in 50.39 are meant primarily to fill out what was implied, but not explicit, in the third poem, vv. 33-38. However, they also indirectly refer back to the first two poems, and in particular, 50.46 connects with 50.2, providing an inclusion for the combined three poems.

The above analysis suggests that Jeremiah 50, far from being poorly organized and thematically sparse, is logically organized and thematically rich. Theologically it expresses the conviction that there is one Lord of history, who is just and powerful and who will punish those who do evil and vindicate those whose cause is just.

STRUCTURE AND REDACTION IN JEREMIAH 2–6

Marvin A. Sweeney

I

As Diamond's introductory essay for this volume demonstrates, current discussion of the book of Jeremiah is heavily influenced by a methodological debate that emphasizes three major reading strategies: (1) author-centered approaches that attempt to read Jeremiah in relation to the historical settings and concerns of the purported author or authors of the text; (2) text-centered approaches that focus on the literary features of the text of Jeremiah irrespective of its supposed historical settings; and (3) reader-centered approaches that emphasize the biases, perspectives and concerns of the readers of Jeremiah as major elements in the interpretation of the book. Each of these approaches has its own strengths and weaknesses. Author-centered approaches correctly emphasize the role that the author and historical setting of a text play in determining its formulation and the concerns that it addresses, but they suffer from the inherently hypothetical nature of the textual, authorial and historical reconstructions that constitute a necessary element of such reading strategies. Text-centered approaches correctly emphasize the literary features of a text as the basis for interpretation, insofar as the text is the only objective element that stands before the interpreter, but such analyses do not account adequately for the determinative roles of the contexts in which the text is formed or read. Likewise, reader-centered approaches correctly point to the role of the reader in setting the agenda and parameters for interpretation, but again they do not account adequately for the role of the writers and the historical contexts of composition and indeed frequently of readings from later historical contexts.

Although it is important to identify these emphases in current interpretation, to some extant, their differentiation leads to a certain element of scholarly polarization as proponents of each approach tend to emphasize the benefits of their respective strategies and to critique alternative approaches. This is an indication of scholarly health in that it facilitates full discussion of the strengths and weaknesses of each strategy that ultimately serve biblical interpretation by pointing to previously unrecognized aspects of biblical literature. But one must also ask to what extent such strategies can be combined in an overall reading of a text. Indeed, all three strategies play an important and necessary role in biblical interpretation, and the insights gained by each approach must be considered in the interpretation of a biblical text. Biblical texts are written by authors with a unique set of concerns in specific historical settings; they display distinctive literary features; and they are read by interpreters, either in the present or in the past, who also bring their unique concerns in relation to their own settings.[1]

Jeremiah 2–6 is a particularly useful text for illustrating the interrelationship of these three reading strategies. Although Jeremiah 2–6 presently forms a major component of the book of Jeremiah that in its present form addresses the issue of the Babylonian exile, scholars have consistently maintained that an earlier form of this material from the reign of King Josiah may be reconstructed.[2] Attempts have been made

---

1. For methodological discussion, see especially, John Barton, *Reading the Old Testament: Method in Biblical Study* (Louisville, KY: Westminster/John Knox Press, rev. edn, 1996); Rolf Knierim, 'Criticism of Literary Features, Form, Tradition, and Redaction', in D.A. Knight and G.M. Tucker (eds.), *The Hebrew Bible and its Modern Interpreters* (Chico, CA: Scholars Press, 1985), pp. 123-65; Robert Morgan with John Barton, *Biblical Interpretation* (The Oxford Bible Series; Oxford: Oxford University Press, 1988); Marvin A. Sweeney, 'Formation and Form in Prophetic Literature', in J.L. Mays, D.L. Petersen and K.H. Richards (eds.), *Old Testament Interpretation: Past, Present, and Future: Essays in Honor of Gene M. Tucker* (Nashville: Abingdon Press, 1995), pp. 113-26; *idem*, 'Form Criticism', in Steven L. McKenzie and Stephen R. Haynes (eds.), *To Each its Own Meaning: An Introduction to Biblical Criticisms and their Application* (Louisville, KY: Westminster/John Knox Press, 2nd rev. edn, forthcoming).

2. For a summary of research on Jer. 2–6, see Mark E. Biddle, *A Redaction History of Jeremiah 2:1–4:2* (ATANT, 77; Zürich: Theologischer Verlag, 1990), pp. 3-29; cf. Siegfried Herrmann, *Jeremia* (BKAT, 12.2; Neukirchen–Vluyn: Neukirchener Verlag, 1990), pp. 93-109, and Klaus Seybold, *Der Prophet Jeremia: Leben und Werk* (Stuttgart: W. Kohlhammer, 1993), pp. 68-80. For general overviews of research on the book of Jeremiah and the prophet, see R.P. Carroll, *Jeremiah* (OTG; Sheffield: JSOT Press, 1989); Siegfried Herrmann, *Jeremia: Der Prophet und das Buch* (Erträge der Forschung, 271; Darmstadt: Wissenschaftliche Buchgesellschaft, 1990); Jack R. Lundbom, 'Jeremiah, Book of', *ABD*, III,

to establish the literary structure of this text and to examine its literary features, but such attempts have frequently been overly influenced by redaction-critical concerns that have hampered such literary analysis. Nevertheless, a full understanding of the text in its present form is the necessary prerequisite for historical and redaction-critical reconstruction. Furthermore, the concerns of the reader must be considered as those concerns delimit and define the issues to be addressed in the interpretation of the text. In the present case, the reader of this text is interested in determining its relevance for reconstructing aspects of King Josiah's reign and reform program and for understanding the early career of the prophet Jeremiah in relation to Josiah's reign.[3]

This essay therefore proposes a redaction-critical analysis of Jeremiah 2–6 that accounts for the author of the text, its literary features and the concerns of its reader. It examines a recent proposal by Biddle for a redaction-critical analysis of the text[4] and argues that although Biddle's idea advances redaction-critical research on Jeremiah 2–6, it is limited by insufficient attention to the literary features of the text in its own right as literature. On the basis of a synchronic examination of the literary structure of these chapters, it argues that a basis for redaction-critical reconstruction emerges. The present form of the text points to an attempt to address the former northern kingdom of Israel with an accusation that its rejection of YHWH led to its punishment. This serves as the basis for a similar address to Judah that establishes an analogy between Israel's and Judah's actions and thereby points to the potential punishment of Judah. Insofar as the material directed to Israel appears in Jer. 2.2–4.2* and that directed to Judah appears in Jer. 2.1-2, 28; 3.6-11; and 4.3–6.30, the essay argues that a text addressed to Israel during the reign of King Josiah was reworked and expanded to address the kingdom of Judah in the face of the later Babylonian threat.[5] Such

---

pp. 706-21; *idem*, 'Jeremiah (Prophet)', *ABD*, III, pp. 684-98; and Seybold, *Der Prophet Jeremia.*

3. See also Jack Lundbom, *The Early Career of the Prophet Jeremiah* (Lewiston, KY: Edwin Mellen Press, 1993), for a discussion of research. Lundbom's proposal for an early dating for Jeremiah's oracles correctly notes thematic elements in various passages that point to Josiah's reign, but it is dependent on an overly literal reading of the reference to Jeremiah's eating of YHWH's words in Jer. 15.16 as a reference to the discovery of the Torah scroll during the reign of Josiah reported in 2 Kgs 22.8-13.

4. Biddle, *A Redaction History of Jeremiah 2:1–4:2.*

5. See also Christof Hardmeier, 'Die Redekomposition Jer 2–6: Eine ultimative

work indicates the dynamic nature of Jeremiah's oracles in that they are read and applied in relation to different historical contexts during the course of his career. It further indicates shifts in the prophet's thinking in relation to the changing sociopolitical and religious circumstances of Judah during his lifetime. This of course does not address subsequent readings and applications of the text—that is the topic of future research.

II

Scholars generally maintain that Jeremiah 2–6 constitutes a distinct collection of Jeremiah's oracles that stem from the earliest periods of the prophet's activity. The present form of this material is addressed to Jerusalem and Judah (cf. Jer. 2.2; 4.3-4, 5-6), and it appears to presuppose the early reign of Jehoiakim, following the death of Josiah, when Judah was threatened by Egypt in the wake of the Assyrian collapse (cf. Jer. 2.18, 36; 3.6). These chapters portray the coming threat that YHWH is bringing against Judah and Jerusalem from the north to punish them for their lack of fidelity to their God. Insofar as the theme of repentance plays a major role in these chapters, they appear to constitute a parenetical composition that is designed to persuade Judah and Jerusalem to return to YHWH before the punishment is realized.

Although the present form of Jeremiah 2–6 is addressed to Judah and Jerusalem, scholars persistently argue that an earlier text form, addressed to the northern kingdom of Israel, lies behind the present form of the text in Jer. 2.1–4.2. The reasons for this contention are quite clear. Although the text as a whole identifies Jerusalem and Judah as its addressee, Jer. 2.1–4.4 frequently identifies 'Israel' (Jer. 2.3, 14, 31; 3.23; 4.1); 'the House of Jacob/Israel' (Jer. 2.4, 26; 3.20); 'apostate Israel' (Jer. 3.12); and 'the sons of Israel' (Jer. 3.21) as its addressee. In addition, it emphasizes the wilderness tradition (Jer. 2.2, 6, 17, 31), typically associated with the northern kingdom of Israel; the return of

Verwarnung Jerusalems im Kontext des Zidkijasaufstandes', *Wort und Dienst* 21 (1991), pp. 11-42; *idem*, 'Geschichte und Erfahrung in Jer 2–6: Zur theologischen Notwendigkeit einer geschichts- und erfahrungsbezogenen Exegese und ihrer methodischen Neuorientierung', *EvT* 56 (1996), pp. 3-29, who argues that these chapters may well contain material that dates to the reign of Josiah, but reads them in relation to the threat posed against Judah by Babylon during the reign of Zedekiah.

the 'rebellious sons' to Zion (Jer. 3.14, 17); and the walking together of the 'House of Judah' and the 'House of Israel' (Jer. 3.18). It likewise compares the apostasy of Israel with that of Judah (Jer. 3.6-10, 11). Furthermore, the superscription of the book (Jer. 1.1-3) states that the prophet was active during the reign of King Josiah, who attempted to bring the territory and people of the former northern kingdom of Israel back under Davidic rule. Finally, the text employs a variety of pronoun forms, including 2nd m. sing., 2nd m. plural, and 2nd f. sing., to designate its addressee, which suggests the hand of a redactor at work. Because of these considerations, many scholars argue that an earlier form of Jer. 2.1–4.4 was composed by the prophet during the reign of King Josiah as part of an effort to convince the people living in the territory of the former northern kingdom of Israel to accept Davidic sovereignty and thus to return to YHWH.[6]

But this consensus can be challenged on a number of grounds. The most important objection involves the chronology of the book and the prophet's career. Although Jer. 1.1-3 states that Jeremiah spoke during the reign of King Josiah, the book contains no text that appears unequivocally to derive from this period. In two instances, the text refers positively to Josiah (Jer. 3.6; 22.15-17), but it views Josiah retrospectively and never suggests that the prophet spoke during his reign. Likewise, the two blocks of text that scholars identify as those that may derive from Josiah's reign are addressed to both Israel and Judah in their present forms. This suggests either that they have been edited or composed to address a later period when Judah was also threatened. Other objections question the relationship of Jeremiah to Josiah's

---

6. Rainer Albertz, 'Jer 2–6 und die Frühzeitverkündigung Jeremias', *ZAW* 94 (1982), pp. 20-47; cf. William L. Holladay, *Jeremiah 1: A Commentary on the Book of the Prophet Jeremiah, Chapters 1–25* (Hermeneia; Philadelphia: Fortress Press, 1986), p. 2. Rüdiger Liwak, *Der Prophet und die Geschichte: Eine literarhistorische Untersuchung zum Jeremiabuch* (BWANT, 121; Stuttgart: W. Kohlhammer, 1987), pp. 303-31, argues that Jer. 2 contains prophetic words from various periods during the reign of Josiah (p. 304), but that the whole of Jer. 2–6 dates to shortly after 586 (p. 312). Contra Taro Odashima, *Heilsworte im Jeremiabuch: Untersuchungen zu ihrer vordeuteronomistischen Bearbeitung* (BWANT, 125; Stuttgart: W. Kohlhammer, 1989), p. 296, who dates the 'pre-deuteronomic' words of Jer. 2–6 to the early exilic period, and Robert Carroll, *Jeremiah: A Commentary* (OTL; Philadelphia: Westminster Press, 1986), pp. 116-17, who maintains that it is possible to date this material to any period of Israelite history.

reform, the historical reliability or referents of these texts, and the meaning of the term 'Israel' in Jeremiah.[7]

On the basis of these objections, Biddle's recent study of the redaction history of these chapters correctly challenges this consensus by pointing to the difficulties that scholars face in their attempts to posit Jeremiah's prophetic activity during the reign of Josiah.[8] Biddle maintains that there is no clear evidence that Jeremiah spoke during the reign of Josiah, and that the ideological character of Jeremiah 36 undermines the basis for reconstructing an *Urrolle* of the prophet's words that might be attributed, at least in part, to the reign of Josiah.[9] Nevertheless, he does not reject the possibility or need for redaction-critical work on the book as a means for reconstructing earlier text forms. He correctly argues that an analysis of the structure of the text must constitute the starting point for redaction-critical reconstruction, insofar as the present structure of these chapters points to various inconsistencies, such as shifts in the addressee, the status of the people, and the presence of smaller textual units on which the present text is based.[10] Following an analysis of the structure of Jeremiah 2.1–4.2, Biddle identifies four

7. For a summary of the primary objections, see Biddle, *A Redaction History of Jeremiah 2:1–4:2*, pp. 16-23.

8. Biddle, *A Redaction History of Jeremiah 2:1–4:2*.

9. Biddle, *A Redaction History of Jeremiah 2:1–4:2*, pp. 16-25. On the ideological character of Jer. 36 which argues that the chapter was composed in order to contrast the 'wicked' Jehoiakim with the 'righteous' Josiah, see Charles D. Isbell, '2 Kings 22.3–23.24 and Jeremiah 36: A Stylistic Comparison', *JSOT* 8 (1978), pp. 33-45. Against Albertz, Biddle (pp. 19-20 n. 53) maintains that the references to Israel in Jer. 2.1–4.2 must be understood in relation to all the tribes of Israel, including Judah, in that the reference to 'all the families of the House of Israel' in Jer. 2.4 is an ambiguous term that frequently refers to both north and south in prophetic literature (cf. Amos 3.1), but this fails to account for the distinction between Israel and Judah in Jer. 3.6-10, 11, 18. He further argues against Albertz's association of the salvation preaching in ch. 3 with that of Jer. 30–31, which is also concerned with the north, because Jer. 3 (and 4) portrays a people already in judgment who are summoned to repentance whereas Jer. 30–31 announces salvation. But this overlooks the rhetorical force of Jer. 3–4, which is designed to motivate the audience to accept a call to return to Zion and YHWH, and that of Jer. 30–31, which announces and looks forward to the realization of that return. For a study of the structure, intention, and redaction history of Jer. 30–31, see my study, 'Jeremiah 30–31 and King Josiah's Program of National Restoration and Religious Reform', *ZAW* 108 (1996), pp. 569-83.

10. Cf. Knierim, 'Criticism of Literary Features', esp. pp. 150-58.

major stages in the composition of this text that encompass the entire
period of the composition of the book of Jeremiah in the exilic and
postexilic periods.[11] Altogether, these chapters constitute a theological
treatise that introduces the entire book.[12]

Insofar as Biddle focuses on the final form of the text of Jeremiah as
a basis for redaction-critical reconstruction, he advances the study of
Jeremiah 2–6 considerably. But despite its methodological sophistication and its well-considered challenge to past scholarship, two major
difficulties appear in his work. The first is his contention that the 2nd f.
sing. address forms constitute the oldest layer of material within this
text and that the 2nd f. sing. *wattô'm⁽ʳî*, 'but you said', verbal forms
constitute the basis for the structure of the text. Unfortunately, this contention cannot be accepted in that it prejudges the historical and structural conclusions that the study attempts to achieve. Furthermore, past
research demonstrates the difficulties in employing the address forms of
this passage as a basis for textual reconstruction, which calls into question the employment of such a procedure as a major criterion for redaction-critical work on this text. The problem is especially evident in the
observation that nowhere in this text is Israel identified with a feminine
appellation, such as the *b⁽tûlat yiśrā'ēl* of Jeremiah 30–31; rather, the
text employs common forms for the designation of Israel as a people
and alludes metaphorically to the role of Israel as a bride (cf. Jer. 2.2-
3). This suggests that the interplay between masculine and feminine
address forms for Israel in this text may be deliberate, in that they refer
respectively to the sociopolitical reality of Israel as a people and to the
metaphorical portrayal of Israel as YHWH's bride. In general, the
address forms are relatively consistent within the constituent textual
blocks of this passage, but at times they mix and demonstrate their
rhetorical, but not redactional, significance. The phenomenon is evident

---

11. Biddle's stages include (1) the *Schuldübernahme* redaction, composed
during the exilic period as a preamble to Jer. 4–6, which argues that the people of
Jerusalem must recognize their guilt as the cause for their own predicament; (2) the
repentance series, which calls for reconciliation based upon the people's repentance; (3) the generations redaction, composed during a later postexilic period when
Deuteronomistic theology had become orthodox, which extended the indictment to
later generations of all Israel and Judah as a means to account for continued hardships; and (4) the final framework redaction which places greater emphasis on the
guilt of an earlier generation from whose sinful history Israel must distance itself.

12. Cf. Liwak, *Der Prophet*, pp. 293-302.

in Jer. 2.31-33 which begins with 2nd m. plural address forms directed to Israel as a people, but shifts its imagery to that of a bride followed by 2nd f. sing. address forms directed to Israel. This suggests that the shift in address forms cannot serve as a reliable indicator of the redaction history of this text or even of its structure.

The second difficulty pertains to his demarcation of this text, its relation to its literary context, and the relative meaning of the term 'Israel'. Biddle does not fully justify the structural demarcation of Jer. 2.1–4.2, although he does provide several hints to his thinking. He notes the occurrence of Jerusalem in Jer. 2.1-2 and 4.3, 5, and argues that Jerusalem is otherwise unnamed throughout the body of the text. Because he maintains that these texts constitute framework materials for the whole, he discounts them as constituent elements of the text to be studied and posits that they facilitate a transition from a collection concerned with Israel's sin in Jeremiah 2–3 to one concerned with the 'foe from the north' directed against Jerusalem in Jeremiah 4–6. Nevertheless, he treats chs. 2–3 and 4–6 as if they are separate textual blocks, overlooking the syntactical connective *kî* which links 4.3-4 to 4.1-2, and which effects the transition between two subunits of a larger text. Because Jacob/Israel is the addressee of Jeremiah 2–3 (cf. 2.4), this forces him to discount the address to Judah in 2.28 as contradictory. He therefore argues that 2.1-3 is secondary 'since it is difficult to imagine a redactor destroying an original unity between 2.2b-3 and 2.5ff' (p. 34), and he dismisses the structural significance of 3.6-12 which distinguishes Judah and Israel. These texts are particularly important in defining the relationship between Judah (and thus Jerusalem) and Israel within Jer. 2.1–4.2 in that they indicate that the distinction between Israel and Judah is fundamental to the concerns of this text. Such a distinction points to the larger literary context in which concern with Israel in chs. 2–3 prefigures concern with Judah/Jerusalem in chs. 4–6. In short, redactional criteria influence his views on the structure and interpretation of the final form of the text and thereby aid in predetermining his results. This suggests that greater attention should be directed to the larger literary context of Jeremiah 2–6, the distinction between Israel and Judah within that context, and the role that the references to Jerusalem and Judah in Jeremiah 2–3 play in relating these chapters and their concerns to Jeremiah 4–6.

On the basis of these considerations, it is therefore necessary to reconsider the redaction history of Jer. 2.1–4.2, both in relation to its internal referents and in relation to the larger literary context of Jeremiah 2–6. This points to the need to establish the structure of Jeremiah 2–6, together with the differing references to Israel and Judah, as the bases for the redaction-critical study of this text.

III

Jeremiah 2–6 is demarcated initially by the YHWH-word transmission formula in 2.1, *way^{e}hî d^{e}bar-yhwh 'ēlay lē'm'ōr*, 'and the word of YHWH was unto me saying'.[13] This occurrence of the formula is the third in a series of the same formula that appears also in 1.4 and 1.11. No such formula appears again until Jer. 7.1 which reads *haddābār '^{a}šer hāyâ yirm^{e}yāhû mē'ēt yhwh lē'mōr*, 'the word which was unto Jeremiah from YHWH, saying'. The correspondence between this formula and the superscription in Jer. 1.1-3, *dibrê yirm^{e}yāhû ben-hilqîyāhû ... '^{a}šer hāyâ d^{e}bar-yhwh '^{e}lāyw ...*, 'the words of Jeremiah ben Hilkiah ... which was the word of YHWH unto him ...', suggests that 1.1-3 and 7.1 mark major divisions within the book. Insofar as the formulas in 1.4; 1.11; and 2.1 are linked syntactically to Jer. 1.1-3 by their waw-consecutive verbal forms, this suggests that a sequence of three interrelated textual blocks in 1.4-10; 1.11-19; and 2.1–6.30, introduced by the superscription in 1.1-3, defines the structure of the initial subunit of the book of Jeremiah. As scholars note, these chapters introduce the reader to the major themes, concerns and perspectives of the book.

Jeremiah 2–6 is defined as a distinct textual block within Jeremiah 1–7 not only by the introductory YHWH-word transmission formulae in Jer. 2.1 and 7.1, but as well by its concerns with both Israel and Judah, the threat of destruction or punishment levelled against them, and the call for repentance. Several observations are pertinent in attempting to define the internal structure of these chapters. First, the interchange between the various address forms (i.e. 2nd m. plural, 2nd m. sing., 2nd f. sing.) cannot serve as an adequate criterion to establish the structure of this text; the various forms are simply too intertwined within the text which suggests that they constitute a rhetorical shift in the means to address Israel and Judah rather than a structural criterion.

Second, the shift in the addressee detected by scholars within the

---

13. On the YHWH word transmission formula in Jeremiah, see Theodor Seidl, 'Die Wortereignisformel in Jeremia', *BZ* 23 (1979), pp. 20-47.

larger framework of Jeremiah 2–6 likewise cannot serve as an adequate structural criterion. The material addressed to Israel in 2.1–4.2 focuses especially on repentance in the wake of punishment, and that addressed to Jerusalem/Judah in 4.3–6.30 focuses especially on the threat from the 'foe from the north'. But the distinction in addressee is not so clear. The Israelite material is placed within a framework that is initially addressed to Jerusalem in 2.2, and that reiterates this perspective with an address to Judah in 2.28. Likewise, material addressed to 'the house of Israel' (5.15) appears in 5.14-19 within the context of that addressed to Jerusalem/Judah. The apostasy of both Israel and Judah are compared in 3.6-10, 11 with the aim of demonstrating that Judah is worse than Israel. Furthermore, both Israel[14] and Judah are addressed together in 5.20 (cf. 5.11), and Jerusalem is defined as 'the remnant of Israel' (*šĕ'ērît yiśrā'ēl*) in 6.8-9. Finally, the address to Jerusalem and Judah which begins in 4.3 is linked syntactically to material addressed explicitly to Israel in 4.1-2 by the connective *kî*, 'because'. This demonstrates that a structural distinction cannot be made at this point, and it suggests that a deliberate transition is made in the text which highlights the importance of the analogy between Israel and Judah made elsewhere in these chapters. Although the distinction between Israel and Judah is fundamental to the purposes of this text, the shift in address is not a criterion for establishing its structure.

Third, the fundamental significance of the analogy between Israel and Judah within this text points especially to 3.6-10, 11, which establishes the analogy most clearly. Jeremiah 3.6-10, 11 is composed in narrative form, and the only other narrative material in this entire text appears in the YHWH-word transmission formula in 2.1. Taken by itself, 2.1 establishes the generic character of this text as a report of YHWH's word to the prophet, insofar as it describes objectively the transmission of YHWH's word to Jeremiah. Furthermore, the 1st c. s. pronoun suffix of *'ēlay*, 'unto me', establishes that it is formulated as a first-person statement by the prophet. Jeremiah 3.6-10, 11 is likewise formulated as 1st c. s. statements by YHWH to the prophet. Likewise, both 2.2 and 3.12 contain commissioning formulae within the speech by YHWH to the prophet which instruct him to speak the following statements by YHWH to the people. These factors indicate that the narrative passages in 2.1; 3.6-10; and 3.11, each formulated as a 1st c. s. narrative report of

14. Lit. 'the house of Jacob'.

YHWH's word to the prophet, mark the basic structural divisions of Jeremiah 2–6. These passages therefore characterize the whole as the prophet's report of YHWH's word to him concerning Israel and Judah.

This, of course, raises the issue of the interrelationship between Israel and Judah within the larger structure of this text. Jer. 3.6-10, 11, plays an especially important role in establishing the analogy between Israel and Judah that defines an essential concern of this text. Because of its central position within the structure of the text, 3.6-10 facilitates the transition between concern with Israel to concern with Jerusalem/Judah. Concern with Jerusalem/Judah appears in the context of concern with Israel in 2.1–3.5, and concern with Israel continues to be highlighted especially in 3.12–4.2, but also in the balance of 4.3–6.30. In both cases, concern with Jerusalem/Judah defines the context in which concern with Israel is raised. Jeremiah 2.2, 28 defines the primary addressee of 2.2–3.5 as Jerusalem/Judah, and Jer. 4.3-4 and the entire context of 4.5–6.30 define the primary addressee as Jerusalem/Judah as well, even though Israel is prominently mentioned.

Obviously, a thematic concern other than the distinction in addressee must define the interrelationship of the textual blocks Jer. 2.1–3.5; 3.6-10; and 3.11–6.30. It is noteworthy that following the establishment of the analogy between Israel and Judah in 3.6-10, 11, the text immediately turns to a concern with the repentance of Israel that continues throughout the balance of the material directed to Israel in 3.12–4.2. In contrast, the material addressed directly to Jerusalem/Judah in 4.3–6.30 does not speak of repentance, but of the threat posed by the 'foe from the north'. At first sight, this appears to be unrelated to the repentance motif, but the nature of the analogy established between Israel and Judah in 3.6-10, 11 requires consideration of the interrelationship of these themes. Prior to the establishment of the analogy, the material directed to Israel in 2.2–3.5 focuses especially on YHWH's judgment against and punishment of Israel expressed metaphorically in terms of a divorce. Israel's guilt or abandonment of YHWH is established as the basis for the divorce decree. Likewise, 4.5–6.30 focuses on Jerusalem's and Judah's guilt as the basis for the punishment at the hand of the 'foe from the north' brought by YHWH. In this regard, the calls for the repentance of Israel in 3.12–4.2 play a very important role in relation to the following announcements of punishment directed to Jerusalem/Judah in that they provide the context for understanding the purpose of such judgment. Based on the analogy of Israel, which YHWH calls to repentance after its 'divorce', Jerusalem/Judah will likewise be called to repentance in light of its upcoming punishment. This concern is hardly evident from 4.5–6.30 itself; only the slightest hint of Jerusalem's repentance appears in 6.8, 'be warned, O Jerusalem, lest my soul be thrust from you, lest I make you a desolation, an uninhabited land'. Rather, it is evident from the literary context and structure of Jeremiah 2–6, in which Israel serves as an analogy for Jerusalem and Judah. It is also evident from the structural relationship between Jeremiah 2–6 and 1.4-10 and 1.11-19, in which the prophet is told respectively that YHWH will both destroy and rebuild (1.10) and that YHWH's punishment will come in the form of a threat from the north (1.13-19). Consequently, the call for repentance to Israel found in 3.12–4.2 also serves as an indication of what YHWH expects from Jerusalem/Judah once the punishment is completed.

The result is a three-part structure for Jeremiah 2–6. Jeremiah 2.1–3.5 constitutes 'The Prophet's Report of YHWH's Word Concerning Israel' in the form of a trial speech or divorce proceeding. Jeremiah 3.6-10 constitutes 'The Prophet's Report of YHWH's Word Concerning Both Israel's and Judah's Unfaithfulness in the Days of Josiah'. Jeremiah 3.6-10 merely states the comparison or analogy between Israel and Judah, that is, both are unfaithful. Jeremiah 3.11 then asserts that the unfaithfulness of Judah is worse than that of Israel as the premise on which the following material will proceed. Jeremiah 3.11–6.30 therefore constitutes 'The Prophet's Report of YHWH's Word Concerning Judah', which employs the analogy of Israel and Judah to call for repentance (3.12–4.4) as a basis for defining the purpose of the punishment announced in 4.5–6.30.

IV

It is now possible to attempt a redaction-critical reconstruction of an earlier form of Jeremiah 2–6. As noted above, the text identifies both the northern kingdom of Israel and the southern kingdom of Judah (or simply Jerusalem) as its addressees. Specific references for the northern kingdom include 'Israel' (2.3, 14, 31; 4.1), the 'house of Israel' (2.4, 26; 3.18, 20; 5.11, 15), the 'sons of Israel' (3.21), the 'house of Jacob' (2.4; 5.20), 'apostate Israel' (3.6, 8, 11, 12), 'repentant Israel' (3.23); specific references for the southern kingdom include 'Judah' (3.18; 5.11), 'treacherous Judah' (3.7, 8, 10, 11), 'Jerusalem' (2.2; 4.3, 4, 5,

10, 11, 14, 16; 5.1; 6.6, 8), 'Zion' (4.6), the 'daughter of Zion' (4.31; 6.2, 23) and the 'remnant of Israel' (6.9). Apart from the indirect references to the northern kingdom that appear in various texts, all but one of the references to the northern kingdom as the addressee of the text (5.15) appear in 2.2–4.2. Although the address to the northern kingdom is relatively consistent throughout Jer. 2.2–4.2, it is set in a framework that identifies Jerusalem and Judah as the addressee.[15] This distinction in addressee is crucial for understanding the redactional character of this text in that the references to the southern kingdom appear primarily at the beginning and end of 2.1–4.4 and in the prose material in 3.6-11. This suggests that a text addressed to the northern kingdom of Israel has been reworked to address the southern kingdom of Judah.[16]

The redactional character of this text is evident in the relationship between the prose material in Jer. 3.6-11, which establishes the analogy between the unfaithfulness of 'apostate Israel' and that of 'treacherous Judah', and the surrounding poetic material that is addressed to the northern kingdom. Since Mowinckel's early source-critical study identified poetic material in Jeremiah 1–25 as source A and the prose sermons as source C,[17] scholars have become accustomed to identifying the source A material as the work of Jeremiah himself and the prose material as the work of a Deuteronomistic redaction.[18] Although the distinction between poetry and prose is not in itself an adequate criterion to define the redactional character of a text, a recent study by McKane demonstrates the exegetical relationship between 3.6-11 and both 3.1-5 and 3.12-13.[19] The prose material in 3.6-11 takes up vocabulary and

---

15. Jer. 2.2, 28; 3.6-10, 11, 18; 4.3-4.

16. Note that the bulk of Jer. 2.1-2aα, including the reference to Jerusalem, is missing in the LXX, which reads only *kai eipe*, 'and he said', prior to the messenger formula in v. 2aα.

17. See Sigmund Mowinckel, *Zur Komposition des Buches Jeremia* (Kristiania: Jacob Dybwad, 1914); cf. Bernhard Duhm, *Das Buch Jeremia* (Tübingen: J.C.B. Mohr [Paul Siebeck], 1901).

18. See, for example, Winfried Thiel, *Die deuteronomistische Redaktion von Jeremia 1–25* (WMANT, 41; Neukirchen–Vluyn: Neukirchener Verlag, 1973); *idem*, *Die deuteronomistische Redaktion von Jeremia 26–45* (WMANT, 52; Neukirchen–Vluyn: Neukirchener Verlag, 1981).

19. William McKane, 'Relations between Poetry and Prose in the Book of Jeremiah with Special Reference to Jeremiah III 6-11 and XII 14-17', in J.A. Emerton (ed.), *Congress Volume: Vienna 1980* (VTSup, 32; Leiden: E.J. Brill, 1981), pp. 220-37, esp. 229-33; see also his *A Critical and Exegetical Commentary*

develops themes from both 3.1-5 and 3.12-13 which demonstrates its redactional character. Thus 3.6-11 takes up the divorce theme from 3.1-5, the appellation *mᵉšubâ yiśrā'ēl* from 3.12, and the phrase *taḥat kol 'ēṣ ra'ᵃ nān*, 'under every green tree', from 3.13, all of which appear in contexts that are addressed to the northern kingdom of Israel, in order to create a text that establishes the analogy between the unfaithfulness of Israel and that of Judah. As noted above, the purpose of this text is to establish that the guilt of Judah is greater than that of Israel. It thereby creates the premise for the final form of this text which warns Judah of the coming punishment from YHWH in the form of an enemy from the north and thus calls for Judah's repentance just as Israel was called to repent. In this manner, the redaction apparent in 3.6-11 transforms a text that calls for the repentance of Israel following its punishment to one that announces the anticipated punishment of Judah as a basis for its subsequent repentance.

A similar concern is evident in the framework material that appears at the beginning (2.1-2) and end (4.3-4) of the material addressed to the northern kingdom of Israel. Following the narrative YHWH-word transmission formula in 2.1, Jer. 2.2 contains a commissioning formula in which YHWH commissions the prophet to speak the following words 'in the ears of Jerusalem' (*bᵉ'oznê yᵉrûšalayim*). This is remarkable in that the following material is addressed to the northern kingdom, not to Jerusalem, as indicated by the address forms discussed in the analysis of the structure presented above. Nevertheless, such a distinction serves the purposes of the redaction evident in 3.6-11; that is, the experience of the northern kingdom of Israel will serve as an analogy and example for Judah.

The same may be said of the juxtaposition of the address to Israel in 4.1-2, which states the conditions of Israel's repentance, and the address to Judah in 4.3-4, which is linked syntactically to 4.1-2 by the particle *kî*, 'for, because'. The address to Judah cannot be considered separately from that to Israel; the command for Judah and Jerusalem to 'plow its own field' and to 'circumcise itself' must be taken as a consequence of the instructions to Israel to remove its filth and to restore righteousness

on Jeremiah. I. *Introduction and Commentary on Jeremiah I–XXV* (ICC; Edinburgh: T. & T. Clark, 1986), pp. 67-69. Cf. Thiel, *Jeremia 1–25*, pp. 83-93, who assigns Jer. 3.6-13 to the basic deuteronomic redaction of the book of Jeremiah during the exile and Jer. 3.14-18 to various postexilic expansions.

and justice; that is, just as Israel must repent, so must Judah and Jeru-salem. Again, the experience of Israel serves as an analogy and model for Judah.

The framework passages in Jer. 2.1-2 and 4.3-4 and the prose mate-rial in 3.6-11 appears to be redactional in that they transform material addressed to the northern kingdom of Israel into material addressed to the southern kingdom of Judah. Two exceptions appear, however, that must be considered. The first occurs in Jer. 2.28 in the form of an address to Judah which appears unexpectedly in the context of an address to the northern kingdom. But v. 28b, *kî mispar 'ārêkā hāyû 'ᵉlōhêkā yᵉhûdâ*, 'for the number of your cities were as the number of your gods, O Judah', appears to be a gloss in that it duplicates exactly the language of Jer. 11.13 which addresses Judah's revolt against YHWH. Such an address is anomalous in an immediate context which addresses the northern kingdom (cf. 2.26, 31) with no indication of a transition. It would appear that the glossator or redactor of this text employed a statement from 11.13 to establish the context of an address to Judah in keeping with the purposes of the overall redaction of this text evident in 2.1-2; 3.6-11; 4.3-4. The second appears in Jer. 3.18, which looks forward to the time when the 'house of Judah' will walk together with the 'house of Israel'. But such a statement is consistent with expectations that the northern kingdom of Israel would reunite with the southern kingdom of Judah under Davidic rule in Jerusalem as a result of its repentance (cf. Jer. 3.14-17). It need not be explained as a redactional expansion of this text.

From these considerations, it becomes apparent that the redaction has transformed a text addressed to the northern kingdom of Israel to one that is addressed to Jerusalem and Judah. Thus the anticipation of Judah's punishment and the expectation of Judah's repentance in the larger framework of Jeremiah 2–6 are based on Israel's experience of punishment and call for repentance evident in Jer. 2.2–4.2.

The redactional material in 2.1-2aα[1]; 2.28; 3.6-11; and 4.3-4 estab-lishes the analogy between Israel and Judah. Once this material is removed, a relatively coherent text remains in which the northern king-dom of Israel is called to repentance. The text begins with the trial speech or divorce proceeding identified earlier in Jer. 2.1–3.5, which identifies Israel as YHWH's bride (2.2aα[2-3]) and continues with the divorce proceeding proper in which YHWH states the grounds for divorce and argues that Israel has no basis on which to argue. The result is a call for repentance in Jer. 3.12–4.2 in which Israel is given the chance to return to YHWH provided the filth is removed and Israel is 'circumcised', or purified from previous wrongdoing.[20]

The setting of such a text must be placed in the reign of King Josiah, who attempted to restore the former northern kingdom of Israel to Davidic rule and thereby to reunite the 12 tribes of Israel. In this case, the repentance and purification of the former northern kingdom articulated in 3.12–4.2 is equated with its reunification with Judah under Davidic rule (cf. Jer. 3.14-18). Josiah's destruction of the former northern sanctuary at Beth-El (2 Kgs 23.15-20), his attempts to centralize worship and royal authority in Jerusalem (2 Kgs 23.1-25), and his marriages to women from Libnah and Rumah (2 Kgs 23.31, 36; 24.18), all demonstrate his intention to bring the territory of the former northern kingdom of Israel under Davidic rule and thereby to strengthen the authority of the Davidic dynasty.[21] Insofar as the superscription to the book of Jeremiah states that the prophet was active during the reign of Josiah (1.1-3), it would appear that this address to the northern kingdom was written by Jeremiah as part of an attempt to support Josiah's policies of reform and restoration. Certainly, the favorable references to Josiah in Jer. 22.13-17 indicate the prophet's support for Josiah.

Likewise, the redaction that established the analogy between the call

20. It must remain uncertain whether Jer. 5.15-17, which is also addressed to the northern kingdom, ever formed a part of this text. Note the address to *bêt yiśrā'ēl*, 'the House of Israel', in v. 15. The vocabulary of this passage suggests that it may allude to Isa. 5.26-30, which also addresses the northern kingdom of Israel in the context of the book of Isaiah. In this case, a warning to Israel would serve the purposes of the composer of the material addressed to Judah in Jer. 4.3–6.30 who built upon the analogy between Israel and Judah established in the redaction of Jer. 2–6.

21. For an overview of Josiah's policies during this period, see Jay Wilcoxen, 'The Political Background of Jeremiah's Temple Sermon', in A. Merrill and T. Overholt (eds.), *Scripture in History and Theology* (Festschrift J.C. Rylaarsdam; Pittsburgh: Pickwick Press, 1977), pp. 151-66. See also R. Althann, 'Josiah', *ABD*, III, pp. 1015-18 and the bibliography cited there; D.L. Christensen, 'Zeph 2:14-15: A Theological Basis for Josiah's Program of Political Expansion', *CBQ* 46 (1984), pp. 669-82; M.A. Sweeney, 'A Form-Critical Reassessment of the Book of Zephaniah', *CBQ* 53 (1991), pp. 388-408; W.E. Claburn, 'The Fiscal Basis of Josiah's Reforms', *JBL* 92 (1973), pp. 11-22; Naomi Steinberg, 'The Deuteronomic Law Code and the Politics of State Centralization', in D. Jobling, P. Day and G.T. Sheppard (eds.), *The Bible and the Politics of Exegesis* (Festschrift N.K. Gottwald; Cleveland: Pilgrim, 1991), pp. 161-70, 336-39; N. Na'aman, 'The Kingdom of Judah under Josiah', *TA* 18 (1991), pp. 3-71.

for Israel's repentance and the warning to Judah would also stem from Jeremiah. Following the death of Josiah in 609, Judah came under threat from Egypt and later from Babylon. The present text of Jeremiah 2–6 certainly indicates fear of a threat from both Egypt and Assyria (cf. Jer. 2.16-18, 36-37), which suggests that, with its warnings of punishment by an 'enemy from the north', it is consistent with Jeremiah's advice to avoid alliance with Egypt and to submit to Babylon as an expression of YHWH's will (cf. Jer. 27–28; 29). Just as Israel was punished and called to repent for its rejection of YHWH, so Judah's attempts to ally with Egypt against Babylon during the early reign of Jehoiakim (609–598 BCE) prior to the Babylonian defeat of Egypt at Carchemesh in 605 would provide an appropriate setting for this text.

V

In conclusion, this essay demonstrates that a synchronic literary evaluation of the structure and themes of Jeremiah 2–6 provides a basis for the redaction-critical reconstruction of an earlier text form. In the present case, it provides evidence for the activity of the prophet during the reign of King Josiah. It demonstrates that the prophet supported Josiah's policy of reunification of the former northern kingdom of Israel with Judah under Davidic rule. It further demonstrates the prophet's conclusion that, in light of Josiah's death and the failure of his program, the case of Israel provides an analogy with that of Judah. Just as Israel was called to repent for its abandonment of YHWH, so Judah will also face punishment for abandoning YHWH. By analogy with Israel's experience in the view of this text, such punishment will also serve as the basis for Judah's repentance once the punishment is complete.[22]

22. This is an expanded version of a paper read at the Pacific Coast Regional Meeting of the Society of Biblical Literature, 31 March 1995, Redlands, CA. An earlier draft was prepared during the term of my appointment as the 1993–94 Dorot Research Professor at the W.F. Albright Institute, Jerusalem, Israel. I would like to thank the Albright Institute, the Dorot Research Foundation, and the University of Miami for making this appointment possible.

APPENDIX

Jeremiah 2–6: Structure Diagram

PROPHETIC SUMMONS TO REPENTANCE DIRECTED TO JUDAH	2.1–6.30
I. Prophet's Report of YHWH's Word concerning Israel: Trial Speech/Divorce Proceeding	2.1–3.5
A. narrative introduction: word transmission formula	2.1
B. report of YHWH's word proper: trial speech/divorce proceeding	2.2–3.5
1. commissioning speech concerning Israel as YHWH's bride	2.2-3
a. commissioning formula	$2.2a\alpha^1$
b. content of commission: YHWH's reminiscence of Israel as bride: basis for trial/divorce proceeding	$2.2a\alpha^2$-3
2. trial speech/divorce proceeding proper	2.4–3.5
a. call to attention directed to Jacob/Israel	2.4
b. messenger speech concerning basis for YHWH's continuing controversy against Israel	2.5-11
(1) concerning Israel's rejection of YHWH's benefits/actions for Israel	2.5-8
(2) announcement of continuing controversy	2.9-11
c. concerning YHWH's accusations against Israel: abandonment of YHWH	2.12-28
(1) YHWH speech accusing Israel of abandonment with call to attention directed to heavens	2.12-13
(2) prophet's elaboration: speech concerning Israel's turn to Egypt/Assur	2.14-19a
(3) YHWH speech concerning Israel's pursuit of other lovers	2.19b-25
(4) prophet's elaboration concerning Israel's reliance on other gods	2.26-28
d. concerning Israel's lack of grounds for argument	2.29–3.5
(1) YHWH speech questioning Israel's ability to contend	2.29-30
(2) prophet's elaboration: confirmation of divorce proceeding/grounds for judgment	2.31–3.5
(a) prophet's quote of YHWH speech stating YHWH's rejection of Israel	2.31-37
(b) substantiation concerning law of divorce	3.1-5
II. Prophetic Report of Conversation with YHWH Concerning Israel's and Judah's Unfaithfulness in Days of Josiah	3.6-10

Part II

READER-CENTERED READINGS OF JEREMIAH

THE BOOK OF J: INTERTEXTUALITY
AND IDEOLOGICAL CRITICISM

Robert P. Carroll

Every discourse has its own selfish and biased proprietor; there are no words with meanings shared by all, no words 'belong to no one' ... When we seek to understand a word, what matters is not the direct meaning the word gives to objects and emotions—this is the false front of the word; what matters is rather the actual and always self-interested use to which this meaning is put and the way it is expressed by the speaker, a use determined by the speaker's position (profession, social class, etc.) and by the concrete situation. Who speaks and under what conditions he speaks: this is what determines the word's actual meaning. All direct meanings and direct expressions are false, and this is especially true of emotional meanings and expressions.

Mikhail Bakhtin[1]

There is neither a first word nor a last word and there are no limits to the dialogic context (it extends into the boundless past and the boundless future). Even *past* meanings, that is, those born in the dialogue of past centuries, can never be stable (finalized, ended once and for all)—they will always change (be renewed) in the process of subsequent, future development of the dialogue. At any moment in the development of the dialogue there are immense, boundless masses of forgotten contextual meanings, but at certain moments of the dialogue's subsequent development along the way they are recalled and invigorated in renewed form (in a new context). Nothing is absolutely dead: every meaning will have its homecoming festival.

Mikhail Bakhtin[2]

---

1.   M.M. Bakhtin, 'Discourse in the Novel', in M. Holquist (ed.), *The Dialogic Imagination: Four Essays* (trans. C. Emerson and M. Holquist; Austin: University of Texas Press, 1981), pp. 259-422 (401).
2.   M.M. Bakhtin, 'Toward a Methodology for the Human Sciences', in C. Emerson and M. Holquist (eds.), *Speech Genres and Other Late Essays* (trans. V.W. McGee; Austin: University of Texas Press, 1986), pp. 159-72 (170).

> We know now that a text is not a line of words releasing a single 'theological' meaning (the 'message' of the Author-God) but a multi-dimensional space in which a variety of writings, none of them original, blend and clash. The text is a tissue of quotations drawn from the innumerable centres of culture ... the writer can only imitate a gesture that is always anterior, never original. His only power is to mix writings, to counter the ones with the others, in such a way as never to rest on any one of them.
>
> Roland Barthes[3]

This essay was first delivered as a paper to the Composition of Jeremiah Consultation meeting at the AAR/SBL Annual Meeting in Washington in 1993. However throughout 1992–93 I had given it in different, evolving forms to various groups in places as far apart as Glasgow and South Africa, as well as in the United States. Two different published versions of it have appeared in quite distinctive publications and, as this version will demonstrate, it is still evolving as a statement of my fundamental understanding of the book of Jeremiah.[4] In spite, however, of its having appeared elsewhere in different forms I feel it ought to be included in this collection of Consultation essays because it represents about the only *major* paper I ever wrote for the Consultation—the minor, occasional papers may not warrant such published exposure—and because of its regularly changing content it reflects my continued thinking about the book of Jeremiah in relation to the many vexed interpretative issues related to explaining the emergence of that particular biblical text. So what appears here will be an admixture of the original paper (in its varied forms) and my *rereadings and revisions* of it in the light of my own current thinking about Jeremiah as the twentieth century comes to an end. I will, however, stick very close to the form and content of the paper(s) as given in Washington (and South Africa) in order to maintain a strong continuity between what I said in the early 1990s and what will appear in this the latest and final version of my thoughts on the two topics of intertextuality and ideological criticism as an approach to the composition of Jeremiah.

---

3. Roland Barthes, 'The Death of the Author', in *idem, Image-Music-Text* (trans. S. Heath; Glasgow: Fontana, 1977), pp. 142-48 (146).

4. See Robert P. Carroll, 'Intertextuality and the Book of Jeremiah: Animadversions on Text and Theory', in J. Cheryl Exum and David J.A. Clines (eds.), *The New Literary Criticism and the Hebrew Bible* (JSOTSup, 143; Sheffield: JSOT Press, 1993), pp. 55-78; R.P. Carroll, 'Jeremiah, Intertextuality and *Ideologiekritik*', *JNSL* 22.1 (1996), pp. 15-34.

In my judgment Jeremiah studies reached an impasse in the 1980s because too many differing points of view had contested the analysis and interpretation of the book of Jeremiah for there to be any hope ever again of reaching a consensus on the reading of Jeremiah. From henceforward there would always be a multiplicity of divergent, even oppositional, readings of the text and explanations for the composition of the book. I tend to think of this period in Jeremiah studies as having been 'a guerilla war' period where no clear winners emerged but many skirmishes led to a sense of real impasse.[5] The polyphonic book of Jeremiah had produced mirroring and conflicting polyphonies in the scholarship on Jeremiah.[6] I would neither expect nor hope that such conflictual differences among scholars, theologians and other readers scrutinizing the book of Jeremiah could or would be resolved, reconciled or generally minimized in the future because I value conflict and difference too much as creative forces in scholarship. We must attend to the conflicts of readers and interpreters in the future and do everything possible to maintain healthy disagreement and a polyphony of readings. My own further contribution to such a gallimaufry[7] of readings here will focus on the twin notions of intertextuality and ideological criticism in an attempt to explore some of the fundamental problems of reading Jeremiah today, while keeping a critical mind open for the

---

5.   I owe the phrase 'guerilla warfare' to a description of some of the historiographical debates in recent French discussions of history and acknowledge here the source of my use of it: see Michel de Certeau, 'A Transitional Epistemology: Paul Veyne', in Jacques Revel and Lynn Hunt (eds.), *Histories: French Constructions of the Past* (Postwar French Thought, 1; trans. A. Goldhammer *et al.*; New York: The New Press, 1995), pp. 310-18 (310).

6.   On the polyphonic nature of the book of Jeremiah see especially Mark E. Biddle, *Polyphony and Symphony in Prophetic Literature: Rereading Jeremiah 7–20* (Studies in Old Testament Interpretation, 2; Macon, GA: Mercer University Press, 1996); Robert P. Carroll, 'The Polyphonic Jeremiah: A Reading of the Book of Jeremiah', in Martin Kessler (ed.), *Reading the Book of Jeremiah: A Search for Coherence* (Winona Lake, IN: Eisenbrauns, 1999).

7.   I use this word here because in my 1986 OTL commentary I used it to describe the book of Jeremiah itself as 'a gallimaufry of writings': Carroll, *Jeremiah: A Commentary* (OTL; London: SCM Press; Philadelphia: Westminster Press, 1986), p. 38. For folk who do not know the meaning of the word, it means 'a jumble, hotchpotch' and I use it with reference to the book of Jeremiah in contradistinction to the New Criticism type of biblical reading which insists on finding neatness and tidyness, structure and signification in every text, including the book of Jeremiah.

problematic of reading which is inevitably entailed when the Bible is approached in our time.[8]

Intertextuality

> The frontiers of a book are never clear-cut: beyond the title, the first lines, and the last full-stop, beyond its internal configuration and its autonomous form, it is caught up in a system of references to other books, other texts, other sentences: it is a node within a network.
>
> Michel Foucault[9]

The word 'intertextuality' (*intertextualité*) was originally coined by Julia Kristeva to describe Mikhail Bakhtin's dialogical notion of texts:

> ... the 'literary word' as an *intersection of textual surfaces* rather than a *point* (a fixed meaning) ... as a dialogue among several writings: that of the writer, the addressee (or the character) and the contemporary or earlier cultural context ... any text is constructed as a mosaic of quotations; any text is the absorption and transformation of another. The notion of *intertextuality* replaces that of intersubjectivity, and poetic language is read as at least *double*.[10]

The essential features of this kind of definitional approach are clear to see: an intersection of textual surfaces, a mosaic of quotations and the fundamental observation that any writing is itself dependent on prior writing. Roland Barthes nicely encapsulates these points in his descriptive account of what a text is:

8. Elsewhere I have discussed something of that problematic of reading in relation to the Bible: see Robert P. Carroll, *Wolf in the Sheepfold: The Bible as Problematic for Theology* (London: SCM Press, 1997) (first published by SPCK in 1991 with a different subtitle; American edition *The Bible as a Problem for Christianity* [Philadelphia: Trinity Press International, 1991]).

9. I found this Foucault citation as the epigraph to Linda Hutcheon, 'Historiographic Metafiction: Parody and the Intertextuality of History', in Patrick O'Donnell and Robert Con Davis (eds.), *Intertextuality and Contemporary American Fiction* (Baltimore: The Johns Hopkins University Press, 1989), pp. 3-32 (3). See Michel Foucault, *Language, Counter-Memory, Practice: Selected Essays and Interviews* (ed. David F. Bouchard; trans. David F. Bouchard and Sherry Simon; Ithaca, NY: Cornell University Press, 1977; paperback edn 1980).

10. Julia Kristeva, 'Word, Dialogue and Novel', in Toril Moi (ed.), *The Kristeva Reader* (Oxford: Basil Blackwell, 1986), pp. 34-61 (36-37: emphases in the original); cf. the original article 'Le mot, le dialogue et le roman', in J. Kristeva, *Semotiké* (trans. A. Jardine, T. Gora and L.S. Roudiez; Paris: Editions du Seuil, 1969), pp. 143-73 (146).

The intertextual in which every text is held, it itself being the text-between of another text, is not to be confused with some origin of the text: to try to find the 'sources', the 'influences' of a work, is to fall in with the myth of filiation; the citations which go to make up a text are anonymous, untraceable, and yet *already read*: they are quotations without inverted commas.[11]

The word 'intertextuality' has now passed into standard usage among literature people, literary critics and theorists—it has even come into biblical studies where a number of biblical scholars have caught up with it and there is now a flourishing use of it among informed biblical critics.[12] In relation to the Bible I would just want to define intertextuality along the lines of Barthes, Foucault and Kristeva and emphasize the factors of 'every text is the intertext of another text ... quotations without quotation marks ... a system of references to ... other texts ... a node within a network ... an intersection of textual surfaces ... a mosaic of quotations'. In other words, every writer of a text is first a reader of (other) texts. That implied interchange (or exchange) of reading and writing captures something of the essential nature of the intertextuality of texts. That is why, in my judgment, the various collections of so-called prophetic texts in the Hebrew Bible are so often capable of being interchanged with one another. Such an interchange reflects the essential intertextuality of the whole enterprise which created the 'prophetic corpus' in the first place.[13]

The notion of intertextuality in some ways reflects one of the oldest

11. Roland Barthes, 'From Work to Text', in *idem*, *Image-Music-Text*, pp. 155-64 (160) (emphasis in original).

12. When I first wrote this piece back in 1992 there was little available on the topic relating to biblical studies (which is why I originally wrote it for the Exum and Clines volume), but that is now no longer the case: see Danna Nolan Fewell (ed.), *Reading between Texts: Intertextuality and the Hebrew Bible* (Literary Currents in Biblical Interpretation; Louisville, KY: Westminster/John Knox Press, 1992). What I did have access to then was Daniel Boyarin, *Intertextuality and the Reading of Midrash* (Indiana Studies in Biblical Literature; Bloomington: Indiana University Press, 1990) and some books from disciplines other than biblical studies.

13. On the formation of this 'sacred library of the prophets' see Charles C. Torrey, 'The Background of Jeremiah 1–10', *JBL* 56 (1937), pp. 193-216. More recently on the formation of the prophetic literature see, among so many other writers, especially Philip R. Davies, *Scribes and Schools: The Canonization of the Hebrew Scriptures* (Library of Ancient Israel; Louisville, KY: Westminster/John Knox Press, 1998), pp. 107-25.

tropings known to readers: that of echo, influence, repetition—of what John Hollander calls 'language answering language'.[14] In the Bakhtinian and Barthesian senses of intertextuality the matter becomes much more complex and complicated than simply that of influence and echo, but the simple forms belong to the intertextual spectrum as much as the theoretical sophistications of post-structuralist writers. Intertextuality also represents 'language's ever-unfolding filiation with itself, its posited objects, its networks of references', as well as signalling 'an *anxiety* and an *indeterminacy* regarding authorial, readerly, or textual identity, the relation of present culture to past, or the function of writing within certain historical and political frameworks'.[15] Those notes of 'anxiety' and 'indeterminacy' are important for contemporary biblical studies because their employment in current biblical criticism signals the huge gap that has opened up between traditional modes of reading the Bible and contemporary ways of reading texts.[16] I doubt if I would be recommending an intertextual approach to reading Jeremiah if more traditional ways of reading the biblical text had proved satisfactory. Anxiety generated by the instability of texts is certainly a feature of current Jeremiah studies, even though such instability allows for the construction of many different networks of meaning and significance for readers. As The Bible and Culture Collective rightly note:

> Text is the product of signifying difference. Text and its related terms
> (such as *writing* and *reading*) are, for deconstruction, complex, fluid, and
> powerful metaphors. Whatever a text is, it is not a stable, self-identical,

14. John Hollander, *The Figure of Echo: A Mode of Allusion in Milton and After* (Berkeley: University of California Press, 1981), p. 21.

15. See Patrick O'Donnell and Robert Con Davis, 'Introduction: Intertext and Contemporary American Fiction', in O'Donnell and Davis (eds.), *Intertextuality and Contemporary American Fiction*, pp. ix-xxii (xiii; emphases in original). For a most useful discussion of the matter see Thaïs Morgan, 'The Space of Intertextuality' in the above volume (pp. 239-79).

16. One comprehensive illustration of this gap would be The Bible and Culture Collective's volume *The Postmodern Bible* (New Haven: Yale University Press, 1995). Even though elsewhere I have criticized severely this volume for its failure of nerve, hypocrisy, double standards and hypercritical attitudes (see Carroll, 'Post-structuralist approaches: New Historicism and postmodernism', in John Barton [ed.], *The Cambridge Companion to Biblical Interpretation* [Cambridge: Cambridge University Press, 1998], pp. 57-62) it provides a brilliant set of essays on the structure, shape and divergencies of newer approaches to reading the Bible when compared with more traditional historical-critical methods.

enduring object but a place of intersection in a network of signification. *Intertextuality*—a term introduced by Julia Kristeva—suggests that each text is situated for each reader in an ever-changing web composed of innumerable texts. There is no extratextual reality to which texts refer or which gives texts their meaning; meaning or reference are possible only in relation to this network, as functions of intertextuality.[17]

In terms of an intertextual approach to the book of Jeremiah I will start at the simplest level of stating the obvious: however we may wish to describe the phenomenon there is a very strong relationship between the language and discourses of Jeremiah and those other biblical books of Deuteronomy and Joshua–Kings. Whether we describe such intertextuality in terms of a deuteronomistic world of discourse or refuse to name the interchangeable prose common to all these books is of less importance than the recognition of the commonplace linguistic world they all share. The interconnections could not be stronger: for example, between Jeremiah and 2 Kings there is the shared final chapter (2 Kgs 25; Jer. 52), so that the two volumes are linked together by the same prose *inclusio* and effectively incorporated into each other. Rabbinic tradition made Jeremiah the author of Kings and Jeremiah, but our modernist and postmodernist approaches to reading the Bible favour abandoning the naïve attribution of imagined authorship to ancient texts. While there are very many explanations on offer by biblical scholars for the similarities between the so-called deuteronomistic literature and the book of Jeremiah I shall save a forest of trees here by simplifying my account of the literary-linguistic network constituted by the scrolls of Kings and Jeremiah.[18]

I do not imagine or believe that the book of Jeremiah was written by the prophet Jeremiah or by the scribe Baruch: that is, I do not believe that Jeremiah 36 provides a model of how the book was written. I have many reasons for such lack of belief: I do not believe that Jeremiah and Baruch went around together during the period when the Roman imperial forces destroyed Jerusalem nor do I believe that Baruch wrote the apocalypse attributed to him. So why should I believe that Baruch wrote the book of Jeremiah? I accept the literary point that the pair of characters, Jeremiah and Baruch, represent a topos in biblical and extra-

---

17. *The Postmodern Bible*, p. 130 (italicized words in original).

18. For an interesting but inconclusive treatment of the issues involved here see Walter Gross (ed.), *Jeremia und die 'deuteronomistische Bewegung'* (BBB, 98; Weinheim: Beltz Athenäum Verlag, 1995).

biblical literature—a sort of Don Quixote and Sancho Panza of such literature![19] I do not think, however, that prophets went about the land of ancient Palestine, accompanied by their amanuenses and dictating to them their oracles, parables or memoirs. This negative faith statement is another way of saying that I have no evidence to warrant such a view of the origins of prophetic scrolls. The anonymous poems constituting the bulk of the book of Jeremiah do not strike me as being the single output of one writer who can in turn be identified as the prophet Jeremiah. The linguistic diversity, formal contradictions and multiple voices resonant in the text do not strike me as coming from one voice, author or source. I think an argument could be mounted for saying that Jeremiah 36 represents an aetiology (or legitimation claim) for claiming that the *written form* of the *spoken words* of Jeremiah constituted 'the words of YHWH'.[20] I think it is arguable that the narrative in Jeremiah 36 may also be an intimation (or claim of legitimation) of the scribal transformation of oral prophecy into inscripturated scrolls, but I would have to admit that there may be many different ways of reading this narrative and allegorizing its signification in the Jeremiah tradition.[21] If we treat the collections of poems in the prophetic writings as anthologies—an approach which I no longer favour because I do not think that there is a huge reservoir of prophetic poetry not included in these so-called anthologies!—then I would have to say that there is a high degree of *leakage* between the different collections. I think the term 'intertextuality' describes this leakage phenomenon better than more traditional readings of it as borrowings or dependence. A sweep of the book of Jeremiah would reveal many such intertextual instances (e.g. read Jer. 48 with Isa. 15–16, or Jer. 49.12-22 with Obad. 1–4, or Jer. 30–31 with Isa. 40–55, or Jer. 11–20 with the book of Psalms[22]).

19. Cf. Carroll, 'Jeremiah, Intertextuality and *Ideologiekritik*', pp. 25-26.

20. See Davies, *Scribes and Schools*, pp. 119-20.

21. Cf. Carroll, *Jeremiah*, pp. 656-68; Carroll, 'Manuscripts Don't Burn—Inscribing the Prophetic Tradition: Reflections on Jeremiah 36', in Matthias Augustin and Klaus-Dietrich Schunck (eds.), *'Dort ziehen Schiffe dahin ...'*: *Collected Communications to the XIVth Congress of the International Organization for the Study of the Old Testament, Paris 1992* (BEATAJ, 28; Frankfurt on Main: Peter Lang, 1996), pp. 31-42.

22. Much of the material and analysis may be found in Pierre E. Bonnard, *Le Psautier selon Jérémie: Influence littéraire et spirituelle de Jérémie sur trente-trois psaumes* (LD, 26; Paris: Cerf, 1960). I would, however, read the data very

Within the book of Jeremiah itself it is easy to recognize many inter-textual strategies at work: the inclusios, chiastic structures, repetitions, meditations on other texts, echoes, borrowings and interweavings of all such echoes, etc. A simple comparison of the Hebrew and Greek texts of Jeremiah will serve to make the intertextual point. Cycles of material in the book reveal a conscious rearrangement and organization of mate-rial—disrupted by time, transmission and further redactional transfor-mations—which can hardly owe anything to the imagined historical circumstances of an equally imagined prophet. The many repetitions (e.g. 6.13-15 = 8.10-12; 11.20 = 20.12; 16.14-15 = 23.7-8; 23.19-20 = 30.23-24) indicate a fair degree of reflectivity going on in the Hebrew version of the book. The interweavings of *Leitwörter* signalled by Jer. 1.10 and used throughout the book suggest an intertextual *Holzweg* (forest path) running through the book of Jeremiah. A reading of the so-called temple sermon in 7.1-15, its reception narrative in ch, 26, the development and closure of ch. 26 in Jeremiah 36, with its intertext of 2 Kings 22, ought to make all readers of the book of Jeremiah reflect on matters narratological and intertextual rather than on matters authorial. Each section looks like and *is* a reading (every reading is a *re*reading) of the previous textual pericope in the development of paradigms of response to the prophetic word. There is even a direct intertext from Mic. 3.12 adduced in 26.18 both to signal the intertextual weave and to make it more interesting. This is all didactic and ideological and it demonstrates the intertextual nature of the construction of the book of Jeremiah.

A further set of examples of intertextual readings may be seen in the treatment of the relevant kings of Judah in the books of Jeremiah and of Isaiah. Here the *intertext* for both prophetic collections may well be the material in 2 Kings 15–25: this claim is based on the view that the colophons which introduce the prophetic books link the activity of the named prophets to the reigns of kings *narrated in the volumes of Kings*. The activity of Isaiah is represented as having taken place during the reigns of Uzziah, Jotham, Ahaz and Hezekiah (Isa. 1.1), with narratives set against such a background (Isa. 6–11; 36–39), and Jeremiah's activ-ities are situated in the reigns of Josiah, Jehoiakim and Zedekiah (Jer. 1.1-3), with a collection of poems associated with these kings (21.11–23.6) and various narratives related to specific kings (Jer. 3.6-10; 21-24;

differently from Bonnard and in pursuit of a fundamentally different hermeneutic of the Jeremiah text.

25-29; 32-36; 37-40; 45). To read all this material intertextually is to undertake a complex reading of very different texts which will bear a considerable degree of interpretative variation according to different readers.[23] All I can say here is this: comparing and contrasting the inter-textualities of Isaiah and Jeremiah on the kings of Judah highlights the essential positiveness of Isaiah's interrelationship with the kings of Judah and the essential negativity of Jeremiah's relations with the kings. There are, of course, some ambiguities in these relationships (Isaiah and Hezekiah, Jeremiah and Zedekiah), but taking the narratives and poetry intertextually I would tend to the opinion that the textualities of the matter are paradigmatic representations of positive and negative responses to monarchic rule. That is, as befits Isaiah's name the kings are associated with salvation (especially Isa. 7–11; 39.8) and as befits Jeremiah's quintessentially negative attitude and message the kings are associated with doom and destruction (with some allowance for ambi-guity and ambivalence). Studying the relationships between the two very different prophets and their teamed monarchs would provide a bright graduate student with a fine study in the intertextualities of biblical prophecy.

What strikes me when reading the book of Jeremiah is the sense that in the first place the writers of the book were readers of other scrolls. That is the nub of intertextuality: writers of texts are first readers of other texts. While the intertext may not always be recoverable, the intertext is 'already read'—to quote Barthes—and that 'al*ready* read' (note the repeated 'read'!) is the key to intertextuality. Reading the book of Jeremiah in intertextual ways makes us switch tracks or change roads in that we stop looking for original speakers whose utterances we would like to think were written down and then transmitted faithfully over millennia. Oral cultures do not work that way. The producers of scrolls were first readers of scrolls and in their scrolls carried on dialogues with other scrolls. A trace of such an activity may be detected in Jeremiah 36 where the burnt scroll is the precedent for writing the second scroll which is represented as an expansion of the previous

---

23. For readings which are very different from my own see Christoph Hard-meier, *Prophetie im Streit vor der Untergang Judas: Erzählkommunikative Studien zur Entstehungssituation der Jesaja- und Jeremiaerzählungen in II Reg 18–20 und Jer 37–40* (BZAW, 187; Berlin: W. de Gruyter, 1989), and Christopher R. Seitz, *Theology in Conflict: Reactions to the Exile in the Book of Jeremiah* (BZAW, 176; Berlin: W. de Gruyter, 1989).

scroll (36.32)—whence came the material for that expansion?[24] It was
certainly not just a copy of the first scroll but an expanded and different
scroll—perhaps including the tale of the first scroll's burning? We are
now into intertextual speculations and forced to recognize the need for
an intertextual account of the composition, redaction, development and
transmission of the scroll we associate with the book of the prophet
Jeremiah. For me that book of Jeremiah is a reading of readings.
The intertextual partners may well have been, *inter alia*, Deuteronomy,
the so-called Deuteronomistic History, lists of kings, other prophetic
scrolls, etc. The story of Jeremiah the prophet may well have been a
level or strand of the book related intertextually to the stories of the
prophets, a metanarrative itself, interwoven into the scrolls forming the
collection Samuel–Kings. The topos 'the fall of Jerusalem'—not so
much the so-called historical 'event' itself: which is barely touched on
except in the briefest forms in 2 Kings 24–25 and Jeremiah 39–40—as
a metaphysical or mythological event in the (distant) past appears to be
a major focus of Isaiah, Jeremiah, Ezekiel and many of the prophetic
scrolls. The readings and interreadings in all the different scrolls, with
their constant intertextual weavings and interweavings, are all discrete,
different and interrelated variations on that single topos 'the destruction
of Jerusalem by the God YHWH by the hand of his servant Nebuchadrezzar'.

A somewhat different intertextual reading of Jeremiah is developed
in William McKane's magisterial commentary on Jeremiah where he
develops the notion of 'a rolling corpus'.[25] This excavative approach to
the text holds good promise for a highly intertextual account of the
composition of Jeremiah and it does seem to me to be one of the (few)
good suggestions to come out of the books written on Jeremiah in

---

24. I must admit to having been disappointed on first reading Marc-Alain
Ouaknin's very fine volume *The Burnt Book: Reading the Talmud* (trans. Llewellyn
Brown [orig. *Le livre brûlé: Lire le Talmud*, 1986]; Princeton, NJ: Princeton University Press, 1995) to find that it had nothing to say about the burning of Jeremiah's scroll. Of course Ouaknin should not be blamed for my disappointment,
after all he was not writing about the Hebrew Bible nor about the unhappy experiences of Jews under Christian hegemony when the Talmud was regularly burned by
godly Christians, but about something quite different.

25. William McKane, *A Critical and Exegetical Commentary on Jeremiah*. I.
Introduction and Commentary on Jeremiah I–XXV (ICC; Edinburgh: T. & T. Clark,
1986), pp. l-lxxxiii.

the1980s.[26] The idea of texts generating other texts is a quintessentially intertextual approach to reading Jeremiah. I would like to see McKane's major idea developed along speculative lines to include some account of a *locus*, most likely in old Jerusalem during the late Persian or early Greek periods (or later than these conservative estimates), where writers worked with and on scrolls producing further scrolls from their own readings of the scrolls to hand. The caves out at Qumran may point to such a location and such an activity, but Jerusalem would make a better location for such scroll-intensive productions. I find McKane's reading of the text of Jeremiah as having given rise to further texts, many without any historical or extratextual referents, a highly imaginative and constructive account of the production of the book of Jeremiah.

Jeremiah is a very long scroll, with a very long history of such scroll-making. We know of shorter scrolls of Jeremiah represented by the Greek versions of the book, so we do have comparative material for discussing the intertextual nature of the production of the Jeremiah tradition in written form. What I would really like to see explored now are questions about *the necessary and sufficient conditions* for the production of scrolls as long and as complex as the scrolls of Isaiah, Jeremiah, Ezekiel and the Book of the Twelve. The province of Yehud, with its ancient town (city?) of Jerusalem, was a small and excessively modest backwater of the Persian Empire. Without the influx of intellectuals and writers from Babylon and other more central areas of the empire, I do not see how the twin luxuries of materials and time—not to mention adequate resources of money—could have been utilized to produce such lengthy scrolls as those of the primary narrative, the so-called Deuteronomistic History and the prophets, not to mention the many editions of Jeremiah. Perhaps the Hellenistic period would be a better time to which such scroll production should be assigned rather than to the Achaemenid era. At the same time, because of all the intertextual

26. I have commented on the main commentaries of the 1980s in 'Radical Clashes of Will and Style: Recent Commentary Writing on the Book of Jeremiah', *JSOT* 45 (1989), pp. 99-114; 'Arguing about Jeremiah: Recent Studies and the Nature of a Prophetic Book', in John A. Emerton (ed.), *Congress Volume: Leuven 1989* (VTSup, 43; Leiden: E.J. Brill, 1991), pp. 222-35; and to some extent in 'Surplus Meaning and the Conflict of Interpretation: A Dodecade of Jeremiah Studies (1984–95)', *Currents in Research: Biblical Studies* 4 (1996), pp. 115-59. For a very different estimation of the 1980s Jeremiah commentaries see Walter Brueggemann, 'Jeremiah: Intense Criticism/Thin Interpretation', *Int* 42 (1988), pp. 268-80.

connections and traces between Jeremiah and the other scrolls in the Hebrew Bible we have to assume a literary centre producing, repro- ducing, maintaining, developing and transmitting such a considerable quantity of lengthy scrolls. We cannot just assume that the kinds of brief, lapidary inscriptions so far found, interpreted and beloved by biblical epigraphists were necessarily constitutive of such huge scrolls. Temple bureaucracies, bourses or taxation centres—if difference there be between these complexes—are the most obvious centres for such scroll production and given long periods of stability, during which materials were readily available with the necessary financial resources, it is possible that the scrolls constituting the Hebrew Bible came into existence.[27] As for the poet-sage-scribes who wrote the scrolls, what can I say? Those who wish Jeremiah to have been such a major poet- sage-scribe will not be deterred from following their own path whatever I say about the intertextual nature of the Jeremiah scroll. But let me remind such interpreters even then of the obvious intertextual nature of any great poet's work, taking my clue from Derek Walcott, a major Western poet of our time:

> Fear of imitation obsesses minor poets. But in any age a common genius almost indistinguishably will show itself, and the perpetuity of this genius is the only valid tradition, not the tradition which categorizes poetry by epochs and by schools. We know that the great poets have no wish to be different, no time to be original, that their originality emerges only when they have absorbed all the poetry which they have read, entire, that their first work appears to be the accumulation of other people's trash, but that they become bonfires, that it is only academics and frightened poets who talk of Beckett's debt to Joyce.[28]

27. For a parallel speculation see Philip R. Davies, *In Search of 'Ancient Israel'* (JSOTSup, 148; Sheffield: JSOT Press, rev. edn, 1995 [1992]), p. 120. In my pub- lished version of this paper 'Jeremiah, Intertextuality and *Ideologiekritik*', pp. 24- 26, I discuss further these matters, but will omit that discussion here for reasons of space.

28. 'The Muse of History', in Derek Walcott, *What the Twilight Says: Essays* (London: Faber & Faber, 1998), pp. 36-64 (62) (original essay 1974). I use this citation from Walcott because it appears in the section 'On History as Exile', so has a nice fit with diasporic literature such as Jeremiah. I am rather conscious that Wal- cott's last clause could be aimed at all those scholars who talk about 'dependence' in relation to Jeremiah and the other prophets. Sorry about that, but truth is where you find it!

Ideological Criticism

> An ideology is really 'holding us' only when we do not feel any opposi-
> tion between it and reality—that is, when the ideology succeeds in deter-
> mining the mode of our everyday experience of reality itself ... An
> ideology really succeeds when even the facts which at first sight contra-
> dict it start to function as arguments in its favour.
>
> Slavoj Žižek[29]

> Ideology and pluralism are incompatible.
>
> John Schwarzmantel[30]

Before space disappears altogether I should move from the intertextual
to the ideological as the second prong of my approach to rethinking
Jeremiah studies. However, I shall not pay as much attention to this
second aspect of my approach to Jeremiah because I have written
frequently elsewhere about ideological aspects of the book of Jeremiah.
I am deeply conscious of the fact that, in spite of the fact that I have
been using the word 'ideology' with reference to the book of Jeremiah
for some 20 years now, American audiences dislike intensely the use of
such a word in conjunction with the Bible and especially in relation to
Jeremiah studies.[31] In recent years I have had to attend to the ideological, both in terms of definitions and in relation to praxis, because so
much of the fuss created in the Composition of Jeremiah Consultation
meetings has focused on the use of this term and my scholarly work
found itself having to deal with such definitions and analyses of the
term as practised by members of the Guild. My trip to South Africa in
1993 to lecture at the universities there involved me in a series of
lectures and seminars on the topic of 'Ideology and the Bible'. There in

29. Slavoj Žižek, 'How Did Marx Invent the Symptom?', in *idem*, *The Sublime
Object of Ideology* (London: Verso, 1998 [1989]), pp. 11-53 (49). See also *idem*,
'The Spectre of Ideology', in *idem* (ed.), *Mapping Ideology* (Mapping; London:
Verso, 1994), pp. 1-33.

30. John Schwarzmantel, *The Age of Ideology: Political Ideologies from the
American Revolution to Postmodern Times* (London: Macmillan, 1998), p. 173.

31. See Robert P. Carroll, *From Chaos to Covenant: Uses of Prophecy in the
Book of Jeremiah* (London: SCM Press, 1981), pp. 13-18 (Xpress Reprints; London: SCM Press, 1996). Mary Callaway has graciously pointed out to me the error
of my ways in doing this, but I guess for me the ideological is demonstrated precisely in such dislike of and refusal to use the term to describe theological attitudes
and masking operations currently dominant in biblical studies.

the heartland and home of the doctrine and practice of apartheid, and its concomitant fundamentalistic aspects of the Christian religion, on what else could I possibly lecture? Some of those lectures and seminars have been published, so this essay should be read as a continuation of that debate in relation to ideological criticism and the Bible.[32] The South African dimension of this essay need not detain us here, but I must say just one thing about the post-apartheid society I found myself lecturing in when I was out there in 1993:[33] it is one thing to talk about ideology and religion or the Bible in the abstract terms typical of academic discourse, but it is an entirely different thing to encounter the actual material results of the praxis of such an ideological interpretation of the Bible. The wretchedness of Black existence in South Africa as a direct result of the implementation of a separatist reading of the Bible provided a far better *Ideologiekritik* of the Bible than anything I could have imagined before my visit.[34] Having learned so much about ideological criticism from Ferdinand Deist, it was a fascinating but terrifying experience to encounter the results of the actual implementation of such an ideological reading of the Bible.[35] After I returned from South Africa I resolved to go on with my insistence that the profession and practice of biblical studies requires the serious attention to the discipline that is

32. For the record see Robert P. Carroll, 'As Seeing the Invisible: Ideology in Bible Translation', *JNSL* 19 (1993), pp. 79-93; 'On Representation in the Bible: An *Ideologiekritik* Approach', *JNSL* 20.2 (1994), pp. 1-15; 'An Infinity of Traces: On Making an Inventory of our Ideological Holdings: An Introduction to *Ideologiekritik* in Biblical Studies', *JNSL* 21.2 (1995), pp. 25-43; 'Jeremiah, Intertextuality and *Ideologiekritik*', *JNSL* 22.1 (1996), pp. 15-34.

33. The universities I lectured in and held seminars included UNISA (Pretoria), the University of Pretoria, University of Natal at Durban-Westville, Gerald West's place at Pietermaritzberg (Natal), University of Stellenbosch and the University of Cape Town.

34. I have tried to say something about this experience in my contribution to Gerald West's forthcoming major volume *The Bible in Africa* (Leiden: E.J. Brill, forthcoming 2000): see Carroll, 'Africa, Bible, Criticism: Reflections on the Rhetorics of a Visit'.

35. Ferdinand Deist's sudden death (of a massive heart attack) in July 1997 while teaching in Heidelberg was a terrible shock for all his many friends and a shattering blow to biblical studies in South Africa. I have acknowledged his great influence on my own thinking by developing my thinking about ideology further in my contribution to his Memorial Volume: see Carroll, 'Biblical Idolatry: *Ideologiekritik*, Biblical Studies and the Problematics of Ideology', *JNSL* 24.1 (1998), pp. 101-14.

necessarily imposed by a thoroughgoing ideological criticism approach to reading the text and its reception history (or its *Wirkungsgeschichte*).

Defining the nature and practice of ideology is open to much discussion and many heated debates, so I will not repeat here matters pertaining to definitions because they can be found spread throughout my numerous articles on the topic and may be read there by all interested parties.[36] While I am aware of the claim that some scholars would make that, in plain-speaking terms, 'texts do not have ideologies', I would be prepared to agree with such a claim provided that we moved the task of ideological criticism to the reception of such non-ideological, meaning-neutral texts.[37] For readers and writers of texts may well possess ideologies which can be inscribed in texts by reading and exegetical techniques and/or put into practice as a consequence of reading strategies allied to prevailing ideological forces in culture. Where ideology is to be located in any society may be debated, but all practical readings of texts ought to be scrutinized for traces of inscribed or imposed ideology.[38] In the West where the Bible has been such an important generator of cultural practices it would be wise to keep a seasoned eye open for the ideological.[39] Wherever traditional and fundamentalistic readings of the Bible flourish there is a strong case for doing ideological criticism of the Bible and its reception because whether we admit it (to ourselves) or not, in the West political

36. In the more recently published paper 'Jeremiah, Intertextuality and *Ideologiekritik*' I have used the writings of Martin Seliger to define ideology (pp. 18-19, 34), but would want to supplement such definitions here with the work of Slavoj Žižek on ideology.

37. See Stephen Fowl, 'Texts Don't Have Ideologies', *BibInt* 3 (1995), pp. 15-34. In my 'Biblical Ideolatry' article I have addressed Fowl's point to some extent: see Carroll, 'Biblical Ideolatry: *Ideologiekritik*, Biblical Studies and the Problematics of Ideology', esp. pp. 102-105.

38. For doubts about the value of ideological criticism and related problems see Raymond Geuss, *The Idea of a Critical Theory: Habermas and the Frankfurt School* (Modern European Philosophy; Cambridge: Cambridge University Press, 1981); Michael Rosen, *On Voluntary Servitude: False Consciousness and the Theory of Ideology* (Cambridge: Polity Press, 1996).

39. It is still too early to find adequate published approaches to the Bible as culture and in relation to cultural studies, but see the excellent volume: J. Cheryl Exum and Stephen D. Moore (eds.), *Biblical Studies/Cultural Studies: The Third Sheffield Colloquium* (JSOTSup, 266; GCT, 7; Sheffield: Sheffield Academic Press, 1998).

authorities frequently use religious attitudes and beliefs to back up their imposition of ideological values on societies. I frequently hear on the radio (less often on television) or read in the newspapers that some repressive proposal or political initiative for oppression or the imposition of imagined values on a section of society is being backed by clerics claiming to have biblical warrants for imposing such tyranny on their neighbours. So uses of the Bible may be ideological in any given society or culture, whatever we as 'sophisticated' scholars may imagine to be the case with reference to the text and its ideological possibilities. Political, cultural and ideological forces in Western societies seldom need to stoop to crude forms of oppression without being able to rely on support from upholders of and believers in the Bible for sanctions and warrants, so the task of ideological criticism in relation to the Bible is unlikely ever to disappear from so-called civilized society in the West as *a necessary scrutiny*.[40]

So how do I imagine the notion of ideology applies in relation to the book of Jeremiah? This is a question about *reading*: how is the book of Jeremiah to be read in our time? This is where the twin notions of intertextuality and ideological criticism meet and mesh together. Recognition of the intertextuality of texts leads on to ideological criticism because in the generation of multiple readings and contested sites of meaning it becomes necessary to ask basic questions about *who* determines any specific reading and *under what conditions* all such readings take place, are produced or constructed—see the first Bakhtin epigraph to this paper. Timothy Beal, in his discussion of intertextuality and the Hebrew Bible, introduces into his analysis the notion of ideological criticism because such basic questions are necessarily directed at 'the reader's ideology':

> ... intertextuality leads quickly from musings on the Hebrew Bible's *surplus* of meaning to serious talk about biblical interpretation as *production* of meaning. The next step from there is to ask who, or what, controls the means of production. And controlling the means of

---

40. If further defining and analytical treatments of ideology are required see The Bible and Culture Collective, 'Ideological Criticism', in *The Postmodern Bible*, pp. 272-308; James H. Kavanagh, 'Ideology', in Frank Lentricchia and Thomas McLaughlin (eds.), *Critical Terms for Literary Study* (Chicago: University of Chicago Press, 2nd edn, 1995), pp. 306-20; Raymond Williams, 'Ideology', in *idem*, *Keywords: A Vocabulary of Culture and Society* (Glasgow: Fontana/Croom Helm, 1976), pp. 126-30.

production is always an ideological activity. Movement from the indeterminate 'general text' to particular practices of intertextual reading demands that one ask about the ideological limits, or 'strategies of containment' (Fredric Jameson 1981: 52-53), that make interpretation possible. It demands, in other words, *an ideological-critical approach to reading readings.*[41]

So while we may transfer the scrutiny of ideological criticism from the text to the practice of reading the text, we cannot avoid using an ideological-critical approach to readings of the Bible. For myself I am not so averse to reading the biblical text from the viewpoint of an ideological critcism approach because I imagine the writers of that text may well have possessed ideologies of their own. There again, perhaps we should locate ideology in the editors, transmitters and canonizers of the biblical text as well as in the reading communities which have received the Bible as part of their own ideological holdings. However the matter is analysed and scrutinized it does seem to me to be the case that there is plenty of work to be done by biblical scholars in pursuit of an ideological-critical reading of the Hebrew Bible.

Among the ideological aspects of the book of Jeremiah to which I would wish to draw attention are matters having to do with representations of the past and with the land. I read Jeremiah 2–20 as consisting of a series of instantiations of, what I have called, 'the writing off' aspect of the book.[42] That is, the past in its various forms—historical, legendary, social, political and religious—are all written off as having failed to maintain the purity of YHWH-worship. All the structures have been proved to be false: temple, kings, priests, prophets, sages and people. Nothing escapes the sweeping condemnatory modes of utterance attributed to the prophet Jeremiah. In effect, the book represents him as having written off all the forces, influences, institutions and structures which led to the destruction of Jerusalem by the Babylonians. Everything associated with the past, its beliefs, practices and institutions, is condemned and subverted by the fate of Jerusalem. There is, of course, an opposing line of thought running through Jeremiah 11–20

41. Timothy K. Beal, 'Ideology and Intertextuality: Surplus of Meaning and Controlling the Means of Production', in Fewell (ed.), *Reading between Texts*, pp. 25-34 (28: emphasis in original). The reference to Fredric Jameson is to Jameson, *The Political Unconscious: Narrative as a Socially Symbolic Act* (London: Methuen; Ithaca, NY: Cornell University Press, 1983).

42. Cf. Carroll, 'Jeremiah, Intertextuality and *Ideologiekritik*', pp. 28-30.

where Jeremiah is represented as speaking for 'the righteous' in the land (compare and contrast 5.1-6 and 12.1-4) and from time to time the edited text deconstructs its main thrust by admitting to the presence of good people in society. Yet a line such as 'because of what Manasseh the son of Hezekiah, king of Judah, did in Jerusalem' (15.4) renders the material on the righteous immaterial because no amount of righteous folk or justice-practising individuals (cf. 5.1-5) could have saved a society doomed because of the actions of *a king who was dead before Jeremiah was born*! Thus Jeremiah is a book crying out for a serious ideological-critical scrutiny in order to determine how its main ideological thrusts should be read.

Other ideological traces inscribed in the book of Jeremiah may be detected in the contrary representations of the Babylonians: Nebuchadrezzar as the servant of YHWH (25.1-14; 27–29) and Nebuchadrezzar as the dragon (50–51).[43] These seem to me to reflect differing (perhaps conflicting) values from a time when Jewish communities flourished in Palestine and in Babylonia and should be linked to the hostilities expressed against Jewish communities in Egypt (Jer. 44). Discourses about land are fundamental to the book, especially in relation to its possession, its loss and its subsequent retrieval. Behind these many textual moments may be traced aspects of land ideology which are so characteristic of the rest of the Hebrew Bible.[44] In the final analysis my reading of Jeremiah would see in the so-called final form of the text traces of ideological support for the communities of Jewish refugees deported from the land and living in Babylon, but not support for such deported communities living in Egypt. That kind of *partisan support* must reflect some ideological elements in the Persian-Greek periods because it makes such a sharp differentiation between discrete communities of deported people (cf. Jer. 24; 29; 44). It is not the case that the

43. I have tried to say something about these conflicting images in Carroll, 'Synchronic Deconstructions of Jeremiah: Diachrony to the Rescue? Reflections on Some Reading Strategies for Understanding Certain Problems in the Book of Jeremiah', in Johannes C. De Moor (ed.), *Synchronic or Diachronic? A Debate on Method in Old Testament Exegesis* (OTS, 34; Leiden: E.J. Brill, 1995), pp. 39-51 (esp. 46-50).

44. On such matters see Norman C. Habel, *The Land Is Mine: Six Biblical Land Ideologies* (Overtures to Biblical Theology; Minneapolis: Fortress Press, 1995), especially Chapter 5, 'Land as YHWH's Personal *naḥalah*: A Prophetic Ideology' (pp. 75-96).

book of Jeremiah represents support for all the groups of people who left Jerusalem during the onsalughts of the Babylonians. On the contrary, the book does not reflect *an ideology of diaspora* as such, but only those deported to Babylon and not those who may have fled to Egypt. In fact, reading the book of Jeremiah today leaves me with a very strong impression that it was produced for and on behalf of those Jewish communities in Babylon. Jews who chose to trace their origins to Babylon (cf. Abraham in the Genesis stories) would find patronage and empowerment in the book of Jeremiah, whereas Jews who traced their origins to Egypt (cf. Moses in the Exodus stories) would find no support in Jeremiah—rather the contrary. So I read the text of Jeremiah as a deeply ideological scroll, as well as a deeply intertextual book.[45]

Conclusion

The writers of the biblical texts produced their texts in conversation with all the other texts available to them and we try to read their texts in conversation with many other texts of our own. While we may scrutinize these texts for their ideological traces or the reception literature for such ideological traces, it is always very difficult for us to become aware of, or even to construct an inventory of, our own ideological holdings—especially when reading the Bible.[46] As Žižek says 'an ideology is really "holding us" only when we do not feel any opposition between it and reality'. Perhaps that is why American audiences have such difficulty recognizing or admitting to the ideological in relation to the Bible: they so comfortably exist within a biblically constructed ideology that they cannot recognize it for what it is. It 'succeeds in determining the mode of our everyday experience of reality itself' (Žižek). Yet without an ideological-critical analysis of the book of Jeremiah I find the text to be virtually unreadable today. This is where

45. In my OTL commentary I treat the ideological aspects of Jeremiah as 'interests' (*Interesse*): see Carroll, *Jeremiah*, pp. 69-82. Even at this distance from that commentary I still think I was on the right lines, though perhaps I could have worded the matter better, with more subtle distinctions and qualifications and at much greater length.

46. I have attempted to produce an inventory of my own ideological holdings *and failed*: see Robert P. Carroll, 'An Infinity of Traces: On Making an Inventory of our Ideological Holdings: An Introduction to *Ideologiekritik* in Biblical Studies', *JNSL* 21.2 (1995), pp. 25-43.

the notion of the unreadability of Jeremiah comes to the fore for me as a nightmare to disturb all our easy readings of the book. While I think I would prefer to continue to struggle to understand the book of Jeremiah in such a way as to respect its alterity and therefore to accept the risk of its unreadabilty rather than join all those well-sighted academics who appear to understand the book to the point where it no longer possesses any alterity at all, I suspect that many readers of Jeremiah would challenge this way of expressing the problem.[47]

To return to the Bakhtinian points with which this paper started, I would like to speculate a little about the implications of Mikhail Bakhtin's trope of the 'homecoming festival'. What Bakhtin had in mind was a notion of the narrative, text, suppressed history or whatever finally being allowed to speak to us. I will need some help here to elucidate Bakhtin's trope, so let me cite Michael Gardiner's reading of Bakhtin's notion of a homecoming:

> Like Walter Benjamin, perhaps the Western Marxist he has the most affinity with, Bakhtin therefore exhorts us to probe the gaps and silences, the fractures and fault-lines that expose the operation of a monologism which seeks to effect an ideological closure in order to 'blast a specific era out of the homogeneous course of history'. Only then can the meaning of a suppressed history have its own 'homecoming festival'; that is, be allowed to speak to us, and we in turn have the linguistic capacity and the cultural resources to answer it in a 'free and familiar' manner, without fear of censure or retribution. But Bakhtin provides no elaborate epistemological or eschatological justification for this stance, he makes no dogmatic appeal to 'science', 'truth', or 'the historical mission of the proletariat'. In short, his is a critical hermeneutics without guarantees. The Bakhtinian justification of critique is a moral one, which is ultimately connected to our immediate ethical concerns in the sphere of practical social intercourse. This is what could be termed Bakhtin's gamble, his 'Pascalian wager'.[48]

---

47. The original form of this sentence reflected a polemical engagement with my critics in Jeremiah Studies ('Jeremiah, Intertextuality and *Ideologiekritik*', p. 31), but my modifications to the original article have excised such disagreements. If there is anything I really regret about my participation in the Consultation on the Composition of the Book of Jeremiah it is the bad feelings ('bad blood'?) generated among the audience. I regret it but there is nothing I can do to make people like my approaches to the biblical text—can or would, that is.

48. Michael Gardiner, *The Dialogics of Critique: M.M. Bakhtin and the Theory of Ideology* (London: Routledge, 1992), p. 194.

This is music to my ears—wonderful stuff! I am not sure that I understand it completely nor that I can apply it immediately to reading the book of Jeremiah, but it does provide me with food for thought and powerfully engages me in a thoughtful and a reflective mood. Various phrases pick themselves out of that commentary on Bakhtin: 'the fractures and fault-lines that expose the operation of a monologism which seeks to effect an ideological closure in order to "blast a specific era out of the homogeneous course of history" '.[49] This is such a fine statement that I could refer it to the book of Jeremiah without having to make any further adjustments for context or focus. Following Gardiner's reading of Bakhtin I would want to say that the notion of an ideological closure is quite apparent in the way the book of Jeremiah removes from history the people of Jerusalem left behind after the destruction and also the people of the various deportations *except to Babylon in 597* and writes out of history the Jews of Egypt. Opposing such a suppressed history is where an ideological-critical reading of Jeremiah has a cutting edge to it and warrants our protest and objection to a text which is so careless with people's lives and hopes. Speaking for myself I would love to be able to read the book of Jeremiah 'without fear of censure or retribution', but that homecoming is a long way off I think. Another phrase which catches my eye and engages my imagination is 'a critical hermeneutics without guarantees'. I think all my work on Jeremiah has been geared to the construction of a critical hermeneutics, but I find the aspect of 'without guarantees' to be the really painful side of hermeneutics. It makes for a *Sisyphean* mode of reading the biblical text, without hope or guarantee that any reading will work itself out in positive or edifying results.[50] It certainly is extremely subversive of contemporary theological readings of the text which are always seeking to be edifying something or somebody and always in pursuit of a hermeneutics *with* guarantees. Other phrases which catch my attention are 'immediate ethical concerns' and 'Pascalian wager'.[51] So from my own

49. This particular phrase puts me in mind of Keith Whitelam's passionately argued thesis in his book *The Invention of Ancient Israel: The Silencing of Palestinian History* (London: Routledge, 1996), even though I would want to take it differently in relation to Jeremiah studies.

50. I am no stranger to Sisyphean readings of the Bible: see Carroll, 'The Sisyphean Task of Biblical Transformation', *SJT* 30 (1977), pp. 501-21.

51. The allusion to Pascal's wager triggers off memories of George Steiner's fine book *Real Presences: Is There Anything in What We Say?* (London: Faber &

point of view I would have to say that a 'homecoming festival' for the book of Jeremiah for me would consist, at least, of a series of readings which were strongly intertextual and ideological-critical, reflecting a critical hermeneutics with attention to our own immediate ethical concerns—including a strongly *ethical* reading of Jeremiah. An *ethical* reading of Jeremiah? Now there would be a challenge worthy of the next century of scholars working in Jeremiah studies. Such an engagement with Bakhtinian values, however, makes me feel that I have hardly begun to read the book of Jeremiah seriously yet.

How then do I think that the twin approaches of intertextuality and ideological criticism can help to progress forward the reading and study of Jeremiah? It would take a further essay to answer this question and, as I have no desire to depart greatly from the original paper given to the Consultation in Washington, I shall not attempt to write that paper here. Suffice it to say, I believe both approaches remove from the agenda the traditional obsessions with authorship and authenticity-hunting around the notions of primary and secondary sources—so that renders the bulk of conventional historical scholarship merely academic! Historical research is fine and dandy as an academic subject but there are other approaches to literature and texts which need not become so obsessive with the search for imagined history. I think notions of intertextuality and ideological criticism take us away from current obsessions with canons and the canonical, rescue the Hebrew Bible from its ecclesiastical captivity—a much more catastrophic captivity than the Babylonian captivity ever was for the people of ancient Jerusalem and Judah—and invite us to contemplate more complex networks of texts and values embedded in such texts than ever seems to be the case among canonical conformists. Much more interesting vistas of scholarship open up for the twenty-first century, among which I would wish to emphasize the fact that any ideology itself is much less well served by intertextuality and even less well served by a pluralism of approaches to reading the text of Jeremiah (see the Schwarzmantel citation at the head of the section 'Ideological Criticism').[52] We may argue about the

Faber, 1989) and the very strong Steinerian influence on my *Wolf in the Sheepfold* book.

52. I would really need the space of a further chapter to explain why ideology is so poorly served by intertextuality and pluralism—in terms of dilution, opposition, construction, etc.—but will not take up that space here. The two previously published versions of my 'Intertextuality and the Book of Jeremiah' paper (see n. 4

relationship between ideology and the text, but I have in mind here the ideologies represented by the reception of the text, the canonizing communities and all the different ways in which contemporary readings of the Bible feed into the dominant ideology of Western religious values and communities. For no matter how much the methodologies and discipline of biblical studies may change, the main beneficiaries of biblical scholarship always seem to remain various mainstream branches of the Christian churches. How that can continue to be the case, *after* so many radical reformations, *after* Spinoza and the subsequent centuries of radical rethinking of everything, *after* Thomas Paine and rationalism, *after* Kant and the Enlightenment, *after* the Einsteinian scientific revolution and *after* two world wars and the death camps of the *univers concentrationnaire*, and even in these postmodern times, beggars belief and defeats my powers of imagination. Ideology must be at work somewhere to have produced such a state of affairs and such ideological forces require serious analytical work in order to be unmasked. That is the promise ideological criticism holds out to (post)-modern scholarship on the Bible and intertextuality represents one way of making good that promise.

above) contain within the concluding section some observations pertinent to this claim.

WHEN METAPHOR BECOMES MYTH:
A SOCIO-LINGUISTIC READING OF JEREMIAH

William R. Domeris

The writings, attributed to the prophet Jeremiah, have shaped our understanding of the socioreligious reality of late pre-exilic and early exilic Israel. Unfortunately, texts rarely mirror their social setting, with any accuracy, but are instead the projection of that reality (as intended or unintended) by the author(s).[1] The power of the writings attributed to the prophet Jeremiah is unmistakable. His vivid language and unforgettable metaphors of cisterns, potters and unfaithful wives create a convincing picture of the social and religious reality of that time. Scarce wonder, therefore, that generations of readers assumed that this was indeed the reality experienced by most Israelites of the time. They were led by the author's literary strategy into an acceptance of the ideology of the text, as a true reflection of the values and norms of the wider society.

Jeremiah, as we shall see, represented not the society at large but rather an antisociety (the Yahweh-alone party) and the text follows the format of an antilanguage. As a representative of the prophetic minority, Jeremiah sought to devalue the dominant ideology of the popular religion. His metaphors, like that of the lusty asses, intentionally skewed the position of his rivals. Consequently, he also left modern scholars with the difficult task of sorting out myth from fact, the apparent promiscuity of the popular religion from vivid metaphor.

---

1. See further T. Eagelton, *Marxism and Literary Criticism* (London: Methuen, 1976), and *The Function of Criticism* (London: Verso, 1984). Also P. Macherey, *A Theory of Literary Production* (London: Routledge & Kegan Paul, 1978), who clearly warns against the simplistic reading of a text as a true reflection of the society in which it came to birth (pp. 105-56, esp. 130).

The composite nature of the text of Jeremiah[2] militates against a simplistic historical reading of the text, and forces us to engage with 'the redactional circles and levels of tradition which have *created* the words and the story of Jeremiah ben Hilkiah of Anathoth!',[3] and to seek out that community whose interests coincided with the writing of the text. But if interpreting the written text is difficult, any attempt to penetrate behind its cover, is even more complicated.[4] The intention of this essay is to show how an understanding of sociolinguistics might enable the critical reader to appreciate the strategy of the author(s) of Jeremiah, and to delve behind the metaphorical flights of fancy. Whether one is closer to the reality of the times is debatable, but at least one is made aware of the creative process upon which the author has embarked.

Language as Social Semiotic

Most social actions have a language component, which enables communication from the most basic of levels to the most abstract. Sociolinguistics recognizes this social dimension of language, its place in social intercourse and its vital role within the regulation and maintenance of one's social order. Language resembles a code, complete with signs and signals. The child learning a language is involved in a social process in which 'an exchange of meanings with significant others' takes place.[5]

The sociolinguist M.A.K. Halliday writes:

> Language does not consist of sentences; it consists of text, or discourse—the exchange of meanings in interpersonal contexts of one kind or another. The contexts in which meanings are exchanged are not devoid of social value; a context of speech is itself a semiotic construct, having a form (derived from the culture) that enables the participants to predict features of the prevailing register—and hence to understand one another as they go along.[6]

2. See further R. Carroll, *Jeremiah: A Commentary* (OTL; London: SCM Press, 1986), pp. 36-47.

3. Carroll, *Jeremiah*, p. 47.

4. So Carroll, *Jeremiah*, p. 81.

5. M.A.K. Halliday, *Language as Social Semiotic: The Social Interpretation of Language and Meaning* (London: Edward Arnold, 1978), p. 1.

6. Halliday, *Language as Social Semiotic*, p. 2.

The child's understanding of reality cannot be separated from the semantic construction of that same reality. In effect, his or her reality is encoded in a semantic system. The 'prevailing register' is the technical term used for the particular list of signs (codes) which makes possible the communication process in a specific societal setting. Failure to read the prevailing register correctly may result in misunderstanding and misinterpretation, which often happens in cross-cultural exchanges. Innocuous terms in one culture may become fiendish traps in another.

Language, according to sociolinguists, should be understood therefore as a *social semiotic*. Halliday writes:

> A social reality (or a 'culture') is itself an edifice of meanings—a semiotic construct. In this perspective, language is one of the semiotic systems that constitute a culture; one that is distinctive in that it also serves as an encoding system for many (though not all) of the others. This is in summary form what is meant by the formulation 'language as a social semiotic'. It means interpreting language within a sociocultural context, in which the culture itself is interpreted in semiotic terms—as an information system ... [7]

Tenor, mood, inflections and gestures all contribute to the complex construct we call language. Each culture produces its own set of linguistic codes, for as human cultures differ one from another so the products of that culture (like language) also differ. Language mirrors the culture in which it plays a part. As Halliday observes, 'Language actively symbolizes the social system, representing metaphorically in its patterns of variation the variation that characterizes human cultures. This is what enables people to play with the variation in language, using it to create meanings of a social kind.'[8] By invoking the subtleties of the language, the speaker or author reinforces the social distinctions of that culture, in the ongoing process of the creation of meaning.

Sociolinguistics, as a branch of linguistics, may be applied, fruitfully, to the study of the Bible.[9] In the first instance, sociolinguistics warns us

---

7. Halliday, *Language as Social Semiotic*, p. 2.
8. Halliday, *Language as Social Semiotic*, p. 3.
9. On the use of sociolingusitics and specifically antilanguage, see M.A.K. Halliday, *Language as Social Semiotic*; *Language, Context and Text* (Oxford: Oxford University Press, 1985); and R.T. Bell, *Sociolinguistics: Goals, Approaches and Problems* (London: B.T. Batsford, 1976). Sociolinguistic studies of the New Testament include N.R. Petersen, *The Gospel of John and the Sociology of Light: Language and Characterization in the Fourth Gospel* (Valley Forge, PA: Trinity

of the gap between ourselves and the world of the Bible. When the language is confined to a text, particularly an ancient text like Jeremiah, the modern reader often loses the ability to predict the 'features of the prevailing register'. Instead we use our own prevailing register, with consequent anachronisms. Secondly, while we have been aware of such stylistic features as irony, metaphor or alliteration, we have not always taken cognisance of the author's role within his or her social context, and in particular of his or her creation of an alternative social reality through the text. We read the text as the mirror of the society of that time, and to some extent that is true. But mirrors, like those of the ancient world, both reflect and distort reality. We gaze through 'a glass darkly' instead of seeing 'face to face', for what we are observing is the author's projected reality, his or her deliberate portrait of their society, and not the historical setting in which that society existed.[10] We ride with the authors on their flights of fancy, at the same time seeking to separate myth from metaphor, truth from literary fiction.

Jeremiah in Sociolinguistic Perspective

Jeremiah (or the authors who write in his name), like all other authors, embarked upon the process of communication and hence the creation of 'meanings of a social kind'. His intention was to convince the reader of the legitimacy of his ideological position.[11] Evidence of this process appears within certain of the layers making up the text of the book. Thus Carroll writes, 'The religious discourses in 2.4–4.4 and the Deuteronomistically influenced sermons reflect a combative ideology designed to denigrate the practices and beliefs of the cultic communities of Judah and Jerusalem (contrast 10.1-16)'.[12]

Such an ideology stood opposed to the hegemonic control of the state religion of pre-exilic times, and it continued as a counter-ideology through the period of the exile. According to Carroll:

Press International, 1993), pp. 89-109; and B.J. Malina, *The Gospel of John in Sociolinguistic Perspective* (Berkeley: The Center for Hermeneutical Studies, 1985), pp. 11-19.

10. As clearly argued by Macherey, *A Theory of Literary Production*, p. 130.

11. Generally on the prophets and ideology, see N.K. Gottwald, 'Ideology and Ideologies in Israelite Prophecy', in S.B. Reid (ed.), *Prophets and Paradigms: Essays in Honor of Gene M. Tucker* (JSOTSup, 229; Sheffield: Sheffield Academic Press, 1966), pp. 136-49.

12. Carroll, *Jeremiah*, p. 11.

Merely as records of the past and 'battles long ago' these strands would have neither value nor significance in the circles which constructed and transmitted them, so they must be read as reflecting interests current in the period of their development. Read as polemics against alternative views of Yahweh and his relation to other gods they would appear to belong to the utterances of the Yahweh-alone party intent on disputing the legitimacy of other Yahwists of a more inclusive type.[13]

The figure of Jeremiah becomes a rallying point around which the ideology of the monists is free to gather. Scarce wonder then that the so-called 'historical Jeremiah' is such an enigma. By contrast the Jeremiah of the text, in the words of Carroll, 'is a protean figure who bestrides all contradictions and overcomes the problems of time and space ... This is not a real person but a conglomerate of many things, reflecting the fortunes of various Jewish communities during and after the Babylonian period.'[14] Legitimation of the prophet, then, served also as the legitimation for the ideology, which undergirded these communities.[15]

The Process of Legitimation

Authority, like honour, is at the behest of society. Jeremiah's first task, therefore, is to establish his credibility, the process of social legitimation. Why should the readers listen to him? Why should the readers align themselves with his version of what is wrong with society? The twin themes of a degenerate society and a corrupt leadership resonate throughout the book.[16] But why should anyone believe this version rather than the official version of the society at large?

In quest of credibility, Jeremiah (or his editors) might have appealed, as Paul did, to his leadership role in the subculture of his readers. Jeremiah did not, but instead used another technique, also employed by Paul, of legitimation by reference directly to God. For this to succeed, the audience would have had to acknowledge such a possibility. If revelation (divine legitimation) was seen to be restricted to the inherited authority of the priesthood, then Jeremiah's appeal would have been without the social legitimacy necessary for success. Fortunately the

13. Carroll, *Jeremiah*, p. 80.
14. Carroll, *Jeremiah*, pp. 63-64.
15. See Gottwald, ' Ideology and Ideologies', pp. 140-45.
16. Carroll, *Jeremiah*, p. 124.

genre of Israelite prophecy, from the time of Amos (if not before) had established a precedent. Jeremiah presumes that an appeal to Yahweh as the source of his authority, will form an acceptable basis for his social legitimation. To this end he chooses to conform to the prophetic genre, and to make use of its semantic configuration (register). In this way his appeal for legitimation will be decoded correctly and given the appropriate social status.

Several scholars draw attention to Jeremiah's use of legitimation motifs, particularly in 1.4-19; 14.10-16; 16.1-9; 20.7-13 and 23.9-40.[17] Legitimation is one of the foci of the prophetic call or commissioning.[18] God has called Jeremiah (1.5) and he is responsible for the message (1.9-10). Berquist writes that 'The prophet is shown to be exercising legitimate authority, received from God, to proclaim the specific message. Both the speaker and the speech are pronounced legitimate because of divine authority.'[19] The call of Jeremiah thus functions to affirm his place as the conveyer of the words of God. The words do not come from within him, but exist externally to him. He has, therefore, no responsibility for the content of the oracles, but acts simply as God's mouthpiece.[20] The authority of Jeremiah was little less, therefore, than the very authority of God.

In using the genre of prophecy, Jeremiah both adopts and adapts its features. He speaks about a prophetic calling, but locates it before his birth (1.5). Moreover, like Amos, to become a prophet was not his intention, rather it was a decision taken on high (1.6). He anticipates opposition and the disavowal of his words, by having God prophesy such scepticism and disbelief (1.17-19; cf. 20.7-13). What could have been a sign of failure is instead turned into a token of success—a masterful stroke of genius.

Apart from affirming one's authority, in this instance as the legitimate bearer of the oracles of Yahweh, there is the opposite process, namely the discrediting of one's rivals. At the heart of Jeremiah's work is the issue of the *locus* of the divine revelation. In the face of both the state religion of the temple in Jerusalem and the popular cultus, Jeremiah claims that the words given to him constitute *the* authoritative

17. So, for example, J.L. Berquist, 'Prophetic Legitimation in Jeremiah', *VT* 39 (1989), pp. 129-39.

18. So Carroll, *Jeremiah*, pp. 94-101.

19. Berquist, 'Prophetic Legitimation', p. 130.

20. Berquist, 'Prophetic Legitimation', p. 132.

revelation. He pours out a bitter condemnation of all other prophets (23.9-40)[21] whose ideology is in conflict with the Yahweh-alone anti-society. Jeremiah's final legitimation, in line with Deut. 18.18-22, is in the historical verification of his prophecies. Destruction and not peace is the true message (Jer. 23.16). Even the tragedy of Jerusalem's fall is used to discredit the opposition parties and in particular their 'claims to control the cult centre because of their association with temple practices of the past'.[22] It 'afforded the first real opportunity for the Yahweh-alone ideologies to reshape the Jerusalem community in the succeeding centuries'.[23]

The process of reshaping an ideology is the primary task of the spokespersons of any antisociety. Jeremiah's appeal to divine revelation may have succeeded in convincing his readers that the correct register for interpreting his words was the prophetic genre, but his task was not complete. In the face of the counter-claims of the religious hierarchy, the ideologues behind Jeremiah needed to convince their society that Jeremiah's definition of orthodoxy and heresy was authentic. No matter how firm the legitimation of a speaker may be, if the message is to be received it needs to evoke a sympathetic echo in the minds and hearts of the audience. In pursuit of this goal, Jeremiah makes use of what sociolinguists have termed 'antilanguage'.

The Concept of an Antilanguage

Sociolinguists define antilanguage as the product of an antisociety. As a society has its language so an antisociety has its antilanguage. Halliday offers the following definitions:

> An antisociety is a society that is set up within another society as a conscious alternative to it. It is a mode of resistance, resistance which may take the form either of passive symbiosis or of active hostility and even destruction. An antilanguage is not only parallel to an antisociety; it is in fact generated by it.[24]

The examples given by Halliday include inner-city subcultures, as

21. See further Carroll, *Jeremiah*, p. 450.
22. Carroll, *Jeremiah*, p. 80.
23. Carroll, *Jeremiah*, p. 126.
24. Halliday, *Language as Social Semiotic*, p. 164.

well as religious groupings, not least early Christianity,[25] and at a more sophisticated level, mysticism.[26]

Antilanguage has some typical features which make it readily identifiable. The first of these is related to the social process of boundary definition. Language and culture are united in the defining of boundaries between insiders and outsiders, including specification of social behaviour, and codes. The classic biblical example is that of Jephthah the Gileadite in the book of Judges (12.4-6). The pronunciation of 'shibboleth' provided the cue for demarcation, and unfortunately for some, death. Such definition of boundaries forms an important part in the self-definition and self-understanding of antisocieties. So, early Christianity evolved a complex system of definitions and markers, allowing for a ready set of distinctions between insiders and outsiders, as Malina's work on John's Gospel illustrates.[27]

Inner-city subcultures use clothing, language and other means to distinguish insiders from outsiders. In the case of language, one notices the variety of terms, many of which are new terms or words used in new contexts. Such changes in vocabulary are most evident in areas of particular concern for the antisociety. For example, Halliday refers to 41 words for police in Calcutta underworld slang. 'The language is not merely relexicalized in these areas; it is overlexacalized.' [28] The consequent humour, secrecy and diversity all contribute to the process of linking insiders together against the society at large, from which they feel estranged. The relexicalization process of the antisociety provides both the means of self-definition and forms a barrier, preventing the access of outsiders. Perceived enemies of the antisociety (like the police in Calcutta) are vilified and demonized.

An antisociety uses antilanguage both to create an alternative reality, by processes like the demarcation of social boundaries, and to maintain such a reality. In effect an antisociety is 'an alternative social structure, with its system of values, of sanctions, of rewards and punishments; and this becomes the source of an alternative reality'.[29] The process of

25. Halliday writes, 'the early Christian community was an antisociety, and its language was in this sense an antilanguage', *Language as Social Semiotic*, p. 171.

26. See the full discussion in Halliday, *Language as Social Semiotic*, pp. 164-82.

27. Malina, *The Gospel of John*, pp. 1-22.

28. Halliday, *Language as Social Semiotic*, p. 165.

29. Halliday, *Language as Social Semiotic*, p. 168; and see P.L. Berger and

resocialization is facilitated by the antilanguage, which enables the new plausibility structure, through the reconstruction of an alternative reality. We use the term 'Reconstruction' because the building blocks of the antisociety, including the antilanguage, are taken from the original society. The grammar remains the same while key terms are either invented or are given a new inflection.

The essence of an antisociety and hence of an antilanguage is not the fact that it exists in alternation to an existing society but that it exists in tension with that society as 'a counter reality, set up in opposition to some established norm'.[30] Consequently social values, which are prominent in an antilanguage, are 'defined by what they are not'.[31]

Antilanguage is itself a metaphorical entity, since it symbolizes the reality of the social order in which it had its origin. Consequently, 'metaphorical modes of expression are the norm'.[32]

The Antisociety of Jeremiah

Jeremiah's task is best understood as an attempt to win over his listeners, or readers, to a minority position within the society at large.[33] The popular Yahwism was apparently an amalgam of various traditions including ideas which, in the mind of Jeremiah, were alien to the true worship of the God of Israel. As a proponent of the Yahweh-alone party,[34] Jeremiah represented a conscious attempt to set up an alternative set of social norms and values. To speak of a conflict between the

T. Luckmann, *The Social Construction of Reality: A Treatise in the Sociology of Knowledge* (New York: Doubleday, 1966).

30. Halliday, *Language as Social Semiotic*, p. 171.

31. Halliday, *Langauge as social semiotic*, p. 172.

32. Halliday, *Language as Social Semiotic*, p. 177.

33. J. Boissevain writes of the typical opposition leader, 'Since he [*sic*] does not have access to the resources controlled by the establishment leader, and thus cannot recruit as many followers through patronage, he is more likely to be attracted by new techniques and ideologies, which he may also develop himself to meet the anti-establishment interests of his potential follower', *Friends of Friends: Networks, Manipulators and Coalitions* (Oxford: Oxford University Press, 1974), p. 230.

34. On the idea of the 'Yahweh alone' party see B. Lang, *Monotheism and the Prophetic Minority: An Essay in Biblical History and Sociology* (The Social World of Biblical Antiquity, 1; Sheffield: Almond Press, 1983). See also Carroll, *Jeremiah*, pp. 126-27; and W.R. Domeris, 'Jeremiah and the Religion of Canaan', *OTE* 7.1 (1994), pp. 7-20.

religions of Canaan (Baal, Asherah and the Queen of Heaven) and absolute Yahwism may be one way of describing the situation, but it presumes too much. The worship which Jeremiah critiques is Israelite. It is the religion of the temple in Jerusalem, and the religion practised by the majority of Israelites. It is the legitimate religion of Israel, not of some anonymous Canaanite group, nor of a particular set of foreign neighbours. Hence, Jeremiah is obligated to establish an antisociety by redefining the boundaries of the religion of Yahweh. His antisociety is set up in opposition to the official religion. The values of his antisociety are defined in contrast to the perceived practices of that religion. Its language is highly metaphorical in order on the one hand to caricature the official religion and on the other, to paint a glowing picture of the monist position.

Jeremiah's Use of Antilanguage

Antilanguage involves extensive relexicalization, including the creation of new terms or the reuse of old terms, but in new contexts. Jeremiah employs a considerable diversity of terms for describing the popular religion of the time, several without parallel even in the prophetic genre. Antilanguage is a metaphorical language, and Jeremiah's writings abound in metaphors. Antilanguage focuses upon social values, as does the prophet's work. Antilanguage is used in the redefining of social boundaries between those who are the insiders and those who are the outsiders.[35] Jeremiah's proclamation centres upon the call to the wider society to become one of the Yahweh-alone group. Antilanguage uses irony and humour especially based on insider knowledge. Jeremiah's use of both stylistic devices is apparent. Finally antilanguage involves a vilification of opponents of the antisociety, as does Jeremiah. Most, if not all, of the prophetic writings make use of antilanguage, but the writings of Jeremiah provide some of the richest examples of metaphor.

The religion of Israel in the late seventh century probably represented a broad spread of religious persuasions stretching from an exclusivist worship of Yahweh, through various forms of popular Yahwism, with increasing evidence of syncretism, to the actual practice of the worship

---

35. For a more nuanced and complex reading of insider/outsider language, see L. Stulman, 'Insiders and Outsiders in the Book of Jeremiah: Shifts in Symbolic Arrangements', *JSOT* 66 (1995), pp. 65-85.

of other deities. While the ends of the spectrum stood in clear polarity, the shades of Yahwism within the middle, for the average Israelite, probably appeared indistinguishable. Jeremiah, because he wishes to redraw the boundaries, lumps together syncretistic Yahwism with the extremes of the worship of Baal, the Queen of Heaven and of Asherah.

Jeremiah creates a false dichotomy, but one which enables him to develop his antisociety and in particular its antilanguage. As he isolates particular forms of the religion of his society, he intentionally lumps them together, so allowing the extremes to colour the more moderate shades of syncretism. In effect he tars all the religious expressions of his contemporaries with the same brush, creating both an artificial division (between his own extreme form of Yahwism, and all other expressions), and an artificial unity (within the other expressions, in spite of their obvious differences). Typical of an antisociety, the expressions closest to his own are seen to be as evil as those furthest away.

The plethora of terms used by the prophet for this amalgam of religious expressions indicates what sociolinguists would term 'over-lexacilization'. Jeremiah describes the religion of his contemporaries variously as 'wickedness' (1.16), 'the forsaking of God' (1.16), 'worshipping the works of their hands' (1.16), 'walking after emptiness' (2.5), 'defiling the land' (2.7), 'making the land an abomination' (2.7), 'walking after things which did not profit' (*hebel*; 2.11), after 'gods which they have not known' (7.9), following 'worthless customs' (10.3), 'a detestable thing which God hates' (44.4). The objects of worship are 'worthless idols' (2.11), 'other gods' (7.18), 'worthless wooden idols' (10.8), 'Baal' (11.13), 'the Queen of Heaven' (7.18), like a 'scarecrow in a melon patch' (10.5), can neither 'walk nor speak, and can do neither good nor ill' (10.5), 'fraudulent images, without breath' (10.14), 'worthless, objects of mockery' (10.15), 'lifeless forms of their vile images', 'detestable idols' (16.18), 'false gods' (16.19), 'detested things' (4.1) and 'abominable idols' (32.34).

Each description carries the specific nuance of the insiders. Humour (the scarecrow in the melon field), deeply felt emotion (the detestable thing, which God hates) and sarcasm (they can neither walk nor speak) are combined: sarcasm, because these are idols representing a deity, and so naturally the idols themselves cannot walk or speak, nor are they expected to do these things. A statue in a church would not be expected to do so either. Jeremiah uses sarcasm to attribute ridiculous claims to the people, in his attempts to ridicule the society and its religion to which he stands opposed. The fact that the phrase 'people worshipping idols' has remained to the twentieth century indicates the persistence of the myth, which grew out of such sarcasm. People do not worship idols, but the power represented by the idol. Jeremiah well knew that, but in typical fashion for antilanguage it suits his purpose to picture the rival religion as composed of devotees of handmade objects of worship. Thus he foreshortens the religious sight of the people to his own advantage.

Jeremiah categorizes the worship of his rivals as foreign, disordered and immoral. The people offer sacrifices (incense) to 'other gods' (19.4). They have as many 'gods as cities' (2.28), and the altars they have set up to burn incense to 'that shameful god, Baal' are as many as 'the streets of Jerusalem'. (11.13). At the high places of the Topheth in the valley of Ben Hinnom, the people 'burn their sons and their daughters' (7.31 cf. 32.35 to Molech, which may be a corruption of the name of a deity); they 'followed', 'consulted and worshipped the sun, moon and stars' (8.2). Even the children attend at 'the altars and Asherah poles beside the spreading trees and high hills' (17.2). These are gods which 'neither they, nor their fathers, nor the kings of Judah ever knew' (19.4 cf. 44.3). At the same time, the worship of Baal is 'as their fathers taught them' (9.14 cf. 23.27). They offer 'their sons in the fire as offerings to Baal' (19.5). They 'burn incense on the roofs to all the starry hosts and pour out drink offerings to other gods' (19.13). Exaggeration and vagueness attend Jeremiah's descriptions. Even the Israelite sacrificial system comes under attack (7.22) as the people follow religious precepts, which according to Jeremiah include things which God not only never commanded, but which never even entered God's head (7.31).

The people, who do these things, are described as a people who 'wash with lye, but their stain of iniquity remains' (2.22), 'the degenerate shoots of a foreign vine' (2.21), 'a swift young camel entangling her ways' (2.23), 'a wild donkey in heat' (2.24), 'a harlot with many lovers' (3.1), 'a treacherous and unfaithful woman' (3.20), 'people of a perverted way' (3.21), 'a people of shame and humiliation' (3.25), 'fools who do not know God', 'senseless children, lacking understanding', 'skilled in evil, without knowledge of good' (4.22). In parody of the objects which they worship, Jeremiah speaks of a 'foolish and senseless people, who have eyes but do not see and ears that do not hear' (5.21). They are 'rejected silver', which cannot be refined (6.30;

cf. v. 29). They are even 'rejected by God' (6.30). They are all 'sense-less' as 'taught by worthless wooden idols' (10.8), 'without knowledge' (10.14), 'goldsmiths shamed by their idols' (10.14). We see deliberate irony as, for example, worship of the stars becomes instead a case of people who 'are terrified of the signs of the heavens' (10.2). Astrology, if that is what the writer has in mind, becomes a nightmare, which the people intentionally bring upon themselves.

Finally, the city of Jerusalem is likened to a 'well that pours out wickedness, full of violence and destruction, sickness and wounds' (6.7). The temple, which bears the name of God (a Deuteronomistic touch), has become a 'den of bandits' (7.11). All of these accusations clearly reflect the ideological position of the monist group, as in graphic detail they draw the line between insider and outsider, between what the book defines as true and false religion.

Jeremiah's Utilization of Metaphor

The text of Jeremiah is a complex tapestry of metaphorical images interwoven with narrative seams, with the figure of the prophet pro-viding the recurrent theme.[36] Perhaps the most striking of all the meta-phors used by Jeremiah, is that of sexual analogies. Some are drawn from the wild, such as the young female camel (2.23), the wild donkey in heat (2.24). Other images come from human society: The harlot with many lovers (3.1) or the 'treacherous and unfaithful woman' (3.20). Colourfully Jeremiah describes Jerusalem, in terms of her 'adultery and lustful neighing' and 'shameless prostitution' (13.27). She is unclean, because of her detestable acts on the hills and in the fields (13.27). The acts here are unnamed but with the sexual innuendo hanging over the verse, one presupposes some shameful act of immorality. The power of the metaphor is its ability to condition the reading of the text, for the specific purpose of denigrating the opposing forms of Yahwistic reli-gion. The people are accused of forsaking fountains of living water for broken cisterns (2.10-13), an act which no one in their right mind would undertake. This prompts Carroll to write:

> For these evaluations to be made in such a fashion requires understand-ing the discourse as a highly ideological statement directed against a different ideology. The critique of the nation's religious history as

36. Carroll, *Jeremiah*, p. 58.

apostate, idolatrous and baalistic is made from the standpoint of a Yahweh-alone group which was not prepared to tolerate certain kinds of syncretistic religion.[37]

Irony and Humour

The classical instance of irony coupled with humour is Jeremiah's deliberate distortion of the worship where he speaks of the people 'praying to wood as father and to a stone as mother' (2.27). Correctly speaking, the reverse is true. The standing stone or *mazzebah* symbolizes a male deity, while a tree or grove with forked branches symbolizes the female. By turning the imagery around, Jeremiah caricatures the worship of the people. They are so stupid that they cannot even discern male from female.

The Vilification of his Opponents

Like Amos, Jeremiah condemns the foreign nations around about, as well as the leaders of his own society. Much of the latter part (chs. 46–51) are diatribes against the nations, but it is his condemnation of other prophets which is particularly striking. Edelman speaks of the creation of 'mythical population groups' as part of the process of the categorization of enemies.[38] The historical Jeremiah probably envisaged a real group of people, which in the present edited compilation have become a 'mythical' symbol for all those religious leaders who oppose the Yahweh-alone ideology. These prophets of the state, who are in effect any prophet who does not belong to the antisociety, are connected directly with the worship of Baal. In similar ways rival Christian groups today are very quick to label 'unorthodox teaching or behaviour' (unorthodox in their view) as demonic or satanic in origin. The prophetic rivals of Jeremiah probably believed in the divine source of their oracles, and would have objected violently to the association with Baal. Indeed one might justifiably question whether Jeremiah is not using the title 'Baal' in a typically antilanguage way and has given the name his own content, quite divorced from the actual deity of that name.

37. Carroll, *Jeremiah*, p. 126.
38. M. Edelman, *Political Language: Words that Succeed and Policies that Fail* (Institute for Research on Poverty Monograph Series; New York: Academic Press, 1977), pp. 29-33.

The prophets, rivals to Jeremiah, prophesy by Baal (2.8, cf. 8.10-11) and have taught the people to swear by the name of Baal (12.16). God did not send these prophets, yet they are saying 'No sword or famine will touch this land' (14.15). They will die by those non-existing swords and famine (14.15). Once again the metaphor of adultery is used. 'The land is full of adulteries' (23.10), the prophets follow an evil course and use their power unjustly (v. 10). Both priest and prophet are godless and even in the temple their wickedness may be found (v. 11). In comparison with the prophets of Samaria who are accused of 'a repulsive thing', namely prophesying by Baal and leading the people astray (v. 13), the prophets of Jerusalem do something equally 'horrible', namely 'they commit adultery and live a lie' (v. 14). The emotive force of such an accusation is self-evident. Adultery was socially considered as the most shameful of crimes. Here Jeremiah enlists the social abhorrence of the act of adultery, in order to denigrate the prophets of Jerusalem.

Jeremiah also accuses the prophets of 'strengthening the hands of evildoers so that no one turns from their wickedness' (23.14). Adultery, living a lie, strengthening the hand of evildoers are all metaphors, but become in themselves the sins of the priests and prophets. Their actual works remain unmentioned, and it may well be that neither corruption, adultery nor the actual worship of Baal were among them. But, for Jeremiah, the comparison with the northern kingdom prophets is a useful one for it enables him to carry over their sin onto the shoulders of his contemporaries. The insinuations of an antisociety quickly take root and grow in that society. The more vague the accusation the more insidious the attack becomes. The shamefulness of the metaphor is allowed to colour the whole perception of the sin of the priests and prophets.

'Ungodliness' has spread from Jerusalem through the whole land, because of the prophets (23.15). They fill the people with false hopes, speaking visions from their own minds (v. 16). Here is the heart of Jeremiah's accusation. It appears that the prophets prophesy the inviolability of Zion, but this is hardly cause for the accusation of adultery, Baal worship, living a lie and strengthening the hands of evildoers.

Sodom and Gomorrah are then enlisted in support (v. 14) of the wickedness of Jerusalem. Again metaphor acts through association with those notorious cities of the ancient world. The insinuations of sexual immorality and the imminent threat of God's punishment all form part of the metaphorical world which Jeremiah enlists in his task to win support for the antisociety. The accusation goes beyond the prophets now living, to their forefathers, who 'forgot my name through Baal worship' (23.27 but cf. 44.4). The present prophets are also accused of trying to make the people forget the name of God. The force of the comparison makes the present prophets appear guilty of Baal worship, but that is not actually said. Yet through effective use of association, Jeremiah leaves the reader with that impression. The power of an anti-language is its ability to create perceptions of reality that stand in direct opposition to existing perceptions, and through metaphor to colour those perceptions in particular ways.

Still in ch. 23, the diatribe continues (vv. 30-32). The prophets steal words from one another, and say they come from God. They 'wag their own tongues' (again note the humour), experience 'false dreams' (how does one do that?) and lead the people astray with 'their reckless lies' (not just lies, but reckless lies).

Carroll writes: 'Precision of meaning is not to be sought in such rhetorical discourses where the gravamen is carried by emotion rather by argument. The leadership is to blame: priests, scribes (cf. 8.8), shepherds (cf. 23.10-2) and prophets (cf. 23.9-40). They have shown themselves to be unsound ideologically.'[39]

Jeremiah in Tension with his Society

The heart of any antilanguage lies in the tension which exists between the antisociety and the society of which it is a product. Powerful symbols such as Yahweh, the temple, priesthood, prophecy, the law and the covenant operate in that society. Jeremiah wages metaphorical war at each of these levels. Perhaps his most vivid and lasting work, in ch. 31, concerns the notion of a new covenant. The force of the argument in this chapter is predicated upon the 'failure' of the old covenant, as perceived from the ideological standpoint of the Yahweh-alone group. They have used 'foreign religions' and 'other gods' as a foil for their depiction of the religion of Yahweh as 'other than' the religion of Canaan. In fact what we have is a series of competing interpretations of Yahwistic worship across a broad spectrum of beliefs.

Carroll writes:

---

39. Carroll, *Jeremiah*, p. 124.

In so far as Israelite religion can be discerned in the Bible in its original form, it conforms to a Canaanite type of belief and practice, but the account of that religion produced by post-587 biblical writers is dominated by their Yahweh-alone ideology. The fall of Jerusalem was the greatest boon to that ideology, for it discredited all other religious and political parties.[40]

Indeed, it was the destruction of Jerusalem that lends credence to the words of Jeremiah, his appeal for a new covenant and his denigration of the popular religion. But we should never forget that he represents an antisociety in tension with the larger community, whose religion he critiques.

When Metaphor Becomes a Myth

In Murray Edelman's book *Words that Succeed and Policies that Fail* he quotes an example of the manner in which a metaphor may become a myth.[41] His example is that of the use of the metaphor 'mental illness' for people who are intellectually challenged, and who fail to fit into society's understanding of normative behaviour. The expression was first used by Teresa of Avila in the seventeenth century and gained a life of its own, as first metaphor, then myth, and eventually as truth. The expression 'mental illness' continues to be used today, even when no illness as such is involved. The power of such a myth is its ability to convince the reader or listener beyond the level of the purely metaphorical.

Jeremiah makes extensive use of metaphor in his depiction of the perspective of his antisociety. In particular, as we have seen, he uses the metaphor of promiscuity to describe the religious persuasion of the greater Israelite society. By a skilful weaving of truth, metaphor, insinuation and comparison, Jeremiah links the popular religion of his time with a promiscuous form of Baal worship. The reader of the book might be forgiven for accepting this picture as a reflection of an actual degenerate cult. But in fact Jeremiah never says that any form of sexual activity is actually involved. His connection is entirely metaphorical. The people, by failing to keep to Jeremiah's definition of true Yahwism, have broken the covenant. In the analogy of a marriage, they have committed adultery. They are the promiscuous donkey in heat, the

40. Carroll, *Jeremiah*, pp. 126-27.
41. Edelman, *Political Language*, p. 17.

unfaithful wife, the lustily neighing male donkey, and one thinks inevitably of cultic prostitution and other forms of promiscuity. However, Carroll adds a caveat: 'The precise degree to which sacred prostitution was practised among Israel's neighbours is impossible to determine, but its presence contributed to making sexual references terms of abuse for Yahwistic ideologies. Since Hosea, religious pornography has become a standard form of abusing opponents ... part of the arsenal of religious denunciations.'[42]

In reading this 'religious pornography', scholars have been tempted to go beyond the metaphorical level and have, in the process, created a myth—the myth of a promiscuous Canaanite cult. The fact that the Baal texts themselves are critical of promiscuity[43] appears to have escaped the attention of the commentators. So the metaphor has become myth and in turn academic consensus. The sociolinguistic reading of Jeremiah can neither prove nor disprove the existence of a degenerate Canaanite cult. What it can show is the presence of an antilanguage which uses the metaphor of adultery in its critique of the religion of the society. It is a true antilanguage in that it is in tension with the society at large, and its metaphors represent a definite bias. To take such a metaphor as an accurate mirror of the society at large is naïve. Elements of truth are undoubtedly present, but outside confirmation is necessary in order to distinguish fact from fiction.

J. Jeremias, in similar vein, has shown how the prophetic speaking of the sin of Baal gradually developed from Hosea, through the various strata of Jeremiah to the Deuteronomistic writer. 'Jeremiah takes up the abstraction of the term בעל from Hosea, but transfers this code to a completely different theme.'[44] Both in Hosea and in the earlier strata of Jeremiah we may discern 'the development towards abstraction' meaning that Baal becomes 'a code for a set of ideas (wrong worship in Hosea, false prophecy in Jeremiah)'.[45] In the Deuteronomistic History 'Baal' has become 'one of the many ways of denoting the absence of

---

42. Carroll, *Jeremiah*, p. 134.

43. See, for example, in Baal II iii 16-19, 'Lo! (there are) two sacrifices (which) Baal, three (which) the rider on the clouds does hate: a sacrifice of shame and a sacrifice of the lewdness of handmaids', in G.R. Driver, *Canaanite Myths and Legends* (Old Testament Studies, 3, Edinburgh, T. & T. Clark, 1956), p. 95.

44. J. Jeremias, 'The Hosea Tradition and the Book of Jeremiah', *OTE* 7.1 (1994), pp. 21-38.

45. Jeremias, 'The Hosea Tradition', p. 30.

Yahweh'.[46] These different meanings attached to the term 'Baal' urge us to take seriously the use of prophetic antilanguage.

Without such a caution, the unwary reader may well fall into the trap of reading Jeremiah's antilanguage as an accurate reflection of the socioreligious context. Instead, by treating the book as the composition of an antisociety, one is able to appreciate its metaphorical flights of fantasy, and to recognize terms like 'Asherah' or 'Baal' as deliberate codes with particular nuances of meaning sometimes quite different from the use of these terms in the broader socio-historical context. In essence a sociolinguistic reading alerts us to the subtleties of the communication process, and lays great emphasis upon the creative work of the text we now call 'Jeremiah'.

46. Jeremias, 'The Hosea Tradition', p. 31.

A ROLLING CORPUS AND ORAL TRADITION: A NOT-SO-LITERATE SOLUTION TO A HIGHLY LITERATE PROBLEM

Raymond F. Person, Jr

The reception of any work of literature is culturally determined. This observation is widely accepted, even by most of us who continue to argue about origins, redactional layers and history. We also accept that the degree of dissimilarity between the culture that produced a text and the reader's culture affects how culturally determined any reading of a text is as well as any subsequent arguments based on this reading. That is, if the reader's culture differs significantly from that of the author, then the reader has a lot of work to do to bridge that cross-cultural gap in order to approach what the text meant to its author and original audience.

This essay concerns such a cultural gap and its adverse affect on the interpretation of the book of Jeremiah. The gap consists of the highly literate world of modern biblical scholars and the primarily oral world of the ancient Israelite scribes/redactors. Each modern biblical scholar has spent thousands of work hours pouring over primary and secondary printed texts in well-lit, air-conditioned libraries and studies. The goal of these many hours of study is to produce yet another tome to be read by our colleagues. We produce these publications so that we can feel good about a job well done and then we go home to relax, reading the newspaper, a magazine or a good book. Although ancient Israel had the technology of writing, the ability to read, copy or write extended pieces of literature was limited to a few. Even these few continued to live in a primarily oral culture.[1]

---

1. I agree with the conclusions reached by David W. Jamieson-Drake, who suggests that writing generally existed within the monarchic bureaucracy and was not widespread (*Scribes and Schools in Monarchic Judah: A Socio-Archeological Approach* [JSOTSup, 109; The Social World of Biblical Antiquity, 9; Sheffield: Almond Press, 1991]).

It is my contention that this cultural gap has adversely affected numerous aspects of our interpretation of biblical texts, one of which is the topic of this paper—that is, the relationship between the LXX of the book of Jeremiah (hereafter LXX-Jer.) and the Masoretic text of the book of Jeremiah (hereafter MT-Jer.).[2] Below, I will demonstrate that the scholarly consensus that LXX-Jer. is generally closer to the original text than MT-Jer. as expressed by Emanuel Tov and William McKane are both highly literate ways of interpreting the evidence. Although I agree with their basic conclusion, they failed to realize that in order to understand the process from LXX-Jer. to MT-Jer. we must take into account the primarily oral culture that produced it. In order to better understand this process, I will draw from the field of the study of oral traditions.[3] First, however, I must explain why the solutions by Tov and McKane are inappropriately, highly literate.

The recognition that LXX-Jer. and MT-Jer. differ is itself a literate observation for differences in oral 'texts' can continue side by side (a visual, literate metaphor) for long periods of time. For example, differences in the two orally transmitted genealogies of a Luo tribe were not detected until a highly literate anthropologist began to write them down.[4] Of course, differences between biblical manuscripts have been noticed at least as far back as the scribes at Qumran, where scribes

---

2. LXX-Jer. refers specifically to J. Ziegler (ed.), *Ieremias, Baruch, Threni, Epistula Ieremias* (Septuaginta Vetus Testamentum Graecum Auctoritates Societatis Göttingensis, 15; Göttingen: Vandenhoeck & Ruprecht, 1957); MT-Jer. to *BHS*.

3. The study of oral traditions is based upon the foundational works of Milman Parry, Albert Lord and Walter Ong. For an excellent introduction to this field of study, see J.M. Foley, *The Theory of Oral Composition: History and Methodology* (Bloomington: Indiana University Press, 1988). Foley's own contributions are highly recommended: *Traditional Oral Epic: The Odyssey, Beowulf, and the Serbo-Croatian Return Song* (Berkeley: University of California Press, 1990); *Immanent Art: From Structure to Meaning in Traditional Oral Epic* (Bloomington: Indiana University Press, 1991); and *The Singer in Tales in Performance* (Bloomington: Indiana University Press, 1995). The most comprehensive application of this field of study to the Hebrew Bible is S. Niditch, *Oral World and Written Word: Ancient Israelite Literature* (Library of Ancient Israel; Louisville, KY: Westminster/John Knox Press, 1996).

4. B.G. Blount, 'Agreeing to Agree on Genealogy: A Luo Sociology of Knowledge', in M. Sanches and B.G. Blount (eds.), *Sociocultural Dimensions of Language Use* (New York: Academic Press, 1975), pp. 117-35.

proofread their own work and the work of other scribes.[5] However, this clearly remains a literate activity.

What makes Tov's and McKane's positions highly literate is the way in which they explain the process that led from the shorter LXX-Jer. to the expansive MT-Jer. Tov maintains that LXX-Jer. and MT-Jer. represent two systematic redactions or 'editions'.[6] In other words, Tov envisions the redactor of MT-Jer. (his 'editor II') taking the 'liberty to add and change many minor and a few major details'.[7] 'Editor II rewrote, re-edited and, in a way, revised edition I [represented by LXX-Jer.], even though edition II does not reflect a consistent rewriting of the previous edition'.[8] Tov's vision appears to be consistent with the process by which I am revising the paper I presented orally into the present essay. On my desk, there is a copy of the paper as given orally with some additional references I am working into the present text. I have rearranged, added, omitted and otherwise revised the previous paper. The process as Tov describes it seems to be too consciously thought out—'Do I want to change this section or not?'—for a redactor in the primarily oral culture of ancient Israel. In fact, Tov's description almost implies that he regrets that 'editor II' was not more 'consistent'—something we certainly expect of ourselves as biblical scholars.

Although he also argues that MT-Jer. is expansive, McKane describes the process leading to MT-Jer. differently. He argues that LXX-Jer. generally preserves an earlier text than MT-Jer, but that the process that produced MT-Jer. was not 'a systematic, comprehensive scheme of editing, but exegetical additions of small scope, operating within limited

---

5. E. Tov, 'The Textual Base of the Corrections in the Biblical Texts Found at Qumran', in D. Dimant and U. Rappaport (eds.), *The Dead Sea Scrolls: Forty Years of Research* (STDJ, 10; Leiden: E.J. Brill, 1992), pp. 299-314.

6. E. Tov, 'Some Aspects of the Textual and Literary History of the Book of Jeremiah', in P.-M. Bogaert (ed.), *Le livre de Jérémie: Le prophète et son milieu, les oracles et leur transmission* (BETL, 56; Leuven: Leuven University Press, 1981), pp. 145-67; E. Tov, 'The Literary History of the Book of Jeremiah in the Light of Its Textual History', in J. Tigay (ed.), *Empirical Models for Biblical Criticism* (Philadelphia: University of Pennsylvania Press, 1985), pp. 211-39; E. Tov, *Textual Criticism of the Hebrew Bible* (Minneapolis: Fortress Press, 1992), pp. 319-27.

7. Tov, 'Some Aspects', p. 151.

8. Tov, 'Some Aspects', p. 151.

areas of text'.[9] He provides numerous examples in which a pre-existing text (poetry or prose) provides the impetus for the addition—that is, as the scribe/redactor was reading the text, a phrase in the text provoked a theological reflection that was incorporated into the text as an addition following the pre-existing text. McKane himself summarizes this idea as follows:

> What is meant by a rolling *corpus* is that small pieces of pre-existing text trigger exegesis or commentary. MT is to be understood as a commentary or commentaries built on pre-existing elements of the Jeremianic *corpus* ... In general, the theory is bound up with the persuasion that the rolling *corpus* 'rolled' over a long period of time and was still rolling in the post-exilic period.[10]

It is as if LXX-Jer. and MT-Jer. were snapshots of a dynamic process in which the significantly different poses in each snapshot could easily be misunderstood as sudden changes occurring moments before the picture was taken rather than the gradual changes that they are.

Some of McKane's comments seem to suggest that the scribes or redactors responsible for MT-Jer. are more or less unthoughtful and arbitrary. He never directly says this, but it seems that he sets up a sharp contrast between a systematic redaction, which he rejects, and his rolling corpus. For example, he writes:

> we err when we suppose that these processes are always susceptible of rational explanation, or that they must necessarily contribute to a thoughtful, systematic redaction.[11]

It seems that the alternative is an irrational, thoughtless, arbitrary redactional process. In his following statement, this is more explicit:

> There is more of accident, arbitrariness and fortuitous twists and turns than has been generally allowed for. The processes are dark and in a measure irrecoverable, and we should not readily assume them to possess such rationality that they will yield to a systematic elucidation.[12]

I sense that McKane himself experienced some discomfort from these conclusions when he writes:

---

9. W. McKane, *A Critical and Exegetical Commentary on Jeremiah*. I. *Introduction and Commentary on Jeremiah I–XXV* (ICC; Edinburgh: T. & T. Clark, 1986), p. lxxxi.

10. McKane, *Jeremiah*, I, p. lxxxiii.

11. *Jeremiah*, I, p. xlix.

12. *Jeremiah*, I, pp. xlix-l.

The objection may be lodged that such an idea of *corpus* is ambiguous, vague and ill-defined, and the only defence which I can offer is that it has helped me to pick my way through the minefield of Jer. 1–25.[13]

McKane's defensive tone here seems to be similar to Tov's regret that 'editor II' was not more consistent—that is, they both appear uncomfortable with the lack of conscious intentionality in the redactional process, the kind of intentionality we expect of ourselves and our colleagues as writers. But we, biblical scholars, live in a print-dominated world, even if some of our contemporaries are moving into media-induced, secondary orality. We can not expect such consistency from a scribe in the primarily oral culture of ancient Israel. Therefore, a deeper understanding of oral cultures may ease us out of our discomfort about the 'inconsistency' and 'arbitrariness' behind MT-Jer.

Our modern, highly literate understandings of what a word is contrasts dramatically with peoples whose culture is primarily oral and traditional. In a primarily oral culture, a 'word'—that is, a unit of meaning—may be equivalent to what we would call a line, a stanza or even the entire epic.[14] This is illustrated in the interview between Milman Parry's assistant Nikola Vujnovic and the Serbo-Croatian oral poet (*guslar*) Mujo Kukuruzovic:

Nikola: Let's consider this: 'Vino pije licki Mustajbeze' ('Mustajbeg of Lika was drinking wine'). Is this a single word?
Mujo: Yes.
Nikola: But how? It can't be *one*: 'Vino pije licki Mustajbeze.'
Mujo: In writing it can't be one.
Nikola: There are four words here.
Mujo: It can't be one in writing. But here, let's say we're at my house and I pick up the *gusle* [a traditional single-stringed instrument]—'Pije vino licki Mustajbeze'—that's a single word on the *gusle* for me.
Nikola: And the second word?
Mujo: And the second word—'Na Ribniku u pjanoj mehani' ('At Ribnik in a drinking tavern')—there.[15]

In this interview we can see a clash of cultures as the literate Yugoslav insists that 'Vino pije licki Mustajbeze' is not one word but

13. *Jeremiah*, I, p. xlix.
14. J.M. Foley, 'Editing Oral Epic Texts: Theory and Practice', *Text* 1 (1981), pp. 75-94 (77-78); Foley, *Traditional Oral Epic*, Chapters 4–6.
15. Cited in Foley, 'Editing Oral Epic Texts', p. 92 n. 11.

four, while the oral poet insists that it is only one word. In fact, the oral poet's conception of the entire phrase being one word even allows for some variation. Notice that Nikola is discussing the phrase 'Vino pije licki Mustajbeze', but, when Mujo imagines playing his *gusle* and singing it, he says, what from a highly literate viewpoint might be considered a different phrase because of the inversion of the first two 'words', 'Pije vino licki Mustajbeze'. For Mujo, the oral poet, both 'Vino pije licki Mustajbeze' and 'Pije vino licki Mustajbeze' are not only one 'word', but the *same* 'word'.

As we have just seen, such an oral traditional understanding of a 'word' or unit of meaning does not require verbatim reproduction, but rather allows for variation. When the oral poet performs an epic, he or she is not simply reproducing something from the past, thereby preserving it for future generations. Rather, the oral poet performs the epic for the present, including certain adaptations to the circumstances of the performance that, from the poet's perspective, does not essentially change the meaning.[16]

Early studies concerning orality emphasized what Werner Kelber has called 'the great divide thesis'[17]—that is, a tremendous gulf was envisioned between oral and literate cultures. It was as if, when an oral epic was written down, it was completely removed from its traditional culture, never again to be influenced by that culture; and even the earliest readers of this new text lived in a literate culture and were ignorant of its traditional-oral setting. However, recent studies have narrowed the supposed gap between oral and literate cultures, especially as it relates to the interaction of orality and literacy in transitional cultures like ancient Greece and medieval Europe.[18] Therefore, it is quite possible that scribes in transitional cultures still approached the scribal process

16. A.N. Doane, 'The Ethnography of Scribal Writing and Anglo-Saxon Poetry: Scribe as Performer', *Oral Tradition* 9 (1994), pp. 420-39 (433).

17. 'Scripture and Logos: The Hermeneutics of Communication', paper presented at SBL Annual Meeting, Kansas City, 1991.

18. For example, M.T. Clanchy, *From Memory to Written Record: England, 1066–1307* (Cambridge, MA: Harvard University Press, 1979); B. Stock, *The Implications of Literacy: Written Language and Models of Interpretation in the Eleventh and Twelfth Centuries* (Princeton, NJ: Princeton University Press, 1983); B. Stock, *Listening for the Text: On the Uses of the Past* (Baltimore: The Johns Hopkins University Press, 1990); R. Thomas, *Oral Tradition and Written Records in Classical Athens* (Cambridge: Cambridge University Press, 1989).

with an oral mentality. For example, both K.O. O'Keefe and A.N. Doane have argued convincingly that Anglo-Saxon scribes understood entire lines as a 'word' or unit of meaning and that they can be understood in similar ways to oral performers.[19] A similar argument is given below for the ancient Israelite redactors/scribes responsible for the transmission of the book of Jeremiah.

As Tov, McKane, and others have noted, the majority of variants between LXX-Jer. and MT-Jer. consist of additions of titles, proper names, adjectives, adverbs, divine names and epithets, and standard prophetic formulae.[20] Below a few examples are given with the MT-Jer. plusses in parentheses:

> addition of titles:
> > 28.5: And Jeremiah (the prophet) said to Hananiah (the prophet).
> addition of proper names:
> > 21.2: (Nebuchadnezzar).
> > 52.16: (Nebuzaradan).
> addition of patronymics:
> > 28.4: Jeconiah (son of Jehoiakim, king of Judah).
> > 36.8: Baruch (son of Neriah).
> addition of divine names and epitets:
> > 29.21: Thus says the Lord (of Hosts, the God of Israel).
> substitution of proper name for pronoun:
> > MT-Jer. 52.8: Zedekiah // LXX-Jer. 52:8: him.

The following comments concerning variants such as these certainly do not account for all variants between LXX-Jer. and MT-Jer. For example, MT-Jer. sometimes adds lengthy sections (e.g. 39.4-13) and the oracles against the nations are located in a different position. These variants may have occurred in a much different way from what I describe below—that is, there probably was more intentionality present in the creation of the variants involving multiple verses.

The way in which I have presented the above variants has already prejudiced us in our reading of them. I have presented them in some cases as one word which is added in M T-Jer. However, given the broader understandings of 'word' in primarily oral cultures, the ancient

19. K.O. O'Keefe, *Visible Song: Transitional Literacy in Old English Verse* (Cambridge: Cambridge University Press, 1990). Doane, 'The Ethnography of Scribal Writing and Anglo-Saxon Poetry'.
20. See also L. Stulman, *The Prose Sermons of the Book of Jeremiah* (SBLDS, 83; Atlanta: Scholars Press, 1986), p. 141.

scribes may not have understood the units of meaning in the same way that we do. In other words, the structure of this very study is dependent upon our highly literate mentality of comparing written texts and analyzing them according to the smallest units of meaning possible.

Given our literate mentality, we are prone to view these variants as unintentional mistakes or what some scribe intended as an improvement upon the text. For example, the addition of 'son of Neriah' following 'Baruch' in 36.8 provides a better, more specific reading, especially for those readers who are further from the time of the events. However, I suggest that, even if they were conscious of these variations, the ancient scribes may not have even understood these variants as *changes*. If the unit of meaning is understood as much larger, then variation *within* that unit is allowed if the *meaning* of the unit is not changed. We saw this above in Mujo's insistence that 'Vino pije licki Mustajbeze' and 'Pije vino licki Mustajbeze' are both *one* and the *same* 'word'. Thus, for example, the variation between a pronoun and proper name (from 'him' in LXX-Jer. 52.8 to 'Zedekiah' in MT-Jer. 52.8) does not change the unit of meaning if that unit is not understood as equivalent to our understanding of a 'word', but is understood as the entire verse:

> But the army of the Chaldeans pursued the king and overtook him in the plains of Jericho; all his army was scattered overtaking him (52.8).

While copying the text, a scribe simply wrote what he knew to be the antecedent of the pronoun 'him', the proper name 'Zedekiah'. Or, a scribe simply substituted the pronoun 'him' for 'Zedekiah'. In either case, the unit of meaning has not changed—'the army of the Chaldeans ... overtook him/Zedekiah'. In fact, since the unit of meaning is larger than this 'word' which he substituted, the scribe may not have even been conscious of what we perceive as an intentional change, providing more specificity.

With our literate mentalities, such variations may seem unintentional and arbitrary because we focus upon our 'words', our units of meaning. Why did they use a pronoun here and a proper name there? Why did they not consistently use the same divine epithet rather than 'the Lord' here but 'the Lord of hosts' there? But if we can begin to think in units of meaning like that of the ancient Israelite scribes, such variation is only natural and expected, because from their perspective they have not changed a 'word'.

If the conclusions reached above are valid, then McKane's conclusion that the redactional process behind MT-Jer. was gradual gains qualified support. In addition, these conclusions can relieve any discomfort that we, literate scholars, might feel about what appears to be a process conducted by arbitrary and inconsistent redactors/scribes. We do not have to choose between Tov's systematic redactions, which even in his own assessment contain inconsistencies, and McKane's 'rolling corpus', which appears even to him to suggest arbitrariness. We can agree with Tov that the redactional process was thoughtful and systematic in relationship to what the ancient scribes may have understood as their 'words'—that is, what appears to us, literate scholars, as 'inconsistent' changes would not even appear to them to be changes; therefore, the majority of our variants would be eliminated, leaving what the ancient scribes would have also considered to be thoughtful changes (e.g. the rearrangement of the oracles against the foreign nations). We can agree with McKane that the redactional process was gradual with what we call 'words' and 'phrases' providing 'additions' to the text, even though what appears to us as 'changes' would not necessarily be changes to the ancient scribes—that is, the majority of variants occurred in a gradual process of change that provides no evidence of a systematic, thoughtful redaction.

In short, when we somewhat overcome the oral-literate cultural gap between us and them, we can see the ancient Israelite scribes as they were, literate members of a primarily oral culture who are still influenced by an oral mentality. Therefore, most of their work that we call 'variants' is simply the result of their oral mentality and its understanding of 'word', which allows variation within the larger unit of meaning; some of their work that we call 'variants' is the result of their literate task of updating, correcting, and improving the text. These two observations together suggest that the changes that occurred between LXX-Jer. and MT-Jer. were primarily 'oral' in character with some 'literate' variants along the way.

THE AMPLIFICATION OF THE EXPECTATIONS OF THE EXILES
IN THE MT REVISION OF JEREMIAH

Roy D. Wells, Jr

Kessler offers a bleak characterization of the account of Jeremiah's
activity among the 'remnant of Judah' (Jer. 40/47.7—chs. 44/51): 'the
rejection of the divine word by these people is sketched in ugly colors'.[1]
Their decision to go to Egypt demonstrates their final contempt for
God's word and their final mistreatment of the prophet that bears it. It is
characterized as a conscious abandonment of their future with God in
favor of the Queen of Heaven. It also, in a variant of the 'myth of the
empty land', is an abandonment of their future in the land for the disastrous future of Hophra. As Carroll has emphasized, this may be identified as an ideological conviction of the returning exiles, and as a
justification for their reassertion of political and economic control under
the Achaemenids.[2] Two major redactional studies have attempted to
identify the voice of this 'remnant of Judah' that has been marginalized
in the present form of the text. Pohlmann identifies an 'original kernel'

---

1. Martin Kessler, 'Jeremiah Chapters 26–45 Reconsidered', *JNES* 27.2
(1968), pp. 81-88 (85). Ronald E. Clements, *Jeremiah* (Interpretation; Atlanta: John
Knox Press, 1988), especially pp. 229-30, sees a narrative transition to the conclusion 'all hope of Israel's restoration had narrowed to and centered upon the community of exiles in Babylon'. See Enno Janssen, *Juda in der Exilszeit: Ein Beitrag
zur Frage der Entstehung des Judentums* (FRLANT, 51; Göttingen: Vandenhoeck
& Ruprecht, 1956), p. 5 n. f; and Ernest W. Nicholson, *Preaching to the Exiles: A
Study of the Prose Tradition in the Book of Jeremiah* (New York: Schocken Books,
1971 [1970]), p. 109.
2. See especially the discussion of the tension between Jer. 40–42 and the
'myth of the empty land' in Robert P. Carroll, 'Textual Strategies and Ideology in
the Second Temple Period', in Philip R. Davies (ed.), *Second Temple Studies, 1*
(JSOTSup, 117, Sheffield: JSOT Press, 1991), pp. 108-24 (113); and his 'The Myth
of the Empty Land', in David Jobling (ed.), *Ideological Criticism of Biblical Texts*
(Semeia, 59; Atlanta: Scholars Press, 1992), pp. 79-94 (80-81).

showing hope for God's continuing presence and activity among those who remained in the land of Judah, and a 'gola-oriented redaction' that transformed the text into a judgment upon the remnant who rejected Jeremiah's word, went to Egypt in a body, and left the land empty.[3] Seitz locates this attitude in an 'Exilic Redaction' that is the end product of a complex scribal process offering new comprehensive presentations of the Jeremiah tradition in new circumstances, particularly after the crises of 597 and 587/586.[4]

This study is a more modest effort in the shadow of the work of Emanuel Tov[5] to describe a late stage of this process, or at least to describe the complexity of the textual basis for such a discussion. He argues (1) that it is possible within limits to reconstruct the Hebrew *Vorlage* behind the Old Greek translation (which lay behind the LXX); (2) that this *Vorlage* preserves, also with limits, a complete and coherent text of the book of Jeremiah; and (3) that the Masoretic Text of Jeremiah represents a 'second edition' that revises and expands, probably tendentiously, this older text of Jeremiah. The principal thesis here is that the point of view of the Babylonian exiles, under some yet unspecifiable circumstances of their history, may be glimpsed within

---

3. See Karl-Friedrich Pohlmann, *Studien zum Jeremiabuch: Eine Beitrag zur Frage nach der Entstehung des Jeremiabuches* (FRLANT, 118; Göttingen: Vandenhoeck & Ruprecht, 1978), pp. 93-182, and the summary in pp. 183-225. He dates this gola-oriented redaction late in the Persian era. See also Sean McEvenue, 'The Composition of Jeremiah 37.1 to 44.30', in W.C. van Wyk (ed.), *Studies in Wisdom Literature* (OTWSA, 15, 16; Hercules, South Africa: N.H.W. Press, 1981), pp. 59-67.

4. Christopher R. Seitz, *Theology in Conflict: Reactions to the Exile in the Book of Jeremiah* (BZAW, 176; Berlin: W. de Gruyter, 1989), especially pp. 5-6, 228-35, 241-45, 282-96.

5. J. Gerald Janzen's 1965 dissertation (available as *Studies in the Book of Jeremiah* [HSM, 6; Cambridge, MA: Harvard University Press, 1973]) lies behind a substantial body of work by Tov, beginning with 'L'incidence de la critique textuelle sur la critique littéraire dans le livre de Jérémie', *RB* 79 (1972), pp. 189-99. See the survey of research in Hermann-Josef Stipp, *Das masoretische und alexandrinische Sondergut des Jeremiabuches: Textgeschichtliche Rang, Eigenarten, Triebkräfte* (OBO, 136; Göttingen: Vandenhoeck & Ruprecht, 1994), pp. 7-16. He assumes that agreements between the LXX and the MT preserve a common basic text. An 'Alexandrinian personal property' is identified by LXX plusses that do not appear in the MT. The 'Masoretic personal property' includes diverse 'pre-Masoretic' local revisions as well as a comprehensive effort to polish the finished book.

the Masoretic variations from a text that survives only as a presumed Hebrew *Vorlage* underlying the Greek translation tradition.[6]

Jeremiah and the Community:
Jeremiah 40/47.1-6 LXXV

In the LXX, the account of the assassination of Gedaliah and its aftermath is the climactic ending of the book of Jeremiah, followed only by the epilogue in ch. 52. It is preceded by 37/44–40/47.7, Hardmeier's 'history of the imprisonment and liberation of Jeremiah'.[7] Introduced by a narrative of the writing and rewriting of a text (chs. 36/43),[8] this is a series of anecdotes about Jeremiah set against the background of the

---

6. The caveats in Max L. Margolis, 'Complete Induction for the Identification of the Vocabulary in the Greek Versions of the Old Testament with its Semitic Equivalents: Its Necessity and the Means of Obtaining It', *ZAW* 25 (1905), pp. 311-19; and Emanuel Tov, 'On "Pseudo-Variants" Reflected in the Septuagint', *JSS* 20 (1975), pp. 165-77, are fundamental. Other analyses of the LXXV (LXX *Vorlage*) of these texts include Louis Stulman, *The Other Text of Jeremiah* (Lanham, MD: University Press of America, 1985), pp. 139-71; Pierre-Maurice Bogaert, 'La libération de Jérémie et le meurtre de Godolias: Le text court (LXX) et la rédaction longue (TM)', in Detlef Fraenkel *et al.* (eds.), *Studien zur Septuaginta—Robert Hanhart Zu Ehren* (MSu, 20; Göttingen: Vandenhoeck & Ruprecht, 1990), pp. 312-22. See also Hermann-Josef Stipp, *Jeremia im Parteienstreit: Studien zur Textentwicklung von Jer 26,36-43 und 45 als Beitrag zur Geschichte Jeremias, seines Buches und judäischer Parteien im 6. Jahrhundert* (BBB, 82, Frankfurt on Main: Anton Haim, 1992), pp. 320-29.

7. Christof Hardmeier, *Prophetie im Streit vor dem Untergang Judas: Erzählkommunikative Studien zur Entstehungssituation der Jesaja- und Jeremiaerzählungen in II Reg 18–20 und Jer 37–40* (BZAW, 187; Berlin: W. de Gruyter, 1990), pp. 174-246. See Rolf Rendtorff, *The Old Testament: An Introduction* (trans. John Bowden; Philadelphia: Fortress Press, 1986), pp. 205-206; Peter Ackroyd, 'Historians and Prophets', *SEÅ* 33 (1968), pp. 18-54, now in *Studies in the Religious Tradition of the Old Testament* (London: SCM Press, 1987), pp. 121-51 (139), and Kessler, 'Jeremiah 26–45', pp. 83-84 for discussions of the broader textual setting.

8. Robert P. Carroll, *Jeremiah: A Commentary* (OTL; London: SCM Press, 1986), pp. 662-68, and his 'Manuscripts Don't Burn: Inscribing the Prophetic Tradition. Reflections on Jeremiah 36', in Matthias Augustin and K.-D. Schunck (eds.), *'Dort Ziehan Schiffe dahin…': Collected Communications to the XIVth Congress of the International Organization for the Study of the Old Testament, Paris, 1992* (BEATAJ, 28; Frankfurt: Peter Lang, 1996), pp. 31-42.

final siege of Jerusalem.[9] These involve both the rejection of the prophetic word before the fall of the city[10] and the rejection of the prophet.[11] Following each of a series of encounters with the imperious Zedekiah of the LXX*V*,[12] Jeremiah 'remains' (יָשַׁב) in prison. In the LXX*V*, which only has 39/46.1-3, 14-18,[13] there is only an allusion to the subtext of the fall of the city. The account is made up entirely of Jeremiah anecdotes. The text only mentions one item on the agenda of the assembled 'officials', שָׂרִים, of the king of Babylon (39/46.3, 14). They (v. 14) 'sent and took Jeremiah from the court of the guard', and released him to Gedaliah, to 'remain [יָשַׁב] among the people'.[14] The narrative proximity in the LXX*V* enhances the contrast with Zedekiah and his 'officials' שָׂרִים,[15] as well as Jeremiah's final destiny among the people left in the land.

9. Peter R. Ackroyd, 'Aspects of the Jeremiah Tradition', *Indian Journal of Theology* 20 (1971), pp. 1-12, especially 2-3. This study has stimulated a considerable body of work.

10. Kessler, 'Jeremiah 26–45', pp. 84-85.

11. Heinz Kremers, 'Leidensgemeinschaft mit Gott im Alten Testament: Eine Untersuchungen der "biographischen" Berichte im Jeremiabuch', *EvT* 13 (1953), pp. 122-40, describes Jer. 37.11–43.6, 45 as a 'Passion Narrative'.

12. A.R. Pete Diamond, 'Portraying Prophecy: Of Doublets, Variants, and Analogies in the Narrative Representation of Jeremiah's Oracles: Reconstructing the Hermeneutics of Prophecy', *JSOT* 57 (1993), pp. 99-119 (104), describes the Zedekiah of the LXX*V* (37-38/44-45) as a 'scheming Machiavellian'.

13. Pierre-Maurice Bogaert, 'Libération', pp. 312-22. His 'texte très court', based on the Old Latin, also lacks 39/46.1-2. Stipp, *Das masoretische Sondergut*, pp. 71-73, criticizes the assumption that this is a 'parablepsis' of extraordinary length.

14. Gunther Wanke, *Untersuchungen zur sogenannten Baruchschrift* (BZAW, 22; Berlin: W. de Gruyter, 1971), pp. 92, 108-10. The 'recurrent stereotype concluding formula' וַיֵּשֶׁב יִרְמְיָהוּ (37.16b, 21b, 38.13b, 28a; 39.14b; 40.6b) expressly establishes the situation of Jeremiah after each episode. The series originally ended with 38.28b + 39.3, 14a + 40.6. The formula at 39.14b connects a redundant 'legendary' account (39.11-12 + 40.1-5) to the series.

15. It has the same effect on the connection between Ebed-Melech's kindness and Jeremiah's 'personal salvation oracle' 39/46.15-18—see Hannelis Schulte, 'Baruch und Ebedmelech—Persönliche Heilsorakel Im Jeremiabuche', *BZ* 32 NS 2 (1988), pp. 257-68 (259-60). See Claus Westermann, *Prophetic Oracles of Salvation in the Old Testament* (trans. Keith Crim; Louisville, KY: Westminster/John Knox Press, 1991 [1987]), p. 160, on its anomalous form. See Louis Stulman, *The Prose Sermons of the Book of Jeremiah: A Redescription of the Correspondences with the Deuteronomistic Literature in the Light of Recent Text-Critical Research*

The longer doublet (40/47.1-6),[16] separated from this brief report of the release of Jeremiah to Gedaliah by the word to Ebed-Melek (39/46.15-18), is set in Ramah, where Jeremiah was '40/47.1 [] in fetters with [] the exiles of [] Judah [גלות יהודה]'. In the voice of Nebuzaradan, the narrator offers a Deuteronomistic[17] interpretation of the fall of Jerusalem and of the deportation as a confirmation of the divine word:

> 40/47.2 The LORD your God threatened this place with this disaster; [3]and the LORD has [] acted [], because all of you sinned against *him* [] and did not obey his voice. []

In the LXX*V*, Jeremiah is granted a unique exemption from the fate of the 'exiles of [] Judah'. Nebuzaradan, the 'captain of the guard' (who does not appear in the LXX of Jer. 39) 'released him' (vv. 1, 5), 'gave him [] a present' (v. 5b), and offered him a choice between two patrons under Babylonian sovereignty:

> 4b If you wish to come with me to Babylon, come, and I will take good care of you; but if [] [5]not, *go away and* return[18] to Gedaliah son of Ahikam son of Shaphan, whom the king of Babylon appointed governor of the *land* [] of Judah, and stay with him among the people *in the land of Judah*; [] go wherever you think it right to go.

The italicized Greek plusses emphasize the connection between the

---

(SBLDS, 83; Atlanta: Scholars Press, 1986), pp. 111-13, for an analysis of the LXX*V*.

16. A long tradition discusses the double accounts in Jeremiah as a problem in historical reconstruction. J. Philip Hyatt, 'The Book of Jeremiah: Introduction and Exegesis', in *IB*, V, pp. 777-1142 (1082-83), anticipates more recent discussions of this as a textual problem within an ongoing tradition. Carroll's sensitive reading, *Jeremiah*, pp. 697-700, of the function of the doublets in their respective narrative settings is extremely helpful here. See Bogaert, 'Libération', pp. 315-16; Ackroyd, 'Aspects', pp. 4-5, 8-10; Diamond, 'Portraying'; and Seitz, *Theology*, pp. 241-45.

17. See J. Philip Hyatt, 'The Deuteronomic Edition of Jeremiah', in Richmond C. Beatty *et al.* (eds.), *Vanderbilt Studies in the Humanities* (3 vols.; Nashville: Vanderbilt University Press, 1951), I, pp. 71-95, now in Leo G. Perdue and Brian W. Kovaks (eds.), *A Prophet to the Nations: Essays in Jeremiah Studies* (Winona Lake, IN: Eisenbrauns, 1984), pp. 247-68; and Stulman, *Prose Sermons*, pp. 31-48.

18. Carroll, *Jeremiah*, p. 698. His sustained attention to the Greek tradition makes this a valuable resource, along with William McKane, *A Critical and Exegetical Commentary on Jeremiah. II. Commentary on Jeremiah XXVI–LII* (ICC; Edinburgh: T. & T. Clark, 1996).

remnant of Judah and the land of Judah.[19] This anticipates and underlines the final and climactic occurrence of the phrase [ירמיהו] וישב in
chs. 37–40.6: '6 he remained (וישב) [] among the people who were left
in the land'.[20] This final disposition of the prophet links chs. 37/44.1–
40/47.6 with 40/44.7–44/51.30 and the reception of the word by these
people. Though Jeremiah does not appear in the narratives set at
Mizpah, this account may offer an implicit presence.

Jeremiah 40/47.1-6 MT

For the expanded version of this account in MT 39/46.4-10, 11-13 +
MT/LXX 39/46.14,[21] the allusion to the release of Jeremiah to remain
'among the people' around Gedaliah (39.14) has an extended preface.
The grievous suffering of the king and people in Jerusalem is described
in the extended agenda of the 'officials' שׂרים of 39.3: the cruel
punishment and exile of Zedekiah, the slaughter of the nobles (חרי)[22] of
Jerusalem, the demolition and depopulation of the city, the deportation
of its population, and reassignment of the fields and vineyards to 'the
poor' (דלים). Finally (39.11-12), the release of Jeremiah is described as
a specific expression of the authority of the King of Babylon (God's
'servant'?).[23] '11 *King Nebuchadrezzar of Babylon gave command concerning Jeremiah through Nebuzaradan, the captain of the guard.*'
Nebuzaradan is introduced into the 'chief officials (רבים) of the king of
Babylon' (v. 13MT) who carry out his orders. The instruction to '12
deal with him as he may ask you' implies a freedom not expressed in
the decree giving him over to Gedaliah (39/46.14 LXX/MT).[24]

---

19. See Stipp, *Das masoretische Sondergut*.

20. Hardmeier, *Prophetie*, pp. 180-83, emphasizes the presence of the prophet
among this population as the climax of the 'macrostructure' of 37.3–40.6, following
Wanke, *Baruchschrift*, especially pp. 91-95.

21. See the detailed analysis in Bogaert, 'Libération', pp. 313-20.

22. There is no reference to the fate of the nobility in 2 Kgs 25.7 LXX, MT. In
Jer. 52.10, MT has שׂרים = LXX ἄρχοντας.

23. Walter Brueggemann, *To Build, To Plant: A Commentary on Jeremiah 26–
52* (Grand Rapids: Eerdmans, 1991), p. 179, has emphasized 'the precise convergence of *Yahweh's covenantal resolve* and *Babylon's foreign policy*' in the canonical form of the book of Jeremiah (emphasis his). His identification of this theological conviction qualifies any discussion of political and economic ideology. See the
discussion of the MT plus, 'Nebuchadnezzar *my servant*', at 43.10.

24. Bogaert, 'Libération', pp. 317-19, suggests that the change from 'to be

In 40/47.1-6, the second account of the release of Jeremiah, the Jerusalemites among the exiles are specifically mentioned in the MT plus: Jeremiah is '*bound* in fetters' at Ramah, along with '*all* the exiles of *Jerusalem and* Judah who were being exiled to Babylon' (v. 1). This added reference to the Jerusalemites and their bondage brings forward the earlier MT plus describing the suffering of Jerusalem and the Jerusalemites. The MT expansions of the theological assessment by Nebuzaradan allow the interpretation of this past suffering as the fulfillment of the preceding divine words[25] to Zedekiah and his officials:

> 2 The LORD your God threatened this place with this disaster; [3]and the LORD has *brought it about, and has* acted *as he said* (for LXX has acted), because all of you sinned against *the LORD* (LXX him) and did not obey his voice. *Therefore this thing has come upon you.*

The MT expansion of Nebuzaradan's instructions corresponds to Nebuchadnezzar's decree of freedom in the expanded doublet (39.12 MT):

> 4b If you wish to come with me to Babylon, come, and I will take good care of you; but if you do not wish to come with me to Babylon, you need not come. See, the whole land is before you; go wherever you think it good and right to go.[26]

Dijkstra interprets the old crux in 40/47.4-5 MT as an 'irrevocable manumission formula',[27] translating v. 5a (וְעוֹדֶנּוּ לֹא־יָשׁוּב) '*As long as*

---

brought out' (LXX) to 'be brought out *to the house*' (v. 14) should be rendered 'to be brought out *to the temple*', noting the absence of 'he burned the house of the LORD' (2 Kgs 25.9; Jer. 52.13) and of the description of the looting of the temple (2 Kgs 25.13-17; Jer. 52.17-23) from Jer. 39. See Seitz, *Theology*, pp. 270-71, who suggests that this cultic continuity is presupposed in the story of the murder of the pilgrims (41.4-7) after the assassination of Gedaliah.

25. Note an analogous rhetorical expansion of conventional words in the *Heilswort* to Ebed-Melech: 39.16 'I am going to fulfill my words against this city for evil and not for good, *and they shall be accomplished in your presence on that day.*'

26. A.W. Streane, *The Double Text of Jeremiah (Massoretic and Alexandrian) Compared* (Cambridge: Deighton Bell, 1896), p. 249, notes the similarity of MT 40/47.4 to Gen. 13.9.

27. Meindert Dijkstra, 'Legal Irrevocability (*lō' yāsûb*) in Ezekiel 7.13', *JSOT* 43 (1989), pp. 109-16. Note the earlier MT plusses: '4 *Now* look, I have released you *today* from the fetters on your hands'. On the crux, see Dominique Barthélemy, *Isaïe, Jérémie, Lamentations* (OBO; Critique Textuelle de l'Ancien Testament, 2; Fribourg: Editions Universitaires, 1986), pp. 736-38: 47.5 εἰ δὲ μή ἀπότρεχε καὶ

he (Jeremiah) *lives, let no one go back* (on this decree)' (for LXX 'but if … not, go away and… '). It is noteworthy that the critical elements of this formula appear only in the MT. This would elaborate the free choice of the prophet to continue the proclamation of the word under Zedekiah within the 'remnant', the community in '*the whole land*'.

In contrast, the jurisdiction of Gedaliah and the remnant over the 'land', emphasized in the LXX, is limited in the MT to the remaining towns and their population: '5b Return[28] to Gedaliah son of Ahikam son of Shaphan, whom the king of Babylon appointed governor of the *towns* (for LXX land) of Judah, and stay with him among the people (omitting LXX 'in the land of Judah'); *or* go wherever you think it right to go'. So the captain of the guard gave him *an allowance of food and*[29] a present, and let him go'. When the prophet elected to go 'to Gedaliah *son of Ahikam* at Mizpah, and [stay] *with him* among the people who were left in the land' (v. 6), Jeremiah cast his lot with the remnant under Gedaliah. The word is now declared to 'the people who were left in the land', interpreted as the urban/town population[30] administered by a native appointee of the king of Babylon.

The Community under Gedaliah:
Jeremiah 40/47.7-12

The opening reference to the leaders of Judah's remaining military force (40/47.7-8) introduces Johanan son of Kareah, who assumes leadership after the assassination of Gedaliah. Gedaliah's jurisdiction and mandate are described to them as a new political order for the inhabitants of a land under foreign control. Two MT plusses in 40.7-12 affect the reader's impression of the remnant under Gedaliah. The first is in 40.7:

ἀνάστρεψον πρὸς Γοδολιαν becomes וְעוֹדֶנּוּ לְעֹ־יָשׁוּב [שָׁמָּה] לֵךְ: 5 … וְאִם [רַע] 4
וְשֵׁבָה אֶל־גְּדַלְיָה (Janzen, *Studies*, p. 125). Paul Volz, *Studien zum Text des Jeremia* (BWAT, 25, Leipzig: J.C. Hinrichs, 1920), p. 277: 'Die beiden Verbalformen von שׁוּב wurden zwar von den Verss. teilweise nicht mit dem gleichen Wort übersetzt, aber doch wohl noch im Text gefunden.'

28. GKC §119s.

29. MT = the provisions for Jehoiachin (Jer. 52.34 = 2 Kgs 25.30).

30. 40/47.10 LXX, MT has the fruits of the trees of the Judean highlands brought into the towns.

The king of Babylon had appointed Gedaliah *son of Ahikam* governor in the land, and had committed to him men, women (LXX and their wives), *and children, those of the poorest of the land* who had not been taken into exile to Babylon.

The MT addition of 'the poorest of the land' evokes an earlier MT plus, making explicit here what was implicit there. 39.10 MT is typically seen as part of an expansion of the Jeremiah narrative from the Deuteronomistic history.[31] *'Nebuzaradan the captain of the guard left in the land of Judah some of the poor people who owned nothing* [העם הדלים אשר אין להם מאומה], *and gave them vineyards and fields at the same time.'* If this is compared with 2 Kgs 25.12 'But the captain of the guard left some of the poorest of the land [מדלת הארץ] to be vinedressers and tillers of the soil', the MT appears to go beyond the Deuteronomistic reduction of the status of those who were 'left' by introducing the question of land tenure (title?).[32]

Note that Jer. 52.16//2 Kgs 25.12 shows the same tendency. Bogaert has argued that the LXX, extracted from 2 Kings 25, represents an early text that contains no reference to the deportation.[33] The last thing Nebuzaradan does, after destroying the citadel and pulling down the walls, is to leave 'the *remnant of the people* [τοὺς καταλοίπους τοῦ λαοῦ = יתר (שארית?) העם][34] to be vinedressers and tillers of the soil'. The MT

31. Martin Noth, *The Deuteronomistic History* (JSOTSup, 15; Sheffield: Sheffield Academic Press, 1991), pp. 116-17, is the exception.

32. Bernhard Duhm, *Das Buch Jeremia* (Tübingen: J.C.B. Mohr [Paul Siebeck], 1901), p. 311, saw a confirmation of the land titles of non-combatants here. William L. Holladay, *Jeremiah 2: A Commentary on the Book of Jeremiah, Chapters 26–52* (Hermeneia; Minneapolis: Fortress Press, 1989), p. 293, does not exclude the possibility of a redistribution of land. See especially Carroll's discussion of the tension between Jer. 40–42 and the 'myth of the empty land' in 'Textual Strategies', p. 113; and his 'Myth of the Empty Land', pp. 79-94, 80-81. *Pace* J.N. Graham, ' "Vinedressers and Plowmen": 2 Kings 25:12 and Jeremiah 52:16', *BA* 47 (1984), pp. 55-58.

33. Pierre-Maurice Bogaert, 'Les trois formes de Jérémie 52 (TM, LXX, et VL)', in Gerard J. Norton and Stephen Pisano (eds.), *Tradition of the Text: Studies Offered to Dominique Barthélemy in Celebration of his 70th Birthday* (OBO, 109; Göttingen: Vandenhoeck & Ruprecht, 1991), pp. 1-17 (3-4, 8).

34. Bogaert's 'provisional' OL text has *residuum populi* = LXX. Raymond F. Person, Jr, 'II Kings 24,18–25,30 and Jeremiah 52: A Text-Critical Case Study in the Redaction History of the Deuteronomistic History', *ZAW* 105 (1993), pp. 174-205 (195, 201), reads יתר־העם = 2 Kgs 25.11 and Jer. 39.9MT. Though he is probably correct, retroversion within a narrow semantic range often results in a *non*

has 'reintegrated' the text with the account in 2 Kgs 25.12, restoring the report that all but 'some of the poorest of the land [וּמִדַּל[וֹ]ת הָאָרֶץ]' were exiled.[35]

The second MT plus introduces a striking feature of the MT redaction. It brings the entire diaspora, except for the Babylonian exiles, into the 'remnant in Judah' at this point.[36] When refugees from the small Trans-jordanian kingdoms arrive at Mizpah, the MT plus expands the summary: '*then all the Judeans returned from all the places to which they had been scattered and* they came to the land of Judah, to Gedaliah at Mizpah.'

Corresponding to this, the introductory reference to Judeans in '40/47.11LXX the entire land/earth'[37] now refers to Judeans in '11MT

liquet, especially where the editorial hand is heavy. Edwin Hatch and Henry Redpath, *A Concordance to the Septuagint and the Other Greek Versions of the Old Testament* (Grand Rapids: Baker Book House, 1983 [1897]), pp. 2, 738ab: κατα-λοίπους = שׁאר[י]ת 58/91—in Jer. 16/20; = יתר 26/91—in Jer. 0/20. This phrase renders שׁאר[י]ת הָעָם (cf. also 41/47.10) 12/21 and יתר הָעָם 8/21, characteristically when the 'people' are armed.

35. In Gedaliah's affirmation of his vassalage to the king of Babylon (40/47.9-10), Seitz has emphasized the confirmation of Jeremiah's admonitions before the fall of the city to submit to the king of Babylon, and the continuation of this admonition within this new situation. See especially *Theology*, pp. 205-207: 40/47.10 'As for me, I am remaining/enthroned [for LXX 'sitting before you'] at Mizpah to represent you before the Chaldeans.' The LXX 'sitting before you' κάθημαι ἐναντίον ὑμῶν = ישׁב לפיכם is rhetorically conciliatory, paralleling the subservience to the Chaldeans (Holladay, *Jeremiah 2*, p. 295) with subservience to the people. See Hatch and Redpath, *Concordance*, pp. 700-701 and Emanuel Tov, *The Septuagint Translation of Jeremiah and Baruch: A Discussion of an Early Revision of the LXX of Jeremiah 29–52 and Baruch 1:1–3:8* (HSM, 8; Missoula, MT: Scholars Press, 1976), p. 59. Without 'before you', the MT ישׁב בַּמִּצְפָּה could be rendered 'enthroned at Mizpah' under the imperial power of Babylon. Ludwig Koehler and Walter Baumgartner, *Lexicon in Veteris Testamenti Libros* (Leiden: E.J. Brill, 1958): ישׁב.

36. See also Stipp, *Das masoretische Sondergut*, p. 129.

37. 40/47.11. Peter Walters, *The Text of the Septuagint: Its Corruptions and their Emendation* (ed. D.W. Gooding; Cambridge: Cambridge University Press, 1973), pp. 188, 288, explains most translations of the plural 'lands' (בכל הארצות = ἐν πάσῃ τῇ γῇ) as a tendency to avoid the plural of γῆ. But plural translations of ארצות are devised in 38/75 cases. In any case, the MT plural is unambiguous, specifically assembling Judeans from all (foreign) lands, consistent with the insertion in vv. 12a. Janzen, *Studies*, p. 53 finds the phrasing of M 47/40.12a 12× in Jeremiah, 5× in MT plusses.

all *the lands'*. In the MT, the community under Gedaliah and Johanan appears to include every 'scattered' (נדח) Judean not 'exiled' to Babylon. At the end, only the Babylonian *gola* is exempt from the judgment on the remnant and its disastrous fate.

The Community under Johanan:
Jeremiah 41/48.10-18

In the account of the rescue of Ishmael's prisoners (41/48.10-18), the aftermath of the murder of Gedaliah,[38] the MT has stronger links with the earlier account of the assembling of the diaspora at Mizpah (40/47.12). In 41/48.10LXX, Ishmael 'takes back (MT deports)[39] all the people left in Mizpah, and the daughters of the king, [] whom [] the captain of the guard had appointed with Gedaliah the son of Ahikam', echoing 40/47.6, where Jeremiah remains 'among the people who were left in the land'. The rhetorical force of the repetitions in MT 41/48.10 is impressive, despite the strength of Janzen's argument that they are conflated variants rather than expansions.[40]

LXX 48.10	MT 41.10
Then Ishmael took back all	Then Ishmael took captive all
^the people	*the remnant of the people*
who were left at Mizpah^	who were in Mizpah
and the king's daughter(s)	and the king's daughters
	and all ^the people
	who were left at Mizpah^,
whom Nebuzaradan	whom Nebuzaradan
the captain of the guard	the captain of the guard
had committed to Gedaliah	had committed to Gedaliah
son of Ahikam	son of Ahikam

38. 40/47.13–41.48.9. See Bogaert, 'Libération', pp. 320-22. Seitz, *Theology*, p. 274: 'at no point in this narrative account is the post-587 remnant … negatively portrayed'.

39. Carroll, *Jeremiah*, p. 710: LXX and Tiberian vocalization are based on the same consonantal text. LXX ἀπέστρεψεν = וַיֶּשֶׁב, anticipating the use of שׁוב in vv. 14, 16. MT וַיִּשְׁבְּ anticipates the use of שׁבה in the MT plusses in vv. 10, 14. Stipp, *Das masoretische Sondergut*, pp. 126, 129; and especially *Parteienstreit*, pp. 184-86, sees an enhancement of the peril to the remnant and their commitment to Johanan in the MT revisions.

40. Janzen, *Studies*, p. 17.

LXX 48.10	MT 41.10
	Ishmael son of Nethaniah
	took them captive
and set out to cross over to	and went beyond
the Ammonites.	the Ammonites.[41]

The same may be said of vv. 14 and 16, also treated as variant readings by Janzen.[42]

> 41/48.13 And when all the people who were with Ishmael saw Johanan *son of Kareah* and *all* the leaders of the forces with him, they *were glad.* 14 *So all the people whom Ishmael had carried away captive from Mizpah turned around and* came back, *and went* to Johanan *son of Kareah,*
> ... 16 Then Johanan *son of Kareah* and all the leaders of the forces with him took all the remnant of the people whom he recovered from Ishmael *son of Nethaniah from Mizpah after he had slain Gedaliah son of Ahikam.*

With all due reservation, the rhetorical effect of the MT emphasizes the statement in v. 16 that everyone who had assembled at Mizpah had been taken away by Ishmael, and now became the community accepting the leadership of Johanan.[43] Now the fatal intention to go to Egypt in the original narrative (41/48.17) involves the entire remnant under Gedaliah, as it is expanded by the MT.

Response to Inquiry:
Jeremiah 42/49.7-22

The inquiry from Johanan, the commanders of the forces, and 'all the people from the least to the greatest' (42/49.1, 8; 2 Kgs 25.16) is

41. The MT, in addition to amplifying the rhetoric, contains echoes of a different pattern of texts. Though the 'remnant of the people' only appears in Jeremiah 41.10M; 41/48.16, it may echo 'the remnant of Judah', connected with the assembly of the diaspora (40/47.11) and with the concerns of Johanan (40/47.15). More important, it is connected with the words of judgment upon the 'remnant of Judah' that went to Egypt (chs. 43–44/50–51).

42. *Studies*, pp. 22-24. See his discussion, pp. 24-25, of peculiarities in the translation of the list of categories of people.

43. Stipp, *Das masoretische Sondergut*, pp. 126, 129, sees in the MT revisions a distancing of the Judean community from Ishmael and a closer connection with Johanan, who now becomes their leader.

followed by a word given through Jeremiah (42/49.7-18). This word has its background in Deuteronomic sermons that present alternatives to the community, promising salvation for obedience and judgment for disobedience.[44] In the LXX and the MT, the only hope for a future with God lies with those who remain in the land.[45] The pattern of rhetorical intensification is visible in the phrases bracketed by McKane.[46] Note especially the citation of the words of the people

> 42/49.13 But if you continue to say, 'We will not stay in this land', thus disobeying the voice of the LORD *your God* [14]*and saying, 'No, we will* go to the land of Egypt.

and the opening formula for the judgment word following this announcement of alternatives:

> 42/49.15 *Now* therefore hear the word of the LORD, *O remnant of Judah*. Thus says the LORD *of hosts, the God of Israel*: 'If you have set your face to *enter* Egypt and go to settle there ... [17]All the people ... who have set their faces to *go into* (LXX + the land of) Egypt to settle there shall die by the sword, (and) by famine, *and by pestilence*' ... [19]The LORD has said to you, O remnant of Judah, 'Do not go to Egypt. Be well aware *that I have warned you today* [20]that you have made a fatal mistake.'

The repetition of '*go/enter*' and '*there*' in vv. 15-17 emphasize the effect of this word upon those who went to Egypt. The address of the divine word to the (v. 15) '*remnant of Judah*' (= v. 19LM) in the MT includes all the people who live in the land, including the returned diaspora from all nations.

---

44. Winfried Thiel, *Die deuteronomistische Redaktion von Jeremia 26–45* (WMANT, 52; Neukirchen–Vluyn: Neukirchener Verlag, 1981), pp. 64-65; John Maclennan Berridge, *Prophet, People, and the Word of Yahweh: An Examination of Form and Content in the Proclamation of Jeremiah* (BST, 4; Zürich: EVZ-Verlag, 1970), p. 203.

45. The salvation oracle to those who remain in the land contains a thematic Jeremianic couplet, used here in a conditional promise: '42/49.9 Thus says the LORD, *the God of Israel, to whom you sent me to present your plea before him*: "10 If you will only remain in this land, then I will build you up and not pull you down; I will plant you, and not pluck you up." ' See Robert Bach, 'Bauen und Pflanzen', in Rolf Rendtorff and Klaus Koch (eds.), *Studien zur Theologie der alttestamentlichen Überlieferungen* (Neukirchen–Vluyn: Neukirchener Verlag, 1961), pp. 7-32, especially pp. 10, 27.

46. *Jeremiah*, II, pp. 1030-31.

Rejection of the Word:
Jeremiah 43/50.1-7

In the MT and the LXX*V*, 'all the people', led by the *'insolent* men'[47] (43/50.2) who challenged the authenticity of Jeremiah's word, left for Egypt, and 'arrived at Tahpanhes' (43/50.4-7). More emphatically, the land is emptied of 'all the remnant of Judah' in the LXX as well as the MT.[48] This fulfillment of the word of Jeremiah is not the creation of the MT elaboration. In the LXX, Jeremiah's words to the community under Gedaliah and Johanan are a continuation of his proclamation under Zedekiah. The MT has only heightened the severity of the word of judgment, and specifically included everyone in the land in the group that went to Egypt. At 43/50.5, the MT repeats a plus associated with the assembly of the diaspora at Mizpah (40/47.12). Though the reconstruction of 4QJer[b/d] from the surviving three letters (two partial) is disputed,[49] there is a strong likelihood that the MT adds those *'from*

47. MT plus הזדים. Note the LXX plus at 42/49.17, καὶ πάντες οἱ ἀλλογενεῖς = הזרים, [ר/ד], discussed in Janzen, *Studies*, p. 65 and Duhm, *Jeremia*, p. 323.

48. Christopher R. Seitz, 'The Crisis of Interpretation Over the Meaning and Purpose of the Exile: A Redactional Study of Jeremiah xxi-xliii', *VT* 35.1 (1985), pp. 78-97 (94): 'the people departed, down to the last soul'.

49. 4QJer[b/d] has ם?[] ?[] שארית כל את. Emanuel Tov, 'The Jeremiah Scrolls from Qumran', *RevQ* 14 (1989), pp. 189-206, argues that the three fragments of '4QJer[b]', first presented as a survival of a text tradition documenting a Hebrew Vorlage of the LXX in Janzen, *Studies*, pp. 181-84, actually come from different scribes, rather than different times in the scribe's work day. 9.22–10.18 is 4QJer[b]; the closely related 43.3-10 is 4QJer[d]; 50.4-6 is 4QJer[e]. In Eugene Ulrich *et al.*, *Qumran Cave 4. X. The Prophets* (DJD, 15; Oxford: Clarendon Press, 1997), p. 203 (Plate XXXVII—See also his 'Three Fragments of Jeremiah from Qumran Cave 4', *RevQ* 15 [1992], pp. 531-41 [538-39]; and *Textual Criticism of the Hebrew Bible* [Minneapolis: Fortress Press, 1992], p. 326), Tov offers a reconstruction that agrees with M:

M את כל־שארית יהודה אשר־שבו מכל־הגוים אשר נדחו־שם לגור בארץ יהודה:

T את כל־שארית] יהודה אשר־שבו מכל־הגוים אש[ר [נדחו־]שם:

Janzen, *Studies*, p. 53 n. 141, pp. 182-83, finds space only for a text similar to L:

L את כל־שארית יהודה אשר־שבו [] לגור בארץ []:

J את כל־שארית]יהודה אשר־שבו לגור בארץ[[מצרי]ם:

Stipp, *Das masoretische Sondergut*, p. 79 n. 51 supports Janzen: Tov's reconstruction of 4QJer[d] 43.5 is an 'Annahme' that rests 'auf schwachen paläographischen

all the nations to which they had been driven [נדח]' to the remnant leaving for Egypt (cf. 40/47.12):

> 43/50.5 But Johanan *son of Kareah* and all the commanders of the forces took all the remnant of Judah who had returned *from all the nations to which they had been driven* to settle in the land *of Judah*—⁶the men, the women, the children, the princesses, and everyone[?] whom Nebuzaradan *the captain of the guard* had left with Gedaliah son of Ahikam *son of Shaphan*; also the prophet Jeremiah and Baruch son of Neriah. ⁷And they came into *the land of* Egypt, for they did not obey the voice of the LORD. And they arrived at Tahpanhes.

The instruction to perform a symbolic action in Tahpanhes (43/50.8-13) is interpreted by a divine word that contains a much-discussed plus in the MT: '10 I am going to send and take *my servant* King Nebuchadrezzar of Babylon'.[50] Without a reprise of this discussion, note that Nebuchadnezzar will not only bring Egypt to an end but also, in this context, any Judean who has decided to go there.

Jeremiah's Response:
Jeremiah 44/51.1-14[51]

Jeremiah's final words in the LXX, following this climactic departure, are an announcement of disaster to '¹all the Judeans living in the land of

---

Indizien'. McKane, *Jeremiah*, II, pp. 1052-53, also sees too little room for a text like the MT without, however, discussing Tov's reconstruction.

For a discussion of the text and lexicography of 43/50.6 (and 41/48.16), see Joseph Ziegler, *Beiträge zur Jeremias-Septuaginta* (Mitteilungen des Septuaginta-Unternehmens der Akademie der Wissenschaften in Göttingen; Göttingen: Vandenhoeck & Ruprecht, 1958), pp. 53, 101; Janzen, *Studies*, p. 24.

50. See also 25.9, 27.6 and Berridge, *Prophet*, p. 125; Adrian Schenker, 'Nebukadnezzars Metamorphose vom Unterjocher zum Gottesknecht: Das Bild Nebukadnezzars und einige mit ihm Zusammenhängende Unterschiede in den beiden Jeremia-Rezensionen', *RB* 89 (1982), pp. 498-527 (523-27) (note his discussion of the changes of person at 43/50.10-13). Thomas W. Overholt, 'King Nebuchadnezzar in the Jeremiah Tradition', *CBQ* 30 (1968), pp. 39-48, and William McKane, 'Jeremiah 27,5-8, Especially "Nebuchadnezzar, My Servant" ', in Volkmar Fritz *et al.* (eds.), *Prophet und Prophetenbuch* (Festschrift Otto Kaiser; BZAW, 185; Berlin: W. de Gruyter, 1989), pp. 98-110. Note that, at 42/49.12, the king of Babylon has become the agent of the restoration (MT) promised in the name of God (LXX).

51. See the reconstruction in Stulman, *Prose Sermons*, pp. 112-17.

[Rahlfs γῆ = MT; Ziegler = 0][52] Egypt', who have come to Egypt with Johanan.[53] The MT plus '44/51.3 *neither they, nor you, nor your ancestors*' is characterized in chilling terms by Thiel.[54] This crisp formula connects the present with a sinful past, and expresses the solidarity of the present generation with its forebears in disobedience and judgment—but now there is no further Deuteronomic / Deuteronomistic call to repentance, and no further prophetic plea (vv. 4-5):

> 44/51.2 You yourselves have seen all the disaster that I have brought on Jerusalem and on *all* the towns of Judah. Look at them; *today* they are a desolation, without *an* inhabitant *in them*, 3 because of the wickedness that they committed, provoking me to anger, in that they went to make offerings *and serve* (LXX to) other gods that they (LXX you) had not known, *neither they, nor you, nor your ancestors.*

The focus on the solidarity of the remnant with its forebears is continued in the awkward addition of '*your own crimes*' in v. 9, underlined by the expansions in v. 10:

> 44/51.9 Have you forgotten the crimes of your ancestors, of the kings of Judah, of *his wives, your own crimes* (LXX your officials) and those of your wives,[55] which they committed in the land of Judah and in the streets of Jerusalem? [10]They have shown no contrition *or fear* to this day, nor have they walked in my *law and my* statutes that I set before *you and before your* (LXX their?) ancestors.[56]

---

52. Joseph Ziegler, *Jeremias Baruch Threni Epistula Jeremiae* (Septuaginta; Vetus Testamentum Graecum, 15; Göttingen: Vandenhoeck & Ruprecht, 2nd edn, 1976). Alfred Rahlfs, *Septuaginta: Id est Vetus Testamentum Graece iuxta LXX Interpretes* (Stuttgart: Privilegierte Württembergische Bibelanstalt, 6th edn, n.d.).

53. Stipp, *Das masoretische Sondergut*, pp. 161-63, finds in the MT tense changes and 'deictic elements' a conscious effort to give the speeches in 43/50.8– ch. 44 a 'Palestinian' setting. Briefly, (1) he has not eliminated the possibility that 'tense changes' are 'pseudo-variants' (Tov), or (2) that the 'deictic particle' שׁם is a side effect of MT efforts to interlock this speech with the earlier speech in the land (beginning with the addition of a phrase from 42/49.15 at 44/51.12 without removing MT שׁם—note also the discussion of שׁם at 42/49.16 and of בוא at 42/49.15, 17).

54. *Jeremia 26–45*, pp. 1069-70.

55. Janzen, *Studies*, pp. 18-19 discusses the array of LXX variant readings, and the perplexing נשׁיו in the MT.

56. Though most of these plusses could be Deuteronomistic, Berridge, *Prophet*, pp. 204-205, says that 44.11 'set His face against [נתן/שׂם פֿנ] (MT = LXX)' reflects Ezekiel or H, not Dtr Dtn. Stipp, *Das masoretische Sondergut*, p. 57, thinks that none of this 'legal terminology' is Deuteronomistic.

The MT plusses in 44/51.11-14, as at 42/49.13-22, considerably amplify the accusation and the threat addressed to the remnant, or in the MT the remnant *of Judah*. The resumption of the word *disaster* (רעה) from LXXV/MT vv. 2-3, 5 is part of an amplification of this final announcement of disaster that goes far beyond the modest expansions in v. 2. The opening of this announcement in the LXXV 'I am determined to [] bring to an end (LXX all) the remnant [] in [] Egypt' (v. 11) seems quite laconic when compared to the MT. In the opening of the judgment word, the characterization and fate of the remnant (now 'all Judah') are expanded *in malam partem*:

> 44/51.11b I am determined *to bring disaster on you*, to bring to an end all *Judah*. [12a]*I will take* the remnant *of Judah who are determined to come to the land of Egypt to settle, and they shall perish, everyone*; in *the land of* Egypt.

In the announcement of judgment, despite uncertainties in the Greek tradition, there is a similar tendency—especially in conventional formulas:

> 44/51.12b They shall fall by the sword and by famine they shall perish; from the least to the greatest, *they shall die by the sword and by famine*; and they shall become an object of *execration and* horror, of cursing and ridicule. [13]I will punish those who live in *?the land of* (Ziegler; Rahlfs = MT) Egypt, as I have punished Jerusalem, with the sword, with famine, *?and with pestilence* (Ziegler; Rahlfs = MT), [14]so that none of the remnant of Judah who have come to settle (LXX settled) there in the land of Egypt shall escape *or survive* (? οὐκ ἔσται σεσῳσμένος οὐθεὶς) or return to the land of Judah. Although they long to go back *to live* there, they shall not go back, except some fugitives.

If the communities under Gedaliah (40.7 *the poorest of the land*; 40.12 *all the Judeans ... from all the places to which they had been scattered*) and Johanan (41.10 *all the rest/remnant of the people who were in Mizpah*; 41.13 *all the people whom Ishmael had carried away captive from Mizpah*) are brought forward into this context, there seem to be no standing claimants to the land—whether it is empty or not.

Final Word and Sign:
Jeremiah 44.15-28, 29-30

The response to the credo (44/51.15-19) of the worshipers of the Queen of Heaven transmutes the accursed land that results from idolatry into a still empty land, that continues to attest the idolatry of the Judeans who went to Egypt:

> 44/51.22 The LORD could no longer bear your evil doings, the abominations that you committed; therefore your land became a desolation and a waste and a curse, *without inhabitant,* as it is to this day. 23 It is because you burned offerings, and because you sinned against the LORD and did not obey the voice of the LORD or walk in his law and in his statutes and in his decrees, that this disaster has befallen you, *as is still evident today.*

This verse forms an *inclusio* in the LXX and the MT, placing the Judeans under Johanan in the situation under Zedekiah before the destruction of the nation: '40/47.3 All of you sinned against *the LORD* (LXX him) and did not obey his voice. *Therefore this thing has come upon you.*' The judgment in the new situation is analogous to the old judgment—the essential annihilation of the Judeans in the land of Egypt, described in a 'doom oracle complex'[57] that climaxes in the MT plus at 44/51.29. Certain of the MT plusses underline the judgment described in the LXX*V*:

> 44/51.24 Jeremiah said to *all* the people and *all* the women, 'Hear the word of the LORD, *all you Judeans who are in the land of Egypt,* [25]Thus says the LORD *of hosts,* the God of Israel: 'You *and your wives* (LXX women[58]) have accomplished in deeds what you declared in words, saying, 'We are determined to perform the vows that we have made, to make offerings to the queen of heaven and to pour out libations to her.' By all means, keep your vows and perform *your vows* (LXX them)! 44.26 Therefore hear the word of the LORD, all you Judeans who live in the land of Egypt: 'Lo, I swear by my great name, says the LORD, that my name shall no longer be *pronounced* on the lips of *any of the people of Judah* (יהודה שׁ אִישׁ־כָל LXX παντὸς Ιουδα) all Judeans) in all the land of Egypt, saying, 'As the Lord GOD lives.' [27]I am going to watch over them *for harm* (LXX to do them harm) and not *for* good; *any of the people of Judah* (LXX 'all Judeans') who *are* (LXX live) in the land of Egypt shall perish by the sword and by famine, until not one is left.

There is no expression of hope for the stray fugitives 'who escape the

---

57. Martin Kessler, 'A Prophetic Biography: A Form-Critical Study of Jeremiah, Chapters 26–29, 32–45' (PhD Dissertation, University of Brandeis, 1965), pp. 326-27.

58. Stipp, *Das masoretische Sondergut,* p. 127 n. 44, connects this variant with Masoretic 'smoothing' of incongruities encountered at 44/51.15 and 19 (Syriac and Lucianic)—v. 25 cites 44/51.17.

sword' in the LXX*V*. Their only function will be to know the outcome
of the conflict between the word of Jeremiah and the word of the worshipers of the Queen of Heaven. This conflict is underlined by the MT
plus *mine or theirs* (v. 29), in a continued focus on the community
under Johanan:

> 44/51.28 And those who escape the sword shall return *from the land of*
> *Egypt* to the land of Judah, few in number; and *all* the remnant of Judah,
> who have come to the land of Egypt to settle, shall know whose words
> will stand, *mine or theirs*!

The LXX*V* of v. 29 offers a future demonstration that this judgment is
of God's making: 'This shall be the sign to you, [] that I am going to
visit (פקד) you [] for evil: 30 Thus says the LORD, I am going to give
[] Hophra, king of Egypt, into the hands of his enemies, those who seek
his life.' The MT plus in v. 29 explicitly makes this defeat a confirmation not only of Jeremiah's prophetic act in 43/50.8-13, but also of his
words of judgment upon the Judeans in Egypt.

> 44/51.29 This shall be the sign to you, *says the LORD*, that I am going to
> punish (פקד) you *in this place, in order that you may know that my*
> *words shall surely stand against you* for evil: [30]Thus says the LORD, I
> am going to give *Pharaoh* Hophra, king of Egypt, into the hands of his
> enemies, those who seek his life, just as I gave King Zedekiah of Judah
> into the hand of King Nebuchadrezzar of Babylon, his enemy who
> sought his life.

Carroll's stark conclusion precisely reflects the major tendency of the
Masòretic revision: 'All the Jewish communities, apart from the one in
Babylon, are written off as objects of Yahweh's implacable wrath.'[59]
    This unobtrusive 'rereading'[60] in the MT shows an overwhelming ten-
dency to echo existing phrases from the Jeremianic, Deuteronomic or
Deuteronomistic tradition, rather than generating striking or original
phrases. The originality lies in combination, repetition and juxtaposition. The traditions being reread are handled with respect, leaving
inconsistencies in viewpoint that do not satisfy an academic sense of

---

    59. *Jeremiah*, p. 743. Brueggemann, *Jeremiah 26–52*, p. 184, notes the 'inter-
play of *vested interest* and *theological affirmation* [emphasis his]', but his view of
the 'canonical process' leads him to emphasize the 'theological faithfulness' (p. 743
n. 75) of these old ideological claims.
    60. See the astute comments in Léo Laberge, 'Jérémie 25, 1-14: Dieu et Juda ou
Jérémie et tous les peuples [LXX vs. MT]', *Science et Esprit* 36 (1984), pp. 45-66
(61-62), who offers a more ambitious schema.

logic. The clarity of Seitz's analysis of the ongoing dialogue between faith and concrete history is a stimulus and a challenge to the less ambitious analysis of the Masoretic editing of Jeremiah,[61] as is McKane's idea of a 'rolling corpus'[62] that mandates closer examination of specific texts and their interrelations, and less concern with global redactional theories. Brueggemann's reading of the subversive force of Jeremiah's theological affirmation of Babylonian power under Zedekiah—'God's counterword'—invites further reflection. When this affirmation is incorporated into the ideology of the victors in an economic and political power struggle behind the canonical form of the text,[63] other issues emerge. The dialogue between the canonical form of Jeremiah accepted by the Roman Synagogues and Latin Christendom and the canonical form accepted by the Alexandrian Synagogues and by Patristic and Byzantine Christendom allows an amplification of the marginalized voices on the other side of the issue, replacing an authoritative conclusion with an ongoing dialogue within the tradition. It is even likely that the Masoretic revisions are better understood as the early stages in Carroll's *Rezeptionsgeschichte*[64] of the book of Jeremiah.[65]

By endorsing, amplifying and supplementing aspects of what appears to be a finished form of the tradition, the MT emphasizes elements of a bleak picture of the apostate 'remnant of Judah', defiantly refusing the prophetic word as their forebears had, and committed to idolatry. In the

61. *Theology, passim,* discussed earlier.

62. William McKane, *A Critical and Exegetical Commentary on Jeremiah.* I. *Introduction and Commentary on Jeremiah I–XXV* (ICC; Edinburgh: T. & T. Clark, 1986), pp. l-lxxxiii. See his remarks in *Jeremiah,* II, pp. 1091-95.

63. Walter Brueggemann, *A Commentary on Jeremiah: Exile and Homecoming* (Grand Rapids: Eerdmans, 1998), pp. 360-64, and especially p. 395 n. 75, p. 366 n. 42.

64. Robert P. Carroll, 'The Discombobulations of Time and the Diversities of Text: Notes on the *Rezeptionsgeschichte* of the Bible', in *idem* (ed.), *Text as Pretext: Essays in Honour of Robert Davidson* (JSOTSup, 138; Sheffield: Sheffield Academic Press, 1992), pp. 61-85, especially pp. 83-85.

65. Samuel J. Pezzillo, my colleague in Classics, has called my attention to the complex problem of the lists of obelized lines from Aristarchus's edition of the Iliad. George Mellville Bolling, in *The Athetized Lines of the Iliad* (Baltimore: Linguistic Society of America, 1944), offers a convenient introduction to his thesis that the longer standard edition of the Iliad was an Athenian master text, expanded tendentiously from the shorter version (associated with Zenodotus) that lacked these obelized lines. Though the structure of the problem is different, much can be learned from his work.

coming judgment upon Egypt, this remnant will be virtually wiped out except for a few who escape the sword and learn too late. Ultimately, they have forfeited any legitimate claim on the land they deliberately abandoned. In this, they appear to be a foil for the exiles. The privileging of the Babylonian exiles consists in the final elimination of all other claimants to a future in the land.

DRESSED TO BE KILLED: JEREMIAH 4.29-31 AS AN EXAMPLE FOR THE FUNCTIONS OF FEMALE IMAGERY IN JEREMIAH*

Angela Bauer

In the book of Jeremiah female imagery appears in central passages. Whether bride, prostitute and wife, or promiscuous woman, woman in labor and woman raped, whether wise women mourners, musicians and teachers, or Rachel weeping for her children, and the women worshiping the Queen of Heaven, these gendered images clash and contend while they sustain the literary-theological movement of the book in remarkable reversals. A closer look at a cluster of female images in Jer. 4.29-31 will provide a lens for reading the gendered constructions and rhetorical strategies, that is the functions of female imagery in the overall composition of Jeremiah.

Jeremiah 4.29-31

Like in the judgment oracles that precede, devastation in Jer. 4.29-31 is portrayed in female imagery. The deity addresses the people as 'Desolate One' and identifies them/her as 'Daughter Zion':

> 29 At the sound of a rider and shooter of a bow,[1]
> > fleeing [is] all the city,[2]
> > they go into thickets,[3]
> > and among rocks they climb;
> > all the city [is] abandoned,
> > and not anyone is dwelling in them.

---

*   An earlier version of this essay was presented at a session of the Composition of the Book of Jeremiah Consultation at the 1993 SBL Annual Meeting in Washington, DC.
1.   Many Mss. have plural. In parallel with פֶּרֶשׁ the singular is consistent.
2.   LXX has πᾶσα χώρα, 'all the land'.
3.   LXX expands reading εἰσέδυσαν εἰς τὰ σπήλαια καὶ ... ἐκρύβησαν, 'they enter into caves and [...] hide themselves'.

30 And you,[4] o Desolate One,[5]
    what are you doing   that [*kî*] you dress up in scarlet;
                         that [*kî*] you adorn yourself in adornments of gold,[6]
                         that [*kî*] you enlarge with paint your eyes?
    in vain you beautify yourself.
    They reject you—[your] lovers;
    your life they seek.
31 Lo [*kî*] the sound as of a woman in labor I heard,[7]
    anguish as of one bringing forth her first child;[8]
the sound of Daughter Zion gasping for breath,[9]
        stretching out her hands,
    'woe to me, for/lo [*kî*] perishing [is] my life before murderers'.[10]

The word for sound (קוֹל) marks the boundaries of the unit, as its content is embodied in the text. The noise of war opens the poem; the pained cry of a woman in labor, of Daughter Zion in agony between life and death stands at its close. In between, sight rather than sound gives

    4.   *Kethib* represents an archaic spelling of 2nd f. sing. pronoun; cf. Judg. 17.2; 1 Kgs 14.2; 2 Kgs 4.16, 23; 8.1; Ezek. 36.13. For archaic spellings of 2nd f. sing. verb forms in Jeremiah see, e.g., Jer. 3.5.

    5.   William L. Holladay, *Jeremiah 1: A Commentary on the Book of the Prophet Jeremiah, Chapters 1–25* (Hermeneia; Philadelphia: Fortress Press, 1986), pp. 144-45, reconstructs the cola, reading the participle with the previous colon, the necessity of which eludes me. The participle is missing in LXX. William McKane, *A Critical and Exegetical Commentary on Jeremiah. I. Introduction and Commentary of Jeremiah I–XXV* (ICC; Edinburgh: T. & T. Clark, 1986), p. 111, refers to Kimchi's observation of the dual use of שָׁדוּד as masculine and as feminine with Israel (cf. GKC §145t), and opts for the deletion of the participle here for lack of grammatical congruence.

    6.   Commentaries disagree on detecting a dittography here. Paul Volz, *Der Prophet Jeremia* (KAT; Leipzig: A. Deichert, 1922), p. 52, suspects dittography; so does Wilhelm Rudolph, *Jeremia* (HAT, 1.12; Tübingen: J.C.B. Mohr, 3rd edn, 1968), p. 36. Holladay, *Jeremiah 1*, p. 145, considers it possible but not necessary.

    7.   MT כְּחוֹלָה with ו suggests a fem. ptc. of the root חלה, 'to be sick'; the parallel כְּמַבְכִּירָה, however, suggests fem. ptc. of חיל, 'to shake, whirl'; thus the translation 'woman in labor'; cf. LXX, Vulgate and Targum.

    8.   LXX reads τοῦ στεναγμοῦ σου, 'of your groaning'.

    9.   תִּתְיַפֵּחַ, htp. of יפח is a *hapax legomenon*. The versions offer several renditions: LXX 'shall be fainting', Vulgate 'who is fainting', Targum 'who is prostrating herself', S 'who is working to exhaustion'. Holladay (*Jeremiah 1*, p. 145) suggests יפח as a by-form of פוח I and נפח, 'blow', thus translating the word as 'panting'.

    10. LXX and Vulgate read ptc. passive, 'the slain'.

access to another image of a woman who is challenged on her appearance and consequently threatened.

Divine first-person speech (4.23-28) has given way to third-person report (4.29-31). Five parallel cola describe the reaction to the קוֹל פָּרָשׁ וְרֹמֵה קֶשֶׁת, 'the sound of a rider and shooter of a bow', the response to the noise of war. The entire city flees. The direction of the flight is specified twice: they go into thickets and they climb among rocks. Also the result of the flight is stated twice: the abandoned city and no one dwelling there anymore. Desolation ensues.

In second-person speech, the deity addresses the 'Desolate One' (4.30). Discrepancy in gender between the personal pronoun (וְאַתְּי, 2nd f. sing.) and the vocative (שָׁדוּד, ptc. m. sing.) alerts the reader to confusion. It seems an appropriate means to mirror the chaotic situation after the hasty departure from the city. A rhetorical question completes the sentence. It moves from a general inquiry regarding the action of the female ('what are you doing?') to a tripartite specification of the alleged behavior.

> what are you doing   that [*kî*] you dress up in scarlet;
> that [*kî*] you adorn yourself in adornments of gold,
> that [*kî*] you enlarge with paint your eyes?
>
> (4.30a)

Three times in a recitative function, the particle כִּי opens each of the parallel cola. Each time a second-person feminine singular active verb follows to paint part of the woman's image: 'you dress-up', 'you adorn yourself' and 'you enlarge your eyes'. So far we see a woman/city who cares for her appearance, putting on special clothing, jewelry and make-up. She does it gradually, carefully. The text uses three separate phrases, stressing the importance of the procedure, and slowing the action with details. The modifiers that follow the three verbs supply the color for the picture.[11] She dresses 'in scarlet'; the clothing is red. She puts on 'gold' jewelry. She enlarges her eyes with paint adding the black of the eye make-up. She looks ready to go out and enjoy herself. Yet, the image is in tension with its context. Against the background of

---

11. Cf. Athalya Brenner, *Colour Terms in the Old Testament* (JSOTSup, 21; Sheffield: JSOT Press, 1982); on שָׁנִי, 'scarlet, crimson', for textiles, Brenner, *Colour Terms*, pp. 143-45; on פּוּךְ, which is 'eye make-up the color of which is determined in the process', a powder 'to blacken the area around the eyes', Brenner, *Colour Terms*, p. 151.

the desolate city this woman appears out of place, overdressed and
heading in the wrong direction (since there is no place left to go out to).
Who is she? The text does not say, but asserts the vanity of her effort:
'in vain you beautify yourself'. In the context of desolation, appearance
does not attract spectators. The sight is not seen. Rather, judgment is
passed on the woman.

> *They reject* you—[your] lovers;
> your life *they seek.*
>   (4.30b)

In chiastic word order, the two cola reveal the woman's fate and give
away her identity. Identified by the existence of her lovers, she is the
promiscuous woman familiar to the reader from the first cycle of
oracles in the book (Jer. 2.20, 25, 33; 3.1-5). Here her destiny is
sealed—literally closed in—by the action of these lovers. 'They reject'
her; moreover, 'they seek' her life. Two verbs that in context forebode
desolation and death surround her, the object. Paradox characterizes
these verbs in their action of rejecting, yet seeking. The object of the
search, the woman's life, turns the isolation of the beginning into a
death threat by the end. Isolated and helpless, the dressed-up woman is
lost in desolation, caught in the male gaze. She is presented to the
voyeurs/readers dressed to (be) kill(ed).

Hitzig and Holladay point to the similarities between this image of
the promiscuous woman and the motif of the woman at the window,
mentioning Jezebel in 2 Kgs 9.30.[12] For both scholars this parallel
underscores the power of judgment against the female. The ideological
bias of such unequivocal readings awaits further exploration.[13] Commenting on the female images of Jer. 4.29-31, Carroll states that
'[s]ome modern readers will take offence at the biblical use of feminine
metaphors to denigrate or describe the collapse of the city'. He claims
that these images 'hardly imply an undervaluing of women in the
society from which they emanate'. With the assertion that the 'metaphorical status [of these images] must be recognized as removing them
from the sphere of direct comment on the valuation of real people', he

---

    12. Ferdinand Hitzig, *Der Prophet Jeremia* (KHCAT, 11; Leipzig: J.C.B. Mohr,
1901), p. 40; Holladay, *Jeremiah 1*, p. 170.
    13. A more sympathetic reading of the Jezebel story, exploring her role(s) in the
narrative on various levels of ideological function, may find that the gender relations in that story, too, are more complex.

launches an attack on feminist interpretations of these metaphors and their impact as 'not only misguided but [...] often exegetically unbalanced'.[14] He cites Ochshorn and Trible as representatives of such feminist readings. To my knowledge, however, neither Trible nor Ochshorn have written on Jer. 4.29-31. In any case, biblical metaphors continue to have power in contemporary discourses and as such need to be explored as to who is helped and who is hurt by their use.[15]

From the image of the woman ironically made-up for death, rather than love-making, the text moves to a third image. Second-person speech shifts to first-person discourse.

> Lo [*kî*] the sound as of a woman in labor I heard,
>> anguish as of one bringing forth her first child;
> the sound of Daughter Zion gasping for breath,
>>> stretching out her hands,
>>>> 'woe to me, for/lo [*kî*] perishing [is] my life before murderers'.
>
> (4.29-31)

An asseverative, emphatic כי opens the verse. Sound characterizes the recently introduced female image (cf. 4.19). The deity reports hearing קול כחולה, 'the sound as of a woman in labor'. From the sight of an overdressed woman, the text has moved to the sound of a mother struggling to give birth. The parallel colon fleshes out the impression even more: צרה כמבכירה, 'anguish as of one who brings forth her first child'. Pain echoes in this woman's voice, but for the sake of life at this special moment of giving birth for the first time. Who is she? Her identity is not yet made clear, though the context of the desolate city is suggestive. The deity hears more, as the force of the divine שמעתי carries over into the second half of the verse. Parallel to the קול כחולה, there resounds קול בת־ציון תתיפח, 'the sound of Daughter Zion gasping for breath'. The intensity of the sound heightens. Is Zion the woman in labor? The sound of a woman gasping for breath would imply that. At

14. Robert P. Carroll, *Jeremiah: A Commentary* (OTL; Philadelphia: Westminster Press, 1986), pp. 172-73.

15. See, e.g., Barbara A. Bozak, CSJ, *Life 'Anew': A Literary-Theological Study of Jer. 30–31* (AnBib, 122; Rome: Pontificio Istituto Biblico, 1991), pp. 157-72; cf. also Sallie McFague, *Metaphorical Theology: Models of God in Religious Language* (Philadelphia: Fortress Press, 1982); Carole R. Fontaine, 'The Abusive Bible: On the Use of Feminist Method in Pastoral Care', in Athalya Brenner and Carole Fontaine (eds.), *A Feminist Companion to Reading the Bible: Approaches, Methods and Strategies* (Sheffield: Sheffield Academic Press, 1997), pp. 84-113.

the same time, it introduces a moment of death into the struggle for new life. The woman is indeed struggling as the next colon emphasizes: she stretches out her hands. The struggle to give birth has become a struggle to survive herself. As the threat to her life seems to approach not only from within but also from without, the bent toward death becomes even stronger. As climax and closure, the final colon comes in the form of a direct quotation. The woman is speaking, crying אוֹי־נָא לִי כִּי־עָיְפָה נַפְשִׁי לְהֹרְגִים, 'woe to me, for perishing [is] my life before murderers'. Subtly, the woman's pain for life has turned into a cry of death. Thus the verse connects back to the beginning of the poem, the deadly war and the desolate city.

Three images representing reversals have been piled on top of each other, the desolate city, the overdressed woman threatened to be killed by her lovers, and the woman in labor who cries for her life.[16] Unified in gender, the images portray female figures as vulnerable, in pain, facing death—desolation engendered. Promiscuous woman and dying mother have joined in a depiction of devastated Jerusalem. Reversing all expectations—fleeing from rather than to the city; dressed not 'to kill' but to be killed; being in labor not to give birth but to die—the rhetorical strategy has become blunt. The triple emphasis leaves no doubt as to the severity of the situation. And female images have carried the literary movement to that point.

Surveying the Book

(Fe)male images and metaphors accumulate especially in the first sections of Jeremiah, the prologue and the first two cycles of judgment oracles (Jer. 1.1–6.30).[17] A female metaphor gives birth to YHWH's first words in the book. The womb, the organ unique to the female, encloses God's creativity to bring forth the origin and destiny of the

16. On the rhetorical figure of 'extended metaphor' here, see Renita J. Weems, 'Sexual Violence as an Image for Divine Retribution in the Prophetic Writings' (unpubl. PhD dissertation, Princeton, NJ, Princeton Theological Seminary, 1989), p. 212 n. 87.

17. For a detailed analysis of the functions of female imagery in the book of Jeremiah, see Angela Bauer, *Gender in the Book of Jeremiah: A Feminist-Literary Reading* (Studies in Biblical Literature, 5; New York: Peter Lang, 1999). Cf. also Kathleen M. O'Connor, 'Jeremiah', in Carol A. Newsom and Sharon H. Ringe (eds.), *The Women's Bible Commentary* (Louisville, KY: Westminster/John Knox Press, 1992), pp. 169-77.

prophet. An ambiguity retained in the text whereby 'in the womb' (בבטן) has no pronominal link to Jeremiah's human mother invites an association of God with the maternal organ. YHWH brings Jeremiah forth and calls the prophet from the womb (Jer. 1.5).

This initial metaphor is soon contrasted by different female images in the oracles of judgment that follow the prologue (Jer. 1.1-19). Marital imagery succeeds parental imagery to represent YHWH's relationship with the people. Images of bride, prostitute, wife and promiscuous woman appear as Jeremiah calls the people to repent in a first cycle of judgment oracles (Jer. 2.1–4.4).[18] Israel as the loving bride of cherished memory (אהבת כלולתיך) provides background contrast for the present picture of Israel as prostitute and promiscuous woman. Under judgment, Israel as female is compared to a cow-camel and a wild ass that are unable to control their sexual impulses. She is exposed, violated and publicly humiliated. Her indictment results in divorce. Her sexual activity is faulted for the pollution of the land. Yet she is still invited to repent. Images of sexual violence against the female underscore the severity of the judgment. Athalya Brenner has called these passages 'Jeremian pornography', poems of male voices abusing metaphorized female sexuality.[19] Alice Keefe's contention that 'the violated body of woman functions as a metonym for the social body as it is disrupted in war' can also apply to these texts.[20]

When the request for repentance gives way to judgment in the next cycle of oracles (Jer. 4.5–6.30), the people, addressed as בת עמי, 'Daughter My People', and בת־ציון, 'Daughter Zion', face destruction. Jeremiah identifies with Jerusalem and takes on a female persona in lamenting her suffering (Jer. 4.19-21), a female voice with

18. For a close reading of the function of gendered images in this section, see A.R. Pete Diamond and Kathleen M. O'Connor, 'Unfaithful Passions: Coding Women Coding Men in Jeremiah 2–3 (4:2)', *BibInt* 4.3 (1996), pp. 288-310. Cf. also Mary E. Shields, 'Circumcision of the Prostitute: Gender, Sexuality, and the Call to Repentance in Jeremiah 3:1–4:4', *BibInt* 3.1 (1995), pp. 61-74.

19. Athalya Brenner, 'On "Jeremiah" and the Poetics of Pornography', in Athalya Brenner and Fokkelien van Dijk-Hemmes, *On Gendering Texts: Female and Male Voices in the Hebrew Bible* (Leiden: E.J. Brill, 1993), pp. 178-93; cf. *eadem*, 'Pornoprophetics Revisited', *JSOT* 70 (1996), pp. 63-86; J. Cheryl Exum, 'Prophetic Pornography', in *idem*, *Plotted, Shot, and Painted: Cultural Representations of Biblical Women* (GCT, 3; JSOTSup, 215; Sheffield: Sheffield Academic Press, 1996), p. 107.

20. Alice Keefe, 'Rapes of Women/Wars of Men', *Semeia* 61 (1993), pp. 79-97.

transgendered resonances.[21] The metaphor of a woman in labor pain depicts the ultimate agony of the people. As we have already seen, in the following prophetic oracle this voice of woman agonizing in labor mingles with the image of a promiscuous woman, overdressed and set up for death rather than love (Jer. 4.29-31). Female imagery continues to embody indictment and judgment.

In the next section of the book (Jer. 7.1–25.38), female images and metaphors continue to surface in various ways. The women worshipping the Queen of Heaven (7.16-20) and the wise women mourners and teachers (9.16-21 [MT]; Eng. 9.17-22) are prominent in the beginning of this movement wherein impending disaster turns into experienced destruction. Women who are not identified by family ties take on leadership roles in the rituals venerating the goddess (7.16-20). Their cultic activity is condemned as apostasy, the reason for inevitable punishment. In the face of destruction, grief and mourning remain the only option. YHWH calls on the dirge-singing wise women to wail and to teach each other and their daughters to lament (9.16-18 [MT]). The ensuing jeremiad continues with the unique divine command to women to listen to YHWH's word, the only time in the Hebrew Bible that the formula is addressed to women: שמענה נשים דבר־יהוה (9.19 [MT]). It results in the divine order for the women to teach their daughters a wailing and each other a dirge in the face of death. Again, women take on leadership roles in a requiem of remembrance (9.20-21 [MT]). The sound of female voices is heard at a turning point in the book of Jeremiah, at a point of reversal in the history of the people.

Beyond the possibility for repentance, in the next part of the second movement the prophet agonizes over his identification with the people. Female imagery provides thematic continuity in the section organized around the so-called confessions of Jeremiah (11.1–20.18). The voice of the prophet, male and female, echoes the devastation that has female faces. The metaphor of woman violated, exposed, and raped with the approval and involvement of the deity (13.20-27) confronts the reader(s) and listener(s) with the cruel fate of the people as female—

---

21. For a close reading of this passage, see Angela Bauer, 'Jeremiah as Female Impersonator: Roles of Difference in Gender Perception and Gender Perceptivity', in Harold C. Washington, Susan Lochrie Graham and Pamela Thimmes (eds.), *Escaping Eden: New Feminist Perspectives on the Bible* (Biblical Seminar, 65; Sheffield: Sheffield Academic Press, 1998).

pornoprophetics in the name of God.[22] Then, the image of a mother
shamed and humiliated (15.8-9) adds to the portrayal of the people
under destruction. In the final confession, the prophet again takes on a
female persona, sounding a female voice when accusing the deity of
seduction and rape (20.7). Jeremiah's wish for his mother's womb to
have been his tomb (20.14-18) echoes the call of the prophet, as the
female organ enfolds origin and destiny.

Once more in the conclusion (21.1–25.38) of this section (7.1–25.38),
female imagery emerges to embody the fate of the people. Sexual
violence against the female and her birthing pain depict the suffering of
exile (22.20-23), which recall *in nuce* female images of judgment
throughout the first part of the book (Jer. 1–25).

Female images and metaphors show distinct variations in the second
half of the book of Jeremiah (Jer. 26–52). In this mainly narrative portion of Jeremiah, female imagery appears in particular sections which
are predominantly poetic. After the destruction of the city has become a
reality, when the future is addressed in the so-called Book of Consolation (Jer. 30–31[33]), female images are omnipresent.[23] The pain of the
present is likened to the birthpangs of a woman, and these are even
attributed to a warrior-male (גבר, 30.6). Then, in the realm of the future,
בתולת ישראל, 'Maiden Israel', is dancing and playing drums (31.4, 13),
mirroring her ancestor Miriam at the Sea (cf. Exod. 15.20-21). The
female, musician and mourner (cf. Jer. 9.16-21), finds her sorrow
reversed to joy. YHWH offers her comfort (31.13), extending the
Divine Self to Rachel who is weeping for her children refusing to be
comforted (31.15). God shows motherly compassion with the divine
womb (מעי) trembling for Ephraim (31.20). Indeed, female imagery
multiplies to embody an eschatological theology of compassion and
new creation. The poem (31.15-22) climaxes in a promise to Israel

---

22. Cf. Exum, 'Prophetic Pornography', pp. 107-108, 115-22; F. Rachel
Magdalene, 'Ancient Near Eastern Treaty-Curses and the Ultimate Texts of Terror:
A Study of the Language of Divine Sexual Abuse in the Prophetic Corpus', in
Athalya Brenner (ed.), *A Feminist Companion to the Latter Prophets* (The Feminist
Companion to the Bible, 8; Sheffield: Sheffield Academic Press, 1995), pp. 326-52,
esp. pp. 328-29; Pamela Gordon and Harold C. Washington, 'Rape as a Military
Metaphor in the Hebrew Bible', in Brenner (ed.), *A Feminist Companion*, pp. 308-
25; esp. pp. 316, 323-25; see also Harold C. Washington, 'Violence and the Construction of Gender in the Hebrew Bible: A New Historicist Approach', *BibInt* 5.4
(1997), pp. 324-63.

23. For a close reading of Jer. 30–31, see, e.g., Bozak, *Life 'Anew'*.

addressed as the rebellious Daughter (31.22). In the creation of something new there is the vision of female surrounding warrior-male (31.22b) which explodes the limits of the gendered imagery in this section of the book. The theological movement from exile to eschatology is mirrored there. Climactically, the new quality of gender relations finds another expression in the promise of a new covenant (31.31-34) which is established in the form of a marriage contract (31.33), yet beyond traditional patriarchal role divisions. Indeed, in the realm of eschatology the female is ubiquitous.

Yet moving from this glimpse into the future back to the reality of the present, from eschatology back to the experiences of exile, the book returns to oracles of judgment indicting Israel and the nations. Jeremiah once more condemns the people for worshipping the Queen of Heaven (44.15-25; cf. 7.16-20). Again, women play a prominent role in the veneration of the goddess, an act denounced by the prophet. Indeed, their voices cannot be suppressed and subsequently are declared the problem. Then, in the oracles against the nations (46–51) some of the same vocabulary and images for the female that served to depict Israel (e.g. a mother shamed and disgraced, or woman suffering birth pangs) illustrate the fate of the nations. The language of judgment in the female images of shame, pain and violation recall the indictment of Israel addressed as female throughout the book.

Indeed, female imagery has substantiated the literary-theological movement of the book of Jeremiah. And while this analysis of the functions of female imagery does not resolve the bigger compositional issues in the book of Jeremiah, it raises questions as to the overarching rhetorical strategies. Attention to the interplay of gendered voices and their various appeals to the audience, the implied male audience of the book as well as its contemporary audiences, male and female, highlights the complexity of the constructions of Jeremiah.

Listening to the Gendered Voices in/of Jeremiah

In the text of Jeremiah as a whole, judgment speech surrounds proclamations of promise. In terms of gendered voices,[24] male voices sur-

---

24. Cf. Bauer, *Gender in the Book of Jeremiah.* For another emphasis on dynamics of voices in Jeremiah, see Mark E. Biddle, *Polyphony and Symphony in Prophetic Literature: Rereading Jeremiah 7–20* (Studies in Old Testament Interpretation, 2; Macon, GA: Mercer University Press, 1996).

round female voices with a few exceptions, notably passages of utmost judgment (e.g. Jer. 13.20-27) and of ultimate promise (e.g. Jer. 31.15-22). There reversals interrupt conventions, when female surrounds male. Indeed, listening to the language of voice (קול) brings female images and metaphors again into focus. The vocabulary appears mainly in three configurations: קול יהוה, the voice of YHWH; קול as it signifies the sounds of war (cries of destruction, clamor of approaching armies, cries of pain, etc.); and קול as the voices/sounds of women.

As for the female voices, there are the ones we have seen in the images above echoing, even embodying war and destruction in images of labor pain and of sexual violation. There is the voice of the prophet lamenting as a woman in labor, who cannot keep silent hearing the קול שופר, the sound of a shophar (Jer. 4.19, 21). There is, as we have seen above, קול כחולה, the sound of a woman in labor (Jer. 4.31) and קול בת־ציון תתיפח, the sound of 'Daughter Zion' gasping for breath (Jer. 4.31), which together embody the sound of war (מקול פרש ורמה קשת, Jer. 4.29).

Then there are the female voices that resound as countervoices in response to war, death and destruction. There is קול נהי, a sound of wailing which is heard from Zion (Jer. 9.18 [MT]) in response to the devastation, the voices of the dirge-singing wise women who teach their daughters and each other songs of mourning in the face of death (Jer. 9.19-21 [MT]). And there is קול which is heard on a height/in Ramah, the sound of Rachel weeping for her children (Jer. 31.15-16). When it comes to war these ancient female voices are strikingly contemporary, as female voices resound in tortured cries and mourning dirges amid a predominantly male context/discourse.

In the shifting layers of competing sounds and echoes, who have been the audiences/readers then and now, and whose voices have they/ we heard? The voice of Jeremiah, the prophet? The voice of Baruch, the scribe? The voice of the narrator(s)? The voices of the Deuteronomistic editor(s)? These all are male voices using female imagery to address a predominantly male audience. They employ rhetorical strategies that urge identification of the male with the female, that appeal to males with the threat of feminized violation, shame and humiliation (as well as occasional hope). And what do such rhetorical strategies achieve? On what levels do they continue to reinscribe gendered power dynamics then and now by playing on male fear of female sexuality, fear of loss of control over possessions/wives, fantasies of sexualized violence with

the stated intention of making the male audience turn around/reverse/
repent? Female images and metaphors are twisted and exposed to the
gaze of the male reader/audience, as men confronting a God portrayed
as male are urged into female positions in a culture of assumed hetero-
sexuality.[25] With the threat of homoeroticism shaping the construction
of intense relations between the audience and the deity, female imagery
abounds. On a socio-historical level female images further refer to
women's realities in Jeremianic times. Given the power dynamics presented, other questions arise. Are the female voices of women's pain
and mourning used to promote the male discourse on war and destruction, theologized as judgment? Indeed, is it too much to hope for that
some of these female voices may echo whispers of resistance? Voices
of hope amidst death? Life nevertheless? In the context of a people
during war, in the context of a rape culture 'that propagates the crime
while denying its reality',[26] what do these contexts of normalized
violence contribute to the rhetorical climate?

Further, the pull of a long interpretive tradition that sides with the
voice(s) of prophet/YHWH against the people/Israel, that sides in most
instances with the male against the female, confronts glimpses of reversals in emerging counter-readings. Yet it continuously threatens their
erasure, as textual and intertextual levels diverge. It is contemporary
feminist and womanist voices that have been critical of dualistic patterns confining women. Yet not so Jeremiah. Israel of the past is
remembered as 'bride' being 'holy' to YHWH (Jer. 2.2-3), or promised
to be 'Maiden Israel', dancing in the future (Jer. 31.4). By contrast, the
people of the Jeremianic present are accused of acting as a promiscuous
woman of uncontrollable sexuality, defiled and defiling (e.g. Jer. 2.20-
22, 23-25, 33-34; 3.1, 2-3, 6-10, 19-20), while at the same time rape, a
crime of uncontrolled sexual violation, is presented as 'justified' (e.g.
13.20-27).

It is contemporary female voices that call for the embracing of
ambiguities. Not so Jeremiah. The use of the childbirth metaphor (e.g.
Jer. 4.19-21; 4.31; 13.21; 22.23; 30.5-7), woman writhing in labor pain,
serves as an image for the suffering of the people. Without bringing

25. See Howard Eilberg-Schwartz, *God's Phallus and Other Problems for Men
and Monotheism* (Boston: Beacon Press, 1994), *passim*; esp. 'Unmanning Israel',
pp. 137-62.

26. Washington, 'Violence and the Construction of Gender in the Hebrew
Bible', pp. 352-57. Cf. esp. Jer. 2.29-37; 13.20-27; 20.7; 22.20-23.

new life into the world, the childbirth metaphor in Jeremiah tips toward death. The image is reduced to the pain and threat of death alone; it does not lead to the joy of new life. Rather, it recalls that the pain of childbirth represents 'women's punishment for disobedience' (cf. Gen. 3.16). The image of the womb as symbol of death (Jer. 20.14-18) underscores the polarized, exclusively negative use of the childbirth metaphor, which adopts an additional nuance when divine and human merge to give birth to Jeremiah (Jer. 1.5). Labor pain is not mentioned as part of the birthing experience of YHWH and/or of Jeremiah's human mother. Yet there, too, the emphasis is on death rather than on life. Jeremiah curses his birth (Jer. 15.10) and wishes for his mother's womb to have been his tomb (Jer. 20.14-18). Indeed, female experiences are presented as polar stereotypes of good and evil, life and death. The female comes to be identified with judgment and punishment. And even the qualities of care, consolation and compassion, which characterize YHWH in Jer. 31.20, are in jeopardy of being appropriated by ideologies of idealized motherhood.

It is contemporary (fe)male voices that search for fluidity of gender, transgression of traditional gender roles, and flexibility of identities, and hear the male prophet speak in a female voice. Not so Jeremiah. Even though the prophet takes on a female persona lamenting in labor pain (Jer. 4.19-21) and accusing YHWH of rape (Jer. 20.7), he does not speak about himself with the respective pronoun references. As the voices in the text come alive through the responses of the readers of various social locations, variations resound in the hearing of yet other sounds and silences.

Thus a reading of the female imagery throughout Jeremiah refocuses perspectives on constructions of the book as a whole. Across various textual divisions, female images and metaphors have substantiated the literary-theological movement through remarkable reversals. Further, attention to the functions of gendered voices, especially in their female manifestations in male contexts, highlights rhetorical strategies operating in a complexity that challenges traditional understandings of Jeremiah.

JEREMIAH IN THE APOCRYPHA AND PSEUDEPIGRAPHA

John Barton

Among the various biblical figures who became the subject of speculative interest in the late Second Temple period and into the Christian
era, Jeremiah has been somewhat neglected. He certainly does not
begin to rival the two great personages of apocalyptic and sapiential
literature, Enoch and Ezra. But, along with his secretary, Baruch, he
enjoyed some fame, certainly greater than that of most of the other
prophets of biblical times with the possible exception of Isaiah. We
might speculate on the reasons for this. My hunch—and it is no more—
is that the explanation lies in Jer. 36.26, where after king Jehoiakim has
burned Jeremiah's scroll, 'the king commanded Jerahmeel the king's
son and Seraiah the son of Azriel and Shelemiah the son of Abdeel to
seize Baruch the secretary and Jeremiah the prophet, *but the LORD hid
them*'. The hint here of a special hiding place prepared by God for these
two faithful servants may well, I believe, have been read as analogous
to what happened to Enoch, who 'was not, for God took him' (Gen.
5.24). Interestingly enough, Josephus's account of this incident glosses
over the phrase 'but the LORD hid them' (LXX: 'and they were hidden') in a way that produces a lame effect:

> Then he ordered that a search be made for both Jeremiah and his scribe
> Baruch and that they be brought to him for punishment. So then [οὖν]
> they escaped his wrath (*Ant.* 10.95).

It looks as though Josephus is slightly embarrassed by the implication
of divine intervention, though it is hard to see why. At all events, both
Jeremiah and Baruch gradually turned, as we shall see, into Enoch-like
figures, little resembling the people we know from the book of Jeremiah, and were seen as recipients of special divine revelations and gifts
and even, in time, as eschatological figures.

A strange feature of this development is the way that Baruch came to
usurp pride of place from his master Jeremiah. There is scarcely any

Jeremiah literature as such among the Pseudepigrapha: most of the works in which the prophet appears are attributed to Baruch. *4 Baruch*, for example, is called in the Greek 'The Things omitted from Jeremiah the Prophet', using the same term, παραλειπόμενα, that is used for Chronicles in the Greek Bible; but by the time of the Ethiopic version it has become 'The Rest of the Words of Baruch'. The editor of the work in Charlesworth's *The Old Testament Pseudepigrapha*, II, sees a historical development from an interest in Jeremiah to Baruch as the focus of attention:

> An originally Jewish composition, 4 Baruch has been interpolated by a Christian and provided with a Christian ending ... [But] the Jewish portion of the document has more than one redactional level. Characteristic of the earlier level of Jewish redaction is an emphasis on the figure of Jeremiah the prophet as the 'chosen one' of the LORD and as the LORD's agent in dealing with Israel. If Baruch figures in the story at this level, it is only as an auxiliary of Jeremiah. This is in harmony with the picture of these events in canonical Jeremiah, 2 Maccabees 2.1-7, and The Lives of the Prophets. The later level of redaction in the Jewish portion of the text is characterized by an emphasis on the importance of Baruch the scribe ... Jeremiah, who completely overshadows Baruch in chapters 1 through 4, is almost totally eclipsed by Baruch in chapters 7 and 8, in which the prophet must accept the mediation of the scribe between himself and God. Moreover, we are told in 7.25-28 that God loved Baruch too much to let him suffer the same fate as Jeremiah.[1]

G. Delling has suggested that this change represents a Pharisaic, pro-scribal and anti-prophetic movement.[2] But the book of Baruch itself already shows a tendency for the secretary to be seen as more important than his employer, the prophet, so perhaps there are further reasons than this which were at work earlier than the time of *4 Baruch*. There could be an analogy with that other famous scribe, Ezra: not even mentioned by Jesus ben Sira in his list of the great men of Israel's past, he rapidly overtakes Nehemiah, who is mentioned there, to become a central figure in apocalyptic literature. Perhaps what was important about scribes was not that they represented the Pharisaic party against prophecy (if so, why is it that what is attributed to Ezra and Baruch *is* mostly prophecy, in the new mode we call apocalyptic?) but simply that, because

---

1. S.E. Robinson, '4 Baruch', in *OTP*, II, pp. 413-25; the quotation is from p. 415.

2. G. Delling, *Jüdische Lehre und Frömmigkeit in den Paralipomena Jeremiae* (Berlin: Alfred Töpelmann, 1967).

they were writers, it made sense to attribute books to them rather than to people like Jeremiah who spoke rather than writing.

The shift of attention from Jeremiah to Baruch can also be seen by comparing *4 Baruch* with the probably later *2 Baruch*, 'The Book of the Apocalypse of Baruch the Son of Neriah'. In *4 Baruch* 1, Jeremiah receives a divine warning of the impending fall of Jerusalem, which he then at God's command goes and shares with Baruch: 'rise up and go to Baruch and tell him these words' (*4 Bar.* 1.10). Baruch receives the message from the prophet, whom he consistently addresses as 'Father Jeremiah': there is no doubt that he is the subordinate figure. In *2 Baruch* 1–2 it is Baruch who is told of the fall of the city, and sent to inform Jeremiah: 'This, then, I have said to you that you may say to Jeremiah and all those who are like you that you may retire from this city. For your works are for this city like a firm pillar and your prayers like a strong wall' (*2 Bar.* 2.1). Baruch duly passes on the message:

> And I went away and took with me Jeremiah and Adu and Seraiah and Jabish and Gedaliah and all the nobles of the people. And I brought them to the valley of Kidron and told them all which had been said to me. And they raised their voices and they all lamented. And we sat there and fasted until the evening (*2 Bar.* 5.5-7).

Nevertheless, a good deal of material about Jeremiah himself remains among the traditions collected in the Baruch literature, as also in the *Lives of the Prophets*, the *History of the Rechabites*, Eupolemus, 2 Maccabees and Josephus. An initial analysis of it suggests that Jeremiah is seen under four aspects, which can be presented in ascending order of divergence from the biblical traditions about the prophet. These are (1) Jeremiah as a historical figure, with the details of his involvement in the events of his time enhanced but not transformed; (2) Jeremiah as a seer, predicting the future, often the distant future—a development common in all presentations of ancient prophets in the Second Temple period;[3] (3) Jeremiah as a wonder-worker and mystagogue; and (4) Jeremiah as a figure of the end-time.

Jeremiah as a Historical Figure

The biblical text preserves much more narrative about Jeremiah than about any other prophet, and for writing the history of Israel this was

---

3. On this see my *Oracles of God: Perceptions of Ancient Prophecy in Israel after the Exile* (London: Darton, Longman & Todd, 1986).

naturally felt to be invaluable. Josephus devotes more than one hundred sections of his *Antiquities of the Jews* to the events surrounding Jeremiah, but in the process changes little and has no new material of his own to add. He is completely dependent on the biblical text, just as is Ben Sira when he summarizes Jeremiah's life in Ecclus 49.4-7:

> Except David and Hezekiah and Josiah
>   they all sinned greatly,
> for they forsook the law of the Most High;
>   the kings of Judah came to an end;
> for they gave their power to others,
>   and their glory to a foreign nation,
> who set fire to the chosen city of the sanctuary,
>   and made her streets desolate,
>   according to the word of Jeremiah.
> For they had afflicted him;
>   yet he had been consecrated in the womb as a prophet,
> to pluck up and afflict and destroy,
>   and likewise to build and to plant.

Another Jewish historian, however, records a legend about Jeremiah not found in the biblical text. This is Eupolemus as quoted in Eusebius's *Praeparatio evangelica*:

> Then Jonachim (became king). During his reign Jeremiah the prophet prophesied. Sent by God, he caught the Jews sacrificing to a golden idol, whose name was Baal. He disclosed to them the coming misfortune. Jonachim attempted to burn him alive, but he said that, with this wood, as captives they would prepare food for the Babylonians, and dig the canals of the Tigris and Euphrates. When Nebuchadnezzar the king of the Babylonians heard the predictions of Jeremiah, he exhorted Astibares the king of the Medes to join him in an expedition. He associated with himself Babylonians and Medes and gathered together a force of one hundred and eighty thousand foot soldiers, one hundred and twenty thousand cavalry, and ten thousand chariots for foot soldiers. First, he subdued Samaria and Galilee and Scythopolis and the Jews living in Gilead. Then he seized Jerusalem and captured Jonachim the king of the Jews. He took as tribute the gold and silver and bronze in the Temple and sent them to Babylon, except for the ark and the tablets in it. This Jeremiah preserved.

Most of this may be simply a garbled version of biblical narratives, rather in the manner of Chronicles; but note the association of Jeremiah with the preservation of the ark, which will concern us again.

For the most part later sources are true to the biblical account in presenting Jeremiah as one who warned the people of destruction to come, even though this gave succour to their enemies—as is clearly implied by Eupolemus. According to the *Apocalypse of Paul*—which is the source of the tradition that Isaiah was decapitated with a saw, mentioned also in the Epistle to the Hebrews—Jeremiah died a martyr's death for his prophecies. When the three major prophets appear to Paul in a vision, Jeremiah says 'I am Jeremiah who was stoned by the children of Israel and killed' (*Apoc. Paul* 49). That Jeremiah sought to help the people of his day through his prophecies, although they cruelly misunderstood and rejected him, is clear in all the sources. In *4 Baruch* 1 he prays for the city, asking God to change his mind when he has decided to destroy it through the Babylonians, and there are overtones of Abraham praying for Sodom:

> Jeremiah answered, saying, 'I implore you, LORD, allow me, your servant, to speak before you.' And the LORD said to him, 'Speak, my chosen one, Jeremiah.' And Jeremiah spoke, saying, 'LORD Almighty, are you delivering the chosen city into the hands of the Chaldeans, so that the king may boast with the multitude of his people and say, "I prevailed over the holy city of God"? (Surely) not, my LORD; but if it is your will, let it be destroyed by your (own) hands.'

We may not think this is the kind of intercession Jeremiah would have uttered if he had not been forbidden to do so (Jer. 7.16): presumably he would really have prayed for the city to be spared altogether. There is a subtle shift in the direction of making Jeremiah more submissive to the divine will than the biblical book sees him as being. In a similar way, Jeremiah's denunciations of the worship of foreign gods is transmuted, in the so-called *Epistle of Jeremiah* (= Bar. 6), into an exhortation to those deported to Babylonia not to be afraid of the gods of the Babylonians, who can do no harm since they are entirely feeble and powerless. Jeremiah thus turns into a prophet after the manner of Deutero-Isaiah: 'like a scarecrow in a cucumber field, that guards nothing, so are their gods of wood, overlaid with gold and silver ... like a thorn bush in a garden, on which every bird sits; or like a dead body cast out in the darkness. By the purple and linen that rot upon them you will know that they are not gods' (Bar. 6.70-72). There is, however, already a Deutero-Isaianic passage (so to speak) in Jeremiah itself, in 10.1-10, which is the source of the joke about the scarecrow in a cucumber field. So although the tradition in Baruch 6 may diverge from what Jeremiah actually taught (always assuming that we can recover that!), it has an antecedent in the book of Jeremiah as it now stands.

More surprising is a tradition in *4 Baruch* 8 in which Jeremiah appears to have a role similar to Nehemiah's in encouraging men to put away their foreign wives, in this case Babylonian women. Those who refuse to divorce them are debarred from entering Jerusalem, but the Babylonians will not allow them back into Babylon either, so they return to Palestine and build a city and name it Samaria—certainly a novel explanation of the origin of the Samaritans. This is the only reference I can find to any success experienced by Jeremiah in his prophetic activity, since he does prevent Jerusalem from being defiled by the presence of partners in mixed marriages. Otherwise he is normally presented, true to the biblical narrative, as a largely unsuccessful prophet, who (as the *History of the Rechabites* puts it) 'rent his garments and was clothed in sackcloth, and sprinkled dust upon his head. And he showed to the common folk the way of goodness; and urged them to return to the LORD' (*Hist. Rech.* 8.2). No-one however paid heed to him.

Jeremiah as a Seer

The earliest reference to Jeremiah as a seer with insight into the remote future can be found in Dan. 9.1-2, the famous passage where Daniel tries to understand what Jeremiah had meant by prophesying a 70-year exile when in fact the Jews are still in bondage to their enemies more than 400 years later. The problem is solved by the device of 'weeks' of years (Dan. 9.24). The passage is important as the first unequivocal evidence for the picture of a prophet as someone who can look into the far distant future and foretell events that have no importance for his own lifetime and that of his hearers, but will come to matter to generations as yet unborn. This is a quite normal perception of ancient prophecy in the late Second Temple period. Josephus also understands Jeremiah in this way, saying that he wrote of 'the misfortunes that were to come upon our city, and left behind writings concerning the recent capture of our city, as well as the capture of Babylon' (*Ant.* 10.80). Presumably this is a reference to the book of Lamentations, which acquired its title 'Lamentations *of Jeremiah*' in the Greek biblical tradition: Josephus assumes that this is a prophecy of the capture of Jerusalem by the Romans, not just of its fall to Babylonian power in the sixth century.

But the perception of Jeremiah as foreseeing the distant future, in a way we should probably describe as more typical of apocalyptic than of prophecy, is plainest in Christianizing additions to various works in the Jeremiah and Baruch literature. In the ninth chapter of *4 Baruch* Jeremiah, who has offered a sacrifice and gone into a trance, receives a revelation of the glorious future which Israel will enjoy in the days of the Messiah:

> Glorify God with one voice! All (of you) glorify God, and the Son of God who awakens us, Jesus Christ the light of all the aeons, the inextinguishable lamp, the life of faith! And after these times there will be another four hundred and seventy-seven years, and (then) he is coming to the earth. And the tree of life which is planted in the middle of Paradise will cause all the uncultivated trees [the Gentiles] to bear fruit, and they will grow and sprout ... And what is scarlet will become as white as wool; the snow will be made black; the sweet waters will become salty, and the salty sweet in the great light of the joy of God. And he will bless the islands that they may bear fruit at the word of the mouth of his anointed one. For he will come! And he will go out and choose for himself twelve apostles, that they may preach among the nations, he whom I have seen adorned by his father and coming into the world on the Mount of Olives; and he will fill the hungry souls (*4 Bar.* 9.14-20).

The *Lives of the Prophets* similarly contains a Christian messianic prophecy attributed to Jeremiah:

> Then Jeremiah gave a sign to the priests of Egypt, that it was decreed that their idols would be shaken and collapse through a savior, a child born of a virgin, in a manger. Wherefore even to this day they revere a virgin giving birth and, placing an infant in a manger, they worship. And when Ptolemy the king inquired about the cause, they said, 'It is an ancestral mystery delivered to our fathers by a holy prophet, and we are to await, he says, the consummation of his mystery' (*Liv. Proph.* 2.8-10).

The Jeremiah of such traditions is very remote from the figure in our biblical book; but he would not have seemed alien to most readers in the days of Josephus or later, when it was taken for granted that a true prophet could foresee not just imminent events—a rather lowly gift—but events of the most distant future.

Jeremiah as Wonder-worker and Mystagogue

With this theme we move further away from the biblical book of Jeremiah and into traditions that may be called free-floating, in which

Jeremiah is simply remade in the image of the spiritual hero of the late Second Temple period. In the *Lives of the Prophets* Jeremiah works a miracle for the Egyptians among whom he has come to live after leaving Jerusalem:

> Jeremiah was from Anathoth, and he died in Taphnai of Egypt, having been stoned by his people. He was buried in the environs of Pharaoh's palace, because the Egyptians held him in high esteem, having been benefitted through him. For he prayed, and the asps left them, and the monsters of the waters, which the Egyptians call *Nephoth* and the Greeks crocodiles. And those who are God's faithful pray at the place to this very day, and taking the dust of the place they heal asps' bites (*Liv. Proph.* 2.1-4).

Jeremiah also heals the sick with some magic figs, in *4 Bar.* 7.37—figs, incidentally, acquired by a very complicated process. Jeremiah's servant Abimelech, while bringing them to him, falls asleep for 66 years during a brief pause under a tree, so that he is spared having to see the destruction of Jerusalem. He sends the figs to Jeremiah, who strangely has been deported to Babylon, by tying them to the neck of an eagle, which can speak and also has the power to raise the dead.

Not only could Jeremiah heal sickness, he could also grant success in battle, as Judas Maccabeus discovers through a dream or vision:

> What he saw was this: Onias, who had been high priest ... was praying with outstretched hands for the whole body of the Jews. Then likewise a man appeared, distinguished by his grey hair and dignity, and of marvellous majesty and authority. And Onias spoke, saying, 'This is a man who loves the brethren and prays much for the people and the holy city, Jeremiah, the prophet of God.' Jeremiah stretched out his right hand and gave Judas a golden sword, and as he gave it he addressed him thus: 'Take this holy sword, a gift from God, with which you will strike down your adversaries' (2 Macc. 15.12-16).

As well as being able to work miracles, Jeremiah is sometimes portrayed as a mystic. We have already seen how in *4 Bar.* 9 he goes into a trance: as he is praying to God at the altar and offering sacrifice, he becomes 'as one of those who have given up their soul' (*4 Bar.* 9.7). But it turns out that he is not dead, and as Baruch and his other companions prepare to bury him, they hear a voice which says, 'Do not bury one still living, for his soul is coming into his body again'; and after three days he revives (*4 Bar.* 9.12-14)—this is one of the Christian passages in *4 Baruch.* Jeremiah's enemies start to stone him while he is uttering the messianic prophecies quoted above, but he causes a stone to become a replica of himself, and the crowd stones that while he continues to prophesy. This done, he reveals himself openly, and dies under a hail of stones.

One of the most complex of the late Jeremiah traditions concerns miraculous activity in connection with the sacred vessels of the Temple. The simplest version of the story is in 2 Macc. 2.1-7:

> One finds in the records that Jeremiah the prophet ordered those who were being deported to take some of the fire, as has been told, and that the prophet after giving them the law instructed those who were being deported not to forget the commandments of the Lord, nor to be led astray in their thoughts upon seeing the gold and silver statues and their adornment. [An allusion to Jer. 10, and perhaps also to Bar. 6] ... It was also in the writing that the prophet, having received an oracle, ordered that the tent and the ark should follow with him, and that he went out to the mountain where Moses had gone up and had seen the inheritance of God. And Jeremiah came and found a cave, and he brought there the tent and the ark and the altar of incense, and he sealed up the entrance. Some of those who followed him came up to mark the way, but could not find it. When Jeremiah learned of it, he rebuked them and declared: 'The place shall be unknown until God gathers his people together again and shows his mercy. And then the Lord will disclose these things, and the glory of the Lord and the cloud will appear, as they were shown in the case of Moses, and as Solomon asked that the place should be specially consecrated.'

There is already here a miraculous element in the concealment of the place of hiding for the Temple vessels, but the elaboration of the story in the pseudepigraphical literature heightens it considerably. In *4 Baruch* the oracle from God which led Jeremiah to hide the vessels is given verbatim: 'Take them and deliver them to the earth, saying, "Hear, earth, the voice of him who created you, who formed you in the abundance of the waters, who sealed you with seven seals in seven periods (of time), and after these things you will receive your fruitful season. Guard the vessels of the (Temple) service until the coming of the beloved one"' (*4 Bar.* 3.10-11). In the *Lives of the Prophets* Jeremiah seizes the ark with its contents himself—nothing is said of an oracle—and causes it to be swallowed by a rock, saying:

> 'This ark no one is going to bring out except Aaron, and none of the priests or prophets will any longer open the tablets in it except Moses, God's chosen one. And in the resurrection the ark will be the first to be

resurrected and will come out of the rock and be placed on Mount Sinai, and all the saints will be gathered to it there as they await the LORD and flee from the enemy who wishes to destroy them.' In the rock with his finger he set as a seal the name of God, and the impression was like a carving made with iron, and a cloud covered the name, and no one knows the place nor is able to read the name to this day and to the consummation. And the rock is in the wilderness, where the ark was at first, between the two mountains on which Moses and Aaron lie. And at night there is a cloud like fire, just like the ancient one, for the glory of God will never cease from his Law. And God bestowed this favor upon Jeremiah, that he might himself perform the completion of his mystery, so that he might become a partner of Moses, and they are together to this day (*Liv. Proph.* 2.14-19).

Finally, there is a tradition in *2 Baruch* in which the hiding of the vessels is effected not by Jeremiah but by an angel, but the angel utters an oracle which begins with a clear allusion to Jer. 22.29, ארץ ארץ ארץ:

He descended in the Holy of Holies and ... took from there the veil, the holy ephod, the mercy seat, the two tables, the holy raiment of the priests, the altar of incense, the forty-eight precious stones with which the priests were clothed [so far as I am aware, nothing is known from elsewhere of these forty-eight stones], and all the holy vessels of the tabernacle. And he said to the earth with a loud voice:

Earth, earth, earth, hear the word of the mighty God,
and receive the things which I commit to you,
and guard them until the last times,
so that you may restore them when you are ordered,
so that strangers may not get possession of them.
For the time has arrived when Jerusalem will also be
delivered up for a time,
until the moment that it will be said that it will be
restored for ever.
And the earth opened its mouth and swallowed them up
(*2 Bar.* 6.7-9).

It would take a lot of detailed work to construct a stemma for these traditions, and I shall not attempt here to decide on a relative dating. But it is clear in all of them that Jeremiah's association with the fate of the Temple vessels is felt to be a close one, and that it is connected both with his penetration into the mysteries of the heavenly sanctuary and with his abilities as a wonder-worker. The peg in the book of Jeremiah on which such traditions hang is Jer. 3.16, 'In those days, says the

LORD, they shall no more say, "The ark of the covenant of the LORD."
It shall not come to mind, or be remembered, or missed', together perhaps with Jeremiah's dispute with Hananiah over the fate of the Temple
vessels in Jeremiah 28. But the traditions grew in a luxuriant way, and
in them Jeremiah turns before our eyes into something approaching a
magician.

I have also used the word 'mystagogue', and this can be seen most
clearly in Philo's occasional reference to Jeremiah. In his section on the
cherubim Philo mentions Jeremiah by name—the only one of the latter
prophets he does name:

> I myself was initiated under Moses the God-beloved into his greater
> mysteries, yet when I saw the prophet Jeremiah and knew him to be not
> only himself enlightened but a worthy minister of the holy secrets, I was
> not slow to become his disciple. He, out of his manifold inspiration gave
> forth an oracle: 'Didst thou not call upon me as thy house, thy father, and
> the husband of thy virginity?' (Jer. 3.4).[4]

Jeremiah as a Figure of the End-Time

Our final category is perhaps as far removed from the figure who
appears in the biblical book of Jeremiah as it is possible to get: Jeremiah not as a prophet but as the subject of prophecy, a figure of the
end-time. He appears in this guise in the little-noticed reference in Mt.
16.14, where people speculate that Jesus may be John the Baptist, or
Elijah, *or Jeremiah*, or one of the prophets. And he is also mentioned,
just as briefly, in *4 Ezra*:

> Do not fear, mother of the sons, for I have chosen you, says the Lord. I
> will send you help, my servants Isaiah and Jeremiah. According to their
> counsel I have consecrated and prepared for you twelve trees loaded with
> various fruits, and the same number of springs flowing with milk and
> honey, and seven mighty mountains on which roses and lilies grow; by
> these I will fill your children with joy (*4 Ezra* 2.17-19).

We might suspect from these allusions that there was a body of
tradition in which Jeremiah, like Elijah, was expected to return to usher
in the end. But it seems not to have survived, or at least not in the
Apocrypha and Pseudepigrapha that I have been able to consult.

---

4. Cited in N.G. Cohen, 'Earliest Evidence of the Haftarah Cycle for the
Sabbaths between בתמוז ז'' and סוכות in Philo', *JJS* 48 (1997), pp. 225-49.

Conclusion

In conclusion, one could describe the after-life of the figure of Jeremiah as a matter of luxuriant growth. Like so many other biblical figures—Moses, Isaiah, Elijah, Enoch—he became the focus for all sorts of legendary accretions that had little or no direct connection with the biblical text. At the same time, it is usually possible (as Professor Walter Brueggemann noted in helpful remarks when this essay was presented as a paper to the SBL) to find some pretext in the biblical book of Jeremiah for the directions that development took. For example, Jeremiah as an unsuccessful prophet is an accurate enough image of the biblical figure. That his message included weal as well as woe is not always conceded by modern commentators, but it is an important element in the traditions about him that the biblical book records. Again, the Bible does not present him as a seer in the sense that term had for Philo—someone initiated into the mysteries—but it does think of him as one with far sight, who could see beyond present disaster to a glorious future. Though made in the image of the prophetic figures known in the late Second Temple period,[5] the Jeremiah of the Apocrypha and Pseudepigrapha is not just an all-purpose holy figure: he is still recognizably the Jeremiah we read about in the book of that name. Those who wrote pseudonymously after the biblical canon was largely closed do not seem to have been entirely random in their choice of biblical figures to whom to attach revelations or histories; though it can hardly be said that they were exactly 'faithful' to the biblical record either.

5.   On which see R.N. Gray, *Prophetic Figures in Late Second Temple Jewish Palestine: The Evidence from Josephus* (New York: Oxford University Press, 1993).

Part III

THEOLOGICAL CONSTRUCTION

THE BOOK OF JEREMIAH IN OLD TESTAMENT THEOLOGY[*]

Leo G. Perdue

To Pluck Up and to Pull Down

A Prophet to the Nations

During the past two decades, approaches to the interpretation of the book of Jeremiah have dramatically changed. In 1979 Brian Kovacs and I set about what we then thought was the not-too-imposing task of assembling a collection of seminal essays in Jeremiah studies which were written between the early 1900s and the late 1970s.[1] As we pursued our quest, we discovered no shortage of wonderful articles and

   *   The original draft of this paper was prepared for the panel discussion ('*The Collapse of History* and its implications for Reading the Book of Jeremiah') of my book (*The Collapse of History: Reconstructing Old Testament Theology* [Minneapolis: Fortress Press, 1994]) during the SBL/AAR Annual Meeting in New Orleans, 1996. Participants in this panel discussion, in addition to me, included Mary Chilton Callaway (Fordham University), Lawrence E. Boadt (Washington Theological Union), Dennis T. Olson (Princeton Theological Seminary), and Thomas W. Overholt (University of Wisconsin, Stevens Point). I wish to thank these panelists for their insightful criticisms of my contribution to Old Testament Theology and the book of Jeremiah. I also am grateful to the co-chairs of the Composition of Jeremiah Group, Kathleen M. O'Connor and Louis Stulman, for inviting me to participate in what was for me a stimulating discussion.

   1.   For a variety of presentations of theological issues in the study of Jeremiah, see Brevard Childs, *Biblical Theology in Crisis* (Philadelphia: Westminster Press, 1970); Leo G. Perdue and Brian W. Kovacs (eds.), *A Prophet to the Nations: Essays in Jeremiah Studies* (Winona Lake, IN: Eisenbrauns, 1984); Walter Brueggemann, *To Pluck Up, To Tear Down: A Commentary on the Book of Jeremiah 1–25* (Grand Rapids: Eerdmans; Edinburgh: Handstel Press, 1988); and *idem, To Build, To Plant: A Commentary on Jeremiah 26–52* (Grand Rapids: Eerdmans, 1991); and Kathleen O'Connor, 'Jeremiah', in Carol A. Newsom and S.H. Ringe (eds.), *The Women's Bible Commentary* (Louisville, KY: Westminster/John Knox Press, 1992), pp. 169-82.

essays by significant scholars whose insights into the book and person of Jeremiah were shaped by the developing methods of historical-criticism, ranging from Mowinckel's literary sources,[2] to Hyatt's Deuteronomic edition,[3] to von Rad's existential, form-critical analysis of the confessions,[4] to Zimmerli's interpretation of the life of the prophet within the typos of the suffering prophet.[5]

In my introduction to this marvelous array of essays,[6] I identified what were then the key issues yet to be resolved in the study of Jeremiah by what I concluded would be the refined application of historical-critical methods that, while never static, appeared adaptable to new, yet not radically contrastive, strategies of discourse. These key issues, largely historical in nature, were the identification of the 'Foe from the North', the date of Jeremiah's call, the authorship and form of the confessions, the character and extent of the Deuteronomistic redaction of the book, the delineation of the book's literary sources, including the scrolls of Baruch, and whether the theology of Jeremiah could best be seen through the old liberal lens of Skinner[7] and Hyatt[8] or the neo-orthodox formulation of von Rad.[9] Skinner and Hyatt interpreted the person of Jeremiah, revealed in the earliest strata of 'authentic', poetic speeches in the first 20 chapters, as something of an Adolf von Harnack, while von Rad traced the history of the theological traditions of the prophet who, in the continuity of his continuing re-presentations

2. Sigmund Mowinckel, *Zur Komposition des Buches Jeremia* (Kristiania: Jacob Dybwad, 1914).

3. James Philip Hyatt, 'The Deuteronomic Edition of Jeremiah', in M.K Spears, R.C. Beatty and J.P. Hyatt (eds.), *Vanderbilt Studies in the Humanities* 1 (Nashville: Vanderbilt University Press, 1951), pp. 71-95.

4. Gerhard von Rad, 'Die Konfessionen Jeremias', *EvT* 3 (1936), pp. 265-96.

5. Walther Zimmerli, 'Frucht der Anfechtung des Propheten', in J. Jeremias and L. Perlitt (eds.), *Die Botschaft und die Boten* (Festschrift Hans Walter Wolff; Neukirchen–Vluyn: Neukirchener Verlag, 1981), pp. 131-46.

6. Leo G. Perdue, 'Jeremiah in Modern Research', in Perdue and Kovacs (eds.), *A Prophet to the Nations*, pp. 1-32.

7. John Skinner, *Prophecy and Religion* (Cambridge: Cambridge University Press, 1961).

8. James Philip Hyatt, *Jeremiah: Prophet of Courage and Hope* (New York: Abingdon Press, 1958).

9. Gerhard von Rad, *Old Testament Theology* (2 vols.; San Francisco: HarperCollins, 1965), II, esp. pp. 50-125, 188-219.

both within the developing text and afterwards, sounded ever so much like Karl Barth.

Now, in retrospect, some 20 years later, all of us can readily see how the landscape of Jeremiah studies has changed, and radically changed it has. New methods of interpretation have arisen that raise fresh questions or approach old ones in different ways, and others, yet to be born, undoubtedly will do the same. These methods provide new insights into our understandings of the ancient prophet from Anathoth and the biblical book that bears his name.

The most pressing question for me nowadays, however, is whether these more recent methods may be adapted to and incorporated within previous historical-critical work, or whether they represent what some of our colleagues call a 'paradigm shift' that, for the most part, tends to dismiss the past in order to make room for the new. Have we indeed, for the first time since the Enlightenment, entered into a scholarly and hermeneutical eschaton of a postmodern 'new heaven and new earth' when most of what existed before us has been swept away? Or do we have instead a continuum where the past prepares the way for and even merges into the present, even as the present awaits its transformation in the not-yet-actual?

The Challenge of Epistemological Fragmentation

I have no doubt that the modern academy and the churches, whose traditions of biblical interpretation, at least in the West, have largely come to be shaped by the epistemological strategies of the Enlightenment, now face the real threat of continuing fragmentation, if not disintegration. Today the cacophony of competing voices attempting to be heard has become a din of dissonance and a Tower of Babel in modern scholarship. This fragmentation (I prefer not to use the term 'crisis'[10]) is centered in epistemology, for in these times we have many ways of knowing, issuing from different genders, sexual orientations, ethnic groups and cultures. Yet one may also ask whether in this time of breaking apart there is the inevitable descent into epistemological and theological nihilism where we may believe nothing that is sure, affirm no virtue as certain, and know nothing to be real outside of the solipsistic world of our own private making, or whether there are instead stirrings of fresh creativity that break forth into new visions of understanding for both the academy and the church.

10. Contrast Childs, *Biblical Theology in Crisis*.

To Destroy and to Overthrow

The Collapse of History

I wrote *The Collapse of History* with several objectives in mind: to describe the salient features of a select number of recent interpretive strategies of biblical interpretation and theology, to evaluate their strengths and weaknesses, to discover grounds for common discourse between their significant representatives, and to use their implications for the study of Jeremiah as a case in point. I concluded with a brief summary of how I would proceed, given the current variety and sometimes competitive approaches in biblical scholarship, with writing my own Old Testament theology that, while using new methods, would maintain some connection with past interpretations.

I suggest it is the case that history, especially the kind formulated in positivistic categories, has indeed 'collapsed', at least in the sense that it today no longer dominates biblical scholarship and thus biblical theology as it did for over a century. However, by 'collapse' I do not mean or even imply, much less suggest, the 'demise' of historical method or of history as a theme in biblical texts. Rather, I argued that we have entered a period of epistemological quandary when the uncertainty of what we know and even how we are to proceed with knowing are not so very clear. However, as in the past, I propose this uncertainty eventually will give birth to new creations yet undreamed and to ways of knowing that are fresh and provocative. It is my contention that recent approaches do not necessarily require the casting aside of past methods and their epistemological foundations, but rather usually, and most often do, build upon and at the very least may incorporate what we have learned from the past. Indeed, new approaches may transform this living tradition, should we so choose, into novel understandings that allow the formative traditions of the academy and the church to experience rebirth.

Let me now briefly summarize a few salient points of a select number of more recent approaches to the Old Testament, their implications for Old Testament theology, and their contributions to our understandings of the book of Jeremiah. Finally, I shall conclude with a response to a recent critique of my book that should sharpen some of the major issues at stake.

History as Liberation
The important work of Norman Gottwald[11] has largely taken place within the framework of much previous historical work, although his own philosophical grounding is no longer the positivism and Euro-centrism of many of his predecessors, but rather neo-Marxism and lib-eration theology.[12] Gottwald's linear tracing of Israelite history moves from revolutionary society to oppressive monarchy to imperial colony. His analysis of Israelite and early Jewish religion and thought is based on a materialist understanding of culture rather than on German ideal-ism. While his historical reconstruction and his theological insights are daring and bold, he does appear largely to reduce Israel's God to a sym-bol and function of its revolutionary social ideology.[13]

For Gottwald, Jeremiah's theology is grounded in the premonarchial, even anti-royal traditions of exodus liberation and covenant obligation. Accordingly, Jeremiah's powerful and penetrating criticism of the monarchy may well have originated and then continued within the traditions of a village and clan society oppressed by and opposed to royal ambitions. Gottwald suggests that the prophet Jeremiah was the spokesman for the 'peace' party that advocated submission to Babylo-nian rule and promoted non-violent reform. Thus, historical triumphal-ism was to be replaced by a righteous community of extended families living out its faith and piety as a royal colony.

Gottwald's major theological insight, it seems to me, is that theology emerges primarily from the fabric of human social life. This is true, not only for the book of Jeremiah and the entire Hebrew Bible, but also for theology as a whole. Gottwald repeatedly drives home the point that theology and culture are entwined and inseparable.

Creation Theology
A second development in biblical theology that has important impli-cations for the study of Jeremiah is renewed interest in creation.[14] It is

11. Gottwald's two most important works are *The Tribes of Yahweh* (Mary-knoll, NY: Orbis Books, 1979); and *The Hebrew Bible: A Socio-Literary Introduc-tion* (Philadelphia: Westminster Press, 1985).

12. For a fuller discussion, see Chapter 4, 'History as Liberation: Social Science and Radical Theology', in *The Collapse of History*, pp. 69-109.

13. See his edited collection of essays in *The Bible and Liberation* (Maryknoll, NY: Orbis Books, rev. edn, 1983).

14. See my more detailed discussion in Chapter 5, 'History and Creation: Myth

no secret that creation theology in recent years has emerged as a major counterpart to redemptive history. This biblical horizon has been viewed through the lenses of various methods ranging from British and Scandinavian myth and ritual approaches to recent cultural anthropology. Insightful studies have been written by Jon Levenson,[15] Rolf Knierim[16] and Claus Westermann.[17] Creation as a legitimate theological theme in the Hebrew Bible has allowed us to reclaim and to see with fresh eyes not only the wisdom corpus, but also other biblical collections and books, including Jeremiah.

The 'Foe from the North' and the 'New Covenant' speeches in Jeremiah are two examples of texts that are replete with images and understandings originating in the theophanic representation of the Divine Warrior and the mythic triumph over the forces of chaos.[18] In addition, the birth oracle in ch. 1 and the concluding confession in ch. 20 draw on

and Wisdom', in *The Collapse of History*, pp. 113-50. Important surveys of the renaissance of interest in this biblical theme include R.J. Clifford, 'The Hebrew Scriptures and the Theology of Creation', *Theological Studies* 46 (1985), pp. 507-23; *idem*, 'Creation in the Hebrew Bible', in Robert Russell *et al.* (eds.), *Physics, Philosophy, and Theology: A Common Quest for Understanding* (Notre Dame, IN: University of Notre Dame Press, 1988), pp. 151-70; H. Graf Reventlow, *Problems of Old Testament Theology in the Twentieth Century* (Philadelphia: Fortress Press, 1985), pp. 134-86; and Hans Heinrich Schmid (ed.), *Altorientalische Welt in der alttestamentlichen Theologie* (Zürich: Theologischer Verlag, 1974).

15. Jon Levenson, *Creation and the Persistence of Evil*: *The Jewish Drama of Divine Omnipotence* (San Francisco: Harper & Row, 1988).

16. Rolf Knierim, 'Cosmos and History in Israel's Theology', in Rainer Albertz *et al.* (eds.), *Werden und Wirken des Alten Testaments* (Festschrift Claus Westermann; Göttingen: Vandenhoeck & Ruprecht, 1980), pp. 59-123; and *idem*, 'The Task of Old Testament Theology', *HBT* 6 (1984), pp. 25-57. See now his recent volume, *The Task of Old Testament Theology: Substance, Method, Cases. Essays* (Grand Rapids: Eerdmans, 1995).

17. Claus Westermann, *Creation* (Philadelphia: Fortress Press, 1974); *idem*, *Genesis 1–11* (Minneapolis: Augsburg, 1984); and *idem*, *Theologie des Alten Testaments in Grundzügen* (ATD, 6; Göttingen: Vandenhoeck & Ruprecht, 1978).

18. For a detailed look at the creation myth of the Divine Warrior and its presence in the book of Job, see my book, *Wisdom in Revolt: Metaphorical Theology in the Book of Job* (JSOTSup, 112; Sheffield: Sheffield Academic Press, 1991), pp. 47-56. For this mythic struggle in Jeremiah's oracles concerning the northern foe, see Brevard Childs, 'The Enemy from the North and the Chaos Tradition', *JBL* 78 (1959), pp. 187-98; and Michael Fishbane, 'Jeremiah IV 23-26 and Job III 3-13: A Recovered Use of the Creation Pattern', *VT* 21 (1971), pp. 151-62.

the anthropological tradition of God's creating and nurturing of life in the womb and predetermining the newborn's destiny (see Ps. 139). A balanced treatment of the theology of Jeremiah should include the intertwining of redemptive history and creation, including both his formation in the womb and divine action in his prophetic life (fictional or historical) and the origin and providential guidance of the world and of Israel.

The Canonical Approach

A third, recent development in biblical studies and biblical theology that provides new insight into Jeremiah is the canonical approach of Brevard Childs.[19] It is here that one finds another movement away from history as both the topic and the method of biblical theology. For Childs, the Bible becomes not a document of history, but rather Scripture for confessing communities. The Canon, not the social setting of ancient communities, becomes the context for interpreting biblical texts.

Childs's work on Jeremiah is helpful at many points. But perhaps his most significant insight is that, through the impact of Deuteronomy, Jeremiah came to understand himself as standing in the long line of prophets who preached repentance on the basis of the law. Thus, instead of contrasting Law and gospel, Childs grounds the proclamation of the prophet Jeremiah in the deuteronomic reformulation of the Torah. Similarly, Childs argues that Deuteronomy, or an earlier form of the book, was beginning to function as authoritative Scripture for Jeremiah in shaping his self-understanding as a preacher of judgment.

Feminist Hermeneutics

A fourth major impact on Jeremiah in recent years has been made by feminist theology in its variety of expressions.[20] The undermining of

19. For a more complete discussion, see Chapter 6, 'From History to Scripture: Canon and Community', in *The Collapse of History*, pp. 153-96. Childs's most important works include *Introduction to the Old Testament as Scripture* (Philadelphia: Fortress Press, 1979); *Old Testament in a Canonical Context* (Philadelphia: Fortress Press, 1985); and *Biblical Theology of the Old and New Testaments: Theological Reflection on the Christian Bible* (Minneapolis: Fortress Press, 1993).

20. For a survey of feminism and especially feminist literary criticism in biblical studies, see Chapter 7, 'From History to Metaphor: Literary Criticism and Feminist Hermeneutics', *The Collapse of History*, pp. 197-227. Key feminist studies of the Bible include: Letty Russell (ed.), *Feminist Interpretation of the Bible*

patriarchy and its ideological undergirding in sexism are important developments in all of biblical scholarship, including theology. The subversion of sexist texts, the utilization of a hermeneutics of suspicion to question the possible ideology of traditions, and the recognition of the silencing of women's voices have resulted in important theological insights. In addition, the recovery of women's stories, feminine images of God, and new readings of ancient texts that subvert patriarchy are important contributions to our collective efforts.

The work of Phyllis Trible has provided significant contributions not only to biblical studies and theology, but also to the understanding of Jeremiah.[21] Her refinement of rhetorical criticism has enabled us to see with new understanding many biblical texts. Her explication of the 'weeping' Rachel in Jeremiah is but one example of her recovery of neglected themes and counter-literature that often lay dormant within biblical texts unless revealed by the craft of the literary artist and insights of a feminist hermeneutic.[22]

In her interpretation of Jer. 31.15-22, Trible builds on her important insight about 'womb' imagery in the Hebrew Bible, noting that *reḥem* in the singular means 'womb' or 'uterus', but in the plural includes the abstract terms of 'compassion', 'mercy' and 'love'. Theologically conceived, God creates and nurtures the fetus in the womb, prepares the uterus for birth, assists in the delivery, receives the infant from the womb, and sustains the newborn's life into the future. Divine compassion is expressed by the metaphor of a mother's experience and stirrings of feelings in carrying a child to term in her womb and in bonding to that life throughout the offspring's and her future existence.

In Jeremiah's magnificent poem concerning the 'weeping' Rachel, Trible calls this text a drama of voices that 'organize structure, fill

(Philadelphia: Westminster Press, 1995); and the multi-volume series of essays on books of the Hebrew Bible by Athalya Brenner (ed.), *The Feminist Companion to the Bible* (Sheffield: Sheffield Academic Press). Phyllis Trible outlines what she sees as the major contours of a feminist biblical theology: 'Five Loaves and Two Fishes: Feminist Hermeneutics and Biblical Theology', *TS* 50 (1989), pp. 279-95.

21. See Phyllis Trible, *God and the Rhetoric of Sexuality* (Philadelphia: Fortress Press, 1977); and *idem*, *Texts of Terror* (Philadelphia: Fortress Press, 1985); and O'Connor, 'Jeremiah'. O'Connor's study is an important feminist reading of Jeremiah that outlines its importance of women's history, its problematic God language (she notes the book's predominantly male language for God), and notes the harmful gender language also present in the book.

22. Trible, *God and the Rhetoric of Sexuality*, pp. 31-59.

content, *and mold* vision to create a new thing in the land, and this new
thing is nothing less than the poem itself and the inbreaking reality it
construes. A confessing Ephraim is surrounded by four feminine voices,
thus interpreting the final clause, "female surrounds man".' The new
creation is a transformed reality in which the virile male is surrounded,
nurtured, and protected by the feminine. It is this feminine compassion
and nurture, expressed by the metaphor of the womb, that will replace
military power and political treaties.

Biblical Story and Narrative Theology
A fifth approach in biblical studies that has impacted Jeremiah studies
and Old Testament theology is narrative theology, or the artistry of
story.[23] Gabriel Fackre has defined narrative in rather simple terms 'as
an account of characters and events moving over space and time'.[24] The
'Passion Narrative' of Jeremiah in chs. 37–44 is, to use the language of
Erich Auerbach, realistic or history-like.[25] Paul Ricoeur's differentiation between productive (i.e. fictional) imagination and reproductive
(i.e. historical) imagination is helpful at this point. According to
Ricoeur, both types of narrative share the same strategy of discourse,
but whereas the first allows the writer greater freedom in shaping the
text, the second is constrained by the requirement of re-presenting what
occurred, or at least corresponds with the data that may be construed
in a realistic fashion. Both types of narrative, however, appeal to
the imagination of the reader for authentication, whether 'real' or
'imagined' as 'real'.[26]

In the 'Passion Narrative' (Jer. 37–44), for example, one discovers
the intertwinement of prophetic word and existence in torment. Here
one finds, through close reading, a theology of creative imagination as

23. For a brief overview, see Chapter 8, 'From History to Imagination: Biblical
Story and Narrative Theology', in *The Collapse of History*, pp. 231-62. For the
impact of the study of story on biblical interpretation and biblical theology, see
Robert Alter, *The Art of Biblical Narrative* (New York: Basic Books, 1981); Hans
Frei, *The Eclipse of Biblical Narrative: A Study in Eighteenth and Nineteenth
Century Hermeneutics* (New Haven: Yale University Press, 1974); and Dale
Patrick, *The Rendering of God in the Old Testament* (Philadelphia: Fortress Press,
1981).

24. 'Narrative Theology: An Overview', *Int* 37 (1983), pp. 340-51 (341).

25. *Mimesis* (Garden City, NY: Doubleday, 1957).

26. See especially Ricoeur's essay, 'The Narrative Function', *Semeia* 13 (1978),
pp. 177-202.

complex characters come to encounter God, the meaning of their own formative traditions, and themselves. It is through entrance into these imaginative worlds of biblical narrative that readers also may experience that same encounter with what are real and true and come to self-understanding.

Of course, the reader's distanciation is a necessary hermeneutical process in which, fully aware of the vast socio-historical and cosmological separation between the Bible's and one's own narrative worlds, one may attempt to enter that strange other reality and experience it to the full or at least in part.[27] The consequence for the reader may be transformation, revulsion, indifference, or some other response.

Narrative theology teaches that it is possible to maintain one's own intellectual integrity and still affirm a text as theologically 'true', perhaps even normative, regardless of whether it is fiction or history.

Imagination

With narrative theology we have already begun to enter into the final approach to be mentioned in this essay, that of imagination. This approach is important, for it offers a way not only of accessing the linguistic and historical realities of the past, but also of engaging them in the present. This approach is called imagination.[28]

Many would agree that Walter Brueggemann's work is among the most insightful in this arena of discourse.[29] He begins, as do most theologians of the church since Gabler, with an underlying affirmation. The Old Testament is a normative collection of texts that moves the

27. See Hans Gadamer, *Truth and Method* (New York: Seabury, 1975).

28. A brief summary is provided in Chapter 9, 'From History to Imagination: Between Memory and Vision', in *The Collapse of History*, pp. 263-98. Some of the most incisive work in this approach to biblical studies has been done by Amos Wilder. See, e.g., his *Theopoetic: Theology and the Religious Imagination* (Philadelphia: Fortress Press, 1976); and his *Jesus' Parables and the War of Myths: Essays on Imagination in the Scripture* (Philadelphia: Fortress Press, 1985).

29. See especially the following studies by Brueggemann: *Living toward a Vision* (Philadelphia: United Church Press, 1982); *Hopeful Imagination: Prophetic Voices in Exile* (Philadelphia: Fortress Press, 1986); *The Prophetic Imagination* (Philadelphia: Fortress Press, 1987). His major essays on Old Testament Theology have been edited and placed into a single volume by Patrick Miller, *Old Testament Theology: Essays on Structure, Theme, and Text* (Minneapolis: Fortress Press, 1992). See now his recently published *The Theology of the Old Testament* (Minneapolis: Fortress Press, 1997).

interpreter beyond critical dissection and historical location to the sphere of contemporary hermeneutics in which the text addresses with authority and guidance the contemporary church. This means that Scripture is a linguistic and historical text that is firmly grounded in the past, and yet also makes normative claims for the faith and practice of the believing church in the present.

Furthermore, Brueggemann contends that a theological statement is not concerned with the activities and character of the text, but rather with the process and character of God in the text. Thus, in Scripture, or in its teaching and proclamation, one encounters the Word through human words that enables us to interpret our own existence, to borrow the language of Rudolf Bultmann.[30]

In the Hebrew Bible, Brueggemann contends that the merging of historical past and contemporary present requires a bipolar dialectic that consists of structure legitimation and the embrace of pain. On the one hand, the Hebrew Bible imagines God participating in the common theology of its world (i.e. structure legitimation), and yet, on the other hand, struggling to be free from that common theology by active engagement in social struggle (i.e. the embrace of pain). Brueggemann, in his new Old Testament Theology, uses the language of sovereignty and pathos mediated by righteousness. God both transcends the conflicts of human life and yet authentically participates in their reality. If there is only structure legitimation, the danger is propaganda and self-serving ideology. If there is only the pathos of pain, then the chaos of dissent and the unruliness of disorder prevail. Alternative theology subverts conventional theological images to shape for the social structures fresh and provocative ones that are more humane and compassionate.

In Jeremiah, Brueggemann sees the prophet providing an alternative theology grounded in the embrace of pain.[31] In Jeremiah, Israel encounters God through the images and claims of the covenant of Sinai that demands faithful obedience. In Jeremiah, the 'pathos of Yahweh' is present in God's yearning to maintain a life-sustaining relationship with even a faithless people. Also, one finds in Jeremiah a radical critique against the royal-temple ideology of divine protection and guaranteed presence. Instead, Jeremiah's oracles and narratives set forth a theology

30. *Jesus and the Word* (New York: Charles Scribner's Sons, 1934).
31. See his two-volume commentary: *To Pluck Up, To Tear Down*; and *idem*, *To Build, To Plant*.

that combines the covenant of Sinai with divine pathos that moves beyond judgment to a hopeful future based on divine grace. In Brueggemann's words: 'the text leads the listener out beyond presently discerned reality to a new reality formed in the moment of speaking and hearing.' This is for Brueggemann the 'prophetic imagination' of Jeremiah.

To Build and to Plant

Does or Should Postmodernism Dismiss Modernism?

In a probing essay, published in a recent issue of the *Journal of Religion*, Burke Long takes Langdon Gilkey and me to task for being unreconstructed modernists largely irrelevant for a postmodern world.[32] He views some of our work as a modernist reaction against postmodern diversity and pluralism that allow for no recognized norms, much less a unifying vision.[33] For Long, modernism's quest to find *the* truth (i.e. an 'objective truth "out there" ') or *the* answer to a host of problems, through the application of Enlightenment's epistemology to texts and their present understanding, is a hopeless effort in a multi-cultural world devoid of any common experiences, traditions and norms. My own very brief sketching out of something of a future (for) Old Testament theology, so Long submits, is nothing more than a reactionary return to an irretrievable if not also undesirable past that disallows by its very nature the reality of pluralism and diversity in the present.

I suggest that Gilkey and I are not quite so naïve as Long intimates we are. What especially troubles Long with my work, it seems, is the

32. Burke Long, 'Ambitions of Dissent: Biblical Theology in a Postmodern Future', *Journal of Religion* 76 (1996), pp. 276-89. For discussions of postmodernism, see David Harvey, *The Condition of Postmodernity* (Oxford: Basil Blackwell, 1989); and Robert Scharlemann (ed.), *Theology at the End of the Century: A Dialogue on the Postmodern* (Charlottesville: University of Virginia Press, 1990).

33. Long's criticisms against norms or what I term 'unifying visions' are largely grounded in Derrida's version of deconstructionism, that in the judgment of many, including myself, borders on epistemological, and thus theological and ethical nihilism, and not in the large number of methods, approaches and views of the great majority of understandings that are found within postmodernism. See Jacques Derrida, *Speech and Phenomena, and Other Essays on Husserl's Theory of Signs* (Evanston, IL: Northwestern University Press, 1973); *Of Grammatology* (Baltimore: The Johns Hopkins University Press, 1976); and *Writing and Difference* (Chicago: University of Chicago Press, 1978).

seven-page conclusion of *The Collapse of History* where I outline the approach I plan to take in composing my own Old Testament theology. This is evidence, he says, that 'in the end' I seem to hold onto my 'modernist soul'. I believe I made it clear from the beginning, that is, the introductory chapter, that this is at least in part correct. Long's criticism holds true, if it means I am an 'unrepentant rationalist' who thinks not that history and historical method have collapsed, but rather their hegemony as the dominant theme and methodology in the study of the Hebrew Bible. However, he is well off the mark if he thinks I have neither disclosed nor attempted to avoid as best I can many of the pitfalls of modernist historicism. He is also wrong if he thinks I have not tried to point to ways that many new approaches, even so-called postmodern ones, outlined in *The Collapse of History,* have not used or cannot be wedded to earlier 'modernist' methodologies.

Long is concerned that I am trying to impose coherence on the disparate nature of the Hebrew canon (a disparity that most Old Testament theologians since the late nineteenth century have recognized), a coherence issuing from a unifying center and systematic categories that allows those who engage the text to come to some understanding of the past and to formulate its meaning or comings for the present. Long is especially opposed to my suggesting that we (i.e. Old Testament theologians who stand, at least to a degree, within the context of the church) need to have a criteriology that seeks to find some basis for unifying the enormously diverse traditions lodged within the Hebrew canon and that allows the many and often diverse hermeneuts in the (post)modern period a way of assessing and articulating these varieties of biblical views so that they may engage in discourse with texts and with each other. This basis for conversation, so Gilkey and I affirm, permits us to get at the matter of normativity that allows judgments about the veracity or falsehood, the pertinence or irrelevance, of truth, even that embedded in ancient texts, for modern lives. Long casts aside normativity as a hopeless and misleading illusion that has lost its meaning in a world of many competing ways of knowing and judging what is right and wrong, true or false. Any truth claims, so he contends, are constructions of human discourse grounded only in the language of the subjective knower and shaped by self- or group interest. There is, then, for Long no truth 'out there' or even 'in here', save that created by the subjective knower and his or her self-interest. He asserts that pluralism is the order of the day, and not the tyranny of coherence where judgments are made and norms become the guides not only for human thinking, but also for moral living. And he argues, following Foucault, that all discourse is political, that is, grounded in the self-interest of people and social groups who through language create the objects of their knowing.[34]

All of this means, then, for Long, that God, in any construction of the human mind, is just that: a mental creation with no objectivity, even though God language or religious metaphor may evoke a powerful response in shaping human culture along the lines of this or that group's self-interest. This absence of objectivity and this creative power of discourse or thinking is also true for human values or virtues, which, while possessing no normative character, still make for the sociability of human living in an ordered scheme possible. Truth for Long has no objective basis outside the human or collective mind of a group, but rather is socially created according to the experience and especially the self-interests of its creator(s). This means then, by its very nature, truth is neither more nor less than ideology.

Interpretation and the Ethical Dilemma[35]

While I do not concede many of his points, perhaps Long is at least partly correct in his assessment of present Western culture. Perhaps we have entered into a historical realm ruled not by Apollo, but by Dionysus, whose powers of ecstasy and madness make reason suspect, while unlicensed passion and blind irrationality cast their spell on all who would fix their gaze too long upon their alluring images. I would never myself affirm that anyone can ever come to a complete and perfect understanding of what is true.[36] But, I do contend, as passionately but also as rationally as I can, that making judgments about right and wrong, true and false are inherently endemic to what it means to be human. I contend that scholars have a moral responsibility to make judgments about things that matter. And I do argue that truth is an

---

34. Michel Foucault, *The Order of Things: An Archaeology of the Human Sciences* (New York: Pantheon, 1970); and *idem*, *The Archaeology of Knowledge* (New York: Pantheon, 1972).

35. Wayne C. Booth, *The Company We Keep: An Ethics of Fiction* (Berkeley: University of California Press, 1988).

36. I am reminded of Aristotle's observation that 'no one is able to attain the truth adequately, while on the other hand, no one fails entirely, but everyone says something true about the nature of things' (*Metaph.* 933b).

object residing, at least in part, outside the human mind of the knowing person. Additionally, truth contains some element of relationship in which some balance between discussants and the object of conversation is maintained. Otherwise we enter into the inescapable solepsism of individual hubris that makes human society and civil existence impossible.

We make rational decisions, grounded in our experience, each and every day, whether of great magnitude or of minor consequence, whether we are seeking to defeat legislation against Affirmative Action or are choosing what color of shoes best matches the clothing we are wearing. Pluralism, whether lodged within the Hebrew canon or within the current heterogeneity of modern culture, presents the danger of an incoherent fragmentation that, unchecked, results in intellectual collapse and the demise of even moral judgments that truly matter. In the postmodern world, if that is where we have taken up dwelling, is just any old ideology as good as the next? How would we *know*? Or perhaps we should not even use the term 'good' for, if I read Long's critique correctly, the word begs the question that, ironically, has no answer. I would submit that it is better to make at least the judgments of great magnitude on the basis of a well-articulated, even rational criteriology grounded in collective, though certainly varied, human experience and embedded in the value systems of human and religious traditions that lay themselves open unashamedly to human reflection and critical assessment, than it is to decide this or that on the basis of whim, caprice, self-interest or a 'good' feeling. Apollo must at least constrain, if not always bring into submission, Dionysus.

I do contend that theology, truth, epistemology and virtue have a subjective-objective binary relationship, that there is something beyond the mere linguisticality of human creation, and that all systems of philosophy, theology and ethics are open to critical sanctions. Without some type of criteriology, whether clearly articulated or only suggestively intimated, how do we ever say that something is right or wrong, true or false? Are skinheads and neo-Nazis right or wrong in their racist ideologies? Are sexists right or wrong in their view of the role and nature of women? Are homophobes right or wrong in their fear and castigation—even persecution—of gays, lesbians and bisexuals? Or, in returning to the Hebrew Bible, is the genocide of Joshua right or wrong? Is the judge Jepthah a model for emulation or an example of revulsion? Were Hananiah (Jer. 28), Haggai and Zechariah court prophets whose nationalistic aspirations and dreams of restoration proved to be wrong-headed, even false prophecies that misled the people of their day into thinking that future glory was at hand? Were not lives lost or futures more than likely ruined by such propaganda? Or were they right and the circumstances not advantageous? Is the sexism, patriarchy and homophobia of the Priestly document bad, while its affirmation of loving the neighbor as well as the stranger as oneself good? Or, how do we, without a reasonable criteriology grounded in some general, collective, human experience and a unifying, theological (or even humanist) vision, say 'yes' or 'no' to the variety of ideologies present in our postmodern world? Dionysus would say we cannot, while Apollo would inquire and then search out a reasonable and coherent answer. Certainly we humans continually make judgments, ones we consider right or wrong, even normative, either knowingly or at least intuitively. But make them we do and decide them we must. In a postmodern world, where competing voices have created a din of dissonance and each one seeks to rise above the crowd to command our allegiance to follow this teaching or that idea, how do we decide, even if we *choose* to listen? Or, even more challenging is the question, 'Why *should* we listen?' After all, the oughtness of the *should* implies a moral imperative that smacks of Kantian epistemology and morality.

In the world of Long, there is no engaging conversation, no normativity, no center, no absolutes, no virtues 'out there', no transcendence and no unifying vision. There is no Apollo. He has drowned in a sea of diversity and even relativity. Rather, in Long's view, Apollo has been replaced by Dionysus. And in changing metaphors (in his many disguises Dionysus especially may do this), we are set adrift, rudderless, in a sea of pluralism and multi-culturalism blown here and there by the four winds of the earth with no course to follow, no storms to outlast, no destination at which to arrive. Even if we did arrive, how would we know it, and how could we say it is the right port? How could we contend that even our survival is good? Good for whom and for what? But then, for Long, there is no 'right' port. 'Any port in a storm', one might say. Or at the very least a 'port' that meets the destination of our self-interest. But why is even self-interest a value? Why not total nihilism, including the self?

It is a serious, even wrong-headed mistake, I contend, to assume that any contemporary ideology, or theology for that matter, is set forth as claiming absolutely nothing. But are we simply claiming that this or that meets either our self-interest or our particular experience and that no one dare challenge what we affirm? And may we simply dismiss understandings without an opportunity for dialogue in order to understand others' views? We live in a world of countless ideologies and theologies, and most (save for deconstructionism and even Derrida, pushed hard here, admits he values life and love, though it is never clear why and on what grounds) issue universal or at least life claiming demands. Their protrepsis is not an invitation to a world of 'So what?' and 'Who cares?' Yet to say there are competing claims from a multi-cultural world is to say nothing new at all. Did not Epicureans and Stoics, Sadducees and Pharisees, National Socialists and Social Democrats, even in the same periods and cultures, compete for the allegiance of others by claiming to have a higher authority or greater grasp of what is true or normative? Were any of them right or wrong, true or false, on or off the mark, and if so, how would one know? Pluralism is no modern phenomenon, no opposition massing itself against the tyranny of a Euro-centric West only in contemporary times, but rather is apparently omnipresent throughout the history of humankind, at least a history that has left behind scattered, though incomplete records, whether oral or written or both. Pluralism has been with us as long as human groups have formed, built, and attempted to sustain their cultures. Save for those groups and their ideologies that are inherently destructive of or that discriminate against others, pluralism, in and of itself, may pose no serious threat, save in the possible failure of human groups to engage in discourse. But then what if Peter Berger is correct in arguing that the 'world hangs together by the thin thread of conversation'? Communication that leads to understanding and mutual learning, possibly even the affirmation of certain fundamental values and beliefs, is the moral imperative I affirm. If we do not reach some common understanding and form alliances grounded in tolerance and the affirmation of core values, will we not fall all too easily victim to fascist regimes and destructive ideologies who recognize that humans crave order, even demonic tyranny, if it saves us from what Thomas Hobbes calls the Leviathan of our own uncontrolled passions and desires?

In his review of *The Collapse of History* in the same issue of the *Journal of Religion*, Brueggemann has noted that it is 'high irony, that whereas old-time historical criticism was at one point daring and inventive (I would also add dangerous, at least for its early practitioners in their culture), it tends now, when taken alone, to become a refuge for the reactionary to fend off the demands and permits of a radically changed world.' Yet he concludes the review with this asseveration: 'It is important to recognize that these newer methods and perspectives are not exchanging one set of interpretations for another but are profoundly changing what *we might* mean by interpretative transactions.'[37]

Have I abandoned modernism? Of course not. Have I even intimated that historical criticism is now an outmoded collage of historical (and literary) methods that have 'collapsed'? No. Have I attempted to rehabilitate historical criticism following the numerous assaults of new ways of reading and understanding ancient texts of Scripture? No, again. Do I think historical criticism is the tool of the privileged, intellectual elite of the West to hold on to power and status? No, though any method that shapes human understanding may certainly be abused when the 'results' of the method applied, in this case to Scripture, are misused by the privileged to oppress marginal groups. I have argued, I thought rather clearly, that historical criticism no longer enjoys the position of privilege it once held for close to a century of important work in biblical studies. My 'agenda' in my work is nothing more and nothing less than to bring theologians, biblical as well as contemporary, into conversation; to seek out, when possible, common grounds for discourse; and at least to regain some measure of civility in our conversation, even when we, as often is true, seriously disagree. My most daring dream is that we might even agree on some common criteria for assessing the construction of meaning, whether that proposed by the interpretation of a text or by the articulation of a fresh cosmology for human dwelling. At the very least scholars working out of a variety of contrasting paradigms would have the occasion for dialogue.

I would prefer to speak of the relationship of the old to the new in this way: the new revives, transforms and thereby continues the old. Or to use the prophet from Anathoth's words, the new enables us 'to build and to plant'. And yet the new is not enslaved by the old, as new formulations of understanding take their place, or at least stand alongside them, in the history of human thought, and dare we say it, provide insight into the Holy, regardless of how very limited or slight.

I confess that what drives my own work is the quest to place old wine into new wineskins, to gain a sense of the Holy, to see even a glimmer of the good in what is contained in earthen vessels, even if this effort is

37. Walter Brueggemann, 'Review of Leo G. Perdue, *The Collapse of History*', *Journal of Religion* 76 (1996), pp. 349-52.

judged (wrongly I contend) nothing more than a remnant of my old, passé, modernist desire. I do search for normativity, not to discover *the* correct interpretation of this or that text, not to silence the voices that disagree, not to construct a tyranny of order, and not to fail to consider new outlooks that awaken and revive old texts, but rather to discover, if only by a brief glimpse, an element of the beautiful, the good, and the true that, offered as gifts by Apollo, become the basis for the reflective and, yes, the moral life. To do so, I contend, requires a carefully articulated criteriology that provides the basis not simply for making coherent interpretations, but also moral judgments. Then perhaps I shall have found, if only for a quickly passing moment, something of a glimmer of the sacred, whether in ourselves or in a transcendent Other. I begin this quest for the good with self-transcendence that is the foundation for my own hermeneutics of suspicion when reading ancient texts and their later interpretations, but, then, this is a thesis for another paper and perhaps the beginning of another book.

THE BOOK OF JEREMIAH AND THE POWER
OF HISTORICAL RECITATION

Lawrence Boadt

There have been more radical efforts to solve the editorial and redactional questions of the book of Jeremiah in recent debate than for any other prophetic corpus. These range from John Bright's arguments that the collection basically mirrors the work and thought of the prophet himself, through William Holladay's elaborate editorial gathering of the materials around seven-year festivals for proclaiming the Deuteronomic Law, or William McKane's 'rolling corpus' of post-Jeremianic development of the tradition, to finally Robert Carroll's general scepticism that anything much remains of the historical Jeremiah that can be safely recovered from a thoroughly theologized postexilic deuteronomic creation.[1]

The Historical Issue in Jeremiah Studies

Bright and Holladay take seriously the importance of the ministry of the historical Jeremiah for shaping the basic message and governing the choice of texts that were collected by disciples such as Baruch, even though there were many subsequent expansions and additions. But McKane and Carroll lean in the opposite direction, and doubt whether the actual message of Jeremiah to exiles and those about to be exiled

---

1. See John Bright, *Jeremiah* (AB, 21; Garden City, NY: Doubleday, 1965); William McKane, *A Critical and Exegetical Commentary on Jeremiah. I. Introduction and Commentary on Jeremiah I–XXV* (Edinburgh: T. & T. Clark, 1986); William L. Holladay, *Jeremiah 1: A Commentary on the Book of the Prophet Jeremiah, Chapters 1–25* (Hermeneia; Philadelphia: Fortress Press, 1986); *idem, Jeremiah 2: A Commentary on the Book of the Prophet Jeremiah, Chapters 26–52* (Hermeneia; Minneapolis: Fortress Press, 1989); Robert P. Carroll, *Jeremiah: A Commentary* (OTL; London: SCM Press, 1986).

are really at the heart of a book that redesigns the prophet for a post-exilic age. Since all of these scholars are careful to explain along the way how much weight they give to the historical likelihood that a text came either from Jeremiah or from a later setting, they clearly recognize the significance that the historicity of prophetic words has played in earlier commentaries.

Nor is this the only issue. The historical question is important, not just for those trained in the historical-critical method, but pre-eminently for the faith communities that have preserved and canonized the book of Jeremiah. If sacred texts contain God's word to humankind in history, it does matter whether prophets spoke the words attributed to them or not. As a problem, this may be more pressing for the Reformation tradition, which highly values divine inspiration to the individual prophets, than it is for Jews or Catholics, who see the community (ecclesial) setting of canonization as more fundamental than individual inspiration. But all insist on the link between historical origin and message if there is to be a sacred text. Perhaps Bright and Holladay are concerned to preserve that connection because they value its importance to faith communities, while McKane and Carroll bend a little to break the connection in order to free the book from a faith context of interpretation.

Jeremiah is a good test case for any discussion about whether recovery of the historical situation and words of the original prophet really does matter for interpreting the book. Jeremiah certainly *appears* to be the most history-like of the prophetic books. It has a large number of autobiographical and biographical literary constructions, it has time markers and names of kings and officials sprinkled throughout the text, and it moves in a general chronological schema from the prophet's early warnings through siege and destruction to aftermath. Without judging how accurately these text claims are, we can at least say that the book of Jeremiah gives us a picture of the times that we can *imagine* very consistently with what we know of the events of the Exile from other sources.

At the same time, the jumble of small units, of prose and poetic forms, and of different outlooks and theological perspectives, found side by side even in a single chapter, makes the evaluation of this book's redaction history among the most controverted. It is difficult to see any current scholarly consensus. The problem can be perhaps illustrated by reformulating my earlier sentence: while we can readily *imagine* what Isaiah and Ezekiel as books propose as a program for postexilic communities to believe in, it is not at all clear what Jeremiah suggests as a relevant program for the actual postexilic world. Bright, Holladay, McKane and Carroll couldn't be farther apart in how they answer this question. So, the dialogue between history and theology or purpose is yet to be satisfactorily resolved for Jeremiah. But there is still tremendous energy available for studying it!

The Effect of New Directions in Interpretation

Current biblical scholarship has shifted dramatically from a primary use of historical-critical methodology towards the application of newer approaches, which can be classified generally as either literary readings or contextual interpretations. Often both are applied together while historical questions or the search for original authorship are bracketed.[2] No one doubts that historical-critical work has been important and remains so in analysis of biblical literature, if for no other reason than that the Bible developed historically in an age far earlier than our own, and one which was prior to any serious critical historical consciousness.

One major achievement of three centuries of historical-critical method has been awareness of the important role that redaction played in ancient texts in order to keep them contemporary. The skill and subtlety of Israel's redactors has been stressed again and again by commentators such as Gerhard von Rad and Walther Zimmerli. They also emphasize how different is the final message of a biblical book from its earlier stages.[3] But the very success of historical critcism in identifying the literary and theological shape of the final text has ironically fueled the arguments of those concerned with literary and contextual readings. They make use of the 'final redaction' to insist that the final *text* is the only text that matters for the *reader*.[4] These interpreters place strong

2. See, e.g., Robert Carroll's remarks on his task as an exegete in his article 'Intertextuality and the Book of Jeremiah: Animadversions on Text and Theory', in J. Cheryl Exum and David J.A. Clines (eds.), *The New Literary Criticism and the Hebrew Bible* (JSOTSup, 143; Sheffield: Sheffield Academic Press, 1993), pp. 55-78; or the explanation of Peter Miscall on why he proposes a literary reading of Isaiah, in his *Isaiah* (Sheffield: JSOT Press, 1993), p. 11.

3. W. Zimmerli, *Ezekiel 1* (trans. R.E. Clements; Hermeneia; Philadelphia: Fortress Press, 1979); *Ezekiel 2* (trans. J.D. Martin; Hermeneia; Philadelphia: Fortress Press, 1983).

4. See Anthony Thiselton, *New Horizons in Hermeneutics* (Grand Rapids:

emphasis either on the unified composition and artistic power of the text in itself, or oppositely on the overwhelming ideological (theological) context of any modern reading of sacred texts, both of which lead to severe doubts whether we should, or even can, recover much of the earlier historical situation of texts or their development before the final redaction took place.[5]

Leo Perdue surveys a particular aspect of this shift in scholarship in his book *The Collapse of History*.[6] He focuses on how Old Testament theology has moved towards newer methods in recent decades, and away from a direct concern with the historical development of Israel's faith represented by both the salvation-history approach of G.E. Wright or John Bright and the tradition-history approach of A. Alt, G. von Rad and M. Noth. He evaluates the opportunities opened up by (a) the use of the social sciences to identify ideological aspects (as in Marxist analyses, liberation theology); (b) an emphasis on myth and creation over history; (c) canonical and intertextual developments; (d) literary insights from metaphor and story theologies; (e) narrative theology; and (f) a theology of imagination. Since Perdue finds positive dimensions to all these new approaches (as well as limitations), he challenges readers to be attentive to the dynamic potential available in constructing a vital biblical theology today, especially by incorporating the perspectives of imagination, narrative and metaphoric theology, but above all the theme of creation, which has been too often neglected.[7]

There is a great deal of wisdom in Perdue's judicious evaluation of the interplay among all the competing methods of text interpretation available to exegetes and theologians at present. He particularly cautions against our loss of interest in the historical-critical gains that have contributed so much to understanding the theological and faith development of ancient Israel even as we explore other methodological approaches.

Zondervan, 1992) for a thorough review of contemporary developments in hermeneutics, chronicling the shifts over the last 30 years.

    5.   See the remarks of Carroll, *Jeremiah*, pp. 34-50.

    6.   Leo G. Perdue, *The Collapse of History: Reconstructing Old Testament Theology* (Overtures to Biblical Theology; Minneapolis, Fortress Press, 1994).

    7.   Except, of course, by Perdue, who has written a major work on creation theology published nearly simultaneously with *The Collapse of History* in 1994: *Wisdom and Creation: The Theology of Wisdom Literature* (Nashville: Abingdon Press, 1994).

It can hardly be an accident then that he chooses the text of Jeremiah as his testing field for doing biblical theology. Certainly few books have been so challenged for their historical claims in recent years as has Jeremiah, perhaps because it was so central to the thinking of biblical history theologians such as John Bright.[8] Jeremiah has also been the center of a great deal of interest in this century over what appears to be its complicated redactional history. The identification of the hand of the deuteronomist at work directed the attention of exegetes towards the *theological* bias of its redaction, and so has generated a rich debate concerning the relationship between the theology of Jeremiah the prophet and that of his redactors, which often included both a so-called 'Baruch' level and a deuteronomistic one.[9] If the book that seems most biographical and 'history-like' is also the most blatantly theological in its final redaction, then it should be the perfect test case for Perdue's efforts to illustrate how a wide variety of methods can be applied towards the development of an Old Testament theology. At the same time, it will bring into high relief the conflicts and discrepancies between the conclusions of many of the newer methods and the historical claims seemingly built into the structure of the text as it stands.

Jeremiah as a Theology of History Based on Creation

Perdue has been particularly effective in reminding scholars of the important role that a creation perspective plays in biblical thinking, as much among prophets as among the wisdom and temple traditions.[10] A creation theology can focus on the cosomogonic and cosmological, that is, the mythological or at least mythopoetic, horizon of biblical thinking, that is strongly present in such texts as Genesis 1–11 and the Psalms of Zion. Or it can focus on the wonder of divine governance and providence and its implications for universal divine kingship over the nations, as found in Second Isaiah, the Oracles against Nations (OAN), and in wisdom speculations such as Proverbs 8 or Sirach 24 or Wisdom of Solomon 9. Both variants play each other off in significant works

---

8. Bright, *Jeremiah*.

9. See Sigmund Mowinckel, *Zur Komposition des Buches Jeremia* (Kristiania: Jacob Dywbad, 1914); also Brevard Childs, *Introduction to the Old Testament as Scripture* (Philadelphia: Fortress Press, 1979), pp. xx-xxx.

10. Perdue, *Wisdom and Creation*; Perdue, *The Collapse of History*, Chapter 5, pp. 113-50.

such as First Isaiah or Ezekiel. For this reason, we should expect to find it present in Jeremiah as well. Von Rad's emphasis on Jeremiah as a preacher of salvation history has often obscured the presence of creation themes as crucial elements in the book.

To understand Jeremiah's theology of divine intentionality, it is necessary to move beyond a descriptive mythopoesis or poems on divine order and wonder, and understand 'creation' as a teleology that builds on the conviction that a single *personal* God is both intervening in and guiding historical events in dialogue with humankind. Philosophically, we can recall the debate between Parmenides' 'the one and the many' and Heraclitus's 'you can never step into the same river twice'. The universal divine governance is interactive with the immanent and particular of human history. Thus the forces of nature, or the myths of polytheism, are useless for Jeremiah's overall message; only the personal encounter with God and recognition of God's wisdom will explain the events of history:

> Learn not the customs of the nations,
> and have no fear of the signs of the heavens,
> though the nations fear them.
> For the cult idols of the nations are nothing ...
> No one is like you, O Lord, great are you,
> Great and mighty is your name.
> Who would not fear you, King of the Nations,
> for it is your due!
> Among all the wisest of nations,
> and in all their domain,
> there is none like you (Jer. 10.1-2, 6-7).

Thus creation and redemption are integrated in Israel's thinking as inseparable parts of a wise God's purposes from the beginning. Scholars such as Knierim, Schmid and Westermann, whom Perdue admires, are on the right track in their descriptive efforts to recover the unitive elements between the two.[11] Stressing dichotomies between the word of salvation and cosmological interests imported from a polluted Canaanite culture have for too long set the prophets against their culture and made a division between wisdom, Torah and the prophets inevitable.

11. Claus Westermann, *Creation* (Philadelphia: Fortress Press, 1974); Rolf Knierim, 'The Task of Old Testament Theology', *HBT* 6 (1984), pp. 25-27; Hans Schmid, *Gerechtigkeit als Weltordnung* (BHT, 40; Tübingen: J.C.B. Mohr [Paul Siebeck], 1968).

There are many themes in Jeremiah that suggest a concern for a wider and longer vision of history than just the immediate call for Judah's conversion in the face of the Babylonian threat in order to preserve its existence. Perdue points to the 'foe from the North' and the salvation oracles of chs. 30–31. But note that structurally we have three stages: (1) Jeremiah's call in 1.10 'This day I set you over nations and and kingdoms, to uproot and tear down, to destroy and overthrow, to build and to plant', followed by (2) the turning point of God's judgment against the nations in 25.15-38, and (3) the actual oracles over these nations in 46–51. Moreover, the beginning and the end are linked by the final climax against Babylon in 51.50-58 where the city shall fall and its idols be destroyed—which picks up 1.15-19, where Jeremiah is to be the symbol of the faithful 'city' that shall stand against both Babylonian idols and their armies.

None of the above passages is normally identified with the strictly deuteronomic layers of Jeremiah but with the poetic material that may be based on the prophet's actual words. The vision of God's universal control of history was undoubtedly compatible with the Deuteronomists' own interest in creation as a basis for God's rule (seen, e.g., in Deut. 4 and 30). Indeed, it is quite possible that the theology of Jer. 45.1-5 and 51.59-64, both redactional passages, represents a deuteronomic reflection on the creation theology of 1.10-19, 25.15-38 and 51.50-58. This could even suggest that there was a basic Jeremian text structured by a creation theology at its key points *before* any deuteronomic editing took place.

Jeremiah as a Theological Narrative

If the book is history-like, then it is 'storylike'. The fact that so many passages in Jeremiah seem to be outside of a strictly chronological sequence does not preclude the intent of the editors to create a story. Several trends may be noted here. One is the recognition that biblical 'stories', like modern fiction, create their own plot world, rather than attempting to report actual incidents in eyewitness form.[12] Even if Jeremiah does not reflect the historical course of events, but instead creates a theological sequence of meaning, the plot will be just as strong and recognizable. Many efforts have been made in the direction

12. See Perdue, *The Collapse of History*, pp. 178-86.

of an ordered narrative function in Jeremiah, from Holladay's *The Architecture of Jeremiah 1–20* to Perdue's own study of the so-called 'passion narrative of the prophet' in Jeremiah 37–44.[13]

I find Holladay's arguments for a complicated rhetorical unity with chiastic elements ultimately forced and not very convincing. But it can be argued that Jeremiah is purposely structured in chs. 1–20 to avoid any specific temporal references. Note, for example, that the temple sermon in ch. 7 does not bear the specific dating that its parallel in 26.1 has. Note also that the only mention of Josiah falls in these chapters (3.6). It has always been a disputed verse among scholars, but its purpose can be more readily understood if it was so labelled to signal that all the oracles in this section were not to be identified specifically with the reigns of Jehoiakim and Zedekiah, thus suggesting that *from the beginning* Jeremiah preached his message as a program beyond individual events and moments. Naming Josiah then in fact offers 1–20 as paradigmatic of a larger schema of history. This in turn fits nicely with the conclusions drawn above regarding the cosmic (creation-oriented) scope of the book's vision (which is possibly that of Jeremiah himself).

The second trend emphasizes the role of the reader in creating the story's meaning. Sternberg and others have pointed to such narrative techniques as gapping and allusion that force the reader to create much of the narrative's inner development.[14] This involves readers and commentators in drawing on their life experiences to interpret the text. The prophetic language of persuasion also challenges the reader at the level of decision making so that an intimate dialogue or confrontation is established between text and reader that cannot be ignored.[15] It also juxtaposes our comfortable religious beliefs, traditions and memories against the shocking proclamation of God's present direction.

No reader of Jeremiah can stop short of reading the whole book, since God's plan transcends in the end even the vindication, and perhaps even survival, of the prophet. But it is also clear that the historical

13. William L. Holladay, *The Architecture of Jeremiah 1–20* (Lewisburg, PA: Bucknell University, 1976); Perdue, *The Collapse of History*, pp. 247-59.

14. See Meir Sternberg, *The Poetics of Biblical Narrative: Ideological Literature and the Drama of Reading* (Bloomington: Indiana University Press, 1987); Robert Alter, *The Art of Biblical Narrative* (New York: Basic Books, 1981).

15. See L. Boadt, 'The Power of Prophetic Persuasion: Preserving the Prophet's Persona', *CBQ* 59 (1997), pp. 1-20.

is very important for making such a 'fiction' work, since the outcome from judgment to vindication has both its lesson and its power from the struggle of the prophet against the tide of events.

Towards a Theology of Imagination

The climactic point of Perdue's evaluation of new directions in biblical theology is an emerging 'theology of imagination'. He builds towards it by appreciating the importance that language as metaphor has come to play in current hermeneutics. Strictly metaphorical language, in which an entire passage carries multiple levels of possible meaning, applies particularly to the prophetic books like Jeremiah. These texts are confessions of faith in which readers interpret themselves through their responses to the text.[16] There is almost no declarative doctrine or fact at stake, but a process of forming concepts that then open up further revelatory processes.[17] *Imagination* is the key to this approach. It is understood by Perdue and his sources to be that juncture in the human intellect where the transcendent and ineffable meet concrete historicity and sensual existence. We create a relationship to God who is both interactive in our world and yet beyond our experience. Jeremiah *as text* challenges us to understand our experience anew in the light of the prophetic message. We imagine the world as Jeremiah experienced it and the book describes it through the concrete images and events of our own conventional experience. But his refusal to accept the standard perception of what God was doing forces the reader to image the living God acting in new ways that we believe are possible but not what we have previously expected. We join with the prophet through the narrative mode of the text which by its juxtaposition of materials evokes a new vision, thus leading us to recast our former religious interpretation of experience and so reimagine how God is to be perceived for the future.

Jeremiah is the perfect model of biblical literature to achieve this result in the reader or hearer since it is framed to imagine the birth of the future from the pain and agony of the present. It is not just the people who suffer because of events and because of their lack of imagination, but the prophet suffers with them and for them. Even

16. Sallie McFague, *Metaphorical Theology* (Philadelphia: Fortress Press, 1982).

17. Perdue, *The Collapse of History*, pp. 201-205.

more, the book emphasizes that God suffers with Israel, and from that grief emerges a renewed commitment to one another (see 8.18-23; 31.15-20). Jeremiah's story is a paradigm. Again, however, we can only understand it as *paradigm* if the actual suffering of the Exile was real enough to force the theological imagination to change its vision about the future. Imagination needs memory: without historical rootedness, the metaphors fly off in a thousand arbitrary directions.

An Ecclesial Theology of Jeremiah

Canon criticism has recalled us to the living context in which Scripture survived past its authors. It reminds us that history in biblical theology is not just originating events behind the text, but the actual life of the text in a community that preserves it and cherishes it. Unfortunately, most of canonical criticism is a glorified extension of redaction criticism, identifying the reasons for the ordering of passages and organization of canons instead of seeing the power of a 'sacred canon'.[18]

Since most modern interpretive developments that we are discussing assume the legitimacy of multiple readings of any given text, they generally pass over any idea of an 'authoritative' reading of the text. But that is precisely the history of the intepretation of the text until now. There may have been multiple readings offered, but the faith communities insisted on governing which readings were acceptable or not. Can one have a totally individual *theology*? Or is theology in fact a result of community participation, involving authoritative teachers, catechesis, liturgical ritual, and deep traditionalism? This is a burning issue in hermeneutics that church-people are only beginning to address. The Academy holds sway with a study of the text outside its faith-effect on the reader. But even if this has worked well in some areas, such as literary appreciation and historical recovery, or even in social critiques of ideologies inherent in the texts' background cultures, it has not proven effective for doing theology of the Bible. If religious metaphorical language and imagination is an expression of faith-confession, can commentators effectively approach the text if they do not know how to

18. So Childs, *Introduction to the Old Testament as Scripture*. No doubt Childs has a deeper faith commitment to canon than the merely descriptive, but he limits his study to the development of the texts themselves and not to the development of their understanding and use in the later communities of faith.

articulate it within a real living community which takes it as a normative and authoritative religious text? One wonders.

To return to Jeremiah as theology, we might ask pointedly whether efforts to divorce the text from the original prophet, as Carroll mostly does, will be successful. My answer is no. I can agree that there is a strong theological construction of the book from what can be loosely styled 'the deuteronomistic school'. However, the logic of the 'story' goes far beyond specific links to Deuteronomy. There is both a passion and a rough-hewn edge to the book that preserves stories in duplicate and in odd sequences and out of temporal order, which clearly signals the effort of the editors to preserve the memory in action of the prophet Jeremiah himself. This is not a constructed prophet, who is more a teacher than a prophet, like the 'servant figure' of Second Isaiah, but an inspired voice in history whose words have effective force because people believed that God was active in those events and in particular had seized Jeremiah to be both the voice and the guinea pig for the divine plan.

Because the context of preservation was the faith community of Israel, that historical memory was important in the formation of the tradition as well as in the design of the book. The power of the prophet lived on in the synagogue and church and guaranteed the sacred status of the book precisely because it was a *historical* recital.

BETWEEN THE TOWER OF UNITY AND THE BABEL
OF PLURALISM: BIBLICAL THEOLOGY AND LEO PERDUE'S
THE COLLAPSE OF HISTORY

Dennis T. Olson

At the outset, I want to express my appreciation for Leo Perdue's helpful and stimulating book *The Collapse of History*.[1] I share many of Professor Perdue's convictions about the importance of theological interpretation of the Old Testament and the promise of more recent interpretive approaches for that task. However, I want to raise some questions and issues for the sake of stimulating further discussion and thinking.

The title of Perdue's book suggests a twofold purpose in his work, one descriptive and the other prescriptive. On one hand, Perdue *describes* 'the collapse of history as the dominant paradigm in Old Testament theology' (p. 7). On the other hand, Perdue's subtitle, 'Reconstructing Old Testament Theology', suggests a constructive proposal, *prescribing* how to move forward once 'history' has 'collapsed'.

Let me first consider the description dimension of this book. Perdue observes early on in his study: 'It is the collapse of the historical paradigm as the singular approach for doing Old Testament theology that is the central problem in present theological discussion' (p. 11). There have been many previous surveys of the field of Old Testament theology. However, Perdue notes that these previous surveys have largely ignored more recent methods or approaches that no longer assume the priority of history as the dominant feature of Old Testament theology. Perdue seeks to fill this gap. Thus Perdue describes a number of alternative approaches to Old Testament theology apart from a focus on

---

1. Leo Perdue, *The Collapse of History: Reconstructing Old Testament Theology* (Overtures to Biblical Theology; Minneapolis: Fortress Press, 1994). All page references to the book will be included in the body of the essay.

history: creation and wisdom, canon and community, literary criticism and feminist hermeneutics, story and narrative theology, and the role of imagination in creating narrative worlds of meaning.

This descriptive task is given some particularity and a shared biblical platform through Perdue's selection of the book of Jeremiah. Jeremiah functions throughout Perdue's book as a common lens through which to view each of the different approaches he analyzes. This strategic move illuminates how different facets of this prophetic book and its theology emerge depending upon the interpretive grid placed upon it.

But this descriptive enterprise of tracing the collapse of history as a dominant paradigm by highlighting numerous other paradigms has an implicit argument, namely, that history *has* collapsed as a dominant paradigm in Old Testament theology. The question I would press here is this: what kind of history does Perdue have in mind as having collapsed in biblical studies? Does history here mean simply the methods of historical criticism? No, it is not historical criticism that has collapsed for Perdue. This is clear when Perdue discusses the epistemological crisis of postmodernism. He notes that some scholars argue that this crisis might lead to the abandonment of historical criticism. But he writes, 'I suggest that reports of the death of this approach, to borrow from Mark Twain, have been greatly exaggerated' (p. 10). Historical criticism is not the 'history' that has collapsed. Moreover, several of the methods Perdue surveys to illustrate 'the collapse of history' explicitly employ historical criticism as an important tool. Historical criticism remains alive and well.

Does Perdue mean by 'the collapse of history' the shift of primary focus from reconstructed events or texts to the present or final form of the biblical text? No, many of the methods he analyzes do not focus on the final form of the text. For example, Gottwald's so-called radical theology uses social-scientific reconstructions to get to events under or behind the text. Studies on the themes of creation and cosmology rely in part on reconstructions using cultural anthropology. Perdue observes, 'Ultimately it is up to the interpreter, including the Old Testament theologian, to decide whether to focus on the reconstructed history behind the text, the text itself, or the interplay between the two' (p. 285). For Perdue, it seems, any of those choices are acceptable.

Does Perdue mean by 'the collapse of history' what postmodernist scholars mean when they speak of a collapse of old notions of history? According to Pauline Rosenau in her book, *Post-Modernism and the*

Social Sciences, postmodernist scholars oppose conventional notions of history and

> question (1) the idea that there is a real, knowable past, a record of evo-
> lutionary progress of human ideas, institutions or actions, (2) the view
> that historians should be objective, (3) that reason enables historians to
> explain the past, and (4) that the role of history is to interpret and trans-
> mit human cultural and intellectual heritage from generation to genera-
> tion.[2]

Does Perdue count himself or those whom he studies in this book as participating in this understanding of the collapse of history? Perdue does make some moves in this direction as he discusses Hayden White's view of history. Perdue writes, 'History is more fictional than positivists would allow. As Hayden White demonstrates ... historians use their imagination in writing history' (p. 280).

Yet it seems Perdue does not want to give up on some sense of objectivity in history. He acknowledges that history involves creative and imaginative redescriptions of reality. Nevertheless, he writes, 'there are norms and criteria of evaluation that may be articulated, including tradition, reason, experience, coherence, compelling engagement, humaneness, and even results' (p. 264). Perdue later confesses he is 'an unrepentant rationalist'. He goes on to list the five historical causes that explain the collapse of history in Old Testament theology, an explanatory and causal strategy that would belie a thoroughly conventional historian. So I continue to wonder what kind of history is Perdue speaking of when he describes 'the collapse of history' in Old Testament theology.

Perhaps we would be helped if we move to consider the *prescriptive* character of Perdue's book, suggested by his subtitle 'Reconstructing Old Testament Theology'. Perdue not only describes the pluralism of many different approaches to Old Testament theology. He not only describes their strengths and contributions. He also critiques what he discerns as the weaknesses in all of them. In these critiques and in his concluding chapters, the reader begins to see where Perdue is heading. As the reader travels through the book, it is interesting to see the pattern of critique: the key issue seems to be avoiding extremes and seeking a middle road. G. Ernest Wright's historical focus and Trible's feminism

---

2.   Pauline Rosenau, *Post-Modernism and the Social Sciences* (Princeton, NJ: Princeton University Press, 1992), p. 63.

are criticized because they are not systematic enough. On the other hand, Perdue faults Rolf Knierim for being too systematic. Knierim's proposal to fit everything in Old Testament theology under one topic, 'the universal dominion of Yahweh in justice and righteousness' is 'perhaps a little too rational and systematic' (p. 128). For Childs, historical particularity gets too little attention (p. 186); with G.E. Wright historical particularity gets too much. Gottwald sees too much ideology behind every theological tree (p. 106); Childs sees too little (p. 189). History is one aspect, but so is creation. Historical-critical work is not sufficient; it must be supplemented by literary approaches. In this quest for balance, Perdue is working hard with the issue of balancing pluralism versus striving for coherence and unity. It is that issue—pluralism versus unity—that will be the focus of my remaining comments which will be spiced with some reflections on Jeremiah.

The structure of Perdue's survey of various methods and approaches to Old Testament theology in light of Jeremiah amply illustrates the pluralism of biblical interpretation in recent decades. For the most part, he writes, biblical theology has become 'a "tower of Babel" with articulations that command no consensus, either clash with or ignore different approaches, and command no overwhelming following' (p. 7). In his critiques, Perdue chides some scholars for being overly systematic in their Old Testament theologies. So does Perdue want to rebuild the tower of Babel in Old Testament theology? Doe he want the discipline to engage in debate and argumentation so that it will lead to a scholarly consensus of the unified and coherent theme and structure for Old Testament theology that then can be applied by various interpreters to their different contexts?

Well, not quite. Perdue wants to maintain a balance or tension between affirming pluralism and driving toward coherence. He writes, 'The systematization of the biblical traditions should not eliminate the pluralism inherent in the text. At the same time, pluralism should not be allowed to paralyze an intelligent rendering of the theology of the biblical traditions in a systematic form' (p. 305). And Perdue is optimistic that this can happen. He writes, 'Through the evaluation of the multiple theologies of the biblical texts by accepted criteriology, an adequate, cogent, and coherent OT theology should emerge' (p. 307). Perdue defines for us what that unifying and systematic theme of Old Testament theology is:

> The unifying principle for this systematic presentation is the sovereignty
> and providence of God who shapes and sustains in righteousness and
> compassion both cosmos and history and the humane and immanent
> deity who is present in the world (pp. 306-307).

I offer four responses to this proposal.

1. This unifying principle sounds much like Rolf Knierim's proposal
for the central theme for Old Testament theology, 'the universal dominion of Yahweh in justice and righteousness' that Perdue had earlier in
the book rejected as 'a little too rational and systematic' (p. 128). Why
is it too systematic for Knierim but properly systematic when stated
with some additions as in Perdue's proposal?

2. What is the community of interpretation that Perdue has in mind
for agreeing upon the 'accepted criteriology'? Who is this community
who should not 'allow' pluralism to paralyze 'intelligent' renderings of
biblical theology? What are the concrete institutional ways that this in
fact happens? The rhetoric of 'accepted criteriology' and 'not allowing'
things to happen suggests functions of policing, enforcing, power, and
saying 'yes' to some and 'no' to others. Does Perdue assume that this
consensus will emerge from the guild of biblical scholars, the Society
of Biblical Literature or some other scholarly organization? Is such an
assumption possible, realistic or desirable?

The deep divides in the book of Jeremiah itself between true and false
prophets both presuming to speak in the name of Yahweh ought to
remind us of the depth of differences in basic assumptions when comparing communities of interpretation. I doubt Jeremiah and his opponents who plotted against his life could have come to a reasoned
consensus. Moreover, it is difficult to find a unifying theological
principle just for the book of Jeremiah itself, never mind the whole Old
Testament. Jeremiah holds together strong words of unconditional
judgment of pre-exilic Judah with seemingly incompatible but equally
strong words of unconditional promise for Judah in exile. If Jeremiah's
theology resists systematization, how much more the entire Old Testament?

3. Is Perdue's unifying principle and structure for Old Testament
theology a timeless and eternal principle and structure for all ages and
cultures? A reader may receive that impression from some parts of the
book. But at one point, Perdue does acknowledge that the theology and
ideology of Scripture 'must be evaluated and assessed by the norms of
the culture and age to which it attempts to speak' (p. 277).

However, is there a unified culture even in the United States from which one could hope to derive unified norms? What is the culture that Perdue has in mind here? A world culture? A national culture? A regional culture? A denominational culture? A racial-ethnic culture? A religious culture? A local community culture? And is there really a unified age, an era, a time when a set of consensual norms function? To speak of a broad unified culture or an age or an era does not take seriously the many cultures of interpretation, the fragmented character of our age, and the deep, fundamental divisions that divide us—academic values versus communities of faith, Jew versus Christian, conservative traditionalism and progressive reimagining of the tradition, issues of race, class and gender, differences among regions of the world, and the myriad denominational differences within Jewish and Christian communities—Orthodox, Conservative, Reformed, Reconstructionist, Roman Catholic, Pentecostal, evangelical, liturgical traditions, confessional traditions and the list goes on. In addition, there is the complex interaction and mutual influence of religion and the larger culture. Most communities and most individuals have multiple shaping influences and multiple allegiances among these and many other communal forces that compete for our devotion. No unifying principle can satisfactorily incorporate and unify the very different ways that such readers work theologically or ideologically with Scripture.

4. Perdue's model seeks to avoid the extremes of a timeless tower of Babel on one hand and everyone doing what is right in their own eyes on the other. But the model strives to avoid those extremes by seeking a unified principle that finally transcends all particular communities of interpretation, seeking a consensus among all parties in a given culture and age. I am reminded of a passage from John Bunyan's *The Pilgrim's Progress* in which a religious pilgrim journeys toward the Heavenly City:

> The way to the Celestial City
> lies just through this town
> where this lusty fair is kept;
> and he that will go to the city,
> and yet not go through this town,
> must needs go out of the world.[3]

---

3. John Bunyan, *The Pilgrim's Progress* (New York: American Tract Society, n.d.), p. 257.

It is only by passing through particular and local towns and communities that progress is made. To do otherwise is to seek to avoid the
realities of this world. Perdue's transcendent, unified principle threatens
to take a detour around the particular in a quest for an abstract idealism.

I would offer a different kind of model for biblical and theological
interpretation. It is a model, I would argue, that is more in keeping with
three important realities that face us in the lusty fairs and diverse towns
that make up our present interpretive landscape. First, the model needs
to take seriously the reality of our interpretive climate that is itself
highly pluralist and divided. Fundamental differences in basic starting
points, methods and assumptions separate us. Secondly, the model
needs to be in keeping with the shape of Scripture itself. Scripture contains strikingly different theological voices. There is simply a different
theological atmosphere that animates Jeremiah as compared to Isaiah,
even though they are both major prophets of ancient Israel. Even with
its diversity, however, Scripture also contains a highly intricate network
of connections that invite conversations and intertextual readings. This
web of relationships encourages juxtaposition, comparison and strivings
for provisional coherence without collapsing into a single unifying
principle. For example, the Deuteronomistic prose sections of Deuteronomy and the Deuteronomistic framing of the book of Jeremiah invite
the reader to ponder the message of the prophet Jeremiah in light of the
Mosaic book of the Torah in Deuteronomy and the other books of the
Deuteronomistic History. Jeremiah is given a Deuteronomistic 'tilt'
even as the distinctive voice of the Jeremiah traditions remain. Thirdly,
the model I propose should be in keeping with the locus of biblical
interpretation over much of the Bible's history, namely, within local
communities with provisional but frequent engagements in preaching,
teaching and study of Scripture.[4] Such engagements have been and continue to be shaped by traditions that function as fruitful 'prejudices',[5]

---

4.   By the term 'local' community, I do not mean only small local communities
(congregations, classes, small groups). By local, I mean communities located in a
specific time and space in a contextual matrix of traditions, influences, time and
space with certain boundaries and limits of influence and authority. A national or
regional assembly can function as a local community as can a small group of four
or five individuals who regularly gather together.

5.   For understanding tradition as a positive and useful 'prejudice' in the interpretation of texts, cf. Hans-Georg Gadamer, *Truth and Method* (New York:
Seabury, 1975), pp. 241-52.

whether the Mishnah, midrash and other traditions of Judaism or the creeds, doctrines, confessions and other common practices of various Christian traditions or the particular interpretive rules shaped by cultural, historical, literary or social-scientific approaches.

The model I suggest is more a web or network of localized interpretive communities than an authoritative pronouncement from one individual or one community of experts. This web of communities would be encouraged in conversation and translation among one another. This web of communities would also be encouraged in self-critical reflection in light of hearing the voices of other people and other traditions in public debate, argumentation and cooperation to seek local and provisional consensus about the meanings of particular biblical texts in light of particular needs, issues and actions. Such local communities and consensus-building suggests a model of truth, reason and debate that is more rhetorical in the broadest and classical sense of that term.[6] There is a kind of provisional truth sufficient for the moment that emerges within the intersubjective interaction of text, interpreter, audience and interpretive tradition.

What would then be the role of the biblical scholar in the discipline of Old Testament theology? The role would entail providing resources that offer some range and analysis of interpretive options for given texts, biblical books, topics and themes. The biblical scholar has a responsibility to provide models and analogies that argue or make a case for particular interpretations of texts. Such arguments are best made, however, in a way that acknowledges their provisionality, that invites critique and conversation, and that is open to the possibility of very different ways of reading. One of many possible ways of reading may include a true interpretation not rooted primarily in the historical-critical method.[7]

---

6. On the relationship of rhetoric and theological truth claims, cf. David Cunningham, *Faithful Persuasion: In Aid of a Rhetoric of Christian Theology* (Notre Dame: University of Notre Dame Press, 1991); and Cunningham, 'Theology as Rhetoric', *TS* 52 (1991), pp. 407-30.

7. A thoughtful reflection on the theoretical foundations of historical criticism in comparison to pre-critical methods of biblical interpretation is provided by David Steinmetz, 'The Superiority of Pre-Critical Exegesis', *TTod* 37 (1980), pp. 27-38; reprinted in Stephen Fowl (ed.), *The Theological Interpretation of Scripture: Classic and Contemporary Readings* (Cambridge, MA: Basil Blackwell, 1997), pp. 26-38.

The question of truth is important for the book of Jeremiah itself, as it is for Perdue. But the accepted criteriology for Jeremiah and his tradition of interpretation is something other than whether or not methods of discerning truth and meaning properly balance an inclusive list of recent approaches and themes. The criteriology is even something more than 'history'.

In the Deuteronomistic tradition, one of the tests of a true prophet was whether the judgment of exile that God promised through Jeremiah would come true. Jeremiah's editors attached the prose account of the Babylonian exile in 2 Kings 25 as a concluding appendix to Jeremiah in ch. 52. The historical appendix was a confirming sign to the reader that Jeremiah's words of judgment had indeed happened in history as Jeremiah had predicted. This represents a kind of historical criticism. But even for the Deuteronomistic tradition and the criteria of true prophecy in Deuteronomy 18, history alone was no guarantee. Even if a prophet's words come true, if that prophet speaks in the name of another god, then that prophet is a false prophet (Deut. 18.20). For Jeremiah, God in the end will have the final word about what is true and what is false. In the meantime, the debates about Old Testament theology and Jeremiah will continue. We should be grateful to Professor Perdue for providing us a valuable resource to help stimulate those ongoing debates.

WHAT SHALL WE DO ABOUT PLURALISM? A RESPONSE
TO LEO PERDUE'S *THE COLLAPSE OF HISTORY*

Thomas W. Overholt

Henry Reed's poem 'Chard Whitlow', a send-up of T.S. Eliot's war-
time radio talks on the BBC, begins:

> As we get older, we do not get any younger.
> Seasons return, and today I am fifty-five,
> And this time last year I was fifty-four,
> And this time next year I shall be sixty-two.

Indeed, seasons do return: this time two years ago we were in Chicago;
and this time last year we were in Philadelphia; and this year we are
in New Orleans. Surely history has not collapsed in any literal sense,
and we are not surprised to find that in the catchy title of his recent
book Leo Perdue is using the term 'history' in a rather specialized and
restricted sense. What has collapsed, or at least come to be seriously
destabilized, is the familiar historical critical paradigm that up to now
has been dominant in biblical scholarship.[1] In this context he observes
that if we broaden our view and see Old Testament theology not simply
'within the rubric of the history of Israelite religion' but as 'a discipline
within theology as a whole', then we will see that a good deal of significant work has taken place in the last 50 years that does not fit neatly
into the dominant paradigm.[2]

One goal of the book is to survey samples of this work, emphasizing
approaches to the Old Testament that focus more on the text and its language than on the history of Israelite religion and wherever possible
using interpretations of Jeremiah to illustrate the various orientations
and methods he describes. The first section is on history, and has

---

1. L.G. Perdue, *The Collapse of History: Reconstructing Old Testament Theology* (Minneapolis: Fortress Press, 1994), p. 4.
2. Perdue, *The Collapse of History*, p. 13.

chapters on G.E. Wright and G. von Rad that illustrate the limitations of the old paradigm and one on N.K. Gottwald's more modern, but still historical, methodology. This section took me back to my graduate school days when the biblical theology movement was in full swing and when the second volume of von Rad's *Theology* was hot off the press and we scrambled to purchase and read it before the translaton appeared, and also of the autumn of 1979 when I procured a copy of the newly released *Tribes of Yahweh* and tried to get it read before the annual meeting in New York.[3] There follow chapters on wisdom (where God is known in creation, not just in history), on canon, on literary criticism and feminist hermeneutics, on narrative theology, and on the theology of imagination. *The Collapse of History* is a wide-ranging book, clearly written and informative.

It is, furthermore, a book generous in spirit. I think many readers will be struck as I was by Perdue's openness to alternative ways of defining and approaching the task of Old Testament theology. He is at one level resolutely pluralistic, searching out, inquiring into, and appreciating different methodologies. At the end of the book he observes that while some might characterize 'this variety of approaches and interpretations ... as fragmentation, suggesting something of a negative image', he prefers to see it 'as diversity, implying a richness of insight that offers many opportunities for conversation',[4] and he laments the lack of 'conversation' between proponents of different approaches.[5]

Turning from this somewhat general description of what's in the book, I'd like to raise another question, namely, What is the book about? Perdue very clearly has an agenda that goes beyond a survey of scholarship. To alter only slightly another line from Henry Reed's poem, 'I think you will find this put, better than I could ever hope to express it, in the words of [the book itself]':

> Pluralism ... should not become a license for legitimating every presentation of biblical theology. Open conversation that frankly engages the variety of approaches to biblical theology and its many particular presen-

---

3. Gerhard von Rad, *Old Testament Theology*, II (trans. D.M.G. Stalker; New York: Harper & Row, 1965); Norman K. Gottwald, *The Tribes of Yahweh: A Sociology of the Religion of Liberated Israel, 1250–1050 B.C.E.* (Maryknoll, NY: Orbis Books, 1979).

4. Perdue, *The Collapse of History*, p. 301.

5. For example, Perdue, *The Collapse of History*, pp. 6, 196, 301-303, 307.

tations needs to proceed along the lines of common criteria of evaluation.[6]

> ... in this age of multiculturalism and diversity, we should celebrate our pluralism and rejoice over our differences. Yet this too only contributes to increased fragmentation and may even lead to the danger of making theology primarily a matter of private taste ... Serious efforts at criteriology need to be undertaken in order to find established procedures for evaluating theological interpretations and approaches ... [this] would not result in only one way of doing Old Testament theology. However, appropriate criteria, carefully applied, could evaluate and assess the quality of an interpretation in important ways and remove it from the realm of subjective preference and preposterous claims.[7]

> ... pluralism should not allow theology to enter into the quagmire of relativity and private preference.[8]

The first of these quotations comes from the Preface, the second from the beginning of the first chapter, and the third from the last chapter. To use a term well-known to and perhaps even dear to the hearts of students of Jeremiah, they form an *inclusio* that frames the entire exposition. Perdue embraces pluralism, but his project is to keep it in check.

The references to 'common criteria of evaluation' and to 'criteriology' caught my attention immediately. I wondered what would pass for such criteria, and kept an eye out for answers to that question. It turns out that quite in contrast to his lengthy and carefully organized expositions of the views of others, Perdue doesn't devote much space explicitly to setting out his own position. One is forced to look for clues in his assessments of the various methodologies he discusses and in a proposed 'paradigm for Old Testament theology' found in the last two pages of the book. In my view Perdue in fact proposes (without specifically differentiating between them) two different sets of criteria, one methodological, the other normative.

Three distinct criteria cluster around the methodological pole. First, Perdue believes that an adequate Old Testament theology must 'posit a center that allows for a systematic presentation'.[9] Thus he judges von Rad's descriptive approach linked to the history of Israelite religion to

---

6. Perdue, *The Collapse of History*, p. xii.
7. Perdue, *The Collapse of History*, pp. 6-7.
8. Perdue, *The Collapse of History*, p. 303.
9. Perdue, *The Collapse of History*, p. 67.

be inadequate, and criticizes P. Trible for opposing 'systematic formulation of Old Testament theology' and J. Sanders for 'embrac[ing]
fragmentation'.[10] Wright's attempt to find a center in the mighty acts of
God in history fails because it is positivistic and untenable. On the other
hand, R. Knierim wins praise for moving beyond the 'paralysis of
pluralism' by seeking 'a monotheistic structure that relates and system-
atizes [the plurality of Old Testament theologies in the text] into a
consistent whole'.[11] In his concluding brief proposal Perdue sums up
the point in this way. After the initial descriptive task of 'articulat[ing]
the meaning that derives from understanding texts in their historical and
cultural context', Old Testament theologians should move on to a 'con-
ceptualization of the multiple images, ideas, and themes that leads to
the systematic rendering of the multiple theologies of [the] texts within
the dynamic matrix of creation and history'.[12]

A second methodological criterion is that a theology of the Old Testament ought to be capable of incorporating all parts of that collection,
a point on which he faults Wright, von Rad and Gottwald.[13] Third, it is
necessary to establish and maintain 'the necessary distance between the
biblical worlds and the modern reader'.[14] We need to be acutely aware
of the chronological and cultural differences that separate us from the
Old Testament world, and thus while no longer in a privileged position,
historical criticism is after all not obsolete. Specific examples of modern literary criticism and narrative theology are found wanting when
judged by this criterion.

There are two normative criteria. First, Old Testament theology
should be 'constructive', that is, it must deal with pressing 'questions
emerging from the contemporary community of faith ... [questions like]
sexism, racism, environment, war, the Holocaust, and social justice'.[15]
It must be broad enough to include the life experiences of many groups,
and should 'lead into contemporary hermeneutics, without completely
sacrificing historical particularity'.[16]

The second normative criterion is a corollary to the methodological

---

10. Perdue, *The Collapse of History*, pp. 226, 189.
11. Perdue, *The Collapse of History*, pp. 128, 126.
12. Perdue, *The Collapse of History*, p. 306.
13. Perdue, *The Collapse of History*, pp. 64-65, 106-107.
14. Perdue, *The Collapse of History*, p. 304.
15. Perdue, *The Collapse of History*, p. 67.
16. Perdue, *The Collapse of History*, pp. 303, 306.

requirement that Old Testament theology be systematic. 'The unifying principle for this systematic presentation is the sovereignty and providence of God who shapes and sustains in righteousness and compassion both cosmos and history and the humane and immanent deity who is present in the world.'[17] The transcendent reality of God must be maintained and not, as in the case of a materialist theology, reduced to ideology or social ethics.[18]

At the end of the book Perdue says, 'pluralism should not be eliminated, but through the evaluation of the multiple theologies of the biblical texts by accepted criteriology, an adequate, cogent, and coherent Old Testament theology should emerge'.[19] I translate that to mean such a theology will be systematic and persuasive, adequate to the needs of a believing community. Well, that may be a worthy goal, but it raises several important questions. For one, what 'believing community' are we speaking of? Surely there are many such communities even within Christianity broadly defined. Which shall have priority? Perdue himself acknowledges this problem, noting the wide variety of available answers to the question of where revelation and the knowledge of God 'reside'.[20]

The existence and nature of God himself is another question the book raises. This is the quintessential theological problem, and I'm uncomfortable with the limits Perdue places on conversation by insisting on the transcendence of this entity known only by the human imagination. Take, for example, his criticism of Gottwald's materialist approach, the 'major theological liability' of which is, he says, 'the loss of transcendence', reducing theology as it does to 'a set of religious symbols expressing the ideology of a social group' and paying scant attention to worship, 'the search for harmony with nature, and sprituality, unless they are intimately part of the fabric of social life'.[21] But when are such human activities not a part of that fabric? He also claims that eliminating transcendence makes it difficult to evaluate how good or bad a given ideology may be.[22]

Ideology is the culprit here. Perdue insists that in order to preserve

17. Perdue, *The Collapse of History*, pp. 306-307.
18. Perdue, *The Collapse of History*, p. 105.
19. Perdue, *The Collapse of History*, p. 307.
20. Perdue, *The Collapse of History*, p. 301.
21. Perdue, *The Collapse of History*, pp. 104-105.
22. Perdue, *The Collapse of History*, pp. 105-106.

God's transcendence and at least 'some measure' of God's Word in the 'human words of Scripture' we must have a 'valid hermeneutic for critically engaging Scripture ... that transcends ideology'.[23] Now consider that 80 pages later in the context of his discussion of B. Childs, Perdue says 'it is reasonable to assume that social groups in ancient Israel, including those to which authors and redactors and tradents belonged, at times shaped ideologies of self-interest that eventually entered the Old Testament'.[24] Well, if the texts can 'at times' be ideological, why can't they be so all the time? And if a given text is not ideological, how can we tell the difference from one which is? More basic, if we understand 'ideology' in a more neutral way to refer to 'the sum of the ways in which people both live and represent to themselves their relationship to the conditions of their existence',[25] then the terms 'ideology' and 'theology' seem to me to be virtually synonymous.

Perdue would keep creation and history as the arenas of God's activity, but he is no positivist. How then would he go about trying to discern divine activity in these spheres? In the end it seems to me he casts his lot with the proponents of theological imagination.[26] Such a move, of course, has its hazards. That a particular product of the imagination seems realistic or plausible or satisfying guarantees nothing with respect to its truth value. And so we have another version of the problem Perdue raised in criticizing Gottwald, namely, how to differentiate between good and bad interpretations. Here he follows the lead of W. Brueggemann, who brings a rich mix of 'historical criticism, social-scientific analysis, and newer literary methodologies' to his study of texts, and who emphasizes the 'corporate character' of, for example, the prophetic imagination encountered in them. This recognition of a 'theology of imagination ... shaped within the context of a historical community' (and, by the way, inviting later interpreters to appropriate it imaginatively in their own time) prevents merely private interpretations by virtue of recognizing 'at least implicit criteria for evaluation. These criteria include the careful inquiry into theological conceptualizations to ensure that ideological formulation is avoided, the analysis of new formulations of theology to see whether they are capable of representing in authentic and convincing ways the faith traditions of collective memory,

---

23. Perdue, *The Collapse of History*, p. 106.
24. Perdue, *The Collapse of History*, p. 189.
25. Catherine Belsey, *Critical Practice* (London: Routledge, 1980), p. 42.
26. See Perdue, *The Collapse of History*, p. 302.

and the more pragmatic evaluation of whether a theology enhances well-being, love, justice, and peace'.[27]

But, again, what counts for ideological formulation? A few pages earlier Jeremiah's 'critique of ideology' is described in terms of 'covenant obligation and divine pathos shap[ing] an alternative consciousness that is in opposition to the ideology of court and temple'.[28] I can't help reflecting that in the old days we described this contest that dominates important sections of the book of Jeremiah as a struggle between two covenant theologies, each of which was firmly rooted in the people's past. From Jeremiah's point of view, his opponents' view may have seemed an 'ideology of self-interest', and vice versa. I've always thought of them as legitimate, if competing, attempts to understand the course of current events. If Jeremiah's opponents seem to us ideologues, it is perhaps because (aided by hindsight) we have cast our lot with the texts' representation of them, that is, with the ideology of those in Jeremiah's camp.

How do we differentiate good from bad? Speaking of 'artistic imagination that goes beyond descriptive representation to new creation', Perdue says that 'canons of evaluation can only derive from what one thinks or believes are common human values. Are the products of the imagination life-enhancing or destructive? Are they liberating...or ...debilitating to the human spirit?'[29] Or, in the terms just used of the prophetic imagination, do these understandings enhance 'well-being, love, justice, and peace'? I am impressed by the necessary ambiguity of these terms: adequate, cogent, coherent;[30] common human values, life-enhancing, liberating;[31] enhancing well-being, love, justice, and peace.[32] I really think this is as good as we can do. Ambiguity—existence in a confusing world and being responsible for what we will make of it—is inherent in the human enterprise. I see nothing in this situation that would privilege one type of Old Testament theology over others. The more the merrier, since we need all the help we can get.

Well, you are no doubt thinking, certainly it's time to bring these remarks to an end, and so I shall after a final reflection. For the 35 years

27. Perdue, *The Collapse of History*, p. 298.
28. Perdue, *The Collapse of History*, p. 295.
29. Perdue, *The Collapse of History*, p. 272.
30. Perdue, *The Collapse of History*, pp. 262, 307.
31. Perdue, *The Collapse of History*, p. 272.
32. Perdue, *The Collapse of History*, p. 298.

that I have been more or less actively engaged in studying the texts of the Old Testament, I had never been particularly troubled by certain statements about God that I repeatedly encountered—how he created the world then destroyed it with a flood, toyed with an aged and childless couple, sought to kill Moses whom he had just commissioned, liberated his people from slavery in Egypt and almost immediately thereafter manifested himself to them at Sinai as a threatening and potentially destructive presence, and the like. The reason, I presume, was that standard historical critical moves presented a number of options for separating out such tales and interpreting (domesticating) them. Recently, however, I have been reading Jack Miles's *God: A Biography*[33] with some students, and suddenly I am aware of a powerful unfolding of theological imagination that takes these grim and grisly stories seriously, in order, and in stride, and interprets them as episodes in the development of God's 'personality'. I doubt it would occur to anyone to argue that Miles's imaginative reconstruction of what he takes to be the Tanakh's imaginative presentation of the personality of God should replace other views, but that's not the point. Nevertheless, can we say that Miles's interpretation is potentially adequate, cogent, coherent and liberating? I think perhaps we can, and certainly that says something about the quest for a firm criteriology.

---

33. New York: Alfred A. Knopf, 1995.

THE 'BARUCH CONNECTION':
REFLECTIONS ON JEREMIAH 43.1-7[*]

Walter Brueggemann

We are only at the beginning of our attempt to understand the canonical shape of the book of Jeremiah. It is clear that the three-source hypothesis of Mowinckel and Duhm continues to hold scholarship in thrall. Not only has 'source analysis' dominated recent discussion, but scholars have most often insisted upon asking not only questions about literary sources, but also questions about the historicity of those who purport to author the sources. Thus the recent comprehensive and impressive commentaries of Holladay and Carroll not only articulate the extreme limits of such source analysis, but they are in fact twinned in their preoccupation with historical questions.[1] Whereas Holladay voices a maximalist claim for the historical Jeremiah, Carroll is concerned to deny any claim for the availability of the historical Jeremiah in the text, in the interest of his larger concern to establish the Deuteronomic shape of the book.[2] While Carroll comes closer to issues of canonical shape than does Holladay, this is largely inadvertent. Carroll has no interest that I can discern in the canonical shape; the reason he comes closer than Holladay is only because of his interest in moving as far away as possible from the historical Jeremiah. Thus he draws more

---

*   Previously published as 'The Baruch Connection', in *JBL* 113 (1994), pp. 405-20, and is reproduced here by kind permission of the Society of Biblical Literature.

1.   William L. Holladay, *Jeremiah 1: A Commentary on the Book of the Prophet Jeremiah, Chapters 1–25* (Hermeneia; Philadelphia: Fortress Press, 1986); *idem*, *Jeremiah 2: A Commentary on the Book of the Prophet Jeremiah, Chapters 26–52* (Hermeneia; Minneapolis: Fortress Press, 1989); and Robert P. Carroll, *Jeremiah, A Commentary* (OTL; Philadelphia: Westminster Press, 1986).

2.   In addition to his commentary, see Robert P, Carroll, *From Chaos to Covenant: Prophecy in the Book of Jeremiah* (New York: Crossroad, 1981).

and more of the text later, closer in time to the final shapers of the book. To be sure, Carroll and Holladay cannot be faulted for not addressing canonical questions, since that is neither their interest nor intention. I begin here only in order to observe that recent scholarship, dominated as it is by these two commentaries, is of little help for the matter before us.[3]

I

Concerning the question of canonical shape, I may mention four pertinent matters. First, Diamond, O'Connor and Smith have begun an investigation of the role of the so-called 'lamentations of Jeremiah' in the canonical form of the text.[4] Unfortunately, they have confined themselves to that part of the book of Jeremiah in which those poems occur, and do not venture into the more comprehensive issues of the canonical shape of the book. Second, I suspect that McKane's notion of 'rolling corpus' is pertinent to our question;[5] it is, however, not very well developed, and thus far McKane pursued canonical issues in any intentional way. Third, Childs has provided a rich but inchoate suggestion about 'two forms of proclamation' concerning early/late, oral/written, poetry/prose, judgment/promise[6] (on which see the paradigm proposed by Clements).[7] But Childs has done little specific textual work

---

3.　The work of Holladay and Carroll, respectively, coincides with the work of Helga Weippert, *Die Prosareden des Jeremiabuches* (BZAW, 132; Berlin: W. de Gruyter, 1973); and Winfried Thiel, *Die deuteronomistische Redaktion von Jeremia 1–25* (WMANT, 41; Neukirchen–Vluyn: Neukirchener Verlag, 1973), *Die deuteronomistiche Redaktion von Jeremia 26–52* (WMANT, 52; Neukirchen–Vluyn: Neukirchener Verlag, 1981).

4.　A.R. Pete Diamond, *The Confessions of Jeremiah in Context: Scenes of Prophetic Drama* (JSOTSup, 45; Sheffield: JSOT Press, 1987); Kathleen M. O'Connor, *The Confessions of Jeremiah: Their Interpretation and Role in Chapters 1–25* (SBLDS, 94; Atlanta: Scholars Press, 1988); and Mark Smith, *The Laments of Jeremiah in their Context: A Literary and Redactional Study of Jeremiah 11–20* (Atlanta: Scholars Press, 1990).

5.　William McKane, *A Critical and Exegetical Commentary on Jeremiah*. I. *Introduction and Commentary on Jeremiah I–XXV* (ICC; Edinburgh: T. & T. Clark, 1986), pp. l-lxxxiii.

6.　Brevard S. Childs, *Introduction to the Old Testament as Scripture* (Philadelphia: Fortress Press, 1979), pp. 345-47.

7.　Ronald E. Clements, 'Patterns in the Prophetic Canon', in George W. Coats and Burke O. Long (eds.), *Canon and Authority: Essays in Old Testament Religion*

to show how the broad claims of a canonical structure work out in detail. Fourth, Christopher Seitz has considered the ways in which the book deliberately juxtaposes tensions with opposing interpretive views.[8] In my judgment, however, Seitz has only identified the materials out of which a canonical reflection must be pursued. Thus, while there are important hints and beginnings in present scholarship, the question of canonical process and shape still awaits a more sustained address.

II

The purpose of this essay is to suggest that the person of 'Baruch', and particularly 'Baruch' in 43.1-7, may be understood as a key to the canonizing process and shape of the material. That is, the interest that seems to be represented by 'Baruch' in the text seems to be congruent with that redactional community which shaped the final form of the text. This congruence makes it possible to see something of canonical intentionality in the character of Baruch.[9] (Here I shall be concerned with the shape of the Masoretic text.[10]) Of course, reference to 'Baruch' is not a new suggestion; I intend, however, to consider Baruch not as an editor, author or redactor, but as a character in the text, whose role may suggest something of the intention of the shapers of the book.

Focus on 'Baruch' is in and of itself problematic, At the outset, by 'Baruch' I do not refer to the so-called 'Baruch source',[11] but to the explicit references to him in the text. On the one hand, Baruch is mentioned infrequently in the book. Of the four references, 43.1-7, my text of focus, is least addressed in scholarly discussion. The other three references include the two narratives about the purchase of Jeremiah's land inheritance (ch. 32), the burning of the scroll (ch. 36), and the oracle concerning the destiny of Baruch (ch. 45). Thus attention to

and Theology (Philadelphia: Fortress Press, 1977), pp. 42-55.

8. Christopher R. Seitz, *Theology in Conflict: Reactions to the Exile in the Book of Jeremiah* (BZAW, 176; Berlin: W. de Gruyter, 1989).

9. On recent developments in 'canonical criticism', see Gerald T. Sheppard, 'Canonical Criticism', *ABD*, I, pp. 861-66.

10. On the matter of the MT, see J.G. Janzen, *Studies in the Text of Jeremiah* (HSM; Cambridge, MA: Harvard University Press, 1973).

11. On the 'Baruch' sources the programmatic discussion of G. Wanke, *Untersuchungen zur sogenannten Baruchschrift* (BZAW, 122; Berlin: W. de Gruyter, 1971).

43.1-7 may be a focus on what appears to be a minor text, even for the character of Baruch.

On the other hand, scholars have not been able to resolve the issue of the historicity of the person of Baruch. Holladay, for example, follows a long-established consensus in taking what seem to be historical allusions to Baruch at face value.[12] In that reading, Baruch and his brother Seraiah (cf. 51.59) may be understood as 'members of a family prominent at the royal court'. That consensus about the historicity of Baruch has been sharply challenged by Carroll who finds in Baruch a fictional character whereby the 'tradition created and developed a subsidiary figure to accompany Jeremiah'.[13] Carroll seems to vacillate between a verdict that Baruch was 'created' out of whole cloth, and a contention that he is a secondary, minor 'aleatory' figure who has been made large by the tradition. Carroll's point, I take it, is that Baruch is to be seen not simply as a historical agent, as though our text is simply reportage, but as a carrier of the ideological interests of the Deuteronomic tradition, Seen in that context, I suspect it does not matter much to Carroll whether Baruch was or was not a historical person, as long as primary accent is given to him as an ideological carrier and cipher.

The most important and serious response to Carroll's dismissal of the 'historical' Baruch is that of Dearman, who asserts that 'there is no good reason historically or culturally to doubt the existence or the actuality of Baruch and certain other scribal officials named as sympathetic to Jeremiah'.[14] I am inclined to think that Dearman's case for 'historicity' is a compelling one. That, however, does not diminish Carroll's main point that Baruch is cast in the text in the service of 'scribal-Deuteronomic ideology'. Indeed, Dearman seems to concede as much at the end of his notes, where he speaks of 'evidence for the circle of scriptural editors/authors commonly known as the Deuteronomistic historians'.[15]

---

12. Holladay, *Jeremiah 2*, pp. 215-16 and *passim*.

13. Carroll, *Jeremiah*, pp. 665, 722-24 and *passim*. See also Carroll, *From Chaos to Covenant*, p. 151.

14. J. Andrew Dearman, 'My Servants the Scribes: Composition and Context in Jeremiah 36', *JBL* 109 (1990), pp. 403-421 (404 n. 2).

15. Dearman, 'My Servants', p. 404 n. 2. On the ideological dimension of Deuteronomic theology, see Patricia Dutcher-Walls, 'The Social Location of the Deuteronomists: A Sociological Study of Factional Politics in Late Pre-exilic Judah', *JSOT* 52 (1991), pp. 77-94; and Norman K. Gottwald, 'Social Class as an

In the end, in my judgment, the issue of historicity is completely unimportant for our purposes. It matters not at all whether Baruch is a fictive vehicle for an ideology or a historical personality, in the background of the present book of Jeremiah. In either case, his presence as a character within the text is in the service of a specific ideology which may stand in tension with the historical Jeremiah, but which pervades the canonical book of Jeremiah. I do not think, however, that simply identifying 'ideology' as a force in the present book of Jeremiah is the end of the matter. Rather, we must scrutinize more carefully the meaning of the term 'ideology', and the substance of this particular ideology, if 'Baruch' is to help us read the book of Jeremiah, in its final form and in its final intentionality.

III

The text of 43.1-7 reflects a dispute in the community about how to respond to the announced threat of Babylon.[16] As it is presented, the debate turns on whether to stay in Jerusalem (which means submitting to the invading power of Babylon) or to flee to Egypt. The dispute about adherence to one superpower or the other was a long-standing one, reflected, as Seitz has shown, in the varying influence of the several sons of Josiah and their respective mothers.[17] It is to be noted that in the book of Jeremiah, the dispute takes two sequential forms. In its earlier form, the issue is whether to *submit* willingly to Babylon or to *stand in resistance* in Jerusalem (38.17-18). The second, later form of the same dispute, reflected in our text, represents a fall-back position after it had become clear that Jerusalem would be taken, that is, after resistance in Jerusalem had become futile. Now, with resistance no longer an option, the debate is whether *to stay* in submission or *to flee* to Egypt (42.9-17). In both phases of the dispute about policy, Jeremiah (the person or the book) takes the position more sympathetic to

Analytic and Hermeneutical Category in Biblical Studies', *JBL* 112 (1993), pp. 3-22 (12-13) and *passim*.

16. Seitz, *Theology in Conflict*, provides a complete review of the disputes, understanding them as rival claims for authority among competing exilic communities.

17. Seitz, *Theology in Conflict*, pp. 52-57. See Jay A. Wilcoxen, 'The Political Background of Jeremiah's Temple Sermon', in Arthur J. Merrill and Thomas W. Overholt (eds.), *Scripture in History and Theology: Essays in Honor of J. Coert Rylaarsdom* (Pittsburgh: Pickwick Press, 1977), pp. 151-66.

cooperation with Babylon, first *not to resist* in Jerusalem, and then *not to flee* to Egypt but to remain in the city. The counter-opinion, reflected by the opponents of the book of Jeremiah, is first *to resist* and then *to flee*. (It is important for our purposes that both of these assertions [38.17-18; 42.9-17] are already cast in prose.)

The two phases of this dispute are evidenced in two heavy-handed oracles placed in the mouth of Jeremiah. The first, concerning whether to submit or resist, is given in 38.17-18 with a double 'if–then' phrasing. The positive outcome of surrender for Zedekiah is that 'your life shall be spared, and this city shall not be burned with fire, and you and your houses shall live' (v. 17). The negative outcome of resistance is massive destruction with no escape (v. 18). The strategic question of policy is cast as a severe theological choice.

In the second policy decision (42.9-17), to which our text of 43.1-7 is a response, the issues are again given in an 'if–then' formulation. The positive 'if–then' formulation in vv. 10-12 concerns remaining in the city and receiving mercy (from Yahweh and from the king of Babylon) and restoration, The negative alternative is more complex, because it contains a subsidiary 'if–then' formula in vv. 15b-17. But the negative outcome is the same, an intense rhetorical effort culminating in death by sword, famine and pestilence (vv. 16-17).

Thus, in both parts of the policy dispute, cooperation with Babylon is given by the Jeremiah tradition as a chance for survival, but resistance to Babylon is given in divine oracle as a sure way to death.

IV

After the demanding options of 42.9-17 given as divine oracle, which is re-enforced by the assertion of 42.18-22 reiterating the threat of sword, famine and pestilence, we arrive at the confrontation of 43.1-7. The opponents to Jeremiah's recommended policy of submission and continuation in the city, the advocates of flight to Egypt (in this partisan rendering called 'insolent' [*zēd*]), respond. They declare that the prophetic counsel to remain in submission to Babylon is a lie, that is, a false policy. The word used here is the same as is the one earlier preferred by Jeremiah in 23.16-22, when he accused his opponents of falseness.[18] There the false prophets are accused of speaking 'visions of

18. See Thomas W. Overholt, *The Threat of Falsehood: A Study in the Theology of the Book of Jeremiah* (SBT NS, 16; London: SCM Press, 1970); and more

their own minds', stubbornly following 'their own stubborn hearts' (23.16-17).

What is most striking in the parallel between the indictment of Jeremiah in our passage with the dismissive term *šqr* and Jeremiah's indictment in 23.16-22,[19] is that Jeremiah is not accused of speaking 'visions of his own mind' nor following his own 'stubborn heart'. Rather the cause of the lie is Baruch! It is the vision of *his* mind and *his* stubborn heart which stands indicted.

As the book of Jeremiah has it, this rejection of Jeremiah's counsel (or the counsel of Baruch, as the opponents put it) and the defiant flight to Egypt lead in 43.8-13, 44.1-23 and 24-30 to a massive prophetic threat against Egypt and against those of Jerusalem who flee there. In 43.10-13, Nebuchadnezzar is specifically named as the 'devastator' of Egypt.[20] In 44.30-31, the destroyer is unnamed, but the destruction in Egypt will happen 'just as' Nebuchadnezzar devastated Jerusalem at the behest of Yahweh. In the imaginative construal of historical reality, as shaped by the canonizers of the book of Jeremiah, this devastating, deathly return to Egypt brings the story of Yahweh's life with Israel full circle from the Exodus, so that this foolish choice is presented as the negation and nullification of the entire story of rescue which constituted Israel.[21] Thus a public crisis, seen in larger theological context, is read as a negative counter-point to Israel's primal credo and self-understanding. (See the Exodus rhetoric used negatively in 21.5.)

generally James L. Crenshaw, *Prophetic Conflict: Its Effect upon Israelite Religion* (BZAW, 124; Berlin: W. de Gruyter, 1971), pp. 62-90.

19. See also chs. 27–28.

20. Though the wording is not the same, the mood evoked is parallel to that of the so-called Scythian Songs of chs. 4–6. The stylized language of v. 11 is equivalent to that of 15.2, which suggests that the curses to be brought against Jerusalem are now extended to Egypt. See also the description in ch. 46 of the damage to be worked against Egypt. At least in the prose interpretive comments of vv. 2, 13, and 26, the agent of that devastation is Nebuchadnezzar. Thus our verses reflect a view championed elsewhere in the book of Jeremiah, and by the use of the same sort of rhetoric extend the work 'from the North' even against Egypt.

21. On the 'return to Egypt', see Richard Elliott Friedman, 'From Egypt to Egypt: Dtr[1] and Dtr[2]', in Baruch Halpern and Jon D. Levenson (eds.), *Traditions in Transition* (Winona Lake, IN: Eisenbrauns, 1981), pp. 167-92. See also D.J. Reimer, 'Concerning Return to Egypt: Deuteronomy xvii 16 and xxviii 68 Reconsidered' in J.A. Emerton (ed.), *Studies in the Pentateuch* (VTSup, 41; Leiden: E.J. Brill, 1990), pp. 217-29.

What interests us here, however, is that the opponents of the warning of Jeremiah given in 42.8-17 refuse the work of Jeremiah, but credit that rejected counsel to Baruch instead, Two questions arise from this exchange, both of which directly concern canonical matters.

First, what does this charge tell us about the relation between Jeremiah and 'Baruch?' (Note that I allow for the role of Baruch to be fictive, following Carroll.) We may take Jeremiah to be a prophetic figure who anguishes over the ruin of Jerusalem, and who discerns in it the hidden but decisive resolve of Yahweh. It is exactly poetic idiom that permits the interpretation of a public event in terms of divine resolve. (Indeed, it is clear that as soon as the elusiveness of poetry is reduced to prose, the theological judgments made are open to a very different kind of political dispute.) The speech most characteristically assigned to the poet Jeremiah (perhaps also fictively constructed) is intensely Yahwistic, imaginatively poetic, and almost completely lacking in specific sociopolitical references. This is not to say that 'Jeremiah' was not aware of political matters or disinterested. But his poetry avoids specifically political commentary or even recommendation. That is, it is plausible that Jeremiah, with a poetic-Yahwistic discernment, was largely 'innocent' of concrete socio-political intent and unencumbered by policy *Tendenz*, so intense was he about the Yahwistic theological crisis, letting the political implications of his words knock themselves out as they will. (I do not suggest that anyone, least of all such a daring poet, is ever completely innocent; relatively speaking, however, the poetry is surely restrained about lending itself to any blatant concrete propagandistic effort. It is important to notice precisely how I mean 'innocent'. The difference between the poetry and prose in this matter is not a subjective or interpretive judgment. It is the case that the poetry lacks political specificity.) While such a poet could not be unaware of the political interests served by the poetry, it is credible to think that the interests thus served neither evoked nor legitimated the prophetic utterance, so fixed was he upon the covenantal tradition and the claims of Yahweh in that tradition.[22]

22. By 'innocence' I do not mean ignorance or naïveté. Rather, I mean that the poetic tradition of Jeremiah sought to cut underneath specific political recommendations to more elemental theological matters, even though those theological matters had important, if unspecific, political implications. It is possible to see in the recent work of Vaclav Havel in Czechoslovakia something of a parallel, when Havel was an artistic figure in protest and before be became politically engaged as a

In contrast to Jeremiah, who in 43.1-7 is not the target of attack, the accusation leveled against Baruch is that Baruch is not an 'innocent', disinterested Yahwist, but is party to the sociopolitical dispute, and an adversary of those here called 'insolent'. That is, we may imagine that Baruch is deeply involved in quarrels about policy that are never disinterested. If this is a correct identification of the (fictive?) character of Baruch, then we have a relation between a poet whose words address metapolitical issues and a much interested political 'user' of his Yahwistic poetry.

The relation between the two characters (which has spin-off value with regard to their conventionally designated literary sources, respectively A and B-C) thus is an asymmetrical one. I therefore suggest more or less politically *'innocent' and unencumbered poetry* of anguish and discernment is taken up and utilized for a *political opinion*. That is, the poetry taken up is understood by its political user not as a distortion, but as an 'application', concrete explication of what is implicit in the poetry. Given the poetry, so the 'users' may have concluded, it can have no other political import than the one they give it. There is

party figure and an office holder. For example, in his letter to Gustav Husak, 'Dear Mr. Husak', *Open Letters: Selected Writings 1965–1990* (New York: Vintage Books, 1992), pp. 52-83, Havel makes no specific political urging, but simply makes evident the destructive power of falsehood in the deceptiveness of the government. Such an exposé has an important political spin-off, but Havel at that point does not articulate it. The evolution of Havel's career from artist to politician may help us to see the very different role of the artist in the political process.

No doubt Jeremiah's commitment to the radicality of the Mosaic tradition and the resultant criticism of dynastic theology have an important political spin-off. The more concrete statements of that political spin-off, however, are expressed in prose, much of which evidences Deuteronomic recasting, i.e., articulation of a more concretely political kind. I do not suggest that Jeremiah is free of 'ideology' for his covenantal Yahwism is an ideology. Indeed, Paul Ricoeur, *From Text to Action: Essays in Hermeneutics II* (trans. Kathleen Blamey and John B. Thompson; Evanston: Northwestern University Press, 1991), p. 207, cf. p. 254, is surely correct in concluding that there is 'no place that is completely outside of ideology'. Such an advocacy as that of Jeremiah, however, is of a different sort from the more blatant political practice of the Deuteronomists whose own benefit in their advocacy is relatively transparent. In a broad sense, every advocacy is 'ideology', but not all 'ideologies' serve 'distortion' which is grounded in pragmatic interest. It is not easy to identify pragmatic interest in Jeremiah's 'ideology'. Thus while the ideology of Jeremiah is 'integrating', it is not 'distorting' in the same sense as is that of the Deuteronomists.

inevitably, to be sure, a very different texture to the unencumbered poetry and the practical usage of it. For the practical usage of such anguished articulation and anticipation is never innocent, unambiguous nor disinterested. It is in the nature of the interpretive maneuver toward specificity that it cannot be otherwise, The opponents of this peculiar, asymmetrical relation between poet and political operative (Baruch) reverse the process and suggest that the poet is not only 'used' by, but is motivated and counselled by the political operative. This polemic against the poet along with the political advocate is a common strategy of 'the opposition', who characteristically misunderstand that such poetry can be innocent and unencumbered, and yet 'useful' for more concrete purposes.

Second, one may wonder why the 'insolent men' take up this form of accusation. Why did they not directly accuse Jeremiah more insistently? It may be that the poet himself is too much beyond reproach for such a charge to be credible, for perhaps he is vindicated by events. Perhaps Jeremiah was so protected as pro-Babylonian that he is unassailable. Or it may be that Jeremiah's own 'non-applied' utterances simply do not justify such a charge. Or it may be that Baruch, and all that he represents, is simply an easier target, and that it is the political operators and not the poet whom they want to get. Such a scenario presses us a second time to the question. Who is Baruch? I intend to bracket out historical issues about his person, and ask what interests he serves and embodies in the text. Here I believe that Dearman helps us greatly. He proposes that the families of Shaphan, who is several times the great public defender of Jeremiah and his disputed message, and Neraiah, whose sons Baruch and Seraiah figure in the scrolls of Jeremiah, are in fact influential scribal families.

Once we are past the historical questions, the arguments of Dearman and Carroll, in my judgment, tend to converge and agree, On the one hand, these families *exercise enormous public influence*. (Here again I allow the textual sketch to be fictive, though no doubt reflective of actual public forces.) On the other hand, they *respond affirmatively to the poetic-Yahwistic discernment of reality offered by Jeremiah*. These families, or the scribal-Deuteronomic forces they embody and represent, occupy a middle position between Jeremiah's poetry (which is not designed to be politically 'useful') and *Realpolitik* (which is not seriously occupied with the religious claims of Yahwism).

V

I suggest that these families, or those interests they represent and embody, occupy a delicate middle ground which refuses both 'innocent religion' and cynical politics. They affirm that Jeremiah's 'innocent' rhetoric speaks a truth which effectively impinges upon the political reality. They accept the poetry as germane to public policy and practice, I imagine, not simply because they are pious, but, as is always the case when religion sounds politically credible, because the poetry at least in part coheres with vested interest and perceived interest.[23]

I do not suggest that this is an act of pre-emptive 'bad faith', but an act of good faith 'realism'. It is for this reason that Jeremiah's words, when 'applied' in more concrete ways by the Baruch party, are contentious, given other political interests with other judgments about what is faithful and pragmatic. Thus, as understood by scribal-Deuteronomic opinion, I do not conclude that staying in Jerusalem rather than fleeing to Egypt is either simply an act of trustful piety without a component of practical politics, or an act of cynical politics without serious attentiveness to Yahwism. Rather, it is exactly a pragmatic act which in good faith is taken to be a Yahwistic intention, deduced from the poetry of Jeremiah, but not in itself recommended by Jeremiah. For that reason, I suggest, the opponents of this view rightly 'blame' Baruch, that agent (fictive or not) who let Jeremiah's theocentric utterance touch concrete issues in a decidedly interested way.

Thus I conclude that Baruch and those whom he purportedly represents—the scribal-Deuteronomic circles who enlisted Jeremiah's poetic-Yahwistic discernment for their own purposes, and who likely completed something approximating the canonical process—were, as Carroll proposes, ideologues. We must, however, be precise on what is meant by this label. Carroll uses the term 'ideology' in this context as a pejorative term, I believe, in a Marxian sense as 'distortion'.[24]

23. On the 'use' of the tradition by the pro-Babylonians, see Else Kragelund Holt, 'The Chicken and the Egg—Or: Was Jeremiah a Member of the Deuteronomist Party?', *JSOT* 44 (1989), pp. 102-22.

24. Carroll, *Jeremiah*, pp. 723, 724, 740, 742, uses the term. It is probable, however, that Marx's understanding of ideology concerns not only 'distortion' but already anticipates the later notion of ideology as a 'strategy of containment'. See Fredric Jameson, *The Political Unconscious: Narrative as a Socially Symbolic Act*

Moreover, Carroll opposes 'rhetoric' to 'analysis',[25] hyperbolic sermon to reality,[26] experience to ideology,[27] thus suggesting an accent on *willful* distortion.

I do indeed understand what Carroll intends. It may be possible, however, to understand the ideological process of 'Baruch' 'using' 'Jeremiah' as a more dialectical process which does not, in any positivistic way, establish such clear opposition between rhetoric and analysis, sermon and reality, and experience and fact. Marx's study of ideology suggests that God-talk always 'reads down' from superstructure to base, from 'heaven, religion, and theology' to 'earth, law, and politics'.[28] Of course, this may be the case and the opponents of Baruch take such

(Ithaca, NY: Cornell University Press, 1981), pp. 49-58, on the notion of 'ideology' in relation to 'totality'.

Michele Barrett, *The Politics of Truth: From Marx to Foucault* (Stanford: Stanford University Press, 1991), has subjected the Marxian notion of ideology to careful critical review. In light of the work of Gramsci, Lacan, Althusser and Foucault, the Marxian notion of ideology is shown to be enormously complex and problematic, if not contradictory. The issue which concerns Barrett is the interrelation of 'class setting' for ideology, and a more general notion of 'mystification' without reference to class situation. Barrett concludes: 'There is, in my view, a useful set of meanings that the term ideology can capture well; they cluster around processes of mystification. The retrievable core of meaning of the term ideology is precisely this: discursive and significatory mechanisms that may occlude, legitimate, naturalise or universalise in a variety of different ways but can all be said to mystify. In such a usage, the term ideology is clearly a general term referring to mystification: it refers to a function of mechanism but is not tied to any particular content, nor to any particular agent or interest. On this definition, ideology is not tied to any one presumed cause, or logic, of misrepresentation; it refers to a process of mystification, or misrepresentation, whatever its dynamic' (pp. 166-67).

Such a conclusion is consistent with the usage of the term 'ideology' in this essay. The conclusion of Barrett suggests, as concerns Scripture study, that the label 'ideology' can as well apply to so-called 'objective' or 'neutral' readings as those which attend to the theological claims of the text.

25. Carroll, *Jeremiah*, p. 242.

26. Carroll, *Jeremiah*, p. 244.

27. Carroll, *Jeremiah*, p. 246.

28. Thus Marx asserts: 'The criticism of heaven is thus transformed into the criticism of earth, the criticism of religion into the criticism of law, and the criticism of theology into the criticism of politics.' Cf. David McLellan, *The Thought of Karl Marx: An Introduction* (New York: Macmillan, 1971), p. 22.

a view. This 'lie' is exactly what Marx means when he discusses ideology in terms of distortion.[29]

But if we entertain ideology in Clifford Geertz's more carefully nuanced way, as 'making sense' in order to counter the stress of non-sense, we need not drive a wedge between the 'religious' and the 'real', or in this case between poetry and its 'use'.[30] We may take as good faith on the part of Baruch the coherence of the two, the poem and its Babylonian 'application', so that the critique by the 'insolent' in 43.23 is never only against Baruch the pragmatist, but also against Jeremiah the (so to say) 'innocent' religionist. In this understanding of ideology, such religious claims are never merely, in Marx's terms, 'earth, law, politics', but have a good faith component of 'heaven, religion, and theology' as well, which the 'insolent' do not want to entertain, That is, the wedge driven between Jeremiah and Baruch by the enemies of Baruch makes it possible to dismiss Baruch as an ideologue who 'uses', but does not take seriously, the poetic vision of the prophet. Such a dismissive reading, I suggest, is simplistic and excessively cynical, for the interface between serious faith and serious politics is never so one-dimensional. The complexity and intransigence of the public process requires us to give the Baruch party more maneuverability as it moves between poetic truth and political realism.

29. On these categories in relation to the Jeremiah tradition, see Henri Mottu, 'Jeremiah vs. Hananiah: Ideology and Truth in Old Testament Prophecy', in Norman K. Gottwald (ed.), *The Bible and Liberation: Political and Social Hermeneutics* (Maryknoll, NY: Orbis Books, 1983), pp. 235-51.

30. Clifford Geertz stands at the forefront of those who seek to reposition 'objectivist' social science to overcome the presumed contrast between 'real' and 'religious'. Thus Geertz, 'Blurred Genres: The Refiguration of Social Thought', *The American Scholar* 49 (1980), pp. 165-79 (178), writes: '... a challenge is being mounted to some of the central assumptions of mainstream social science. The strict separation of theory and data, the "brute fact" idea; the effort to create a formal vocabulary of analysis purged of all subjective reference, the "ideal language" idea; and the claim to moral neutrality and the Olympian view, the "God's truth" idea—none of these can prosper when explanation comes to be regarded as a matter of connecting action to its sense rather than behavior to its determinants'. And in 'Religion as a Cultural System', in William Lessa and Evon Vogt (eds.), *Reader in Comparative Religion: An Anthropological Approach* (New York: Harper & Row, 1965), p. 215, Geertz asserts that our sense of God or the 'really real' colors our sense of 'the reasonal, the practical, the humane and the moral'. See also the discussion of Judith Plaskow, *Standing Again at Sinai: Judaism from a Feminist Perspective* (San Francisco: Harper & Row, 1990), p. 126.

I suggest that this alternative approach to the ideological factor in the text, not in order to defend or to value Baruch and his ilk, but in order to understand the canonical process, is what is evidenced here. If 'ideology' moves beyond Jeremiah in a more pragmatic and partisan direction, as is charged by Baruch's opponents, I propose the following. Penultimately, and this will be my main argument, the Baruch-community believed passionately in the coherence and identification of Yahweh's intention (which Jeremiah uttered) and Babylonian foreign policy. It is that coherence which gives the words of Jeremiah such usefulness and credibility in the Baruch community, made up as it was of shrewd pragmatics. It is that coherence, between poetry and pragmatic application, which illuminates the place and function of the assaults upon the pro-Egypt party in 43.8-13, 44.1-23 and 44.24-30.

Moreover, as an abrupt and abrasive counterpart to 43.8–44.30, this coherence greatly illumines the placement of ch. 45, the oracle promising a rescue for the person of Baruch.[31] It is Baruch after all—or the party he represents and embodies—who risked, for good-faith as well as pragmatic reasons, support of Jeremiah's rhetoric in the public arena, As Seitz has seen, this oracle in ch. 45 closely parallels 39.15-18, the oracle concerning Ebed-Melek, the other case wherein Jeremiah receives public support at great risk. In the oracle concerning Baruch, the counter-theme to the well-being of Baruch involves Yahweh's intention to bring 'disaster'. The great verbs of destruction 'break down and pluck up' are used once more, thus reiterating Yahweh's largest purpose. Thus the oracle of ch. 45 focused on Baruch—or the Baruch community he represents and embodies—acts as a foil for the larger purpose of the book of Jeremiah, namely, the devastation upon a community of deep disobedience.

The canonical process in the MT tradition, as is well known, has juxtaposed to ch. 45 the Oracles Against the Nations in chs. 46–51. These oracles are rarely studied in canonical context, but are most often examined for their historical reference points or as a part of the genre of 'oracles against the nations'. It is to be noticed, however, that in first place among the oracles stands the oracle against Egypt (46.1-28). The Egypt condemned in 43–44, the Egypt taken by Baruch as a counter to

---

31. See the shrewd argument of Marion Ann Taylor, 'Jeremiah 45: The Problem of Placement', *JSOT* 37 (1987), pp. 79-98. Taylor sees in the chapter a promise to the person of Baruch, but the larger intention, indicated by placement, is a massive announcement of judgment, i.e. 'the fourth year of Jehoiachim'.

Yahweh's intention for Babylon, this Egypt is now in first place for condemnation in the oracles of chs. 46–51. Indeed, in 46.19, it is the 'sheltered daughter of Egypt/Memphis' who will be ruined and exiled. Moreover, as the text stands, it is Nebuchadnezzar who will work the devastation (46.13, 26), thus linking the text to 43.10. The culmination of this denunciation of Egypt is a statement of rescue for 'Jacob' (46.27-28). Thus, across the canonical sequence of 43.8–44.30, 45.1-5 and 46.1-23, very different genres with different redactional histories, the main point stands: Yahweh's Babylonian policy cannot be resisted. This message coheres with Jeremiah's elusive 'foe from the north', and serves Baruch's pragmatic policy.[32] (It will be evident that something is missing in the swift move to the rescue of Judah in 46.27-28, for the primary problem for 'Jacob' is not Egypt but Babylon, which at this point still survives in awesome, brutal power.)

I have said, however, that this coherence of Yahweh and Babylon, of theological intention and practical policy, is a *penultimate* coherence treasured by the Baruch community. I use the word penultimate, of course, because in 50.1–51.58, at the end of the Oracles Against the Nations, the ultimate judgment is that the alliance between Yahweh and Babylon falls apart, as inevitably it must. In the end, so the text asserts, Yahweh turns against Yahweh's own established ally, Babylon, and destroys it. The reason for such a turn, after such a rhetoric of alliance, is (a) that Yahweh makes no permanent alliances which would permit the absolutizing of any historical structure or institution, and (b) the rhetoric of Jeremiah is characteristically twofold, even if the wording is Deuteronomic; Yahweh not only plucks up and tears down, but plants and builds.[33] There can be, as it now stands, no Jeremiah message that does not make both moves (cf. 31.28).

---

32. Apart from the prose commentary, the destroyer in ch. 46 is of course unnamed. The ominous threat created by the rhetoric is parallel to that of the so-called Scythian Songs, for which the intended subject seems deliberately opaque. On the latter, see the papers by Henri Cazelles, Brevard S. Childs and C.F. Whitley in Leo Perdue and Brian Kovacs (eds.), *A Prophet to the Nations: Essays in Jeremiah Studies* (Winona Lake, IN: Eisenbrauns, 1984), pp. 129-49, 151-61, and 163-73.

33. On this programmatic set of words, see Carroll, *From Chaos to Covenant*, pp. 55-58, and Prescott H. Williams, Jr, 'Living Toward the Acts of the Savior-Judge: A Study of Eschatology in the Book of Jeremiah', *Austin Seminary Bulletin* (1979), pp. 13-39.

VI

Of course, it is easy enough to say that chs. 50–51 come later from a different group who saw the next historical turn, that is, the move of Cyrus against Babylon (which evoked Second Isaiah). Even Carroll, however, observes that chs. 50–51 are an exception to the *Realpolitik* of the tradition.[34] This large, relentless judgment about Babylon, against the pro-Babylonian weight of much of the Jeremiah tradition, can indeed be an exception to *Realpolitik*, if we do not begin with a flat, positivistic notion of *Realpolitik*. I propose that the Baruch community, in its 'ideology' which is informed by Jeremiah but processed through its own interests, hopes and fears, never practiced simple *Realpolitik*. (See especially 26.16-19 for something other than *Realpolitik*.) Thus that community, I propose, held together a *penultimate alliance* of Yahweh and Babylon, and an *ultimate confession* that Yahweh has no permanent allies.

Given such a theological norm, albeit not innocent and perhaps not disinterested, this interpretive community could see or anticipate that Yahweh's rule will win out against all pretenders, including a long-standing ally of Yahweh. This conclusion may have been in the service of an interest, but such a nuanced Yahwistic judgment is, I submit, unavoidable in a community in any way serious about Yahwism. This may of course assign to the canonizers too much 'theology' which flies in the face of pragmatism. I suggest, however, that this move from the destruction of Egypt in ch. 46, to the destruction of Babylon in chs. 50–51, from the penultimate to the ultimate in this context, is neither simply an act of *Realpolitik* nor simply an abrupt departure from *Realpolitik*, but that this canonizing community was always practising more than *Realpolitik*. That is, the factoring of Yahweh into the public process is a real and serious move on its part, and not simply disguised code language for interest and preference, as a more positivistic interpretation would insist. The vision of the anguish and buoyancy of

---

34. Carroll, *Jeremiah*, p. 240. Carroll moves almost without pause from 'ideology' (by which he seems to mean distortion) to *Realpolitik*. Indeed, in Carroll's presentation, there seems to be no third alternative to ideology and *Realpolitik*, thus by definition precluding the attribution of any seriousness to the assertions of Jeremiah or what purport to be the faith claims of the Baruch community. They are in principle nullified.

the poet made available and even decisive this other 'actor' (Yahweh) who is not a pawn of flat political interest.

What is practiced by the Baruch community (which utilizes Jeremiah) is indeed 'ideology'. I want, however, to follow Frederic Jameson and Paul Ricoeur in their use of Mannheim's category of ideology, twinned as it is with utopia. Ideology in any of its senses—distortion, stress-management or integration—is geared to an intended defense of the *status quo*. Agreed. But Jameson and Ricoeur, working with Mannheim's categories, have suggested that even the most zealous practitioners of ideology, in this case the community of Baruch, tend to turn ideology beyond itself and spill over into utopia, that is, into a future which is based on a valued *status quo*, but which runs well beyond that *status quo* into something richer, even beyond vested interest and beyond present 'doable' circumstance. Thus Jameson asserts:

> All class consciousness—or in other words all ideology in the strongest sense, including the most exclusive forms of ruling-class consciousness just as much as that of the oppositional or oppressed classes—is in its very nature Utopian.[35]

If we assume that the Baruch community is in some way the 'ruling class' in the exilic period, we may expect, in my judgment, that its hope would move past its protective interest in the *status quo*.

In like manner, Ricoeur concludes:

> As for myself, I assume completely the inextricable role of this utopian element, because I think that it is ultimately constitutive of any theory of ideology. It is always from the depth of a utopia that we may speak of an ideology.[36]

More recently, Ricoeur has asserted:

> Every society ... possesses, or is part of, a sociopolitical *imaginaire*, that is, an ensemble of symbolic discourses. This *imaginaire* can function as a rupture or a reaffirmation. As reaffirmation, the *imaginaire* operates as an *'ideology'* which can positively repeat and represent the founding discourse of a society, what I call its 'foundational symbols', thus preserving its sense of identity ... Over against this, there exists the *imaginaire* of rupture, a discourse of *utopia* which remains critical of the powers that be out of fidelity to an 'elsewhere', to a society that is 'not

---

35. Jameson, *The Political Unconscious*, p. 289.

36. Paul Ricoeur, *Lectures on Ideology and Utopia* (New York: Columbia University Press, 1986), p. 251.

yet' … In short, *ideology* as a symbolic confirmation of the past and *utopia* as a symbolic opening towards the future are complementary; if cut off from each other they can lead to a form of political pathology.[37]

In our case, it is the 'utopia' of Yahweh's ultimate concern for Judah that lies in, with, and under the ideological alliance with Babylonian policy on the part of the Baruch community.

In the case of Jeremiah's canonizers, I submit that in chs. 43–44, 45 and 46, ideology as advocacy of an interest does indeed operate. Finally, only late, in chs. 50–51, ideology pushes beyond itself to daring hope, for God's awaited action. I suggest that this move in chs. 50–51 is not an add-on, not superfluous, not a concession to a tamer faith, but a cogent next move in rhetoric which may be interested and pragmatic, but never reductionist to the exclusion of the very faith that made the scribes advocates of the large theological vision of Jeremiah.

VII

This move from penultimate Babylonian policy to the ultimate expectation of Babylonian defeat, this move from ideology to utopia, is evidenced in two ways which, in conclusion, I wish to identify. First, the anti-Egypt/pro-Babylon construal of Yahweh's will has run its course by ch. 50. The long poem demolishing the Babylonian Empire is capped in the prose 'report' of 51.59-64. According to the 'report' itself, the functionary to carry out the destruction of Babylon is Seraiah, son of Neraiah, and therefore brother of Baruch.[38] The instigator of the action of Seraiah, however, is none other than Jeremiah. As presented here, the prophet finally turns against Babylon. Jeremiah does two things. He dispatches this voice of the Baruch community; he writes the 'disaster' on a scroll which is to be read, and instructs the scribe to throw the scroll into the Euphrates, to sink as Babylon will sink.

The substance of Jeremiah's instruction is to announce (and enact?) the end of Babylon, as willed by Yahweh. The actual sequence of words attributed to Jeremiah is more than a little curious. In vv. 61 and 63, instructions are directly given to Seraiah. In v. 62, however, the

---

37. Paul Ricoeur, 'The Creativity of Language', in Mario J. Valdes (ed.), *A Ricoeur Reader: Reflection and Imagination* (Toronto: University of Toronto Press, 1991), pp. 463-81 (475).

38. Dearman, 'My Servants', pp. 408-21, identifies the generations of this family and situates it in the work of Deuteronomic, scribal circles.

speech is presented as a reminder to Yahweh. And in v. 64, the first-person verb has no clear subject, though we may infer that the subject is Yahweh, In any case, the intention is clear. The culmination of the book of Jeremiah is the sharp distinction between the plans of Babylon and the intention of Yahweh.[39] (See 29.11 and Isa. 55.8-9 on contrasting 'plans'.)[40]

What interests me most is the connection of this act of the counter-scroll to the family (and community) of Baruch. In this concluding assertion, the scribal family moves beyond its pragmatic commitment to Babylon, and embraces the more radical note of Yahweh's destructive hostility toward Babylon, a hostility which will in time permit Jews to return home from Babylon. The intense ideological commitment which has driven much of this literature is now superseded. That overriding of a provisional commitment may of course be the next step in a larger ideology; it may, however, also be a break with ideology that places the future in the hands of Yahweh, a utopian anticipation beyond the terrible hand of Babylon.[41]

The second variation of this theme of hope beyond ideology I identify in 50.41-42. The long poem against Babylon in chs. 50–51 contains a curious allusion back to 6.22-23, in what is conventionally catalogued as a 'Scythian Song'.[42] With slight variation, the later poem utilizes the form and wording of the earlier poem. The decisive phrase used in both cases is 'no mercy'. In the first usage, an unnamed people 'from the

39. This judgment of course fails to account for ch. 52. A concern to identify the canonical intention of this chapter lies beyond the scope of this essay and remains for further consideration.

40. On the notion of 'plans' in these texts, see Walter Brueggemann, 'Genesis 1.15-21: A Theological Exploration' (VTSup, 36; New York: E.J. Brill, 1985), pp. 40-53.

41. Whether this anticipation of a return home is 'utopian' or more 'ideological' depends upon the interpreter's extrapolation. There is, however, no built-in tilt toward ideology. For that reason, I read with the grain of the text. There is a temptation given the reader's propensity for ideology, to read the text as ideology, even when the text intends otherwise.

42. The Scythian Songs have been intensely studied. Because of scholarly attention to form analysis, it is conventional to study the 'Oracles Against the Nations' in chs. 46–51 as though they are completely separated from the earlier poetry. Attention to canonical intentionality requires and permits breaking out of such a 'form'—controlled analysis. The result is a fresh field of enquiry concerning the intertextual relation of the earlier and later poetry.

north' (presumably Babylon) is dispatched by Yahweh in destructive ways against Jerusalem. Such an assertion stands at the center of Jeremiah's dread-filled message. There is coming a threat that will show 'no mercy'. In the second poem, the same rhetoric is used, again asserting 'no mercy', but this time against Babylon (50.43). Thus the canonizers have reused the rhetoric of the prophet, indicating that God's alliance with Babylon is taken as an interim arrangement.[43]

This capacity to hold tentatively but tenuously to a concrete political force, and yet to see that force as deeply problematic indicates the way in which the scribal canonizers did indeed make use of Jeremiah for their own purposes. Finally, even their political purposes, however, were overcome by the tenacity of a theological vision.

In the end, the fall of Egypt (ch. 46) and the fall of Babylon (chs. 50–51) are, as the book is cast, not simply turns of *Realpolitik*. Nor is this sequence fully comprehended as a statement of vested interest and ideology. In, with and under the capacity of the scribal community for both *Realpolitik* and ideology, it is Yahweh's sovereignty which prevails and which causes the text to run beyond more managed horizons. That decisive conviction at play in the text reiterates at the end of the canonizing process and the canonical corpus the main claims made at the outset by the 'prophet to the nations'. The end of the book is, to be sure, a considerable distance from the anguish and wonder of the prophet, for the wildness of the prophet has been toned down. Even at that distance, nonetheless, the interested claims made by the canonizing community of Baruch are not incongruous with the theocentric casting of the public process already at work in the first dangerous utterances which have seeded the larger corpus.[44]

---

43. On the theme of 'no mercy', see especially Isa. 46–47. See Walter Brueggemann, 'At the Mercy of Babylon: A Subversive Rereading of the Empire', *JBL* 110 (1991), pp. 3-22.

44. I am grateful to Tim Beal for his suggestions concerning this essay.

THE TEARS OF GOD AND DIVINE CHARACTER IN JEREMIAH 2–9[*]

Kathleen M. O'Connor

The character of God in the book of Jeremiah is multiple and unstable. Images and metaphors about the deity tumble over and contradict each other in a poetics of divine proliferation and profusion. This multiplicity appears to undermine any consistent characterization or portrayal of the divine and creates by linguistic abundance a language of a God who is multiple and multifaceted.

For historical-critical interpreters, Jeremiah's proliferation of theological language was the logical consequence of the book's complex process of composition. Understood as an amalgamation of disparate literary pieces, the book inevitably portrayed God in a variety of ways. Inconsistencies in divine portrayal resulted from the unruly process of mixing of sources, genres and traditions.[1] But as Jack Miles has cogently observed, such an approach 'conveniently overlooks the fact God is the speaker throughout'.[2] Seemingly contradictory messages all come from the same divine subject.

Recently, a variety of literary studies of Jeremiah have begun to challenge views of the book as an unreadable amalgamation. Brueggemann, Biddle, Liwak, Diamond and O'Connor, and Stulman,[3] among others

*   Reprinted by permission from Tod Linafelt and Timothy K. Beal (eds.), *God in the Fray: A Tribute to Walter Brueggemann* (Minneapolis: Augsburg Fortress, 1998).

1.   For summaries of the discussion, see Seigfried Hermann, *Jeremia* (BKAT, 12: Neukirchen–Vluyn: Neukirchener Verlag, 1986); and William McKane, *A Critical and Exegetical Commentary on Jeremiah.* I. *Introduction and Commentary on Jeremiah I–XXV* (ICC; Edinburgh: T. & T. Clark, 1986), pp. xv-lcii.

2.   Jack Miles, *God: A Biography* (New York: Alfred A. Knopf, 1995), p. 195.

3.   Walter Brueggemann, 'The Baruch Connection: Reflections on Jeremiah 43.1-7', *JBL* 113 (1994), pp. 405-20; Mark Biddle, *Polyphony and Symphony in Prophetic Literature: Rereading Jeremiah 7–20* (Macon, GA: Mercer University Press, 1996); A.R. Pete Diamond and Kathleen M. O'Connor, 'Unfaithful Passions:

have begun to locate synchronic coherence in the book, irrespective of historical origins of materials. Diamond and O'Connor find a loose narrative unity in 2.1–4.2 that emerges from the metaphor of YHWH's broken marriages with Israel and Judah. Mark Biddle locates a 'polyphony' of voices in Jeremiah 7–20, created by the juxtaposition of speakers that include YHWH, the prophet, personified Jerusalem, and the people. Rather than progressing in linear argument, the book resembles a musical composition in which voices, speak, fade, reappear, overlap and grow quiet. Although Biddle does not study metaphorical groupings of material, poetic cycles in chs. 2–9 gain further unity from the presence of organizing metaphors and images.

Three poetic cycles or metaphorical groupings follow the introductory call narrative (Jer. 1): the broken marriage, or more accurately, the broken family metaphor (2.1–4.2), the mythic battle (4.5–6.30; 7.1–8.3), and the weeping (8.18–9.22). After 4.2, the marriage/family metaphor recedes but does not disappear. It remains in the background as divine discourse on the mythic battle moves to the foreground (4.6–6.30).[4] In chs. 8–10, both marriage and mythic battle are decentered and language of weeping becomes prominent (8.18–9.23). This essay studies divine characterization in the poetic cycles of Jeremiah 2–9, giving particular attention to the weeping God in 8.18–9.2. Divine depiction varies greatly among these poetic cycles.

Timothy Beal shows the instability of the divine character in Micah 1 in part by intertextual readings with other passages.[5] That YHWH is not unified, not one, but a destabilized character is evident within the poetic cycles of the book of Jeremiah itself. Three characterizations of the deity emerge from this study that are difficult to ascribe to the same speaking subject. In Jer. 2.1–4.2, Yahweh is the Divine Husband, angry, jealous, petty and abusive. In 4.5–6.30 Yahweh is the Military

Coding Woman Coding Men in Jeremiah 2–3 (4:2)', *BibInt* 4 (1996), pp. 280-310; R. Liwak, *Der Prophet und die Geschichte: Eine literar-historiche Untersuchung zum Jeremiabuch* (Stuttgart: W. Kohlhammer, 1987); Louis Stulman, 'Insiders and Outsiders in the Book of Jeremiah: Shifts in Symbolic Arrangement', *JSOT* 66 (1995), pp. 65-85.

4. The prose temple sermon serves as a parenthetical comment on the battle, in which insiders not the foe from the north threaten Jerusalem's destruction. See Stulman, 'Insiders and Outsiders'.

5. Timothy K. Beal, 'System and Speaking Subject in the Hebrew Bible', *BibInt* 2 (1994), pp. 171-89.

General, the fiendish but troubled initiator of the mythic battle and destroyer of creation. In 8.22–9.3 Yahweh is a weeping God who grieves unceasingly over the destruction of the people. In all three depictions, Yahweh's behavior responds to the poetic presence of the female persona as symbolic representation of the unfaithful people.

Divine Husband (2.1–4.2)

As divine husband[6] YHWH appears as broken-hearted and abandoned spouse, dumbstruck and enraged by the collapse of a relationship in which he thinks he has done everything possible to make the marriage flourish. In that material he rails at his unfaithful wife with a rhetoric of shaming in accusatory, blaming terms, and he finally casts her aside once and for all.

Jeremiah 2.1–4.2 combines previously separate materials to create a metaphorical and narrative drama of the broken family told almost entirely as a divine monologue. YHWH's speech alternates in addressing male Israel (2.4-16, 26-32; 3.14-18) and female Judah/Zion (2.17-25; 2.33–3.5; 3.12-13). This alternation of addressee between the male and female personae serves to identify the two literary figures as one entity, and in 2.1-3 and 3.19-20 YHWH explicitly equates the two as one people. YHWH accuses male Israel and female Judah/Zion of similar offenses. Both turn away from him and to other lovers or deities. YHWH uses the same rhetorical devices of direct address, rhetorical questions, and quotation of their speech to interrogate and accuse each of them. These poetic devices further identify the male and female personae with one another.

One function of the female persona is to present her infidelity in the most shameful sexual, intimate terms possible in a nearly unthinkable betrayal of her spouse. A second function of the female is to symbolize or encode the whole nation. The metaphor uses a female to shame male Israel.

Across this material, YHWH portrays himself as a fully sympathetic figure, wronged by treacherous adulterers who have forsaken him and 'loved strangers' (2.25). Divine discourse is a one-sided harangue and dominates not only the poetry itself, but also the speech of the others whom YHWH quotes simply to accuse them with their own words.

6. Arguments by Diamond and O'Connor, 'Unfaithful Passions', forms the basis for study of the divine husband.

YHWH focuses on his own pain and betrayal (2.4-16) and on his astonishment that he could be treated so badly by someone for whom he had done so much (2.4-8, 21, 31-32). The husband's pride is hurt, and the husband is publicly shamed (3.1). In 3.1-5 he divorces her and their relationship is over.

For ancient readers this husband would be a figure of sympathy. He has been doubly unfortunate in his choice of wives for in 3.6-10 YHWH reveals that he had had a previous wife who had also betrayed him. Modern readers, by contrast, might get suspicious of this Husband and his dominating ways, and wonder if there are other stories hidden in this metaphor, if the wives could speak.[7] But they do not.

Because the first wife appears in retrospect to have been less faithless than the second, YHWH sends Jeremiah to win her back. But she does not reply to the invitation (3.12-13). Only the children of this broken family, to whom the husband/father makes glowing promises and from whom he does not demand repentance (3.14-18), only they repent and return to him (3.21-25). The children signify and encode the implied readers in exile who are invited to return and are provided here with a model of liturgical repentance.

The broken family metaphor describes symbolicly the history of YHWH's relationship with Israel and Judah. The narrative thread of the marriages, divorces, invitations to return, and the acceptance, not by the wives but by the children, constructs a version of the nation's past, present, and hoped-for future. It explains the nation's fall as deserved punishment for idolatry; it appeals to the exiles to repent in the present, and it gives hope for a restored future.

The highly emotional language of the divine husband, his nostalgia, anger, and jealousy create a character in search of exoneration from blame, one who cannot be charged with injustice or capriciousness for clearly his wives deserve what they get. In the ancient world, such a character would gain the empathy of readers, presumed to be male, by bringing them to the side of the betrayed husband. But the metaphor

---

7. For feminist critiques of the metaphor see Diamond and O'Connor, 'Unfaithful Passions'; Renita J. Weems, *Battered Love: Marriage, Sex, and Violence in the Hebrew Prophets* (Overtures to Biblical Theology: Minneapolis: Fortress Press, 1995; and Tikva Frymer-Kensky, *In the Wake of the Goddesses: Women Culture and the Biblical Transformation of Pagan Myth* (New York: Fawcett Columbine, 1992).

tricks them for they discover that they are the wanton, treacherous female, doubly shamed by being identified as a woman and a whore.

Architect of War

In 4.5–6.30 (and less abundantly 8.4–10.27) a military metaphor replaces the domestic one, and a rhetoric of terror overtakes the rhetoric of shaming. Leo Perdue has recognized the cohesiveness of these poems in their blending of creation traditions with the mythic battle of the foe from the north.[8] Perdue places all the poetry in 4.5–6.30 under the rubric of mythic battle and includes much of the poetry in 8.4–10.27 as well. Interest in historical origins of individual poems and the generic grouping of the poetry in chs. 2–25 as 'accusations against Judah and Jerusalem' has in the past obscured the predominance of battle language.[9]

Symbolically, the mythic battle constructs a *post facto* reflection on the nation's collapse as a military, political and theological upheaval that destroyed a world. The highly dramatic poetry in which the mythic foe from the north attacks Daughter Zion brings readers into a time and space outside of history that interprets history. The battle's poetic enactment discloses divine ordination of Jerusalem's destruction, its inevitability and totality, and the rightness of divine decision to destroy. Yahweh remains the principal, though not sole speaker,[10] and a female, identified here as Daughter Zion, appears as the object of attack.

The literary unity of this poetic cycle is neither narrative nor sequential as is the episodic drama of the broken family (2.1–4.2). Rather the military poetry repeatedly announces the battle's approach (4.5-22; 5.14-17; 6.1-12, 16-26; 8.14-17; 9.17-25), describes its status as cosmic event (4.23-28), and provides reasons why YHWH cannot avoid executing the divine plan of attack and destruction (5.1-13, 20-31; 6.13-16, 27-30; 8.4-13; 9.3-8 Heb.). Poems of battle create the constant and noisy backdrop against which YHWH ruminates about

8. Leo G. Perdue, *The Collapse of History: Reconstructing Old Testament Theology* (Overtures to Biblical Theology; Minneapolis: Fortress Press, 1994), pp. 141-46.

9. Robert P. Carroll, *Jeremiah: A Commentary* (OTL; Philadelphia: Westminster Press, 1986), is a notable exception.

10. The people (5.10-11, 19), Jeremiah (4.10, 19, 23-26a; 5.4-5, 10-11; 6.26), the enemies (6.4-5) and female Jerusalem/Zion speak (4.20b, 31).

sending the foe from the north and expresses his efforts to avoid the disaster. The impressionistic depiction of war across these chapters evokes the chaos of battle and creates high drama by the inequity between attackers and attacked. The poetry discloses a divine character who threatens, oversees and engineers war in fearsome ways, even as he is at war within the divine self about doing it.

The battle poems use metonomy to create by details of sight and sound the feelings of terror at the imminent approach of the army about to attack and destroy Jerusalem. Trumpet and standard (4.5-6, 19, 21; 6.1, 17) signify mustering of troops and their preparation for attack. Sounds of horsemen and archers (4.29), voices of enemies planning the siege (6.4), the noise of approaching cavalry 'like the roaring of the sea' (6.23), the snorting and neighing of horses (8.16)—all conjure up warfare, making it vividly present in the imagination, and creating terror by the invocation of its nearness.

The initiator, designer and director of battle is YHWH himself. In this rhetoric of fear, divine agency is paramount, 'for I am bringing evil from the north and a great destruction' (4.6). The evil from the north is a lion, a destroyer of nations who has set out purposefully 'to make your land a waste' (4.7). The coming of the enemy is due to the 'fierce anger of YHWH' (4.8). 'I am going to bring disaster on this people' (5.19a).

The mythic power of the enemy, either the foe from the north or YHWH himself, is clear from his supraterrestrial approach. 'He comes like clouds, with chariots like the whirlwind, his horses swifter than eagles' (4.13). The enemy's might is not human, but incomparable and terrifying. It is a 'great nation' with bow and javelin, cruel and without mercy; their 'sound is like the roaring of the sea', they come on horse, 'equipped as a warrior for battle' (6.22-23).

Not until 20.4-6 is the foe from the north historicized and Jerusalem's attacker revealed to be Babylon. Although critics have sought to find a historical enemy behind the foe, Childs[11] and Perdue[12] are surely correct in seeing its mythic nature. To do so is to see the poetry's power. The foe is superhuman, sent by God, and described in hyperbolic, transcendent terms. They are 'an enduring nation', 'from far away', 'their quiver is like an open tomb', all of them are mighty warriors who

---

11. Brevard Childs, 'The Enemy from the North and the Chaos Tradition', *JBL* 78 (1959), pp. 187-98.

12. Perdue, *The Collapse of History*.

will eat, eat, eat, the population, the animals and the fruit of the land itself (5.15-17). This is the language of terror.

By contrast with the monstrous power of the foe from the north is the weakness and vulnerability of the one attacked. The object of invasion is Daughter Zion (4.14-18, 19-20, 29-31; 5.7-11; 6.2-23; 10.19-24). In the book of Jeremiah, gendered language constructs not only the broken family metaphor but also the mythic battle, for it is against a woman that Yahweh amasses the invading army. Jerusalem's personification as female is a conventional gender designation of cities in antiquity,[13] but within the symbolic world of the mythic battle, Daughter Zion's gender heightens the unequal possession of power and resources among the opponents.[14] The one is demonic, possessed of might, weaponry and an army that surpasses human experience and requires supraterrestrial language to be described as opposed not only to the merely human but to a female whom the ancients agreed needed protection. She is defenseless as the foe approaches. She laments the destruction of her tents (4.19-20; 10.19-20), panics before the attack (4.19) and faints before killers (5.31).

Daughter Zion's portrayal in the battle cycle is consistent with the characterization of Yahweh's wife Judah/Jerusalem in 2.1–4.2, although there she is unnamed and untitled. Daughter Zion is rebellious (4.17) and faithless (5.10-11). She behaves like a whore (4.30) and her inhabitants do not 'know' YHWH (4.22). To avert disaster, she is to wash herself clean, but the besiegers are already at hand (4.14-17). Yahweh turns to her directly and accuses of her of bringing doom upon herself (4.18). In the battle cycle, however, language of broken intimacy is conspicuously absent. Yahweh speaks to her with disgust (6.8) and only briefly recalls her past loveliness (6.2). Daughter Zion's personification as female, whatever, its ancient roots, here underscores the extreme inequity between the city and the mythic forces unleashed against her by YHWH. What drives the divine warrior is not an attack to suppress a bellicose bully or an arrogant aggressor but the desire to avenge himself and to punish an impotent weakling.

13. See F.W. Dobbs-Allsopp, *Weep, O Daughter of Zion: A Study of the City-Lament Genre in the Hebrew Bible* (BibOr, 44; Rome: Pontificio Istituto Biblico, 1993); Julie Galambusch, *Jerusalem in the Book of Ezekiel: The City as Yahweh's Wife* (SBLDS, 130; Atlanta: Scholars Press, 1992).

14. D. Bourguet, *Des metaphores de Jérémie* (EBib, 9; Paris: LeCoffre, 1987), p. 117.

But YHWH wavers in his resolve. He hesitates and questions. To avoid invasion, he sends Jeremiah to play Diogenes or Abraham, to run up and down the streets of Jerusalem in search of one righteous inhabitant so that he may pardon Jerusalem (5.1-6). But no righteous ones can be found, since they all behave as YHWH's wife who 'broke the yoke' and 'burst the bonds' (5.6, cf. 2.20). Using second feminine singular forms, YHWH then plaintively asks Daughter Zion, 'How can I pardon you… Shall I not punish them for these things?' (5.7-9, 29). It is as if the divine warrior has weighed the options and decided that he cannot pardon, forgive or turn back the advancing foe. It is not within his character to ignore her crimes.

The onslaught of the mythic army will cause cosmic upheaval and the 'uncreation' of the earth (4.23-28). At first glance, the poem of uncreation appears to change the subject from the mythic battle. The poem depicts, instead, the cosmic effects of the war as a total, world-destroying onslaught that will leave a bombed-out place of chaos.

The poem contains two voices, Jeremiah's in 4.23-26 and YHWH's in vv. 27-28. Jeremiah witnesses the reversal of creation, step by step, in a cosmic upheaval. The land returns to *tōhû wābōhû* ('waste and void'). Light is extinguished in the heavens, mountains and hills quake, and the earth is emptied of all its inhabitants. The land returns to desert, cities lie in ruins, before YHWH's fierce anger (4.23-26). Massive and total annihilation, the grieving of the earth, and darkening of the heavens occur because of the divine word, purpose, and unrelenting resolution. The mythic battle destroys the cosmos as Judah knew it. And the one who designs, executes, and presides over this demolition is the Creator himself.

In the cycle of the mythic battle poems, YHWH is the military general who prefers not to go to war, who seeks other courses of action, but is ultimately driven to it. He has the resolve, the power and the furious rage that enables him to complete his purpose. He is the Creator who disassembles creation. At his disposal is an army of unsurpassed power and cruelty for whom he calls and sends against the woman, Daughter Zion. The divine character disclosed here is not inconsistent with the divine husband in 2.1–4.2, but the tenderness and broken-heartedness of the family drama is completely absent. Instead, this deity is a killer, a hesitant one, but a killer nonetheless. He determines that Zion's character is irredeemably flawed so destruction must follow. The warrior's rage and resolution emotionally separates him from Daughter of Zion and she is doomed.

The poetry of the mythic battle is not randomly placed in the book, nor is divine characterization as warrior arbitrary. The battle poems could not appear before the divine husband casts off his recalcitrant wife. If the book began with the mythic battle cycle, YHWH's summoning of the foe from the north and his decision to destroy the nation would characterize him as a capricious destroyer, a cold, distant, killer, destroyer and uncreator. The book would create an attack on YHWH, a protest against his cruelty, rather than a theodicy that seeks to win readers to YHWH's side and defend him from charges of capriciousness in the national tragedy for he is a wronged lover and husband.

The Weeping God (8.18–9.22)?

In sharp discontinuity with the God who executes war and the God who casts off his unfaithful spouse is the God who weeps (8.18–9.22).[15] In this cluster of poems about weeping, YHWH weeps (8.18–9.2) and orchestrates the weeping of others (9.10-11, 17-22). These poems function as dramatic response to the ineluctable coming of the mythic battle (8.15-16). Since death has come up to the windows (9.20), since the enemy cannot be turned back, there is nothing to do now but mourn, shed tears, and grieve the nation's death publicly and privately.

That divine laments are prominent in the book has long been recognized, but usually interpreters have assigned the tears in 8.18–9.2 to Jeremiah.[16] Indeed, speakers, demarcation of units, and meaning of these verses find no consensus among interpreters.

8.18 My cheerfulness is gone, grief is upon me,
      my heart is sick.
8.19 Listen (*hinnēh*), the cry of the daughter of my people from far and
      wide in the land:
            Is YHWH not in Zion?
            Is her king not in her?

---

15. Because the English text numbers 8.23 of the Hebrew as 9.1, the English verse numbers are one verse ahead of the Hebrew in ch. 9.

16. J.J.M. Roberts ('The Motif of the Weeping God in Jeremiah and its Background in the Lament Tradition of the Ancient Near East', *Old Testament Essays* 5 [1992], pp. 361-74), and Biddle (*Polyphony*, p. 30) have both made similar claims to mine.

Why have they provoked me to anger with images and with their
foreign idols?

8.20   'The harvest has past, the summer is ended and we are not
        saved.'

8.21   For the crushing of the daughter of my people I am crushed,
        and I grow leaden in spirit,
        and dismay has seized me.

8.22   Is there no balm in Gilead?
        Is there no physician there?
        Why then has the health of the daughter of my people not been
        restored?

8.23   O that my head were waters and my eyes a fountain of tears,
        that I might weep day and night for the slain of the daughter of my
        people.

9.1   O that I had in the wilderness a traveler's lodging place
        that I might leave my people and go away from them!
        For they are all adulterers, a band of traitors.

9.2   They bend their tongues like bows:
        they have grown strong in the land for falsehood and not for truth;
        for they proceed from evil to evil and do not know me, says YHWH
                                    (my translation).

Particularly disputed is the principal speaker in 8.18–9.2(3). Who is
the 'I', and who grieves over 'the daughter of my people' (8.19, 21, 22,
23)? A sampling of commentators reveals vast disagreement. Carroll
assigns these verses to personified Jerusalem, whereas Condamin
attributed them to the people, and Craigie *et al.* and Clements make
Jeremiah the speaker.[17] Holladay finds three voices in the poem and
limits divine speech to 19b and 22a.[18] Even Fretheim who has written
beautifully about the suffering of God, assigns these lines to Jeremiah
as the embodiment of divine pain.[19]

By contrast, Brueggemann's observation that divine pathos structures

---

17. Carroll, *Jeremiah*, p. 255; A. Condamin, *Le livre de Jérémie* (Paris:
Librairie Victor Lecoffre, 1920), p. 84; Peter Craigie, Page Kelley and J.F.
Drinkard, *Jeremiah 1–25* (WBC, 26; Dallas: Word Books, 1991), p. 136; Ronald E.
Clements, *Jeremiah* (Interpretation; Atlanta: John Knox Press, 1988), p. 59.

18. William L. Holladay, *Jeremiah 1: A Commentary on the Book of the Prophet
Jeremiah, Chapters 1–25* (Hermeneia; Philadelphia: Fortress Press, 1986), pp. 288-
89.

19. Terence E. Fretheim, *The Suffering of God: An Old Testament Perspective*
(Overtures to Biblical Theology; Philadelphia: Fortress Press, 1987), p. 135, though
later, p. 161, he proposes that vv. 18-19 might be divine speech.

the poem[20] gains specificity from a number of speech markers that indicate that YHWH is the poem's principal speaker. At the end of the poem the speech formula *n^e'um YHWH* ('says YHWH', 9.2), ascribes the preceding verses to Yahweh. The only possible speaker of the rhetorical question 'Why have they provoked me to anger with their images and foreign idols?' (8.19d) is YHWH. YHWH frequently uses the rhetorical device of direct quotation of the accused in 2.1–4.2, as may be the case in 8.19bc and possibly 8.20.[21] Typically, YHWH is speaker of the phrase, 'my people' that appears in 8.18, 19, 21, 22, 23 and 9.1 (cf. 2.11, 13, 32; 6.14, 30; 8.7, 11; 9.7; 15.7; 18.15 ; 23.22; but less clearly, 6.26; 14.17). Biddle adds to this list of divine speech markers, the observation that 8.23 resembles YHWH's statement in 14.17-18.[22] In addition, extra-biblical evidence indicates that a weeping deity is not an anomaly in the ancient world. J.J.M. Roberts provides a long list of weeping gods and goddesses in Mesopotamia who shed tears over the destruction of their cities as does YHWH over the 'crushing of Daughter Zion' (9.2).[23] With the clear exception of 8.20 and 8.19bc[24] (indented above in the translation), YHWH is the poem's principal speaker. YHWH is the one who weeps.

The poem is a monologue of divine grief, interrupted by speech of 'the daughter of my people', or her inhabitants. She is personified Jerusalem, that is, Daughter Zion in the poems of the mythic battle, and YHWH's divorced wife in 2.1–3.5. The literary structure of the poem is not rigidly symmetrical, but it does contain repeated patterns. There are two first-person statements of divine grief (8.18, 21), two sets of three rhetorical questions[25] (8.19b-d, 22), a first-person plural statement of terror and despair, two syntacticly parallel divine wishes (8.23, 9.1)—all culminating in the reason for YHWH's behavior in this poem (9.1b-2).

---

20. Walter Brueggemann, *To Pluck Up, To Tear Down: A Commentary on the Book of Jeremiah 1–25* (Grand Rapids: Eerdmans; Edinburgh: Handsel Press, 1988), p. 88.

21. See Diamond and O'Connor, 'Unfaithful Passions'.

22. Biddle, *Polyphony*, p. 30.

23. Roberts, 'The Motif of the Weeping God'.

24. In 8.20 a first-person plural pronoun *wa'anahnu* and verb *nosa'nu* indicate a corporate voice and in 8.19bc YHWH is referred to in the third person.

25. See Walter Brueggemann, 'Jeremiah's Use of Rhetorical Questions', *JBL* 92 (1973), pp. 358-74.

In YHWH's opening expressive burst of pain, first-person verbs spiral downward in the direction of despair.[26] His cheerfulness disappears, grief descends upon him, sickness invades the heart of God (8.18). With urgency (*hinnēh*), YHWH announces the sound of a female voice, literally, 'the sound of a cry for help (*qôl saw$^{e^t}$at*) of the daughter of my people' (8.19a). The two questions that follow may contain the content of the daughter's cry, expressed either in her own voice or as YHWH's quotation of her speech. 'Is YHWH not in Zion? Is her king not in her?' (8.19bc). The import of the daughter's questions is not clear. The questions may express her arrogant confidence[27] that YHWH is in Zion and she must therefore be safe. But YHWH heard a cry for help not of confidence. Viewed this way her cry probes divine abandonment of the city. YHWH is not in Zion but has departed and she is in mortal peril.

The third question is YHWH's and it poses a counter-charge to the daughter's questions: 'Why have they provoked me to anger with their idols?' (19.d). He has not abandoned the inhabitants of Zion; they have abandoned him for other loyalties and provoked his righteous anger just like wife Judah/Jerusalem (2.1–4.2) and Daughter of Zion (4.5–6.30). The city's inhabitants respond to YHWH's question in seeming desperation. Time is up, and 'we are not saved' (8.20). Something awful is happening, presumably the invasion, and YHWH does not act.

Using language reminiscent of clinical depression, YHWH trades his anger for sinking despair in the poem's second statement of grief: 'For the crushing of the daughter of my people, I am crushed, I grow leaden in spirit, horror has seized me' (8.21). First-person verbs identify YHWH with Daughter Zion. As she is broken (*šeber*), he is broken (*hašbārtî*). His spirit grows leaden (*qadartî*), horror seizes him (*heh^{e}zi-qatnî*). His life dims; he is wounded by her wounds and seized by feelings that overwhelm him. In a remarkable poetic turn, the distance between YHWH and the Daughter has dissolved. YHWH participates in and is emotionally intertwined with the miseries that afflict her.

With three further rhetorical questions, constructed like the previous three (8.19b-d, *'ên ... 'ên ... madû'a*), YHWH declares his amazement that her crushing, her woundedness, goes untended. 'Is there no balm in Gilead? Is there no healer there? Why is the daughter of my people not

---

26. See Holladay, *Jeremiah 1*, pp. 287-88 and McKane, *Jeremiah*, I, p. 194 on translation problems.

27. Holladay, *Jeremiah 1*, p. 293.

healed?' (8.22). Yahweh inquires sympathetically about her health and wholeness. His questions reveal inner helplessness, desperation and sorrow. That YHWH is the inflicter of wounds, the warrior who orders and designs the attack on her (8.16-17), the husband who cast her off does not appear within the world of this poem. Instead YHWH weeps with her.

Divine sorrow leads to two wishes (8.23; 9.1). YHWH is so immersed in Daughter Zion's pain, the boundaries between them have become so permeable, that his first wish is to weep forever. With glorious hyperbole he wants to become tears on her account. 'O that my head were waters and my eyes a fountain of tears that I might weep days and nights over the slain of the daughter of my people' (8.23). The weeping God, with a head turned to waters, eyes become a fountain, desires to go on a crying bout for days and nights over Daughter Zion and her dead. So much sorrow overtakes God that an endless river of tears is required to express it.

YHWH's second wish (9.1) is syntacticly parallel to the first.[28] Both wishes begin with the idiomatic expression *mi-yitnēnî* ('who will give me', translated here as 'O that'). What YHWH yearns for now is escape. He wants to run from the sorrow and to abandon the cause of tears. 'O that I had in the wilderness a traveler's lodging place that I might abandon my people and go away from them (9.1). The deeply troubled deity wants to return to the wilderness where his relationship with his bride flourished (2.1-3). Two verbs emphasize the leaving. *'Āzab* is a verb of separation, of forsaking and abandoning; *hālak* is a verb of action, of motion, of walking out. YHWH's two wishes express profound inner disturbance.

The poem's conclusion provides the reasons for the tears of God and God's desire to escape to the wilderness (9.2b-3). In terms that summarize the sins of the faithless wife (2.1–4.2), YHWH declares them all adulterers, traitors, liars, evildoers who 'do not know me' (9.2). Within the imaginative confines of this poem, betrayal does not lead to violence, warfare or vengeance. It brings out, instead, divine empathy, vulnerability and profound sorrow. Grief overtakes anger; sympathy replaces fury. In Brueggemann's language in another context, the tears of God portrays a divine character who 'enters hurt'. And in 9.11-12

---

28. Arguing against J.A. Thompson, *The Book of Jeremiah* (NICOT; Grand Rapids: Eerdmans, 1980).

and 17-23 Yahweh invites the earth and the whole people to weep with him.

The rhetorical function of the weeping poems at this juncture of the book is to mark the tragedy, to lament it, and to dwell on the funeral for the world of Jerusalem and Judah that is no more. But as divine characterization, the tears of God convey something more.

A Semiotics of Divine Tears

The resistance of biblical scholarship to poetic characterization of God as a weeping deity may be because such a deity appears too vulnerable, powerless and embodied, or perhaps insufficiently macho, to accord with the jealous husband and angry warrior from the book's earlier poetry. Recognition of the divine identity of the weeping in 8.18–9.2 is, however, theologically crucial. To recognize that YHWH speaks and weeps in this poem is to see a temporary but massive turning in the book.[29] God's tears recall the broken-hearted husband, but rather than keeping YHWH at a distance as does the drama of the divorce of his wife (2.1–3.25), these poems unite YHWH with the personified Zion (8.18–9.2) and the people in their weeping (9.17-22). God's tears mean that there may be a balm in Gilead, healing may be possible because God draws near, abandons fury, leaves aside honor, and joins in the people's suffering.

Tears heal because they bring people together in suffering, and reveal them to one another in their vulnerability. In the words of C.S. Song, tears 'stir all living souls'.[30] In Song's parable of political theology on the building of the great wall of China, only the tears of Lady Ming have strength enough to cause the wall's collapse and to reveal the bones of the oppressed who built it. Tears are a political language that opposes language of power. In Jeremiah, God's tears are more powerful even than the armies under divine command because, for a poetic moment at least, God, people and cosmos articulate a common suffering and God changes sides.

Brueggemann has written profoundly on the imagery and rhetoric of pain in the Old Testament in general and in Jeremiah in particular. He

29. I am grateful to Columbia Theological Seminary graduate, Mark Gray, for several ideas expressed here.

30. C.S. Song, *The Tears of Lady Meng: A Parable of the People's Political Theology* (Risk, 11; Geneva: The World Council of Churches, 1981), pp. 38-45.

notes that Jeremiah 'brings the tradition of lament to intense personal speech'.[31] But the theme of weeping, the river of tears that runs through the book, though related to lamentation, stands outside the tradition of protest inherent in lament. Punishment, rage and resistance are missing from it. When the mourning women, Jeremiah, the earth and forlorn Rachel weep, their weeping signifies the imminence and inevitability of the destruction and recognition of profound, irrevocable loss. But the poetry of divine weeping connotes something more. The tears of God are part of the imaginative literary enterprise that ruptures theological language. The book's lead character breaks from his role as dominating, proud male, cruel architect of war, and for a brief poetic interlude embodies and participates in the pain of the people.

The tears of God offers an alternative interpretation of the suffering of the exiles. Divine tears put aside punishment, eschew questions of causality, and characterize God in radically different terms from much of the rest of the book. This is a God who is fluid, unstable, changing and active, and whose external relations to the humans parallels the same dynamics.[32] Language of divine tears offsets language of the divine punisher and wrathful judge, for it posits vulnerability in God to the conditions of the other. It provides a glimpse of another kind of deity, a non-predictable, unknown and uncontainable being with a fluid inner life who expresses it in biological, material tears. Tears are the mighty act of a God who, in this poem, is deeply relational, infinitely active, and 'radically multiple'.[33] Divine tears suggest a deity who vacates sovereignty and hierarchical transcendence, at least temporarily, and relates in vulnerability to the other, the daughter of my people. The incommensurable other is not so by excessive, transcendent might, but by a woundedness, a sorrow, a lack. The God of tears interrupts theological discourse and offers a glimpse of relationship without violence. Without such disjunction in the divine character, healing would not be possible.

31. Walter Brueggemann, 'A Shape for Old Testament Theology, II: Embrace of Pain', *CBQ* 47 (1985), pp. 395-415 (404).

32. Serene Jones, 'This God Which is Not One: Irigaray and Barth on the Divine', in C.W. Maggie Kim *et al.* (eds.), *Transfigurations: Theology and the French Feminists* (Minneapolis: Fortress Press, 1993), pp. 109-41.

33. Jones, 'This God', p. 132.

Part IV

RESPONSE

NEXT STEPS IN JEREMIAH STUDIES?

Walter Brueggemann

These present essays unmistakably exhibit the fact that Jeremiah studies are off in new directions with a great deal of vigor and energy. It is a commonplace that the three great commentaries of 1986 provide a key marker in the turn of Jeremiah studies. While the work of William Holladay does not figure greatly in newer methods and approaches, his prodigious effort serves the important purpose of pushing historical critical study as far as can now be imagined.[1] While few would now go that route, Holladay has provided a reliable and stable baseline and foil for newer ventures. It is the important merit of Robert Carroll that he has irreversibly introduced the category of 'ideology' into Jeremiah studies, so that neither historical-critical nor innocently theological interpretation is any longer credible.[2] Carroll's move in that direction has now become a usage at the center of our common work. It appears to be a major contribution of William McKane, without neglecting his important and dense textual work, to provide the notion of a 'rolling corpus' as a way of understanding the thematic constancy of the book of Jeremiah together with what appears to be its disjunctive develop-ment.[3] The present conversation draws heavily upon these commen-taries, though it is of course informed as well by the larger interpretive

---

1.   William L. Holladay, *Jeremiah 1: A Commentary on the Book of the Prophet Jeremiah, Chapters 1–25* (Hermeneia; Philadelphia: Fortress Press, 1986). See also *idem, Jeremiah 2: A Commentary on the Book of the Prophet Jeremiah, Chapters 26–52* (Hermeneia; Minneapolis: Fortress Press, 1989).

2.   Robert P. Carroll, *Jeremiah: A Commentary* (OTL; Philadelphia: Westmin-ster Press, 1986).

3.   William McKane, *A Critical and Exegetical Commentary on Jeremiah*. I. *Introduction and Commentary on Jeremiah I–XXV* (ICC; Edinburgh: T. & T. Clark, 1986). See also *idem, A Critical and Exegetical Commentary on Jeremiah*. II. *Commentary on Jeremiah XXVI–LII* (ICC; Edinburgh: T. & T. Clark, 1996).

currents that are at work in Old Testament studies, most especially a move away from an innocent positivism to what is conventionally termed a postmodern perspective.

The rich and supple interpretive possibilities are evident in the valuable summary of options in theological exposition by Leo Perdue.[4] Along with attention to the major scholarly ventures and emerging new models for biblical theology, Perdue's study has the special merit of illustrating those large possibilities by particular reference to what may be done in Jeremiah interpretation. Perdue's focus upon Jeremiah indicates that Jeremiah is not only a fruitful focus for scholarship but is also a pivotal point of dispute in interpretive matters, and likely also to be a principle datum for biblical theology at the beginning of the twenty-first century. In the final section of this essay, I will consider some reasons why and how this may be so.

I

It is not news any longer that scholarship has moved decisively from *diachronic* to *synchronic* ways of reading. And while some scholars may be polemical about the matter, most are inclined to adopt something of a both/and approach.[5] The reason for this is simple. While sympathies are characteristically in a synchronic direction, it is obvious to everyone that the voices sounded in the book of Jeremiah are profoundly in touch with real historical realities in the seventh and/or sixth centuries, so that one cannot be purely synchronic, as though the 'book' floated in the air. It is of course not clear about the extent or character of the 'contact points' between this literary piece and historical reality,

---

4.   Leo G. Perdue, *The Collapse of History: Reconstructing Old Testament Theology* (Overtures to Biblical Theology; Minneapolis: Fortress Press, 1994). In this volume, see Perdue's essay and Thomas Overholt's response to it.

5.   See the comment of Rolf Rendtorff, 'The Book of Isaiah: A Complex Unity: Synchronic and Diachronic Reading', in Roy F. Melugin and Marvin A. Sweeney, *New Visions of Isaiah* (JSOTSup, 214; Sheffield: Sheffield Academic Press, 1996), p. 40, who speaks of 'a reversal of scholarly priorities: 'The latter reading, which I am sympathetic with, does not imply a denial of diachronic questions but a change—and perhaps a reversal—of scholarly priorities.'

See also Johannes C. de Moor (ed.), *Synchronic or Diachronic: A Debate on Method in Old Testament Exegesis* (OTS, 34; Leiden: E.J. Brill, 1995); and J. Noble, 'Synchronic and Diachronic Approaches to Biblical Interpretation', *Literature and Theology* 7 (1993), pp. 130-48.

but one cannot proceed without an awareness of the large context of emergency in which the literature is set.

Leo Perdue, first in his book *The Collapse of History* and now in his essay in this volume, has performed an especially important service in reviewing, summarizing and assessing the important critical issues related to the question of *diachronic* and *synchronic*. He makes it clear that this general rubric (that revolves around the vexed question of 'history') generates a host of problems, a variety of approaches, and rich possibilities for interpretation that were not available in the old monolithic approach of 'historical criticism'. Specifically issues of (a) ideology and interpretive stance, and (b) pluralism, are deeply at stake in our new interpretive environment. As the responses to Perdue by Lawrence Boadt, Dennis Olson and Tom Overholt make clear, we still have hard work in front of us that as of now admits of no consensus.

I have come to the conclusion that while the deep interpretive crisis present in Jeremiah studies and in theological interpretation more generally can be characterized as the vexed relation between 'modern' and 'postmodern' perspectives, the reality of how scholars work is very different from that. The direction the interpretive work of a scholar takes, so it seems to me, depends upon a *felt threat* and a *felt need* that are quite personal, subjective and existential, even if they are presented in more erudite fashion. (This is perhaps indicated by the way in which seemingly scholarly questions can generate adrenalin and acrimony that seem oddly disproportionate to the question.) On the one hand, if the felt threat is taken to be *fragmentation* of interpretation (as seems to be the case for Perdue), then the felt need is for some coherence that yields a modernist perspective, that sustains something of a core of interpretive stability. If, on the other hand, the felt threat is *reductionism* (as seems to be the case for Burke Long), then the felt need is for openness and freedom in interpretation that embraces postmodern pluralism as a way of keeping the process open. While Perdue suggests his own propensity in this regard, the great merit and gain of his work is to lay out with clarity the taxonomy of current interpretation. It seems important, in my judgment, that while different scholars, out of particular felt threats and felt needs, focus upon a certain direction of interpretation, we keep before us the map of the entire enterprise, entertaining the thought that we may learn from each other, and in the meantime act attentively and with respect toward each other.

At the moment, the future of scholarship is clearly in a synchronic direction. There is nonetheless still a great deal unsettled about what that means. Earlier studies by Kathleen O'Connor, Pete Diamond and Mark Smith are enormously suggestive about the synchronic shape of Jeremiah 11–20, and the intentional placement of the so-called 'Confessions' in a grid of the larger text.[6] More recently Ronald Clements has extended such reflections concerning the theological grid of the entire unit of chs. 1–25.[7] It remains of course to see how such arguments can be further extended.

The most influential advocate of synchronic interpretation is Robert Carroll who has not paid primary attention to the niceties and symmetries of the synchronic, but has been primarily concerned to show that any access to the historical is impossible. That is, the final form of the text is a literary-rhetoric-imaginative constant that stands at an important distance from anything we might regard as 'history'. When Carroll pursues this notion of rhetorical distance plus his accent on ideology, he concludes that the text characteristically is axe-grinding in ways that heretofore have been regarded as theological, though Carroll tends to reduce such to sociopolitical tendentiousness.

In the present volume, Diamond has considered the theoretical inadequacy of historical critical to address the problems of the text it has helped us to see.[8] Synchronic contributions include that of Stulman on chs. 1–25, Holt on chs. 37–44, and Wells on chs. 40–44.[9] The discussion of Diamond and O'Connor, though not preoccupied with synchronic method, clearly appeals to such a perspective.[10] All of these seek to read without reference to conventional historical considerations.

In a very different way from that of Carroll, with a theological interest Carroll would eschew, Brevard Childs purposes that the book of Jeremiah concerns a theology of God's word that issues variously in

---

6.   A.R. Pete Diamond, *The Confessions of Jeremiah in Context: Scenes of Prophetic Drama* (JSOTSup, 45; Sheffield: JSOT Press, 1987); Kathleen M. O'Connor, *The Confessions of Jeremiah: their Interpretation and Role in Chapters 1–25* (SBLDS, 94; Atlanta; Scholars Press, 1988); and Mark S. Smith, *The Laments of Jeremiah and Their Contexts: A Literary and Redactional Study of Jeremiah 11–20* (Atlanta: Scholars Press, 1990).

7.   Ronald E. Clements, 'Jeremiah 1–25 and the Deuteronomistic History', in *idem, Old Testament Prophecy: From Oracles to Canon* (Louisville, KY: Westminster/John Knox Press, 1996), pp. 107-22.

8.   A.R. Pete Diamond, 'Introduction', pp. 16, 32.

9.   See their essays in this volume.

10.   See their essay in this volume.

assertions of *judgment* for rejection of the word and a summons to repentance and *promise* what 'was part of the divine plan from the outset'.[11] In a way with more nuance, Ronald Clements argued some time ago that the prophetic literature has been edited to focus primarily upon themes of judgment and promise:

> It is rather precisely the element of connectedness between the prophets, and the conviction that they were referring to a single theme of Israel's destruction and renewal, which has facilitated the ascription to each of them of the message of hope which some of their number had proclaimed after 587 BC.[12]

Clements's more recent discussion shows how the accents of Deuteronomic theology has shaped Jeremiah, a theology in its own way concerned with judgment and promise.[13]

It is clear that *synchronic reading* and *canonical interpretation* are not to be equated. Nonetheless, an important convergence may be seen in these approaches. One important accent in synchronic approaches is a negative one, namely, to loosen the text from 'history'. But once it is loosened from history as a principle of explanation, one is driven to 'intentional meaning', whether Childs's 'theological' or Carroll's 'ideological'. Thus I suggest that we may see something of a general agreement about the synchronic, even if it receives different scholarly valuations. In a recent brief note to me, Carroll has suggested that in fact the 'earlier' material of 'judgment' is further removed from the actual voices of the text (the text being later) and so the 'later' material of 'hope' is to be taken as a more reliable and exact claim of the text. This, so it seems to me, is an important move in the direction of the theological calculations of Childs and Clements. The conclusion I draw is that once a move is made to the synchronic, it is almost inevitable that the material will be taken as statements of intentional memory in some larger pattern of meaning, whether that larger meaning is taken to be theology or ideology.

---

11. Brevard S. Childs, *Introduction to the Old Testament as Scripture* (Philadelphia: Fortress Press, 1979), p. 351.

12. Ronald E. Clements, 'Patterns in the Prophetic Canon', in George W. Coats and Burke O. Long (eds.), *Canon and Authority: Essays in Old Testament Religion and Theology* (Philadelphia: Fortress Press, 1977), pp. 42-55 (48).

13. See n. 7.

II

The move from diachronic to synchronic is marked by a move from *historical analysis* to *rhetorical study*. Attention to *synchronic interpretation* and *rhetorical analysis* overlap, but they are not the same. And therefore it is important to recognize that we are only at the beginning of rhetorical analysis. Perhaps it is correct to observe that synchronic perspectives tend to deal in larger units and ask about the interface and interaction between texts or larger collections of texts that seem to be disjunctive.

By contrast rhetorical criticism tends to focus on smaller units and to ask about the intentional operation of the text. There is no doubt that James Muilenburg is the progenitor of such an approach, and the unavailability of his draft of a Jeremiah commentary continues to be an aggrieved loss to us all. Here I wish to make only a single point about the character of rhetoric, particularly as it is practised in ancient Israelite-Jewish materials such as Jeremiah. This rhetoric is endlessly plurivocal, subversive and deconstructive.[14] It does not admit of a single meaning and evokes ongoing interpretation that is never finally settled. In part, this is the character of poetry and thus pertains especially to the poetic sections of the material. In part, it has to do with the elusive quality and character of Hebrew articulation that is evocative and venturesome, but seldom conclusion drawing. And in part, so far as Jeremiah is concerned, the literature is a reflection within a community that must speak, but must speak about an unutterable *Tremendum*.

I have been helped by the juxtaposition Philip Fisher makes between *myth* and *rhetoric*:

> *Myth* ... is always singular, *rhetorics* is always plural. Myth is a fixed, satisfying, and stable story that is used again and again to normalize our account of social life. By means of myth, novelty is tamed by being seen as the repetition or, at most, the variation of a known and valuable pattern ... Rhetoric, in contrast, is a tactic within the open questions of culture. It reveals interests and exclusions ... Rhetoric is the place where language is engaged in cultural work, and such work can be done on, with, or in spite of another group within society. Rhetorics are plural because they are part of what is uncertain or potential within culture. They are servants of one or another politics of experience. Where there is

14. See Mark Coleridge, 'Life in the Crypt or Why Bother with Biblical Studies?', *BibInt* 2 (1994), pp. 139-51.

nothing openly contested, no cultural work to be done, we do not find the simplification into one and only one rhetoric. Instead we find the absence of the particular inflammation and repetition that rhetoric always marks. We find no rhetoric at all, only the ceremonial contentment of myth.[15]

I find this statement illuminating of Jeremiah. There is clearly 'cultural work' to be done, both in response to enormous displacement and in response to contested and competing futures.

To be sure, in Jeremiah studies we do not use the term 'myth', but it occurs to me that our term 'ideology' comes close to what Fisher means by 'myth'. Indeed, Fisher continues to say about myth and rhetoric:

> Within the term *ideology* we are right to hear a combination of calculation, cynicism about social truth, a schoolteacher's relation to the pupils, indoctrination, and propaganda. Whether as reality or hope, ideology implies that one part of the legitimacy of authority is a monopoly on representation, and this is exactly the condition in which rhetorics become irrelevant.[16]

It appears to me that much talk about ideology (myth!) in Jeremiah studies is premature, precisely because there is no monopoly of representation, and surely rhetoric is not yet 'irrelevant'. It is precisely the contested character of the future in Judah, as Christopher Seitz has best explicated, that precludes our flattening the rhetoric into ideology or myth.[17] There is no doubt that the Jeremiah tradition inherits and utilizes 'mythic' material, for example, the broken marriage, the foe from the north, God as patron of the city. But these standard thematics are handled in the Jeremiah tradition in supple ways with imagination and freedom. Thus what is 'mythic' is made into rhetoric that remains open in interpretation. It is important to attend to this suppleness and not impose a *closure* that belongs to the reader and not to the text. Evidently Jeremiah is not yet beyond 'the particular inflammation and repetition' that rhetoric always marks. To be sure, such advocacies as we have in the material might wish they had become 'fixed, satisfying, and stable', but they had not,

---

15. Philip Fisher, 'American Literary and Cultural Studies since the Civil War', in Stephen Greenblatt and Giles Gunn (eds.), *Redrawing the Boundaries: The Transformation of English and American Literary Studies* (New York: The Modern Language Association of America, 1992), pp. 232-33.

16. Fisher, 'American Literary and Cultural Studies', p. 233.

17. Christopher Seitz, *Theology in Conflict: Reactions to the Exile in the Book of Jeremiah* (BZAW; Berlin: W. de Gruyter, 1989).

- because things were not settled;
- because the community is endlessly contentious; and
- because the several advocacies claim to appeal to a 'Holy One' whom even they know cannot be reduced to fixity.

Thus we may expect and exercise close attentiveness to rhetoric in the recognition that settlements are elusive, and what we have at best are 'bids' and not conclusions.[18] We may welcome the essays in this volume, focused on rhetorical analysis, including those of Diamond and O'Connor, Nancy Lee, Alice Ogden Bellis and Marvin Sweeney, even though Sweeney's discussion parses the rhetoric with some attention to radactional development.[19]

III

Such a contrast between rhetoric and myth, or alternatively rhetoric and ideology, leads us naturally to consider the role of *ideology* in Jeremiah studies. Carroll's introduction of the term into our common work is to insist, surely rightly, that the several advocacies in the text, including 'God-advocacies', are not innocent, but are highly tendentious, intentional and characteristically self-serving. It is Carroll's intention, in substituting 'ideology' for 'theology', to bring God-claims in the text into social-scientific confines and so to nullify the 'privilege' of God talk.

It is of course well known that 'ideology' may be understood simply in a Marxian sense as *distortion*, or in a non-Marxian way, as in Clifford Geertz, as an attempt to state a communal, shared *meaning*, an affirmation that contains no pejorative or polemical intent.[20] When we

18. On the notion of 'bids', see Rowan Williams, 'The Literal Sense of Scripture', *Modern Theology* 7 (1991), pp. 121-34.

19. See individual essays. The essay of Raymond F. Person, Jr, in this volume suggests a different kind of sensitivity to oral rhetoric to which attention must be paid.

20. Clifford Geertz, 'Ideology as a Cultural System', in *idem, The Interpretation of Cultures: Selected Essays* (New York: Basic Books, 1973), pp. 193-233. For a helpful review of the topic, see Paul Ricoeur, *Lectures on Ideology and Utopia* (New York: Columbia University Press, 1986). Norman K. Gottwald, 'Ideology and Ideologies in Israelite Prophecy', in Stephen Breck Reid (ed.), *Prophets and Paradigms: Essays in Honor of Gene M. Tucker* (JSOTSup, 229; Sheffield: Shef-

are all on our good behavior, we may intentionally accept 'ideology' in this second way, as simply a sober, fair-minded recognition that a communal shared meaning is offered. In such a usage, 'ideology' is not more than a mode of 'social construction of reality'.[21] And in the book of Jeremiah, we may imagine that the Deuteronomic teaching that is prominent in the final form of the text is a social construction of reality that especially prizes Torah obedience, that takes seriously the God who is said to authorize the Torah and to summon obedience, and to acknowledge the obedience of a particular segment of the community. So far so good.

I have come to think, however, that in strongly felt interpretive situations like that of Jeremiah studies where we interpreters seem as passionate as our forebears in the literature, it is impossible to adhere to a non-Marxian usage, because there is always ready at hand a bootlegging of 'distortion' in a polemical way. Thus even in his present essay that is greatly refined from his initial use in the commentary, Carroll's non-Marxian usage cannot finally refrain from 'a power group over the rest of the community' concerning 'who controls past and future'.[22]

None of this is problematic except to notice that such usage of the term 'ideology' is gratuitously reductive. The trade-off of 'ideology' for 'theology' of course reduces 'Yahweh' simply to a cipher for a greedy, intentional program of land acquisition. In this collection, the article by Wells makes a comparable and well-said argument. What happens is that Yahweh is reduced in the most extreme Feuerbachian way. That may indeed be correct. Except that such a flatness will never permit us to understand what the voices in Jeremiah intend to be saying or doing. It is my impression that Geertz and other anthropologists resolved to try to understand cultures on their own terms as much as possible, rather than on modernist 'scientific terms' that can easily show such cultures to be 'silly'. One cannot, I suggest, simply reduce Yahweh to a social

---

field Academic Press, 1996), pp. 136-49, has helpfully reconsidered the theme with reference to the prophets.

   21. See Peter L. Berger and Thomas Luckmann, *The Social Construction of Reality: A Treatise in the Sociology of Knowledge* (Garden City, NY: Doubleday, 1967).

   22. Robert P. Carroll, 'Jeremiah, Intertextuality, and Ideologiekritik', *JNSL* 22.1 (1996), pp. 26, 27.

function in an Israelite text and eliminate Yahweh as agent, and yet hope to understand what is being done and said.

I have no wish to polemize against Carroll and have participated enough in that. Carroll is surely right in his polemic against excessive privilege for theological claims. But an easy move to 'ideology' is not very effective, because a non-Marxian 'ideology' would need to accept Yahweh as a key factor in meaning, Yahweh understood as more than illusion or projection. My point is that there is no easy or innocent settlement of categories of 'ideology' and 'theology', and to project one's own reservations of certain categories of utterance (or one's own enthusiasms) is hardly helpful or scholarly. I suspect we shall continue to barter about this matter. Those who prefer 'theology' cannot expect privileged claims. Those who prefer 'ideology' cannot pretend scientific detachment when the usage is reductionist. We must make sure that we offer arguments based in the text and not simply dismissive name-calling driven by current resentments. It may well be that we need yet to find a better word that is free of the accumulated freight of time.

IV

The larger categories of *rhetoric* and *ideology* invite a distinct comment concerning feminist interpretation in Jeremiah studies. As in every aspect of our field, feminist undertakings have not had a smooth entry into Jeremiah studies. At the outset of this phase of scholarship, Carroll applied the term 'ideology' in a catch-all usage concerning such advocacy positions, with special reference to the work of Trible. Since that time, of course, we have learned a great deal and refined the categories of both 'ideology' and 'feminist'.

It seems unmistakable that we have a great deal of work remaining to be done in this regard, especially in the poetic materials where the use of metaphor and image is not only elusive but enormously venturesome. The several studies of Kathleen O'Connor, following the lead of Phyllis Trible, suggest ways in which materials can now be read afresh to great advantage.[23] Our concern is not simply with the role of women

23. Phyllis Trible, 'The Gift of a Poem: A Rhetorical Study of Jeremiah 31:15-22', *ANQ* 17 (1976), pp. 271-80; *God and the Rhetoric of Sexuality* (Overtures to Biblical Theology; Philadelphia: Fortress Press, 1978), pp. 41-50; Kathleen O'Connor, 'Jeremiah', in Carol A. Newsom and Sharon H. Ringe (eds.), *The Women's Bible Commentary* (Louisville, KY: Westminster/John Knox Press,

in the literature, but the ways in which feminist imagery in the text permits the most elemental, painful and wondrous of interactions to be voiced beneath conventional modes of reportage. Here I may mention three lines of investigation that will be of great benefit in time to come:

Gale Yee, with reference to Hosea, has considered how feminine imagery not only reflects patriarchy, but in important ways subverts the very claims of patriarchy that it reflects.[24]

Renita Weems has shown how violent sexual imagery is in substance a social practice of violence that may indeed evoke violent human practice, reflective of the rhetoric of divine abusiveness.[25] There is no doubt a great deal more of this to pursue in the traditions of Jeremiah, as Angela Bauer's essay in this volume makes clear.

Most important, so it seems to me, is the notion of 'antilanguage' on the part of William Domeris (see his essay in the present volume). If, as seems likely, the dominant rhetoric of ancient Israel in the seventh–sixth centuries is patriarchal, then the risky sexual metaphors that pay attention to female-Israel may indeed be seen as 'antilanguage' that gives voice to counter-reality, or in the terms of Domeris, antireality. If that is so, moreover, then the old and intractible problem of relating poetry to prose becomes substantively urgent, for that interface becomes an interface between *rhetoric on its way to ideology* (Dtr) and *anti-utterance* in the poetry that Deuteronomic editing did not nullify but preserved. Such antilanguage, apparently valued by would-be ideologue, testifies to the quite provisional claims of would-be ideology, a provisional quality perhaps dictated both by the ambiguity of circumstance and by the elusiveness of the Key Player in this ideological-theological articulation. Such antilanguage that pervades the tradition warns us against taking the final form of the text as too settled or stable. Whether the use of such antilanguage is happenstance or intentional, it bespeaks an openness that no amount of loudness or firmness can easily overcome.

1992), pp. 169-77, and 'Speak Tenderly to Jerusalem: Second Isaiah's Reception and Use of Daughter Zion', forthcoming in *Princeton Seminary Bulletin*.

24. Gale A. Yee, *Poor Banished Children of Eve: The Symbolization of Women as Evil in Biblical and Related Texts* (New York: Continuum, forthcoming).

25. Renita J. Weems, *Battered Love: Marriage, Sex, and Violence in the Hebrew Prophets* (Overtures to Biblical Theology; Minneapolis: Fortress Press, 1995).

V

There is a great deal of evidence now to suggest that the book of Jeremiah in final form is a literature that is intensely *future oriented*. By that I do not mean that we can substantively identify 'eschatological themes', for that is a much-too-cognitive approach. Rather, the shape and texture and character of the text intends to be generative into the next generations of text-preservers and text-readers and text-hearers.

If, as seems clear, there is a movement from early to late, at least ostensively from pre-587 to post-587, as the Jeremiah tradition keeps 'growing' and being restated after the demise of Jerusalem and after the lifetime of the prophet and after the displacement of leading citizens, then it does not surprise that the movement of the text toward 'final form' is indeed generative and is itself a practice and a product of such ongoing generativity.

While matters are not yet sorted out, it seems clear that the pivotal role of ch. 25,[26] the corpus of Oracles Against the Nations that anticipates the overthrow of the nations, the particular narrative enactment of 51.59-64 concerning the 'sinking' of Babylon, and the prose addendum of ch. 52 with particular reference to 52.31-34 all indicate that the process of the book continues to ponder how to end, and in light of a literary ending to wonder what comes next. It is not yet clear, if it ever will be, how this convoluted material is internally related nor can it be said that there is an agreed-upon ending for the future, even in the MT without reference to the different arrangement of the Greek version. Rather, the literature and its framers are restless about what comes next and care greatly about it.

What seems important to me in this regard is that McKane's 'rolling corpus' is not 'rolling' aimlessly and without direction. Rather the 'roll' of the tradition is on a steady trajectory toward new possibility. It is altogether possible that 'roll' toward new futures may be understood (a) *geopolitically* as exilic Israel moves into the Persian defeat of Babylon that in turn permits some rehabilitation of the community, (b) *ideologically* as the Babylonian community of Jews asserts hegemony in reshaping Jerusalem, or (c) *theologically* as Yahweh is reckoned to be a God of fidelity. I do not imagine that these dimensions of the future are mutually exclusive, but rather that the shapers of the book of

---

26. See the essays of John Hill and Martin Kessler in this volume.

Jeremiah—geopolitically, ideologically, theologically—cannot and will not believe that termination is the final fact. Carroll's suggestion that the promise is in fact closer to the lived reality of the final form than is the judgment, is an important acknowledgment of that remarkable affirmation about the future. It is not at all necessary (or possible) to distinguish the pragmatic and fideistic elements in that decision, but only to notice that the bracketing of 'captivity' (1.3) and 'captivity' (51.28-30, 31-34) contains within it a remarkable resolve that 'captivity' is indeed provisional. And so the scroll keeps 'rolling'.

VI

In the end, the book of Jeremiah is an effort to construe and imagine the defining emergency of Israel-Judaism with reference to Yahweh as the agent of both judgment and possibility. Having recognized that the terms 'theology' and 'ideology' are in their different ways problematic, it seems important to me, in the end, to recognize as well that the book of Jeremiah, without reference to Yahweh, is no book at all and its sustained act of imagination is emptied of any force if Yahweh is flattened out to be only a code-term for aggressive land acquisition. Thus I finish with the anticipation that our future work in Jeremiah inevitably will be in some way theological, if we take the material of the book seriously.

The reference to Yahweh in the book seems to be pervasive and indispensable. We do not know how naïve, innocent or fideistic the framers of the book are, but given their sophistication about other matters, we may imagine that they were not simpletons about uttering the name of Yahweh, but meant by the utterance to point to the inscrutable mystery at the center of public life that would not be tamed but that may in some important way be known by reference to antecedent experiences and articulations. It is a commonplace to say that in that ancient world 'atheism' was no real option, but that 'idolatry' is an endless agenda, by which I mean a dispute about what is true and reliable and what is false and fickle about the intransigent mystery that pervades human, public life.

Whether a belated modernist or postmodernist reader happens to agree with this naming of that Holy Intransigence seems to me of almost no interest or merit. Of course there is a temptation in some circles to want with excessive eagerness to subscribe to what the text seems to affirm or even to press it further so that the God voiced in this material becomes the more established God of the orthodox, hegemonic Western tradition. Such a domestication and familiarity predictably evokes an adamant skepticism, seeming to be most acute among those nurtured in authoritarian fundamentalism who readily spot authoritarianism wherever it surfaces in interpretation and wherever it seems present in the text. Such belated fideism and complementary skepticism seem to me beside the point and inadmissible in our study, for our work is not to impose or to expose, but to hear what is here imagined. The proper procedure, so it seems to me, is to explicate the claims of the tradition as best we can, without reference to our own readiness or resistance, and then, only then, at the end, to assess our own engagement with or distance from these claims. I understand, of course, that such attentiveness to the claims of the tradition is never innocent or pure. But a proximate effort can be made that does not begin in either exuberant embrace or polemical rejection. Without denying interest and bias, it is important that they are not, at the outset, given completely free rein. A premature certification or dismissal of claims seems only to block our capacity to entertain the material.

It is commonly remarked that the book of Jeremiah is 'unreadable', that is, that it is so filled with disjunction that it makes no coherent sense. But then, it seems to me, that the judgment of 'unreadability' is a common judgment made in Greek reading of Jewish texts that proceed by a different voice.[27] The judgment 'unreadable' may be more a judgment on the reader than on the material.

I wonder then if it could be that 'unreadable' is not a profound *problem* in the book of Jeremiah but rather a *core datum* to be attended to as a crucial part of the book's *testimony*.[28] It occurs to me that 'unreadability' may reflect

27. See Susan A. Handelman, *The Slayers of Moses: The Emergence of Rabbinic Interpretation in Modern Literary Theory* (Albany: State University of New York Press, 1982).

28. As much as anyone, Elie Wiesel has shown the possibility of 'testimony' as a legitimate alternative mode of knowledge. Wiesel is of course concerned for the evidence of the death-camps that depends, finally, upon the witnesses. More generally on testimony as a reliable mode of knowledge, see C.A.J. Coady, *Testimony: A Philosophical Study* (Oxford: Clarendon Press, 1992).

And with reference to testimony in Scripture study, see Walter Brueggemann, *Theology of the Old Testament: Testimony, Dispute, Advocacy* (Minneapolis: Fortress Press, 1997).

1. *the experienced Tremendum* of history, the loss of treasured, guaranteeing Jerusalem and the ensuing displacement that required a disjunctive voicing;[29]
2. *the contested shape of life and faith* and the competing claims of vying communities which means that no voice can effect a smooth hegemony, but that the political, interpretive situation of necessity is a cacophony of claims and counter-claims.
3. The experience of the *Tremendum* and the political contestation together may be witnesses, so that they attest to the *disjunctive character of Yahweh*, the one who defeated the city, authorized the empire, and summoned the interpreters. It is this Holy One, so the material suggests, who legitimated the political and literary practice of disjunction. The book cannot be made 'readable', perhaps, without violating this Holy One who refuses conformity to such contained sense-making.
4. Those of us who practise Jeremiah interpretation as a goodly company, I propose, cannot spend all our energy on our intra-guild disputes, important and interesting as they are to us. Thus I suggest that Jeremiah studies has a special, public responsibility, not only to popularize our research, but to permit this 'unreadable' material to be an opening for the 'unreadable' quality of our own time and place.

Somewhere Elie Wiesel has commented that Jeremiah is that part of the Bible that we now need to be reading. He does not specify why that is so. It takes no great imagination, however, to suggest what he may mean. Specifically, the barbarity of the twentieth century—with special but not exclusive reference to the Shoah—might suggest that the *Tremendum* of sixth-century Israel has an analogue in our time. More generally, one might ponder the collapse of the 'known world' of the West at the end of the twentieth century to be a parallel to that primal collapse of Israelite life and faith shadowed in the book of Jeremiah. Cultural analogues and parallels, however, are not an adequate access point for our contemporary reading of Jeremiah. We finally, in the end, must push beyond cultural issues to theological wonderment. Here I may identify three facets of the question of God in that ancient text that

---

29. I intend to refer deliberately to Arthur Allen Cohen, *The Tremendum: A Theological Interpretation of the Holocaust* (New York: Crossroad, 1981).

in contemporary life, in my judgment, belong to the serious reading of Jeremiah:

1. As much as anyone, Weisel has insisted that the only valid form of knowledge that counts in deep human emergency is testimony, whereby exposed human agents, without institutional credibility or authority, give an account of human reality that attests to the reality of God. Testimony is a lean mode of knowledge, but may indeed be the only serious offer of meaning and hope in an environment like that of the sixth century or our own. Whatever may be said of the person of Jeremiah and whatever may be said 'historically' about Jeremiah 36, the book of Jeremiah is indeed offered as testimony to a rereading of reality at the behest of God.[30] In a social environment wherein conventional positivism has failed—the positivism of science or of theology—ours may be a moment of reading that is left with only testimony. And if so, Jeremiah constitutes a witness of great durability and generativity.

2. The God given in this text, and offered by testimony from that text to our context, is indeed an elusive, holy figure who will not be captured, caught, domesticated or reduced by way of our explanations. The quality of Yahweh is nicely voiced in 23.23-24

> Am I a God near by, says the Lord, and not a God far off? Who can hide in secret places so that I cannot see them? says the Lord. Do I not fill heaven and earth? says the Lord.

This is a God from whom no secret can be kept, but a God who may be kept secret. I take it that the elusive language of the book is because Yahweh is not directly and fully available by utterance or in any other way.[31] In that text and in our context, perhaps, the holy one inhabits but also haunts in ways past inhabiting. And while conventional theo-ideology may want the habitation, what is most given here is the haunting. The haunting God among this haunted people is sure to be unreadable, precisely the proper God for an unreadable time like ours.

3. But there is more here than holy elusiveness. As Abraham Heschel

---

30. I fully share the judgment that the narrative of ch. 36 is a fictive construct designed to authorize the book and the voice of the prophet who speaks there. Of course the fictive character of the narrative does not diminish its importance for the processes and claims of authority for the literature.

31. This quality of 'knowledge' of Yahweh has been well probed by Samuel Terrien, *The Elusive Presence: Toward a New Biblical Theology* (San Francisco: Harper & Row, 1978).

has seen best, the God who haunts is the God who is uttered and given in deep pathos, so that sovereignty comes as generative suffering.[32] It is exceedingly important that this recognition of suffering is not projected backward by Christians from the cross of Jesus, but receives its best voicing from that quintessential Jewish voice of Heschel. As he has seen, the suffering of the poet and the poet's preservers echoes and embodies the suffering of Yahweh. And were Heschel doing his study today, moreover, he would surely say that some presence-in-suffering is the primary claim, practice and assurance of the book of Jeremiah that might now claim our attention.

Our time, like that time, is seduced by deep denial (6.14; 8.11):

- We imagine certitudes better than risky testimony.
- We imagine holiness available in tamed categories.
- We imagine sure scriptings free of suffering.

But of course, none of this is given. This script keeps insisting otherwise, in censoring and in generative ways. If this book now is not read, the book is not damaged. It is rather the unreading time that is diminished ... and it need not be so.

I am aware of the hazards of theological 'contemporeneity' in appropriating a text. I share the common reluctance of our discipline about easy connections and I propose none. In my judgment, Carroll is right in his insistence on responsible, contemporary reading that depends on two conditions:

> For those prepared to do the hard work entailed, and who live in circumstances out of which such a project naturally arises, there is material in Jeremiah which may be beneficial for our time.[33]

Carroll's reference is to Czechoslovakia post-1968. I do not romanticize, but given the crisis of Western culture, many folk qualify, in my judgment, for the right circumstance where hard work may be usefully done. The issue in that ancient text and in our present context, so it seems to me, is that of *relinquishing* what is being ended by holiness

---

32. Abraham Heschel, *The Prophets* (New York: Harper & Row, 1962). See also Kazo Kitamori, *Theology of the Pain of God* (Richmond: John Knox Press, 1965).

33. Robert P. Carroll, *From Chaos to Covenant: Prophecy in the Book of Jeremiah* (New York: Crossroad, 1981), p. 279.

and the even more demanding work of *receiving* what is being given in suffering love.

In the end, the contemporary public question is: What kind of material is this in the book of Jeremiah? Some time ago I gently chided colleagues who were keen on criticism but thin on interpretation.[34] Since I wrote that, I am helped greatly by distinctions already made in 1979 by George Steiner who distinguishes *critic* and *reader*. He observes that the critic rightly engages in a *distancing* process whereby one may arrive at *objective* meaning.

But the reader, unlike the critic, has a different stance. The reader

> inhibits the provisional—in which manifold term he recognizes as relevant the notions of 'gift', of 'that which serves vision', and of that which 'nourishes' indispensably ... The reader proceeds *as if* the text was the housing of forces and meanings, of meanings of meaning, whose lodging within the executive verbal form was one of 'incarnation' ... As lived by the true reader, the text is irreducible to, inexhaustible by, even the most penetratively diagnostic, explicative visions—be they linguistic, grammatological, semiotic, historicist, sociological, 'deconstructive', or what you will.[35]

In the end, Steiner observes:

> The critic prescribes a syllabus; the reader is answerable to and internalizes a canon.[36]

I have no resistance about our work of prescribing a syllabus; it is our proper critical work. If, however, that is all, we shall have missed the scroll. The 'canon' here is not the rigid, reductionist 'canonical' to which Childs is obligated. The term here, I take it, means a normative script invested with presence. Our work is to move, I propose, through and beyond syllabus, when syllabus is well done, to canon, to a normizing voice that refuses to be 'readable' precisely because readability produces domestication.

One other phrase from Steiner instructs me: 'A syllabus is taught; a canon is lived.'[37] Canon is the embrace of a generative text beyond the regime of thought and analysis to where the claims must be faced and

---

34. Walter Brueggemann, 'Jeremiah: Intense Criticism//Thin Interpretation', *Int* 42 (1988), pp. 268-80.

35. George Steiner, 'Critic/Reader', *New Literary History* (1979), pp. 423-52 (442).

36. Steiner, 'Critic/Reader', p. 445.

37. Steiner, 'Critic/Reader', p. 447.

lived. Jeremiah as canon is an authorization to live in lean testimony to a holy, pathos-filled presence. The aim of such scholarship that is demanded by the material, in my judgment, is to move through the paces of criticism so that this unreadable script may rescript our unreadable lived reality.

The outcome of such reading-living is the emergence of an anti-community, or we might better say a counter-community, counter in good times to *self-deception*, counter in lean times to *despair*. Such a stance of 'anti' is a tough one—whether in Jerusalem or in Babylon. It may issue in doxology (20.13) that shades immediately to despair (20.14-18). Or it may be weeping (31.15) that culminates in mercy (31.20). Either way, an 'anti' stance studies the syllabus carefully, and then moves to subversive authorization, in jeopardy, everywhere accompanied.

SOMETHING RICH AND STRANGE: IMAGINING A FUTURE FOR JEREMIAH STUDIES

Robert P. Carroll

> Full fadom five thy father lies;
> Of his bones are coral made;
> Those are pearls that were his eyes:
> Nothing of him that doth fade,
> But doth suffer a sea-change
> Into something rich and strange.
> Ariel's Song[1]

> What is now proved was once only imagined.
> William Blake[2]

I think of myself as approaching the end of my serious work on Jeremiah, so the future of Jeremiah studies is not one in which I would expect myself to play a very big part at all. The bulk of my work on Jeremiah is, in my opinion, now done and if I have not made a sufficiently strong case for my own distinctive approach to reading the book of Jeremiah in my previous writings on Jeremiah, then I do not expect to be able to make such a case with any further writings. In the 1980s I wrote three books on Jeremiah.[3] By the 1990s my academic career had

---

1. William Shakespeare, *The Tempest*, Act I, Scene 2, lines 399-404. For this form see Frank Kermode (ed.), *The Tempest* (The Arden Shakespeare; London: Methuen, 1966 [1954]), pp. 35-36; cf. Stanley Wells and Gary Taylor (eds.), *William Shakespeare: The Complete Works* (The Oxford Shakespeare; Oxford: Clarendon Press, 1986), p. 1322.

2. 'Proverbs of Hell' from 'The Marriage of Heaven and Hell', in Geoffrey Keynes (ed.), *Blake: Complete Writings with Variant Readings* (Oxford: Oxford University Press, 1969), Pl. 8, p. 151.

3. See Robert P. Carroll, *From Chaos to Covenant: Uses of Prophecy in the Book of Jeremiah* (London: SCM Press, 1981 [Xpress Reprint, 1996]); *Jeremiah: A Commentary* (OTL; London: SCM Press, 1986 [pb repr., 1996]); *Jeremiah* (OTG; Sheffield: JSOT Press, 1989).

become subverted by academic administration and such administrative duties at the University of Glasgow started to take their heavy toll on my writing career.[4] So I limited myself to articles in journals and collections, chapters in other people's books, and conference papers (invited and volunteered). I should, of course, also single out for mention whatever I have managed to contribute over the years to the SBL Composition of Jeremiah Consultation.[5] I have, however, kept in touch with Jeremiah studies, mostly because other people have kept me in touch with it by inviting me to contribute to projects on Jeremiah. Writing from time to time on Jeremiah and still having to review books on Jeremiah have allowed me to keep a weathered eye on the Jeremiah scene.[6]

I would not wish to flatter myself unduly or unreasonably, but I do know that among various *individuals* around the world, especially from the next generation of biblical scholars working on Jeremiah—what I would want to insist on calling 'the younger generation'[7]—I have had

---

4. After a stint as Head of the Department of Biblical Studies (1986–89), I became Dean of the Faculty of Divinity (1991–94), Head of the Divinity Planning Unit (1991–94) and, finally, a governor of the University of Glasgow (1996–2000), as an *elected* Senate Assessor (for the faculties of Divinity, Engineering, Law and Financial Studies) on the University Court. So much administration, allied to the very heavy teaching load typical of academics at Scottish universities, finally put paid to my book-writing career—hence the lack of books since *Wolf in the Sheepfold: The Bible as a Problem for Christianity* (London: SPCK, 1991) was written in 1990 before the onslaught of administration.

5. I would like to put on record here my deepest gratitude for the amount of support I received from Kathleen O'Connor and Louis Stulman at these Consultation meetings and also to Pete Diamond for friendship, support and stimulation. Jeremiah studies is secure in their sound keeping and the next generation of scholars should be a fine achievement in the field.

6. For example, Robert P. Carroll, 'Surplus Meaning and the Conflict of Interpretations: A Dodecade of Jeremiah Studies (1984–95)', *CRBS* 4 (1996), pp. 115-59; a follow-up article will appear in the same journal in 1999 (provisional title: 'Century's End: Jeremiah Studies at the Beginning of the Third Millennium').

7. It may not be politically correct to use the term 'younger', but as an Irish-European white male I insist on my right to be politically incorrect. That is because people in Europe know from bitter experience this century that the evils of the Thought Police control are greater than the minor infelicities entailed in rhetorical alterity. I (we?) tend therefore to view with suspicion all interferences with language usage because we suspect that the masking operations of ideological distortion may be at work in the machinations of such oligarchic ideologues (cf. Soviet and Nazi uses of *Sprachregeln*).

some small influence. I know because these individuals have informed me of that influence—Marduk bless them! I doubt if it would be wise, or if I am entitled, to have had more influence than that. As the physicists say, new theories do not take over from old theories, it is just that old theoreticians die! Among the previous generation of Jeremiah commentators I can read the writing on the wall and know quite accurately how much I have been weighed by them and by how much I have been found wanting by virtually every writer on Jeremiah of that generation.[8] So I shall have to wait for the generations to come to find out about my ultimate status in Jeremiah studies in the twenty-first century. As befits a writer on Jeremiah I have had to learn to live with *fierce* opposition and, as a target of unending criticism from some of the senior members of the 1980s generation (especially at the Consultation meetings in the States throughout the 1990s), I have come to find a new sympathy for and identification with the Jeremiah character as represented in the biblical text. With a wry smile, even a grimace, I read such a statement as 'Woe is me, my mother, that you bore me, *a man of strife and contention to the whole land*. I have not lent, nor have I borrowed, yet all of them curse me' (Jer. 15.10: my personal emphasis) and wonder about what I can have done wrong in a previous existence to be so spoken against by so many of the older members of the Guild for my work on Jeremiah. So for me the future of Jeremiah Studies will be one in which I shall find a much easier time by not contributing to the discussion, though there are still a few items from my study which have yet to see the light of published day. After that the dark and the light—all at once—and I can move on to pastures new and fresh woods.

I recall a Panel Discussion for the theme 'Jeremiah: Where Do We Go from Here?' in the 'Israelite Prophetic Literature Section' at the Annual Meeting in New Orleans on 18 November 1990 when I shared that Panel with two of the current giants of Jeremiah studies (William

8.   In spite of his disagreement with my general approach to Jeremiah, I would still want to enroll Willie McKane, especially the McKane of *A Critical and Exegetical Commentary on Jeremiah. II. Commentary on Jeremiah XXVI–LII* (ICC; Edinburgh: T. & T. Clark, 1996), among the few senior scholars working on Jeremiah who have treated my work fairly and given it a reasonable representation in their work. For such practical support I am deeply grateful to the doyen of Jeremiah studies, wishing him continued good health, long life and more power to his continued book-writing skills.

Holladay and Walter Brueggemann) and two of its outstanding performers (Ronald Clements and Thomas Overholt). I felt so very small
in that company and so very much out of place. It was not the greatest
Discussion Panel I have ever served on, but it was a very interesting
study in different styles and forecasts of the future of the genre. I made
notes on an index card for delivery at that Panel, but time has hidden
that card from me and my memory cannot make good what time has
spoiled. I do recall, however, that I said something about the need for
attending to the reception history of the text, the importance of looking
at the feminine metaphors in the text and probably something pious
about the need for utilizing an ideological criticism approach. Since
then I have done something along each of those lines and I shall take
them up here briefly, while making some further remarks on a few other
desiderata for the coming century (and millennium) in Jeremiah studies,
as my contribution to imagining a future for Jeremiah studies in the
Guild. Space does not permit an adequate or comprehensive treatment
of the notion of 'imagining a future for Jeremiah studies', so I will con-
fine my attention to a number of factors which I think I signalled in the
New Orleans Panel Discussion session at the beginning of the 1990s.

Feminism

I cannot say that the trickle of work on Jeremiah which I have produced
since that meeting in New Orleans has used the above as any kind of
programme, but I have developed some of those aspirations, especially
the stuff about feminism, in further writings.[9] I knew at the time and
have had many reasons since for thinking that it was always going to be
a most unwise decision to have discussed feminism in the OTL
commentary at all, especially in terms of a critical take on the subject.[10]

9.	See Robert P. Carroll, 'Desire under the Terebinths: On Pornographic Rep-
resentation in the Prophets—A Response', in Athalya Brenner (ed.), *A Feminist
Companion to the Latter Prophets* (The Feminist Companion to the Bible, 8;
Sheffield: Sheffield Academic Press, 1995), pp. 275-307; 'Whorusalamin: A Tale of
Three Cities as Three Sisters', in Bob Becking and Meindert Dijkstra (eds.), *On
Reading Prophetic Texts: Gender-Specific and Related Studies in Memory of
Fokkelien van Dijk-Hemmes* (Biblical Interpretation, 18; Leiden: E.J. Brill, 1996),
pp. 67-82.

10.	See Carroll, *Jeremiah: A Commentary* (OTL; Philadelphia: Westminster
Press, 1986), pp. 132-34, 142-44, 153, 157-59 (cf. 249-52), 172-73, 178-80, 303-
305, 595-605.

To criticize feminism as a male *resistant reader* is to ask for trouble and to invite dismissal and denunciation of oneself. Graeme Auld did comment negatively on this aspect of the commentary, though Hugh Williamson was surprised by the critical aspect of it.[11] However, I honestly thought it would be wiser and hermeneutically more responsible to introduce the topic and even to criticize aspects of feminism as applied to the Bible because I genuinely wanted to engage with such an important dimension of contemporary biblical interpretation and also because I did want to have a place in my commentary for such a discussion. I do not think that commentators can any longer have the luxury of ignoring what is happening on the hermeneutic front when they are writing their commentaries.[12] Given the response by some feminist critics and their male supporters to my remarks in the Jeremiah commentary, I would have to say that I was wrong to think that *a critical but sympathetic reading* of some feminist appropriations of the biblical text would go unattacked or would not provide grounds for the dismissal of virtually all of my work on Jeremiah.

A good example of such *totalizing* dismissive criticism appears in Walter Brueggemann's masterly volume *Theology of the Old Testament*. I would have to admit to having experienced a *frisson* of puzzled shock when I first read a footnote in this major volume which contained a sideswiping blast against my OTL commentary for its attack on feminism. I knew I had criticized certain feminist approaches to reading the text, but I had absolutely no idea that by such criticism I had in effect marginalized one particular feminist. Here I should cite Brueggemann's footnote in full so that readers can judge the matter for themselves:

11. See 'Review of R.P. Carroll, *Jeremiah*', by Auld, in *SJT* 41 (1988), pp. 415-17 ('too many ripostes to feminist protests against sexism found in Jeremiah's sexual metaphors') and 'Review of R.P. Carroll, *Jeremiah*', by Williamson, in *VT* 38 (1988), pp. 502-503 ('[but note that surprisingly he directs a number of pointed remarks against feminist theology]'). Ah, my sins have found me out!—but I hear the criticism and will attend to it.

12. Yet I notice the way that a series such as the ICC can produce volumes such as McKane's *Jeremiah* and Macintosh's *A Critical and Exegetical Commentary on Hosea* (ICC; Edinburgh: T. & T. Clark, 1997) without attending to the issues raised by feminism for the text. I guess philology has privileged access to the past without having to take contemporaneous issues into account—I wish I had been as smart as they were!

> Trible's marginality is indicated both in general by the dismissive tendency of Brevard Childs concerning a feminist hermeneutic, and in particular by the gratuitous attack on her work by Robert Carroll in *Jeremiah: A Commentary* (OTL; Philadelphia: Westminster Press, 1986). Whether Trible and other feminist interpreters are right or wrong on any particular point is not at issue. What matters is that such a considerable scholarly perspective can be so lightly dismissed out of hand, without any serious engagement, thus making unmistakable the marginality of the enterprise.[13]

It was true there had been a critical engagement with feminist thought, but the work of Phyllis Trible had been taken, along with Judith Ochshorn's book *The Female Experience and the Nature of the Divine*, as paradigmatic of feminist readings, in order to provide a shorthand engagement with what was, by any standards, a major field of hermeneutic endeavour opening up then in biblical studies.[14] So Brueggemann's remark made me go back to my commentary and read what I had written in it about the work of Phyllis Trible. I could not find any attack as such on her or her work, though I suppose my critical engagement with feminist thought in the commentary could be read, by a suspicious reader, as 'a gratuitous attack' on the grounds that any critical reading whatsoever of feminism is not to be tolerated because criticism is imagined to be an operation of the (so-called) powerful against the so-called powerless. If my criticizing feminist readings of the Bible is evidence of 'the marginality of Trible', then what does my use of her work in the first place or my quoting her with approval indicate? For my positive use of her work in the commentary cannot be

---

13. Walter Brueggemann, *Theology of the Old Testament: Testimony, Dispute, Advocacy* (Minneapolis: Fortress Press, 1997), p. 98 n. 101. Apart from two footnotes alluding to my *From Chaos to Covenant* book, that is the *sum total* of Brueggemann's use of my work on Jeremiah in his *magnum opus*! As such it concerns me that readers of his *Theology of the Old Testament* may gain the impression that Carroll on Jeremiah is only notable for an imagined swipe at Trible's work and therefore may be safely dismissed for being politically incorrect. What a *thin reading* of Carroll that would be—not only thin but unscholarly *and untrue*!

14. See Judith Ochshorn, *The Female Experience and the Nature of the Divine* (Bloomington: Indiana University Press, 1981). The generalized criticism (always a mistake) of certain sexist attitudes among feminist writers which characterized my commentary should not be read as a denigration of the high quality of Ochshorn's book—*au contraire*.

ignored as easily as Brueggemann's reading of my book would suggest.[15]

In the commentary I thought to engage with feminism, taking it seriously enough to use aspects of it and even to criticize it *as if it were a genuinely serious enterprise*—which I did and do think it to be—hence its appearance in and engagement with in the commentary.[16] If I used Trible's work as paradigm for a feminist reading of the biblical text, then I would have thought she was being treated as mainstream and certainly not as marginal. Had I thought of her work as marginal I would not have mentioned it at all, instead of citing it with such approval (cf. Carroll, *Jeremiah*, pp. 597-601).[17] I think this is just a misreading of my book by Brueggemann. As for regarding Phyllis Trible as a marginal figure, I would regard this charge as a piece of nonsense. I have no rational explanation for what I can only regard as a grossly unsubtle misreading of my commentary. In my commentary on Jeremiah (as in my work in general) feminism is never silenced by non-reference or dismissed without thought: criticized, yes, disagreed with, yes, argued with, yes—but never ignored. I do think that the future of Jeremiah Studies will be rich in, and enriched by, many feminist readings and critiques of the book of Jeremiah.

15. Other feminist writers had already noted my engagement in the commentary with such issues and had not read my treatment as marginalizing at all: e.g. Renita J. Weems, 'Gomer: Victim of Violence or Victim of Metaphor?', *Interpretation for Liberation*, Semeia 47 (1989), pp. 87-104 (n. 8).

16. See Carroll, *Jeremiah*, pp. 178-80 (see n. 10 above), I wonder how many other major, mainstream commentaries of the 1980s (or later) on Jeremiah engaged as much as I did with feminism? That was the whole point of the exercise, so I am surprised (am I?) to find the experts incapable of reading the subtext of a contemporary book. If this is the extent of their competence with reading a modern work, how much less will their competence be for reading ancient texts?

17. It is arguable that Trible is criticized on p. 173, but not elsewhere and certainly cited with approval on p. 600. If I had wanted to criticize Trible it would have been terribly easy to do so because most academics are vulnerable to criticism about the paucity of their published output, the inadequacies of their relations with colleagues and their failure to maintain graduate studies by encouraging research students to complete their theses. But not a word of any such focused criticism appears in my commentary, so Trible is not under attack. Auld's sense of my vexation with feminism is I'm sure a correct one, but that has to do with logical flaws in some feminist readings of the text: e.g. the claim that only the feminine terms of prophetic critique are focused on, when the biblical text is impartial in its criticism of male and female, using metaphors of either or both genders.

Ideological Criticism

I read the book of Jeremiah as a series of stringent critiques of the past, so when I read the text of Jeremiah itself I necessarily read it *critically*. I am therefore bound to take issue with any easy, comfortable or slack readings of the biblical text.[18] I would like to think that in the future participants in Jeremiah Studies will *engage critically with* the text and its reception rather than with its current readers. So much of what I read in books and articles on Jeremiah represents *in my opinion* either the paraphrasing of the text itself or the internalization of values imagined to be in the book of Jeremiah. So that there is no place for a critical engagement with the text or assessment of such textual values (*Sachkritik*) or room for allowance for the *Rezeptionsgeschichte* (reception history) of the tradition raising questions about text or tradition. For example, Brueggemann, who is currently one of the (if not *the*) outstanding American readers of Jeremiah sides with the textual representation of the Jeremiah character, so that he lacks any critical distance from the text itself: 'Jeremiah is exactly right' (*A Commentary on Jeremiah*, p. 495).[19] In my opinion that is far too easy a way of reading the text and *for me* it fails at every point to appropriate the text *critically*. Given the way the world (out there) is I think the Guild of Biblical Studies has a duty to be true to its post-Enlightenment heritage and to engage *critically* with all claims to power or to the exercise of

18. For an example of how I read Jeremiah synchronically see Carroll, 'The Polyphonic Jeremiah: A Reading of the Book of Jeremiah', in Martin Kessler (ed.), *Reading the Book of Jeremiah: A Search for Coherence* (Winona Lake, IN: Eisenbrauns, 1999); for criticisms of synchronic approaches to reading Jeremiah see Carroll, 'Synchronic Deconstructions of Jeremiah: Diachrony to the Rescue? Reflections on Some Reading Strategies for Understanding Certain Problems in the Book of Jeremiah', in Johannes C. de Moor (ed.), *Synchronic or Diachronic? A Debate on Method in Old Testament Exegesis* (OTS, 34; Leiden: E.J. Brill, 1995), pp. 39-51.

19. If in this article I appear to dissent mostly from Walter Brueggemann's work on Jeremiah, that is because I judge his work on Jeremiah to be currently among the most approachable, interesting, readable and important writings on Jeremiah *in the States*. I suspect that, for all our very many differences, we share some interests and even seek to occupy some of the same space at times in the matter of Jeremiah Studies. Disagreement here does not mean or entail disparagement or denigration. It is out of respect and attention that I write here and yet also out of the deep pain and regret of harshly voiced disagreements in the past.

power represented by the traditional authorities. If texts can be said to possess or represent ideology, then a thoroughgoing ideological criticism (*Ideologiekritik*) is warranted and required of readers of such texts. If the biblical texts can be cleared of the charge of being themselves ideological, then the critique must be (re)directed at the canonizing communities and at the reception of such texts.[20] As elements of canonical collections texts participate in power structures (cf. Bruns on canon), so I would like to see in the future a much greater engagement with this aspect of the reception of texts and I would also have to add that it is one of the benefits of the feminist scrutiny of texts that such issues have come to the fore in recent biblical studies.

If I were writing a programme for Jeremiah studies in the twenty-first century I would want to place the issue of ideological criticism very near the top of the list of desiderata. For example, questions along the lines of whose interests are served by this book in the form(s) it has come down to us and whose interests have been served by the predominant interpretations of Jeremiah through time and, especially, in the twentieth century, ought to be asked. I have already stated my own convictions of what the book of Jeremiah means ideologically: see quest for land, entitlement, diasporic interests, etc., but I would like to see the investigation carried on much further than that by others in the future.[21] A further concern must be: if the original Jeremiah was such a radical critic of the Jerusalem community, culture and cultus how could he have been incorporated, without serious and severe transformations, into the canon? What hidden agendas did tradition find in his work or *create there in the first instance* that made his story so amenable to the

---

20. I have touched on the relation of ideological criticism to Jeremiah Studies in my study in this volume (see above 'The Book of J: Intertextuality and Ideological Criticism') and my contributions to *Ideologiekritik* in *JNSL* 19–22 (1993–96) (see p. 234 n. 32 above) and in Carroll, 'Clio and Canons: In Search of a Cultural Poetics of the Hebrew Bible', in Stephen D. Moore (ed.), *The New Historicism: BibInt* 5 (1997), pp. 300-323 (esp. 308-15). On the viewpoint that texts do not possess ideologies see Stephen Fowl, 'Texts Don't Have Ideologies', *BibInt* 3 (1995), pp. 15-34.

21. The motif of the possession of land issue is fundamental for any reading of Jeremiah: see Norman C. Habel, *The Land Is Mine: Six Biblical Land Ideologies* (Overtures to Biblical Theology; Minneapolis: Fortress Press, 1995), pp. 75-96 (on the prophetic ideology of land). My own convictions on this matter can be found expressed in the various pieces I have written on the subject of ideology in the Bible (see n. 20 above).

Jerusalem authorities? While I could offer many speculations here, I shall stick to the simpler explanation of asking for account to be taken of the *doctoring* of the text. The text is after all, what Gerald Bruns has called, 'a doctored text', for how else would it have been incorporated into the power structures of text production in later Jerusalem?[22] As to the questions of who did the doctoring and why, we may answer according to our own analytical studies of the book's composition, with a strong presumption in favour of the deuteronomists.[23] In my judgment we cannot get back behind the text to an imagined original Jeremiah who uttered his words before Baruch, the scribes, the deuteronomists, the redactors or whoever got to them and transformed them by addition, subtraction, redaction and supplementation.[24] If I may cite myself on the book of Jeremiah, in my judgment the book as it now stands represents a case of 'The prophet is lost to the scribe'.[25] There are so many different ways of making this fundamental point—Mark Biddle's simple statement that the book 'is *several steps removed* from the career of the prophet' will do nicely [26]—but it seems to need to be made time and time again in order to keep the Guild honest in Jeremiah Studies. We may dispute the implicatures of such a state of affairs, but I have chosen

22. See Gerald L. Bruns, 'Canon and Power in the Hebrew Bible', in *idem*, *Hermeneutics: Ancient and Modern* (New Haven: Yale University Press, 1992), pp. 64-82 (the phrase 'a doctored text' appears on p. 76) (original publication in *Critical Inquiry* 3 [1984], pp. 462-80).

23. I do recognize here that voices such as Graeme Auld and Roy Porter have been counselling us to avoid such presumptions about the existence of a (pan)deuteronomistic influence on the prophetic texts, but until I can find a better explanation I shall stay with the compact majority point of view. On this matter see Walter Gross (ed.), *Jeremia und die 'deuteronomistische Bewegung'* (BBB, 98; Weinheim: Beltz Athenäum Verlag, 1995).

24. Here I do think that Brueggemann is on to something in his discussion of the role of Baruch in the book: see Brueggemann,'The Baruch Connection: Reflections on Jeremiah 43.1-7', *JBL* 113 (1994), pp. 405-20.

25. Robert P. Carroll, 'Manuscripts Don't Burn—Inscribing the Prophetic Tradition: Reflections on Jeremiah 36', in Matthias Augustin and Klaus-Dietrich Schunck (eds.), *'Dort ziehen Schiffe dahin ...': Collected Communications to the XIVth Congress of the International Organization for the Study of the Old Testament, Paris 1992* (BEATAJ, 28; Frankfurt on Main: Peter Lang, 1996), pp. 31-42 (40).

26. Mark E. Biddle, *Polyphony and Symphony in Prophetic Literature: Rereading Jeremiah 7–20* (Studies in Old Testament Interpretation, 2; Macon, GA: Mercer University Press, 1996), p. 128 (emphasis in the original).

to make of it a *thick description* of the transformations brought about in the story of Jeremiah as mediated by the scribes (symbolized by Baruch?) who constructed the tradition we now know as the book of Jeremiah and as further transformed by matters having to do with canonization and the ideologies of such canonizing communities.

The doctored text is all that we have and therefore historical investigation will inevitably leave us in the dark. It is in such darkness that we all do our work on Jeremiah and any future I could imagine for Jeremiah studies would not necessarily wish to relieve that dark of its darkness. Whether the dark is light enough I do not know. But what I would like to see more of is the scholarly acknowledgment of such darkness because the concept or image of scholars working *on* the darkness which is the tradition and *in* the dark helps to prevent every one of us from making grandiose claims beyond our station as academics or as commentators on the past. I recall counsel from a learned source given some years ago when summing up another scholar's life's work and I would like to use it here in application to Jeremiah Studies:

> ... ask the big questions and get the big picture; be sceptical about every generalization including this one; hold up every fashion to the mirror of history; and ... acknowledge the extent to which we are in the dark rather than pretending that we have seen the light.[27]

Of course some writers will imagine that they have lightened their own darkness and the darkness of the tradition somewhat whereas other writers will be less convinced that their own work illuminates much. However, I want that acknowledgment of limited knowledge and restricted insight to go on before us into the future in order to keep us humble, realistic and struggling. Otherwise we will have rushed to closure in the matter of reading Jeremiah and will convey to future generations a false picture of the matter. After some 20 years of working on the Jeremiah tradition I remain inclined towards that opinion of the matter, even though very many people may well be dissatisfied with a

---

27. Raymond John Vincent, 'Order in International Politics', in R.J. Vincent and J.D.B. Miller (eds.), *Order and Violence: Hedley Bull and International Relations* (Oxford: Clarendon Press, 1990), pp. 38-64 (64). Vincent uses this summary form as a description of the legacy of Hedley Bull's intellectual style and I used it as a citation in my paper ('No Peace for the Wicked') given in the 'Prophets and History Consultation' at New Orleans on 19 November 1990. I feel that it will bear repetition here in published form, even though in a different context.

point of view which will not admit that illumination is necessarily on tap in the Bible.[28]

Reception History

Where Jeremiah thundered, there are topless bars.[29]

However important a feature the element of reception history may be, I do not quite share the enthusiasm for it that so many other commentators seem to express for it. That is because I think it is much more complex, even more complicated, than most commentators give any sign of imagining. My own brief treatment of examples of how such a reception history of Jeremiah might be done used Edgar Allen Poe's poem 'The Raven', one of Gerard Manley Hopkins's 'Terrible Sonnets' and the poetry of Allen Ginsberg, but the exercise was a mere scratching of the poetic surface of the matter.[30] To do a proper reception history study of Jeremiah ideally would take many volumes and, because in the West our whole culture since the sixteenth century has been suffused with biblical metaphor and metonym, allusion and allegory, there would be no end to dissecting language, literature and speech for uses of and allusions to the book of Jeremiah. For example, apart from the fact that the word 'jeremiad', common in English usage, indicates both a complaining, kvetching attitude to anything and incorporates an allusion to the biblical prophet Jeremiah, weekly serious newspapers refer to Jeremiah when they wish to criticize a critical or whingeing

28. See 'Appendix II', in Carroll, *From Chaos to Covenant*, pp. 275-79.

29. George Steiner, *Errata: An Examined Life* (London: Weidenfeld & Nicolson, 1997), p. 54. I would like here, once again, to acknowledge the range and depth of George Steiner's work and its influence on my thinking for more than 30 years now. I doubt if I could really begin to acknowledge adequately or realistically the seminal influence of his work on my work—full fathom five, I think!—but see Carroll, *Jeremiah*, p. 668 (why, even Brueggemann himself was able to use my OTL in order to be able to cite this brilliant *aperçu* of Steiner's [citing my commentary as source]) and my *Wolf in the Sheepfold*, *passim*.

30. I have merely played with the complexities of the matter in my contribution to the Robert Davidson Festschrift which I edited some years ago: see my 'The Discombobulations of Time and the Diversities of Text: Notes on the *Rezeptionsgeschichte* of the Bible', in Carroll (ed.), *Text as Pretext: Essays in Honour of Robert Davidson* (JSOTSup, 138; Sheffield: JSOT Press, 1992), pp. 61-85 (77-80 on Jeremiah). See the much more interesting volume, Adrian H.W. Curtis and Thomas Römer (eds.), *The Book of Jeremiah and its Reception: Le livre de Jérémie et sa réception* (BETL, 128; Leuven: Leuven University Press/Peeters, 1997).

attitude to current politics or life as we know it. How could one possibly keep track of all such references? When I discovered on the West Coast of the States (San Francisco: well, Palo Alto to be exact), courtesy of that renowned biblical scholar and culture critic Alice Bach, the coffee blend called 'Jeremiah's Pick'[31] I knew that reception history was over for me! I could not possibly keep up with the multitudinous myriad uses of and allusions to Jeremiah in the contemporary world— let alone throughout the history of Western and world cultures—I will forbear to mention the priest called *Jeremiah Carroll* who used to work in Clydebank in the West of Scotland because that is another man's story rather than part of my story.

I have cited George Steiner's passing observation on the way modern Israel has transmogrified its ancient past as a concrete example of just one more example of how complex and wide-ranging a reception history of Jeremiah might turn out to be. I do often wonder when I read advocacies of the importance of doing reception history of the Bible whether such advocates have more than the slightest idea of how wide-ranging and comprehensive such a topic would be if practised properly and not just confined to a *few* favourite major theologians—and all the usual suspects at that too (e.g. Augustine, Luther, Calvin, Barth, etc.). It is not the case that I think it should not be done, it is just that I am not very keen on it being done so badly or so inadequately. But of course it must be attempted, even though invariably it will be done badly and inadequately. As Rabbi Tarphon said: 'it is not for you to complete the work, nor are you free to desist from it'.[32]

Theological Readings

> Yet Freud and Kafka in their very denial of all transcendence appear as the heirs of a Jewish revolt against outwardness and authority that goes back as far as Jeremiah. Kafka's covenant of pure writing emerges as the late, bleak corollary of Jeremiah's New Covenant of inwardness.
>
> Ernest Bernhardt-Kabisch[33]

31. Jeremiah's Pick [Jeremiah Pick] (1495 Evans Avenue, San Francisco, CA 94124). Of course I know that this is only a proprietary brand name, but everything is grist to the hermeneutic mill and everything feeds into the construction of an adequate reception history of a text.

32. Rabbi Tarphon in *P. Ab.* 2.21.

33. In his review of Harold Bloom's *Ruin the Sacred Truths* in *JAAR* 58 (1990), p. 482.

I deliberately eschewed the theological in favour of the ideological in my OTL commentary because having read so many theological readings of Jeremiah, especially Christianized theological readings, I felt I desperately needed to escape from the throttling suffocation of piety and its domestication of the text.[34] The only bearable 'theological' reading of the text for me would be a hermeneutical-ideological reception history which had incorporated the constant transformation-transcendence (*Aufgehoben*) of the text through time and tradition. But others think very differently (e.g. Brueggemann's commentary and the Word Commentary two-volume work),[35] so I had better engage with the demand which such works are designed to meet and imagine a future for Jeremiah Studies in the century about to dawn which would include the theological. It would have to be one which had taken the Enlightenment project seriously into account and which, perhaps moving towards and beyond the postmodern, would also have incorporated the ever-changing ways of reading the text. For a start it would have to have come to terms with or have entered into dialogue with the extremely pertinent remarks made by McKane in his commentaries in relation to the metaphor 'the word of YHWH/God'.[36] All the tensions, contradictions, contrarieties in the text of Jeremiah require a much more sophisticated and informed approach to the textual conventions governing the representation of the reception of the divine word in Jeremiah. McKane is right—'God does not speak Hebrew'.[37] God(s) do not possess larynx(es). I would have thought that this was Philosophy or Theology 101 stuff, but McKane is *one of the very few* contemporary commentators on Jeremiah who has seen fit to start from the foundations of thought. Without such a discussion of first principles I see little hope of advancing the theological dimension of Jeremiah Studies towards anything meaningful in the next century.

At the other end of the spectrum from McKane are so many commen-

34. While nobody spotted this point, it was implicit in my writing the commentary under an intertext supplied by lines from a George Seferis's poem ('An Old Man on the River Bank').

35. P.C. Craigie, P.H. Kelley and J.F. Drinkard, Jr, *Jeremiah 1–25* (WBC, 26; Dallas: Word Books, 1991); G.L. Keown, P.J. Scalise and T.G. Smothers, *Jeremiah 26–52* (WBC, 27; Dallas: Word Books, 1995).

36. McKane, *Jeremiah*, I, pp. xcvii-xcix.

37. W. McKane, *The Book of Micah: Introduction and Commentary* (Edinburgh: T. & T. Clark, 1998), p. 23.

tators (especially Brueggeman, Craigie *et al.*, Holladay, Jones, McConville, etc.) for whom there appears to be a direct link between the words of the text and whatever they imagine to be the transcendental. I find all such simplistic assumptions, which neither argue their corner nor make any allowance for the transmogrifications of time, to border on a fundamentalism in the reading of ancient texts. As I read him it seems to me that Brueggemann just engages with the text of Jeremiah theologically but uncritically. The engagement is extremely good as far as it goes, but I can see nothing in his commentary which would hint at any distance—critical, historical or whatever—between the location of his reading and the text. It is as if 2500 years had never happened or had only ever contributed 'nice thoughts' to the enhancement of the text's exposition. In his work the text has been domesticated quintessentially by his own ecclesiastical theology and brought into an easy, comfortable fit with his own domestic theology.[38] Such an approach has certainly no real interest for me as a way of reading Jeremiah *at the end of the twentieth century*, so I do not find in Brueggemann's very able theological treatment of Jeremiah any sense of what I think I find in my reading of that text: of the word being in crisis[39] or of the profound denial of form and structure inherent in Jeremiah's critique of everything ('all your structures are false'). I would like to see a future for Jeremiah studies where the traces of Jeremiah's contribution to negative theology would be picked up and pursued through the awfulness of the

38. I hope this observation will not be misunderstood by readers, especially by Walter Breuggemann, because I have no wish to denigrate his fine commentary (reviewed favourably by myself in *Scottish Journal of Religious Studies* 1999 and *invariably* recommended by me to the students in the Jeremiah text course I teach at Glasgow University) which is fine as far as it goes, but which does not appeal to me *personally* as a way of reading Jeremiah.

39. I have only touched on this issue in my 'The Polyphonic Jeremiah: A Reading of the Book of Jeremiah' for the Martin Kessler volume (*Reading the Book of Jeremiah*), but having read through the book of Jeremiah many times since writing my OTL commentary my sense of the book is that above all else the very notion of 'the word of YHWH' itself is profoundly in crisis. After Jeremiah no more word of YHWH? Just as in our own time after Auschwitz no more theology (the *implicitum* of Paul Celan's poetry)? I think it is time for readers of Jeremiah to peer into the Abyss, rather than to look away. In the matter of a polyphonic reading of Jeremiah I would recommend highly Mark Biddle's fine monograph *Polyphony and Symphony in Prophetic Literature: Rereading Jeremiah 7–20*.

twentieth century to take up the insights of Freud and Kafka and to
touch on the awful silence of god so much associated with the various
destructions of Jerusalem and all those death camps so graphically
symbolized by the name Auschwitz.[40]

By my way of thinking there is a strong line from Jeremiah to
Auschwitz, but not one in terms of popular or conventional theology.
Klaus Seybold captures something of the point when he identifies
Jeremiah as the Paul Celan of the prophets: 'The zone of death is his
territory ... Jeremiah was the Celan of the prophets. He writes death
fugues.'[41] I also recall lines from a poem by Nelly Sachs:

> O die Schornsteine!
> Freiheitswege für Jeremias und Hiobs Staube—[42]

This makes obvious (textual) connections between the biblical
characters of Jeremiah and Job and the awful experiences of the death
camps of the Third Reich. Both the biblical figures are legendary as by-
words for suffering and therefore both feed as *figura* into contemporary
representations of the death camps. As witness of the destruction of
Jerusalem at the hands of the Babylonians Jeremiah makes a fine symbolic figure for discourses about the destruction of the European Jews
by the Germans in the twentieth century. I can also see some interesting
possibilities in exploring the tensions and dialectical problems in the
book of Jeremiah between the representation of Jeremiah as 'witness
for the prosecution' and also as 'speaker for the defence' (that is, in the

40. When writing my commentary I found symbolic links between the rhetoric
of the Jeremiah tradition and the rhetoric of reports of the awfulness of that *univers
concentrationnaire* (Carroll, *Jeremiah*, pp. 168-70, citing Elie Wiesel's 'Jeremiah',
in Wiesel, *Five Biblical Portraits* [Notre Dame: University of Notre Dame Press,
1981], pp. 125-26).

41. Klaus Seybold, *Der Prophet Jeremia: Leben und Werk* (Urban-Taschen-
bücher, 416; Stuttgart: W. Kohlhammer, 1993), pp. 169, 203.

42. 'O the chimneys! Freedomway for Jeremiah and Job's dust', Nelly Sachs,
'O die Schornsteine', in Sachs, *Fahrt ins Staublose: Die Gedichte der Nelly Sachs*
(Frankfurt on Main: Suhrkamp Verlag, 1961), p. 8. I have used the published
translation of Michael Roloff from Abba Kovner and Nelly Sachs, *Selected Poems*
(Penguin Modern European Poets; Harmondsworth: Penguin Books, 1971), p. 79 (a
volume I have known and loved a long time). For a positive use of Jer. 31.15-16
(also a critique of Christian uses of Jer 31.31-34) with reference to the Shoah see
Emil L. Fackenheim, *The Jewish Bible after the Holocaust: A Re-reading* (Bloomington: Indiana University Press, 1990), pp. 71-99.

conflict between the judgmental oracles and the self-justifying laments). Also, like the textual character of the prophet Jeremiah himself I would want any future work on Jeremiah to continue to seek to rob readers of their certainties, their securities and their cherished fetishes in relation to the text and to their own time.[43] The notion of a prophet who speaks against all certainties and against every object or institution which might make for security is an instrument of subversion against all religious values, institutions and hopes.

Queering Jeremiah

I am not a proponent of 'the historical Jeremiah' approach to reading the text of the book of Jeremiah and I hope I have made my negation of that position clear in the various books and articles I have written about Jeremiah. Yet I am deeply aware of how much so many commentators and even more readers wish to find in the book of Jeremiah some clues for a portrait (if not a biography) of the ancient prophet Jeremiah. When writing the commentary I was regularly struck by how much the text lent itself along historical lines to the production of a 'queering of Jeremiah' approach (e.g. the trace of homosexual rape in popular readings of 20.7). As a historical personage it would be easy enough following a number of textual clues to construct an account of Jeremiah which would give positive flesh to the question 'Was Jeremiah queer?' All historical approaches must be prone to this question and I am surprised that the suggestion has not appeared in book-form before now. So I look forward to the future when some rising academic stars pursue this matter and using queer theory as a reading strategy demonstrate that Jeremiah too was (is) 'a friend of Dorothy's'. At that point Jeremiah studies will have come to full mature adulthood and biblical commentators will be able to commit to the task of reading and commenting on Jeremiah facing the future rather than, as always, facing the past.

I would have to admit that on the possibility of queering Jeremiah there are some clues in my commentary along these lines, but nothing was articulated or spelled out because I was awfully conscious of the kind of rage which such a reading can produce and besides I am no good at theorizing.[44] And yet Thomas Hanks did spot certain allusions

43. Such a sentiment functioned as one of the subtexts of my own two books on Jeremiah: *From Chaos to Covenant* and the OTL commentary (1986).

44. See Carroll, *Jeremiah*, p. 178; the reference to John Boswell's work was one

within my commentary and here I would like to congratulate and thank him for such a percipient reading of my commentary. I wish all my readers were as sharp a reader as he is or, at least, that I had more percipient readers of my commentary. I will not go into queer theory here, but the future I can imagine for Jeremiah studies in the next century is one which will include a considerable amount of 'queering of Jeremiah' in order to explore one of the most pressing needs of ecclesiastical-theological communities—the incorporation of gayness into the theological enterprise.[45] I am here of course out of my depth—as I always am when it comes to sophisticated theory and theorizing— because I am, at best, only a jobbing academic who is an old-fashioned textualist and a historical-critical hermeneut trained in what are now probably regarded by many contemporary biblical scholars as out-moded techniques of reading and *explication de texte* strategies. I can just about imagine the map I would like to have drawn of reading Jeremiah in the next century, but as I am no cartographer it is highly unlikely that I shall ever construct such a map of the future of Jeremiah studies. The future of Jeremiah studies which I can imagine (or would like to see) will have to be constructed by other writers and commentators.

Conclusion

So what kind of future of Jeremiah studies does the above discussion amount to? A modest one I would have to say. Yet I would also hope that the notion of 'something rich and strange'—which I have used as a titular trope for this article in order to signal the very rich transformations which have taken place in the reading and understanding of Jeremiah over the millennia of its reception—would have a role to play in the future of Jeremiah studies because it would indicate that surface

such clue. Given the rage that the OTL commentary produced in some readers I'm glad I did not pursue this aspect any further in it.

45. This is one of the more important subtexts of my *Wolf in the Sheepfold* book: see the preface to the new edition (London: SCM Press, 1997 [p. xiii]). I really do think that theological readers of the Bible are going to have to bite this bullet in the upcoming century, because the legitimacy of gayness is currently the stumbling-block over which so many ecclesiastical and theological communities are stumbling and falling to the ground. It will be a highly contested site of legitimation in the twenty-first century, but I hope Jeremiah studies will make a contribution to such a vexed debate.

readings of the text had given way to the more oblique and indirect ways of reading texts in contemporary thinking about literature and the past.[46] Elsewhere in this volume I have already indicated my hopes for a future where *a critical hermeneutics* might lead to an *ethical* reading of the book of Jeremiah.[47] On the other hand, I have no doubt that the *actual* future of the subdiscipline is more likely to follow the paths beaten out by Brueggemann, Clements, Jones, Holladay, McConville, Thompson than those made by Carroll or even McKane. I think the more radical approaches of a Mark Biddle will have some impact on how future work on Jeremiah is done, as will the work of the many feminists who have turned their scrutiny to the prophetic texts. I fully expect that the sterling work on Jeremiah done by Pete Diamond, John Hill, Kathleen O'Connor and Louis Stulman will bear fruit in the next century. I also hope that McKane has a major contribution yet to make *by way of influence* because his textual work on Jeremiah is superb.[48] Of my own commentary's fate I used to have hopes and fears in the past, but now I have a fairly good idea how mainstream scholarship will actually go in that matter. I recall Simon de Vries interrupting from the floor at one of the Consultation's meetings and saying that he thought Holladay and McKane were the important commentaries and that Carroll's was interesting but not important (that was the gist of what he said or of how I remember him as saying). I think he was right about the relative merits of the different 1986 commentaries, but I would like to think (author's utopian incorrigibility perhaps) that my work on Jeremiah will, in the future, constitute a limiting case in the discussion.[49] It may be too much to expect that in future people will

46. This is not the place to venture into the territory of postmodernism and new historicism, but as an introduction to how things have changed see Frank R. Ankersmit, 'Historiography and Postmodernism', in *idem, History and Tropology: The Rise and Fall of Metaphor* (Berkeley: University of California Press, 1994), pp. 162-81 (original article in *History and Theory* 28 [1989]); also Stephen D. Moore (ed.), *The New Historicism, BibInt* 5 (1997). To this point I shall return in subsequent work on Jeremiah.

47. See the Conclusion to my 'The Book of J: Intertextuality and Ideological Criticism', above.

48. See my various reviews of McKane's two-volume commentary: *JTS* 38 (1987), pp. 446-50 (vol. 1) and *JTS* 50 (1999), vol. 2.

49. As an earnest of his point the fact that my commentary is out of print in the States and will remain that way is indicative of the shrewd truth of de Vries's judgment. I have still to write a further book on Jeremiah, picking up all the many

refer to 'Jeremiah' in inverted commas because they will recognize that 'Carroll on Jeremiah' has made a mark of some kind on their thinking, but I would still hope that before launching into disquisitions on 'the historical Jeremiah' there will be, at least, a slight hesitation. I would settle for that moment of hesitation, the size, as it were, of a little cloud like a man's hand on the horizon.

I do recall William Blake's observation about how what used to be only imagined is now accepted everywhere as gospel truth—hence its appearance as an epigraph to this paper as a gesture of hope about the prospects for current Jeremiah studies. I would like to be able to think of my work on Jeremiah in such a fashion—as the unthinkable made thought (perhaps). It may not be much, but realism is also called for in imagining the future because if there is anything I have learned from decades of working on Jeremiah it is this: trust nobody (a good *X-Files* injunction), distrust all structures, scale down all expectations, moderate hope, learn to live with scarcity and, above all else, prepare to live in exile.[50] And yet ... I still hope to have made a real contribution to Jeremiah studies in the last quarter of the twentieth century, however subtle, however much spoken against and however much vilified that imagined contribution may be. So when a major but conservative theologian of the calibre of Walter Brueggemann can write in the following way in the updated introduction to his Jeremiah commentary

> Now it is clear, given current perspectives, that the book of Jeremiah is not a 'record' of what happened, but rather a *constructive proposal of reality* that is powered by *passionate conviction* and that is voiced in cunning, albeit disjunctive *artistic form*. This means that the book of

unused bits from the commentary's preparation period. I also wish to write a piece on all the self-denying ordinances which governed my writing of that commentary ('Metacommentary on Jeremiah') and something on the reception of the OTL commentary ('The Gap on the Shelf'). All these will constitute my farewell to Jeremiah Studies and I hope to get them all written by the time the century is giving way to the next millennium.

50. It just so happens that I am an Irish *economic exile* living in self-imposed exile in Scotland (part of Britain but not of Ireland), so for me this injunction is not a metaphor but a reality—even though it is a self-imposed exile for economic reasons rather than a deportation for th/ideological reasons! For a comprehensive treatment of the notion of exile see James M. Scott (ed.), *Exile: Old Testament, Jewish, and Christian Conceptions* (JSJSup, 56; Leiden: E.J. Brill, 1997) and my own contribution to that volume: 'Deportation and Diasporic Discourses in the Prophetic Literature', pp. 63-85.

Jeremiah is a rich and open field for venturesome interpretation, none of which can claim to be 'objective' and none of which is likely to dominate or defeat alternative perspectives[51]

then I feel a little more cheerful and begin to suspect that Carroll on Jeremiah may have had a subtle (whether acknowledged, liked or whatever) but definite influence on the subdiscipline of Jeremiah Studies and I know that I shall rest content with that knowledge. What other kind of future for Jeremiah studies could *I* possibly imagine or could I ever hope to end on a more cheerful personal note than that?

---

51. 'Recent Jeremiah Study', in W. Brueggemann, *A Commentary on Jeremiah: Exile and Homecoming* (Grand Rapids: Eerdmans, 1998), p. ix (emphases in the original). I use the term 'conservative' to describe Brueggemann here because I would rather not use the term 'reactionary'. My justification for placing him towards the right-wing end of the hermeneutic-ideological spectrum is simply that in contrast to my own Irish-European way of thinking his reading of Jeremiah represents for me a deeply reactionary approach to Scripture. Everything is, of course, relative, so this point of view is my own subjective reading of Brueggemann's place in current American Biblical Studies seen from an Irish-European perspective on Jeremiah Studies. *C'est tous*!

INDEX OF AUTHORS